Contents

How to use this book

STRUCTURE

This book covers Route F of the Edexcel A Level and AS Level History qualifications. Route F consists of three papers which are linked by the theme 'Searching for rights and freedoms in the 20th century'.

- Paper 1: In search of the American Dream: the USA, c1917–96
- Paper 2a: India, c1914–48: the road to independence
- Paper 2b: South Africa, 1948–94: from apartheid state to 'rainbow nation'

To take Route F, you must study Paper 1, plus **one** of the two Paper 2 options. You do not need to study the other Paper 2 topic for your exam, but you might like to read it for interest – it deals with similar themes to the topics you are studying.

If you are studying for A Level History, you will also need to study a Paper 3 option and produce coursework in order to complete your qualification. All Paper 3 options are covered by other textbooks in this series.

AS LEVEL OR A LEVEL?

This book is designed to support students studying both the Edexcel AS Level and A Level qualifications. The content required for both qualifications is identical, so all the material in the papers you are studying is relevant, whichever qualification you are aiming for.

The questions you will be asked in the exam differ for the two different qualifications, so we have included separate exam-style questions and exam preparation sections. If you are studying for an AS Level, you should use the exam-style questions and exam sections highlighted in blue. If you are studying for an A Level, you should use the exam-style questions and exam sections highlighted in green.

AS Level Exam-Style Question Section B

How accurate is it to say that Congress consolidated its position in the 1920s? (20 marks)

Tip
Think about the re-structuring of Congress and also the ways in which Congress operated in practice.

A Level Exam-Style Question Section B

How far do you agree that the car changed the face of the USA in the years 1917–80? (20 marks)

Tip
Think of factors other than car ownership and think of those the car did not affect (be careful to consider knock-on effects though).

The 'Preparing for your exams' section at the end of each paper contains sample answers of different standards, with comments on how weaker answers could be improved. Make sure you look at the right section for the exam you are planning to take.

FEATURES

Extend your knowledge

These features contain additional information that will help you gain a deeper understanding of the topic. This could be a short biography of an important person, extra background information about an event, an alternative interpretation, or even a research idea that you could follow up. Information in these boxes is not essential to your exam success, but still provides insights of value.

EXTEND YOUR KNOWLEDGE

The space race
Without the Cold War, it is unlikely that Congress would have voted to spend money on space exploration, but many people felt the next war could be won from space. The country that 'controlled' space was likely to win. Also, in the war of 'hearts and minds' between East and West, it was important to show other countries you were better than the competition. The USSR scored a political win when it launched the first spacecraft, Sputnik 1, on 4 October 1957. In 1958, President Eisenhower set up the National Aeronautics and Space Administration (NASA) to explore space. The USA and the USSR also set up, secretly, space programmes to investigate waging war from space and spying using satellites. On 20 July 1969, the USA put the first man on the moon, scoring a huge propaganda victory at a cost of $25 billion.

Knowledge check activities

These activities are designed to check that you have understood the material that you have just studied. They might also ask you questions about the sources and extracts in the section to check that you have studied and analysed them thoroughly.

ACTIVITY
KNOWLEDGE CHECK

The Cold War

1 Write a version of Truman's 1947 speech (Source 7), making the Truman Doctrine clear to a younger student.

2 Draw a diagram to show how the Cold War affected the powers of the president.

3 Read the paragraph 'The armed services' (previous column): what do you think the 'hawks'/'doves' divide was and why do you think it was an important split?

Summary activities

At the end of each chapter, you will find summary activities. These are tasks designed to help you think about the key topic you have just studied as a whole. They may involve selecting and organising key information or analysing how things changed over time. You might want to keep your answers to these questions safe – they are handy for revision.

ACTIVITY
SUMMARY

1 List the ways in which black American civil rights tactics were similar/dissimilar before and after 1950.

2 Write notes for an essay on how far you agree with the statement: 'The civil rights movement **was** Martin Luther King. It took off with him and it died down after his assassination.'

3 You are going to take part in a debate on the statement: 'The achievements of civil rights campaigners were not worth the price paid for them.' You don't know whether you will be arguing for or against the proposal. Make notes on arguments that could support either side, giving specific examples.

4 Write at least a page to explain how far you agree with the statement: 'Minority rights campaigners just copied the tactics of the black American civil rights movement, they did nothing unique.'

Thinking Historically activities

These activities are found throughout the book and are designed to develop your understanding of history, especially around the key concepts of evidence, interpretations, causation and change. Each activity is designed to challenge a conceptual barrier that might be holding you back. This is linked to a map of conceptual barriers developed by experts. You can look up the map and find out which barrier each activity challenges by downloading the conceptual map from this website: www.pearsonschools.co.uk/historyprogressionapproach.

conceptual map reference

 THINKING HISTORICALLY Evidence (3b)

It depends on the question

When considering the usefulness of a piece of evidence, people often think about authenticity in the case of artefacts, reliability in the case of witness statements, or methodology and structure in the case of secondary accounts. A better historical approach to the usefulness of a piece of evidence would be to think about the statements that we can make about the past based on it. Different statements can be made with different degrees of certainty, depending on the evidence.

Work in small groups and answer the following:

1 Look at Source 5.

  a. Write three statements that you can reasonably make about the Greensboro sit-in based solely on Source 5.

  b. Which of the statements can be made with the greatest degree of certainty? Why is this? Which statement can be made with the smallest degree of certainty?

  c. What else might you need to increase your confidence in your statements?

2 Source 5 is an artefact and Source 4 is a witness statement. Which is more useful to the historian studying the impact of the Greensboro sit-in?

3 Look at Extract 3. How would the historian have gone about constructing this piece? What kinds of evidence would he have needed?

Getting the most from your online ActiveBook

This book comes with three years' access to ActiveBook* – an online, digital version of your textbook. Follow the instructions printed on the inside front cover to start using your ActiveBook.

Your ActiveBook is the perfect way to personalise your learning as you progress through your AS/A Level History course. You can:

• access your content online, anytime, anywhere

• use the inbuilt highlighting and annotation tools to personalise the content and make it really relevant to you.

Highlight tool – use this to pick out key terms or topics so you are ready and prepared for revision.

Annotations tool – use this to add your own notes, for example links to your wider reading, such as websites or other files. Or, make a note to remind yourself about work that you need to do.

*For new purchases only. If the access code has already been revealed, it may no longer be valid. If you have bought this textbook secondhand, the code may already have been used by the first owner of the book.

Introduction
AS/A Level History

WHY HISTORY MATTERS

History is about people and people are complex, fascinating, frustrating and a whole lot of other things besides. This is why history is probably the most comprehensive and certainly one of the most intriguing subjects there is. History can also be inspiring and alarming, heartening and disturbing, a story of progress and civilisation and of catastrophe and inhumanity.

History's importance goes beyond the subject's intrinsic interest and appeal. Our beliefs and actions, our cultures, institutions and ways of living, our languages and means of making sense of ourselves are all shaped by the past. If we want to fully understand ourselves now, and to understand our possible futures, we have no alternative but to think about history.

History is a discipline as well as a subject matter. Making sense of the past develops qualities of mind that are valuable to anyone who wants to seek the truth and think clearly and intelligently about the most interesting and challenging intellectual problem of all: other people. Learning history is learning a powerful way of knowing.

WHAT IS HISTORY?

History is a way of constructing knowledge about the world through research, interpretation, argument and debate.

Building historical knowledge involves identifying the traces of the past that exist in the present – in people's memories, in old documents, photographs and other remains, and in objects and artefacts ranging from bullets and lipsticks, to field systems and cities. Historians interrogate these traces and *ask questions* that transform traces into *sources of evidence* for knowledge claims about the past.

Historians aim to understand what happened in the past by *explaining why* things happened as they did. Explaining why involves trying to understand past people and their beliefs, intentions and actions. It also involves explaining the causes and evaluating the effects of large-scale changes in the past and exploring relationships between what people aimed to do, the contexts that shaped what was possible and the outcomes and consequences of actions.

Historians also aim to *understand change* in the past. People, states of affairs, ideas, movements and civilisations come into being in time, grow, develop, and ultimately decline and disappear. Historians aim to identify and compare change and continuity in the past, to measure the rate at which things change and to identify the types of change that take place. Change can be slow or sudden. It can also be understood as progressive or regressive – leading to the improvement or worsening of a situation or state of affairs. How things change and whether changes are changes for the better are two key issues that historians frequently debate.

Figure 1 Fragment of a black granite statue possibly portraying the Roman politician Mark Antony.

Debate is the essence of history. Historians write arguments to support their knowledge claims and historians argue with each other to test and evaluate interpretations of the past. Historical knowledge itself changes and develops. On the one hand, new sources of knowledge and new methods of research cause *historical interpretations* to change. On the other hand, the questions that historians ask change with time and new questions produce new answers. Although the past is dead and gone, the interpretation of the past has a past, present and future.

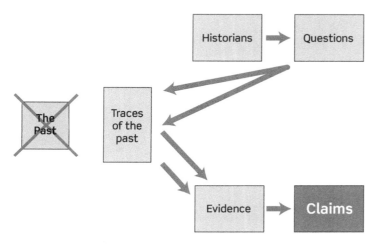

Figure 2 Constructing knowledge about the past.

THE CHALLENGES OF LEARNING HISTORY

Like all other Advanced Level subjects, A Level and AS Level history are difficult – that is why they are called 'advanced'. Your advanced level studies will build on knowledge and understanding of history that you developed at GCSE and at Key Stage 3 – ideas like 'historical sources', 'historical evidence' and 'cause', for example. You will need to do a lot of reading and writing to progress in history. Most importantly, you will need to do a lot of thinking, and thinking about your thinking. This book aims to support you in developing both your knowledge and your understanding.

History is challenging in many ways. On the one hand, it is challenging to build up the range and depth of knowledge that you need to understand the past at an advanced level. Learning about the past involves mastering new and unfamiliar concepts arising from the past itself (such as the Inquisition, Laudianism, *Volksgemeinschaft*) and building up levels of knowledge that are both detailed and well organised. This book covers the key content of the topics that you are studying for your examination and provides a number of features to help you build and organise what you know – for example, diagrams, timelines and definitions of key terms. You will need to help yourself too, of course, adding to your knowledge through further reading, building on the foundations provided by this book.

Another challenge is to develop understandings of the discipline of history. You will have to learn to think historically about evidence, cause, change and interpretations and also to write historically, in a way that develops clear and supported argument.

Historians think with evidence in ways that differ from how we often think in everyday life. In history, as Figure 2 shows, we cannot go and 'see for ourselves' because the past no longer exists. Neither can we normally rely on 'credible witnesses' to tell us 'the truth' about 'what happened'. People in the past did not write down 'the truth' for our benefit. They often had clear agendas when creating the traces that remain and, as often as not, did not themselves know 'the truth' about complex historical events.

A root of the word 'history' is the Latin word *historia*, one of whose meanings is 'enquiry' or 'finding out'. Learning history means learning to ask questions and interrogate traces, and then to reason about what the new knowledge you have gained means. This book draws on historical scholarship for its narrative and contents. It also draws on research on the nature of historical thinking and on the challenges that learning history can present for students. Throughout the book you will find 'Thinking Historically' activities designed to support the development of your thinking.

You will also find – as you would expect given the nature of history – that the book is full of questions. This book aims to help you build your understandings of the content, contexts and concepts that you will need to advance both your historical knowledge and your historical understanding, and to lay strong foundations for the future development of both.

QUOTES ABOUT HISTORY

'Historians are dangerous people. They are capable of upsetting everything. They must be directed.'

Nikita Khrushchev

'To be ignorant of what occurred before you were born is to remain forever a child. For what is the worth of human life, unless it is woven into the life of our ancestors by the records of history?'

Marcus Tullius Cicero

1 In search of the American Dream: the USA, c1917–96 – Introduction

THE AMERICAN DREAM

The historian James Truslow is usually credited with coining the term 'the American Dream', in his book *The Epic of America*, written in 1931. He said the Dream was of America as a country where life would be better, richer and fuller for everyone. The phrase was new, but the idea wasn't. The Pilgrim Fathers had sailed to America in search of religious freedom in 1620. The American colonies declared independence from Britain in 1776, stating that all men were created equal, with God-given rights that included 'life, liberty and the pursuit of happiness'. The pledge of allegiance, first used in US schools in 1896 and still used today, refers to 'one nation, under God, indivisible, with Liberty and Justice for all'.

The phrase 'the American Dream' was taken up by many people. Politicians, from presidents to city mayors, used the phrase when they wanted to promise people that they would protect their rights and freedoms and fight for equal opportunities, regardless of gender or race. The phrase was also used in songs, novels and advertising. People used it to win votes, inspire soldiers and sell cars. It was such a deeply ingrained idea that it must surely, as Source 1 suggests, have created 'the most decent nation on earth'.

SOURCE 1

A recruitment poster for the US military printed in 1942 during the Second World War. Notice the race and sex of the young people shown.

This is America...

... where every boy can dream of being President. Where free schools, free opportunity, free enterprise, have built the most decent nation on earth. A nation built upon the rights of all men ★ This is your America

... Keep it Free!

1917	**6 April:** USA enters First World War (ends 11 November 1918)
1919–20	First Red Scare; Summer race riots
1921	**19 May:** Emergency Quota Act restricts immigration and sets a numerical limit on entry
1933	**4 March:** Inauguration of President Roosevelt; Start of New Deal
1941	**7 December:** Japanese attack US fleet at Pearl Harbor; **8 December:** USA declares war on Japan; **11 December:** Germany declares war on USA
1946	**5 March:** Ex-British prime minister (Winston Churchill) speaks in the USA on the 'iron curtain' separating communist countries and democratic ones; **5 December:** Truman's President's Committee on Civil Rights is set up
1950–53	Korean War
1954–75	War begins in Vietnam between South Vietnam and the communist North
1963	**10 June:** Equal Pay Act
1965	**6 August:** Voting Rights Act; later extended to cover more minority groups including Hispanics and Native Americans
1972	**22 March:** Equal Rights Act is passed; not ratified by enough states
1981	**29 January:** Fuel prices are deregulated and wage and price regulations are removed; **13 August:** Economic Recovery Tax Act (ERTA) and Omnibus Budget Reconciliation Act (ORA) are passed
1986	**22 October:** Tax Reform Act is passed

1919	**January:** 18th Amendment to the Constitution introduces Prohibition
1920	**18 August:** US women get the vote
1929	**October:** Wall Street Crash, which kick-starts the Great Depression
1939	**September:** Outbreak of Second World War (ends in Europe 8 May 1945); women into war work
1945	**August:** USA drops atom bombs on Hiroshima (6 August) and Nagasaki (9 August); end of war in the Pacific
1947	**12 March:** Truman explains his Truman Doctrine Second Red Scare begins
1954	**17 May:** *Brown v Board of Education* decision to desegregate schools
1955	**5 December:** Montgomery Bus Boycott begins (ends 21 December 1956)
1964	**2 July:** Civil Rights Act; includes sexual equality
1969	**20 July:** US astronauts land on the moon
1977	**4 November:** Hostages are taken at US embassy in Tehran
1982	**15 October:** Savings and Loan institutions are deregulated (government bailout 1987)

The reality was different. Ideas of liberty, freedom and justice were all very well, but for whom? Abraham Lincoln made much of humble origins and regularly said 'anyone' could be president, if they worked hard and had the right opportunities. Yet it was 2009 before the USA had a non-white president and it has not yet elected a woman to the presidency. A person's best chance of attaining liberty, equality and justice was to be a white, educated man. Throughout the period 1917–96, opportunities, of all kinds, were weighted in favour of **WASP**s, especially the men. Minority groups had a long, hard fight for legislation to make their rights clear – let alone the enforcement of this legislation.

The search for the American Dream was not just a search for equal rights. It was a search for a better way of life. The ups and downs of the economy and the political and social issues that came to the boil at various times were all obstacles to Americans achieving a better way of life. Throughout the 20th century there were technological innovations that changed the way people lived, from the way they travelled to the way they got their news, and changed their vision of the American Dream. These changes helped to bind the various states into one nation, but also made the issues that divided the nation, such as race, more evident. These changes also had a dramatic impact upon the politics of the nation. Looming over events of the period was a distrust of communist nations, especially the **Union of Soviet Socialist Republics (USSR)**. Despite a brief alliance during the Second World War, the divide between the capitalist/democratic countries of the West and the **communist/totalitarian** countries in the East created a **Cold War** that affected US government policy decisions, both internationally and within the USA.

KEY TERMS

WASP
White, Anglo-Saxon, Protestant.

Union of Soviet Socialist Republics (USSR)
Russia became a communist country after the 1917 revolution. In 1922 it began to call itself the USSR.

Communist
Political ideas of thinkers such as Karl Marx who want a revolution of the workers to overthrow a capitalist society based on individual wealth.

Totalitarian
A system of government where the government, seldom fairly elected, demands total obedience to the state.

Cold War
A time when two hostile sides try to defeat each other by political propaganda, economic restrictions and agreements, and military intervention in other wars, but not direct conflict between the countries concerned.

US PRESIDENTS, 1913-2001		
1913–21	Woodrow Wilson	Democrat
1921–23	Warren G. Harding	Republican
1923–29	Calvin Coolidge	Republican
1929–33	Herbert C. Hoover	Republican
1933–45	Franklin D. Roosevelt	Democrat
1945–53	Harry S. Truman	Democrat
1953–61	Dwight D. Eisenhower	Republican
1961–63	John F. Kennedy	Democrat
1963–69	Lyndon B. Johnson	Democrat
1969–74	Richard M. Nixon	Republican
1974–77	Gerald R. Ford	Republican
1977–81	Jimmy Carter	Democrat
1981–89	Ronald Reagan	Republican
1989–93	George H.W. Bush	Republican
1993–2001	Bill Clinton	Democrat

1.1 The changing political environment, 1917–80

KEY QUESTIONS

- How did the presidency change from 1917 to 1980?
- What influenced the political landscape between 1917 and 1980?
- What impact did war have on domestic politics in the years 1917–1980?

These themes will be looked at across each of three periods in turn: 1917–33, 1933–45 and 1945–80.

INTRODUCTION

The political environment of the USA changed significantly over the years 1917–80. The president's powers increased as society, its problems and ideas about dealing with those problems, changed. Various factors influenced the political landscape: changing ideas about the role of government in society, pressures put on government by wars and the reaction of Americans to government actions. To understand the changes, it is important to understand how the government, set up by the American Constitution in 1789, worked.

The system of government

The US government is a multi-level system: federal (the whole country), state and local (counties and cities/towns in each of the 50 states). Most officials are elected. The Constitution did not set up a party system: people voted for the candidate whose views they preferred. In practice, however, a two-party system emerged: **Republicans** and **Democrats**. Most representatives, especially at federal level, belong to one of these parties. The Constitution sets down what the federal government can pass laws on, and what it can't. It lays down the federal laws that states have to obey. It also makes it clear that the Supreme Court has the final say in interpreting laws and whether federal or state lawmakers have broken the rules of the Constitution.

At each level of government, the '**separation of powers**' system is in place. The tensions over federal and state law-making in 1917–80 were especially strong in the area of equality – with some states resisting federal legislation that gave certain groups political, social or economic equality. Problems over state and federal ruling on segregation (see Chapter 2), for instance, underline the yawning gap between the making of a law, enforcing it and the law actually working for the people it is trying to help.

The president is head of the executive arm of government, head of state and commander-in-chief of the army. In the UK, the prime minister is the leader of the party with the most votes in the House of Commons. In the USA, presidential elections are held separately from Congressional elections to preserve the separation of powers. Voters vote for electors in each state and these electors (the Electoral College) elect the president. Presidents have to balance the needs of both parties in **Congress** (the legislative arm), so they agree legislation. This can be difficult when the president comes from one party, while either house in Congress is dominated by the other party. Opponents will want to oppose the president rather than work with him, or, at best, not seem to be agreeing to everything he wants.

1941
7 December Japanese attack US fleet at Pearl Harbor
8 December USA declares war on Japan
11 December Germany declares war on the

1918
11 November First World War ends

1929
October The Wall Street Crash kick-starts the Great Depression

| 1915 | 1920 | 1925 | 1930 | 1935 | 1940 | 1945 |

1917
6 April USA enters the First World War
October Russia becomes communist

1919–20
First Red Scare
18 January 1919
Amendment to the Constitution introduces Prohibition

1939
September Outbreak of Second World War in Europe

1945
8 May Second World W ends in Europe
August USA drops atc bombs on Hiroshima a Nagasaki; the war in th Pacific ends

The political environment

How the government deals with, or fails to deal with, social, economic and political problems affects the response of the American people to that government as, time after time, a significant number of its citizens fail to achieve the American Dream. The success of government depends on the relationship between the president and **Congress**; the relationship between the president and the media; the effect of internal influences (e.g. changing ideas about welfare provision) and the effect of external influences (e.g. wars).

KEY TERM

Congress
The law-making body of the USA (see Figure 1.1). It has two elected bodies, the Senate and the House of Representatives, that both have to agree laws before they become active. The president can veto any laws agreed by Congress.

FEDERAL GOVERNMENT

Legislature
Law-making body

CONGRESS

Senate — House of Representatives

Senate and House of Representatives can both pass laws, but each law has to be passed by both houses. The president can veto their laws with the agreement of two-thirds of Congress. Congress must agree taxation and going to war. Senate can veto presidential appointments.

Executive
Carries out laws

PRESIDENT

Cabinet — Vice president — Armed forces

The president is head of state, so leads foreign policy, and head of the executive. In emergencies, he can issue Executive Orders (laws not confirmed by Congress) but the Supreme Court can override them.

Judiciary
Applies and interprets laws

The Supreme Court can declare any laws illegal if it thinks they break the rules of the Constitution.

SUPREME COURT

Court of appeals

Supreme Court judges are appointed by the president and confirmed by Congress.

District courts

STATE GOVERNMENT

Legislature
Law-making body

Name varies by state: e.g. legislature, general assembly

Usually 'Senate' — Usually 'House of Representatives'

Law-making and the governor's veto follow the same pattern as the federal legislature above. State legislature can affect international policy (e.g. war) or federal taxes.

Executive
Carries out laws

GOVERNOR

Usually a lieutenant-governor — State National Guard

Judiciary
Applies and interprets laws

STATE SUPREME COURT

State court of appeals

Trial courts

LOCAL GOVERNMENT

Local government varies, reflecting the way that the original state government varied when each state was set up.

Each state is divided into counties, and these counties run their own local services (water, power, rubbish collection, etc.) and local officials have some power over local planning. Cities have their own municipal governments, as do some, but not all, towns.

Local officials get their powers from the state, but are elected by the people in their district.

Key
↑ is part of
↑ advises, reports to
↑ can be overruled by

Figure 1.1 How the US government works. Most officials (apart from Supreme Court judges) are elected.

1947–54
Second Red Scare

1957
4 October USSR first to put a satellite in space

1969
20 July US astronauts land on the moon

1950 — 1955 — 1960 — 1965 — 1970 — 1975

1950–53
Korean War

1962
First US troops into Vietnam

1975
Complete American withdrawal from Vietnam

IS THIS TOMORROW

HOW DID THE POLITICAL ENVIRONMENT CHANGE, 1917–33?

US PRESIDENTS, 1917–33		
1913–21	Woodrow Wilson	Democrat
1921–23	Warren G. Harding	Republican
1923–29	Calvin Coolidge	Republican
1929–33	Herbert C. Hoover	Republican

What impact did the First World War have?

Woodrow Wilson took the USA into the First World War in 1917 (despite campaigning to keep out of it), after several German attacks on US shipping and the discovery that Germany was sounding out Mexico as an ally against the USA. When the war ended, despite the boost it had given the US economy, many Americans felt that involvement in the war had been a mistake. They liked even less the way that President Wilson had tried to involve the USA even more closely in international affairs once the war was over.

The return to 'normalcy'

President Harding, who became president in 1921, promised the American people a return to 'normalcy'. What was 'normalcy'? While black soldiers might have been hoping for greater equality, many WASPs understood 'normalcy' to be a return to things as they had been before the war; this probably looked attractive to many Americans. Between the end of the war and 1921, when Harding took power, there had been a short, sharp economic depression, caused, in part, by the end of the war. Unemployment rose from 950,000 in 1919 to 5,010,000 in 1921. There was a lot of social discontent: protests, strikes and riots. Returning to pre-war life would mean removing these problems. Harding himself defined 'normalcy' as a stable, steady way of life. He didn't want to turn the clock back; he just wanted to shift the focus back to the USA again. He said that the government had to do several things straight away: balance the government's books; reduce taxation on the American people (set high for the war); introduce **tariffs** to protect US trade and industry; provide countrywide radio – this last move as a boost to US industry and as a method of communication. He also said there should be a committee set up to study 'the race question' and how best to solve it, as well as looking after the least well off, possibly through a Department of Public Welfare to direct state efforts.

Isolationism

Harding expressed many people's views after the war when he said the USA should be supportive of other nations, but not become 'entangled' with them. The USA had to focus on itself – 'buy American' became a significant watchword. Isolationism had supporters, and opponents, among both Republicans and Democrats. It meant introducing trade tariffs that favoured US businesses; not joining the **League of Nations**; not setting up colonies. Isolationism also meant cutting back on the numbers of immigrants coming into the country. The 1921 Emergency Quota Act restricted immigration to 357,000 a year. This was revised to 150,000 a year in 1924, with quotas within this of immigrants from different countries. Between 1935 and 1939, Congress also passed a series of Neutrality Acts that restricted the help the USA could give to other countries if they went to war. The USA was not entirely isolationist. It helped Europe rebuild economically and brokered the Washington Conference of 1921–22, which set limits on national navies. It is possible that, without the **Great Depression** of 1929, the USA would have become more internationalist; the Depression forced many people to focus on the problems in their own countries instead of looking outwards.

Tariffs on imports, such as the Fordney–McCumber Tariff Act, did encourage people to 'buy American'. As parts of the economy prospered, so did consumerism. New technology produced consumer goods far more cheaply; **hire purchase** allowed people to buy these goods over a period of time. All this contributed to a 'boom' period that suggested that Republican policies were working.

KEY TERMS

Tariffs
Taxes put on goods going into, or out of, a country to encourage or discourage trading abroad.

The League of Nations
An organisation formed at the end of the First World War, set up for international co-operation and to help its member states to settle their differences peacefully, rather than by going to war. Member states had to agree not to go to war over issues, but to resolve them with the help of the League.

The Great Depression
The economic collapse that hit the USA in 1929.

Hire purchase
Buying goods on credit: taking them at once but paying for them in regular instalments over a set period of time.

ACTIVITY
KNOWLEDGE CHECK

The First World War
1 Write a short paragraph defining 'normalcy'.

2 List three important components of isolationism.

How did the presidency change?

Woodrow Wilson, who took the USA into the First World War in 1917, was only the second Democrat to become president since the **Civil War**. However, many people quickly came to feel that he took far too big a part in government decision-making. He took America into the war despite campaigning to keep out of it and didn't consult Congress about promoting the League of Nations. Wilson also believed that presidents should be involved in law-making. He drafted bills and introduced them to Congress himself. The leader of the Democrats in the House of Representatives was seen as speaking for the president and expected the House to fall in line with Wilson's wishes. For many politicians, this was an unwelcome change in presidential behaviour and came close to breaking the separation of powers principle.

The appeal of Republicanism

Reaction to Wilson's behaviour as president, and to the First World War and its effects, led people to turn to Republican ideals. Even some Southern Democrats (who saw the Republicans as the party of their Civil War enemies) responded in this way. Wilson was replaced as president by Harding, whose slogan was 'Less government in business and more business in government'. This encapsulated the Republican notion of *laissez-faire*: it was not the job of government to control the economy or to manage social problems. The government's job was to keep its own spending under control, rather than spending to help those who were failing. It also fixed the Republican Party as the party of big business – not willing to control wages, working hours or prices. Harding's campaign aims were nicely vague; he looked as if he would be a president who didn't interfere. He didn't. He did not try to draft laws, nor did he try to drag the USA into international politics. Unfortunately, Harding, while not himself corrupt, gave jobs to friends who were. Several of them exploited their positions to make money, making the administration look corrupt.

A Democrat might have been elected after Harding, but the Democrats could not agree on a candidate. The Republican candidate, Calvin Coolidge (who had been Harding's vice-president), combined *laissez-faire* with a dignity and morality that Republicans hoped would restore faith in their party after the Harding years. He let Congress go its own way – when a new Democrat congressman asked how to vote in the Senate, Coolidge told him to ask the leader of the Democrats there. During Coolidge's presidency, the USA entered a period of recovery and prosperity; people began to feel Republicanism was working. The 'boom' economy of the 1920s had serious flaws, but they were not clear at the time. Only with hindsight can we appreciate how much of a problem they were. However, by the time the next Republican president, Herbert Hoover, took over, it was clear to many people that the USA had growing economic and social problems. Despite this, Hoover's election campaign announced that the Republicans had eliminated poverty, encouraged equality and restored the economy, while the Democrats would ruin all of this.

> **AS Exam-Style Question Section A**
>
> Were Republican ideas the main reason for the fact that there was a Republican president and a Republican majority in Congress in the years 1921–31? (20 marks)
>
> **Tip**
> *Consider the alternatives to the Republicans and reactions, other than approval of Republican ideas, that might lead people to vote Republican.*

KEY TERMS

American Civil War, 1861–65
Fought between the Northern states (Yankees) and the Southern states (Rebs), over the issues of slavery and whether to become one nation or continue as separate states. The Southern states wanted to stay separate and continue slavery.

Laissez-faire
French for 'leave well alone', this policy meant minimal government interference: for example, not regulating businesses and not providing welfare for the poor.

ACTIVITIES
KNOWLEDGE CHECK

Changes to the presidency
List the essential differences between Woodrow Wilson and the Republican presidents who followed him.

What influenced the political landscape?

The First Red Scare, 1919–20

From 1905 to 1917, Russia went through a series of revolutions. The monarchy was toppled and replaced by a communist government in 1917 (the Soviet Union or USSR). The revolutions sent shockwaves round the world; particularly as communism encouraged worldwide revolution by the workers against their capitalist masters. This made many people in the capitalist USA very disturbed, especially when workers went on strike in large numbers.

KEY TERM

Anarchist
A person who believes in overthrowing established governments and letting people run their own lives without a formal government.

During the First World War, workers in the USA had not gone on strike over wages, hours or working conditions. When their conditions did not improve post-war, the workers began to strike. The Communist Party of America (CPUSA) was founded, as was the Communist Labor Party of America (CLP). **Anarchists** distributed pamphlets in many cities, urging revolution. In 1919, there were more than 3,600 strikes, with one in four workers (about four million people) on strike. On 21 January 1919, 35,000 shipyard workers went on strike in Seattle. On 6 February, this escalated to a general strike of 60,000. Police and strikers did not clash, but rumours of a communist revolution spread. The strikes (and the supposed communist takeover) became national news. People began to accuse each other of communism; 'Red hunting' began to break out.

EVENTS LEADING UP TO THE FIRST RED SCARE

February 1919
Mayor of Seattle says he will use the city police force, and federal troops if necessary, to break the shipyard strike

11 February 1919
The strike leaders call off the Seattle strike

28 April 1919
The US post office discovers 36 bombs addressed to various state officials

1 May 1919
Workers' rallies across the country; riots in several cities, including Boston and New York

8 May 1919
American Legion founded, as an organisation for veterans of the First World War. However, some of its members also carry out 'Red hunting'. By the end of the year, it has over a million members

2 June 1919
Bombs explode in eight cities; public officials targeted, including the new Attorney General (head of the Judiciary), A. Mitchell Palmer

1 August 1919
New 'Radical Division' set up by Palmer to seek out communist conspiracies. It collects names of 'dangerous' people

9 September 1919
Bombs explode in various cities, said to be planted by 'red' groups. Boston police go on strike. Very little actual violence, but the media spread tales of huge riots and federal troops shooting rioters. Four days later, all the police are sacked and a new police force is appointed by the governor of Massachusetts, Calvin Coolidge

22 September 1919
Pittsburgh steel workers go on strike; strike spreads across the country to become nationwide. Violence erupts in various parts of the country between strikers and local militia

January 1920
Steelworkers' strike ends with no gain for the strikers. The country is now full of anti-communist feeling

FBI raids in 33 cities, somewhere between 5,000 and 10,000 arrests of 'communists' made

Anti-communist feeling escalated. Some businesses sacked employees they suspected of left-wing views. People began to suspect their neighbours. People also began to worry about being suspected of communism. They no longer felt free to express their opinions, if these opinions were left-wing. In some parts of the country, there was considerable violence, especially from groups such as the **Ku Klux Klan**, which targeted all groups they considered 'Un-American'. Of the thousands of people arrested as suspicious, only 556 were deported once their cases were considered. Attorney General Palmer's prediction of a 'Red revolution' on 1 May 1920 failed to occur. The government, the media and most people began to react to communism in a more balanced way. However, anti-communist feeling never went away.

Rugged individualism

Herbert Hoover gave the Republican *laissez-faire* policy a spin that dwelt less on inaction and more on allowing people to take responsibility for themselves. This was a shift in emphasis, rather than a change of direction, for the presidency. In *American Individualism*, a pamphlet he wrote in 1922, Hoover outlined the ideas he would bring to his presidency. By his election campaign of 1928, he had developed this into the theory of 'rugged individualism', where people who could look after themselves would make their own way in the world and prosper, realising the American Dream.

Those who believed in rugged individualism felt that:

- people, even the poor and homeless, were weakened by government support, because it sapped their self-reliance. The government should not interfere to help those with jobs and homes, either. It should not regulate working hours, pay or working conditions, or fix the bank interest on mortgages and other loans. Businesses had to be free to run themselves, even if they exploited the workforce.

- the USA should isolate itself from other countries.

- the USA should restrict immigration. When the USA had needed workers, immigrants had been encouraged to think that they could come to the USA to realise dreams of equality and freedom. At the end of the war, with rising unemployment, unlimited immigration made things worse. Most immigrants were moving to improve their lives, not, in the main, to bring wealth into the country.

The Great Depression

In 1929, the underlying problems with the 'boom' combined with out-of-control share trading to produce the **Wall Street Crash**. This triggered the Great Depression that hit the USA, then the rest of the world, very hard. Unemployment soared, people lost their homes, banks and businesses failed. While we can see, with hindsight, how bad the Depression would get, and how long it would last, most people at the time thought it would improve far sooner than it did. There had been a depression immediately after the First World War that had lasted for just 18 months, so Republicans favoured leaving the economy to sort itself out; Hoover began following this policy.

SOURCE

From *American Individualism*, written by Herbert Hoover in 1922.

Our American individualism has received much of its character from our contacts with the forces of nature on a new continent. It evolved government without official emissaries to show the way; it plowed and sowed two score of great states; it built roads, bridges, railways, cities; it carried forward every attribute of high civilization over a continent. The days of the pioneer are not over. There are continents of human welfare of which we have penetrated only the coastal plain. The great continent of science is as yet explored only on its borders, and it is only the pioneer who will penetrate the frontier in the quest for new worlds to conquer. The very genius of our institutions has been given to them by the pioneer spirit. Our individualism is rooted in our very nature. It is based on conviction born of experience. Equal opportunity, the demand for a fair chance, became the formula of American individualism because it is the method of American achievement.

EXTEND YOUR KNOWLEDGE

The problems with the boom
The boom was based, to a large degree, on credit. Banks were lending too much money and people and businesses were borrowing too much. The situation was made worse because a significant number of people were also buying shares on the stock market on credit.

Meanwhile, slowly but steadily, the prices of farm produce were falling. This put the farmers who had borrowed money (and many had, either to buy their farms or to buy equipment and supplies) in a difficult situation. When they produced more, in order to cover their debts, prices fell still further. At this point, whatever the farmers did, they made their situation worse. They either borrowed more, to cover the drop in prices, or grew more, to try to make more money.

Finally, there was the fact that much of the buying of the boom period was of consumer goods, such as radios and fridges. When, eventually, those who could afford to buy these things had them, the goods began to pile up in warehouses, and businesses began to cut down their workforce, leading to a rise in unemployment.

The decline of Republicanism

In 1929, following the Wall Street Crash, Hoover persuaded Congress to set up the Federal Farm Board to help farmers who found it hard to sell their goods abroad because of government isolationist tariffs, but that was seen as a special case. Hoover did come to realise that *lassez-faire* wasn't working. However, he believed the answer was for private charities, set up by businesses and the wealthy, to offer help on a local, personal level. He felt that the most government should do was to encourage people to do this. In 1930, Hoover set up the President's Emergency Committee for Employment, a temporary organisation to find work projects for the unemployed and to persuade businesses to create more jobs on a local, voluntary, basis. It was overwhelmed. He encouraged businessmen to invest in the economy by setting up similar organisations. In the end, he realised that federal intervention was needed. Between 1930 and the presidential elections in 1932, Hoover moved from encouraging private help to giving federal help to the states, first advising them on projects and then giving them money to fund at least some of the help. When this, too, fell far short of what was needed, he reluctantly asked Congress to pass laws to give direct federal help. This was a significant and, to many people in Congress and the country, unwelcome change of direction. Indeed, Hoover tried to put through more federal measures, many of which Congress rejected. Even those he did get passed took the government into debt, rather than keeping the government debt down, as he was expected to do. In the last year of his presidency, the government received $2,000 million and spent over $5,000 million, but it was too little, too late. And, despite his attempts to change government thinking on welfare provision, Hoover was the person whom many people blamed for the economic crisis. They even named the huge shanty towns of homeless people that sprang up around many cities 'Hoovervilles' after him.

HOOVER'S LEGISLATION

1929
Agricultural Marketing Act sets up a Federal Farm Board that could buy up key crops to stabilise prices

June 1930
Hawley–Smoot Tariff Act increases existing tariffs on foreign imports

January 1932
Reconstruction Finance Corporation (RFC) set up with $300 million to lend to states for relief projects

1930
Committee for Unemployment Relief (to co-ordinate, and advise on, state efforts for the unemployed) and President's Emergency Committee for Employment set up

1931
National Credit Corporation (NCC) funded by healthy banks and businesses to help failing ones; it starts with a budget of $500 million; by the end of the year, the NCC has lent just $10 million

July 1932
RFC lending can also be given to farmers and public works can be set up

Federal Home Loan Bank Act has a federal fund to lend money to people in trouble with their mortgages

SOURCE 2

This photo of a Hooverville in Seattle, Washington state, was taken in 1934. It was set up in 1931 and remained there for ten years. At its biggest, it covered nine acres and held over 1,000 residents.

The Bonus Army

In 1924, the US government gave those who had fought in the First World War a bonus payment calculated on their years of service. They paid veterans who were owed just $50 at once. The rest of the money went into a fund to pay out in 1945. As the Depression bit, many veterans asked for their money early. The government refused. Many veterans who wanted their bonuses were unemployed, some were homeless. In June 1932, they marched to Washington to make their demands in person. Estimates of their numbers range from 150,000 to 200,000 and they camped on various sites around the city – including within sight of the White House. There were fears of riots. The police tried to break up the camps, with little success and some violence on both sides. On 28 July, troops were sent in with tear gas, bayonets, cavalry, and even tanks and machine guns (although only the tear gas and bayonets were used). The camps were dispersed and a report published later suggested that many of those in the camps were communist agitators and criminals, in an attempt to make the incident seem less blameworthy. Despite the fact that he had urged the commander of the 12th Infantry to use restraint, Hoover lost a significant amount of popularity as a result of the way the Bonus Army was treated.

SOURCE 3

Studs Terkel, a radio broadcaster and author, wrote *Hard Times,* a collection of interviews about the Great Depression, in 1970. This extract comes from an interview with A. Everette MacIntyre, a government official, who saw US troops attack the Bonus Marchers in 1932.

The 12th Infantry were in full battle dress. Each had a gas mask and his belt was full of tear gas bombs. They were given a 'right face', which caused them to face the camp. They fixed their bayonets and also fixed the gas masks over their faces. At orders, they brought their bayonets at thrust and moved in. The bayonets were used to jab people to make them move. Soon, almost everybody disappeared from view, because tear gas bombs exploded. The entire block was covered by tear gas. Flames were coming up, where the soldiers had set fire to the buildings to drive these people out.

SOURCE 4

From a government report, prepared for President Hoover, on the attack on the Bonus Marchers in 1932.

There is no difference of opinion about the fact that the presence of troops was necessary to and did prevent further disorder and bloodshed. In their absence, further rioting would have occurred with further bloodshed among bonus marchers and police, and possibly innocent bystanders.

The troops arrived and, with the use of practically no weapons except tear gas, restored order and cleared the area and put an end to the disturbance.

5. Casualties.

Two bonus marchers were killed in the disturbance. They were shot by police in self defense, not by troops. A full investigation by a coroner's jury established that the police shot in necessary self defense to save themselves from threatened fatal injury. After the troops arrived, no serious injuries to anyone followed. A few of the troops were stoned and slightly injured, and one bonus marcher had his ear cut, but no other casualties were suffered after the troops came.

A changing mood

The Congress that met for the last two years of Hoover's presidency was a sign of things to come. Since 1921, the Republicans had had a majority in both Houses of Congress. But, as they failed to cure the problems of the Depression, people began to vote Democrat. In 1931, the Democrats were in the majority in the House of Representatives, and gaining seats in the Senate. Also, Hoover was increasingly unpopular with voters. In 1928, he had campaigned under the slogan of 'a chicken in every pot' – even stating that the Republican Party was the poor man's party. It was now clear to almost everyone that they weren't. He was also becoming unpopular with some Republicans, who disliked the steps he was trying to take to end the Depression, as a break from the principles of rugged individualism. Despite this, Hoover still won the Republican nomination, as there was no opposition candidate who seemed any better.

In the 1932 presidential campaign, Hoover's Democratic opponent, Franklin D. Roosevelt, offered the American people a 'New Deal' and a new attitude to government. His election campaign song was 'Happy Days Are Here Again' and, not only was he an excellent communicator, he had also been an effective Governor of New York. Roosevelt's snappy campaign pointed to Hoover's Republican campaign as being led by the new Four Horsemen of the Apocalypse: 'Destruction, Despair, Delay and Doubt'. Hoover's speeches had none of the vitality of Roosevelt's and his claims that the Depression would have been still worse without his government's measures did not gain him much support. In the election that followed, Hoover only won six states. More than 40 million voters went to vote – the largest number ever recorded in American history.

With Roosevelt as president, the Republican Party unravelled even more. Republicans were so busy contesting a stream of legislation introduced by the Roosevelt administration that they weren't able to plan their own policies to make themselves seem a viable alternative government. In the 1936 presidential election, they won only two states.

THINKING HISTORICALLY Evidence (4a-b)

Evidence in context

Study Sources 3 and 4. These sources could be used by the historian to build up a picture of the breaking up of the Bonus Army on 28 June 1932.

1 Explain why Sources 3 and 4 offer two views of the breaking up of the Bonus Army camp. How might this affect their value as pieces of evidence appraising the event? Explain your answer.

Discuss the following in groups:

2 Suppose the historian had ten more accounts that agreed broadly with Source 3 and only four that agreed with Source 4. What would that tell them about the event?

3 How far should the balance of evidence play a role in constructing written history? What else must the historian consider about the evidence being used before drawing conclusions?

THINKING HISTORICALLY Causation (3c–d)

The complexity of causes

1 Work on your own or with a partner to identify as many causes of the decline of Republicanism as you can. Write each cause on a separate card or piece of paper.

2 Divide your cards into those that represent:

   a) the actions or intentions of people

   b) the beliefs held by people at the time

   c) the contextual factors (i.e. political, social or economic events)

   d) states of affairs (long- or short-term situations that developed in particular ways).

3 Focus on the intentions of some of the key people, or groups of people, in the run-up to the 1932 presidential election. For each person (e.g. Hoover, Roosevelt, the people), draw on your knowledge to fill in a table, identifying:

   a) their intentions

   b) the actions they took to achieve these

   c) the consequences of their actions (both intended and unintended)

   d) the extent to which their aims were achieved.

Make sure you use detail to back up your statements.

4 Discuss the following questions with a partner.

   a) Did the Republicans intend to alienate the voters?

   b) How important are people's intentions in explaining the decline of Republicanism?

AS Exam-Style Question Section A

How far do you agree that it was Hoover's policies that lost him the 1932 presidential election? (20 marks)

Tip

Consider the other factors, including those beyond Hoover's control and the impact of Roosevelt and his promises.

ACTIVITY
KNOWLEDGE CHECK

Rugged individualism

1 How was rugged individualism different from *laissez-faire* in the way it presented its central idea?

2 Prepare for a debate on whether rugged individualism is fair to those in need. You are to argue for rugged individualism being fair. Prepare your points, but also think of the points that could be used against you and decide on the best way to counter those arguments.

The First Red Scare

3 Draw a flow diagram to show how the following contributed to the First Red Scare: strikes, bombing, the creation of the Soviet Union, communist ideas.

EXTEND YOUR KNOWLEDGE

Voting for Franklin D. Roosevelt

The huge swing towards Roosevelt in the 1932 elections was, in many ways, a reaction to the attitudes of the candidates for the presidency, as well as their actions. Hoover was unfairly unpopular with many people. They said he hadn't acted to stop the Depression, whereas he had proposed federal intervention policies, many of which Congress had blocked (see page 16). They also blamed him for the attack on the Bonus Army (see page 17) whereas he had urged MacArthur, who was in charge of the 12th Infantry, to use restraint. However, it can't be denied that he disapproved of federal intervention and was reluctant to use it, whereas Roosevelt saw federal intervention as a tool to fix the economy. The election began the swing of black voters away from the Republican Party (which they had traditionally supported as the anti-slavery party) towards the Democrats.

HOW DID THE POLITICAL ENVIRONMENT CHANGE, 1933-45?

US PRESIDENT, 1933-45		
1933-45	Franklin D. Roosevelt	Democrat

What influenced the political landscape?

New Deal thinking

Roosevelt came to power promising a 'New Deal' for the American people, one where federal government, and the president, would do whatever it took to save the country from disaster. He asked Congress for special powers to deal with the economic situation, as if it was a war, and they granted him those powers. New Deal thinking was very different from rugged individualism. Hoover had tried, but failed, to balance the federal budget. Roosevelt promised he would balance the budget. However, once in power he put this promise aside. He saw providing government help as more important, even if that left the government in debt. New Deal thinking was also different in other ways.

Firstly, it insisted that the government was responsible for the welfare of the people, no matter what the principle of rugged individualism insisted. People needed help to get back on their feet. Then, they could manage for themselves again. This was not so different from Hoover's thinking by the end of his presidency. Certainly, the relief that New Deal agencies provided was the absolute minimum, and the tests people had to pass to qualify for relief were so demeaning that some people in need chose not to take them.

Secondly, and far more contentiously, New Deal thinking stressed the importance of rapid, national action. This meant federal government had to take over some policy-making that was, under the Constitution, the role of individual states. Roosevelt got Congress to accept this because his 'war' rhetoric suggested that this increase in federal powers, and the federal institutions set up to administer his policies, were only temporary. Also, some of his plans, such as the development of the Tennessee Valley (which covered seven states), could only happen with a federal agency co-ordinating activities in several states. A series of such agencies, called the 'Alphabet Agencies' after their abbreviated names, were set up.

- The National Recovery Administration (NRA) set up and enforced codes of practice for businesses, including setting working hours and a minimum wage. Businesses could choose not to join the NRA; however, the public were encouraged to support businesses that displayed the NRA symbol of a blue eagle in their windows.

- The Agricultural Adjustment Agency (AAA) regulated the major crops, such as wheat, cotton and milk. It bought up surplus crops and subsidised farmers to grow less of crops that were being overproduced.

- There were agencies to provide work and to help different sections of society. They provided their help on a state-by-state basis and, theoretically, states still had some control. But they were all accountable to the federal agencies that provided them with money.

The National Recovery Administration (NRA)
The NRA made many businessmen furious. It did what the previous, Republican, governments had directly avoided: it told businessmen what to do. While businesses could refuse to join the NRA, while it was running (1933-35) many people dealt with businesses in the NRA as much as they could. So businessmen felt that their businesses suffered either way - through NRA interference or through loss of custom. Find out more by searching online for: National Archives FDR fireside chats.

How did the presidency change?

Roosevelt was confident, charming and persuasive. He knew his own mind and was very pragmatic – he freely admitted he was prepared to work with anyone to get things done. He was a great communicator and determined to restore confidence to the American people. In his **inaugural speech**, on 4 March 1933, he laid down his policies for the first few months, assuring people that: 'the only thing we have to fear is fear itself'. He then said the Depression was crippling, but could be fought, and explained about the powers Congress had given him. Roosevelt understood how to manipulate Congress. He hadn't intended to pass huge amounts of legislation in his first hundred days, but the ease with which Congress accepted his first banking bill led him to keep going, pushing through laws on banking, taxation, economic help for farmers and home owners in difficulty, and unemployment.

KEY TERM

Inaugural speech
The first speech made by an incoming president. In this speech, the president is expected to outline the broad policy he hopes to follow while in office.

EXTRACT 1

From *Franklin D. Roosevelt and the New Deal*, by D.K. Adams, published in 1979.

Even before the 1932 [presidential] election the contrast between the attitudes of the administration in Washington and those of the New York State government in the person of Roosevelt were startling. The Governor, in calling for state aid to the unemployed in 1931, stated that such help should be given 'not as a matter of charity, but as a matter of social duty'. It seems impossible to avoid the conclusion that for Hoover, despite his compassion, the relationship between government and society was one in which the role of government should be minimal and remote from the individual citizen. Society was a collection of individuals who should help themselves and help each other. Roosevelt, on the other hand, was primarily interested in government, and in principles of government, for the sake of those governed. The state existed for the direct benefit of its citizens: principles should therefore be thrown out of the window whenever the situation demanded a change of policy.

ACTIVITY
KNOWLEDGE CHECK

Rugged individualism and New Deal ideas

1 Write a paragraph to explain how Source 1 (page 15) shows how Hoover's ideas about individualism related to the American Dream.

2 Do you think Hoover would agree or disagree with the interpretation of the differences between his policies and the New Deal presented in Extract 1?

Increasing the importance of the presidency

Roosevelt created a significant White House staff to make increased federal intervention in government work (Hoover had had just three assistants and some secretaries). He set up a separate Executive Office of the President, which had several departments to deal with the administration. Where Congress wasn't helpful, he used presidential executive orders, designed for use only in emergencies, to push laws through. Roosevelt was more concerned with general policy than detail; he did not understand economic theory very well, so some of his economic measures created inflation, while others had a deflationary effect; they cancelled each other out.

However, Roosevelt understood managing people. He instituted a series of radio broadcasts, known as 'fireside chats', in which he explained policies to people as if he was chatting to them in their front rooms. He was the first president to receive sackfulls of letters from ordinary people, both asking for help and thanking him for giving help. It wasn't just ordinary people he understood. He understood the power of the media and the need for their support. He not only used radio broadcasts and speeches, but also held 'off the record' press meetings twice a week with selected reporters at the White House. He told them what was going on and sometimes threw them an 'on the record' piece of information. These briefings meant that, while the press could not always quote him directly on policy, they all had the same understanding of what was going on and felt involved and on his side.

Roosevelt was elected for an unprecedented four terms (a term is four years; presidents traditionally served only two terms), so he was clearly hugely popular. However, he wasn't popular with everyone. Wealthy business people disliked his policies; Republicans disliked his enlarging of the powers of the president, as did some Democrats. During the 1940 presidential campaign, some opponents compared him to dictators such as Hitler, Mussolini and Stalin. From 1936, the Supreme Court, which initially accepted many of his federal agencies and laws that infringed state rights as temporary emergency measures, began to rule against them as unconstitutional. Both the NRA and the AAA were ruled as unconstitutional in 1937. This made things so difficult for Roosevelt that, in 1937, he proposed to increase the number of Supreme Court judges, in order to 'pack' the Court with his supporters. He proposed adding a new judge for every existing judge over 70 (six out of nine). This was such an extreme violation of the theory of 'separation of powers' that it shocked even his most ardent supporters, and he was forced to abandon it.

SOURCE 5

A cartoon from the *Richmond Times Despatch*, 8 January 1937.

Roosevelt's legacy

Roosevelt died in 1945. His successor, Harry Truman, inherited a presidency that was very different from the one that Roosevelt inherited from Hoover. The president was expected to be involved in the forming of policy and legislation. The White House had many more federal boards and committees, both to run the country as a traditional executive and also to discuss policy and draft laws. The White House was expected to tell the media, and the public, about policy. The government and the president were now seen as responsible for welfare throughout the country. Presidents who followed Roosevelt also presented welfare reform packages with names that deliberately referred to his New Deal, such as Truman's Fair Deal and Kennedy's New Frontier. Many people looked to the president to solve all their problems. He was credited when things went well and, when things went badly, there was a tendency to blame his advisors, not the president himself.

However, not everything had changed. The theory of separation of powers still held. The Supreme Court had upheld state rights against a great deal of federal legislation. The president did take part in policy and law-making, but (apart from Executive Orders) needed the agreement of Congress for them to become law. The personality of the president still affected how much he could do and how people reacted to what he did, as did the way the media presented the president and his ideas.

ACTIVITY
KNOWLEDGE CHECK

The role of president

1 Give three important ways in which Roosevelt changed the presidency and explain their importance.

Cartoons

2 Cartoons often give a particular view of a situation, and the date of a cartoon is therefore important. Study Source 5.

   a) Write a paragraph to explain the message of the cartoon.

   b) Is it reliable as evidence of how people at the time felt about Roosevelt?

   c) What more would you want to know about the cartoon before using it as evidence?

Support for Roosevelt

3 Prepare for a radio interview about Roosevelt as if you were a wealthy businessman who opposed the New Deal policies.

   a) List the main points you would want, as a businessman, to stress.

   b) List the other arguments you might use for support.

   c) List the arguments that could be used against you and how you would counter them.

What impact did the Second World War have?

The Second World War (1939–45), as much as New Deal policies, hauled the USA out of the Depression. Roosevelt was a wholehearted supporter of the Allies. However, he knew that reaction to the First World War meant that there were many people, politicians and ordinary citizens alike, who did not want to go to war in Europe. So, in a 'fireside chat' after the outbreak of war, he assured people that the USA would remain neutral. However, he did add that he could not ask every American to remain neutral. These both showed where his sympathies lay and implied to young American men, without openly saying so, that if they went to fight in Europe they were unlikely to be punished. (US Neutrality Acts said a citizen could lose their citizenship if they went to fight abroad.)

Without taking the USA into the war, Roosevelt geared the USA up for war production, technically to supply the Allies. Goods were supplied on a 'cash and carry' basis: Britain, where most war supplies went, did not get credit to buy the supplies. Providing war supplies on credit was forbidden by the US Neutrality Acts. War production boosted industry and farming, and led to a significant rise in employment, which grew as the war went on. Farmers grew more food and factories churned out increasing amounts of weapons and ammunition.

By June 1940, Europe had been overrun and Britain was fighting alone, depending on war supplies from the USA. In December 1940, Winston Churchill told Roosevelt that Britain could no longer pay for its war goods. Roosevelt knew that he was unlikely to get Congress to approve his overruling the Neutrality Acts to let Britain have the supplies on credit. Instead, he proposed a 'lend-lease' scheme, theoretically lending Britain the supplies, to be returned after the war. Congress accepted this and the Lend-Lease Act was passed in March 1941. By the end of the war, the value of lend-lease supplies was about $51 billion. Another scheme of Roosevelt's was the destroyers-for-bases deal, which allowed Roosevelt to give Britain 50 naval destroyers in return for the use of bases in British-held countries.

The USA entered the war on 8 December 1941, after the Japanese, allies of Germany, bombed the US fleet at Pearl Harbor in the Hawaiian Islands. After this, unemployment dropped steeply as men joined the armed services and women stepped in to take their place in farming and industry. Within a year of the outbreak of war, the USA had produced $47 billion worth of war goods. Industry profits rose from $17 million in 1940 to $28 million in 1943. The working week extended and wages rose. The war was good for the economy, but the human cost was high. Of over 16 million who went to fight, just over 400,000 died and nearly 600,000 were wounded or captured.

ACTIVITY
WRITING

The language of change

1 Which of the following phrases do you think best defines the New Deal? Make your choice and then write a justification of your choice. Choose from:

   a) a significant change of policy

   b) a distinct change of government

   c) a radical change of policy

   d) a long-term shift in government thinking

   e) a sudden change in voting behaviour.

ACTIVITY
KNOWLEDGE CHECK

The Second World War

1 List the steps by which Roosevelt led the USA into the Second World War.

2 List the three indicators that Roosevelt wanted to join the war that you think are most important, explaining the reasons for your choice.

HOW DID THE POLITICAL ENVIRONMENT CHANGE, 1945–80?

US PRESIDENTS, 1945–80		
1945–53	Harry S. Truman	Democrat
1953–61	Dwight D. Eisenhower	Republican
1961–63	John F. Kennedy	Democrat
1963–69	Lyndon B. Johnson	Democrat
1969–74	Richard M. Nixon	Republican
1974–77	Gerald R. Ford	Republican
1977–81	James Earl 'Jimmy' Carter	Democrat

How did presidential leadership styles change, 1945–72?

Defining presidential style

The years 1945–72 saw five very different presidents in the White House. Three were Democrats, two were Republicans. Their leadership styles were very different and affected by their personalities, as well as their politics. Figure 1.2 analyses their leadership styles in the following key areas:

- personality

- relations with the media

- communications with the public

- ability to organise/administrate

- ability to manage Congress and other political bodies.

EXTRACT

2 From *The Presidential Difference: Leadership Style from FDR to Barack Obama*, by Fred I. Greenstein, revised and published in 2009. It highlights the importance of the leadership styles of presidents when thinking about the changing political environment in the USA and the place of the president within it.

If some higher power set out to design a democracy in which the individual on top mattered, the results might well resemble the American political system. America's chief executives have placed their stamp on the nation's policies since the founding of the Republic [independence from Britain], but until the 1930s, Congress typically took the lead in policymaking, and the programs of the federal government were of modest importance for the nation and the world.

Then came the emergence of what is commonly called the modern presidency. Under the stimulus of the New Deal, World War II, and the entrepreneurial leadership of Franklin Delano Roosevelt, there was a vast expansion of the scope and influence of the federal government. Meanwhile the United States became a world and then a nuclear power, and the presidency underwent fundamental changes that increased the likelihood that the personal attributes distinguishing one White House incumbent from another will shape political outcomes.

The chief executive [the president] became the principal source of policy initiative, proposing much of the legislation considered by Congress. Presidents began to make an increasing amount of policy independent of the legislature, drawing on their sweeping administrative powers in an era of activist government and global leadership. The president became the most visible landmark in the political landscape, virtually standing for the federal government in the minds of many Americans.

A Level Exam-Style Question Section B

How far do you agree that the personality of the president was the most significant factor in the changes in the presidency in the years 1917–80? (20 marks)

Tip

Present evidence to show that the personality of the president mattered – but be careful to weigh that against other elements that affected the presidency.

PRESIDENTIAL STYLES

Harry S. Truman (1945–53)

Personality: not charismatic, not very confident; could be overwhelmed by the importance of the job and make mistakes under pressure – resulting in some people using the phrase 'to err is Truman'

Media: saw working with media as important; gave careful briefings with flipchart and pointer (economic policy); sometimes didn't explain enough (Korean War)

Public: didn't instantly appeal; didn't try to connect; didn't try to explain strategy (Korean War); set speeches wooden, in ad-lib speeches he sometimes made serious mistakes

Organisational ability: worked well with White House administration; didn't always choose the right people

Congress, etc.: worked less well with Congress, despite the fact that there was a Republican majority in Congress after 1946, they blocked many reforms he wanted; had fewer contacts and was less able to network and charm

Dwight D. Eisenhower (1953–61)

Personality: deliberately cultivated optimistic, friendly manner

Media: saw working with media as important; but often obscured or minimised a problem (the USSR being first into space; the missile gap issue)

Public: good public manner; accessible, used clear imagery in his speeches (explaining the knock-on effect of a communist takeover in terms of knocking over a line of dominoes)

Organisational ability: exceptional organisation: set up regular briefings and long-term planning sessions; had everyone concerned in to debate a decision

Congress, etc.: worked well with Congress, good at political bargaining and persuasion

John F. Kennedy (1961–63)

Personality: from a political family, understood the importance of charm; worked hard on speech-making style and self-presentation

Media: saw working with the media as important (learned names, had personal chats); used television really well ('presidential family' publicity)

Public: good public manner; accessible, attractive

Organisational ability: poor, advisors competed for attention, not working together; Robert Kennedy and Theodore Sorensen did much of the work and reported; abandoned Eisenhower's regular meetings for meetings as needed; didn't always consult the right people (Bay of Pigs disaster); less long-term planning

Congress, etc.: worked very well with Congress, good at political bargaining and persuasion; family connections a big help

Lyndon B. Johnson (1963–69)

Personality: had been in politics a while, understood the importance of winning people over; could change his style and opinions to get what he wanted

Media: not a natural with the media, but was careful to keep them informed

Public: patchy: could give good speeches (speech on voting rights) or stiff, awkward ones; best with smaller groups

Organisational ability: Kennedy's organisation didn't suit him, but he kept it; his own organisation was good (so blocked legislation before taking it to Congress)

Congress, etc.: worked very well with Congress, had political background, really understood how to use connections and persuade; good at creative thinking to make things happen (when school funding became a problem because of the issue of funding religious schools he had the funding go to the children)

Richard M. Nixon (1969–74)

Personality: clever, capable; but suspicious, hated people disagreeing with him; could make spur-of-the-moment decisions then backtrack

Media: distrusted the media, very bad at managing it (Watergate)

Public: not good with people; worked at it, but often seemed awkward and insincere

Organisational ability: reinstated the system of regular meetings and briefings with White House staff; but not good at taking advice

Congress, etc.: awkward with Congress due to his suspicious nature; did find it easy to manage Congress because he found it hard to make personal connections and persuade

Figure 1.2: Presidential styles, 1945–72.

KEY TERM

Korean War, 1950–53
A war that began when North Korea (supplied and advised by the USSR) invaded South Korea. The USA aided the South Koreans and communist China joined on the side of North Korea.

What influenced the political landscape?

The Second Red Scare, 1947–54

The Second Red Scare followed the Second World War. The USSR joined the USA and its allies towards the end of the war, having first fought with Germany against the Allies. Once the war ended, many Eastern European countries occupied by the USSR during the war emerged with Soviet governments, increasing fears of communist takeovers in other countries. The scare took place within the context of the Cold War and the **Korean War**.

SOURCE

The front cover of a 48-page anti-communist comic book distributed by the Catechetical Guild Educational Society of St Paul, Minnesota, USA (a right-wing church organisation) in 1947. It was reprinted, with several different covers; over four million copies were printed.

A climate of fear

The Second Red Scare had more basis than the first. The USSR was spying on the USA; it was especially keen to get hold of atomic weapons secrets. On 31 July 1948, government employee Elizabeth Bentley told **HUAC** she had been part of a Moscow-led spy ring and named other government employees involved in it. Three days later, Whittaker Chambers (also a government employee) told HUAC of more government employees involved with Moscow. Both accusers named people in important government jobs. The trials of Alger Hiss (1949; retrial 1950), who had been an advisor to Roosevelt, and the Rosenbergs (1951) were especially high-profile. The first Hiss trial resulted in a mistrial because the jury could not agree. He was found guilty in the re-trial. The Rosenbergs were found guilty. In both cases, the evidence was conflicting. In 1949, China became communist and the USSR held its first nuclear weapon test. While the 'loss' of China to communism was not something Truman could have stopped, members of the 'China Lobby' accused Truman of being responsible because he did not give enough support to Chiang Kai-Shek, the leader of the Chinese government, against the communist rebels. Truman had been advised not to give more support to Chiang, because his government was corrupt and the advisors thought the rebels just wanted change in China, not worldwide communism, as the Soviet Union wanted. When the communist Chinese helped the communist North Koreans during the Korean War, critics of Truman's China policy said this confirmed their fears. The media began to question whether the government was doing enough to fight communism and protect its citizens – a significant factor in the blowing up of the Second Red Scare, as in the first one in 1919–20.

EXTEND YOUR KNOWLEDGE

HUAC and Loyalty Boards

The House Un-American Activities Commission (HUAC) was set up in 1938 to investigate 'un-American' activities. It focused on communism. The Federal Bureau of Investigation (FBI) carried out the investigations; then suspects appeared before HUAC. Suspicion could be enough to lose someone their job. Suspects came from all walks of life: union leaders, teachers, even movie stars. In a famous case in 1947, ten directors, scriptwriters and other Hollywood workers took a stand. They refused to answer questions when called before HUAC. They were blacklisted (listed as suspect, and not to be employed) and never worked again. Many movie stars marched in protest to support them; hundreds of them were blacklisted too.

On 21 March 1947, President Truman used an executive order to set up Loyalty Boards to investigate the loyalty of government employees. Their activities ran alongside those of HUAC. Every government employee, or job applicant, was investigated by the FBI. If the FBI found 'reasonable grounds' to believe a person might be disloyal, they were either sacked or investigated further. Membership of any of a list of 'suspect' organisations could lead Loyalty Boards to dismiss people without further investigation.

KEY TERM

HUAC
House Un-American Activities Commission (HUAC), set up in 1938, made permanent in 1945, investigated people for all 'un-American' activities, but focused on 'communists'.

Joseph McCarthy: Between 1950 and 1954, Senator Joseph McCarthy headed the Second Red Scare. On 9 February 1950, he made an anti-communist speech to a Republican women's group, announcing he had the names of 205 known communists working in the State Department. When reporters asked to see the list (which he didn't have), he pretended to have left it on an aeroplane. He gathered some support for his assertion, but the next day he revised the number of communists to 57. When called to the Senate, he changed the number again, to 81. Despite this muddle of ill-substantiated facts, he had a lot of support; the Tydings Committee was set up to investigate his charges. In the months that followed, he led a series of investigations of suspect communists and his apparent conviction and use of speeches, interviews and television appearances carried many ordinary people along with him. In many parts of the country, vigilante groups of 'red baiters' hounded people at work and at home, often violently. On 14 July, the Tydings Committee issued a majority report (the Republicans would not sign it) saying McCarthy's accusations were a muddle of half-truths and lies. Even so, he remained powerful until he turned to investigating the army in 1953. These investigations were televised and some 20 million people watched them. His treatment of the interviewees was so unreasonable that he lost support, the Senate passed a vote of censure against him and the Red Scare died down.

Anti-communism, 1954–80: The Red Scares changed the political scene because they led to a significant curb on civil liberties. The FBI was given powers to investigate people and bring them to be questioned by Loyalty Boards or HUAC on very little evidence. It was allowed to open letters, tap phones and bug offices and homes. Its behaviour was moving towards that of the repressive communist regimes that the government condemned. At the height of both scares, people had their freedom of speech and freedom of expression severely limited by worries about what would happen if they expressed even vaguely liberal views. In the late 1950s, a third of librarians removed books such as the works of Karl Marx from their shelves, to avoid being accused of having communist sympathies for stocking them. When Nikita Khrushchev, leader of the USSR, visited the USA in 1959, he was met with large anti-communist demonstrations – one placard read 'THE ONLY GOOD COMMUNIST IS A DEAD COMMUNIST!' Anti-communism was one of the few policies that united many Republicans and Democrats; between 1953 and 1962, not one Senator publicly supported a softening of attitude to the USSR or China. Various groups were set up from the 1950s to press the government to take a hard line in relations with communist countries. One of the most powerful of these was the Committee on the Present Danger, first set up in 1950. It was reformed in 1976 and had many powerful government advisors as members.

EXTRACT 3

From *The USA and the Cold War*, by Oliver Edwards, published in 1997.

The 'Red Scare' was irrational, in that it targeted an enemy which did not really exist. In the mid-1950s membership of the CPUSA [American Communist Party] stood at only 5,000, many of whom were FBI infiltrators. Communism had never commanded much support in the United States. A survey at the height of the 'Red Scare' in 1954 found that only 10 per cent of Americans had known people they even suspected of being a communist. McCarthy also lacked mass public support. Only once, at the beginning of 1954, did more than 50 per cent of Americans say they backed him.

ACTIVITY
KNOWLEDGE CHECK

Attitudes to communism

1 Compile a list of the similarities and differences between the First and Second 'Red Scares'.

2 Read Extract 3 and think about Source 6. Write a paragraph to explain the impact of the scares on politics, referring to both the source and the opinions in the extract.

Liberalism

The Second Red Scare and increasing violence against black civil rights campaigners, especially in the **Deep South**, had made many people uneasy about the political climate in the USA. A new liberalism took off under President Kennedy. While campaigning for president, he discussed the meaning of 'liberal'. He said that, if it meant forward-thinking, flexible, concerned about the welfare of the people and willing to try to be less suspicious abroad, then he was very happy to be classed as one. Many other people felt the same way, both Democrats and Republicans. These were the values of the American Dream. Liberals were usually educated and middle class, or even wealthy. Their views might have got them into political trouble during the Red Scares. They supported equality, civil rights and social welfare. They believed that government intervention could improve things and were prepared to limit individual liberties to help those in need. Liberal politicians produced the idea of **positive discrimination** for what they defined as the 'five minorities': American Indians; Asians; Blacks; Hispanics; women. In this, they were following a move in public opinion. Support for liberal measures, including civil rights, equal opportunities and legalising abortion, all increased in the 1960s.

KEY TERMS

Deep South
There are different interpretations of this phrase, but most historians see it as those parts of the South mainly given over to cotton plantations and so heavily dependent on slave labour before the American Civil War of 1861–65: Georgia, Alabama, Mississippi, Louisiana and Tennessee. Some historians also include parts of Texas and Arkansas, but not the whole states.

Positive discrimination
Preferential treatment in employment, education, social welfare or other areas of life, given to minority groups that have suffered from discrimination in order to redress inequality.

Liberal politicians were more likely to align themselves with people who thought in a similar way than along party lines and they were happy to be involved in protests. In 1968, the Democratic National Convention met in Chicago to decide policy. They were divided about the war in **Vietnam**. There were anti-war protests in the parks outside the hall and the police moved in to break them up, violently, with tear gas and batons. The following day, Donald Peterson, one of the delegates, led a 2,000-strong march against police brutality, calling on young protesters to join in. The Civil Rights Act, the Voting Reform Act and President Johnson's Great Society welfare reforms could only have been passed by a Congress that was liberal-minded. This doesn't mean that all Americans felt this way. Civil rights campaigners and other campaigners for equality faced a great deal of violent opposition in the 1960s and 1970s.

KEY TERM

The Vietnam War, 1954–75
A war between the communist North Vietnam (supported by the USSR and communist China) and its non-communist neighbour, South Vietnam (supported by the USA).

Counter-culture

While liberal politicians were trying to change the face of politics from within, many young people were trying to remake society altogether: rejecting the values of their parents' generation and distrusting the political machine. They wanted to change society by changing the culture – if people began to live differently, then they would behave differently, without government telling them what to do. While these groups all wanted to change society, the society they wanted and the methods they used were vastly different. They often split and reformed as they argued out their ideological differences. Major movements were:

- **Hippies** wanted to loosen the tight family system and live in communal societies. They believed in peace and a simple way of life, rather than working hard within the system to earn money to buy more and more goods. Some smoked dope and took other mind-altering drugs, and many supported a wider sexual freedom than marriage gave. While they wanted to change society, they were prepared to live according to their beliefs separate from others, in communal groups. The most famous hippie gathering of the 1960s was the Woodstock Festival (15–18 August 1969). Just under 200,000 tickets were sold for this combination of music and alternative culture. Somewhere between 400,000 and 500,000 people came – roads leading to the site were closed because the traffic heading there was so heavy. The music was loud, there were drugs freely available and sexual freedom was expected. It summed up everything that opponents of the movement feared.

- **Radical student groups** wanted to change society in the USA to produce a more equal world, closer to their view of the American Dream. They wanted to change everything from the way their courses were organised to ending the war in Vietnam. One of these groups was Students for a Democratic Society (SDS), set up in 1960. SDS's Port Huron statement (1962) denounced conventional politics as having forgotten the principle that all men are created equal, and urged a return to equality.

The SDS rejected all forms of bigotry, including racism and anti-communism, and protested, often violently, against the war in Vietnam. It was the SDS that organised the first mass rally against the war in 1965. The Free Speech Movement was a radical group that led a campaign on the University of California campus at Berkeley in 1964. The group used sit-ins, peaceful protest and other tactics also used by the civil rights movement to push for free speech on campus. When a student was arrested for campaigning for the civil rights group CORE, students took over the main square. Protest escalated; during the two months it ran, over 700 students were arrested for sit-ins and other activities. While radical students were not always in the majority on university campuses, they were the most noticeable and so affected how many people reacted to all students. At first, they protested peacefully, drawing on the non-violent protest methods of the civil rights movement. When this had little effect, an increasing number resorted to violence, as did the police sent to control them. The violence spiralled out of control and, across the country, state National Guards were called in. On 4 May 1970, Ohio National Guardsmen shot four unarmed students and injured nine during a student protest at the invasion of Cambodia, during the Vietnam War. Small, extremely radical, student groups planted bombs at military targets. On 24 August 1970, a bomb was detonated outside an army research base in Madison, Wisconsin. It killed one researcher, injured four and caused $60 million of damage.

Conservative reaction

Many older Americans were bewildered by the counter-culture and the problems they saw it creating. It challenged family values; it rejected the consumer culture they embraced; it rejected the values of hard work and striving for success; it rejected traditional Christian religious values and patriotism. Many people who had not had the chance to go to university thought students were being ungrateful. When some students went even further and resorted to violence, it added to the feeling that liberal government wasn't working.

As the spiralling violence that accompanied protests showed little sign of dying down, many politicians, Republican and Democrat alike, began to campaign as the 'New Right' to restore law and order and traditional values. On 3 November 1969, Republican candidate Nixon campaigned for president on New Right policies, gaining support from many Americans, some of whom had previously voted Democrat, who found the campaign promise of uniting society appealing. There were also young people who, while they might have wanted more equality and more freedom, felt that they didn't want society to change as much as either the hippies or radical students did. From the late 1960s, religious groups, especially evangelical ones, held campus campaigns. Bill Bright was an evangelical preacher whose 1967 'Campus Crusade for Christ' went to campuses all over the USA, including the extremely radical Berkeley, California. During the 1970s, a religious right movement emerged that campaigned for a return to traditional family values, with a move away from 'liberal' policies such as abortion and contraception. Many of these groups also campaigned to keep laws against homosexuality and to remove from office people found to be homosexual.

ACTIVITY
KNOWLEDGE CHECK

Liberalism, counter-culture and conservative reaction

1 List three ways in which hippies were different from radical student groups; list three ways in which they were similar.

2 Which do you think was the most important conservative objection to the counter-culture of the 1960s and 1970s? Explain your answer.

What was the impact of the Second World War on domestic policy?

The Cold War begins

The Second World War led to more US involvement abroad, unlike the isolationism that followed the First World War. It was clear that world events had an impact on the USA, so it was important for it to become a leading world power in order to affect these events. The USA had rejected the League of Nations; it was a founding member of **the UN** in 1945.

KEY TERM

The UN
The United Nations, formed at the end of the Second World War. Member states of the UN agreed to solve any disputes peacefully with, if needed, help from the UN to resolve problems. The UN also had the power to call an army to intervene if members did go to war, or invade each other.

The USA and the USSR had fought together during the Second World War. But their ideological differences were always there; President Truman was very anti-communist and Stalin was very anti-capitalist. The ideological divide soon became a Cold War when countries that had been occupied by the USSR during the war set up communist governments. The two main powers were always the USA and the USSR; even when China became communist, it did not seem as great a threat to the USA as the USSR. On 12 March 1947, Truman told Congress that the USA represented one way of life and the USSR another: they were in competition. The USA needed a policy of 'containment': stopping communist influence spreading by helping countries that might otherwise end up in communist hands. This 'Truman Doctrine' was soon followed by the Marshall Plan – a system of aid to war-torn countries, to prevent their takeover by communist regimes. When the USSR blockaded Berlin in 1948, the USA broke the blockade by airlifting food into the city. In 1949, the USA was one of the member countries of NATO (the North Atlantic Treaty Organisation). One of the key points of this alliance was that members all agreed to respond to an attack on any one of them. The Cold War now drove all US foreign policy; it also had an impact on domestic politics.

LEADERS OF THE USSR, 1922–80	
1922–53	Joseph Stalin
1953–64	Nikita Khrushchev
1964–82	Leonid Brezhnev

SOURCE 7

Part of the speech President Truman made to Congress in 1947, asking it to grant economic aid to Greece and Turkey to avoid them taking communist aid.

The peoples of a number of countries of the world have recently had totalitarian regimes forced upon them against their will. The Government of the United States has made frequent protests against coercion and intimidation, in violation of the Yalta Agreement [1945] in Poland, Rumania, and Bulgaria. I must also state that in a number of other countries there have been similar developments.

At the present moment in world history nearly every nation must choose between alternative ways of life. The choice is too often not a free one. One way of life is based upon the will of the majority, and is distinguished by free institutions, representative government, free elections, guarantees of individual liberty, freedom of speech and religion, and freedom from political oppression. The second way of life is based upon the will of a minority forcibly imposed upon the majority. It relies upon terror and oppression, a controlled press and radio; fixed elections, and the suppression of personal freedoms.

I believe that it must be the policy of the United States to support free peoples who are resisting attempted subjugation by armed minorities or by outside pressures.

I believe that we must assist free peoples to work out their own destinies in their own way.

I believe that our help should be primarily through economic and financial aid which is essential to economic stability and orderly political processes.

Nuclear defence: Once it was clear that the USSR also had nuclear capability, the US government had to be seen to be preparing for a nuclear attack. In the early 1950s, the Federal Defense Administration was set up to organise evacuations and give out pamphlets with advice, such as wearing wide-brimmed hats to protect from the blinding light of nuclear explosion. Schools ran regular 'duck and cover' exercises, where children practised responding to a nuclear attack. The 1956 Interstate Act road network was designed for rapid evacuation of cities, but the federal/state legislative divide made a national system of defence difficult. The government advised, some states acted and people were expected to look out for themselves. In 1958, you could buy a fallout shelter for about $1,300; the average family income was $5,100 a year.

The arms race: Between June 1947 and June 1948, the US holdings of atomic bombs rose from 13 to 50. When the USSR also began to make atomic weapons, it started an arms race that cost both countries huge amounts of money and resulted in both sides stockpiling enough nuclear weapons to cause massive devastation if they were ever launched (MAD – Mutually Assured Destruction). The funding of the arms race became a political bone of contention whenever it came up for debate.

The armed services: The creation of a large, permanent military force affected the domestic economy. The military cost money to run, but it also provided jobs and was a major customer for many businesses, from food to fabric. The existence of this army, the arms race and the Cold War itself created not just a Democrat/Republican divide in politics, but also a 'hawks'/'doves' divide that crossed political boundaries.

EXTEND YOUR KNOWLEDGE

The space race
Without the Cold War, it is unlikely that Congress would have voted to spend money on space exploration, but many people felt the next war could be won from space. The country that 'controlled' space was likely to win. Also, in the war of 'hearts and minds' between East and West, it was important to show other countries you were better than the competition. The USSR scored a political win when it launched the first spacecraft, *Sputnik 1*, on 4 October 1957. In 1958, President Eisenhower set up the National Aeronautics and Space Administration (NASA) to explore space. The USA and the USSR also set up, secretly, space programmes to investigate waging war from space and spying using satellites. On 20 July 1969, the USA put the first man on the moon, scoring a huge propaganda victory at a cost of $25 billion.

ACTIVITY
KNOWLEDGE CHECK

The Cold War

1 Write a version of Truman's 1947 speech (Source 7), making the Truman Doctrine clear to a younger student.

2 Draw a diagram to show how the Cold War affected the powers of the president.

3 Read the paragraph 'The armed services' (previous column): what do you think the 'hawks'/'doves' divide was and why do you think it was an important split?

What was the impact of the Cold War on the presidency?

The growth of the USA as a Cold War power changed the position of the president in several ways:

- The power of the president to go to war or make treaties without Congress grew with the USA's involvement with NATO and the UN. The size and wealth of the USA made it a world power from the start. Its increasing nuclear weapons arsenal made it the only superpower that could stand against the USSR, which meant, in turn, that it felt committed to doing so.

- After the war, the 1947 National Security Act reorganised US military forces under a new Defense Department based at the Pentagon. The size of the armed forces was greatly enlarged after 1950 and, as commander-in-chief, the president could move forces around without the permission of Congress.

- The National Security Act also created the Central Intelligence Agency (CIA) and the National Security Council; both reported to the White House, not to Congress.

- The existence of nuclear weapons meant a nuclear war might begin without warning – the president had to have the power to react at once, and not wait to ask Congress for permission.

After the war, Truman, without consulting Congress, made treaties to place permanent US bases in other countries. He also ordered the Berlin Airlift in 1948 and went to war in Korea without Congress's consent. Later presidents also did this (Kennedy didn't tell Congress about the Bay of Pigs invasion of Cuba in 1961).

What was the impact of the Korean War (1950–53) on domestic policy?

On 25 June 1950, North Korea invaded South Korea, with the help of supplies and advisors (but not troops) from the USSR. From the start, Truman was concerned to fight a 'limited war', keeping the North Koreans in North Korea, rather than entering a full-scale war. The war was taking place in the context of the Second Red Scare, and he wanted to stop hysteria and calls for all-out war. In an early press conference, he stressed that it was not the USA going to war but the UN; a reporter asked if it was just a UN police action. Truman agreed; the phrase haunted him all through the war as he was criticised for not doing enough.

EXTEND YOUR KNOWLEDGE

The Korean War

The Korean War was a UN operation. The UN troops fighting with the South Koreans were from 16 countries – but most were American (260,000 US troops and never more than 35,000 from the other 15 countries). The war was led by an American. At the end of the war, the US death toll (in combat) was 33,629. The border between North and South Korea did not change.

General MacArthur

MacArthur was in charge of the war in Korea from the start, and, from the start, he had wanted a very different war from Truman. He criticised Truman's 'limited war' policy and advocated nuclear bombing of North Korea, and even China, both publicly and privately, at a time when members of an administration were expected to support that administration's policy, no matter what they personally thought. His views were used to support the Republican backlash. He didn't stop at criticism. He disobeyed orders, on several occasions, in ways that could have led to all-out war. For example, on 5 November 1950, he bombed the bridges over the River Yalu (despite orders not to bomb within five miles of the border) and then took troops to the river despite orders to halt.

Korea emphasised the way the Cold War shifted presidential attention away from domestic policy and towards international policy. All domestic policy had to go through Congress; presidents had more freedom to act alone in foreign affairs. Also, in the way the New Deal changed expectations about government involvement in social welfare, the Cold War led to an expectation that the USA should be involved in world affairs, as it was the only country capable of maintaining a balance of power with the USSR. The reins of domestic policy-making therefore began to shift back towards Congress.

As the Second World War ended, many Republicans were tired of being part of a co-operative Congress. They wanted to become a real opposition force again. They felt this even more when they lost seats in the 1949 elections. Truman lost some key Republican allies in Congress, and a combination of the Second Red Scare and the Korean War (and Truman's handling of it) gave the Republicans their opportunity. They were critical of government policy, and of Truman, at every opportunity; in the 1951 elections, they gained five seats in the Senate and 28 in the House of Representatives. It was the start of a move in the Republicans' favour. One criticism that the Korean War encouraged was the cost, to the USA, of the Cold War in general as well as the Korean War itself. Defence spending hit a peak at 14 percent of US **GNP**. Some of the money for this came from government borrowing; however, Truman's administration did raise taxes. Every US government since has had problems balancing the tax/borrowing contribution to the defence budget.

KEY TERM

GNP
The Gross National Product: the value of all the goods and services produced by the people in a country in a year, plus income from abroad.

What was the impact of the Korean War on the presidency?

The Korean War marked a shift in the way the media dealt with the presidency. The media began by promising Truman support, expecting the kind of access and information from the president that they had had under Roosevelt and during the Second World War. Truman made the mistake of holding back with the media, because he didn't want to inflame anti-communist feeling. The media, desperate for news, took their information from other sources, including the Republicans; they became more critical and even indulged in pure speculation. On 7 July 1950, headlines announced that the president wanted to increase troops (true), using the draft (not true), and was considering using the atomic bomb (not true).

In August 1950, Truman began television briefings; then he arranged for over 200 reporters to go to Korea. However, he found it hard to regain media support for 'limited war'. This made it hard to gain public support, as he was not a president who communicated well with the public. When he sacked General MacArthur, in April 1951, he had little support, even though MacArthur had openly criticised and disobeyed direct orders from Truman, his commander-in-chief. Truman came under pressure from both Republicans and Democrats to scale up the war in Korea, to help nationalists in Taiwan to fight the Chinese and to take a harder line on communism everywhere. When the issues with the USSR needed peaceful resolution to avoid a world war, his opponents said this didn't sound like the Truman Doctrine – even though the Truman Doctrine had stressed economic and financial aid, not fighting. Congress and the White House, and members in Congress, had always bickered; this was now conducted in the glare of media publicity. One of the cornerstones of the American Dream was that the USA had a government that was co-operative, self-regulating and fair. The behaviour of the various parts of the government over the Korean War contributed to the beginnings of disillusionment with the presidency and government in general, which deepened under later presidents.

What was the impact of the Vietnam War (1954–75) on domestic policy?

EXTEND YOUR KNOWLEDGE

The Vietnam War

The Vietnam War began when the French were driven out of the country by communist Vietnamese rebels in 1954. The UN intervened to divide the country into a communist North and a democratic South (the USA helped with the elections). Unfortunately, Ngo Dinh Diem, the elected leader, was corrupt and his government was seen by many Americans as almost as bad as the communist regime. The friction between North and South meant that the USA spent the 1950s giving South Vietnamese troops training, advice and supplies. The first troops were sent in by President Kennedy in 1961. From then on, the war escalated and became more and more unpopular. The USA was fighting a guerrilla war, where it often could not distinguish allies from enemies, and where some of the population were involved in helping the rebels and some were innocent. The final withdrawal from Vietnam came in 1975, troop withdrawals having started in 1969; it was the first war the USA had lost, and it had looked bad while it was losing it.

The Vietnam War created similar defence budget concerns as the Korean War. Spending on the war was said to have contributed to the rising inflation of the period. It also created a significant loss of credibility for the presidency and the government, as they introduced unpopular policies and the war escalated out of control. One of the most unpopular policies was the draft. On 1 December 1969, a lottery was held to select men aged 18–26 to fight in Vietnam. These men were sent 'draft cards' and were told to report for duty on the date shown on the card. Some of these men were too young to drink and too young to vote; yet they were expected to go to war. The draw had radio, film and television coverage; the 'game show' element of the draw was said to make the selection fair. In fact, WASPs used the system to get their sons exempted or to send them abroad when they should be serving. It became symbolic for young men with draft cards to burn them during anti-war protests, even though this was a crime (they could be fined up to $10,000 or spend five years in prison). Draft-dodging (not reporting for service) became more and more common as opposition to the war grew.

Who protested against the war?

Mutual distrust grew between officials (e.g. the police) and certain groups in society (e.g. demonstrators). Old and young, black and white, rich and poor, famous and unknown, all protested against the war. Vietnam Veterans Against the War (VVAW) began when six veterans marched together in a peace demonstration in New York City in 1967. It soon had a membership of over 30,000. It campaigned to show the horror of the war and the shabby way many veterans were treated when they returned home, often with disabilities or stress-related illnesses that meant they found it hard to keep a job. No-one understood post-traumatic stress disorder, so most veterans, no matter what their problems and disabilities, were told by the military, and in some cases friends and family too, to put it all behind them and get on with their lives. Many faced abuse for the atrocities that people read about and saw on television, even if they had not been involved in them.

What role did the media play?

Media coverage of the war was intensive. At the start of the war, the media reported events as White House press conferences, or their military press officers in Vietnam, described them. However, as the war went on and they saw the war up close, reporters increasingly reported shocking stories: soldiers going into battle high on drugs; the massacre of an entire village of civilians at Mai Lai; spraying the toxic defoliant Agent Orange on villages, not empty fields; the rewarding of soldiers with ice cream and beer if their mission had a high kill count. This was not just because the stories made news (a mission that wasn't a massacre was not very newsworthy), but because the media were shocked by the ethos prevailing in Vietnam. This was not a war to be fought honourably; their opponents were 'just **Gooks**'. On 27 February 1968, news reporter Walter Cronkite returned from Vietnam after the Tet Offensive and broadcast a scathing criticism of the way the war was being run. Cronkite was a highly influential and respected television reporter. His programme increased public reaction against the war; President Johnson was heard to say after it that he had lost the support of 'middle America' for the war.

KEY TERM

Gooks
A racist word used to describe someone of South East Asian descent.

What was the impact of the Vietnam War on the presidency?

The conflict in Vietnam cast a shadow over four presidencies and drove successive presidents into unpopular domestic policies. Because of the power of the presidency in foreign affairs, presidents were seen as driving policy in the war, and so as more responsible for it than for domestic policy. For example, protests against the war in 1968 (during Johnson's presidency) were often accompanied by the chant: 'Hey! Hey! LBJ [Johnson]! How many kids did you kill today?' This was placing responsibility firmly on the shoulders of the president. US presidents found themselves more and more involved in a war that a growing number of Americans opposed – although even in 1967 about 75 percent of Americans opposed anti-war demonstrations. It became increasingly difficult to leave the war without putting many South Vietnamese (not just the South Vietnamese government and army but all those who could be seen as having 'collaborated' with America) in danger. The final withdrawal did not reflect well on the government, and with it the presidency. Despite the notion of 'planned withdrawal', the American people saw footage in 1975 of a shambolic helicopter evacuation of Saigon, taking out US citizens and some South Vietnamese, leaving many more for North Vietnamese reprisals. People were relieved the USA was out of the war, but they were also humiliated to have fought a 'dirty' war, lost it and left it in such a scramble, leaving many South Vietnamese in the lurch. Vietnam was the first war that the USA had lost, and the first which was seen by so many to have been fought less than honourably and ended humiliatingly. Many people were now likely to look more critically at the role and behaviour of the president in any future wars.

SOURCE

8 Members of VVAW giving back their medals, ranging from campaign medals (that showed they had fought) to purple hearts (awarded for bravery) in an anti-war demonstration on 23 April 1971, outside the Capitol, where Congress met.

War in Korea and Vietnam

1 In what ways were the Korean War and the Vietnam War similar?

2 In what ways were the Korean War and the Vietnam War different?

3 What implication did the setting up of Vietnam Veterans Against the War have for domestic politics and why?

4 In what way did the media shape public response to Vietnam?

THINKING HISTORICALLY   Causation (3a–b)

The human factor

1 'Our lack of control'. Work in pairs.

   Describe to your partner a situation where things did not work out as you had intended. Then explain how you would have done things differently to make the situation as you would have wanted. Your partner will then tell the group about that situation and whether they think that your alternative actions would have had the desired effect.

2 'The tyranny of failed actions'. Work individually.

   Think about Hoover's actions in response to the Great Depression.

   a) Write down three ways that Hoover could have acted differently.

   b) Now imagine that you are Hoover. Write a defence of your actions. Try to think about the things that you would have known about at the time and make sure that you do not use the benefit of hindsight.

3 'Arguments'. Work in groups of between four and six.

   In turn, each group member will read out their defence (from 2b above). Other group members suggest ways to reassure the reader that they were not a failure and that, in some ways, what happened was a good outcome.

4 Think about Roosevelt and the New Deal.

   a) In what ways were the consequences of the New Deal not anticipated by Roosevelt?

   b) In what ways did the New Deal turn out better for Roosevelt than the intended consequences?

5 Think about Eisenhower sending advisors to South Vietnam in 1955. Answer the following:

   a) In what ways were the consequences of intervention in Vietnam not anticipated by Eisenhower?

   b) In what ways did the situation in Vietnam turn out worse for Eisenhower than his intended consequences?

6 To what extent are historical individuals in control of the history they help to create? Explain your answer, with reference to specific historical examples from this topic and others you have studied.

Why did confidence in government decline, 1968–80?

Many historians see the 1960s as the decade when Americans came to lose their faith in their president, their government and themselves. In 1960, 70 percent of Americans said they trusted the government most of the time; by 1974, less than 40 percent said this. There were several factors in the decline of confidence in the presidency. Most boiled down to a lack of trust in the administration, and many of these factors show up in events during 1968.

KEY EVENTS IN 1968 THAT DAMAGED CONFIDENCE IN GOVERNMENT

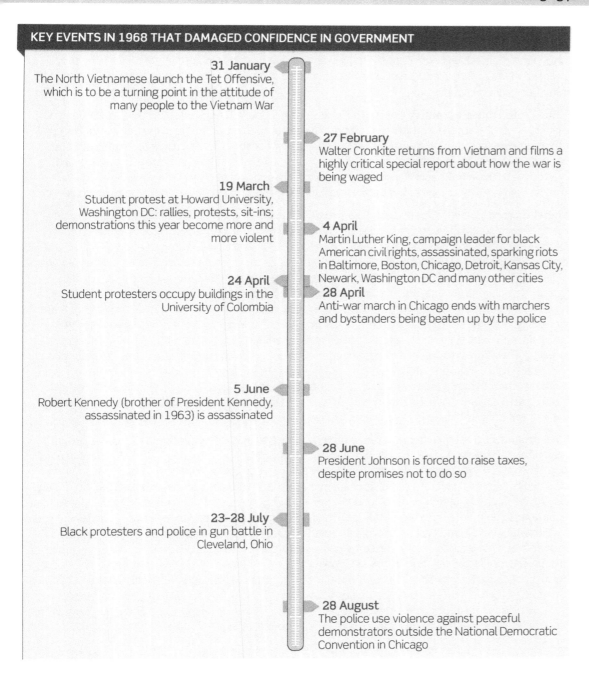

31 January
The North Vietnamese launch the Tet Offensive, which is to be a turning point in the attitude of many people to the Vietnam War

27 February
Walter Cronkite returns from Vietnam and films a highly critical special report about how the war is being waged

19 March
Student protest at Howard University, Washington DC: rallies, protests, sit-ins; demonstrations this year become more and more violent

4 April
Martin Luther King, campaign leader for black American civil rights, assassinated, sparking riots in Baltimore, Boston, Chicago, Detroit, Kansas City, Newark, Washington DC and many other cities

24 April
Student protesters occupy buildings in the University of Colombia

28 April
Anti-war march in Chicago ends with marchers and bystanders being beaten up by the police

5 June
Robert Kennedy (brother of President Kennedy, assassinated in 1963) is assassinated

28 June
President Johnson is forced to raise taxes, despite promises not to do so

23–28 July
Black protesters and police in gun battle in Cleveland, Ohio

28 August
The police use violence against peaceful demonstrators outside the National Democratic Convention in Chicago

The media: People had wider access to the media than in earlier years; radio, television and newspaper reporters changed their views of their relationship with the president and the government. Under Roosevelt, the media saw their job as explaining policies. From 1953, when the Korean War began and Truman mishandled the media, criticism grew. The media took to Kennedy and his government but, from 1968, the media came increasingly to see their job as uncovering government deception. Media stories focused more on showing that the government and the president were telling only part of the story, keeping things from the American people.

Scandal: Public confidence was even more seriously shaken by evidence that they couldn't trust the government. The Watergate scandal (1972–74) showed that the White House and President Nixon were guilty not only of burglary, but also of surveillance of political opponents. Tapes of discussions in the White House showed Nixon in a terrible light; he swore, was suspicious of everyone and made it clear that he was perfectly happy to lie to the American people. Public confidence hit rock bottom. The media had uncovered the crime and the cover-up. They hadn't trusted the Nixon administration – and they had been right not to do so.

Mishandling of events: The government could not avoid responsibility for the conduct of the war in Vietnam. Because presidents were more involved in decision-making after Roosevelt, presidents who found themselves bogged down in the war could not avoid responsibility either. As the media exposed army scandals and government mishandling of the war, public opposition grew. Again, the issue became one of trust.

The White House administration: Roosevelt enlarged the White House staff and created bureaus that reported to the president, not to Congress. As the presidential staff grew, the number of groups reporting directly to the president also grew. Staff members acted in the president's name without consulting him; some took bribes and made deals. The costs of staffing and campaigning rose, so presidential campaigns needed more money, becoming dependent on those who donated funds. Donors were usually unions or big businesses: both expected to have influence if their candidate won.

Social factors: Social problems, and how they were handled at local and state level, contributed to the decline in confidence. Violent police reaction to protests had happened in the South well before 1968; the level of violence and its spread across the country escalated. There were riots in cities countrywide following the death of Martin Luther King, in many cases sparked by an incident involving racial injustice by the police. Some places, such as Chicago, became notorious for police violence against demonstrators. The police and the National Guard became increasingly violent with student protesters. In 1970, the National Guard killed four students and seriously wounded nine at Kent State University, during a large student protest at the invasion of Cambodia, as part of the Vietnam War. Between 1968 and 1980, many white middle-class Americans also became disillusioned with 'liberal' thinking. They began to feel that the government was doing too much to help the poor and not enough for them. The 1965 Voting Rights Act (which actively stopped Southern states from preventing black Americans from voting) led to many white Democrats in those states voting Republican. Some civil rights protesters became increasingly violent when the gap between laws underlining their rights and the enforcement of those rights showed no sign of closing and they still faced discrimination.

The presidents: All presidents in office during the years 1968–80 contributed to the decline of confidence. Johnson put US troops into Vietnam, without Congress's approval. He communicated poorly with both the press and the public. Nixon's public communication style was forced, and few warmed to him as a person. His mismanagement of the Watergate scandal shocked people deeply. So did the later corruption in the administration that was revealed. Public reaction to this meant that Americans could not forgive Gerald Ford (who took over as president when Nixon stood down) when he pardoned Nixon, rather than taking him to a trial that would last years and corrode confidence further. The public didn't elect Ford at the subsequent presidential elections. Instead, they supported Jimmy Carter. Carter was one of the least politically experienced presidents ever, and it showed. He won because he was clearly a very moral man – his main campaign point was that he would never lie to the people. However, he couldn't manage Congress and his presidency was marked by poor decisions and a lack of flexibility. He had come to power by being very moral, but he was also very stubborn and didn't consult enough or look at political realities.

EXTEND YOUR KNOWLEDGE

The Watergate scandal

Early in 1971, President Nixon arranged for the White House to be bugged, so that conversations at the most senior levels would be recorded. Later in the year, he set up an undercover group to discover the source of the leaks that had plagued the White House for years. In June 1972, presidential election year, four men were arrested for breaking into the Democrat headquarters in the Watergate building. One of the burglars was on Nixon's staff.

The *Washington Post* began to investigate and discovered that $25,000 from the president's re-election campaign was in one of the burglar's bank accounts. The FBI found links between the re-election campaign and the burglars. The White House kept denying involvement. Nixon was re-elected. If it had not been an election year, the government might have confessed at the start and the *Washington Post* investigation might not have happened. It was the extent of the cover-up and Nixon's behaviour during it that was most shocking.

In January 1973, the Watergate burglars were convicted and, questioned in a Senate investigation into illegal activities during the re-election campaign, named people close to Nixon as involved. In April, three of these men resigned; the fourth was sacked; Nixon was seen as willing to get rid of anyone to keep himself out of trouble. The committee asked for the White House tapes as evidence. First, Nixon refused to hand them over and then he handed over edited transcripts. The tapes he finally produced were clearly edited too. Nixon resigned.

Three Mile Island

The Three Mile Island nuclear power plant was near Harrisburg, Pennsylvania. At 4 a.m. on 28 March 1979, one of the reactors automatically shut down because of a minor fault. Then an instrument led workers to believe the nuclear core was being cooled by water when there was, in fact, no water in the unit. The core was severely damaged and, at 6.56 a.m., the plant supervisor declared an emergency. Federal and state press conferences gave conflicting reports: both were thought to have played down the problem. Over the next two days, vents were opened to allow gas to escape.

While there was, in fact, no danger, people living near the area fled. People feared health problems from nuclear contamination. They were not reassured by government assurances that the leak was not dangerous – it had already become clear that the accident had been made worse by the lack of maintenance of equipment and training of workers as to how to behave in an emergency. The fact that the government was either covering up or unable to control the situation led to increasing fears about the safety of nuclear power and a loss of confidence in the government.

What was the next step for the government?

In 1981, President Reagan came to power as the candidate with old-fashioned Republican views on welfare, government involvement, law and order and giving business its head. He was against 'Big Government' and all for being financially responsible, reducing government borrowing rather than spending money the government didn't have on welfare. The reaction against liberalism had elected a president and a government that would govern very differently. It wasn't possible for the government to revert entirely to *laissez-faire*; the public still expected some social welfare and Congress still had Democrat and liberal-thinking members. But the tone of government changed from that which had prevailed since the New Deal of taking responsibility for those at the bottom of the heap.

ACTIVITY
SUMMARY

Changing political environment

1 Draw a flow chart to show how the role of the president changed between 1917 and 1980.

2 a) Write a brief description of the differences between 'rugged individualism' and New Deal ideas.

  b) Draw a graph to show how Hoover's policies aligned with each of these.

3 Write a paragraph to explain how each of the following had an impact on domestic politics:

  a) the Red Scares

  b) the liberalism of the 1960s

  c) war.

4 Draw a spider diagram to show how the following were connected:

  a) the Second Red Scare/the Cold War/the wars in Korea and Vietnam

  b) the Cold War/the growth of presidential power/the decline in confidence, 1960–80.

5 How far do you agree that the Vietnam War was the main cause of student protest in the 1960s and 1970s?

WIDER READING

Adams, D.K. *Franklin Roosevelt and the New Deal*, Historical Association (1979)

Greenstein, F.I. *The Presidential Difference: Leadership Style from FDR to Barak Obama*, Princeton University Press (2009)

The Sacco and Vanzetti case of 1921–27 demonstrates how the fear that caused the First Red Scare was still bubbling along after it was 'over'. Search the names online to find out more about the case.

Recordings of Roosevelt's fireside chats, Truman's 'Truman Doctrine' speech and Eisenhower's 'Domino Theory' speech can be found online.

1.2 The quest for civil rights, 1917–80

KEY QUESTIONS

- How and why did black Americans fight for civil rights, 1917–55?
- What was the impact of black Americans' fight for civil rights, c1955–80?
- How and why did minority rights become significant, 1960–80?

INTRODUCTION

The American Dream promised equality of opportunity but, in reality, many groups were denied that equality. People were supposed to be equal under the law: equally protected and equally controlled. In fact, many groups have struggled, and are struggling still, for that equality.

- On 31 January 1865, Congress passed the 13th Amendment to the Constitution, abolishing slavery in the USA.

- On 9 July 1868, the 14th Amendment made all people born or naturalised in the USA, including those who had been slaves, US citizens.

- On 3 February 1870, the 15th Amendment declared that all US citizens had the same voting rights.

So, by 1870, black Americans were supposedly free and equal. Yet, when Fannie Lou Hamer went to register to vote in Ruleville, Mississippi in 1962, she was sacked from her job and told that people weren't 'ready' for her to do this. Why? Because she was black. This illustrates the difference between the existence of a law and its enforcement. When campaigning for their civil rights, black people had a great deal of trouble getting laws passed to help them. They had even more trouble getting those laws enforced in many places.

Black Americans campaigned for civil rights in different ways at different times and places. They did not all move from one type of campaign to another, although different methods attracted more campaigners at different times. They campaigned by using legal challenges: by non-violent protest and also by more violent protest. Alongside their struggle for equality, there were times when various movements advocated giving up the struggle and living separately from white people, so they could be free of violence and discrimination.

While the black American struggle for civil rights was going on, other groups also campaigned for equality. Black Americans were not the only people discriminated against because of their race. Native Americans had long been deprived of rights and subjected to racist treatment, as had **Hispanic Americans**. From the 1960s, they too became more vocal in their campaigns to be given their civil rights and have them enforced. Many of their tactics were modelled on and inspired by the tactics of earlier black American campaigns.

The civil rights movement worked against other forms of discrimination as well, not just racism. The 1960s also saw the rise of groups to campaign for equality for women and for the rights of gays.

KEY TERM

Hispanic American
Defined by the US census as also 'Latino' and applying to a person of Mexican, Cuban, Puerto-Rican and other originally Spanish-speaking ethnic groups.

1929
October The Wall Street Crash kick-starts the Great Depression

1941
May Over 100,000 black protesters ready to march on Washington; demands met
7 December Japanese attack US fleet at Pearl Harbor
8 December USA declares war on Japan
11 December Germany declares war on the USA

1946
5 December
Truman's Preside
Committee on Ci
Rights set up

1915	1920	1925	1930	1935	1940	1945

1919–20
First Red Scare
1919 'Red Summer' race riots

1931
Scottsboro Case

1939
September Outbreak of Second World War in Europe

1945
8 May Second World War end Europe
6–9 August USA drops atom bomb on Hiroshima and Naga
2 September End of the Seco World War in the Pacific

HOW AND WHY DID BLACK AMERICANS FIGHT FOR CIVIL RIGHTS, 1917–55?

In 1900, black Americans didn't know that they would still be struggling for their rights in 2000. Many hoped that, if they worked hard and showed their worth, white people would accept them and allow them the equality they had been granted in law.

Why fight for civil rights?

After the end of the First World War, black Americans found that they still had to struggle for equality. They still faced discrimination, **segregation** and violence. These things were more extreme in the South, especially the Deep South, but even in the North and West black Americans were unofficially segregated and discriminated against. They were expected to live in their own part of town (the worst part), living, shopping and schooling their children there. In most places, they were 'last hired, first fired' and were expected to do the lowest-paid jobs. This segregation was helped by the fact that having the worst jobs and being less well paid automatically pushed people into the poorest parts of town. There were exceptions, but discrimination reached to the very top of government in some cases. In 1913, President Wilson even introduced segregation in government offices and the White House. Violence was common too. In 1919, there were about 25 anti-black race riots, often set off by police injustice, in which hundreds were killed. The worst of these 'Red Summer' riots was in Chicago, not the South.

> **KEY TERM**
>
> Segregation
> The enforced separation of racial groups in many aspects of life.

What was life like in the South?

Life in the South in 1917 was hard for many black Americans. They faced legal restrictions at every turn. Booker T. Washington was a famous black American who advocated accepting segregation. He had a significant following, especially among better-off black Americans. He also had white support; they felt he saw how many Southern whites feared black Americans gaining equality. Under segregation, black Americans were educated in black schools and colleges. Black teachers were paid less and schools were often dilapidated and poorly equipped. However, black children did learn and went on to become doctors, lawyers and teachers, proving that black people were as intelligent as whites, which many Southerners denied.

What was the impact of Jim Crow laws?

With slavery gone, Southerners felt less in control of the black population in the South. So they introduced laws on segregation as a different form of control. By 1917, the South had a large number of laws, known as Jim Crow laws, which segregated every aspect of life. It was called 'the permanent system' or 'the final settlement'. There were laws about where to sit on the tram, where to live, where to send children to school. There were separate public facilities – even drinking fountains. Many workplaces segregated their workers; some even had different staircases to move around the building. States also introduced discrimination against black people more subtly. Voters had to pass a literacy qualification to vote. In some places, black people were given harder passages to read.

1947–54
Second Red Scare
1948
26 July Truman desegregates the military by Executive Order 9981

1955
5 December
Montgomery Bus Boycott begins (ends 21 December 1956)

1965
6 August Voting Rights Act extended to cover more minority groups including Hispanic Americans and Native Americans

1977
8 November Harvey Milk, a gay rights campaigner, elected to office

| 1950 | 1955 | 1960 | 1965 | 1970 | 1975 | 1980 |

1954
17 May *Brown v Board of Education* decision to desegregate schools

1963
May Protests to desegregate Birmingham, Alabama

1964
2 July Civil Rights Act

In many states, voters had to be home owners; most blacks were not. Some states held all-white elections to select the candidates for the actual election. On top of all this, many polling stations were surrounded by whites waiting to beat up any black person who turned up to vote. By 1917, the number of black Americans registered to vote had dropped considerably – in Louisiana, it fell from 130,334 in 1896 to 1,342 in 1904.

EXTEND YOUR KNOWLEDGE

Background to Jim Crow legislation
After the Civil War, the federal government freed slaves and created the Freedmen's Bureau to set up schools and to help people find work and register to vote. It also sent in troops to enforce the freeing of slaves. Some 700,000 registered – and many voted. Politically, things improved. About four million slaves were freed, creating an economic problem, because the South depended on labour-intensive plantations that relied on slaves. In practice, many free slaves returned to plantations to work. The social problems were harder to solve. Slavery had controlled black people – how could Southerners control them once they were free?

From 1865, Southern states reacted by introducing, not just the tacit segregation of the North, but legal segregation. This was done with Black Codes that varied from state to state. Even then, black people protested. In 1864, New Orleans segregated its trams. There were many demonstrations against this and they erupted into a full-scale riot in 1866, after which the trams were desegregated.

Once federal troops left the South, in 1877, states made more and more segregation laws and were less likely to have them overturned. When Louisiana segregated its railways in 1890, black civil rights suffered a huge setback. There were protests against the railway segregation and Homer Plessy, a shoemaker and civil rights activist, took the matter all the way to the Supreme Court. In 1896, in *Plessy v Ferguson*, the Court ruled that, despite the 14th Amendment, segregation was possible as long as provision was 'separate but equal'.

Lynching and the Ku Klux Klan

KEY TERM

Lynching
A mob taking the law into its own hands to punish someone, almost always a man, for what it sees as a crime. In the South, it was most usually white people lynching a black man. The victim was usually hanged, although some were burned alive.

Some whites felt that segregation wasn't enough, that black people needed terrorising into obedience. Between 1915 and 1930, there were **lynchings** of 65 white men and 579 black men, mostly in the South. They did not need to have committed a crime; sometimes those doing the lynching didn't even feel the need to produce a specific accusation. Southern lynchings were often advertised beforehand. There are photographs of crowds of men and women grinning happily beside the corpses. In 1955, 14-year-old Emmett Till, visiting relations in the South from Chicago, was lynched for talking with a white woman, allegedly asking her for a date. He hadn't understood the Southern rules. The lynching attracted a lot of publicity and caused shock, even in the South.

The Ku Klux Klan (KKK), a white supremacist organisation revived in 1915, was against any non-WASP group, but especially black people. Members lived all over the USA; by 1925, estimates of membership ranged from three to eight million. In the South, it was more likely to include people with real political power (even state governors) and social power (state policemen and the army). KKK members wore white robes and hoods, supposedly to keep their identity secret. In fact, most people knew who the Klan members were, but the hoods allowed them to claim that they couldn't identify individual Klansmen. Women Klan members seldom took part in the more violent Klan activities, such as lynchings. They brought their children up as white supremacists and, especially in rural communities, created an anti-black environment that even non-Klan people felt too intimidated to reject.

Did the federal government intervene in the South?

Black people lost political power as they lost their chance to vote, and this took them a step back from achieving equality. The federal government also hindered black equality. In 1896, the Supreme Court, in *Plessy v Ferguson*, had ruled that, despite the **14th Amendment**, segregation was possible if provision was 'separate but equal'. Not everyone agreed with the decision, but, once made, the ruling was used to support many other cases of segregation. The problem was that 'separate' was very seldom 'equal'; the only way to prove it was to take each case of inequality to court. President Wilson, a Southerner, had no problem with segregation. President Harding spoke out against lynching and broadly in favour of civil rights. He even addressed 30,000 (segregated) people at the University of Alabama on the evils of segregation. However, both he and then President Coolidge were committed to a policy of *laissez-faire*. They could express an opinion and try to influence behaviour, but would not enforce it by legislation. When the Depression hit America, the federal government was focused on correcting that and civil rights issues slid even further out of sight.

KEY TERM

14th Amendment
This amendment to the US Constitution made all people born or naturalised in the USA, including those who had been slaves, US citizens.

What was the impact of moving North, 1917–32?

Between 1917 and 1932, there was a wave of black migration from the South to the North and East, mainly to the cities, which became known as the Great Migration. By 1920, almost 40 percent of African Americans in the North were living in Chicago, Detroit, Cleveland, Cincinnati and Columbus, Ohio. The Eastern cities with the biggest population growth were New York, Philadelphia and Pittsburgh. They were mostly industrial towns and black Americans were drawn there for the work, as well as to escape the South.

The black migration began because the USA entered the First World War, producing a rising need for workers in the munitions factories in the North. Factory owners advertised in Southern newspapers for workers. They offered housing, free transport north and good wages. People were encouraged to migrate by friends and family who had already migrated north, who could offer them a place to stay, or help finding work.

SOURCE

Black populations of New York, Detroit and Chicago, 1910–30. Based on data from the US Department of Commerce, Bureau of the Census, *Negroes in the United States*.

Date	Population		
	New York	**Detroit**	**Chicago**
1910	91,709	5,741	44,103
1920	152,467	40,838	109,458
1930	327,706	120,066	233,903

Segregation varied from city to city, but migrants generally found a level of segregation that they might not have expected, especially later in the period. Once they had arrived, most migrants' lives followed a similar pattern. They found somewhere to live and a job. The job was low paid, sometimes replacing white workers who were pushing for higher wages. The accommodation was in the most crowded and run-down part of the city. It was cramped and often in disrepair; the rent was higher than a white person would be charged. There were, of course, variations. Not all landlords exploited migrants, and not all black people were forced to live in the worst parts of the cities. Some black professionals lived in their own black communities, in better parts of the cities; some poorer black Americans moved to their own areas of rich white suburbs, within reach of families that needed nannies and domestic servants. Black people could vote and black people were elected to local and federal government. Not all black people had low-paid jobs; some did very well for themselves, but most of the migrants were poor and even skilled migrants often had to take unskilled jobs. The pattern shows the worst that could happen. It happened a lot.

What was the impact of the migration?

The impact on the cities that had large levels of black migration was significant. The populations of these cities rose sharply. In cities where black migrants settled in areas that coincided with voting wards (e.g. Chicago), black people came to have significant political influence. Once it became clear, as it did in the elections for mayor of Chicago in 1919, that the black vote could keep a mayor in power, black people were listened to more and a powerful business-oriented black elite grew up that had a vested interest in segregation. Segregation made it more likely that they could try for positions in politics, because a black American campaigning in a black ward was very likely to sweep the whole black vote.

In cities such as New York, where the black population was more evenly distributed and white politicians had a tight hold on the politics of the city, black Americans did not gain political power and influence. However, they still tended to live, if not in just a few parts of the city, in smaller segregated groups all over the city with their own businesses, schools and churches. The churches were to become significant bases for organising civil rights protests and many later black American leaders of the civil rights movement were preachers. Black migrants dislodged white workers, especially those who were members of unions and pushing for better conditions. This enabled businesses to put pressure on white workers to leave unions or lose their jobs.

What impact did the migration have in the South?

The black migration had an impact on the South too. The labour force shrank and the farming areas of the South, already having economic problems, struggled to get by. The poorest farmers suffered the most and most of them were black. A significant impact was that Southerners tended to see the migration as black people 'voting with their feet' over Jim Crow laws. There was a tendency to assume that those black Americans who remained in the South were accepting Jim Crow.

SOURCE 2

This photo was taken in Harlem, New York, in 1931. The black couple have a car and fur coats, despite the country being in the grip of the Great Depression. To us, the photo illustrates the exception that proves the rule. The sight of such people offered poor black people at the time a glimpse of what might be possible for them, under the right circumstances.

AS Exam-Style Question Section B

How far do you agree that the impact of the Northern migration (1917–32) can only be considered in terms of the migrants themselves and the cities they moved to? (20 marks)

Tip
Weigh the impact discussed against the impact on the South, such as Southern attitudes to black Southerners.

ACTIVITY
KNOWLEDGE CHECK

Conditions in the South

1 Prepare for a debate on Jim Crow laws in the South. You don't know if you will be arguing for or against the legislation. Think of four points to make for each side, with supporting material for each point.

Northern migration

2 List eight ways in which the Great Migration had an impact on the North and the South.

3 Draw a diagram to show the 'push' and 'pull' factors behind the Great Migration – that is the factors that made people want to leave the South and the factors attracting them to the North.

What was the impact of the New Deal?

During the 1930s black voters shifted from mainly voting Republican (the party that had abolished slavery) to voting Democrat (the party promising a New Deal). Their vote was a significant part of the Roosevelt landslide. President Roosevelt did appoint some black advisers, but he needed the support of many people who were against equal rights, so did little to advance civil rights and often restricted the number of black workers on a project if a donor to the project wanted this. However, when war broke out, he did issue Executive Order 8802, banning racial discrimination in the defence industry, in order to get as many people into war-work as possible, regardless of colour.

Roosevelt's New Deal measures were supposedly colour-blind; the agencies he set up to provide relief and work said they put people onto work projects 'by merit' alone. In fact, black people were constantly moved off projects to make way for whites, despite denials that this was happening. Black farm workers were sacked in their thousands during agricultural reforms and black workers were often sacked to make way for white workers. The social security provisions of the New Deal did not apply to farm workers or those who worked in other people's homes; many of these were black Americans. Black officials in the government protested and advised; sometimes they got results, as when they persuaded the National Recovery Administration, which regulated wages and working conditions, to set the minimum wage for black and white people at the same rate. More often, they were ignored. Some New Deal measures did help black Americans simply because of their situation (e.g. one-third of the low-income housing built had black tenants, because many of the poorest people eligible for this housing were black).

EXTRACT

1 From *We Ain't What We Ought To Be*, written by the historian Stephen Tuck in 2010.

The Agricultural Adjustment Act compensated farmers for planting less cotton, and thus increased prices. Southern landlords duly pushed 100,000 black tenants off the land, without passing on the [federal agency] cheques. The National Recovery Act, which mandated a minimum wage, did not apply to domestic or agricultural work. Where black workers did qualify, most found themselves working fewer hours (at less pay) to accomplish the same tasks, and some half million of black workers lost their jobs altogether to unemployed white men and women. Some called the NRA the Negro Removal Act, or Negroes Roasted Again. Emergency relief was distributed via local agencies, and much was lost in transmission, especially in the South. None of the early New Deal agencies contained anti-discriminatory enforcement provisions. Indeed, the only measure that explicitly called for action on race actually reinforced discrimination. Federal Housing loans were required to preserve racial composition of neighborhoods – in effect, they built walls around black slums. To add insult to injury, Roosevelt ignored black calls for anti-lynching legislation, for termination of the poll tax, and for an end to segregation.

Protesting against the New Deal

Black Americans protested about their treatment during the New Deal. Sometimes they had more support from communist and other left-wing groups that supported equality than from black civil rights organisations. In 1931, the **National Association for the Advancement of Colored People (NAACP)** turned down the case of nine young black men framed for raping two white girls on a train near Scottsboro, Alabama. Communist lawyers took the case, uncovered a conspiracy and the men were found not guilty. In the early 1930s, Birmingham, Alabama had six black American members of the NAACP and over 3,000 black American communists. Communists in the Northern cities also championed the cause of all workers and demanded that relief funds should be allocated equally between blacks and whites. The black press followed these campaigns and often applauded them. The association with communists gave opponents of black civil rights another stick with which to beat the civil rights movement.

As well as protesting, black church organisations set up support systems for black citizens during the Depression. There was more of this support in the North and mostly in the cities, because there were more churches and more people to donate to their relief work. In Harlem, Father Divine of the Peace Mission church group set up restaurants and shops that sold food and supplies to black people at a lower cost than white-run stores. Women's organisations were set up, such as the Housewives Leagues that began in Detroit and spread across the country. The Housewives Leagues mounted 'Don't Buy Where You Can't Work' campaigns to boycott stores in black districts until they hired black workers. It was activism within segregation, but it was taking the initiative, nevertheless.

KEY TERM

National Association for the Advancement of Colored People (NAACP)
The NAACP, established in 1910, organised many of the legal actions against segregation in the USA.

Another depression hit the USA in 1937, and it hit black workers hard. Equality of relief provision slid again and, even where there was help, it was nowhere near enough. The Resettlement Administration was set up by Executive Order 7027 in May 1935 to resettle low-income families in new housing and to lend money where needed. It gave black farmers who had lost their homes a fair share of the money available in loans – but it still only helped 3,400 of over 200,000 farmers. Things were so bad that, in 1939, around two million people signed a petition asking for federal aid to move to Africa.

What was the impact of the Second World War?

In September 1939, the Second World War broke out in Europe. Roosevelt gave the Allies who were fighting Germany help, but did not bring the USA into the war. However, he prepared for war, just in case the USA decided to join later, pushing the USA's first ever conscription bill through Congress in 1940 and putting federal money into research projects, one of which came up with the atom bomb. On 7 December 1941, the Japanese bombed the US fleet at Pearl Harbor. The USA went to war with Japan. Germany declared war on the USA; now the USA was at war in both the Pacific and Europe.

Gains for black Americans

Black Americans did not benefit much from the war-induced boom that began in 1939; white workers were given preference. In May 1941, A. Philip Randolph, who had led a successful protest by railway workers, threatened a 100,000-strong all-black march on Washington unless Roosevelt banned discrimination in the army and in defence factories. Roosevelt's Executive Order 8802 for non-discrimination in defence work, overseen by a Fair Employment Practices Committee, stopped the march. While many complaints were made to the committee, equality was only patchily implemented, due to pressure from opponents of equal rights. The order did not deal with military segregation but, as the war went on, the military and the factories needed more people, so black Americans could push for equality. In the summer of 1942, only three percent of defence workers were black; two years later, this had risen to eight percent. Wartime migration to the cities of the North was even higher than the migration of the 1920s. However, this influx of black workers was resented: 1943 saw outbreaks of racist violence and strikes by white people over having to work with them. This led several towns to set up race relations committees to investigate improvements, because the strikes and riots were damaging the war effort. The shortage of workers also meant that white skilled workers had to allow black people to be trained in these skills. As black and white people worked side by side, some whites saw that black people could do skilled work, could think, could be friends. This affected their reaction to post-war civil rights efforts, but a survey at the end of the war showed that many white Americans were still racist, supporting housing segregation and saying that jobs should go to whites before blacks.

What impact did President Truman have?

President Truman supported civil rights. He proposed anti-lynching, anti-segregation and fair employment laws in 1954, but failed to push them through Congress. Civil rights measures were always difficult to get through; they were almost always blocked by opposition from Southern delegates and lukewarm support from many Northern ones. In 1946, Truman set up the President's Committee on Civil Rights, which called for equal opportunities in work and housing; it also urged strong federal support for civil rights. Truman urged Congress to act on this; it dragged its feet. Black Americans wanted to keep their wartime gains and push for greater equality. Truman was on their side, but his Cold War focus meant he concentrated more on fighting communism than on fighting for civil rights. Earlier collaboration between blacks and communists meant that at least one black organisation, the National Negro Congress (a black civil rights group which had some communist members when it was set up, but pursued civil rights issues not communist ones), ended up on the government's list of suspect organisations. Even so, in 1948, Truman issued executive orders desegregating the military and all work done by businesses for the government. He was, it is true, in an election year and aware of the value of the black vote, but he was also severely shocked by the outbreaks of racist violence against returning black soldiers across the country, some even still in the uniform in which they had fought for their country.

Fighting for civil rights: from legal challenge to direct action, 1917–55

Black Americans used a variety of tactics in their fight for civil rights. The various tactics never went away, but some were more prominent at certain times than others. They depended on time, place, circumstance, the beliefs of those involved and the amount of support available. Black American protestors used non-violent protest, picketing, boycotting and sit-ins to draw public attention to discrimination. They went to the law, hoping to get their rights enforced. All of this needed organising, and some groups were set up in the first decade of the 20th century, such as the NAACP and the National Urban League, that grew and prospered and are still at work now.

Smaller, local organisations were often based around church groups – it is not accidental that many civil rights leaders were churchmen, including Martin Luther King Jr. The number of civil rights groups, and membership of them, took a leap after both the First World War and the Second World War. NAACP membership went from 9,000 in 1917 to 90,000 in 1919 and 600,000 in 1946.

Running alongside the fight for civil rights was the separatist movement. Separatists said black Americans were never going to have true equality with whites. That being the case, they should stop fighting for it. They should embrace segregation and fight for equal conditions within it, because this was more feasible. Separatism would also mean black children would grow up without being made to feel inferior all the time; they could feel proud instead. Some separatists, such as Marcus Garvey in the early 1920s, even suggested that the answer was to do just what white racists were telling them to do – go back to Africa.

SOURCE

3 An NAACP demonstration in Houston, Texas, in 1947. NAACP members travelled to various parts of the country to demonstrate. They always made sure that they dressed neatly to look 'respectable'.

Legal challenges

The NAACP's aim, when it was set up in 1910, was to gain black Americans their legal rights. It began by mounting a campaign against lynching, feeling that many people had no idea of the scale of it, especially in the South. It published pamphlets about lynching, demonstrated, held marches and petitioned Congress. Laws against lynching were brought to Congress, but blocked by Southern politicians. The NAACP also took cases of segregation to court. It was a tough fight, because the 1896 Supreme Court ruling in *Plessy v Ferguson* had said that segregation was permissible, if it was 'separate but equal'. An early NAACP tactic was to argue that the separate provision wasn't equal, so it couldn't be overruled by the 1896 Supreme Court ruling. The NAACP also provided lawyers to defend black people on trial who it felt had been unjustly accused.

The success of legal challenges

The NAACP won some cases in the 1930s and 1940s, and every case it fought in the 1950s. To that extent, it was a success. However, the Supreme Court didn't enforce its rulings and weakened the force of the rulings by not setting time limits for desegregation, or using vague phrases such as 'with all deliberate speed' – as in *Brown II*, a revised ruling of the *Brown v Board of Education* case. Some schools, in some places, were integrated within the year. Other schools, especially in the Deep South, took 'with all deliberate speed' to mean 'not for many years yet'. Ten years after the ruling, only one black child in every 100 in the South

was in an integrated school. The ruling spurred the formation of the White Citizens Council in 1954 to fight desegregation and civil rights for black Americans. By 1956, it had 250,000 members. This was just one of many organisations formed in the South in response to *Brown v Board of Education*. Legal challenges were working, in that they were getting legal support. However, just like the Amendments to the Constitution that gave black Americans equality, they were useless unless they worked in practice. Also, integrating schools was less than helpful if families were still living in segregated neighbourhoods. For this reason, the NAACP targeted housing next, having helped to set up the National Committee Against Discrimination in Housing in 1950.

EXTEND YOUR KNOWLEDGE

Brown v Board of Education

In 1951, NAACP lawyers took several cases to court to desegregate schools. They were overruled in state courts by the 'separate but equal' Supreme Court ruling in the *Plessy v Ferguson* case (1896). The NAACP bundled the cases together and took them to the Supreme Court to challenge the *Plessy* ruling there. Judge Earl Warren was the Supreme Court judge in the case, in 1954, and said that it was clear from the evidence presented that segregated schooling was not 'equal'. He said that 'separate but equal' had no place in education and that schools and colleges should be desegregated. However, he set no timescale for desegregation. The following year, he had to add to his decision that desegregation should be carried out 'with all deliberate speed'. This was still vague enough to allow states that wanted to drag their heels to do so.

SIGNIFICANT NAACP LEGAL CASES

1926 Sweet trial
Doctor Ossian Sweet and his family move to a house in a predominantly white area in Detroit in 1925; the house is surrounded by an angry mob two nights running; on the second night, windows are broken and, fearing an attack, one of Sweet's friends fires a gun and shoots a young man; all the men in the house are put on trial for murder; NAACP lawyers take up the case and win, setting up a legal defence fund to fight segregation

1936 *Murray v Maryland*
University of Maryland's law school is desegregated

1938 *Gaines v Canada*
Supreme Court orders the University of Missouri to take black students

1946 *Morgan v Virginia*
Supreme Court overturns a Virginia state law segregating buses and trains that moved from one state to another

1948 *Shelley v Kraemer*
Bans regulations that bar black people from buying houses in an area in any state

1950 *Sweatt v Painter* and *McLaurin v Oklahoma*
Desegregates graduate and professional schools in Texas and Oklahoma

1954 *Brown v Board of Education of Topeka*
Desegregates schools: first use of evidence that, as well as unequal provision, segregation was psychologically harmful for black schoolchildren

Direct action

The NAACP and other organisations stepped up direct action in the 1940s and 1950s, as their membership grew and they saw that legal rulings were not enough. Marches were not new – there had been a march of over 10,000 black people in New York on 28 June 1917, called the Silent Protest Parade, organised in response to both lynching and anti-black riots in that year. However, protests developed in a different way.

There were more local protests and they happened more often. Influenced by the peaceful, passive resistance of Mahatma Gandhi in India, protesters targeted segregation and deliberately challenged 'illegal' state legislation. There were boycotts and picketing of shops that would not serve black people. **The Congress of Racial Equality (CORE)** held a series of sit-ins in the Northern cities of Chicago (1942), St Louis (1949) and Baltimore (1952) to desegregate public facilities. In 1947, a group of CORE members, and another group called the **Fellowship for Reconciliation**, went on the Journey of Reconciliation, riding inter-state buses through the Southern states of Virginia, North Carolina, Tennessee and Kentucky to desegregate them. Thousands of black people took it into their hands to be the first to move into all-white housing blocks or business districts, often putting themselves in very real danger to do so.

The rules of non-violent protest

A set of rules was developed by civil rights organisations, such as the NAACP, for these demonstrations. Demonstrators dressed as well as they could, to look respectable. They weren't loud or abusive. They didn't fight back if attacked. They tried to show that they supported the government and were looking to the government to support them. So, for example, they collected petitions and took them to local and federal government representatives. They tried, by their protests, to show up the evils of segregation and persuade white people, both ordinary and important in government, to change their views about black people, share their outrage and fight for change. The demonstrators of this period were of all ages, but they were predominantly black. CORE was unusual, at the start, in deliberately having black and white members working together.

KEY TERMS

CORE
The Congress of Racial Equality, set up in 1942 to campaign for civil rights by non-violent means, pioneered the tactics of sit-ins, jail-ins and freedom rides.

Fellowship for Reconciliation
A peace-based organisation founded in 1914. Many of its members were Quakers.

ACTIVITY
KNOWLEDGE CHECK

The New Deal

1 List the ways in which black Americans were at a disadvantage during the New Deal, the Second World War and Truman's presidency.

2 List the ways in which things improved for black Americans in the same period.

3 Turn your lists into a progress graph.

From legal challenge to direct action

4 Write a paragraph to explain why black Americans might move the focus of their activities from legal challenge to direct action after the Second World War.

5 Start a timeline on civil rights activities, using the timeline on page 44 as a start, then add events from this section that are not on the timeline.

A Level Exam-Style Question Section A

How far had legal action advanced the position of black Americans between 1917 and 1955? (20 marks)

Tip

Consider what the legislation says and how that helped. Also consider previous legislation (such as the Plessy case) that might restrict advancement. Consider the difference between legislation and implementation.

WHAT WAS THE IMPACT OF BLACK AMERICANS' FIGHT FOR CIVIL RIGHTS, c1955–80?

The 1955 Montgomery Bus Boycott brought a new civil rights leader to prominence and began a shift in the way civil rights campaigns were run. Civil rights became a major issue in the USA, and events and tactics moved swiftly and caught the eye of the world more – at least in part thanks to the medium of television. It was one thing to read about police beating up black protesters; it was quite another thing to see it.

Changing patterns and approaches, 1955–68

From 1955 onwards, civil rights campaigners were very aware of the issue of putting themselves in the public eye and choosing their causes, and the people involved in them, very carefully. In 1955, a piece of local action in Montgomery, Alabama suddenly became big news. Why? The media's imagination was caught by the combination of a stubborn city government, a charismatic leader and a determined black population.

The Montgomery Bus Boycott

Campaigners had challenged the segregation of buses in Montgomery at regular intervals since a boycott in 1900. Black passengers had to sit at the back of the bus, standing if their allocated seats were full, even if there were empty seats in the whites-only part of the bus. They had to give up any seat on their part of the bus to a white person. In 1954, the Women's Political Council (WPC) in Montgomery warned the mayor that several local organisations, including the NAACP, were considering a bus boycott. They chose their case carefully. Two women were arrested for refusing to give up their seats in 1955, but were rejected by the NAACP because of the use the opposition might make of their circumstances: Claudette Colvin, a 15-year-old girl arrested in March, was unmarried and pregnant; Mary Louise Smith, an 18-year-old woman arrested in October, came from a poor family and her father had a drink problem. Many black people in Montgomery felt that their cases should be taken up, however.

On 1 December, Rosa Parks, a respectable, dignified 42-year-old woman and NAACP member, was arrested for sitting at the front of the bus. The NAACP's lawyer took her case. The following day, the Montgomery Improvement Association (MIA) was formed to organise the boycott. A newly appointed Baptist minister, Martin Luther King Jr, was chosen as leader. He was the right man in the right place at the right time. The MIA leafleted and held meetings to publicise the arrest and the boycott. It organised taxis and other transport to get people to work if they couldn't walk in. The boycott began on 5 December. Over 75 percent of bus users were black and 90 percent of them stayed away from the buses. The boycott lasted for 380 days. King was careful to follow the rules of non-violent protest and to keep the media informed about events. Media interest grew as the boycott carried on. The city government penalised taxi drivers for taking fares; the MIA organised car pools. The homes of King and the NAACP leader E.D. Nixon were fire-bombed; they begged protesters to stay calm and not riot. The city government imprisoned King and several others for conspiracy to boycott; the boycott carried on. Some of the boycotters lost their jobs; they carried on. By this point, the boycott had a huge amount of publicity. The Supreme Court had to act. On 13 November 1956, it ruled bus segregation unconstitutional. On 21 December, over a year after the boycott started, black people began riding the buses again – desegregated buses. The boycott had worked. However, the long fight had hardened the racial divide. In the next local elections white candidates who favoured segregation were elected. Just three days after the buses were desegregated King's home was firebombed and snipers shot at black passengers sitting in white seats (at least one, a pregnant women, was wounded in both legs). Black people went on riding. It took several years for the violence against the bus desegregation to calm down.

 THINKING HISTORICALLY Causation (4a-b)

Inevitability

Nothing that happens is inevitable. There are causes of change which did not have to develop as they did. Something could have altered or someone could have chosen differently. What actually occurred in the past did happen but it did not have to be like that.

Work on your own and answer the questions below. When you have answered them, discuss the answers in groups.

Perceived reasons for the success of the Montgomery Bus Boycott

State of affairs	Event	Event	Development	Development
Long-term feeling in Mongomery's black community against segregation	The choice of Rosa Parks for the case	The choice of Martin Luther King as leader	The support of the black people of Montgomery for the boycott	Media interest and coverage of the case

1 Consider the long-term feeling in the black community in Montgomery against segregation.

   a) How did the arrest of bus protesters affect this feeling?

   b) Had there been no concerted feeling, would there still have been a bus boycott?

   c) What other aspects of the situation existing in 1955 would have been affected had there been no racial tension?

2 Consider the selection of Rosa Parks for the case.

   a) How important was Parks as a person to the success of the boycott, locally and nationally?

   b) What might have happened had Claudette Colvin been chosen instead?

3 What other consequences came about as a result of the information in the table above? Try to identify at least one consequence for each.

4 Choose one factor. How might the Montgomery Bus Boycott have developed differently if this factor had not been present?

Martin Luther King Jr

Martin Luther King Jr became the face of black American civil rights. Some people saw this as unfair. He worked hard, but so did many other civil rights leaders. He spoke well, but so did many of them. Somehow, he got the media attention and they didn't, and the more attention he got, the more prominent he became. He was very media-conscious. In 1957, he set up the Southern Christian Leadership Conference (SCLC). King refined the non-violent protest rules with an eye to creating the best possible impression in the media.

- It must always be clear who is the oppressor, who the oppressed; never give the media the image of a violent black American, it harms the cause.

- Getting arrested, as publicly as possible, and going peaceably, is good publicity. King was arrested many times, and wrote articles and gave interviews from jail about the civil rights cause. Before a protest, campaigners were taught how to go limp if the police tried to move them from a sit-in.

- Accept as many white people as you can on your protests. King was happy to meet with white officials who might help the civil rights cause, even though some black people criticised this.

Campaigning in the South

The focus of civil rights campaigning shifted to the Deep South, where it was often very clear who was the oppressor and who was the oppressed. Many Southerners, especially those in the Deep South, saw nothing wrong with racism or with violence against black Americans. The campaigners wanted to exploit this, and expose the results of these attitudes to the government in Washington and to the world. The campaign focused on integrating those schools, universities and colleges that were still, despite the Supreme Court's ruling on *Brown v Board of Education*, segregated. Particular schools were targeted, in areas where the NAACP had a strong following and the local black communities, as in Montgomery, had dedicated leaders and members. Families were chosen carefully to apply to these schools. In most cases, the school boards chose a few black children out of the many who applied. The same applied to colleges and universities.

Little Rock, Arkansas

Arkansas had a racist governor, Orval Faubus, but there were integrated schools in some towns. Little Rock itself integrated buses in 1956. In 1957, nine black children were selected to attend the previously all-white Central High School. On 4 September, the first day of school, Faubus sent the state National Guard to stop these children going in 'for their safety'. Eight of the children went to school by car, with the NAACP organiser; the ninth, Elizabeth Eckford, didn't get the message and went on her own. The National Guard turned her away and she was surrounded by a screaming mob, many of them women, some shouting 'Lynch her!' She bravely walked through them to the bus stop to go home. Photographs of the incident (there were over 250 reporters and photographers there) shocked the world. King managed to get a meeting with President Eisenhower, in which he pointed out the political damage this was doing to Eisenhower

and his administration, and urged federal intervention. Eisenhower reluctantly sent in federal troops to guard the children going to and from school, and in the school corridors. In the classrooms, the dining halls and at home, the children were subjected to years of taunts and violence. The homes of local NAACP leaders were firebombed several times, but Central School was integrated. Faubus closed the school for the whole of the following year, supposedly to 'let things cool off', but the school was eventually integrated for good.

There were similar scenes at schools and colleges all over the South and many people were killed in the rioting that accompanied integration.

The Greensboro sit-in

On 1 February 1960, four black students went into a Greensboro department store, bought some supplies, went to the segregated **lunch counter** and waited to be served. They kept waiting until the store shut. This kind of protest wasn't new; what happened next was the students came back. The next day, about 30 students joined them; the day after, nearly all the seats were occupied by black students. White youths came to heckle and the media filled with images of calm, well-dressed black students sitting waiting to be served while a crowd of white louts yelled at them, blew smoke in their faces or poured food over them. The shop finally shut due to a bomb scare, but it was too late. The issue wasn't education, housing or schooling. It was freedom and equality for black Americans in their daily lives.

> **KEY TERM**
>
> **Lunch counter**
> A place in a department store where people could get drinks and something to eat. Many lunch counters in the South were segregated, even if the department store was not.

The Student Nonviolent Coordinating Committee (SNCC)

The Student Nonviolent Coordinating Committee (SNCC) was set up in Raleigh, North Carolina on 15 April 1960. It was a racially integrated organisation of young people. The SNCC believed in non-violent direct action and students all took training sessions in how to cope with abuse and violence from whites during demonstrations. The SNCC sent out 'field secretaries' to live and work in dangerous parts of the South; one of their most important tasks was to encourage voter registration – they knew black people needed the political power of the vote to get government attention. There had been local pushes for voter registration before, for example, in Atlanta in 1935 and 1936, where the mayor, asked for adequate street lighting in black areas, said that he would provide it if the people in those areas would vote for him and vote the way he told them to in other elections. The SNCC took King's ideas a step further – it took non-violent protest into places where there was likely to be violence. CORE was also involved in the protest that followed the Greensboro sit-in; the NAACP followed more slowly, uncertain about the shift in emphasis, but won over by its youth councils. Through all of this, Martin Luther King threaded his way, speaking, advising and encouraging.

SOURCE

4

Samuel Jones was a student at the same college as the four students who sat at the lunch counter in Greensboro in 1 February 1960. In an interview in 2015 he described what happened after the store closed for the night on the day of the first sit-in.

When they returned to the college, a big discussion was held among the rest of the students. It was decided we would go back en-mass to the lunch counter the next day. It was a grand sight to see approximately thirty-five Black students marching up Market Street, the main street from A&T College to downtown Greensboro. When we got there, some of us took a seat at the lunch counter, in an orderly fashion. After a while the ones at the counter were asked to leave. When they left their seats, the rest of us sat down in them. This scenario was repeated daily, until July 26, 1960. When we first started, none of us had an inkling of what we were getting into or the impact we would make on history.

EXTRACT

2

From *We Ain't What We Ought To Be: The Black Freedom Struggle from Emancipation to Obama*, written by Stephen Tuck in 2010.

Soon there were wade-ins on the beaches, pray-ins in churches, read-ins in libraries, and piss-ins in restrooms. Whereas African Americans in Montgomery had protested segregation by staying away, this was protest by confrontation. By August 1961, over seventy thousand people had participated in some kind of direct-action protest. Hundreds of thousands more joined economic boycotts supporting the sit-ins. Within a year, over one hundred communities had desegregated their lunch counters some – starting with San Antonio, Texas, in March – to pre-empt sit-ins from even starting. On July 25, 1960, after renewed demonstrations, the lunch counter in Greensboro's Woolworths served its first black customer.

SOURCE

5

Part of the Greensboro lunch counter, on display in the Smithsonian museum. The rest of the counter is part of the International Civil Rights Museum in Greensboro. The person eating his lunch in front of the exhibit is Dr Franklin McCain, one of the original four Greensboro sit-in protesters.

THINKING HISTORICALLY Evidence (3b)

It depends on the question

When considering the usefulness of a piece of evidence, people often think about authenticity in the case of artefacts, reliability in the case of witness statements, or methodology and structure in the case of secondary accounts. A better historical approach to the usefulness of a piece of evidence would be to think about the statements that we can make about the past based on it. Different statements can be made with different degrees of certainty, depending on the evidence.

Work in small groups and answer the following:

1 Look at Source 5.

  a) Write three statements that you can reasonably make about the Greensboro sit-in based solely on Source 5.

  b) Which of the statements can be made with the greatest degree of certainty? Why is this? Which statement can be made with the smallest degree of certainty?

  c) What else might you need to increase your confidence in your statements?

2 Source 5 is an artefact and Source 4 is a witness statement. Which is more useful to the historian studying the impact of the Greensboro sit-in?

3 Look at Extract 2. How would the historian have gone about constructing this piece? What kinds of evidence would he have needed?

Freedom rides

In 1961, CORE and the SNCC carried out a series of freedom rides in the South, organised by James Farmer of CORE. These rides were to test whether bus restroom facilities had been desegregated, as they should have been after a 1961 Supreme Court ruling. The freedom riders knew that, the deeper into the South they went, the less likely it was that this would have happened and the more likely it was that they would meet with a violent reception. Farmer said they planned the rides with the intention of provoking a crisis, knowing that the publicity would affect the way the world looked at the USA. They felt that desperate measures like these seemed to be the only way to get the government to enforce legislation, not just pass it. The first two buses were attacked and riders, black and white, were beaten up at several stops. Worse followed. At Anniston, Alabama, one of the buses was firebombed after the bus had been chased by about 50 cars, some of them police cars. All the riders got off the bus alive, but the media coverage showed shocking levels of violence. The buses kept coming. Freedom riders were imprisoned in Birmingham and beaten up in Montgomery; three were killed, but others kept on riding.

Birmingham, 1963

Birmingham, Alabama was nicknamed 'Bombingham' for the regularity with which black homes, businesses and churches were firebombed. In 1963, King and the SCLC led a push to desegregate, not buses or lunch counters, but the whole town. King knew it would provoke violence, but had seen, from CORE and SNCC protests, that it worked. The campaign began on 3 April and the protesters' leaflets made specific reference to the American Dream. One tactic was to get arrested and fill the jails; by the end of the month, the jails were full. Children were trained in protest tactics and, when they marched, the racist chief of police, 'Bull' Connor, ordered his men to use high-pressure fire hoses and dogs on them. Again, shocking pictures went worldwide. President Kennedy, seeing them, admitted he felt ashamed. He sent in federal troops to restore calm on 12 May. Following that, Birmingham was desegregated. Birmingham and the publicity it produced was a significant factor in Kennedy pressing forward on civil rights legislation, as was a poll after Birmingham showing that 42 percent of people thought race was the USA's most pressing problem (only four percent had said this in 1962). The March on Washington (August 1963) showed the scale of civil rights activism, with speakers like King joined by famous white singers such as Joan Baez and Bob Dylan. Hundreds of thousands of people marched; and King's 'I have a dream' speech became instantly famous.

SOURCE 6

This photo of a police dog attack on 17-year-old Walter Gadsden was taken on 3 May 1963 in Birmingham, Alabama. It was frequently used in reports of the campaign. At the time, Gadsden was said to be one of the demonstrators. Recent articles have claimed he was just a passer-by, and that the policeman wasn't hauling him towards the dog but trying to rescue him.

Freedom Summer, 1964

In 1964, an election year, the SNCC decided on a push for voter registration, sending large numbers of volunteers to the South. They had had some volunteers in the South from the start, to encourage black people to register and to train them to pass the voter registration tests, but it was slow going. They sent 45 volunteers, mostly young, white and able to pay their own way (and afford bail to get out of jail), to Mississippi. The SNCC volunteers teamed up with local organisations for the task; most local volunteers were black. On 20 June, the first batch of students set out. The next day, three volunteers disappeared, two white, one black. They were found dead six weeks later. By the end of the summer, there had been three more murders, 35 shooting incidents and countless beatings. About 17,000 black people tried to register to vote that year. Only 1,600 were accepted.

AS Exam-Style Question Section A

Were the media the main reason for the increasing sympathy for the civil rights movement in the early 1960s? (20 marks)

Tip

Consider how the media reported the civil rights movement in the 1960s, but also consider other factors (e.g. the police tactics, rather than the reports of them; the way the demonstrators behaved).

ACTIVITY
KNOWLEDGE CHECK

Campaigning for civil rights, 1950–80

1 Write a paragraph to explain the significance of the Montgomery Bus Boycott.

2 List three ways in which the Greensboro sit-ins changed civil rights tactics.

3 List three ways in which civil rights campaigning did not change.

4 Explain how the events of 1963–64 might have contributed to growing militancy in civil rights campaigning.

5 a) Study Source 6. In pairs, discuss whether it matters if Gadsden was a demonstrator or not.

   b) How would you use this photo as evidence?

What was the impact of black militancy?

The SNCC had changed the face of campaigning – most of its members were young and intellectual, and many were white. Many people who fought for civil rights for black Americans disliked this turn of events. There had always been groups and people who advocated black militancy, the most famous being Malcolm X, but in 1965 a new organisation was set up that sparked the Black Power movement.

EXTEND YOUR KNOWLEDGE

Malcolm X (1925-65)

Malcolm X was born Malcolm Little, in Michigan. His family was among many black Americans terrorised by the Ku Klux Klan and his father was murdered (he believed by racist whites). The fatherless family moved to Harlem, in New York, and Malcolm got into trouble and went to prison. There, in 1952, he joined the Nation of Islam, a black Muslim group, and took the name Malcolm X.

He believed that non-violent protest had had its day and that, in the words of one of his speeches, it was the ballot or the bullet. He said that he didn't advocate violence except in self-defence, but it was the slogan that held people's attention. Malcolm X didn't believe white people should be involved in the civil rights movement, nor did he believe white politicians would ever do more than they were forced to do to advance it. He saw King's cultivation of white politicians in the hope of getting legislation passed as useless. He was one of the first people to stir up militancy in black Americans countrywide.

He was assassinated in 1965 and, in the months before that, he was beginning to shift his position. He had several meetings with King and his radicalism seemed to be softening. Shortly before his assassination, he remembered having once told a young white woman who offered help that she was a white devil, who could do nothing; now he would tell her to work to change white opinion.

Black Power

In 1965, Stokely Carmichael, leader of the SNCC, set up the Lowndes County Freedom Organisation in response to black feeling that, even if they had a vote, why vote for white Southerners? The group used the panther symbol and the slogan 'Vote for the Panther, then go home'. In June 1966, James Meredith (who integrated the University of Mississippi as a student in 1962) led the March Against Fear through Mississippi. He was shot on the second day. King took over, urging multiracial non-violent behaviour. Carmichael said non-violent protest wasn't working. He wanted the SNCC and the civil rights movement to radicalise and exclude white campaigners. He suggested a slogan to replace the now-traditional cry of 'Freedom'. The cry was 'Black Power!' Its symbol was a raised arm and a clenched fist. This salute was famously used in 1968 by some of the black American athletes who won medals at the Olympics.

From 1965, the movement split. There were no marches where all the civil rights movements worked together. The Black Power movement wasn't a coherent force. There were many groups, some more radical than others. The panther symbol was adopted by the Black Panthers, set up in 1966. The Panthers worked in black communities, keeping order, but also organising community projects such as free breakfasts for schoolchildren. Their ten-point programme included decent housing and black history courses at university. Not surprisingly, it was the fact they wore a uniform and carried guns that attracted the government's notice, not the community work. Some radical groups wanted separation, either within the USA or by leaving the country altogether (as the Back to Africa movement advocated). Most worked on a local level, and this was where they got the best results. Black Power students pressed for more black staff and courses on black history. Black Power workers set up radical trade unions to push for black jobs, equal pay and equal job opportunities. More than this, the ideas behind Black Power radicalised many of the long-established civil rights groups in the longer term, even the NAACP. If these groups didn't always radicalise, they became more pragmatic, seeking local solutions, such as when the leader of the NAACP in Atlanta accepted the slowing of segregation in 1973 in return for more control over black schooling. It was an acceptance that white attitudes to integration meant a generation of black children were integrated in schools, but not getting an education. What was needed was to improve things then, not just to work for the long term and the future.

ACTIVITY
KNOWLEDGE CHECK

Effect of the Black Power movement

The Black Power movement was fragmented and worked best on a small-scale, local level. Does this mean it wasn't as useful as the non-violent campaigns?

Riots

In 1964, there were major riots in New York, Chicago and Philadelphia, each set off by an instance of police brutality, but with the long-term problems of city life for blacks as their root cause. It is no coincidence that these riots, and the riots in every year afterwards up to 1971, took place in summer, when tempers in overcrowded areas with poor facilities were at their worst. The impact of the riots was significant. Government intervention to calm the violence became seen as acceptable, whereas violence by state police and guardsmen in the early 1960s had been seen by many as excessive. Media coverage of the riots meant that the image of non-violent black people assaulted by whites was replaced by the image of burning cities and a young black man with a petrol bomb. It helped hasten civil rights legislation, but brought a white backlash, not helped when riot-torn areas were given federal government aid (in 1965, the Watts district of Los Angeles got $18 million after the August riots there).

The Northern Crusade, 1966

After 1964, King began to focus on the North, visiting the badly provided, overcrowded black **ghettos**. In the summer of 1966, there were 20 major riots in city slums all over the USA. King announced a 'Northern Crusade' to improve slums by setting up tenant unions, improving working conditions and teaching young people about non-violent protest. He began with Chicago, where over 800,000 black Americans lived, mainly in ghettos (which Mayor Daley had denied existed in 1963). The campaign focused on Chicago, as it had focused on Birmingham in 1963. The Northern Crusade petered out; King claimed significant gains, but many others felt it had been a failure because it brought no permanent change. In some ways it was harder to get political support for social issues than it was for issues of segregation. King's relationship with the media was also turning sour; he accused them of trying to make non-violent campaigners like himself make militant statements, like Carmichael, or they wouldn't be reported. In 1967, he took up issues of poverty in general, beginning to plan a Poor People's Campaign with a march and a camp in Washington (similar to the Bonus March camps of 1932). As part of his support for the rights of poor workers, he supported a strike of Memphis sanitation workers in March 1968. He was assassinated while on this campaign, on 4 April 1968.

KEY TERM

Ghetto
Part of a town or city where a certain racial group is expected to live, set apart from the rest of the town or city.

The impact of civil rights legislation

Two major pieces of civil rights legislation were passed between 1955 and 1980: the 1964 Civil Rights Act and the 1965 Voting Rights Act. The timeline on page 53 shows the main civil rights legislation, 1917–80. It does not include the rulings in cases brought to enforce the legislation, just the laws themselves. Notice the **extensions**, which were made in attempts to make the laws work in practice.

FURTHER SIGNIFICANT CIVIL RIGHTS EVENTS, 1955–65

25 November 1955
Segregation on interstate buses is banned all over the USA

12 March 1956
102 Southern Congressmen sign the Southern Manifesto, condemning *Brown v Board of Education*

11 June 1963
Governor of Alabama stops two black students desegregating the university; Kennedy takes over state troops to make it happen

28 August 1963
March on Washington is biggest civil rights protest up to that date; estimates of numbers involved range from 200,000 to 500,000

2 July 1964
Civil Rights Act is passed banning discrimination in voting, public services and work

January–February 1965
Civil rights voter registration campaign in Selma, Montgomery; mass arrests; on 18 February a campaigner is shot by a state trooper

February–March 1956
Autherine Lucy becomes the first black student to go to the University of Mississippi; the white riots are so bad she is expelled

30 September 1962
James Meredith integrates the University of Mississippi, but only with the help of 3,000 federal troops and in the face of rioting

12 June 1963
Medgar Evers, a leader of the Mississippi NAACP, is shot

15 September 1963
Black church Sunday School is bombed in Birmingham; four girls are killed (21st firebombing in eight years)

10 December 1964
Martin Luther King is awarded the Nobel Peace Prize

7 March 1965
Selma to Montgomery March in response to shooting; more arrests and violence; march eventually finishes with federal troop escort

KEY TERM

Extension
A change to a law that adds something, usually to tighten it up. So *Brown v the Board of Education* said schools should be desegregated, but gave no timetable. The following year, *Brown II* was ruled – it was the same as *Brown v Board of Education* but with an added timescale (which was, however, far too vague): 'with all deliberate speed'.

These legal changes came after decades of struggle and protest. After 1955, it became more and more likely that civil rights campaigners would be arrested, beaten up or even killed. Even if places were forced to desegregate, it didn't make black Americans welcome, let alone safe. Civil rights campaigners in the Deep South could almost expect to have their homes, offices and churches firebombed. Black children and adults who were integrated in its schools and colleges had to face hatred and violence and didn't get anything like a 'normal' education. The price of this legislation was very high. Even in places in the South where desegregation was not violently resisted, there were still many problems. In 1965, the NAACP took the town of Charlotte to court because its schools reorganisation by area meant that, as many black people lived in the poorest areas, just as in the North, there was an 'informal' segregation. The NAACP pushed for busing black children to schools in other areas, to integrate them. The courts turned this down but, in 1971, the Supreme Court upheld the idea of busing. Other cities were able to introduce busing after this, often against local resistance. So what did the legislation achieve?

MAIN CIVIL RIGHTS LEGISLATION 1917–80

29 August 1957
Civil Rights Act sets up a Civil Rights Commission and gives the federal justice department more rights to supervise voter registration

6 May 1960
Civil Rights Act makes it a crime to obstruct federal orders (such as school desegregation) by threat or force and authorises federal 'referees' for voting

20 November 1962
President Kennedy's Executive Order 1106 bans discrimination in the allocation of federal housing

2 July 1964
Civil Rights Act bans discrimination for sex or race in hiring, firing and promoting; Equal Opportunities Commission is set up to enforce this

6 August 1965
Voting Rights Act is passed banning any attempts to stop people voting because of their race; provisions are put in place for five years for federal enforcement of this; the enforcement provisions have to be reconfirmed, with extensions, in 1970, 1975, 1982 and 2007

21 May 1970
Emergency School Aid Act gives funding to schools that are desegregating or struggling after desegregating; there is a second of these acts two years later

20 April 1971
Swann v Charlotte-Mecklenburg Board of Education upholds the policy of busing children out of poor areas to desegregated schools

23 June 1972
Education Amendments Act restricts busing by giving more money to inner-city schools for improvements

Achievements

Legally, in 1980, black Americans were full citizens, just as they were in 1917. In 1980, there was more pressure from federal government to make equality actually happen. For example, since 1961, there have been a series of presidential executive orders to introduce 'affirmative action', giving preference to black interviewees for jobs in government and in businesses generally. By 1980, after huge amounts of campaigning against the violence and discrimination they faced, bringing more of both down upon themselves in some cases, the circumstances of black Americans had changed.

- A black American upper and middle class had developed to a significant extent. Black upper classes tended to be based in cities such as New York and Washington and to model themselves on white society. They were proof of the equality of blacks and whites – but many radicals felt that they had sold out by trying to fit in to white society. Black professionals had, if not equal, significant access to work in the higher levels of business, education, government, the law – all the professions. There were a significant number of black politicians, at local, state and federal level.

- On a socio-economic employment score that runs from 7 for a servant or day labourer to 75, professional black American men moved from an average of 16 in 1940 to 21 in 1960 and to 31 in 1980. In the same periods, the score for black women went from 13 to 21 to 36. Black Americans had several routes to success via sport or entertainment, as well as through the professions. Black people featured more on television and in the cinema; there were more of their books in bookshops and their magazines in paper shops. Home ownership among blacks increased and the number of black graduates went up too.

- More black Americans voted, although voter registration slowed after 1968. In 1966, government census figures show 58.2 percent of black Americans were registered to vote; in 1980, it was 60 percent.

Limits to success

However, there were limits to the improvements that the legislation and civil rights campaigning brought. Maybe some black people were now able to reach for the American Dream; hardly any of them were doing it on an equal level with white Americans. Even the wealthiest of black Americans were made to feel unequal by white people in the same social sphere. The passing of the Civil Rights Act and the Voter Registration Act meant that many people now felt that the issue of civil rights had been dealt with. Affirmative action orders were followed – however, not all blacks thought this was an advance. It resulted in a 'minority quota' way of thinking that created its own limits ('we've got enough minority employees now') and made those black people who got jobs (and some white co-workers) feel they were not there on merit. The radicalisation of some parts of the movement combined with the rioting in the cities to make many people less sympathetic to the rights of black Americans. Quite unreasonably, the death of King made some people turn from black civil rights to other issues; the big spokesman had gone and the war in Vietnam was becoming a bigger issue.

Although significant upper- and middle-class groups had emerged, the poor were getting poorer and more of them were falling below the poverty line than in 1959. There were more black children in schools, but most of these schools were still in the poorest areas and some were still segregated. Poor living conditions continued to affect every aspect of the lives of black Americans. Black babies were more likely to die and black schoolchildren were less likely to succeed and more likely to drop out of education. Gang culture had begun to dominate the ghettos of the big cities, especially Los Angeles; crime rates were higher. In 1980, 75 percent of black high school drop-outs, aged 25–34, had criminal records.

EXTRACT

3

From *The American Dream: From Reconstruction to Reagan*, written by Esmond Wright in 1996.

If faith in integration has waned since 1954, so too has faded the belief that ensuring civil rights is the key to narrowing the divide between blacks and whites. Though affirmative action and other legal strategies designed to expand minority opportunity have enlarged the black middle class, such programs offer less practical help to African-Americans trapped in poor neighbourhoods. As Drew S Days, solicitor general at the Justice Department, acknowledged in 1994, not even 'massive enforcement' of all existing civil rights laws 'would alter significantly the lives of millions of black and other minority people who live at, or beyond, the margins of mainstream America.'

EXTRACT

4

From *Blacks in the 1970s: Did They Scale the Job Ladder?* a Bureau of Labor Statistics report written by Diane Nilsen Westcott in 1982.

The growth of black employment in the expanding skilled craft area was particularly important, in that blacks were able to move into some of the better-paid positions, and, for the most part, were able to increase their earnings relative to their white counterparts in the blue collar occupations. Overall, shifts by blacks into the higher-salaried occupations were rather limited; this was most apparent for those who resided in the central city areas. The majority of blacks lived in central cities, which have high concentrations of office and other business district-type activities. Yet, by 1980, central city blacks had made little progress in increasing their proportion in white collar occupations. Most of the occupational upgrading occurred among the smaller number of blacks who resided in suburban areas.

ACTIVITY
KNOWLEDGE CHECK

How the media affected civil rights campaigns

1 Draw a flowchart to show how media attention benefited or hindered civil rights from 1955 to 1970.

2 Read Extract 3.

   a) How does the extract suggest that civil rights legislation is not enough?

   b) The solicitor-general doesn't explain why he feels massive enforcement of civil rights legislation would fail. Think of three reasons why it might.

3 Draw a diagram to show the achievements and limits to success of the civil rights legislation.

THINKING HISTORICALLY Change (4b–c)

The bird's-eye view

The event	Medium-term consequences	Long-term consequences
Passing of the Civil Rights Act	Positive feeling of achievement and expectation among black Americans Some government moves to support equality (e.g. affirmative action) Diminishing support for civil rights movement among some whites; movement runs out of steam	Disenchantment with lack of progress among black Americans Slowing of government support White impatience with the demands of minorities, especially black Americans, for 'preferential treatment'

Imagine you are looking at the whole of history using a zoomed-out interactive map like Google Maps. You have a general view of the sweep of developments and their consequences, but you cannot see much detail. If you zoom in to the time of the passing of the Civil Rights Act, you can see the event in detail but will know nothing of its consequences in the medium or long term. If you zoom in to look at the medium- or long-term consequences, you will know about them in detail but will know very little about the event that caused them.

Look at the table above and answer the following questions:

1 What were the immediate consequences of the event?

2 In what ways are the medium-term consequences different from the long-term consequences?

Work in groups of three.

Each student takes the role of the teacher for one of the above (the event, medium-term consequences or long-term consequences) and gives a short presentation to the other two. They may comment and ask questions. After each presentation, the other two members of the group write a 100-word paragraph showing how the presentation links to their own.

Answer the following questions individually:

3 What happens to the detail when you zoom out to look at the whole sweep of history?

4 What are the advantages and disadvantages of zooming in to look at a specific time in detail?

5 How could you use the map in order to get a good understanding of history as a whole?

HOW AND WHY DID MINORITY RIGHTS BECOME SIGNIFICANT, 1960–80?

From the 1960s, minority groups pursued claims for equal opportunities, many using tactics similar to those of black Americans in the civil rights movement. This section considers three of these.

Native Americans

Native American civil rights activities during 1960–80 must be seen against the background of hundreds of years of patchwork policies and violence. Government policies towards Native Americans, managed by the federal Bureau of Indian Affairs (BIA), shifted between breaking up or supporting tribal existence. Roosevelt reversed the trend of assimilation under his Indian New Deal, but wanted Indian tribes run in a 'constitutional' way, under tribal councils. After Roosevelt, federal policy became assimilation again; the BIA encouraged Native Americans to move to towns and cities for work, offering job training and housing, but disrupting tribal culture. In 1953, the House of Representatives passed a resolution for '**termination**'. Many Native Americans resisted termination; under a later ruling, termination needed the tribe's consent. By 1970, about half of all Native Americans lived in towns or cities. It was from these groups that the civil rights campaigners came.

KEY TERM

Termination
A policy by which Native Americans were freed from federal control and protected (and policed) by US federal and state laws, but tribal lands once held in trust for them by the government would now be open for sale.

The issues

The Native American fight for rights covered the following main issues.

- **Tribal homelands:** Many Native Americans had been driven from their homelands in the forced relocation of the 1830s, following the Indian Removal Act of 1830. The federal government made treaties (many by force) with individual tribes, giving land and money for their removal. By the 1960s, it was widely agreed, even in government, that the treaties had been unfair. Many Native Americans wanted new treaties, maybe even to return to their homelands and sacred sites where possible.

- **Self-determination:** The tribes had long had an unusual position in the USA. They were independent nations under federal government. Tribes ran their own affairs, but only in their own reservations and only under the control of the BIA. The BIA had, over the years, very heavy-handedly implemented regulations to break up Indian culture and damage tribal cohesion. It oversaw the setting up of Indian Boarding Schools from 1893 onwards. These schools made the children speak nothing but English, cut their hair, dress in 'proper' clothes and give up their native customs. Older children were placed as farm workers in the East and Midwest. Years of actions like this had made Native Americans mistrustful of the BIA; they certainly felt it didn't have their interests at heart. They wanted respect for the tribal organisation, freedom to run their own affairs and a change of BIA personnel.

Organised protest

In 1968, the Indian Civil Rights Act banned tribes from restricting the civil rights of tribal members. It didn't do anything to redress issues Native Americans had with federal government. In the same year, the American Indian Movement (AIM) was set up. Its members were mostly young urban people. Unlike the only other big Indian organisation, The National Congress of American Indians (NCAI) (which worked within the system), AIM took a more radical, anti-federal stance and the slogan 'Red Power'. It consciously adopted the direct action techniques of black American civil rights groups, including sit-ins, demonstrations and occupations. It had a specific issue with its homelands, so groups often targeted disputed land for occupation, although they also occupied federal buildings. AIM also specifically targeted the demeaning of Native American culture by white people in their 'Red Indians' pastiches of the culture.

EXTEND YOUR KNOWLEDGE

The Voluntary Relocation Programme
This federal scheme began in 1952 in order to encourage assimilation. The 1956 Indian Relocation Act encouraged Native Americans aged 18–35 to move to specified towns and cities for work. Many did, but very few found the lifestyle the government brochures suggested they would. By 1961, the BIA estimated that between 25 and 33 percent had returned; other sources suggested this was well over 50–90 percent for some tribes. However, the initial dislocation meant that, while some Native Americans returned, others left and the tribal structure was dislocated.

MAJOR NATIVE AMERICAN PROTESTS

20 November 1969
The Alcatraz Red Power Movement (ARPM) takes over Alcatraz Island (a former US prison) and occupies it until 1971

1971
AIM membership is now 4,500 (total Indian population about one million); violence when AIM protests at white Boy Scouts performing 'Indian Dances' in Topeka, Kansas; protests at Fort Snelling, Minnesota and the Black Hills of Dakota

1972
AIM Trail of Broken Treaties, a protest drive to Washington to protest outside the BIA about BIA management of many issues, including its not renegotiating the many government treaties that originally took over Native American land; BIA building is occupied

February 1973
AIM occupies the village of Wounded Knee and declares independence as the Oglala Sioux Nation; unlike all other occupations, this time the government resorts to sending in US marshalls and the state police; the siege lasts 71 days and AIM only withdraws once the government agrees to an investigation of its demands and grievances

February–July 1978
The Longest Walk from San Francisco to Washington to protest about the forced removal of American Indians from their homelands and against Congress' unwillingness to renegotiate treaties

Gains and limitations

President Nixon sympathised with Native American rights campaigners and felt that it should be possible to make positive changes for about 830,000 people that it wasn't possible to do for the 22,600,000 black Americans. He rejected both termination and forced assimilation. His advisors consulted tribal leaders on solutions. Nixon brought bills to Congress for Indian autonomy. By 1980, Congress had passed the 1972 Indian Education Act (funds for tribal schools), the 1974 Indian Financing Act (which lent tribes funding) and the 1975 Indian Self-Determination Act (which kept the BIA but contracted out services such as health and education), giving tribes much more control. In the same year, the Voting Rights Act was extended to cover more racial groups, including Native Americans, and to provide language assistance when voting. The 1978 Indian Child Welfare Act gave Native Americans more control over the adoption of Native American children.

In 1970, Congress returned land at Blue Lake to the Taos Pueblo tribe. In 1971, the Alaska Native Claims Settlement Act transferred 40 million acres of land and $462,500,000 to Native Alaskans. All through the 1970s, there was a dribble of land returns, often, as with the Kootenai tribe in Idaho, after occupation of the area. However, Nixon's administration didn't reform the BIA, nor did Nixon renegotiate about Native American sacred sites. There was no overall solution to the land issues and various states, for example, Hawaii in 1971, continued to evict Indians from land if the state wanted it for building or other use.

ACTIVITY
KNOWLEDGE CHECK

Native Americans

Explain elements of the Native American situation that might make it (a) harder and (b) easier to solve.

Hispanic Americans

'Hispanics' is usually used to mean Americans with a Spanish-speaking background, mostly from Mexico, Puerto Rico and Cuba. Nixon was the first politician to use the term consistently. Hispanic people tended to cluster together in different parts of the country. As a generalisation, Puerto Ricans tended to live in the poor areas of Northern cities, especially New York and Chicago. Cubans tended to live in Florida. Mexicans tended to settle in California and Texas, often working on the land. The *bracero* **programme** guaranteed incoming Mexicans the same wages as existing workers, but this didn't always work. When Mexicans were forced to work for lower wages, other farm workers resented it, seeing the Mexicans as taking their jobs.

KEY TERM

Bracero **programme**
A Mexican immigration programme run by the US government, 1942–64. Mexicans signed contracts to work, usually on the land, in the USA for a set period of time in return for a guaranteed level of housing and working conditions. During that period, 4.6 million contracts were signed.

The issues

The Hispanic fight for rights covered the following main issues:

- **Land:** The 1846–48 American–Mexican war was ended by the Treaty of Guadalupe Hidalgo. It settled the border between the USA and Mexico, also allocating land in other states. Mexicans living in areas that became American could become US citizens or relocate to Mexico. The issue of land rights in what became New Mexico became a focus of protest.

- **Workers' rights:** Hispanic farm workers, especially those in the *bracero* programme, often had appalling living and working conditions. When workers returned after the Second World War, farmers adopted a 'take it or leave it' attitude to worker complaints. Most workers had no unions and there was a large pool of illegal migrant workers to call on.

- **Discrimination:** Hispanics faced the same problems of racial discrimination as black Americans. In towns and cities, they lived in Spanish-speaking areas (*barrios*) in the worst parts of town, with poor government provision. Often the two groups lived side by side, sometimes peacefully, sometimes not.

- **Deportation:** The US immigration services, from 1953 onwards, deported millions of Hispanic people (3.8 million, including US citizens who were active in protest, in **Operation Wetback** during 1953–58).

KEY TERM

Operation Wetback (1953–58)
A US government drive to find illegal Mexican immigrants and return them to Mexico.

Fighting for rights

Hispanic groups fought for rights in different ways. There was interaction between many of the groups. For example, Cesar Chavez, whose main concern was workers' rights, spoke to rallies to mobilise Hispanic voters in Los Angeles (LA) and two of his organisers in the farm workers' union moved to LA to work at *La Raza*, the most significant of the Hispanic movement's newspapers.

- Cesar Chavez fought a non-violent campaign for the rights of farm workers, focusing on working conditions. He set up a farm workers' union and organised strikes, marches and protests. He also gained publicity by fasting in protest. He travelled widely, speaking to large rallies in cities such as LA.

- Reies López Tijerina organised protests about Mexican land rights in New Mexico. He started with legal protests but, when these seemed to get nowhere, held marches, mass demonstrations and camp-ins on National Forest land. He and Black Power leaders signed an agreement to work together. In 1967, López Tijerina and others went into a county courthouse to make a citizen's arrest of an abusive district attorney. Things went wrong, they took hostages and a gun battle followed.

- Rodolfo Gonzales focused on race. At first, he worked for Hispanic rights within the system, for instance, he was director of the Denver War on Poverty campaign, but he came to favour more radical methods. His Crusade for Justice offered a version of black pride, stressing the importance of racial identity and the need to fight for Hispanic rights at once, locally and by direct action. Crusade for Justice influenced a student walk-out in LA in 1966 and much of the direct action by urban youth that followed, including the Young Citizens for Community Action (YCCA), which had contacts with the Black Power movement.

- Some Hispanics decided to work through political influence. Led by José Angel Gutiérrez, the *La Raza Unida* party set out to encourage Hispanic people to register to vote, and then to provide them with party candidates to vote for, who would support their interests if elected. It campaigned for better work, housing and education. Begun in Texas, it spread to California and Colorado.

- The Brown Berets was a young, militant organisation, set up in 1967 in East LA. Members wore uniform, like the Black Panthers (who also wore berets), campaigned against police brutality and led school walk-outs. By 1968, there were Brown Beret members in most urban centres with a Hispanic population.

EXTEND YOUR KNOWLEDGE

Cesar Chavez (1927–93)

Cesar Chavez was one of seven children from a family that lost its home in the Great Depression, joining the flood of migrant workers to California. He served in the US Navy during the Second World War, then settled in San Jose. He joined the Community Services Organisation (CSO) in 1952 and rose to become its leader. In 1962, he moved to Delano and set up the National Farm Workers Association (NFWA), the farmers' union. His commitment impressed people (e.g. his personal protest fasts, modelled on Mahatma Gandhi). He died in 1993; 40,000 people came to his funeral.

EXTRACT

5 From an article in an American law journal about the LA Thirteen and Hispanic resistance, written by Ian F. Hanley López in 2001.

By 1968, the year of the first major protests in East Los Angeles, the African-American struggle had held the attention of the nation for years. Nightly television brought protest marches, sit-ins, freedom rides, swinging police clubs, snarling dogs, and spraying fire hoses into the homes of the Southwest. Place names like Selma, Montgomery, Birmingham, and Jackson evoked images of marches and police lines, demonstrations and mass arrests, protests and repression. Events in Detroit, Newark, and Watts also entered the public imagination, juxtaposing enraged faces, clamorous voices, milling mobs, and burning buildings with riot police, national guardsmen, sirens, and tear gas, all against a background of desperate urban poverty and extreme segregation. America seemed to be reduced to a place of rioting minorities, flame-engulfed cities, and massive police intervention. Then, in April 1968, a month after the East Los Angeles walkouts, Martin Luther King, Jr., was assassinated in Memphis, Tennessee. And in June, days after the East Los Angeles indictments and arrests, Robert Kennedy, who had supported the walkouts and who had walked arm-in-arm with Cesar Chavez, was shot to death in Los Angeles. As Chicanos in East Los Angeles mobilized around conditions in the schools and later around the arrests of community leaders in the spring of 1968, they did so in the midst of social upheaval and increasing violence.

MAJOR HISPANIC AMERICAN PROTESTS

1962
Cesar Chavez sets up the National Farm Workers Association (NFWA)

1965
Luis Valdez sets up *El Teatro Campesino*, the first farm workers' theatre, using entertainment to educate workers about their rights

1967
UFWOC urges national boycott of grapes

3 December 1967
Brown Berets organisation is set up in East LA

1 June 1968
Over 10,000 students walk out of mainly Mexican schools in East LA, protesting the conditions (walkouts had been happening since May); 13 activists are arrested

1969
Young Puerto Ricans in Chicago set up the Young Lords Organisation, modelled on the Black Panthers, even down to providing breakfast clubs for local schoolchildren

1971
Brown Berets march 1,000 miles from Calexico to Sacramento to protest against police brutality and all forms of discrimination

1973
1970 farm worker contracts are not renewed; widespread strikes, demonstrations, thousands are arrested, two are killed

1975
California's Agricultural Labor Relations Act recognises the right of farm workers to unionise

1965
Delano grape strike of the mostly Mexican NFWA and the mostly Filipino Agricultural Workers Organising Committee (AWOC)

1966
Farm workers march 300 miles from Delano to Sacramento; NFWA and AWOC unite as the United Farm Workers Organising Committee (UFWOC); Rodolfo Gonzales founds Crusade for Justice; Schools in East LA form Young Citizens for Community Action (YCCA)

1968
Chavez goes on a 25-day hunger fast; Robert Kennedy joins him for the end of the fast

2 June 1968
About 200 people protest outside the School Board offices about arrests; the next day about 2,000 protest outside the LA police station

1970
UFWOC negotiates a settlement of the grape strike with a three-year contract for good conditions

1972
Chavez fasts in Arizona against its farm labour laws

1974
First Southwest Voter Education Project; over two million voters register by 1994

1975
Voting Rights Act extension provides language assistance at polling stations and extends rights (which the initial Act only gave to blacks and Puerto Ricans) to Native Americans, Asian Americans and Hispanic groups

Gains and limitations

Legal acceptance of Hispanic rights was slow coming; it wasn't until 1954 that the Supreme Court ruled that Hispanic people were equal citizens. In 1966, Congress's Cuban American Adjustment Act said all Cubans who had lived in the USA for a year were permanent residents. No other Hispanic group was given this right. In 1968, the Mexican American Legal Defense and Education fund was set up to pursue civil rights in the courts. In 1973, the Supreme Court upheld an 'equal provision of education' case against a Texas school. Hispanics were covered by legislation such as the 1974 Supreme Court ruling on the rights of Limited English Proficient (LEP) students in *Lau v Nichols* (Chinese students were not getting equal education opportunities in an integrated classroom because they had not been taught sufficient English). This case led to the 1974 Equal Opportunities Act, which provided for more bilingual teaching in schools. In 1975, a Voting Rights Act extension provided language assistance at polling stations and extended rights (which the initial act only gave to blacks and Puerto Ricans) to Native Americans, Asian Americans and Hispanic groups.

Civil rights campaigns did produce changes within the states: Chavez's campaign made a significant difference to the conditions of farm workers. Local campaigning did improve schools and housing, just as it did for black Americans, but, as for black Americans, the level of change varied from place to place, as did the levels of enforcement of these legal rights. The land issues raised by protesters have still not been settled.

> **A Level Exam-Style Question Section B**
>
> To what extent did Hispanic Americans draw on the tactics and resources of black Americans in their struggle for civil rights? (20 marks)
>
> **Tip**
> *Consider the similarities, but consider what was unique about the Hispanic situation.*

ACTIVITY
KNOWLEDGE CHECK

Hispanic rights

1 Write a paragraph giving your views on why Hispanic rights were a complicated issue.

2 List various tactics employed by Hispanic rights campaigners.

Gay rights

Unlike black, Native and Hispanic Americans, gay Americans were not part of a visible racial group. That didn't stop people discriminating against them; some restaurants and bars wouldn't serve them, some hotels wouldn't put them up. Their very invisibility made some people fearful, just as they feared communism – another invisible 'disease'. In the 1950s, Congress said that homosexuality was a mental illness. A 'Lavender Scare' ran parallel to the 'Red Scare' to root out homosexuals; thousands lost their jobs. One problem gays faced, like other minority groups, was that legislation was a state matter, not a federal matter. Until Illinois repealed its anti-gay laws in 1962, homosexuality was illegal in every state in the USA. Homosexuality was not decriminalised across the country until 2003. Campaigners for gay rights had to use human rights law or argue that the 1964 Civil Rights Act, which said no discrimination for race or gender, also applied to gays.

The gay rights movement

The gay rights movement was formed after the incident at the Stonewall Inn in Greenwich Village, New York on 28 June 1969. Police raided the bar, which they did regularly, supposedly for breaking some liquor licensing laws, but actually because it was known as a gay bar. People who went to the bar were used to the raids and had a routine for slipping away, but that night something snapped when a policeman was too rough with one of the customers. About 400 people began to fight back, throwing things and yelling at the police (who were forced to barricade themselves in the bar for safety). For several nights running, there were protests and clashes with the police in the area around the bar. Over the next few weeks, the issue of gay rights exploded: the Gay Liberation Front was set up and a spate of large, peaceful protests for gay rights and against gay oppression were organised.

Before Stonewall, there had been many individual stories of people, or groups of people, targeting discrimination against gays. Afterwards, it was found possible to gather enough people to have a sizeable protest march, and that marching and visible protest gained gay rights organisations more and more support. Gay Pride marches were held in several cities on 28 August 1970; the New York march alone had about 10,000 marchers.

Taking to the streets

Gay liberation groups sprang up all over the USA. The Gay Liberation Front was set up in the weeks following the Stonewall Inn riots. Many people joined, while others set up their own local gay rights groups. These groups worked both individually and together in an initial climate of mutual acceptance. They took to the streets in protest, and a combination of public support and the predominantly liberal climate of the late 1960s and 1970s meant that the gay rights movement expanded very rapidly. Highly visible gay communities sprang up in cities such as San Francisco, New York, Chicago and Seattle. They tended to form in, or near, areas with a significant counter-culture community, such as Greenwich Village, New York; these were areas where levels of welcome and acceptance were high. The pressure this exerted had an effect on both public opinion and government reaction. Partly this was because most people discovered that people whom they knew and liked were gay, and many of the prejudices against gays dissolved in the light of what they knew about actual gay friends and acquaintances. As early as 1977, polls suggested that over 50 percent of people believed in equal rights for gays. However, certain groups were still very anti-gay, the Ku Klux Klan being one of the more extreme of them, and there was a lot of hostility to gays in parts of the country such as the rural 'Bible Belt' (much of the South) where religious fundamentalism fuelled hostility.

EXTRACT

6 From *The Meaning of Gay*, written by J. Todd Abercrombie in 2010.

African American Civil Rights movement and gay men's identification with blacks provided a framework for conceiving of themselves as a community and as an oppressed minority. The radical movements, especially in Berkeley, furnished the fertile ground for intellectual critique and for political organizing. And finally, the counterculture and hippie movement provided a model for how to live outside the norm and inspired many gay men with the idea that gayness might be part of an 'authentic' self that they had to seek out and express. Obviously, the cultural and social milieu of San Francisco between 1961 and 1972 served as a rich ground out of which gay men could create a meaningful gayness.

SOURCE

7 This photograph of Harvey Milk shows him taking part in San Francisco's gay freedom parade on 26 June 1978, the year after he was elected to a local government job in San Francisco.

Success

The mid- to late 1970s were, for many, the heyday of the gay rights movement. In 1974, Kathy Kozachenko became the first openly gay candidate elected to public office. In 1977, Harvey Milk was elected to office in San Francisco. He was not only openly gay, he also supported many other kinds of minority rights (e.g. setting up non-white women's groups to work for equality) and took an open stand against **Proposition 6**: this was a move at state level that proposed firing gay teachers and teachers who spoke out in favour of gay rights. Milk was the first gay official who made it clear that his being gay affected his political activities as well as his private life. Milk and the pro-gay mayor of San Francisco were both assassinated on 27 November 1979.

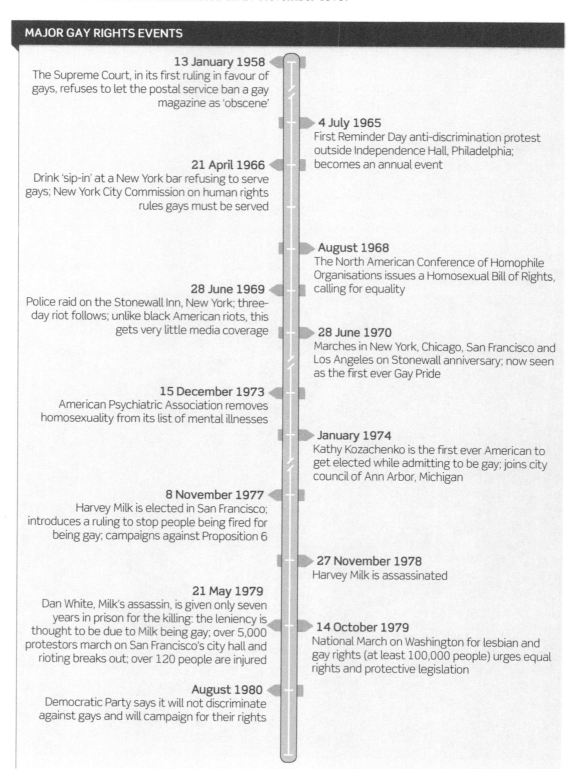

MAJOR GAY RIGHTS EVENTS

13 January 1958
The Supreme Court, in its first ruling in favour of gays, refuses to let the postal service ban a gay magazine as 'obscene'

4 July 1965
First Reminder Day anti-discrimination protest outside Independence Hall, Philadelphia; becomes an annual event

21 April 1966
Drink 'sip-in' at a New York bar refusing to serve gays; New York City Commission on human rights rules gays must be served

August 1968
The North American Conference of Homophile Organisations issues a Homosexual Bill of Rights, calling for equality

28 June 1969
Police raid on the Stonewall Inn, New York; three-day riot follows; unlike black American riots, this gets very little media coverage

28 June 1970
Marches in New York, Chicago, San Francisco and Los Angeles on Stonewall anniversary; now seen as the first ever Gay Pride

15 December 1973
American Psychiatric Association removes homosexuality from its list of mental illnesses

January 1974
Kathy Kozachenko is the first ever American to get elected while admitting to be gay; joins city council of Ann Arbor, Michigan

8 November 1977
Harvey Milk is elected in San Francisco; introduces a ruling to stop people being fired for being gay; campaigns against Proposition 6

27 November 1978
Harvey Milk is assassinated

21 May 1979
Dan White, Milk's assassin, is given only seven years in prison for the killing: the leniency is thought to be due to Milk being gay; over 5,000 protestors march on San Francisco's city hall and rioting breaks out; over 120 people are injured

14 October 1979
National March on Washington for lesbian and gay rights (at least 100,000 people) urges equal rights and protective legislation

August 1980
Democratic Party says it will not discriminate against gays and will campaign for their rights

Gains and limitations

Gay support at federal level was slow coming. However, gay pressure in some states led to positive gay initiatives at state and local level on issues both political and personal. Between 1979 and 1981, the governor of California appointed four openly gay state judges. In 1980, a gay teenage boy in Rhode Island sued his high school for the right to bring a male date to the school prom. He won.

However, in the 1970s, as part of the conservative backlash, people began to campaign against gay rights. In Dade County, Florida, in 1977, a law was proposed to stop discrimination in housing, public facilities (e.g. hotels and restaurants) and employment. Anita Bryan, famous as the spokeswoman for the Citrus Commission in Florida, set up Save Our Children (SOC) and collected petitions against the law – saying gay integration meant 'normal' children would become corrupted. The law was rejected and several similar laws proposed in other states were rejected after action by SOC or similar local groups. These groups projected an image of gay people as, not self-contained, but actively recruiting by preying on the young. From this sprang the 1978 Proposition 6 (Briggs Initiative). It was rejected by voters in California but set off a spate of similar local proposals. Also, the religious right became more outspoken in its opposition and gained more outspoken support from conservatives, and increasing support from some Republicans, including (the later president) Ronald Reagan.

ACTIVITY
KNOWLEDGE CHECK

Gays

1 How do the following show a shift in direction in gay rights campaigning and responses to it:

a) The Stonewall riots

b) The career of Harvey Milk

c) Proposition 6?

General

2 Draw a Venn diagram to show how the issues in minority rights campaigns were similar and different.

ACTIVITY
SUMMARY

1 List the ways in which black American civil rights tactics were similar/dissimilar before and after 1950.

2 Write notes for an essay on how far you agree with the statement: 'The civil rights movement **was** Martin Luther King. It took off with him and it died down after his assassination.'

3 You are going to take part in a debate on the statement: 'The achievements of civil rights campaigners were not worth the price paid for them.' You don't know whether you will be arguing for or against the proposal. Make notes on arguments that could support either side, giving specific examples.

4 Write at least a page to explain how far you agree with the statement: 'Minority rights campaigners just copied the tactics of the black American civil rights movement, they did nothing unique.'

WIDER READING

Chavez, Cesar and Stavans, Ilan, *An Organiser's Tale*, Penguin Classics (2008) is a collection of the speeches of Chavez. Speeches by King and other activists can be easily found in most libraries.

Recordings of speeches by Martin Luther King Jr, Malcolm X and Stokely Carmichael (black American civil rights), Russell Means (Native American rights), Cesar Chavez (Hispanic American rights) and Harvey Milk (gay rights) can be found online.

The Black Power Mixtape 1967–1975 is a 2011 documentary, extracts can be found online.

The History Channel has articles and podcasts on several topics, search the topic (e.g. Stonewall riots).

1.3 Society and culture in change, 1917–80

KEY QUESTIONS

- How significantly did the position of women change, 1917–80?
- How much was society affected by immigration in the years 1917–80?
- To what extent did popular culture and news media impact on society, 1917–80?

INTRODUCTION

The American Dream was a dream that many members of its society shared, no matter who they were or where they originally came from. But the shape of the Dream shifted and the extent it was available to people changed too, over the years, in just the same way as attitudes to black Americans and minority groups changed and their opportunities shifted. Some social groups, such as women and immigrants, cross racial divides; yet reactions to them as members of these groups could be just as prejudiced as racist reactions.

Despite promises and legislation, the gap between legal rights and what was achievable was sometimes enormous, and always there.

Between the years 1917 and 1980, one group of Americans faced, at least to some degree, the following problems in the workplace:

- They were paid less than white men for doing exactly the same job, even if they had more experience.
- They were less likely to get a job than a white male applicant.
- They were more likely to get fired, if jobs needed cutting, than a white man.
- They were constantly passed over for promotion in favour of white men.
- They were unlikely to reach the top level of their work environment.
- They were seen as less committed and more unreliable than white men.
- They were not given credit for their intelligence and ideas.

Can you spot the group? It is quite difficult, because these problems could be applied to many minority groups: black Americans, Hispanic Americans, Native Americans and other ethnic groups, immigrants or not. Here is one more problem that this particular group faced:

- They were turned down for work or refused promotion on the grounds that they would get pregnant and leave.

Does the fact that women faced these problems throughout the period mean that their situation didn't change at all? That is what the first part of this chapter will consider. It then goes on to consider the situation of immigrants and the problems they had achieving the Dream. Finally, we look at how popular culture and media fed society images of the Dream and also shaped how members of society thought about their government and each other.

1929
October The Wall Street Crash kick-starts the Great Depression

1941
8 December USA declares war on Japan
11 December Germany declares war on the USA

| 1915 | 1920 | 1925 | 1930 | 1935 | 1940 | 1945 |

1919–20
First Red Scare
1920 Emergency Quota Act restricts immigration for the first time and sets a numerical limit on entry
18 August 1920 Women in the USA get the vote, with the same conditions as men

1939
September Outbreak of Second World War in Europe; women into war work

1945
8 May Second World War [...] in Europe
6 August USA drops atom[...] bomb on Hiroshima
2 September End of the Second World War in the P[...]

HOW SIGNIFICANTLY DID THE POSITION OF WOMEN CHANGE, 1917–80?

The impact of the First World War

Before the First World War, women in the USA were still struggling to get the right to vote. The war gave them a chance to work, although their wages were often less than what a man would be paid for the job. Once the war ended, most women were fired, to open jobs to returning men. One gain from the war was that Congress passed the 19th Amendment to the Constitution, giving women the vote under the same state rules as men. It was ratified on 18 August 1920. So, now women could vote; as long as they voted in large numbers, politicians would address the broader issue of women's rights in order to gain their votes. In 1920, the League of Women Voters was set up to conduct the equivalent of the civil rights movement's voter registration drives: to encourage women to vote. However, many poorer women did not vote, or voted the way their husbands told them to. Few black women voted, especially in the South. It was mainly educated white women who felt that the vote was a significant change.

The Roaring Twenties

The 1920s were later called the 'Roaring Twenties' because an economic boom meant that many people were better off than ever before. Mass production made consumer goods cheaper and hire purchase made them easier to buy. Road building meant cars could travel further, faster. Widespread electrification meant that more people could run electric appliances, making housework quicker.

How did this affect the position of women? Once the war ended, there was an expectation that things would return to 'normal', including women resuming their traditional roles as wives and mothers. Many people believed women's war work had been an exception for exceptional times and that women should not take work away from men returning from the war. Pre-war, single women had worked while married women had stayed home and raised a family, unless the family could not manage financially without the wife working too.

Most married women who had to work were obliged to work at home for very low wages. Some jobs, such as teaching, were barred to married women and many employers made it a rule not to employ them. It was the lives of single, well-off, mostly (but not entirely) white women that were most open to change. Changing industries had created many more office jobs, such as working in a typing pool, which became accepted as women's work. A Women's Bureau of Labor was set up in 1920, to improve women's working conditions and campaign for the wider employment of women. Between 1910 and 1940, the number of working women went up from 7,640,000 (8.3 percent of the population) to 13,007,000 (9.8 percent of the population). Women in the same jobs as men were usually paid less, and they often found themselves in the 'last hired, first fired' situation that black Americans would recognise, but at least they were earning their own living.

Flappers

Some young women, nicknamed 'flappers', made the most of their independence. They worked. They cut their hair short, and wore short dresses and silk stockings. Some smoked and drank in public and even drove their own cars. In short, they behaved like young men, even going to male-dominated sporting events (e.g. boxing matches) without a male escort. Some people were shocked by flappers, assuming that, along with all their other freedoms, flappers allowed themselves sexual freedom too. Sometimes this was true. Some went to the jazz clubs and **speakeasies** that were seen as places where no 'lady' would go alone. Flappers shifted public perceptions of women, but they were only a small percentage of the female population and many adopted a more traditional role once they married – the way employers behaved made sure of this.

> **KEY TERM**
>
> **Speakeasy**
> A place where, when alcohol was banned during Prohibition (the years when it was illegal to make, sell or transport alcohol in the USA, 1920–33), people could buy alcohol illegally and often gamble too. Some restaurants or hotels also sold alcohol secretly.

1947–54
Second Red Scare

1957
4 October USSR first to put a satellite in space

1961
President Kennedy sets up a Commission on the Status of Women

1965
Immigration and Nationality Act abolishes quotas, but keeps a numerical limit

1972
22 March Equal Rights Act passed; not ratified by enough states

1979
4 November Hostages taken at US embassy in Tehran

1950 — 1955 — 1960 — 1965 — 1970 — 1975 — 1980

1950–53
Korean War

1962
First US troops into Vietnam

1964
2 July Civil Rights Act

1975
Complete American withdrawal from Vietnam

1963
10 June Equal Pay Act

The impact of the Great Depression

The Depression affected people across class rather than gender, bringing unemployment, falling wages and rising prices. Well-off people managed best, unless they lost everything on the stock market. Middle-class people mostly got by, unless they owned a failing business or an over-mortgaged farm. Poor people had few, if any, reserves to fall back on, so suffered most. If husbands kept their jobs, women with families managed, or looked for work to supplement their husband's income. Women who were widowed, divorced or deserted had to take any work they were offered. A 1932 Women's Bureau of Labor report on women workers in slaughtering and meat packing found that about 97 percent of them were working as the only wage earner in the family, or to boost the husband's wage, not because they wanted to work.

The Women's Bureau was largely ignored within the Bureau of Labor, because of its focus on women. Some women thought it was hindering women's progress, both when it supported government legislation (e.g. the Supreme Court's 1908 *Muller v Oregon* ruling that women's working hours should be no more than ten hours a day) and when it pushed for legislation (e.g. when it pressed for a minimum wage: men had no minimum wage). Restricting working hours often forced the poorest women to break the rules or lose their jobs. Work in places such as meat packing plants often required workers to work more than a ten-hour day. Labour regulations often applied only to industrial work, not to farming or domestic service where a large proportion of the labour force was black and female. Those in work were luckier than those forced to apply to relief programmes, if their state had any, or those who found themselves flung into the migrant labour market. The migrant labour pool was enormous, with Mexican Americans, Mexicans, black Americans and whites all competing for badly paid, back-breaking work in appalling conditions. Women with families faced significant difficulties raising their children in these circumstances.

The Roaring Twenties

1 Prepare for a debate about how the First World War changed the position of women. Choose three points that might show that the change was significant. Choose three points to oppose that point of view.

The impact of the Depression

2 Study the employment data for 1900-30 (Source 1).

a) Draw a graph to plot the total number of women employed against the total number of married women employed.

b) The data used were census data, compiled as part of a general survey of those with homes, rented or owned. What data will this table not show? Is this a problem?

SOURCE 1 Female employment, 1900–30. Based on data from the US Bureau of the Census.

Date	Total age over 16 employed	Total married employed
1900	5,000,000	769,000
1910	7,600,000	1,800,000
1920	8,300,000	1,900,000
1930	10,600,000	3,000,000

The impact of the New Deal

The New Deal administration understood that many families were under immense pressure in the 1930s and that the burden of feeding them fell mostly on the women in the family. The New Deal's Aid For Families with Dependent Children provided some benefits for the poorest families, but, as a rule, men came first in New Deal policies on unemployment and working conditions. For example, the Civilian Conservation Corps (1933–42) found work for young men aged 17–23. They lived in army-run camps replanting forests and digging reservoirs; about 2.5 million young men were employed. Eleanor Roosevelt (the president's wife) wanted something similar for jobless young women to work in forestry. In 1933, the first camp, Camp Tera, was set up, funded largely by private donations. On 30 April 1934, Eleanor Roosevelt held the White House Conference for unemployed women; after this, camps were federally funded. By 1936, there were 36 camps, taking about 5,000 women a year. However, they only took women for two or three months and provided no work or wages. Their only training was in budget management. Black Americans benefited less from the New Deal than whites (see page 41). Black women were edged out of even the worst jobs by desperate whites. Even when she had a job, a black woman earned less. For every dollar a white man earned, a white woman earned 61 cents and a black woman earned 23 cents, on average. One black woman, Fannie Peck, set up a series of Housewives Leagues in Detroit in 1930. These organisations worked to encourage women to shop in black-run stores and to organise local help for those in need. They soon spread to other towns and did help local people on a small scale.

New York State and aid for families

In November 1931, with federal aid, New York State set up the Temporary Emergency Relief Administration (TERA). Over the next seven years, it ploughed $234 million in aid into helping families who were, literally, starving. TERA's research showed that 7.8 percent of all families in the state needed relief in December 1932; in December 1933 it was 8.4 percent; and in December 1934 it was 17.7 percent.

Flora Rose, a nutritionist, drew up a budget for TERA to show people how to feed a family of five on $5 a week. These budgets were publicised by Eleanor Roosevelt. At the height of the Depression, nearly one in five families needed help from TERA. Unfortunately, because TERA had to act quickly, it could not always send trained social workers or nurses to see families. It used volunteers whose sympathy and even-handedness varied widely. Some of them favoured Republicans; others gave more food to some families than others.

Dorothea Lange took this photo in 1936; it was published the next day. Lange was one of the many officials reporting on the Depression and New Deal measures for the government. The woman is Florence Owens Thompson, aged 32, a Native American. In 1930, her family lived in California. Her husband lost his job and they became migrant workers. He died in 1932, leaving Florence with ten children. By 1936, three had died. Six of the remaining seven travelled with her from camp to camp. When Lange met her, her car had broken down. The pea crop had failed at the farm she was on. Those still at the camp were starving.

The impact of the Second World War

The Second World War rescued the USA from the Depression. Once again, women showed they could do men's work well. The iconic image of Rosie the Riveter rolling up her sleeve on a well-muscled arm, saying 'We can do it', was the most famous of many posters urging women to war work. Even before the USA went to war, the 1940 Selective Training and Service Act prepared to draft men into the military and to train women to fill their places, including in shipbuilding and aircraft assembly. Only 16 percent of married women worked in 1940, because of childcare problems. The 1941 Lanham Act's childcare provision was extended: by 1944, there were 130,000 children in day care.

The percentage of married women in the workforce rose from 15 to 23 percent. The Women's Land Army of America (formed during the First World War) re-formed to provide farm workers countrywide. It held workshops and meetings and had its own publication, *The Women's Land Army Newsletter*. Exact numbers are difficult to locate because of issues of illegal migrant labour and also the number of women who took over running the family farm when their husbands went to work; however, the Labor Bureau gave a rough estimate of about three million women working in agriculture in June 1943. Non-white women, especially black women, had a different experience. Worker shortages meant black women could train for professions where they had previously not been welcome, so the number of black women on nursing courses rose from 1,108 in 1939 to 2,600 in 1945. However, in some places, employers refused to employ black women, saying they were bound to have, and spread, sexual diseases. Some employees were equally difficult: in one Detroit rubber plant, white women workers refused to share toilets with black women.

Post-war changes

Once the war was over, many women were not re-employed by factories that changed from making war goods (e.g. munitions) to other goods (e.g. electrical appliances). Not all men returned to their old jobs (some took advantage of GI bills that guaranteed an education to returning soldiers), but most wanted their old jobs back. About half the married women who worked during the war left work when it ended, through choice, social pressure or because federally funded day-care centres closed down in 1946. Some states funded the centres for about a year longer, mainly to cover the period while soldiers returned home and found work. Some men did not come back and some marriages did not survive the war. Widowed, divorced and separated women had no choice but to work.

After a dip immediately after the war, the female employment rate rose again, particularly for married women 45–54 years old. This was a significant change, and very different from the situation after the First World War. The percentage of married women in this age group in the workforce rose from 10.1 in 1940 to 22.2 in 1950. The Second World War contributed to this. Before the war, married women were barred from many jobs; these restrictions were lifted during the war and rarely reinstated after it, so a wider range of jobs was open to women. Black and non-white women who had been trained (e.g. as nurses or office workers) often continued to work after the war and so they moved into a wider range of work than domestic and farm work, which had been their predominant employment pre-war. However, more white married women wanted to enter the workforce, and they were often employed before non-white women. More generally, the war significantly changed the attitudes of husbands (and society) to married women working. In 1936, 82 percent of people thought married women should not work; in 1938, it was 78 percent; in 1942, it was only 13 percent. The percentage rose fairly steadily after the war, to 38 percent in 1978. Finally, the attitude of many married women changed. Many of them had acquired skills during the war that enabled them to work, and they developed both an aptitude and an appetite for work; they wanted to go on working.

However, while more women, married and single, worked after the war, they were still paid lower wages than men for the same work. This might have been a factor in employers choosing to employ them post-war. Their work remained mainly clerical, domestic or shop work. How much this was to do with preference, or what was offered, it is hard to say. A small proportion of women, usually white, moved from clerical work in offices into the main business of that office, such as insurance or advertising. In many cases, they faced hostility from both the clerical group they had left and the predominantly male world they had entered. The hostility was nothing compared to the hostility black people faced on desegregating, but it could be relentless and prevent them from achieving as much as they might have.

ACTIVITY
KNOWLEDGE CHECK

The Second World War
Explain the factors that influenced whether a woman's life would be significantly affected by the Second World War and the ways in which her life could be changed.

What changes did suburban living make, 1941-60?

It was not until after the war that the suburbs offered a significant number of middle-class and upper-working-class Americans the lure of home ownership. Suburbs sprang up in a post-war economic and building boom that made homes more affordable. Suburbs were in commuting distance of the cities. Because they tended to be built with similar-sized houses and plots, they were usually socially segregated (see page 95). Black Americans lived very similar lives to white women in white suburbs, only in black suburbs, although some low-cost black suburbs grew up within reach of very expensive white suburbs – to provide a convenient pool of maids, cooks, nannies, gardeners and other staff. Happily integrated suburbs were rare, though not unknown. Often, black Americans who chose to buy in a white suburb, and could find someone willing to sell to them, faced similar dangers to those trying to integrate schools and other facilities (see pages 46–50).

EXTEND YOUR KNOWLEDGE

Integrating a Pennsylvania suburb
In 1957, William and Daisy Myers, who were black, bought a house in a 17,300-home white suburb. The day they moved in, 3,000 'neighbours' surrounded the house and threw stones through the windows. Burning crosses were put up on their front lawn. The Myers repaired the windows and stayed.

State officials upheld their right to stay and banned large gatherings to prevent mobs forming. They were still harassed by some. Others tried to be welcoming. Daisy was invited to join the neighbourhood association of women. She was later invited to give talks to groups of women about how to integrate white suburbs.

In the 1950s, suburbs grew rapidly: in 1960, 19 million more people lived in suburbs than in 1950. Many suburbs had schools, leisure facilities (such as drive-in movie theatres and tennis courts) and shops. The pattern of suburban life was similar across class and race. Usually, the wage-earning husband went out to work while his wife stayed at home, looking after the house and children. If both parents worked, childcare was needed, which made suburban living more expensive. Suburbs created their own social networks and social life. If women worked, they were often excluded from the friendship groups of those who did not. However, housewives could be excluded too, if they did not conform either to the demands of the group or to those of the development: some developments did not allow fences and even had rules about cutting the grass and babies' nap time. Most suburban housewives had labour-saving devices (e.g. washing machines). Better-off women had cleaners or maids; some had cooks and gardeners too.

The suburbs created a subset of women with too much time on their hands, especially if they had once worked. But this life was portrayed on billboards, in magazines and on television (in advertisements and programmes such as the popular *I Love Lucy* show) as the lifestyle to aspire to, the American Dream of any American woman of any race (although the women in media images were usually white). One advertisement showed a husband returning to a candle-lit dinner, with the slogan: *A tempting table for His Highness.*

Suburban living also had an impact on women who didn't live in the suburbs. First, all the advertising made the suburbs something to aspire to for someone who didn't live there. Secondly, as people left the inner cities for the suburbs, those who remained were, largely, those who couldn't afford to move out. The long-term effect of this was that inner cities became locked into a downward spiral that was almost impossible to prevent (see page 54). Non-white ghettos grew and grew – caused by, and fostering, racism. The education and job opportunities available to girls and women who lived in these areas meant that they were going to have to be exceptional, and work exceptionally hard, to change their situation.

The suburbs had very little impact on those living and working in rural communities, until they developed large out-of-town shopping centres (malls), which then became a focal point for many rural housewives, providing a greater variety of goods at a better price than local stores. The first of these shopping malls was built in 1954 in the Detroit suburbs. From 1917 to 1980, women who lived and worked on farms were cut off, physically by distance and also economically, from many of the changes and opportunities that urban women were more able to seize.

AS Exam-Style Question Section B

To what extent was the US involvement in the Second World War responsible for improvements in the position of women in the years 1945–60? (20 marks)

Tip
Before you start your answer, list the improvements and the factors contributing to them, and then decide if they can in any way be related to the war. For example, you might want to give the economic boom as a separate factor, but it was tied to the war and should be discussed as such.

The impact of the women's liberation movement, 1961–80

The politics of equality

In 1961, President Kennedy, influenced by Eleanor Roosevelt, set up a Commission of Enquiry on the Status of Women. In 1963, it published its results, praising the Equal Pay Act (which passed Congress in that year) and the wider job opportunities for women in federal government, following a presidential directive of 1960. This was a positive and significant change for those women affected. However, the Commission also found that the Equal Pay Act was badly needed and needed enforcing. Women accounted for one in three workers, but were discriminated against in access to training, work and promotion. Their wages were uniformly lower and minimum wage regulations did not apply to the low-paid work that many women did, for example, hotel work or domestic work. There wasn't enough day care to help married women work effectively. The report also said that non-white women were in a worse position than whites because of racial discrimination.

The 1963 report noted that, from infancy, girls were not encouraged to think about careers. Parents, even those who could afford it, seldom encouraged their daughters into higher education. The 1958 Education Act had said schools should have job counsellors to work with students. There were too few counsellors – only about 12,000 for all states schools in the USA, very few in low-income areas. Few counsellors were trained: their advice was described as patchy and even dangerous, especially in not considering the abilities and needs of the girls they counselled. This report had some effect on government thinking. In 1964, the Civil Rights Act included sexual equality, as well as racial equality, in its provisions. Women, like all non-white Americans, soon found there was a wide gap between the passing of a law and its enforcement.

Betty Friedan

In 1963, Betty Friedan, a psychologist and journalist, published a book called *The Feminine Mystique* about the constraints of suburban life and the problems of white, educated, married women. Friedan's book got many women thinking about women's rights, and their own lives, in a new way. The controversy it provoked ensured it was widely read and argued about, including on television. This spurred some women (especially educated, middle-class, white women) to organise themselves and work more actively for women's rights. The first and biggest national movement was the National Organization for Women (NOW), set up on 30 June 1966. Friedan was one of its founder members. The national organisations aimed to work within the political system to get equality and better enforcement of the Civil Rights Act and the Equal Pay Act. Since 1923, Congress had regularly been asked to pass an Equal Right Act (ERA). Congress had failed to do this, and women's groups wanted to put pressure on Congress to change its mind. They held meetings, collected petitions and data, demonstrated and lobbied politicians (federal, state and local) for change. They saw themselves as needing to work steadily for change; while they hoped it would come sooner, rather than later, their work was educating people and campaigning about the problems, and providing services and support for working women.

SOURCE

3

From *American Women*, the 1963 report of the Commission of Enquiry on the Status of Women. Many of the remarks below could have been reprinted in 1980.

Seven million non white women and girls belong to minority racial groups. Discrimination based on color is morally wrong and a source of national weakness. Such discrimination currently places an oppressive dual burden on millions of Negro women. The consultation held by the Commission on the situation of Negro women emphasized that in too many families lack of opportunity for men as well as women, linked to racial discrimination, has forced the women to assume too large a share of the family responsibility. Such women are twice as likely as other women to have to seek employment while they have preschool children at home; they are just beginning to gain entrance to the expanding fields of clerical and commercial employment; except for the few who can qualify as teachers or other professionals, they are forced into low-paid service occupations.

Hundreds of thousands of other women face somewhat similar situations: American Indians, for instance; and Spanish-Americans, many of whom live in urban centers but are new to urban life and burdened with language problems.

While there are highly skilled members of all of these groups, in many of the families of these women the unbroken cycle of deprivation and retardation repeats itself from generation to generation, compounding its individual cost in human indignity and unhappiness and its social cost in incapacity and delinquency. This cycle must be broken, swiftly and at as many points as possible. The Commission strongly urges that in the carrying out of its recommendations, special attention be given to difficulties that are wholly or largely the products of this kind of discrimination.

EXTEND YOUR KNOWLEDGE

Betty Friedan (1921–2006)

The women's rights leader and activist Betty Friedan was born in 1921 and trained as a psychologist at the University of California, Berkeley. She became a suburban housewife and mother in New York, supplementing her husband's income by writing freelance articles for women's magazines.

In 1957, she planned a book on women and work. She started by interviewing women with whom she had been in college. Many were also suburban housewives; most were disenchanted. This changed the focus of her book; in 1963, she published *The Feminine Mystique*, showing the dissatisfaction of her generation of independent young women.

MOST SIGNIFICANT NATIONAL WOMEN'S LIBERATION ORGANISATIONS

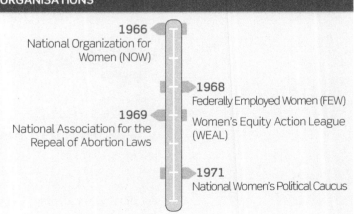

1966
National Organization for Women (NOW)

1968
Federally Employed Women (FEW)

1969
National Association for the Repeal of Abortion Laws

Women's Equity Action League (WEAL)

1971
National Women's Political Caucus

EXTRACT

From *A Century of Change: The U.S. Labor Force, 1950–2050*, a report for the Bureau of Labor Statistics. Published in 2002, the author predicts changes that will take place by 2050.

Among the factors that have contributed to the growth and development of the U.S. labor force; none has been as pronounced as the rise in the participation of women in the labor force. In the two decades after World War II, the U.S. economy enjoyed a major expansion, coupled with increases in productivity, higher standards of living, and rapid acceleration in the growth of college enrolments.

Rapid economic growth vastly increased the demand for labor. The civil rights movement, legislation promoting equal opportunity in employment, and the women's rights movement [another phrase for women's liberation movement] created an atmosphere that was hospitable to more women working outside the home. The combination of all of these factors created strong inducements for women to join the workforce, significantly affecting their participation rate. The dramatic increase in the labor force participation rates of women during the period was accompanied by many other social, economic, and demographic changes in the status of women:

- Women remained single more often.

- Of those who married, many did so later in life, and the median age at first marriage increased substantially.

- Women elected to stay in school longer, achieving higher educational attainment than in the past and pursuing better paying careers.

- Women postponed childbirth to older ages and had fewer children than in previous decades. As a result of improved child care, women tended to enter the labor force even before their children started school, and they were able to maintain a longer job tenure than in previous periods.

- Women got divorced more often; this in itself increased their labor force participation rate.

EXTRACT

From *The Politics of Women's Liberation*, written by Jo Freeman in 1975. In it, Freeman, a white woman, describes her experience of discrimination while looking for work in 1967–68.

My career choice at the time was journalism and I put in several months of unpaid apprenticeship on a local Chicago community paper. After accumulating a substantial file of stories and photographs, I assaulted the local media. If they had simply told me I wasn't good enough I might have accepted their judgment and gone to journalism school, but the level of sophistication about sex discrimination was very low in those days. I was bluntly told, before I even opened my file, that all the papers had a quota of no more than 5 percent women on the city desk and there were rarely any openings. When I questioned this limit, the reply was that women couldn't be sent to cover riots. (I never quite got up the courage to ask why they thought rioters would be more likely to attack white women than white men, since they certainly weren't refusing to hire the latter in favour of black reporters.)

During the next few months of answering ads and signing up at employment agencies I experienced the many subtle and not-so-subtle forms of sex discrimination for any job paying more than that of a clerk-typist. Time and time again I was told that, despite my competencies and the then high need for skilled personnel, I could not be offered a good job because I would soon leave to get married (or to have a baby, or just to leave). Initially I felt I could persuade interviewers of my 'exceptionality'. Other women might leave but not I. My record spoke for itself. Only slowly did it dawn on me that they simply didn't want to listen. The fact that I was female obscured everything else. I might be exceptional in my own eyes, but to the world of potential employers, I was a walking stereotype. After months of having this reality drummed into my head I finally realised that there was no escape. Some women might have it better than others, if the circumstances were right, but the prejudices against all women affected the lives of every woman.

THINKING HISTORICALLY Change (4a)

Significance

1 Read Extracts 1 and 2.

 a) How does the Bureau of Labor Statistics report view the changes in the position of women?

 b) Does it see the changes as significant?

 c) How does Jo Freeman view the position in 1967?

 d) Why do you think these views differ so greatly?

Young radicals

There was a second strand to the women's liberation movement. Its members were predominantly under 30, white, middle-class and college educated. Some had jobs, but often working at a lower level than the men they went to college with, even if they had better qualifications. Many had also worked with black American civil rights groups, or with radical groups such as the Student Non-Violent Co-ordinating Committee (SNCC) or Students for a Democratic Society (SDS). Some had tried to raise the issue of women's equality within these groups, but, despite their radical ideas, the men who dominated these movements were often sexist (e.g. seldom letting women speak at public meetings). At best, women's attempts to raise their issues were met with condescension; at worst, they were met with actual hostility and abuse. So they set up local, radical groups to push for women's liberation and equality. They wanted immediate change and many drew direct parallels between their situation and the situation of black Americans. It was the smaller, radical groups that first used the phrase 'women's liberation'. The national magazine that spread news from all groups, started in March 1968, was called *Voice of the Women's Liberation Movement*. Run by volunteers, it began by selling about 200 copies. The next year it was selling 2,000, but collapsed under the workload. It had set the ball rolling, however, and other magazines and news sheets followed. Unfortunately, the media focused on the more extreme and inflammatory elements of feminism, just as Martin Luther King had complained the media had focused on the more radical arm of the civil rights movement in the late 1960s.

Both strands of the movement wanted broadly the same things. They wanted women to have equal rights, opportunities and pay. They wanted them to have the right to decide about their own bodies: to be able to use contraception, married or not; to choose to have an abortion; to choose with whom to have sex. They did work together. In 1970, almost every feminist group, including NOW and much smaller groups such as the National Coalition of American Nuns, participated in a strike of women on 26 August 1970, the 50th anniversary of women getting the vote. Some women just didn't go to work. Many more took part in countrywide marches and demonstrations, with slogans like 'Don't Iron While the Strike Is Hot'. They all presented the same three demands: equal opportunity in jobs and education; free childcare, community controlled; free abortion on demand. The strike got a lot of publicity for the movement and membership of NOW rose by over 50 percent (NOW's membership rose from 1,000 in 1967 to 40,000 in 1974). The women's movement brought the issue of equality into the public eye. Unfortunately, the radical groups drew the most publicity because they were easier for men to dismiss and make fun of than the NOW campaigners. Kate Millet's *Sexual Politics* (1970) tackled the dominance of men in literature and their attitudes to women. She went to extreme lengths to criticise the 'patriarchy' in literature. On the other hand, Gloria Steinem's *Ms* magazine (first issued in January 1972) was widely praised as catering to the real needs of modern, professional women. It is possible that, in the liberal atmosphere of the 1960s and 1970s, legislation to change the position of women would still have been passed. However, it is unlikely. The campaigns of black Americans and other minority groups seem to show that changes in the law, the first step to changes in reality, were only gained after considerable campaigning and publicity for the cause.

Opposition

The women's liberation movement attracted a lot of opposition, especially among men, even radicals. Some radical women's groups declared that all men were the enemy. This didn't help the cause at all. Conservatives of all kinds rejected the movement, stressing even more strongly the 'un-Americanness' of its demands and the abandonment of traditional roles. As the swing away from 1960s liberalism kicked in, demands for women's liberation lost support, along with many other liberal demands. Opponents, just like the local movements, had different agendas. Some didn't mind the equal rights arm of women's liberation, but objected to the calls for free contraception and abortion. Others, such as Phyllis Schlafly, objected to demands for an Equal Rights Act and set up a group called STOP ERA (STOP stood for 'Stop Taking Our Privileges') to campaign against it in 1972.

EXTEND YOUR KNOWLEDGE

Phyllis Schlafly (1924–present)

Phyllis Schlafly was a conservative who opposed the ideas of the women's liberation groups. She set up STOP ERA to stop the Equal Rights Act being passed. She also set up Eagle Forum, a conservative organisation to support family values and campaign against equal rights and abortion. Among the reasons she gave for her opposition to ERA were the following:

- Women were designed to have babies; they shouldn't be equal in the matter of work, they would need the support of a husband when having a family.

- She didn't want her daughters to be able to choose some jobs, for example, to join the army.

- Women would lose various tax and benefit privileges under equal rights.

Her campaign is one of the main reasons that ERA was still, in 1980, not ratified by all the states.

Gains and limits to advancement

The movement did make some gains on top of the Equal Pay Act and the Civil Rights Act. In 1967, President Johnson extended his executive order calling for affirmative action to improve employment conditions for those discriminated against on the grounds of race, creed or colour to cover sexual discrimination as well. The order only covered federal employees or businesses working for the federal government, however. From 1970, a few states allowed for abortions in very tightly specified circumstances. In 1972, the Supreme Court ruled on the *Eisenstadt v Baird* case, allowing access to contraception to unmarried as well as married women. Abortion was federally legalised on 22 January 1973, by a Supreme Court ruling in the case of *Roe v Wade*, although there were rules about the timing and the health of the mother.

On 22 March 1972, the Equal Rights Act was finally passed as an amendment to the Constitution by Congress. All it needed was ratification by 38 of the 50 states; Congress set a deadline of 1982, ten years, for the ratification. Fifteen states were still refusing to ratify ERA in 1982. There still isn't an Equal Rights Act.

The USA did not sign up to the 1979 United Nations policy of introducing non-discrimination against women in all aspects of life. It was still very difficult to enforce legislation and employers became much more practised at finding 'acceptable' reasons to discriminate against women in the workplace. The women's liberation movement disintegrated, partly because of the conservative opposition it faced and the growing conservatism of the country, but also because it fragmented. All women did not need, or want, the same things and, although the broad aims of the groups were similar, the local issues they took a stand on varied. The fact that so many of them were middle-class white women meant they didn't seem to represent women as a whole either; many working-class and non-white women felt excluded. They set up their own campaign groups, such as the Congress of Labor Union Women (the CLUW, which focused on the rights of working women, especially in industrial work), the Mexican American Women's Organization and the National Alliance of Black Feminists.

> **A Level Exam-Style Question Section A**
>
> How far do you agree that women had made significant gains in their fight for equality by 1980? (20 marks)
>
> **Tip**
> *Make sure you are clear in your mind about both the gain, and the limits there were on those gains, before you answer the question. Also consider the level of generalisation in the question.*

> **ACTIVITY**
> **KNOWLEDGE CHECK**
>
> **Suburban life**
> 1 Draw a spider diagram to show how the various elements of suburban life might make women feel isolated.
>
> 2 Explain how far you agree with the statement: 'After the Second World War, married women found that their position had changed significantly, and for the better.'
>
> **Women's liberation movement**
> 3 Construct a women's liberation timeline, including legislation, groups, events and opposition where appropriate.
>
> 4 Think of three points to support the idea that the women's liberation movement helped to change the position of women and three points against.

HOW MUCH WAS SOCIETY AFFECTED BY IMMIGRATION, 1917–80?

How far did earlier immigration affect reactions to immigrants in the 1920s?

Before the First World War, the USA had operated an 'open door' policy to immigration. There had been only three Acts to restrict the types of immigrants allowed into the country, from the disabled to anyone who was Chinese (1882), and no restrictions were placed on yearly numbers of immigrants or where they came from. Traditionally, the USA welcomed immigrants. The poem on the base of the Statue of Liberty reflects this (see page 74). For roughly 100 years after the nation broke away from British rule, an average of 170,000 immigrants every year entered the USA, which saw itself as the welcoming land of the free. Then the numbers of immigrants rose sharply (in 1882, just under 650,000 immigrants arrived in the USA; in 1907, it was 1.2 million). These immigrants came increasingly from southern and eastern Europe rather than northern Europe, unlike earlier immigration. In 1882, 13 percent of immigrants were from southern and eastern Europe; this rose to 81 percent in 1907. Not only were there more of them, they could not integrate into a group of established US citizens with immigrant roots.

The vast majority of the new immigrants went to live and work in the cities. Cities were growing rapidly, thanks to industrialisation, and the immigrants joined a stream of migrants heading that way – black Americans heading there from the South and people from all over the rural areas of the USA, where many farmers were struggling to adapt to post-war conditions, having spent the war supplying war-torn Europe as well as the USA.

The Dillingham Commission

The Dillingham Commission investigated the impact of immigration on the USA from 1907 and made its report in 1911. The report said immigration was beginning to pose a serious threat to American society and culture. It distinguished between the 'old' immigrants from England, Ireland and Germany (seen as having adapted to life in the USA) and the far greater numbers of 'new' immigrants from southern and eastern Europe (seen as 'racially inferior' and not adapting). The Commission's findings made no concession for the shorter span of time the new immigrants had had to adapt. Despite this, the findings were used to justify Immigration Acts in the 1920s, including the Emergency Quota Act of 1921, which set limits on the number of immigrants.

The Immigration Restriction League
Anxiety about the rising number of immigrants had been growing since the 1850s. In 1894, the Immigration Restriction League was set up to campaign to restrict immigration. Members wrote books and pamphlets on the dangers of the flood of immigrants from southern and eastern Europe, setting more people against them. League members included politicians in the Senate and the House of Representatives. In 1896, Congress passed an immigration restriction bill that included a literacy test and a list of 'undesirable' immigrants. President Grover rejected the bill as against US traditions and values. Congress passed the bill regularly; presidents kept rejecting it. Finally, in 1917, Congress overrode President Wilson's third veto and the bill became law.

Why legislate?

The immigration legislation of the 1920s was set off by a variety of factors. There was post-war isolationism: the government wanted less contact with the rest of the world; immigration was a controllable point of contact. There was the Dillingham report. There was the Red Scare of 1919–20 (see pages 13–15), which led to fears that many of these same immigrants might be communist, anarchist or worse. There was the spike in unemployment. Public reaction was extreme, but, on the other hand, there were bombings by anarchists; there were strikes where some of the strike leaders had communist sympathies. There were riots in some cities: who, people muttered darkly, were behind those? The years immediately after the war had people in a swirl of hostility to anarchists, black people, Catholics, communists, immigrants – anyone who posed a threat to WASPs and their values. The government tried to control the rising hysteria with immigration laws and **deportation**; thousands of people were deported during the Red Scare.

What was the effect of immigration in the 1920s?

With each new wave of immigration came a wave of hostility from many more established communities. This was especially true in the rapidly expanding urban areas. The newcomers would create competition for everything – jobs, housing, facilities of all kinds – just at a point where rural migrants, black and white, were also moving to the cities. For example, in 1910, 1.2 percent of the US urban population was black; by 1920, this was 4.1 percent. At the same time, the percentage of those who were foreign born or with foreign-born parents went from 74 to 85 percent.

The focus of 1920s legislation was on immigration from Europe and Asia. The quota system didn't apply to South America. In the late 1920s and early 1930s, a combination of the Great Depression and immigration restrictions slowed European immigration to a trickle, far less than the quotas set. Immigration from South America, especially Mexico, increased rapidly in the late 1920s to fill the need for cheap labour in states such as California and Texas, in agriculture, mining and railroad building. Some of these immigrants were 'official' immigrants, registered with the Bureau of Immigration. Others crossed the border illegally. The demand for workers meant that employers didn't ask too many questions. The status of the illegal immigrants meant that employers could exploit their fears of deportation, paying them very little and giving them terrible living and working conditions. Once the Depression hit, and many Americans lost their homes and work and migrated towards California in search of work, officials began to deport Mexican workers. Numbers are hard to estimate because of a combination of poor record-keeping and the number of unregistered Mexicans, but historians think that about 400,000 Mexicans were deported during the Depression.

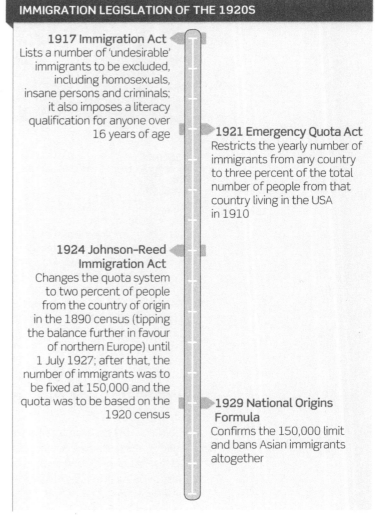

IMMIGRATION LEGISLATION OF THE 1920S

1917 Immigration Act
Lists a number of 'undesirable' immigrants to be excluded, including homosexuals, insane persons and criminals; it also imposes a literacy qualification for anyone over 16 years of age

1921 Emergency Quota Act
Restricts the yearly number of immigrants from any country to three percent of the total number of people from that country living in the USA in 1910

1924 Johnson–Reed Immigration Act
Changes the quota system to two percent of people from the country of origin in the 1890 census (tipping the balance further in favour of northern Europe) until 1 July 1927; after that, the number of immigrants was to be fixed at 150,000 and the quota was to be based on the 1920 census

1929 National Origins Formula
Confirms the 150,000 limit and bans Asian immigrants altogether

SOURCE **4** A cartoon from about 1920.

SOURCE **5** From President Coolidge's first annual message, 6 December 1923.

American institutions rest solely on good citizenship. They were created by people who had a background of self-government. New arrivals should be limited to our capacity to absorb them into the ranks of good citizenship. America must be kept American. For this purpose, it is necessary to continue a policy of restricted immigration. It would be well to make such immigration of a selective nature with some inspection at the source, and based either on a prior census or upon the record of naturalization. Either method would insure the admission of those with the largest capacity and best intention of becoming citizens. I am convinced that our present economic and social conditions warrant a limitation of those to be admitted. We should find additional safety in a law requiring the immediate registration of all aliens. Those who do not want to be partakers of the American spirit ought not to settle in America.

What impact did immigrants have on urban life, 1919–41?

In the 1920s, cities in the USA were growing for a variety of reasons. Industry was expanding and needed workers. Immigrants were a significant factor in their growth – but not in all towns and cities. Immigrants, especially those who could speak little English, had a tendency to gravitate to towns and cities that already had immigrants from their place of origin – sometimes family or friends, but often just people with a language connection. New York, as the city most immigrants reached first, landing at Ellis Island, always had a large immigrant population, but other cities did too. Source 6 shows the percentage of foreign-born people living in seven of the biggest cities in the USA from 1920 to 1940.

THINKING HISTORICALLY Evidence (3a)

The value of evidence

Study Source 4 and read Source 5, then work through the tasks that follow.

1 Write down at least three ways in which Source 4 is useful for establishing attitudes to immigrants in the 1920s.

2 Compare your answers with a partner, then try to identify at least two limitations of each source for establishing attitudes to immigrants in the 1920s.

3 Discuss with a partner whether you think Source 4 or Source 5 is more useful for establishing attitudes to immigrants in the 1920s.

4 Now consider how the sources might be used to answer the question 'What reasons were there to restrict immigration?' Complete the diagrams below to show the usefulness and limitations of Sources 4 and 5 for answering this question and two questions of your own.

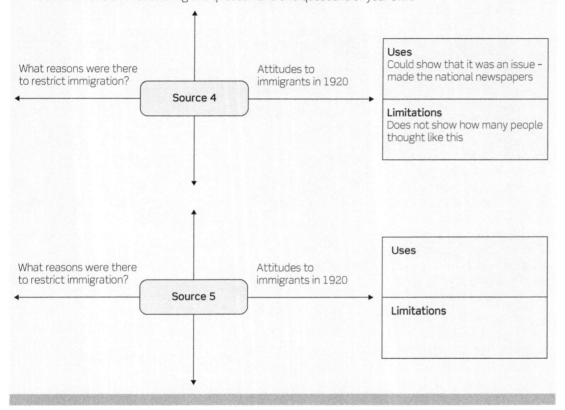

SOURCE 6

Percentage of population that was foreign born (Fb) for seven cities, 1920–40. Based on data from the US Bureau of the Census.

City	1920		1930		1940	
	Population	Fb (%)	Population	Fb (%)	Population	Fb (%)
New York	5.6 million	36	6.9 million	34	7.5 million	29
Chicago	2.7 million	30	3.4 million	26	3.4 million	20
Philadelphia	1.8 million	22	2 million	19	1.9 million	15
Detroit	994,000	29	1.6 million	26	1.6 million	20
Cleveland	797,000	30	900,000	26	878,000	21
St Louis	773,000	32	822,000	10	816,000	7.3
Boston	748,000	32	781,000	30	771,000	24

A melting pot?

The USA is often called a 'melting pot' because of the various immigrant nationalities living there. But the Reverend Jesse Jackson put it more accurately in *Ebony* magazine in 1970, when he described it as a soup with the chopped ingredients visible as separate bits: all in the same soup, but not all the same. US towns and cities were rather like that soup. Most urban areas broke down into informally segregated sections, not just ghettos for black people but separate districts for most ethnic groups of any significant size. These areas had shops selling groceries, and churches following the religious practices of 'the old country', as well as newspapers reporting the local news and news from back home. For example, many towns and cities had areas nicknamed 'little Italy', constantly topping up with incomers. These areas kept the Italian language, many Italian customs and a strongly Catholic religious life. There were also many 'Chinatowns', although immigration from China had been banned since 1882. The Chinese community was one of the most rigidly self-isolating because of its significant cultural differences. However, as the years passed and foreign-born immigrants had American children, 'the old country' and the old traditions did become less important. In 1914, there were about 1,300 foreign-language newspapers published in the USA; by the 1960s, there were just 75.

Source 6 shows how the foreign-born population rose. It doesn't show where the immigrants came from, so it isn't possible to tell what cultures were having an effect on the cities. Detroit, the site of the Ford Motor works, had a large immigrant labour force in 1920. Ford's breakthrough use of mass production techniques led to a rapid growth of car ownership, creating a higher demand and a need for greater production. Most of the workers in Ford's factory came from eastern Europe. The three largest groups in Boston's 1920 foreign population were 24 percent Irish, 17 percent Canadian and 16 percent Italian, whereas in New York the three largest groups were 24 percent Russian, 19 percent Italian and 10 percent Irish.

The impact of immigration on the cities acted on more than one level. The percentage of foreign-born immigrants entering the USA was controlled by the legislation, but the children of immigrants, born in the USA, were also adding to the population, without entering the records as 'foreign-born'. Most of these children were more integrated than their parents, depending on the encouragement they had been given to be so. Many immigrant parents encouraged their children to get an education, work hard and improve their lives – after all, every immigrant had come to the USA hoping to improve their own lives. They may have hoped for more on arrival than they found, but their children knew the situation and could set the right targets.

The bottom of the heap?

Many immigrants arrived in the USA expecting to be welcomed; they expected less hostility and more chances to rise. The newest arrivals mostly tended to end up at the bottom of the heap in the cities they settled in, with the worst jobs, lowest wages and worst living conditions. Those 'fresh off the boat' worked for those who had managed to set up a small family business; in turn, their children got an education and moved further up the social tree if they could.

EXTEND YOUR KNOWLEDGE

Integrating Ford's workers

Detroit's population grew from 465,766 in 1910 to 993,678 in 1920.

In 1914, Henry Ford told the *New York Times* newspaper that 70.7 percent of his 12,880 workers were foreign born and most of them came from south or east Europe; only 29 percent were American. Ford, unlike some employers, went out of his way to 'Americanise' his immigrant labour force, in order to make working relations easier. They were taught English: in 1914, only 59 percent of Ford's workers could speak English; in 1917, it was 88 percent. They were also encouraged to adopt American ways and be patriotic about their new home country, not the old one (e.g. flying the American flag from their windows on celebration days). English classes even had graduation ceremonies.

SOURCE

7 Part of *The New Colossus*, written by Emma Lazarus in 1883 and inscribed on the base of the Statue of Liberty in 1903.

Not like the brazen giant of Greek fame,

With conquering limbs astride from land to land;

Here at our sea-washed, sunset gates shall stand

A mighty woman with a torch, whose flame

Is the imprisoned lightning, and her name

Mother of Exiles. From her beacon-hand

Glows world-wide welcome; her mild eyes command

The air-bridged harbor that twin cities frame.

'Keep, ancient lands, your storied pomp!' cries she

With silent lips. "Give me your tired, your poor,

Your huddled masses yearning to breathe free,

The wretched refuse of your teeming shore.

Send these, the homeless, tempest-tost to me,

I lift my lamp beside the golden door!"

By 1920, there were examples of Irish politicians, lawyers and policemen in Boston, and Italian ones in New York, to show newer immigrants that getting an education and working hard could get you somewhere. Contacts, too, were important in getting on, and ethnic communities allowed immigrants to develop these more quickly and use them to find work and somewhere to live.

Immigrants, because of their numbers, had an influence in politics, local, state and federal. Their votes could change an election result. During the Depression immigrants voted, and campaigned, for Franklin D. Roosevelt in large numbers. Republican *laissez-faire* policies had hit urban areas hardest, because that was where business and industry were concentrated and so where people, many of them immigrants, were being worked too hard for too little money – under the policy that let free enterprise run business and let businesses exploit the workers. In local government, it was especially important to people campaigning for office to appeal to the voters who came from the largest ethnic groups.

The impact of immigration

1 Study Source 4.

   a) Write a paragraph to explain what opinions you think it is trying to express about immigration and why you think that.

   b) What further information would you like about the cartoon before you used it as a source about immigration?

2 Explain how restricting immigration as a policy would seem to the government a way to keep several different groups of voters happy.

3 **a)** Draw a flow diagram of the usual progress of an immigrant in their first years in the USA.

   b) What factors would make it easier for them to fit in?

4 Study Source 6. Draw a bar graph for each city. To what extent was there an emerging pattern?

What impact did the Second World War have on immigrants?

Once the USA entered the war, Americans of Italian (14.2 percent of foreign-born immigrants), German (10.8 percent), and Japanese (fewer than one percent) nationality were classed as enemy aliens. Although there were far fewer Japanese, they were treated most harshly, because the Japanese had bombed the US fleet at Pearl Harbor. About 120,000 Japanese (about 75 percent of them US citizens) were shut up in internment camps. Their property was confiscated and they could only take what they could carry with them. Fewer than one percent of Germans and Italians were interned. However, they had to obey many restrictions – no matter who they were. As the war progressed, attitudes to the 'enemy' immigrant population worsened, even if families had lived for several generations in the USA and saw themselves as American. Some businesses owned by people with Italian- or German-sounding names (no matter what their country of origin) had their windows broken, or found that customers decided to shop somewhere else.

At the same time as they came under suspicion, hundreds of thousands of young men who were technically enemy aliens volunteered for the US military. Some second-generation Japanese men and women were allowed to join the army and served in segregated units. The men were sent to fight in Europe, not against Japan. Young men from all other immigrant groups fought in the war, including Italians and Germans. They were not asked to fight fellow countrymen, although some did. Germans serving in the US military included Admiral Chester Nimitz, who commanded the US Pacific fleet.

EXTEND YOUR KNOWLEDGE

Absurd restrictions
The Italian scientist Enrico Fermi immigrated to the USA in 1938, because he disapproved of the Italian government. He worked for the US government on the secret atomic bomb project. Even though he had been investigated before he joined the project, it took up to ten days for him to get the paperwork to travel from one research site to another.

Government policy and its consequences

Removing the quota system

After the Second World War, the government passed the 1952 Immigration and Nationality Act, which still used quotas. Many people thought that the quota system had outlived its usefulness. One of the problems was that it did not allow for refugees. So, as the Cold War set in, and the USA wanted to help refugees from communism, it had to pass a new refugee law each time. From 1953 onwards, a variety of 'refugee Acts' allowed a set number of refugees into the USA outside of the quota. The government also had difficulty in coping with large numbers of refugees, as when Fidel Castro seized power in Cuba in 1959. The USA opposed Castro and, over the next three years, 200,000 Cubans fled to the USA. The government had to set up a Cuban Refugees Program to deal with the numbers. Very few politicians supported a return to the 'open door' policy that had operated before the First World War, but many of them thought the quota system ought to be replaced by a more sensible system of immigration regulation. After the 1960s, European immigration to the USA slowed and many people became more accepting of European immigration.

President Kennedy was a firm opponent of the quota system and pressed Congress to make changes even before he became president. In 1958, he wrote a book called *A Nation of Immigrants*, outlining how – from the first Europeans to land in 1607 – the USA had been a nation of wave after wave of immigrants.

He said that immigrants should be seen as enriching the country, rather than being viewed with suspicion. Kennedy pointed out that 1950s attitudes to immigration made a mockery of the poem on the base of the Statue of Liberty (Source 7). He said immigrants were only welcome in 1958 if they met certain criteria and there weren't too many of them. When he was assassinated, he was working on a new immigration law which would abolish quotas and had published a new edition of his book to coincide with this. President Johnson brought the bill to Congress after Kennedy's death and it became law in 1965.

Asian immigrants

Immigrants from Asia applied in large numbers for entry to the USA. In the first five years after the 1965 Act, immigration from Asia (especially Vietnam and Cambodia) quadrupled. The Vietnam War was responsible for much of this immigration. After the fall of Saigon in 1975, the USA took in 130,000 Vietnamese refugees. As communism spread, the USA passed additional refugee legislation to take more refugees in – by 1985, there were over 700,000 of them. This changed the ethnic make-up of many US cities.

Immigrants from Central and Southern America

Immigration laws didn't apply to people from the western hemisphere, especially Mexico, although in 1954 the Immigration and Naturalisation Service began to try to control immigration by deporting illegal immigrants from Southern and Western states in what became known as 'Operation Wetback' (see page 56). The number of Hispanic immigrants and their families in the country, both working in agriculture in the South and West of the country and also moving to the cities (83 percent of the Hispanic population was in cities by 1980), became a matter of serious concern for the government. The introduction of a 20,000 limit on entry into the USA in 1976 put measures in place to slow immigration. However, that didn't stop people from coming. People who had long been used to no numerical limits still wanted to join their families and to find work, so they crossed the border secretly and became **'illegals'**.

> ### KEY TERM
>
> 'Illegal'
> An illegal immigrant who entered the country without passing through the immigration process; such people had no visas and the immigration services had no record of them.

Illegal immigrants

Because they entered the country illegally, there is no exact record of the number of illegal immigrants after the 1976 restrictions. The largest number of illegals came from Mexico, averaging over 60,000 a year in the 1970s. Most went to California and Texas, working in agriculture or in factories. In the 1970s, there were 645,000 jobs created in Los Angeles County; about one-third of those jobs were taken by Mexicans. The Immigration and Naturalization Service (INS) along the border did its best to stop illegal immigration, but the border measures 3,169 km and, even with guards and electrified fences, it was impossible to stop smugglers sneaking illegals into the USA. In 1980, about one million illegal aliens were found, arrested and deported.

SOURCE 8

A photo, taken on 29 April 1975, of South Vietnamese people climbing the walls of the US embassy in Saigon, desperate to get onto the last helicopter flight out of the city as the North Vietnamese advanced upon it. Some of the South Vietnamese who made it out found they were the object of suspicion when they arrived in the USA. People would say things along the lines of 'All gooks look the same, how do I know you aren't the enemy?'

However, many more had arrived, helped out by employers happy to have cheap, exploitable labour with no questions asked. Policing the border and tracking down illegals was expensive and the issue became more public in political debates over the cost. This, in turn, meant people were more likely to feel that illegal immigrants were a significant problem. Once in the USA, they were open to exploitation by unscrupulous employers and could not claim any help – healthcare, education for their children, unemployment benefit. Illegal immigrants came from other places too, such as the Philippines. The INS in the mid-1970s estimated there were about seven million illegal immigrants in the USA; they were finding and deporting about 600,000 a year.

IMMIGRATION LEGISLATION 1940–80

1940 Alien Registration Act
Requires non-citizens to register with the federal government; it is a wartime measure, but after the war it is normalised as the 'green card' system; if a non-citizen has a green card, it entitles them to live and work in the USA indefinitely; in 1950, a vetting procedure makes sure that green cards only go to 'legal' immigrants – those processed and registered by the Immigration service

1948 Displaced Persons Act (extended 1950)
Allows for the immigration of 415,000 people displaced by the war over four years, but within the quota limit (President Truman had argued for the admissions to be separate from the numbers administered by the quota, but failed to convince Congress)

1952 Immigration and Nationality Act (also called the McCarran–Walter Act)
Revises the terms of immigration; retains both a limit to the number of immigrants to be admitted (150,000) and the quota system, although many argue against quotas; the balance, based on the 1920 census, means that about 85 percent of immigrants come from northern and western Europe; the Act allows for 100,000 Asian immigrants and introduces a preference system for skilled workers; it still doesn't apply to the western hemisphere

1953 Refugee Relief Act
Extends the 1948 Displaced Persons Act, allowing for 214,000 refugees from Europe; this time, they are dealt with outside the set numerical limit

1954
'Operation Wetback' begins deporting 'illegal' immigrants (those who entered the country without being registered); these are mostly Mexican

1957 Refugee-Escapee Act
Refugee legislation is expanded to cover people escaping from communist countries

1965 Immigration and Nationality Act (also called the Hart–Celler Act)
Abolishes quotas; sets a limit of 170,000 immigrants a year and allows for more Asian immigration; immediate family members of US citizens are allowed in outside this limit; the law still does not apply to the western hemisphere

1966 Cuban Adjustment Act
Gives citizenship to Cubans entering the country after 1959

1968 Armed Forces Naturalisation Act
Amends the 1965 Act to make anyone a US citizen who has fought for the USA in the First World War, the Second World War, Korea or Vietnam (or any other war)

1976 Immigration and Nationality Act expanded
Expands to include the western hemisphere for the first time; the number of immigrants allowed in is 20,000

SOURCE

9 Percentages of foreign-born immigrants by country of origin, 1960–80; 1930 given as a comparison. Based on data from the US Bureau of the Census.

Year	Europe	Asia	Africa	Oceania	Latin America	Canada
1930	83	1.9	0.1	0.1	5.6	9.2
1960	75	5.1	0.4	0.4	9.4	9.8
1970	61.7	8.9	0.9	0.4	19.4	8.7
1980	39	19.3	1.5	0.6	33.1	6.5

Shifting attitudes to immigrants

Both the government and public attitudes to immigration shifted during 1941–80. Attitudes tended to shift with government policy. Republican, conservative governments were more likely to want to restrict immigration and control immigrants. Liberal politicians, such as Kennedy, were keener to accept and adapt to immigrants and their varying cultures. People had different attitudes in different parts of the country, depending on levels of immigration. However, as many people became more conservative, they began to think, not in terms of immigrants enriching the culture (as Kennedy suggested), but in terms of them destroying it. When the economy was doing badly, as in the 1970s, people were most likely to react against both blacks and immigrants who were at the bottom of the heap, because they were seen as a drain on the economy. They were almost always among the first to lose their jobs and become dependent on welfare, so people complained that their taxes were being spent on welfare payments to immigrants. By 1980, attitudes had shifted towards a desire to control immigration, both legal and illegal. It was a swing back towards what some analysts called 'nativism': a form of the isolationism of the 1920s. In 1980, in response to housing and job shortages in Cuba, the Cuban government gave people permission to leave from the port of Mariel (leaving and entering Cuba was usually restricted). The government sent a boatful of refugees to nearby Florida and many others left on hired ships. The ships were packed full by government officials; 14 people died on one boat that capsized. The arrival of these refugees was, for many Americans, the last straw. The Carter administration handled things badly. Officials could not keep the refugees out; they kept those whom they rounded up in awful conditions in refugee camps and prisons.

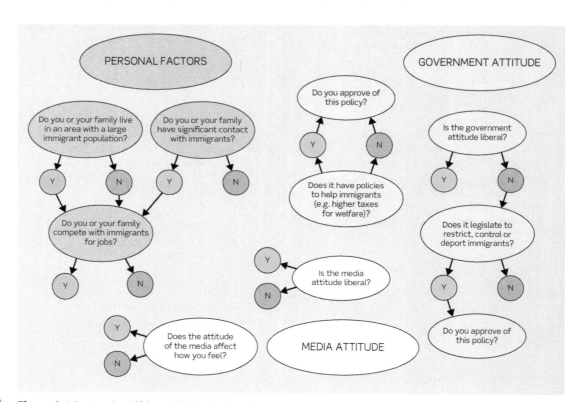

Figure 3.1 Factors in shifting attitudes to immigrants, 1941-80.

A level Exam-Style Question Section B

How far do you agree that the number of immigrants entering the country was the most significant factor in public reactions to immigration between 1917 and 1980? (20 marks)

Tip

Consider other possible factors, such as public spending on immigrants.

ACTIVITY
KNOWLEDGE CHECK

1 Consider the government legislation of 1940-80. Explain which you think had the greatest impact.

2 Explain how each of the following might affect attitudes to immigration:

   a) the politics of the federal administration

   b) where a person lives

   c) the ethnic roots of a person.

WHAT IMPACT DID POPULAR CULTURE AND NEWS MEDIA HAVE ON SOCIETY, 1917–80?

'Popular culture' is usually defined as forms of music, drama or other artistic expressions that have a large following among the people of a country. Before the 1920s, the nation was connected by early movie theatres and the newly emerging record industry. That changed when regular, licensed radio began broadcasting in 1920. There were local radio stations, but there were national ones too; more and more people were listening to the same music and songs and programmes at the same time. Politicians and advertisers were quick to realise that they could use radio to communicate with the public. President Roosevelt used the popular tune 'Happy Days Are Here Again' when he was on the campaign trail for the presidency. He then introduced the people to the reform policies of the New Deal, not via interviews to newspapers, but via a series of radio talks that became known as 'fireside chats'. The power of radio meant that many people felt he was sitting in the room, talking to them personally, making a connection.

The social impact of cinema, 1917–45

Movies had a significant influence on society in this period. By 1917, they were the biggest entertainment media in the USA. Until the 1920s, movies had no sound recording, so these 'silent' movies had pianists (or even orchestras, depending on the budget of the movie theatre) playing music to accompany the mood of the scenes. In 1927, the first 'talkie', *The Jazz Singer*, was shown. It shook up the movie industry because there were many stars who looked good but just didn't sound right. The industry ruthlessly jettisoned stars who could not cope and created new ones who could.

After the war, movies boomed, especially during the 1920s. Movie theatres gave the public an entire evening out. In the 1930s, most changed their 'feature' movie at least twice a week. There was a B-movie, a short cartoon or travelogue, trailers and a newsreel. Some theatres threw in popcorn and ice cream too. By 1941, there were nearly 10,500,000 movie theatre seats, one seat for every 12.5 people.

Movies went out to major theatres in the cities first, moving out from there into areas with smaller and smaller populations. Movies were reviewed in magazines and there were magazines devoted to the lives of the Hollywood stars. In the late 1930s, there were about 20 fan magazines, each with a circulation of 200,000 to one million readers. The gossip columnists on these magazines had real power over the studios. The movies gave people escapism, and fed their fantasies by developing **genre** movies, with significant stars famous in each genre. Clara Bow, known as the 'It' girl ('It' being sex appeal), specialised in 'flapper' roles. Many young women, having seen the movies, wanted to dress like her, have their hair cut like her and behave like her. It was usual for women to go to the hairdressers and ask for a Clara Bow cut. A few years later, men would be asking for a Clarke Gable.

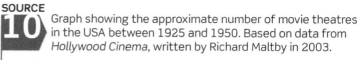

SOURCE 10 Graph showing the approximate number of movie theatres in the USA between 1925 and 1950. Based on data from *Hollywood Cinema*, written by Richard Maltby in 2003.

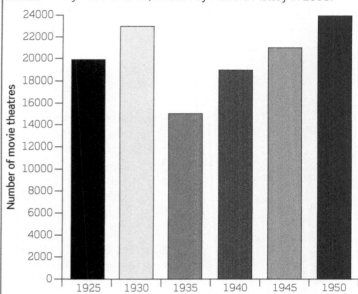

SOURCE 11 Weekly attendance at movie theatres, 1925–50. Based on data from *Hollywood Cinema*, written by Richard Maltby in 2003.

Year	Attendance (millions)
1925	49
1930	80
1935	54
1940	66
1945	81
1950	55

EXTEND YOUR KNOWLEDGE

Early movie-going

Movies began as 15-minute films shown in Nickelodeons, in concert intervals, or in small touring 'theatres'. They grew to films of over an hour, shown in movie palaces with cloakrooms, toilets, plush seats and ushers. Movie palaces could be huge and very profitable. In 1913, the Regent in New York held 3,500 people in seats that cost 10, 15 and 25 cents. Contemporary estimates were that theatres holding about 175 people (at 5 cents each) could make up to $300 a week. The Regent must have made thousands of dollars a week. Black people sat in a separate part of most movie theatres – usually the balcony. In Southern towns, there were separate theatres for blacks and whites.

KEY TERM

Genre
A particular style of book, art or film, e.g. thrillers or romance.

The studio system

Movies cost a lot to make, but showing them could make even more money. In the 1930s and 1940s, about 90 percent of all films worldwide were made in Hollywood. While people went to the movies to see the stars, the real power in Hollywood lay with the studios. There were eight companies that worked together and had almost total control of stars, staff and the industry as a whole. They chose what movies were shown where and classified them according to their own suitability ratings. They set the budget. The cheapest movies, B-movies, had a budget of $50,000–$100,000. They had no stars and made up about half the major studios' output during and immediately after the Depression. Star-studded A-movies cost $200,000–$500,000 to make.

The influence of the stars

Movie stars were tied to a particular studio and had to make a lot of movies. In 1925, her busiest year, Clara Bow made 15 movies. Clarke Gable made two movies in 1924 and became a success. He made eight movies in 1925 and 12 in 1931. Stars were expected to behave in a way that fitted their screen image, even down to 'handsome bachelors' not marrying, in case it put their female fans off. Admitting to being gay was unthinkable, for the same reason. However, not all stars obeyed studio policy. Some regularly went to parties and clubs where drinking, taking drugs and having casual sex were commonplace. Sooner or later, some of this was reported in all the gossip magazines.

Big stars could earn a fortune. Shirley Temple was earning $5,000 a week in the 1930s, when the average wage was under $2,000 a year. However, ordinary actors earned closer to, or even less than, the average wage. Stars could also earn money by advertising products; again, these were carefully chosen to suit their image. Studios also made deals with 'sponsors'; MGM made a $500,000 deal with Coca Cola that its stars would drink Coke during breaks from filming and during interviews for magazines. The major studios' choke-hold on the industry meant that, if anyone in the industry was blacklisted (as happened during the Red Scare after the Second World War) by one studio, it was almost impossible for them to find work anywhere else.

Regulating the movies

While the movies made a big impact on society, not everyone saw that impact as positive. There were many complaints about the movie industry towards the end of the 1920s. Its opponents said many female stars were too scantily dressed and they drank and smoked all the time, while the gangster genre of film made both crime and violence look attractive. Then there were several scandals involving the stars that led the movie studios to act before the government could step in and force control on them. They produced the Motion Picture Production Code (also called the Hays Code) in 1929–30. From 1930 to 1966, all movies had to conform to the code, although fewer of them conformed to the driving idea behind it, that movies should improve society by being morally improving films. However, the studios also began to build a 'morality clause' into their contracts with the stars, whereby they had to sign up to good living.

EXTEND YOUR KNOWLEDGE

The Hays Code

The Hays Code had very clear rules for behaviour in the movies. These included:

- Crimes, for example, safe cracking, dynamiting trains or murder, should not been shown in enough detail to be copied.

- Drug trafficking should never be shown, nor methods of smuggling.

- The white slave trade should never be shown.

- Family life should be portrayed as a good thing; adultery, if it had to be in the plot, should be shown as a bad thing.

- Lustful kissing should be kept to a minimum; perversion, seduction and rape should be avoided; childbirth should not be shown; sex between couples of different races should never be suggested.

- No swearing, not even 'damn'.

- No nudity; no undressing; no indecent exposure; no dancing that suggested sex.

ACTIVITY
KNOWLEDGE CHECK

Movies

Look at the information about movie theatres and movie-going, 1925-50 in Source 11.

1 Explain which were the years when most people went to the movies and why.

2 What does the information tell you about the limitations of statistical evidence?

The social impact of popular music and radio, 1917-45

Popular music

In the 1920s and 1930s, some people still listened to the old music and songs that had been popular before and during the war. However, in the cities, the music that swept everyone off their feet was **jazz**. Thanks to record players and radio, the jazz sound spread to all parts of the USA. Jazz, rather like the movies it was used in, was considered morally lax by many more conservative people in the 1920s. Jazz dances, such as the Charleston and the Black Bottom, were very sexually suggestive. Also, many jazz and swing (a form of jazz played by bigger bands) players were black, which gave some people racist reasons for disliking it. By 1929, almost 50 percent of homes had a gramophone and the industry that made the records to play on them was booming; $75 million-worth of records was sold in that year. There were even specialist record labels, such as 'race records', providing jazz and blues music by black performers. However, by 1935, sales had dropped alarmingly. Radio sales had taken off, and radios played popular music for free. It wasn't the same as owning a gramophone, where people could play what they wanted, when they wanted, but this was the time of the Great Depression and there was less money for everything. Records had become more of a luxury.

> **KEY TERM**
>
> **Jazz**
> Music which had its roots in black American music and which became popular in the early 20th century. 1920s jazz was usually played on piano and brass instruments.

SOURCE 12

Record sales, 1900-35. Based on data from the US Bureau of the Census.

Date	1900	1921	1929	1935
Record sales (millions)	3	140	150	25

Radio

In the 1920s and 1930s, radio ownership grew rapidly. The first commercial radio station, KDKA, began broadcasting on 2 November 1920. It was presidential Election Day and radio broadcast the results before the newspapers could print them, a powerful advertisement for radio. By 1924, there were 600 commercial stations. At first, radio stations were independent, airing whatever the stations wanted to put out. However, they needed money to keep going and so sold advertising. The first radio advertisement aired in August 1922, in New York City. Soon programmes, even whole radio stations, were supported by sponsors, who were regularly mentioned. In 1926, the first national radio station, NBC, opened with an American football game. After this, so many radio stations started up that the airwaves became jammed and the federal government had to pass the Radio Act of 1927 to set up federal licensing of radio stations and share out the airwaves.

Politicians and religious speakers were just a few of the people who used radio to get a message to the nation. Father Coughlin was a priest who broadcast a series of sermons criticising the Ku Klux Klan; by 1930, he had about 40 million listeners. During the Depression, he criticised bankers and supported Roosevelt, saying the New Deal was 'Christ's deal'. When Roosevelt didn't go far enough for him, he criticised Roosevelt and cost the president some support.

While the number of households taking a newspaper rose fairly steadily with the population, radio ownership rose rapidly. Mass production made radios cheaper and hire purchase made them more affordable. Radio brought the world to people's front rooms: music, drama, news, debates. On NBC at least, everyone with a radio heard the same thing at the same time. People felt part of a mass culture, all listening together. As car ownership and an expanding road system allowed people to travel further than ever before, they felt they were travelling in the same country, whistling the same tunes and quoting the same radio show punchlines.

SOURCE

13 Radio ownership and newspaper circulation, 1920–50. Based on data taken from the US Bureau of the Census.

Date	1920	1930	1940	1950
Radio ownership (percentage of population)	n/a	39	73	91
Households taking a newspaper (millions)	27.8	39.6	41.1	53.8

EXTEND YOUR KNOWLEDGE

War of the Worlds

On Halloween 1938, *The War of the Worlds* by H.G. Wells was dramatised on CBS. About six million people tuned in. The director and actor Orson Welles updated the novel to suggest an alien invasion of Princeton, New Jersey and an alien march on New York. Welles used the technique of 'interrupting' the radio broadcast with news of this invasion. The public were used to news broadcasts interrupting scheduled programmes; they weren't used to 'realism' of this kind.

In a survey by Princeton University immediately after the broadcast, about 1.2 million listeners said they had been frightened by the programme. Some people in the supposed path of the aliens even left their homes to escape the alien invasion. Welles ended the broadcast by reminding people that it was Halloween.

The newspapers blew the reaction out of all proportion, with headlines that spoke of hysteria and panic and articles about the need for radio to behave 'responsibly'. It was too good a chance to miss, considering that radio news was providing serious competition for their newspapers.

The social impact of television from the 1950s

At the 1939 World's Fair, RCA demonstrated the first commercial television. It also filmed the opening of the Fair by Roosevelt, who became the first president on television, although the audience was only in the RCA demonstration area. After the Second World War, the government gave media businesses tax breaks to develop and sell television sets. The Federal Communications Commission regulated television, as well as radio. It deliberately allowed unlicensed development in the years 1948–50. So, just like radio, television developed on a local level first; three of the major television companies were radio companies as well.

The 1950s

Television was sponsored, just as radio was. Its advertisements and programmes created a 'national culture' even more than radio did. Advertising was a big part of television, right from the start. Early programmes and advertisements showed very few black Americans (the first television advert with a black American wasn't until 1963). A new departure, driven by the post-war 'baby boom', was that advertisements targeted the growing number of children and began to sell goods using 'special offers' related to popular television series (e.g. encouraging children to ask their mothers to buy a cereal that had coupons to collect, for a gift that was related to the *Lone Ranger* television series).

Political parties quickly saw that they could use television too and bought 'air' time for their politicians. Eisenhower used it in his 1952 campaign for the presidency and Kennedy consciously exploited it as a politician. Television meant that Americans could see their politicians in action. This worked well for Kennedy, who was good looking and a persuasive speaker. It worked less well for Nixon, who was uncomfortable on air and showed it. Suddenly, it became important that a political candidate looked right and interviewed well live.

EXTEND YOUR KNOWLEDGE

The Kennedy–Nixon debates, 1960

In 1960, CBS aired a series of debates between the two presidential candidates, Kennedy and Nixon; the debates were also broadcast on radio. There were four debates and the first one reached a record audience of about 70 million people. It was unusual in that it was broadcast without breaks for advertisements. These debates were one of the reasons Nixon became more wary of the media when he did become president; Kennedy looked better and spoke more confidently, so seemed more in control.

Kennedy won the first debate and the election. Some historians think that the televised debate was what made people vote for him. A poll of people who watched the show on television, taken just after the show, suggested they thought Kennedy was the more impressive. A poll of radio listeners, taken at the same time, suggested Nixon had won, so appearance probably did matter. Fewer people watched the later debates; it was as if they had already decided whom to vote for.

EXTRACT

 3

From *Brought to you By*, a book about post-war advertising, written by Lawrence R. Samuel in 2001.

Between the years 1946 and 1964, American television – and much of American culture – was brought to you by television advertising. …Television advertising is especially fertile ground to study the social and cultural dynamics of post-war America because it was the perfect medium for and a perfect metaphor of the times, steeped in the values of consensus, conformity, and, of course, consumption. Television advertising quickly emerged as a new vocabulary all Americans could share, a common language that often crossed the social divisions of gender, race, class, and geography. By the early sixties, both doctors and construction workers could tell you that Ajax was stronger than dirt and that every litter bit hurts, and people in Casper, Wyoming knew just as well as New Yorkers that Timex watches could take a licking but still keep ticking. Television advertising was thus part of the larger standardization of American consumer culture in the post-war era, when national brands, retailers, franchises, and chains flattened out regional differences and bridged demographic diversity. …

Most important, however, was commercial television's role in reviving the national mythology of the American Dream, that is, every citizen's birthright to achieve success, realise prosperity, and enjoy the fruits of consumer culture.

SOURCE

 14

Weekly attendance at movie theatres, 1950–80. Based on data from *Hollywood Cinema*, written by Richard Maltby in 2003.

Year	Attendance (millions)
1950	55
1955	59
1960	30
1965	20
1970	19.5
1975	20
1980	20

SOURCE

15

Television ownership as a percentage of the population, 1950–80. Based on data from the US Bureau of the Census, *Statistical Abstract of the United States*.

Year	Television owners (%)
1950	9
1955	63
1960	85
1970	95
1980	98

The expansion of television

Television developed very rapidly. Recording techniques improved, as did sets and special effects, so programmes seemed more 'real' to people. Broadcasts aired for longer each day and there were more channels and more shows. This meant that people could, and did, watch more and more television. Many more shows were pre-recorded. This allowed programme-makers to edit what was shown and shape the message they wanted to give the public. Television companies could also show re-runs of favourite shows. In 1953, 80 percent of television was recorded live; by 1960, it was 36 percent. By the 1970s, news and sport were almost the only programmes shown live. It wasn't all positive. Standards on commercial television were criticised in the late 1960s, especially by conservative and religious groups, who disliked the way that many series glamourised crime and violence. There was also criticism of the way that programmes were manipulated: for example, quiz shows were accused of telling contestants the answers to questions beforehand. The public wanted the programmers to be straight with them.

Non-commercial television

The 1967 Public Broadcasting Act set up the government-funded Corporation For Public Broadcasting (CPB), which set up the Public Broadcasting Service (PBS) in 1969. PBS was a national station, made up of groups of local stations, mostly not run for a profit – with education as their main aim. PBS channels were free from the influence of sponsors, but had their own messages. PBS had a liberal agenda, with a brief to educate and entertain, and to 'restore standards'. Educational television took off with PBS, as well as educational programmes on the main channels. The biggest success in children's education was the PBS programme *Sesame Street* (1969–present), which all through the 1970s taught children about racial tolerance and sharing, as well as counting and reading. It was one of the first shows to have a racially balanced cast. Its popularity meant that children watching it in well-off, all-white suburbs absorbed a positive view of other races. In 1981, on the conservative backswing, its government funding was withdrawn.

- More serious documentaries began to be made in the 1960s, following the huge audience for the Kennedy–Nixon presidential debates in 1960. This meant that people were more informed about major issues. Television ownership was widespread and people who might not buy a newspaper to read about issues of the day were happy to sit and watch television programmes about them. The danger of this was that they would accept the slant given to the issues by the programme-makers.

- In the 1970s, however, real life began to seep into entertainment. For example, *M*A*S*H* was a drama series set in the Korean War, which actually considered issues that were very relevant in the war in Vietnam. This was deliberate on the part of the programme-makers. Again, this made the war a discussion point for people. It contributed to the popular feeling against the war – although it was less significant than the news programmes.

- Some series started that reflected black family life. They were comedy shows, so they were just as unrepresentative as were comedy shows of white American life. However, they showed black families in their own homes, leading normal lives. This was better than black people being largely presented as servants or criminals. Some white people who had little or no contact with black people (e.g. those in rural communities in the North East) came to see black Americans as normal people, not exotic, foreign and dangerous.

- Political satire became more popular. *Rowan and Martin's Laugh-in* (1968–73) was one of the first sketch shows openly to make fun of, and criticise, politicians. *Laugh-in* drew on aspects of the counter-culture and many of its punchlines fed into everyday language. Making fun of politicians in this way reached many more members of the public than criticism in serious newspaper, radio or television debates. It also meant that people began to look at politicians in a different light. They were both less respectful and more on the look-out for mistakes. Books and films, as well as television programmes, began to focus on government conspiracies and cover-ups in the 1960s and 1970s. These theories covered a wide range of events, from the assassination of President Kennedy to covering up alien landings.

- News programmes got more prime-time broadcasting and lasted for longer. They also did more in-depth analysis, not just reporting what was happening. Again, this meant that people who watched these programmes became more politically aware and more interested in the issues. Issues raised on the news could become a talking point at work, as well as at home.

ACTIVITY
KNOWLEDGE CHECK

Popular music and radio

1 Draw a graph to chart the relationships between radio ownership, buying records and buying newspapers.

Television

2 a) Draw a graph to chart the relationship between television ownership and movie-going, 1950–80.

   b) Explain the advantages and disadvantages of television over the movies.

3 How did television influence popular culture after 1950? Consider how factors other than sponsorship (for example, the political climate) might have influenced programming.

The influence of broadcast news, 1920–80

From the advent of radio, broadcast news was a quicker, and therefore better, way of getting news to people than newspapers. A voice also seemed more authoritative than newsprint, so made a deeper impression. However, newspapers fought back, providing what radio could not: pictures. The *Daily News*, a New York newspaper, was the first tabloid format newspaper with a camera as its logo and photographs (not engravings) as illustration. Radio news played an important part during the Depression. Reports of the stockmarket crisis fuelled fears about the falling share prices. This caused people to panic and sell their shares, making the crisis worse. That said, the newspapers were full of stock price scares too. It is certainly true that radio helped to settle the crisis. Roosevelt's radio talks helped him to restore confidence and trust in the banks. Radio played an important part in reporting the Second World War more thoroughly and quickly than movie newsreels. Ed Murrow made his name as a radio news reporter during the Second World War. He and his team were based in London, but they also reported from the front line; Murrow accompanied over 20 bombing missions.

Back in the USA after the war, Ed Murrow became co-producer and presenter of the CBS news series *See It Now* in 1951. On 20 October 1953, Murrow broadcast a story on the Red Scare, about a young airman losing his job because of possible family communist sympathies. On 9 March 1954, *See it Now* did a whole show on McCarthy, mostly using film and audio clips, and exposing him as a liar and a bully. The show helped to produce a huge shift of public opinion away from McCarthy.

Through the 1960s, there was live news coverage of events such as the Cuban Missile Crisis and the Moon Landing. While radio still covered the news, many people preferred television news, because of the advantage of pictures. Even politicians who were part of the negotiations over the Cuban Missile Crisis were glued to their screens as ships from the USSR came closer to the 'line' they could not cross without being attacked by the US Navy. It was the television version of controversial issues that most members of the public believed. The coverage of the Watergate hearings in the Senate was vital in the change of public opinion about the presidency and government.

EXTEND YOUR KNOWLEDGE

The Watergate hearings, 1973
Public television played all 250 hours of the Watergate hearings, live. This was the first time anything like this had been done. Not everyone watched all 250 hours live. However, dramatic edited events were broadcast on the news, so people heard important White House officials testifying that President Nixon knew all about the burglary that he had denied knowing about – and that there were tapes to prove it. Jim Lehrer, one of the two presenters, introduced the first programme on 17 May 1973 by announcing that the whole trial would be broadcast, unedited, day by day. He said that this was being done so people had a chance to see the whole thing and make their own judgements.

Shaping opinion

More and more, broadcast news not only showed what happened, it gave its own interpretations of what was happening, shaping how it presented the news. The interpretations often began as the views of the programme-makers. However, the broadcasting company had the final say over what was broadcast. News reports had anchormen who explained the situation generally, with maps if needed. They became seen as the 'teacher' figures – the ones who were explaining things to the public, the ones people could trust. Walter Cronkite's 1968 critical documentary on Vietnam, aired after the 1968 Tet Offensive, was shocking to many people because someone they trusted was criticising a government they were uncertain about. He was confirming their fears. Even worse, he showed that the government was not just pursuing a war that people didn't want, it was doing it wastefully and incompetently. Unlike the Korean War, the war in Vietnam had televised reports, as well as radio reports or newspaper reports with photos. Even before 1968, some news reports told of shocking incidents and the footage showed it in detail. In August 1965, CBS news showed marines burning the village of Cam Ne to the ground. This South Vietnamese village, like many other villages, was suspected of helping the rebels. No rebels were found. The coverage was critical of the impact on South Vietnamese loyalty. However, critical reports were just a small part of the overall, much more 'neutral', reporting.

After Vietnam

More and more, after Vietnam, broadcast news gave its own interpretation of events, shaping its presentation of the news to fit the interpretation. Many Americans were unaware of the extent to which the news was giving an interpretation – often simply by its selection of which news items to run.

The media and Jimmy Carter

The media's relationship with Jimmy Carter demonstrates how its story selection could influence public opinion. At first, the media presented Carter in a positive light and Carter responded well. In the early months of his presidency he had high levels of support in the media and with the public (he had a 60 to 70 percent support level in his first months) However, once it became clear that his administration was managing both policy-making and Congress badly, the media began to withdraw support. Eventually, the media decided that Carter was incompetent and seized upon events that underlined this.

Although the media could find no evidence of presidential wrongdoing, Carter's brother was involved in various scandals with the Internal Revenue Service. His brother became the story and it reflected badly on Carter. In October 1979, Carter was shown collapsing in a marathon, which he later admitted probably contributed to his losing re-election. People didn't want a president who was weak, morally or physically. In the same year, while fishing from a boat in the middle of a lake, Carter was 'attacked' by a rabbit, which he got rid of with his paddle. This hit the news, and captured the public imagination, as another symbol of weakness. It is interesting to compare the way the media treated these incidents – using them to mock Carter – with the way they treated Roosevelt's illness: they never photographed Roosevelt in a way that showed he had polio. This difference was partly due to Carter's actual presidential weakness. It also reflected the way the media felt the presidency could now be mocked. When, in November 1979, 52 US diplomats and citizens were held hostage in the US embassy in Tehran, Carter's inability to deal with the situation put paid to all chances of re-election. The hostages were held for 444 days and were released minutes after Reagan took the presidential oath in 1980.

Hanoi Jane

It wasn't just the government in the media spotlight over Vietnam. Jane Fonda was one of many stars who spoke out against Vietnam. She said she was against the war, not the soldiers. She visited Vietnam veterans and their families and, at anti-war demonstrations, she urged the public not to take their hatred of the war out on returning soldiers. However, the image of Jane Fonda in people's minds after her 1972 visit to Hanoi was of her sitting, smiling, on the seat of a North Vietnamese anti-aircraft gun used against US pilots. The press gave her the nickname 'Hanoi Jane', saying she had shown disrespect for the US military in Vietnam. Extremist groups invented stories about horrific things she did and said to the POWs she visited. She was, and is still in some circles, hated for her visit and her 'support' for North Vietnam.

SOURCE 16

This photo, taken in 1972, shows the actress Jane Fonda with North Vietnam troops in Hanoi. Fonda was against the war and went to Vietnam, invited by the North Vietnamese, to visit POWs with letters and take the letters back. Fonda claimed that she didn't realise how the photo would look. A large section of the media and the public never forgave her for, as they saw it, her disrespect for the soldiers fighting in Vietnam.

EXTRACT

4 From *Media Spectacle* by Douglas Kellner, written in 2003. Kellner discusses the wish of the media generally, including news broadcasts, to present presidential politics as if it was a movie.

Carter, in fact, was never popular with the press, which began to present him as a *Hee-Haw* hick, and this country movie did not sell well in terms of presidential image and narrative with Washington and New York sophisticates.

Nor did Carter's moralism play well with the media or broad segments of the public. However decent and competent Carter appears in retrospect, and he looks good in comparison with what came later, his administration just did not produce a good political narrative or spectacle. Moreover, Carter was condemned by the dramatic display of the Iran hostage crisis that helped to undo his presidency. The popular late-night talk show Nightline featured a logo with dramatic music 'America held hostage! Day X.' As the days went by, and the American hostages remained captives of Iranian students and radicals, Carter was portrayed as ineffectual and incompetent.

A national popular culture grew up in the USA encouraged by radio and television. After the Second World War the media began to have more and more influence over the way that the public viewed issues of the day and also how they viewed politicians [see pages 82–86]. Many Americans reacted to issues such as women's liberation and immigration in direct relation to the way the media presented these issues, just as they had accepted media representations of black American civil rights campaigns. Not everyone reacted in this way. However, enough people were affected by the media to mean that politicians became increasingly concerned about their media image. Carter's loss of public support was a clear illustration of the damage a negative media image could do.

ACTIVITY
KNOWLEDGE CHECK

Broadcast news

1 Explain why television news might be more influential than newspaper or radio reports.

2 In what ways might the way television came to dominate political life be non-beneficial to politics and government?

ACTIVITY
SUMMARY

Government and the media

1 Explain how the media's attitude to government changed between 1920 and 1980.

2 Draw a spider diagram to show as many different industries as you can think of that would be affected by the influence that stars had on movie-goers.

3 Compile a series of bullet points to address the question: 'How far do you agree that attitudes to immigrants barely changed between 1917 and 1980?'

4 How far had women gained equality by 1980?

WIDER READING

McCarthy, Anna, *The Citizen Machine*, New York University Press (2010) is a an academic book about the influence of television in the USA.

Hallin, Michael, *The Uncensored War*, University of California Press (1989) is a thorough analysis of the role of the media reporting the war in Vietnam.

Silent movie clips can be found online and by searching the names of individual stars. News footage, such as Walter Cronkite's Tet Offensive broadcast, can also be found online.

Grieveson, Lee and Kramer, Peter, *The Silent Cinema Reader*, Routledge (2003) is a collection of articles on early cinema.

BBC People's Century: Episode 6, *Great Escape,* looks at Hollywood in the 1920s

1.4 The changing quality of life, 1917–80

KEY QUESTIONS

- What was the impact of economic change, 1917–80?
- To what extent did living standards change, 1917–80?
- How significant were changes in leisure and travel to life in the USA, 1917–80?

INTRODUCTION

The photos in Sources 1 and 2 were taken in 1932 and 1936. Clearly the lives of these people were very different. Was this because there had been an economic crisis? Was life in the cities just better than life in rural areas? Was the white woman wealthy in 1932? Was the black couple worse off in 1936? This chapter doesn't answer all these questions, but it looks at the wide range of living standards in the USA between 1917 and 1980 and some of the factors that brought them about.

SOURCE 1

A black American couple in New York, 1932.

1915	1920	1925	1930	1935	1940	1945

1929
October The Wall Street Crash kick-starts the Great Depression

1941
8 December USA declares war on Japan
11 December Germany declares war on the USA

1947
March First Levittown homes on sale

1919–20
First Red Scare

1933
4 March Inauguration of President Roosevelt and start of New Deal

1939
September Outbreak of Second World War in Europe

1945
8 May Second World War ends in Europe
2 September End of the Second World War in the Pacific

SOURCE
2   A white American mother and her children in California, 1936.

1949	1955		1965	1968	
Cold War	5 December		August Watts riots	4 April	
alignments	Montgomery Bus		6 August Voting	Assassination of	1979
hardening	Boycott begins (ends		Rights Act	Martin Luther King Jr	Fuel crisis
	21 December 1956)				

1950   1955   1960   1965   1970   1975   1980

	1953		1964	1968–69	1972–73		1980–81
	May Protests		2 July Civil	Inner city riots	Fuel crisis		Economic
	to desegregate		Rights Act				recession
	Birmingham,						
	Alabama						

RAVEL BY AIR

EASTERN AIR
TRANSPORT SYSTEM

WHAT WAS THE IMPACT OF ECONOMIC CHANGE, 1917–80?

Boom, bust and recovery, 1917–41

Immediately after the First World War, the US economy entered a brief depression. War production stopped: both manufacturing and producing crops for war-torn Europe and for the USA.

Post-war depression

Farming: During the war, farmers were urged to produce more wheat and were given subsidies to do so. Some took out loans to buy farmland and machinery. Mechanisation meant fewer workers were needed, so some workers became unemployed. During the war, wheat farmers made a profit. After the war, they produced too much; prices fell. Some farmers produced yet more to make enough to cover their loans. Prices continued to fall. Some farmers had to sack workers, others went bankrupt. Farmers who were growing cotton did not escape trouble, due to the **boll weevil**.

Industry: There were many strikes in 1919 and 1920, local and nationwide. Most failed to get better working conditions for the strikers and some caused businesses to fail, increasing unemployment. Meanwhile, many older industries (especially in the north and east) were in decline. For example, the coal industry lost out to other fuels, including water power and electricity. Although electricity plants were fuelled by coal this did not make up the overall drop in demand. In 1900 coal had produced almost 90 percent of energy supplies in the USA. By 1930 this figure had dropped to 60 percent.

Government reaction: The Republican government of the time believed in *laissez-faire* policies, so did not try to stop the depression. However, the isolationist tariffs it put on foreign goods led other countries to introduce similar tariffs on US goods; US exports fell. Tariffs pushed Americans to buy more US goods, but not always the same goods as had lost exports. The government felt that the depression would soon right itself. The economy did adjust and this had a significant impact on government thinking in 1929, when another depression struck.

Boom

The USA came out of its post-war depression and hit a boom cycle. Several factors contributed to this.

Mass production: The mass production technique of breaking manufacturing down into a series of steps and making one worker responsible for one step in the process was developed before the war. Henry Ford's car factories were the most effective example of this. Mass-produced goods were produced more quickly and cheaply, so they could be sold at a lower price. This made them more affordable and so manufacturers sold more of them and people bought more goods – especially cars and radios. In 1917, there were 4,727,468 passenger cars registered in the USA; by 1929, there were 23,060,421. Mass production had significant knock-on effects. Everything from cars to fridges needed raw materials, outlets to sell them, transportation for deliveries, as well as spare parts and specialists to fit them.

EXTEND YOUR KNOWLEDGE

The Ford Model T

In 1914, a Ford Model T cost $825. Henry Ford paid his workers $5 a day; most industrial workers were getting half that. Ford streamlined the production and produced only black cars. This brought the price down, as did increased production. By October 1924, a Ford cost $260.

The Model T was the success story of the boom years. The fact that Ford's success relied on his banning unions, to keep his workers more under control, was brought up less often than this success. Many businesses were banning unions at this time, taking advantage of the government's *laissez-faire* policies.

However, Ford production also demonstrates the problems of the boom. The boom was driven by consumer spending. When everyone who could afford a Model T (or a fridge or a radio) had one, demand dropped. On 26 May 1927, the last (15,000,000th) Ford Model T came off the production line.

New management techniques: Some employers, Ford among them, began to use 'scientific management' ideas (as set out by Frederick W. Taylor) to make the production line worker as effective as the production line itself. Each task was broken down into a series of movements and the worker was trained in the most effective way to do the task. The system worked best when trained workers stayed at the factory, so scientific management advised paying good wages and creating good working conditions, even benefits for those who stayed a long time. These workers benefited, but only if they fitted into the system.

Federal policies: While the government generally avoided intervention in business, it kept some of the wartime subsidies to farmers in place and also cut taxes for businesses to encourage 'buying American'.

Hire purchase and loans: Before the war, borrowing was seen as a last resort and only banks and loan companies lent money. In the 1920s, companies pushed hire purchase (paying the company for goods in a series of fixed payments) as the practical way to buy. Companies such as Sears sent out huge catalogues, promising 'easy payments'. As a sense of prosperity rose, more people bought homes and farms on mortgages that banks were more willing to lend. Between 1920 and 1929, consumer debt rose from $3.3 billion to $7.6 billion. People were not only borrowing, they were borrowing more: before 1920, people borrowed, on average, 5 percent of their income; by 1929, this had almost doubled.

Changing industry: New industries were more efficient and used a higher level of mechanisation. Older industries, such as textile manufacture, became less important than newer industries that manufactured consumer goods. Many of the new industries, and the goods they produced, ran on electricity. The boom could not really take off until the electricity grid was reaching a significant number of consumers. In 1917, there were 7,889,000 homes and businesses wired for electricity; in 1930, there were 24,555,732.

The stock market

In the 1920s, the price of shares in the new industries rose rapidly. Share trading had previously been something that only banks and wealthy people did. They bought shares for the long term, for the **dividends** they paid out. But as share prices rose so rapidly, the media began to point out that it was possible to make money even if you bought just a few shares and sold them a short time later. Suddenly, some ordinary people, egged on by the media, began to buy and sell shares too. Shares went into their own boom cycle, called a **bull market**. People bought shares, they went up in price and then people sold them, making a profit. The demand for shares ensured that prices rose because people wanted to get in on this 'sure thing'. People began to borrow money to buy shares, **buying on the margin**. They felt comfortable with borrowing to do this because they expected to make a profit selling the shares and so be able to repay the loan. Banks were also affected by the bull market and began to use customers' investments to trade in shares. The government did nothing to stop this.

SOURCE 3

Shares sold on the New York stock exchange, 1923–33. Based on data from the US Bureau of the Census.

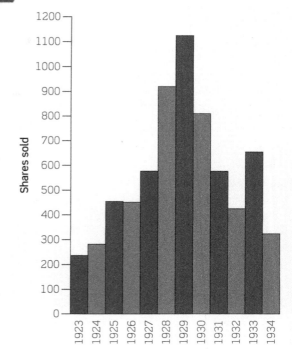

Bust

In 1929, the boom cycle went bust when the Wall Street stockmarket collapsed in what is now called the Wall Street Crash. There were warning signs that the boom was over. Most people who could afford consumer goods had bought them, so demand began to fall. Companies did not cut production enough, so goods piled up in warehouses. By 1927, unemployment was rising. As it did so, employers cut wages and working hours. This had happened before the post-war depression of the early 1920s. The Republican government, still in favour of *laissez-faire*, did nothing. It argued that the economy had put itself right in 1919 and would do so again. They did not consider that, unlike the earlier depression, many more people, businesses and banks were in debt and the stock market was dangerously overheated. The **Federal Reserve Board's** (Fed) earlier attempts to control the boom by tightening the money supply made the depression worse.

In September 1929, some investors, feeling share prices were dangerously high, sold and kept the profit. Stock prices began to fall and kept on falling as more investors sold. The media began to talk of a crash. If people had kept their heads, the market might have stabilised with lower, but not catastrophic, prices. This didn't happen. Too many people had invested heavily on credit and feared losing even more if prices kept falling. They rushed to sell. A **bear market** replaced the bull market. On 29 October, the stock exchange closed. When it reopened, things were calmer, but prices continued to fall until 13 November, by which time many small investors had lost everything. Banks that had gambled with their customers' money went bankrupt; about one-third of all banks in operation before the crash were bankrupt in 1933.

THINKING HISTORICALLY   Causation (5a)

Inter-relations

Causes never simply come one after another. They are often present simultaneously and have an effect on one another. Sometimes new causes develop and interact with existing ones.

Think about the following causes of the collapse of the boom economy:

- too many shares being bought on credit
- media reportage of share prices
- businesses and farms overproducing
- prices falling
- rising unemployment
- Wall Street Crash
- no government control of bank lending or share buying with customers' savings.

Work in groups to produce a diagram of causes and the links between them.

1 On an A3 piece of paper, write all the causes of the collapse of the boom economy. Write these in boxes, the size of which will reflect how long they were a relevant factor. For example, if you argue that 'rising unemployment' had been an important factor since the end of the war, then it will be quite a big box, whereas 'Wall Street Crash' would be a lot smaller. Spread these boxes over the page.

2 Make links between all the causes. Draw lines between the boxes and annotate them to explain how the causes are connected and in what ways each affected and altered the others. For example, between 'too many shares being bought on credit' and 'no government control...' you could write something like: 'If the government had not believed in *laissez-faire*, it might have intervened to control borrowing.'

Answer the following questions:

1 How do the causes differ in their nature? (Think in terms of events, developments, beliefs, states of affairs.)

2 How do the causes differ in the roles they played in causing the collapse of the boom economy? (Think about whether each cause created the right conditions, was a trigger for events, or acted in some other way.)

3 Write a 200-word paragraph explaining how important it is to recognise the relationships between causes. Give examples from your diagram. Try to include connective phrases such as: 'this created conditions conducive to...', 'this triggered an immediate reaction...', 'this made the development of that situation more/less likely'.

The Great Depression

The Wall Street Crash significantly worsened the depression. As businesses and banks went bankrupt, unemployment shot up. Many people lost their jobs and those who could not keep up payments on mortgages lost their homes too. As people stopped buying, prices dropped and more businesses failed. The outcome was homelessness and poverty for many people. At first, the government did nothing. When President Hoover tried to push for federal action, the mainly Republican Congress was unwilling to agree. Some measures were put in place (see page 16), but not enough. Hoover lost the 1932 election to Roosevelt and his New Deal promises.

Recovery

Roosevelt's first action as president was to close all the banks, have FED officials inspect them and then only reopen the 'healthy' ones. This, and using federal agencies to create employment and help those in trouble with loans, began to re-establish confidence (see pages 19–20). Natural disasters hampered recovery (e.g. droughts in the early 1930s made the Great Plains a dust bowl; many farmers lost their farms and became migrant workers). Roosevelt ran up huge government debts funding the New Deal. Recovery was slow and bumpy, with an economic decline (the 'Roosevelt Recession') in 1938–39, but confidence held. In 1937, the Wagner–Steagall National Housing Act set up the Federal Housing Administration to oversee slum clearance and the building of housing for low-income families. The Second Agricultural Adjustment Act, like the first, provided subsidies for farmers to produce less. Recovery still wasn't certain in 1940. There were still more unemployed and homeless people, white and non-white, than federal agencies could help. Then, in 1939, the Second World War broke out. Roosevelt didn't take the USA into the war at once, but moved to war production in order to help the Allies. The USA joined the war in 1941, which had the effect of creating employment in factories and the military.

SOURCE

 4 Number of unemployed and percentage of workforce unemployed, 1917–41. Based on data from the US Bureau of the Census.

Year	Unemployed	Percentage of workforce unemployed
1917	1,848,000	4.6
1918	536,000	1.4
1919	546,000	1.4
1920	2,132,000	5.2
1921	4,918,000	11.7
1922	2,859,000	6.7
1923	1,049,000	2.4
1924	2,190,000	5.0
1925	1,453,000	3.2
1926	801,000	1.8
1927	1,519,000	3.3
1928	1,982,000	4.2
1929	1,550,000	3.2
1930	4,340,000	8.7
1931	8,020,000	15.9
1932	12,060,000	23.6
1933	12,830,000	24.9
1934	11,340,000	21.7
1935	10,610,000	20.1
1936	9,030,000	17.0
1937	7,700,000	14.3
1938	10,610,000	19.0
1939	9,480,000	17.2
1940	8,120,000	14.6
1941	5,560,000	9.9

SOURCE 5 US federal government spending, 1930–41. Based on data from the US Bureau of the Census.

Year	Spending (billions of dollars)
1930	3.3
1931	3.1
1932	1.9
1933	2.0
1934	3.0
1935	3.6
1936	3.9
1937	5.4
1938	6.8
1939	6.3
1940	6.5
1941	8.7

SOURCE 6 Shares traded on the New York stock exchange, 1910–45. Based on data from the US Bureau of the Census.

Year	Shares traded (millions)
1910	164
1920	227
1929	1125
1933	655
1935	382
1940	208
1945	378

ACTIVITY
KNOWLEDGE CHECK

Post-war economy

Draw a graph to show the shifts of the economy from 1917 to 1941, with years on the *x*-axis, 'boom' at the top of the *y*-axis and 'bust' at the bottom of the *y*-axis.

SOURCE 7 A queue for help after the great Ohio flood of 1937. The Depression didn't affect everyone alike. By 1937, many white middle-class families were saving and spending again. 'The American Way' was a phrase used to encourage spending and confidence.

The Second World War, post-war affluence and growth, 1941–69

The Second World War boosted the US economy and, unlike in the years immediately after the First World War, the economy continued to prosper after the war. This boom was fuelled by several factors.

- A huge demand for the consumer goods people had done without during the war made the move from wartime industries to civilian ones easier. Production increased (from $213 billion-worth of goods in 1945 to $284 billion-worth in 1950), which helped keep unemployment low.

- The business boom encouraged employers to expand their workforces and to raise wages, thus encouraging even more spending.

- The government came down hard on strikes for higher wages as prices rose. When coal miners went on strike, President Truman took control of the mines. The rail workers went on strike to support the miners. Truman took over the railways. When rail workers walked out (marooning 90,000 passengers and stopping 25,000 goods trucks, many loaded with perishable food), he asked Congress to draft strikers into the army. The strikers backed down and there were very few strikes after this.

- A post-war 'baby boom' meant a growing demand for child-centred goods and foodstuffs (in 1947, nappy sales were $32 million; in 1957, they were $50 million). Toy manufacturers made $1.6 billion in 1959. By 1961, their profits had risen to $2 billion. In 1940, there were 2,559,000 live births in the USA. In 1950, there were 3,632,000; in 1955, it was 4,104,000. It stayed at the four million mark until 1965 (3,760,000), when the fertility rate began to decline. More babies meant more toddlers and more teenagers to come. They would create a need for more schools and colleges, and would become consumers themselves.

- Even some farmers managed to do well, thanks to continued farm subsidies and the demand for farm produce at home (as consumers spent more on food) and abroad (especially in war-torn Europe).

- Government spending rose steadily throughout the period under Truman's 'Fair Deal' policies. Immediately after the war, the government provided support for all those leaving military service. This included a leaving payment, unemployment pay for a year, loans to buy a home or business, and medical and health care. It also provided education or training through the GI bill (over 12 million did this). The government also increased the amount of social security benefits and expanded them to cover more people. The 1949 National Housing Act introduced slum clearance and the building of 810,000 low-income housing units to replace the slums. This provided work for the building industry and better conditions for some urban poor.

Inflation and growing affluence

The most obvious cloud over the post-war economy was inflation. Prices were rising, sometimes faster than wages. The government's Office of Price Administration (OPA) had controlled prices during the war. When it shut down in 1946, farmers and businesses wanted to exploit the demand for goods and food. Prices jumped 25 percent in two weeks.

However, after the initial jump, prices settled to a steadier rise. Truman passed the 1946 Employment Act (so called because it set a goal of full employment), which set up a Council of Economic Advisers (CEA) to advise the president on managing the economy. It also said the president had to give a strategy report to a Joint Economic Committee of the House of Representatives and the Senate after each federal budget. The government was careful to keep taxes low and the fact that buying on credit was rising meant that inflation didn't damp down spending in the 1950s. The Fed put controls on the **money supply** to keep inflation low.

> **KEY TERM**
>
> Money supply
> The amount of money in circulation in a country. The government can affect this by printing more money.

The 1950s

The 'baby boom' of the 1950s was fuelled by men returning from the war, fewer women working and the buoyant economy. The economic boom of the 1950s and 1960s made people confident about 'the American Way' as opposed to the communist ideas of their Cold War opponents. Consumerism was positively patriotic. However, it was not all steady economic growth. Sometimes both inflation and unemployment increased sharply for a year or so. It is also important to remember that, while the economic climate was good, there were always people who were not a part of the rising affluence. One reason for the growth of the suburbs was that people moved to leave inner cities they saw as increasingly dangerous and slum-ridden. Even so, consumer confidence was vital to the growth of the economy. It also hid the economy's underlying problems.

> **EXTEND YOUR KNOWLEDGE**
>
> The baby boom
> The statistics of the baby boom can be considered in various ways.
>
> The birth rate (for every 1,000 women of childbearing age) was 80 in 1940, 86 in 1945, and hit a high of 113 in 1947. From 1947 to 1959, when it began to fall, the birth rate ran at between 105 and 123, with the three highest years being 1956–58. By 1965, it was back to 97.
>
> In 1950, there were 42.6 million children under the age of 15 in the USA: 27 percent of the population. In 1960, there were 57.4 million children under the age of 15; 30.8 percent of the population.

The suburbs

The suburbs were a visible sign of the impact of economic change in the USA. Factories, colleges and universities moved outside the cities, where there was more land. The government funded the building of roads and homes (e.g. the 1956 Highways Act allowed for 41,000 miles of interstate highways). The boom economy meant builders were willing to invest in building suburbs and running the necessary facilities, such as electricity, water and sewage, to them. The Levitt company specialised in mass-produced, prefabricated houses. They were quick and cheap to build and led to an explosion of 'Levittowns' in the North East, where the firm was based.

One such development, on Long Island, had 17,000 homes for 82,000 residents, the cheapest of which (washing machine included) was just under $7,000. Cheaper homes, added to the fact that people could afford cars and could get a mortgage from banks easily, meant many more people could afford to buy a home – if they moved to the suburbs. Levitt refused to sell to black Americans, as did some other developers. This led to the building of black suburbs: yet another example of Northern segregation.

SOURCE 8

Levittown, Pennsylvania, photographed from the air in 1957. This was the largest Levittown suburb and is still lived in today. The size of Levittowns shows just how many people were buying homes for the first time thanks to the boom.

ACTIVITY
KNOWLEDGE CHECK

The economic boom

1 a) Draw a spider diagram with interconnecting arrows to show how the various factors behind the growth of affluence in the 1950s affected each other.

  b) Is any one factor more significant than the others? Explain your answer, being sure to consider the relationship between factors as shown in your diagram and the effect that removing one factor might have.

2 Explain how the growth of the suburbs might lead to urban decay.

AS Exam-Style Question Section A

Was the Second World War the main reason for post-war affluence in the 1950s? (20 marks)

Tip
Consider other reasons for economic growth, e.g. the baby boom and its relationship to the war.

Continuing economic changes and shifts

While people were spending more on consumer goods, there was a shift in where those goods came from. By the end of the 1950s, the USA was losing its place as the country of technological innovation and its hold on world markets. This would have a growing impact on the economy. For example, Americans designed the first transistor radio, but didn't improve and miniaturise it. The Japanese did. US businesses had to buy Japanese parts to assemble in the USA. By 1958, there were 45 million transistor radios in the USA.

There was a shift in industry from the North and East of the country towards the South and West (the area now called the Sunbelt). Much of the shift was due to wartime investment for the war production industry, including aircraft manufacture and military bases. The move was made because land, goods and services were cheaper in the South and West. After the war, the military bases stayed and the new factories began producing peacetime goods. The development of good air-conditioning made the area more attractive and more people retired there. This sizeable population shift towards areas where there was work and better weather contributed to the emptying of the inner cities and to the problems that developed in them.

In the 1950s, the government shifted its economic strategy. Previous economic thinking, from the New Deal onwards, was that high government spending, even if it created a budget deficit, would keep the economy stable and prices down. After the war, this didn't work. The government wanted to keep interest rates low, so increased the money supply, thinking this would hold inflation down. In 1952, there was $169.7 billion in circulation (not counting savings, shares, etc.). By 1960, it was $215.8 billion.

The 1960s
During the 1960s, the USA finally lost its place as the world's most important exporter. The Vietnam War was draining government finances, as were social welfare payments. The government was still increasing the money supply (with the consent of the Fed), but inflation was still rising. Increasing the money supply helped the government meet increased welfare costs and other bills and, in the short term, helped the economy. But the amount of gold held by the government kept falling, so the balance between gold reserves and paper money was increasingly out of balance. This was a significant problem. The 1944 international Bretton Woods agreement had made the dollar the currency to be backed by a gold reserve (other currencies were then valued against the dollar). The government saw that the falling gold reserve was a problem. In 1966, it slowed (but did not stop) increasing the money supply. There was an almost immediate downturn in the economy and inflation kept rising. The government wanted to control prices, rather than letting business have its head, so it increased the money supply more, slowing inflation but creating problems for the future in terms of the gap with the US gold reserves.

SOURCE 9

Increase in the money in circulation in the USA, 1961–68. Based on data from Statistical Abstract of the United States.

Year	Increase in money in circulation (billions of dollars)
1961	16.9
1962	17.9
1963	18.3
1964	24.7
1965	28.1
1966	15.2
1967	36.6
1968	36.7

SOURCE 10

Price index in the USA, 1939–69. Based on data from the US Bureau of the Census.

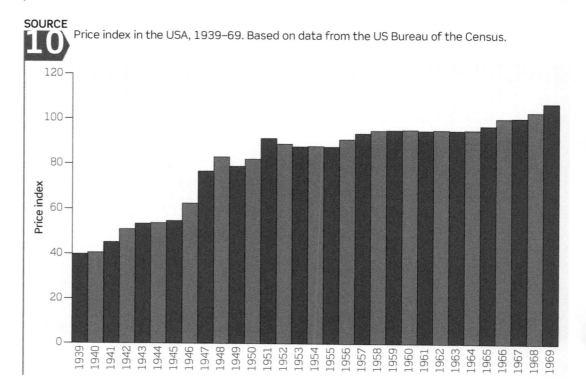

SOURCE
11

Average wage in the USA, 1939–69. Based on data from the US Bureau of the Census.

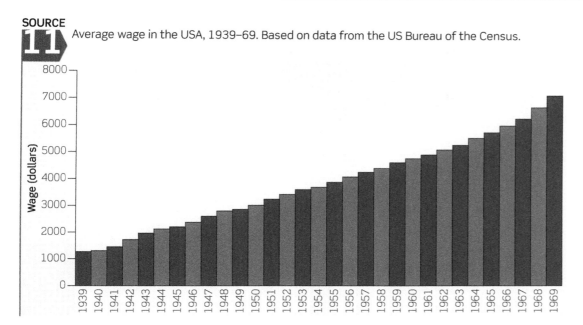

SOURCE
12

Unemployment in the USA, 1939–69. Based on data from the US Bureau of the Census.

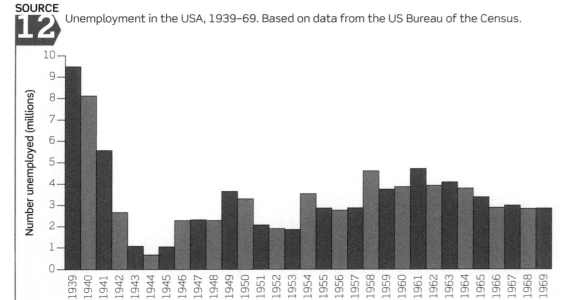

SOURCE
13

Percentage of the workforce unemployed in the USA, 1939–69. Based on data from the US Bureau of the Census.

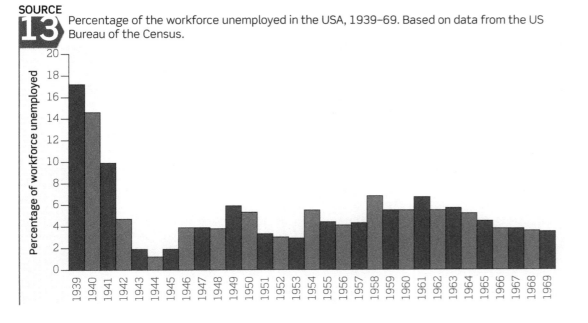

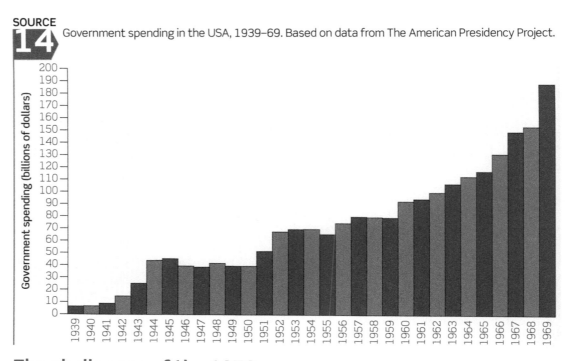

SOURCE 14 Government spending in the USA, 1939–69. Based on data from The American Presidency Project.

The challenges of the 1970s

The 1970s saw the economy move into a new phase, '**stagflation**'. Previously, when businesses stopped expanding, wages stopped rising – or even fell. So people spent less and prices fell. In the 1970s, prices didn't fall. Instead, inflation carried on and people came to see rising prices as normal. Those who could afford to carried on spending. Some workers were less well off, but managed. Some workers (e.g. those in the coal industry) had their wages linked to the **Consumer Price Index (CPI)**. This kept their wages in line with inflation. However, the rising number of unemployed, and those on a fixed income (from those on benefit to pensioners on a fixed pension), found their money could buy less and less.

Why stagflation?

The shift in position of the USA in the world economy was a significant factor in business stagnation. In the early 20th century, the USA had led the world in developing technology for goods such as cars, fridges and televisions. By the 1950s, some other countries (e.g. Japan, the UK and Germany) had overtaken the USA in technological development. Japan rapidly came to dominate electronics. In 1953, the USA's share of the world's export of manufactured goods was 29 percent. In 1963 it was 17 percent and in 1973 it was 13 percent. Meanwhile, business taxes were rising (taxes were not linked to inflation). Costs of raw materials rose with inflation, so businesses had less to invest in improving technology. Falling productivity was also becoming a significant problem. Failing businesses meant cutbacks and a rise in unemployment.

EXTRACT 1 From 'Reaganomics and economic policy', written by Joseph J. Horgan, in *The Reagan Presidency*, published in 1990.

In the 1970s Washington policymakers found it impossible to tackle successfully an upward rise in stagflation that was largely induced by energy and food supply shocks. During the heyday of 'New Economics' in the Kennedy–Johnson era, economic policymakers were confident that they could manipulate the budget to stabilise the business cycle and avoid high inflation or unemployment. In the 1970s this belief that the budget can direct economic growth gave way to the view that the economy shapes the budget. ... The combination of unemployment and inflation certainly weakened the capacity and the political will of the federal government to deal with the policy problems that seemed to be so strongly and intractably involved in fighting stagnation. If the government went after inflation by restricting the money supply, then unemployment increased before the economy deflated. The rise in unemployment quickly caused political problems, which led the government regularly to switch its policy objective to stimulating the economy at the expense of inflation. The 'stop-go' approach failed therefore to arrest the rise in the 'misery index' during the 1970s.

Government action

The government couldn't cope with the economic problems of the 1970s. Rather than the steady ups and downs of the 1960s, the 1970s saw three big economic crises caused by rising food and fuel prices. Federal spending was very high, driven up by linking social security payments and some pensions to the Consumer Price Index in 1972 and 1974. The end of the war in Vietnam saved money that would have been spent on the war, but returning soldiers added to the unemployed and the drain on social and medical benefits. When the government tried to control the economy, it was too nervous of public reaction. When the public reacted badly to sharp increases in inflation, or a sharp rise in unemployment, the government didn't leave control of the money supply in place. Linking wages, pensions and benefits to inflation helped those people it affected, but put the government deeper in debt. Many more people were either falling deeper into debt or cutting back on their standards of living to cope with inflation. Some people failed to cope with credit payments, their homes were repossessed and they became homeless and dependent on government welfare. In 1979, the money supply was contained – but by the Fed, not the government.

Energy problems

There were two fuel crises in the 1970s. They brought fuel shortages, long queues for fuel, a speed limit of 55 mph and (during the first crisis) fuel rationing with ration books, just as in the Second World War.

- In the 1973 Arab–Israeli War, the Organisation of the Petroleum Exporting Countries (OPEC) supported Palestine. OPEC put up prices by 70 percent and then embargoed oil exports to the USA and other countries that supported Israel. It kept prices high even after the war ended. By January 1974, world oil prices were four times higher than before the crisis. Fuel prices never returned to earlier levels.

- In 1979, there was another fuel shortage, from May to July. Shortages were as bad as in 1973, although, as it only lasted three months, there was no fuel rationing. However, there were worries about a heating fuel shortage that winter.

The lack of immediate access to cheap fuel was horrifying to car-dependent Americans. People as young as 15 years old (the age varied between states) could learn to drive. This was years before they were allowed to drink alcohol (21) or vote in elections (18). Both crises created high levels of discontent with the government, which people felt had made the 1979 shortages worse by ordering stockpiling at the start. People began to feel that the government was not only failing to deal with the economic crisis – it was making matters worse. A significant number of people changed their car-buying habits, changing from big American 'gas-guzzling' cars to smaller Japanese and European cars that used less fuel.

The confidence crisis

Soaring fuel prices set inflation rising sharply and a significant depression set in. Unemployment levels rose from 5.8 percent of the workforce in 1978 to 7.1 percent in 1979. People were scared to spend; businesses were scared to spend.

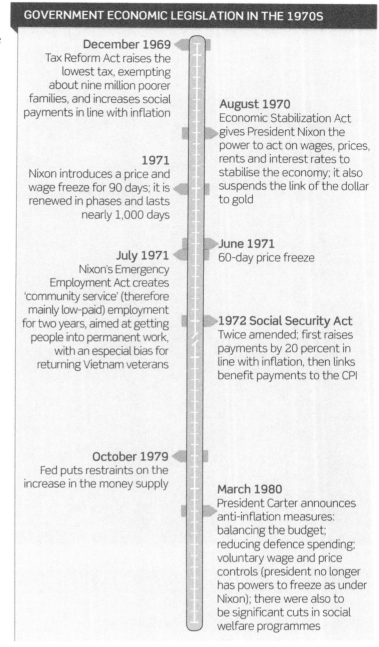

GOVERNMENT ECONOMIC LEGISLATION IN THE 1970S

December 1969
Tax Reform Act raises the lowest tax, exempting about nine million poorer families, and increases social payments in line with inflation

August 1970
Economic Stabilization Act gives President Nixon the power to act on wages, prices, rents and interest rates to stabilise the economy; it also suspends the link of the dollar to gold

1971
Nixon introduces a price and wage freeze for 90 days; it is renewed in phases and lasts nearly 1,000 days

June 1971
60-day price freeze

July 1971
Nixon's Emergency Employment Act creates 'community service' (therefore mainly low-paid) employment for two years, aimed at getting people into permanent work, with an especial bias for returning Vietnam veterans

1972 Social Security Act
Twice amended; first raises payments by 20 percent in line with inflation, then links benefit payments to the CPI

October 1979
Fed puts restraints on the increase in the money supply

March 1980
President Carter announces anti-inflation measures: balancing the budget; reducing defence spending; voluntary wage and price controls (president no longer has powers to freeze as under Nixon); there were also to be significant cuts in social welfare programmes

In July 1979, President Carter addressed the nation and discussed the crisis the nation was facing. He said the biggest crisis the nation faced was not the energy crisis, but a crisis of confidence. He was, almost certainly, trying to reproduce Roosevelt's confidence-inspiring 'fireside chats' of the 1930s (he had tried this before, with a televised fireside chat about the energy crisis in 1977). However, Carter didn't have Roosevelt's way with the public. He also had a history of failing to cope with the economy. Americans had very little confidence that the austerity measures Carter proposed would work. So they were unlikely to support him when he asked them to cut a standard of living that they felt had already dropped considerably. The rising homelessness and unemployment reminded people of the Great Depression. At the next presidential election, in 1980, people voted for a Republican, Ronald Reagan, and a very different economic policy.

SOURCE
15) People in Detroit in 1980, queuing to register as unemployed. Detroit manufacturing was hit hard by the recession of the late 1970s, as it was a major car manufacturing city. Unemployment levels there were several percent higher than average.

ACTIVITY
KNOWLEDGE CHECK

Stagflation

1 Explain how stagflation is different from inflation.

2 a) Give three economic measures Nixon's government put in place to help the economy.

   b) Explain why they were not effective.

3 Why were the fuel crises of the 1970s such a problem for Americans?

4 Explain how Carter's economic policies at the end of his presidency were different from previous policies.

A Level Exam-Style Question Section A

How far do you agree that confidence was the most significant factor in both the affluence of the 1950s and the crisis of the 1970s? (20 marks)

Tip
Consider other factors, such as the oil crisis or the drop in exports (external factors).

TO WHAT EXTENT DID LIVING STANDARDS CHANGE, 1917–80?

Living the American Dream for most Americans meant having a certain standard of living. In 1917, this would have meant having somewhere to live, a job and a family. It would also have meant a wage that covered more than the basic necessities of living. As the decades went by, the 'necessities' increased to include home ownership, a car and a significant number of consumer goods, such as radios, fridges, washing machines and televisions. It also included leisure time to enjoy the Dream. Between 1917 and 1980, people accumulated a lot more 'stuff', from furniture to sports equipment. The richer they were, the more they bought – and the more expensive those items were.

While standards of living changed considerably over the period, there were some constant features. For example, average life expectancy rose, but the fact that white people had a higher life expectancy than non-whites did not change. In 1915, white men had an average life expectancy of 48 years, for non-white men it was 33 years. In 1980, the figures were 74.4 years and 69.5 years. The same is true of the average wage. In 1939, the average wage for a white man was $1,234.41; a man of any other race would earn on average $537.45. In 1979, the figures were $28,894.69 and $19,417.03. These figures reflect the fact that many more white men were in higher-earning jobs. The situation for women followed the same pattern, although women in general lived longer than men and earned less.

The standard of living, 1917–41

There are many different measures of the standard of living. The economy went through boom and bust with several dips in between. Sources 10 and 11 show the relationship between wages and spending during these years. Sources 12, 13 and 14 show unemployment and the level of federal government spending (partly to cover social welfare). As well as this information, it is important to consider other factors.

Home ownership

In the 1920 census, about 6,700,000 people owned their own homes, while about 12,900,000 rented. The 1940 census listed about 19,600,000 renting homes and 15,200,000 home owners, a very steep rise in home ownership. The 1940 census, unlike that of 1920, also listed other facilities of homes. This suggests that these things were seen as important by 1940 (all the data below are from the 1940 census).

- **Running water, bathrooms and toilets:** Only about 2.6 percent of homes had no toilet of any kind, while 59.7 percent had an indoor flushing toilet for their own use. Of these homes, 69.9 percent had running water in the house and 56.2 percent had a bath or shower. Non-white people in rented housing in cities were most likely to have shared facilities and most likely to have plumbing in need of repair.

- **Lighting:** 78.7 percent of homes had electric light, while 20.2 percent still relied on oil lamps. The rest used gas, candles or nothing at all.

- **Cooking:** 48.8 percent of homes cooked by gas and only 5.4 percent by electricity. There were still 0.4 percent of homes with no way of cooking at all.

- **Heating:** 42 percent of homes had central heating; for those homes without central heating, the most usual method of heating was a stove, although 11.3 percent of homes had no heating at all.

- **Refrigeration:** 44.1 percent of homes had an electric fridge, while about 27.4 percent did not even have an ice box to keep food cool.

- **Radios:** 82.8 percent of people said they owned a radio.

Spending money

As the 1920s went on, more and more people shopped in chain stores rather than small, local stores. By 1929, retail chains were selling 21.9 percent of all goods sold in the USA. They were expanding too. Early chains had one or two stores in one state and then moved into several states. Some chains, such as J.C. Penney, spread to all states. There were homeware chains that sold furnishing, clothing and household goods (J.C. Penney was one of these). Chains selling cars and tractors also grew, and there were restaurant and food store chains. They all helped to create an 'American' culture that made people at home in any state. They also began a decline in 'mom and pop' shops: family-run businesses that could not offer the discounted prices of chain stores.

- **Food:** The 1930 census showed that people spent 23.9 percent of their income on food. They spent 13.4 percent of their food-spending money on eating out. By 1933, during the Great Depression, they were spending 25.9 percent of their income on food, but only 12.9 percent of their food-spending money on eating out. By 1940, the standard of living had clearly risen. People only needed to spend 21.1 percent of their income on food. What is more, 15.1 percent (a greater proportion) of that money was spent on eating out, which cost more than eating in.

- **Household appliances:** The household appliance market boomed in the 1920s and 1930s. Most of these appliances (e.g. fridges, radios, toasters, washing machines, irons and vacuum cleaners) ran on electricity. It is no accident that Roosevelt set up the Rural Electrification Administration (REA) in 1935, to get electricity (and so radio, to spread his message) to rural areas. In 1939 alone, the REA ran over 100,000 miles of new power lines. By 1940, newly electrified homes were buying almost as many electrical appliances as more long-established ones – and they were buying the same things. In 1940, over 80 percent of all homes with electricity had an iron and a radio and over 50 percent had a washing machine, a fridge and a toaster.

Other standard of living indicators

- **Health:** The nation's health was improving. The death rates for diphtheria, smallpox, tuberculosis, whooping cough and polio all dropped steadily, with the exception of a rise in the early 1930s, when people couldn't afford to pay medical bills. The government invested more in providing free healthcare for those who could not afford it – making them more likely to go to the doctor. In 1917, it spent $3,100,000 on healthcare. By 1930, spending had reached $11 million and, by 1940, it was $32,700,000.

- **Education:** In 1917, just 27.1 percent of all children aged 14–17 were going to school. By 1929, the figure was 51.5 percent and, by 1940, it was 73 percent. This is a significant indication of a rise in the standard of living. This was before the baby boom, so suggests that, by 1940, many more children were being sent to school than sent out to work as soon as possible to contribute to the family income. In 1920, 8.5 percent of all children under 15 were working. Labour legislation in 1938 included stopping children under 14 working in most non-agricultural jobs. The census data after that did not include children under 14 in the labour force. This suggests that there were very few of them – farming was probably an exception, as children in farming families worked while being registered for school.

Life at the bottom

The monthly wages of farm workers (Source 16) are a reminder that the standard of living varied widely. From these data, a farm worker would earn $298.32 a year, with only very basic food and board provision. This is significantly less than the average wage of a non-white person for the same year and about one-quarter of the average earnings of a white man.

EXTRACT

2 From *The American Dream: From Reconstruction to Reagan*, written by Esmond Wright in 1996.

As they entered the second half of the twentieth century, Americans were enjoying great material prosperity. National income was enormous, well over $200 billion a year. Employment was high, around 60 million. Farmers were doing well; working men – thanks to the war – were obtaining some of the security which they had long desired. Improved educational opportunities, especially grants for veterans, were making it possible for an increasing number of Americans to satisfy their ambitions to enter the professions. Business earnings were at peak levels. Americans had more mechanical conveniences, more cultural opportunities, more leisure than before.

SOURCE

16 Farm worker, monthly wages (with food and lodging provided). Based on data from United States Department of Agriculture, Economics, Statistics, and Market Information System.

Year	Monthly earnings ($)
1928	35.75
1929	33.04
1930	32.29
1931	26.03
1932	19.77
1933	14.77
1934	15.74
1935	17.04
1936	18.54
1937	20.68
1938	25.18
1939	24.86
1940	25.33
1941	26.88

ACTIVITY
KNOWLEDGE CHECK

1 Draw a graph to show how you think the standard of living fluctuated between 1917 and 1941.

2 a) Why do you think the census asked the questions that it did in the 1920 and 1940 surveys?

   b) Compile a table of the information from the 1940 census and leave an empty column for 1960 (to be completed later).

3 Why do you think the farm workers' standard of living was so much worse than the average?

The Second World War and the growth of the consumer society, 1941–60

The war reduced consumer spending, as industry shifted to war production. During the war it was, suddenly, not the American Way to consume. Instead, it was patriotic to scrimp and save, to eat less bread so more wheat could be exported to the Allies in Europe, to save fuel for military use. Once the war ended, industry returned

rapidly to the production of peacetime goods. Americans needed no encouragement to start consuming again. The American Way was back on track. The post-war economic boom led to a burst of consumerism that made the consumerism of the 1920s look insignificant. Manufacturers offered consumers an ever-widening range of choice of goods. Ford's idea of one model of car in one colour vanished. Now an increasing number of products was offered in a huge variety of styles and colours. Manufacturers realised that constantly updating their goods made people buy more often. They also introduced a new policy, built-in obsolescence. They made less sturdy machines that wore out more quickly and so needed replacing more often. Advertisers and businesses began selling 'new' and 'improved' products to encourage even greater spending. They also targeted different groups of people more strongly than before. In this they had a new ally – television. This ran on sponsorship, just as radio did, so advertisements were an integral part.

The impact of television

To begin with, televisions were very expensive (about $200 in 1948), the screens were small (about 15 cm × 12 cm) and you could only get reception in the New York area. By 1950, nine percent of homes had a television; in 1955 it was 65 percent and by 1960 it was 85 percent. It was a massive growth. This can partly be explained by the fact that, by 1950, most homes had electricity and installation wasn't complicated. Televisions did need reception and broadcasting stations grew rapidly. In 1948, there were 16 broadcasting stations; by 1954, there were 354. Television brought entertainment into the home and meant that families went out less. Many buyers lived in the suburbs. Staying in saved finding a babysitter and saved the journey to the movies, theatres, bars and restaurants in town and city centres. As more people stayed home to eat dinner and watch television, pre-cooked 'TV dinners' that could just be heated and eaten in front of the television were developed.

Consumers as targets

Manufacturers became increasingly specific in targeting consumers. They extended their range of goods widely. For example, the toy industry grew rapidly (see page 94), helped by developments in the plastic industry (plastic toy cars were cheaper to make than steel ones). Products aimed at children were advertised around children's programmes on television and radio, targeting children for their 'pester-power' with their parents, not the parents themselves. In 1955, Davy Crockett was a television hero. In just five months, the company making Davy Crockett outfits made $100 million from sales of just the racoon-skin caps of the outfit.

Women were also targeted for their 'pester-power' in major purchases (from kitchen units to washing machines), although men were targets for car advertisements. Women, especially working women, were targets for 'labour-saving' devices. Washing machines, vacuum cleaners, wipe-clean floors and worktop surfaces – all these things made housework faster and easier. Women were also targets for everyday domestic shopping. Throughout the 1950s, they bought more food, drink and domestic supplies than ever before. Women chose the brand of milk, juice and coffee. They decided which grocery chain store to visit regularly (research showed many women had a 'favourite' store rather than shopping around).

Pre-prepared meals were also a time-saver, as were part-prepared items, such as ready-mix cakes. Cake mix providers, such as Betty Crocker, sold the American Dream of a woman baking for her family, quickly, easily and with a reliable result.

Health and nutrition

During the Second World War, food was rationed. After the war, people ate and drank more than before. They craved the foods they had been deprived of during the war: fat, sugar and meat. However, they also ate much more synthetic food (e.g. artificial sweeteners). Sweets and flavoured drinks were big business; Coca Cola made $55.7 million before tax in 1950 and $79.1 million in 1959. People also smoked more (many got into the habit during the war). People were eating far less healthily than before the war. The 1950s saw the first big studies into the effects that food, drink and smoking had on health. By the early 1960s, there were reports about the health effects of smoking and too much cholesterol in the diet. Women were much more likely to feed their babies formula milk, especially the type that had vitamins added. It made it easier for working women to share the care of their babies, but even non-working women were encouraged to use formula because of the added vitamins and because it was easier to measure a baby's intake.

Teenage consumption

Teenagers were significant consumers in the 1950s. A 1959 survey showed that teenagers spent about $10 billion a year, mostly on (in order of spend):

- **Transport 38 percent:** Most of this was car-related. In 1959, there were 1.5 million teenage car owners. This was helped by the growing number of families trading in the family car for a newer model every few years – there were more second-hand cars for the teenage market.
- **Clothing and sports 24 percent:** Teenage girls consumed more clothing and cosmetics than the boys ($20 million on lipsticks alone), but boys spent more on sporting equipment and trips to sporting events.
- **Food and drink 22 percent:** Teenagers ate and drank a significant amount outside the home. Teenagers ate about 20 percent more than adults and, when eating out, they ate huge amounts of ice cream and drank a lot of milk, giving a huge boost to the dairy industry. They also ate in the new drive-ins that produced cheap, fast food.
- **Entertainment 16 percent:** Teenagers spent $75 million on records. From the 1950s, movie-makers began to target teen audiences with high school films and a range of cheap horror and sci-fi movies such as *The Blob* (1958).

EXTEND YOUR KNOWLEDGE

Transistor radios and the teenage market
When transistor radios were invented, they made a huge impact because of their portability. The biggest consumers were teenagers, who primarily wanted them to listen to pop music. The first widely available transistor radio was the TR-1, which went on sale for the first time in 1954. At $49.95 for the cheapest model, it was expensive and it wasn't very small. Thousands, rather than millions, were sold, which wasn't a lot for a teenage market. Then a Japanese company miniaturised the transistor radio by using tubes, not radio transistors. These miniature radios were far more popular; in 1959 alone, the USA imported six million.

THINKING HISTORICALLY   Change (5a)

Complex change

Changes leading up to growth of a consumer society

Strand	Explanation of how the strand links to the growth of a consumer society
People's increasing confidence in the economy	Willingness to spend money, often on credit
The spread of television ownership	Advertising, targeting children, teenagers, women and men
	Television programmes achieving cult status
Manufacturers increased productivity, wider range of goods and changed aims	Manufacturers offering more choice
	The idea of built-in obsolescence, rather than built to last
Second World War	Brought employment and encouraged manufacturing
	Wartime economising meant that people wanted to spend once the war was over

Make two copies of the graph below.

1 On the first, plot the individual strands against the y-axis. Use a different colour for each. You don't need to label it with the events.

2 On the second graph, plot a single line which is a combination of all four strands. (For example, at a given point, two of the four strands are plotted high up on the y-axis, while two are plotted lower. The combined strand would have to be plotted somewhere in the middle to represent a summary of those four individual strands.)

Answer the following:

1 How have the strands combined to make change less or more likely?

2 Why did the consumer society arrive in the 1950s and not before?

Better off than in 1940?

The census measures changed in 1960. They still measured home ownership. In 1960, about 62 percent of all people owned their own homes compared to 43.6 percent in 1940. In 1960, 93 percent of homes had running water in the house; 86 percent of all homes had an indoor flushing toilet for their own use, while 85 percent had a bath or shower. Electricity supplies were no longer recorded and 30.8 percent of homes now cooked with it. Only 1.7 percent of homes had no heating at all. Fridges were no longer recorded, but freezers were recorded instead; 18.5 percent of homes had a freezer in 1960. About 92 percent of homes had at least one radio. Newly registered goods were washing machines (40.3%), telephones (78.5%), televisions (85%) and air conditioning (1.7%).

ACTIVITY
KNOWLEDGE CHECK

1 Explain why each of the following were, or were not, good consumer targets for producers in the 1950s:

   a) a teenage boy with two sisters living in a small rural town

   b) a pregnant woman who works part-time in an office and whose husband works on a production line

   c) a five-year-old child whose father runs a small-town business and whose mother is a housewife

   d) a wealthy man, with a young wife and two grown-up children, who lives in New York

   e) a single man living in Los Angeles, who has just started his first job as a technician in Hollywood.

2 a) Add the 1960 census data to the living standards table you began for the Knowledge Check Activity on page 102.

   b) Write a magazine article explaining the extent to which the standard of living changed between 1940 and 1960.

Anti-poverty policies and economic divisions, 1961–80

During the 1960s, the gap between rich and poor became more marked. In 1949, the richest one percent of the population had controlled 20.8 percent of the country's wealth. By 1956, it was 26 percent. In 1968, a production worker earned, on average, $6,370 a year. The chief executive of the company he worked for was taking home, on average, in wages and bonuses, about $157,000. This seems a big difference, but the difference escalated to $12,962 against $373,000 in 1978. This illustrates the difference between a white production worker and a white manager. But there were other, wider divisions.

Problems facing non-white Americans

Throughout the 1960s and 1970s, it was harder for non-white Americans to get hired and, if they were hired, they were automatically paid less than a white colleague doing the same job. In 1960, the average income for a white family was $5,835. The average income for a black family was $3,230. Affirmative action, proposed by presidents from Roosevelt onwards, was slow coming and often caused resentment. Many non-whites found it unhelpful. They were often seen as chosen for their race, not their abilities. Non-white Americans could advance in professions such as law, accountancy and university teaching. The black middle class made up 27 percent of all black workers in 1970 and there were non-white Americans living in the suburbs. This was still a small percentage of the suburban population as a whole. The most significant non-white suburbs were black American suburbs, at just over 4 percent. Hispanic groups were still moving largely into the inner cities, while many Native Americans remained in the government relocation areas, such as Pico Boulevard, Los Angeles.

In 1966, about 12 percent of white Americans and 41 percent of non-white Americans were living below what the government defined as the poverty line, the equivalent of a family of four living on $3,000 a year. Many lived in the inner cities, although there were also still areas of extreme rural poverty. When better-off whites moved to the suburbs in large numbers in the 1950s, non-white Americans moved to the cities (there was a significant migration of black Americans to the cities in the 1950s). If they were unlucky, the non-whites moving to the cities ended up in the inner cities. The situation in many inner cities was grim. Much inner-city housing was subdivided and rented out and some landlords, as rents fell, began to fail to repair their properties and even burned them down to claim the insurance or left them to rot. These changes can be tracked in the census, where areas such as South Side Chicago had an increasing number of people living in the 'housing units' and the plumbing was often listed as 'in need of repair'.

Most residents of these areas did their best to keep their living standards up, but others, feeling angry or helpless at their situation, turned to crime, drugs or both. By the 1970s, some inner-city areas were locked in a hopeless downward spiral. For example, the South Bronx in New York was in a Hispanic ghetto. In the 1970s, well over half the families there were on welfare. Between 1960 and 1974, the number of deliberate fires (most set by landlords to claim the insurance and federal rebuilding grants) tripled. The Housing Commissioner, Roger Starr, set out a policy of 'planned shrinkage' – closing subway stations, police stations, fire stations, hospitals and schools in these areas, leaving people even worse off. Planned shrinkage was also adopted in other inner cities.

Federal government anti-poverty policies

Kennedy outlined anti-poverty (New Frontier) policies but these were not passed before he was shot. Johnson introduced his 'Great Society' policies to fight 'the war on poverty'. He set up an independent agency, with a staff of over 130 and a budget of over $960 million, to run the policies, reporting directly to him. Johnson stressed that poverty was the enemy (and the problem), not poor people. Congress did not pass all the welfare bills that the Johnson administration presented. However, social welfare programmes were extended to cover more people and pay out more benefits. Other anti-poverty measures were also introduced. The Great Society laws were well intentioned and more wide ranging even than the New Deal. However, the scale of the problem was immense and the funding, though significant, was not enough.

The Community Action Programs (CAPs) could make a big difference. Often the organisers of these projects were women. They collected data on the biggest local problems and presented projects to solve them. One successful project in Memphis focused on high infant mortality and worked with medical professionals to set up free clinics to provide care and advice before and after birth. The scheme was then used all over the country. However, some projects failed. The competition to gain project funding could lead to greater racial tension, even violence (as it did between black and Hispanic communities in Los Angeles).

SOURCE 18

After the inner city riots of 1967, the government set up the Kerner Commission to report on what happened, why it happened and what could be done to stop it happening again. Its report, published in February 1968, was a long, detailed document, but summed up its stark conclusion on the first page, as below.

This is our basic conclusion: Our nation is moving toward two societies, one black, one white – separate and unequal. Reaction to last summer's disorders has quickened the movement and deepened the division. Discrimination and segregation have long permeated much of American life; they now threaten the future of every American. This deepening racial division is not inevitable. The movement apart can be reversed. Choice is still possible. Our principal task is to define that choice and to press for a national resolution. To pursue our present course will involve the continuing polarization of the American community and, ultimately, the destruction of basic democratic values. The alternative is not blind repression or capitulation to lawlessness. It is the realization of common opportunities for all within a single society.

SOURCE 17

Federal troops patrol the Watts district of Los Angeles after the 1965 riots, sparked by police violence while arresting a young black man, but driven by living conditions and constant police harassment. The government responded to the riots in the cities by putting federal money into urban regeneration. This added to the vision that developed during the 1970s of the inner cities as a huge sponge, soaking up federal money: both redevelopment funding and social welfare payments.

EXTRA ANTI-POVERTY MEASURES, 1961-70

21 January 1961
Kennedy issues an executive order that the food made available to people in areas of chronic unemployment (usually agricultural surplus in the area) should be of a more varied type (to satify nutritional needs) and greater quantity

30 June 1961 Housing Act
Extended funding (over $3 billion) for urban renewal, low-income housing and low-interest loans for housing

15 March 1962 Manpower Development and Training Act
Sets up work training programmes for the unemployed

29 August 1964 Economic Opportunity Act
Creates the Office of Economic Opportunity and gives it $947.7 million to fund projects in 'pockets of poverty'; these set up: training and work schemes for the unemployed young; basic adult education; over 1,000 Community Action Programs (CAPs), based in deprived areas working with local volunteers to improve them; it also provides help in rural areas

31 August 1964 Food Stamp Act
Sets up a pilot food stamp system: people could exchange the stamps for food; this was expanded in 1974 to reach 15 million people

30 July 1965 Medicare Act
Takes a small contribution from people's social security payments and guarantees them free medical care in old age; it also sets up Medicaid, which provides free medical care to those on welfare

11 October 1966 Child Nutrition Act
Funds schools that cannot provide lunches because of lack of cooking and eating equipment; extends lunch provision to preschools; starts a breakfast programme for schools in deprived areas; extends the provision of free school milk

Different policies, different aims

By the end of the 1960s, there was growing criticism that 'Great Society' programmes were not helping people out of poverty – they were encouraging them to stay on welfare. Criticism was particularly vindictive against non-white single parents (seen as having babies for welfare) and young black men (seen as the driving force behind the inner-city riots in the late 1960s). Critics also pointed out that all the CAPs were set up by and for non-whites (not surprising, given that they had the most problems).

When Nixon came to power, in 1969, he shifted the focus of federal aid to the working poor, the old, children and people with disabilities, all of whom received extra aid. In his first year, Nixon set about dismantling the Office of Economic Opportunity.

This was a long process, because many programmes were funded for several years. When their funding expired, it was not replaced and many local groups could not find enough local support to keep going. While not in favour of OEO policies, Nixon did pass anti-poverty legislation, enlarging the food stamp programme and making federal government administer it. It became more efficient and this was a real benefit to those relying on the stamps. Nixon also linked social security payments to inflation, which meant that the buying power of benefit payments stayed at the same level, rather than falling with inflation.

To encourage the poor to find work, Nixon emphasised 'workfare' not 'welfare'. His Earned Income Tax Credit gave working poor with children up to $400 a year, linked to their earning in the year. However, this only helped those who could find work, and finding work was a problem for many. The Nixon administration set up family planning advice and resources for the poor. However, this relied on people wanting smaller families and using the contraception provided. Nixon also cut welfare benefits while seeming not to. For example, in the Family Assistance Plan of 1970, he 'rationalised' welfare benefits by combining them. However, the sum of the benefits he combined was often greater than the revised benefit. This meant those claiming benefits lost out – losing the advantage that linking benefits to inflation had given them. There was growing public support for reducing welfare payments. Nixon had tried to replace the Great Society with a work-focused welfare programme. Even this seemed to be too much welfare for some people.

EXTEND YOUR KNOWLEDGE

Johnnie Tillmon (1926–95)
Johnnie Tillmon was a welfare campaigner in the Watts district of LA. She led the National Welfare Rights Organisation (NWRO), campaigning for the rights of mothers on welfare. It was NWRO that pointed out that benefits under Nixon's Family Assistance Plan (FAP) would actually fall. The NWRO protested against the stereotype of the single parent as a welfare scrounger. Tillmon gave evidence to Congress about the problem of tying welfare to work, when single parents were often seen as undesirable workers (so work was harder to find) and had trouble getting childcare. One unsympathetic Congressman said the campaigners should be picking up litter, not marching.

While the NWRO didn't get the FAP overturned, it did get changes at state level, with protests that used civil rights tactics such as sit-ins. For example, it persuaded many states to agree that officials could not raid a home unannounced. Its local support organisations probably had the most impact, prompting tens of thousands of eligible mothers to apply for welfare and helping them form groups to support each other.

When Carter was elected in 1976, he told his administration to work out a plan to help both working and non-working poor, without raising budget costs. This wasn't possible and even a much reduced plan didn't get through Congress. Some reforms were passed. In 1978, the National Consumer Cooperative Bank was set up, to give low-interest loans to co-operative organisations, largely in urban areas. It lent money to small local groups who would otherwise have trouble raising the money to start businesses or buy homes. As such, it helped the working poor to improve their position – it didn't help the very poorest. This bank began work in 1980 with a $184 million budget. The Rural Development Loan Fund was set up just before Carter's defeat in the 1981 election.

It extended various forms of help available to farmers by giving low-interest loans to rural communities to provide electrification, clinics, farm equipment for communal use – whatever was needed. Again, this helped only the working poor and only in areas that received grants from the fund. However, there were many communities that benefited from both projects.

In the last two years of his administration, Carter tried a different tactic. He introduced tax cuts, hoping they would help the economy where trying to manipulate the money supply had failed. His measures might have worked, but the public had lost confidence in his administration and in him as president. He might have been honest, a relief after Nixon, but he seemed less and less competent as his term wore on, and he was very unpopular in Congress. This was exploited by his opponent in the 1980 presidential elections, Ronald Reagan, who had plenty of political experience as governor of California and was popular with many Americans, including politicians and businessmen. Reagan offered the American people change at a time when they desperately wanted it – just as Roosevelt had in 1932. He was elected.

ACTIVITY
CONSOLIDATION

The war on poverty

1 List three ways in which the anti-poverty measures of the 1960s distinguished between different types of poverty.

2 Prepare to debate the question: 'To what extent did Johnson's "Great Society" programme fail to win the war on poverty?' Make at least four points to support and four points to contradict the statement.

HOW SIGNIFICANT WERE THE CHANGES IN LEISURE AND TRAVEL, 1917-80?

After the short period of unrest that followed the end of the First World War, many workers settled into jobs with shorter hours and a higher hourly rate than pre-war jobs, giving them a significant amount of leisure time. However, it was not until 1938 that the Fair Labor Standards Act made a 40-hour week (usually eight hours, five days a week) a legal maximum. It also set a minimum wage and overtime rules. In 1920, there were still many people who had very little leisure time, working long hours or, sometimes, doing more than one job to make ends meet. Many more were unemployed, especially in farming and industries such as the coal industry (which was declining with the growth of the use of electric power). However, there were enough people with increased leisure time to create a growing leisure industry.

No leisure time

During the 1920s and 1930s, many people had very little leisure time; it was a benefit for the middle classes and the better-off working classes. Most poor people still worked long hours, if they had a job at all. Working or not, they had little money to spare for leisure pursuits. During the Great Depression, the situation of many people got worse. People lost their jobs; some lost their homes too. Men and boys, some only in their early teens, left the family home to wander the country, looking for work.

Many families who lost their homes lived and travelled in their cars, searching for work. Farmers made homeless on the Great Plains tended to drift West, looking for seasonal farm labour. Workers from other trades tended to head for towns and cities, as the growing number of 'Hoovervilles' in the 1930s demonstrates.

The leisure industry, 1917–45

Movie theatres, theatres and sports stadiums sprang up in and around cities and towns. Eating out became a popular leisure activity – as did visiting the illegal speakeasies where people could gamble and drink (gambling was illegal and drinking alcohol was illegal until 1933). The amount of choice available varied from place to place, not just in terms of the size of a town but also where it was in the country. Taking movie-going as an example: by 1930, New York had literally hundreds of cinemas, ranging from tiny 50-seaters in black areas to the luxurious Roxy, built to hold over 5,000 people. Other parts of the country were less well served. Of all the towns and cities of North Carolina in the 1930s, only three had more than one movie theatre. In the South, movie theatres were segregated, with black people sitting in the balcony seats, unless the town had more than one movie theatre. In that case, the theatres themselves were segregated. In the North, as in many other respects, unofficial segregation applied. The popularity of movies led to a huge expansion of the movie industry, especially in Hollywood. This created an employment boom for workers in the movie industry, the building industry and the service industries that fed and housed the workers.

EXTEND YOUR KNOWLEDGE

A few lives changed spectacularly

The movies were big business in the 1920s and they transformed the lives of the few people who became stars. Stars earned very large salaries, even during the Depression. However, that is only one side of the story. In 1933, the Screen Actors Guild (the actors' union) estimated that, of all of their members working, earnings were:

Over $50,000	4 percent of members
$10,000–5,000	12 percent of members
Less than $5,000	71 percent of members

There are two further things to consider. First, the average yearly industrial wage at the time was just under $1,000 a year. Secondly, there were many actors who did not belong to the union and many more, in the union or not, who were unemployed.

Growing car ownership and better road systems meant people could get to National Parks to hike and camp. National Parks provided a safe 'back to nature' experience. They had camping grounds, hiking trails and Park Rangers. For days out, rather than longer holidays, a growing number of amusement parks competed to give people the most fun and the scariest roller coaster ride. Kiddie parks became increasingly popular (the first one was built in San Antonio, Texas), providing gentler rides for small children as well as more daring rides for older children and adults. As for leisure time at home, the radio industry grew rapidly (see pages 81–82), but the book market also grew, especially with the arrival of cheap paperbacks in the late 1920s. In 1929, book sales were $117 million; by 1939, they had fallen to $74 million, because of the Depression.

Spectator sports

Spectator sports became a very popular leisure activity. Sports coverage in the newspapers increased as it became clear that sport sold papers. Even before 1917, cigarette manufacturers were producing cigarette cards of famous baseball teams for fans to collect. As more people had more leisure time, the numbers of spectators for all kinds of sports grew (e.g. the American football Rose Bowl stadium, built in 1922 for an audience of 57,000, had to be enlarged in 1928 to hold 76,000). In the 1920s, Americans could watch professional baseball, college football, horse racing, dog racing and boxing. They could watch basketball and hockey matches and they could watch wrestling matches too, although these were already becoming seen as more theatre than sport.

Baseball was the most popular spectator sport and radio broadcasts of baseball games led to more people wanting to watch a game, not just listen to it. Baseball was organised into major and minor leagues. Most major league baseball stadiums held about 35,000 people in the 1920s, but the New York Yankees stadium was rebuilt in 1923 to hold 53,000, then considered the biggest audience it could hope to expect. The Yankees were the most popular team, almost entirely because of their star player, Babe Ruth. In 1917, attendance at Yankees games was just over 330,000 for the whole year. In 1920, it was just over 1,290,000 for the year.

Was radio good for spectator sports?

Radio coverage sold sport and sport sold radios. In September 1926, there was a world heavyweight boxing match between the famous boxers Jack Dempsey and Gene Tunney. The unanimous decision was that Tunney had won. However, there were persistent rumours that the match had been fixed because the Chicago gangster Al Capone had placed a large bet on it. A rematch was agreed the following year and it was to be broadcast on the radio. In the week before the match, just one New York department store sold over $90,000-worth of radios. In 1934, the baseball league sold the rights to broadcast its games to the Ford Motor Company for $10,000. However, some teams (for instance, both the St Louis baseball teams) began to refuse to allow local radio companies to broadcast their matches, thinking that people would stay home and listen to the game on the radio to avoid paying the price of a ticket. Ticket sales for both the St Louis teams did go up once the radio station stopped broadcasting matches (although this could have also been because both teams played better in 1934 than 1933).

Sports stars

Babe Ruth, the Yankees baseball star player, was such a draw that his salary rose from $20,000 a year in 1920 to $80,000 in 1930. Ruth was an example of the way success in sport could change lives, in the same way as the movies changed the lives of a few star actors. Ruth's family background meant that, without his baseball success, he could not have expected to earn one-tenth as much a year as his lowest income in baseball. A significant number of sportsmen came from working-class families. Gene Tunney, the boxer, was the son of an Irish immigrant dock worker and Jack Dempsey came from a farming family.

Black baseball

Black Americans were not allowed to play in white baseball teams until the 1940s. They had their own leagues, such as the Leland Giants in Chicago. In 1920, the Texan black American baseball star, Rube Foster, set up the National Negro Baseball League: the first professional baseball league for black American teams.

The Second World War

The Second World War helped to pull the USA out of the Depression. However, during the war, leisure time came second to the war effort. Also, there were significant restrictions on leisure imposed by wartime conditions (e.g. night-time baseball games were stopped to save electricity). National football and baseball teams were told by President Roosevelt to carry on playing to keep up morale, as long as their players joined the military if they were called up. Many players did not wait to be called up; they volunteered. The quality of the games suffered during the war as the players went off to fight. Travelling to games became more difficult too, with wartime restrictions. While the men were away at war, women took over their roles at home, and this included forming their own sporting teams. The All American Girls Professional Baseball League played from 1943 to 1954 and games drew audiences of about 1,600 a game, on average. Smaller local teams sprang up all over the country. However, once the men returned and the old sports teams started playing again, the women's teams collapsed.

The leisure industry, 1945–80

In the 1950s and 1960s, most working Americans had more time and money to spend on leisure. Paid holidays, the 40-hour working week and wage regulation boosted leisure time and spending power. There were more **white collar workers** than blue collar workers in 1960 (35 million as opposed to 32 million) and about 40 percent of married women were working, raising the family income. Labour-saving devices (e.g. wipe-down surface and floors) cut down on housework, creating more leisure time. Changes in manufacturing (e.g. mass production) made goods cheaper, so wages went further. On average, Americans spent about one-sixth of their income on leisure – either leisure products (such as televisions) or leisure pursuits (such as tickets to the movies or to a baseball game). This was an average statistic from the census – many people were still not part of the consumer culture (see page 101). The very poor and the homeless had little chance of leisure, but poorer working families could listen to sport on the radio or even buy cheap tickets to sports events or the movies. The growth of relatively cheap fast food chains meant they could eat out sometimes too.

White collar worker

A white collar worker is an office worker (named after the white shirt he wore to work), as opposed to a 'blue collar worker' (named after the blue collar of a factory worker's overalls and covering all people who worked with their hands, not just in factories). White collar workers were usually paid better and had shorter working hours.

As the decades passed, there was constant growth in the kinds of leisure pursuits available to Americans. The baby boom meant that family leisure activities became increasingly popular and theme parks and water parks sprang up across the country. Disneyland opened in 1955 with a 90-minute television slot presented by the famous actor Ronald Reagan. The suburbs sprouted family entertainment facilities such as bowling alleys, golf courses and tennis courts. Because the suburbs tended to be segregated by income as much as class, even some of the least expensive suburbs had some of these facilities in their cheapest form. Shopping became a leisure activity; people would go to large shopping malls for a day out, browsing the shops, spending money, and eating and drinking in the food concessions.

By 1980, the technology for home computers and internet connection had been developed. However, computers were expensive, slow and needed to be self-programmed. Bill Gate's Altair 8800 cost $297 ($395 if in a metal case to keep it clean and safe). People who bought it had to learn BASIC (a computer programming language) before they could use it. Computing was a leisure activity for some people, but using the computer was an end in itself, it wasn't seen as a tool. By the 1980s, there were home computers, but only middle-class families or those even better off could afford them. Home use of the internet did not take off until the 1990s.

Spectator sports and new audiences
After the war, football and baseball leagues, which, like industry, had been mainly in the North and East of the USA, began to move South and West. New stadiums were built for larger audiences. All sports benefited from the advent of television at first. The television companies spent a lot of money on the rights to televise sport. In the late 1940s, baseball television rights were selling for about $1,000 a game. By the 1980s, a vast range of sports was televised, not just big stadium sports. This brought a significant drop in sports attendance, which had been getting worse all through the 1970s. Television let people see the games as well as hear them: they could be spectators in their own homes. All but the very poor had a television, so could watch the games for free and, as filming techniques improved, with a better view of the games than many in the stadiums. Sport sponsors helped to raise audience numbers by corporate entertaining, family days and other kinds of special offers. The efforts of the sponsors worked. Major baseball league attendance rose from just under 330 million in the 1970s to just over 460 million in the 1980s.

What was the impact of the USA becoming a car-owning culture?
From the 1920s, American life was increasingly dependent on the car. This was particularly true when the suburbs started to boom in the 1950s. The car also had an effect on business and industry. Car production had one of the most wide-reaching sets of knock-on effects of any technological development before the computer.

Knock-on effects
- **Industrial effects:** Once there was a significant market for cars in the early years of the car industry, car factories expanded and employed more workers. They also started producing spare parts. The industries that produced raw materials for cars (steel, rubber, glass, leather) also increased production (and employed more workers). The need for workers pushed wages up and car prices went down. This meant more people could afford them, so demand increased.

- **Associated supplies:** Cars needed petrol to run and mechanics to maintain them. In 1929, there were 121,500 filling stations that made $1,800 million that year in petrol sales. By 1967, there were 216,000 filling stations that made $22,709 million that year. Meanwhile, car mechanics' workshops and car dealerships sprang up along the roads, often with filling stations attached.

- **Roads:** Roads were improved and expanded. In 1917, the USA had 2,925,000 miles of public road; in 1980, there were 3,860,000 miles of public road. In 1960, 21.5 percent of people in the census had no car; by 1980, it was 12.1 percent.

- **Mobility:** People could travel more widely once car ownership grew and there were more roads. Diners and motels sprang up along the growing number of roads (by 1958, there were about 56,000 motels and they made $850 million a year). National travel was possible before the car explosion – by train. The drawback was that trains didn't always take people exactly where they wanted to go. Cars helped people travel further, faster and more cheaply. This led to a huge rise in the number of travelling salesmen, who worked over larger and larger areas. This helped manufacturers of all kinds of goods to reach a greater number of customers and made door-to-door deliveries by lorry easier too, rather than relying on goods trains. The car (and the removal truck) also made it easier to move home.

SOURCE 19 Number of passenger cars in the USA and miles of public road, 1917–80. Based on data from the US Bureau of the Census.

Year	Number of cars	Miles of public road
1917	4,727,000	2,925,000
1920	8,132,000	3,105,000
1930	23,035,000	3,259,000
1940	27,466,000	3,287,000
1950	40,339,000	3,313,000
1960	61,671,000	3,546,000
1970	89,244,000	3,730,000
1980	121,601,000	3,860,000

- **Shopping:** The car allowed for the development of shopping malls. Southdale, Minneapolis, which opened in 1956, was the world's first covered, air-conditioned mall. It had a wide range of shops and services. People could buy a book, buy clothes, buy furniture, have a meal and get their hair cut. Once there was one mall, they mushroomed. Between 1960 and 1980, about 30,000 malls were built, the average size of them growing each year.

- **Entertainment:** In the 1950s and 1960s, there were a growing number of national drive-in restaurant chains, as well as fast food chains. Drive-in restaurants catered to families. People didn't have to dress up, as at a more conventional restaurant. Some people even took their children in their pyjamas and then put them to sleep on the back seat of the car. There were often play areas for children and the food was child friendly. There were also drive-in movie theatres, where people watched the movies from their cars. They were very popular with young people and usually showed low-budget movies for teenage audiences. Some drive-in movie theatres served food to the movie-goers. By 1954, there were 3,800 drive-ins making 16 percent of all the cinema box office receipts. Drive-in movies did well even though the industry as a whole was losing out to television. Weekly cinema attendance figures overall fell from 40 million in 1960 to 19.7 million in 1980. There were disadvantages, the main ones being the climate. Drive-ins thrived more in places where it was warm and dry most of the year, such as California.

- **Tourism:** The car (and the expanding road system) was vital to the development of the tourism industry within the USA. People could make trips to major cities. They could go to big attractions (e.g. theme parks such as Disneyland). They could go hiking and camping in national parks. No matter what they wanted to do, someone, somewhere, would provide what they wanted. Following this was the growth of hotel, motel and restaurant chains in tourist areas. People began to look for their favourite chain motels and diners (e.g. Dennys, which opened as Danny's Coffee Shop in 1953, grew into a nationwide diner chain, changing its name to Dennys to avoid confusion with another chain).

A car a year

By the 1950s, the American Dream wasn't just car ownership, it was new car ownership. The manufacturers' aim was to move people to buying a new car each year and they began to bring out new models every year – different colours and shapes, different accessories and 'new and improved' performance. To an extent, it worked. The number of cars in the USA kept growing and the number of cars per household grew too.

EXTRACT

3 From *The Motel in America*, written by John A. Jackle, Keith A. Sculle and Jefferson S. Rogers in 2002.

Until the 1960s, motels catered largely to white middle-class Americans. Most car owners and operators were of the same class; excluded were black Americans and, in certain parts of the United States, members of other minority groups as well. Gaining access to motel services and entrée to the economic opportunities of ownerships and management came with the civil-rights movement. Indeed, it could be said that the cause of civil rights was advanced substantially from motels as leaders travelled across the country coordinating activities. It was in the Lorraine motel in Memphis that Martin Luther King Jr was assassinated.

SOURCE

20 Number of cars per household, 1960–80. Based on data from the US Bureau of the Census.

Year	No car (%)	One car (%)	Two cars (%)	Three or more cars (%)
1960	21.5	56.9	19	2.5
1970	17.5	47.7	29.3	5.5
1980	12.9	35.5	34.0	17.5

Problems

Car ownership did bring problems. As cars got cheaper, it was the poorest Americans, who couldn't afford even a cheap car, who suffered most. Life for someone without a car became increasingly difficult, as the non-car transport infrastructure shrank. Rail travel was only convenient if you wanted to go from city to city on fast trains. Getting somewhere rural, even if it was on the railway network, could be time-consuming. Rail travel was also expensive, so was seldom an option for the poor. While fuel prices were low, the car was significantly cheaper than the train, as well as more convenient. Buses carried people to more places and the most significant company, Greyhound Buses, carried millions of passengers every year. But conditions were crowded, the buses were slow and their only passengers were non-drivers – mostly people who could not afford a car. This increased the divide between the poorest Americans, many of them non-white, and the rest.

By the 1970s, the cities had too many cars. Driving was slow, pollution was rising and protests against the pollution were rising too. The two fuel crises of the 1970s led to fuel rationing, rising prices, long queues for fuel and even fights at the pumps. Prices never regained their old, low levels, which meant that many people at the bottom of the car-owning ladder were pushed off it and onto public transport.

EXTEND YOUR KNOWLEDGE

Greyhound Buses

Greyhound Buses began as a small Minnesota bus company in the 1900s. By 1929, it had bought other companies and extended to a nationwide service under the name 'Greyhound', running radio advertisements for its service. It was chosen as the official transport of the 1933 World's Fair in Chicago and, by selling a combination of tickets and hotel rooms, it made over $500,000, despite the Depression. It became the biggest bus company in the USA. By 1939, it had 4,750 bus stations and over 10,000 employees.

After the Second World War, Greyhound bought 1,500 new buses and expanded with the new highways that were being built. In 1954, it ordered over 1,000 new buses with toilets on board and luggage space underneath. By 1959, it was making over $300,000 million in ticket sales and money from the bus station restaurants. It kept expanding and hit an all-time high of $1,045 billion takings in 1980.

What was the impact of increased air travel?

Mass passenger travel by aeroplane came later than car travel, but it had many similar effects on Americans. Aeroplanes of various kinds offered flights from 1915, when a seaplane flew from St Petersburg to Tampa, Georgia (18 miles in 23 minutes), carrying one passenger at a time for $5. Early air travellers had to be very hardy. The cabins were unpressurised, so aeroplanes were banned from flying higher than 10,000 feet because passengers became too dizzy or even fainted.

Smoking was allowed, and caused fires and accidents. Many people were too scared to fly. Then, in 1925, the Kelly Act laid out national routes for mail delivery. Many of the companies that were contracted to take the mail put in seats for passengers. The number of air routes, and passengers, rose rapidly.

As people began to travel more regularly on the mail planes, more people took to flying. The more people who flew, and survived, the more people took to flying. For example, Western Air Express carried 267 passengers in 1926 and over 25,000 in 1929. By 1940 there were so many passengers trying to book seats on scheduled airlines that it took a travel agent 90 minutes, on average, to book a flight. Air travel increased mobility for those who could afford the air fare. However, cost was still a significant factor, as were the limitations of airline routes. It was not until after the Second World War that commercial air travel really took off.

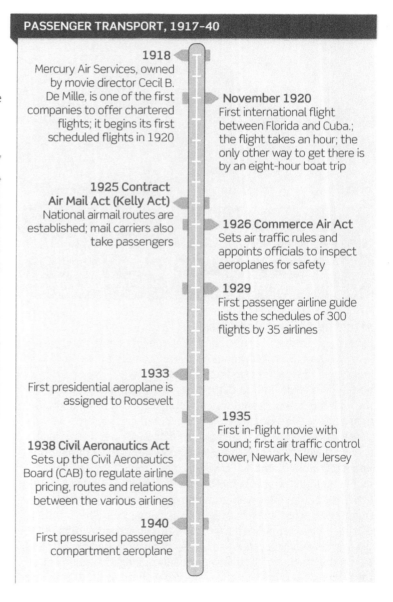

PASSENGER TRANSPORT, 1917-40

1918
Mercury Air Services, owned by movie director Cecil B. De Mille, is one of the first companies to offer chartered flights; it begins its first scheduled flights in 1920

November 1920
First international flight between Florida and Cuba.; the flight takes an hour; the only other way to get there is by an eight-hour boat trip

1925 Contract Air Mail Act (Kelly Act)
National airmail routes are established; mail carriers also take passengers

1926 Commerce Air Act
Sets air traffic rules and appoints officials to inspect aeroplanes for safety

1929
First passenger airline guide lists the schedules of 300 flights by 35 airlines

1933
First presidential aeroplane is assigned to Roosevelt

1935
First in-flight movie with sound; first air traffic control tower, Newark, New Jersey

1938 Civil Aeronautics Act
Sets up the Civil Aeronautics Board (CAB) to regulate airline pricing, routes and relations between the various airlines

1940
First pressurised passenger compartment aeroplane

This poster for Eastern Airlines shows the routes covered by its aeroplanes. Most early airlines focused on serving a relatively small area. This was more practical given the need for refuelling. Flights outside a company's route involved changing aeroplanes, often with long trips between airports.

After the Second World War

By the end of the Second World War, the jet engine had been invented and radar had been discovered to help pilots fly 'blind' in bad weather conditions. A system was developed for bombers to refuel in mid-flight, using a 'tanker' aeroplane. After the war, the tanker design was adapted to become the first US passenger jet, the Boeing 707, which could carry up to 181 passengers at speeds of 550 miles an hour. Money was available for this development because the Cold War led to competition between the USA and the USSR in many technological fields, including flight. These planes could fly more people faster, so the scheduled airline network grew rapidly. However, the rise in the number of aeroplanes and flights was dangerous. The collision of two passenger airliners over the Grand Canyon in 1956 led the government to set up the Federal Aviation Administration (1958) to run the air traffic control system and manage the needs of all the airlines. As more and more people wanted to fly, airlines tried to get as many of them in the air at the same time as possible, because that was the most cost-efficient way to fly people. Early planes had held about a dozen passengers. The first Boeing 747 (first flight 1969) could carry up to 450 passengers.

Who benefited from changes in air travel?

The huge increase in air traffic and falling ticket prices meant middle-class professionals could fly regularly, as well as the wealthy. Journeys that had taken days by car now took hours, people could sleep and were fed in-flight. By the 1970s, air travel no longer had the glamour attached to the early days of flying. However, it was having an impact on how a significant number of Americans lived their lives: some people took jobs farther away and commuted to them by plane; people travelled further around the country.

As international travel became more popular, the number of foreign tourists entering the USA went up. While aeroplane travel wasn't cheap, the only other way to holiday in the USA was by means of a long and expensive boat journey. Not many people could afford the time involved for the journey there and back. Far fewer Americans were inclined to visit the rest of the world; they explored the rest of their own country instead. In 1970, 5,260,000 Americans went abroad and the USA had 2,288,000 visitors. By 1980, 8,163,000 Americans went abroad and there were 8,200,000 foreign visitors.

From *The Growth of the American Republic*, a multi-volume history of the USA, first written in 1930 and regularly revised and reprinted. The extract comes from the 1969 edition.

As the automobile, the bus, the truck and the airplane took over much of passenger and freight service, railroads, which had long dominated the economy of the nation, fell into desperate straits. Between 1940 and 1960 total railway mileage actually declined by 17,000, and many parts of the nation which had been well served by the railroads in 1890 found themselves isolated in 1960. The railroad companies, which had once fought Federal intervention, now appealed, almost desperately, for aid from Washington; the Federal Government, which had once frowned on combinations as 'conspiracies in restraint of trade', now encouraged mergers. In the meantime, air service expanded rapidly; every city had an airport and some needed two or three to handle the traffic that filled the skies. Transatlantic air freight even threatened transatlantic shipping.

Scheduled airlines in the USA, 1928–80. Based on data from the US Bureau of the Census.

Year	Passengers carried (millions)
1928	0.1
1930	0.4
1935	0.8
1940	3.0
1945	7.1
1950	19.2
1955	41.7
1960	62.3
1965	102.9
1970	169.9
1975	205.1
1980	296.9

Deregulation

The 1978 Airline Deregulation Act ran down the Civil Aeronautics Board (it was closed in 1984). This ended federal government control over the various airlines, including ticket pricing, routes, buyouts and mergers. While the CAB had controlled pricing and routes served, airlines had had to compete in the service they provided (quality of food, etc.) and how often they flew. By the 1970s, many aeroplanes were flying half full in order to offer a large number of flights a day. Deregulation meant many airlines could lower their prices and cut services. They flew full aeroplanes with cheaper seats and still made money. They could also organise their own routes and equipment. New 'low-cost' airlines could also set up in competition with the established airlines, which helped to pull ticket prices down still more after 1980. Some of the benefits were already being felt by the time of the 1980 election and Reagan could give the airlines as an example of the benefits of removing government controls. However, in the long term, deregulation had its problems, which will be discussed in Chapter 5.

ACTIVITY
KNOWLEDGE CHECK

Increased leisure time

1 Not everyone had more leisure time in 1917–80. Explain how far the increase in leisure time was significant to the country.

A car-owning culture and air travel

2 Draw a flow chart to show the effects of car ownership on Americans; remember to consider those who did not own a car.

3 Draw a graph to show the number of passengers carried by air in 1928–80. Mark on it events from the timeline and the text that might have caused a shift in the speed of change (if any).

ACTIVITY
SUMMARY

Write notes on how you would answer a question on how far you would agree with the following statements:

1 The 1950s was a time when it looked as if everyone was achieving the American Dream.

2 Air travel had much less impact on Americans than the car.

A Level Exam-Style Question Section B

How far do you agree that the car changed the face of the USA in the years 1917–80? (20 marks)

Tip

Think of factors other than car ownership and think of those the car did not affect (be careful to consider knock-on effects though).

 THINKING HISTORICALLY   Change (5b)

Changes that brought the USA together as a nation

Growing car ownership after 1917	The rise in radio ownership in the 1920s and 1930s	The rise in television ownership since the 1950s
The post-war affluence of the 1950s and 1960s	The growing support network of roads, diners and motels that spread across the country	The growth in air travel after the Second World War

Patterns of development consist of changes which, at given times, converge and have a bearing on one another and, at other times, diverge and have little in common. In the above example, the changes come together to form a pattern of development that tends towards the USA having more of a national identity.

In groups, write each change on a small piece of paper and arrange them on a large A3 sheet as you think best. Then link them with lines and write along the line what it is that links those changes. Try to make sure that you think about how those links may have changed over time.

Answer the following questions individually or in pairs:

1 What effects of the Second World War helped to unite the USA as a nation?

2 What changes did the spread of car ownership bring that helped to unify the country?

3 In what way did radio pave the way to unify the country and how did television build on this?

4 Why was the growing support network a vital component for unity?

WIDER READING

DiBacco, Thomas V., *Made in the USA*, Beard Books (2003) considers the standard of living of Americans and how it contributed to the growth of business.

Brogan, H. *The Penguin History of the United States of America*, Penguin (2001)

Cullen, Jim, *The American Dream*, Oxford University Press (2003) discusses the changing standard of living.

Quinn, Kevin G., *Sports and their Fans*, McFarland and Co (2009) has useful sections on the rise of sport.

Google search on 'Great Society' will find the text of President Johnson's speech introducing his welfare reforms and also film footage

History Channel, www.history.co.uk, search on a topic (e.g. 'baby boomers')

Online, *The Fire This Time*, is a documentary that considers the problems that led to the inner city riots in Los Angeles.

1.5

The impact of the Reagan presidency, 1981–96

KEY QUESTIONS

- What effect did Reagan's economic policies have?
- To what extent was 'big government' reduced?
- What was the nature and extent of social change?
- To what extent were the presidency and US politics revitalised?

INTRODUCTION

Ronald Reagan won the 1980 presidential election campaign with 489 electoral college votes against Jimmy Carter's 49. He came to power promising change and to lead, not just to crisis manage, as Gerald Ford and Carter had, in his view, done. Reagan wanted a shift away from the 'Great Society' policies of liberalism that he said were weakening the USA, by encouraging people to rely on welfare rather than looking for work. Reagan vowed that his domestic policies would fix the economy, lower taxes and reduce '**big government**'.

During the presidential campaign, Reagan asked people if they felt better off than they had been four years previously. It was a simple question and the answer, as he suspected and could use to his advantage, was that they didn't. The confidence that had buoyed people through the 1950s was gone. This loss of confidence was the result of a combination of factors: the USA had lost a war for the first time (Vietnam) and the presidency had been tarnished by the Watergate cover-up; the economy seemed to be in decline and many crises were badly dealt with by the administrations that followed Nixon (such as the oil crises in the 1970s). Many people agreed with Reagan that it was time to go back to the values of individualism that underpinned the American Dream.

How far did Reagan live up to his sweeping promises? What impact did his presidency have on the USA up to 1996 (the end of President Clinton's first term)? Different interpretations can be advanced to answer these questions. They depend on the promises under consideration, what they are weighed against and even the political point of view of the person making the assessment. The time the assessment is made is also important – an analysis of the impact of Reagan's administration made just after he left power in 1989 will be different from one made now, with more knowledge about the long-term effects of his presidency.

20 January 1981 Reagan sworn in as president

29 January 1981 Fuel prices deregulated and wage and price regulations removed by Presidential executive orders

3 August 1981 PATCO air traffic controllers' strike

13 August 1981 Economic Recovery Tax Act (ERTA) passed

13 August 1981 Omnibus Budget Reconciliation Act (ORA) passed

1980	1981	1982	1983

4 November 1980 Reagan elected president

30 March 1981 Assassination attempt on Reagan; he is wounded in the chest

5 June 1981 First reported AIDS cases in USA

September 1981 Reagan appoints Sandra Day O'Connor as first female Supreme Court judge

15 October 1982 Savings and Loan institutions deregulated

Reaganism and Reaganomics – a new departure?

Ronald Reagan presented himself as the face of change. He was certainly a change from the administrations of the 1960s and 1970s. However, in general terms, there were ways in which the Republican government of the 1980s was strikingly similar to the Republican government of the 1920s.

- The reduction of 'big government' that Reagan wanted was a stripping away of the interventions made by successive liberal governments since Roosevelt. It was, in many ways, a return to *laissez-faire*.

- They were both hard line anti-union. Under both administrations, union membership fell and the government, and many businesses, portrayed union membership as 'un-American'. In August 1981, 13,000 air traffic controllers went on strike. Reagan said their strike was illegal (unions of people employed by federal government were not supposed to strike) and threatened to fire the strikers if they didn't go back to work within 48 hours. They didn't. He sacked them, despite protests that it would be dangerous to replace that many experienced people all at once.

- They both allowed for the creation of big business corporations which could then **monopolise** areas of industry.

- They both believed in significant tax reductions; both reduced top-level personal tax rates from around 70 percent to around 25 percent and made business tax concessions.

- In both governments, new industries flourished (car industry and computing, respectively), while farming and mining suffered.

- They both created economies where the wealth was concentrated at the top.

- They both encouraged financial speculation and had stockmarket crashes as a result of this, resulting in depression (1929 Wall Street Crash; 1987 crash and a significant wobble in 1989).

- They both believed in 'rugged individualism' and created an economy where such people could flourish (Henry Ford and Bill Gates, respectively). They both mentally divided the poor into 'worthy' poor and 'feckless', offering help to the former and discouragement to the latter.

The backlash against the liberalism of the 1960s and 1970s helped Reagan to power. So did public feeling that widespread federal expenditure on social projects, and the high level of federal involvement at state and local level, was ineffective and 'un-American' (changing the system set up by the Constitution). Carter, the liberal Democrat, was seen as having made things far worse, letting the economy get out of control. People wanted a change of direction, just as they had in 1932, when Republican policies had seemed not to be working.

KEY TERM

Monopolise
When a business has a monopoly of something, it is the only business dealing in that thing. This tends to mean that the business can set its prices higher and put more demands on its suppliers, because there is no other business to buy from the suppliers or to sell to the consumers.

---

6 November 1984 Reagan wins a second term as president, aged 73

2 October 1986 Tax Reform Act passed

8 November 1988 Republican candidate George H.W. Bush elected president

26 June 1990 Bush breaks his 'no new taxes' promise

| 1984 | 1985 | 1986 | 1987 | 1988 | 1989 | 1990 | 1991 | 1992 |

1985 Protests by garment workers over foreign imports

1987 Extent of Savings and Loan crisis clear; government bailout

11 January 1989 Reagan gives his farewell speech to the nation

3 November 1992 Democratic candidate Bill Clinton elected president

The political scene when Reagan came to power

In 1979, President Carter had referred to the USA as having a 'malaise', an indefinable discontent. It had, and it showed in many different ways. A 1979 public opinion poll showed that, for the first time, a majority of Americans thought their children's lives would be worse than their own. Even during the Watergate scandal, only 30 percent of people had thought that. It showed that people not only doubted the government, they had severe doubts about the future as well. Carter saw this, but his answer was to discuss the problems at length, appeal for austerity and all pulling together to fix the problems. His outlook and speeches were pessimistic. Reagan, on the other hand, stressed what the USA had achieved before and what it could achieve again; he promised to fix things. When it came to vote for the president in 1980, people didn't vote for Carter's 'let's all pull our socks up and work together to fix it' speeches. They voted for Reagan's 'I can fix it' ones.

Reagan's beliefs

Reagan, like Carter before him, was a committed Christian. A significant amount of the conservative coalition support that helped him to power came from the religious right: Christians who believed strongly in traditional family values and compulsory prayer in schools. They opposed homosexuality and abortion; many opposed most forms of birth control. Reagan believed many of these things too. He certainly believed in traditional family values and prayer in schools. He also spoke out against abortion. However, he always made it clear in his speeches on, say, abortion or prayer in schools that he was discussing his personal beliefs. He gave jobs in the White House to members of the religious right. He also tried to pass a law severely restricting access to abortion. However, a combination of opposition in Congress, and concern about the acceptability of the laws suggested to him by the religious right, meant that his government was not as conservative as many of the religious right who had supported him would have hoped.

EXTRACT

 From *More Equal Than Others: America from Nixon to the New Century*, written by Godfrey Hodgson in 2004. Hodgson has worked in Britain and the USA as a journalist, radio and television presenter, university lecturer and author who writes mainly about American history.

The proportion of Americans who called themselves 'liberal' had been declining even before 1980. By 1990 it was 16 percent. Since the 1970s, substantial majorities disapproved of affirmative action for minorities. There was a broad and growing assumption that government was often not the right agent to provide solutions for social problems. Instead, there was a new consensus that the 'free market' – a term loosely used to describe extremely complex phenomena, and even more loosely invoked to propose solutions that were often unproved – was the place to find answers. ...

From the 1970s on there was a huge shift in voters' attitudes to government, on the one hand, and to corporate business, on the other. Since 1932 the great majority of Americans had accepted the idea of a welfare state. That implied, at least in principle, willingness to pay taxes that would enable government to provide the services people could not provide for themselves. By the middle 1970s, that fundamental assumption was already under attack.

EXTEND YOUR KNOWLEDGE

Another Franklin D. Roosevelt?
Many historians and political analysts have likened Reagan's election in 1980 to Roosevelt's election as president in 1932. There were some basic similarities:

- both campaigned on a promise of radical change

- both campaigned with a tight focus on the economic situation

- both promised to control federal government spending (and both failed)

- both were charismatic people, campaigning to replace a president who was neither charismatic nor popular.

However, they had deeper differences. Unlike Roosevelt, Reagan wanted:

- to reign in federal spending on those in need

- to reduce federal government intervention.

Federal spending and federal agencies were the key to Roosevelt's New Deal policies, policies that were aimed at helping those at the bottom of the heap to get back on their feet.

Evaluating interpretations of history

Historians do write narrative history that outlines events. However, most of them also provide interpretations of the events they are describing: for example, why something happened, what effects it had and how significant one person's actions were in determining the course of the events discussed. These interpretations are a matter of opinion, but this does not mean that we cannot evaluate them or that we should discard an interpretation that is clearly based on the point of view of the historian. Most historians come to their subject with a point of view on the issues involved. Sometimes they clearly state this, and also state other points of view that can be taken. Sometimes they don't do this but, even so, their point of view is usually clear. There is nothing wrong with historians having a point of view. What is important is that they present the evidence to support that point of view and explain the methods they used to collect this evidence, arguing logically for their point of view.

The interpretations of historians who present no evidence and show no clear methodology will be less valid than clearly supported ones. Their interpretations might be valid ones, but we have no way of knowing unless they show us how they arrived at them. Bear the following considerations in mind when reading each of the extracts in this section:

- Is it giving an interpretation or just information?

- Is there evidence to support any interpretation given?

- Is there any sign of the methods used?

THINKING HISTORICALLY   Interpretations (5a)

Historical methodology

Below are three descriptions of the perspectives of very famous historians.

Herodotus	Leopold von Ranke	Karl Marx
• Research consisted of conversations • Identified that accounts had to be judged on their merits • Some believe that certain passages in his writing are inventions to complete the narrative	• Believed in an evidence-based approach and relied heavily on primary sources • Desired to find out the 'facts' and discover the connections between them • Stressed the role of the individual in shaping history	• Believed that history would go through stages leading to a state where everybody was equal • Believed that historical changes were ultimately determined by changes to the economy • Was often driven by political considerations and looked for evidence to support his point of view

Work in groups of between three and six. Within each group, each member or pair should take the perspective of one of the above historians and argue from that perspective. Work through the questions as a group and answer the last one individually.

1 Herodotus did not use written evidence to construct his history. Does this mean that his history is less useful than the others?

2 Ranke based his writing almost exclusively on primary sources from the time he was investigating, rather than secondary sources. How might this affect his ability to see larger patterns in history compared with the other two?

3 Marx put his philosophy of history, and perhaps politics, first and research second. Would this make his history weaker than the others?

4 'Colourful' individuals populate the writing of Herodotus and Ranke, while Marx concentrates on the difference between classes. Write three historical questions that each historian might ask.

5 The three historians all had different methods and motivations and yet their writing has been valued ever since it was created. Explain how the prior knowledge that we bring to the history that we write does not invalidate it.

WHAT EFFECT DID REAGAN'S ECONOMIC POLICIES HAVE?

SOURCE 1

From President Reagan's inaugural speech, 20 January 1981.

The business of our nation goes forward. These United States are confronted with an economic affliction of great proportions. We suffer from the longest and one of the worst sustained inflations in our national history. It distorts our economic decisions, penalizes thrift, and crushes the struggling young and the fixed-income elderly alike. It threatens to shatter the lives of millions of our people.

Idle industries have cast workers into unemployment, human misery, and personal indignity. Those who do work are denied a fair return for their labor by a tax system which penalizes successful achievement and keeps us from maintaining full productivity.

But great as our tax burden is, it has not kept pace with public spending. For decades we have piled deficit upon deficit, mortgaging our future and our children's future for the temporary convenience of the present. To continue this long trend is to guarantee tremendous social, cultural, political, and economic upheavals.

You and I, as individuals, can, by borrowing, live beyond our means, but for only a limited period of time. Why, then, should we think that collectively, as a nation, we're not bound by that same limitation? We must act today in order to preserve tomorrow. And let there be no misunderstanding: We are going to begin to act, beginning today.

The economic ills we suffer have come upon us over several decades. They will not go away in days, weeks, or months, but they will go away. They will go away because we as Americans have the capacity now, as we've had in the past, to do whatever needs to be done to preserve this last and greatest bastion of freedom.

ACTIVITY
KNOWLEDGE CHECK

Reagan's economic policies

List Reagan's four main aims for his economic policies, saying how, if at all, each aim differed from the aims of President Johnson's 'Great Society' (see page 105).

to set up new advisory groups, reporting directly to him, on how to cut down 'big government'. This made him look a very active new broom, but the financial savings were small and advisory groups don't actually make changes: would he take their advice?

KEY TERM

Supply-side theory
Supply-side economic theory emerged in the late 1970s. Supply-siders argued that the economy wasn't driven by consumer demand but by keeping up production and encouraging saving and investment. They believed restraints on production (government regulation, high taxes and strong unions) should be removed. They argued that the better-off would benefit and the benefits would 'trickle down' to even the very poorest.

EXTEND YOUR KNOWLEDGE

The argument for cutting taxes
The supply-side argument for cutting taxes was that high tax rates were the reason productivity fell in the 1970s. The argument said: Imagine a banker wanted his house painted. He asks a painter for a price and works out how many hours he has to work to pay the painter *after tax*. When tax rates are high, he might have to work quite a few hours, so might decide to paint the house himself.

If the banker paints his house, the government loses on two levels: the banker doesn't do the extra work, his productivity doesn't rise, nor does he pay the tax he would have paid on the extra hours. Also, he doesn't employ the painter, whose productivity doesn't rise and she doesn't pay any tax either, because she didn't get the job.

On the other hand, if the banker was paying less tax, he would be more likely to employ the painter and his wealth would trickle down to her.

ACTIVITY
KNOWLEDGE CHECK

Supply-side theory

Explain how supply-side economic theory was different from supply and demand theory.

Immediate action

Reagan's domestic policies focused on the economy: the issue that brought him to power. Roosevelt's New Deal had shifted from Republican *laissez-faire* policies, increasing federal control and responsibility and letting the budget go as far into deficit as was needed. Later administrations felt obliged to keep up federal involvement in social welfare and funded it with higher taxes and federal borrowing. Reagan was clear that he wanted to control government spending, to reduce government involvement and to cut taxes. He was influenced by '**supply-side**' economic theories.

Reagan swung into action as soon as he became president. In the three days following his inauguration, he sacked many White House staff members and put a federal government hiring freeze in place. He then told all departments there was a freeze on office furnishing and equipment and that they had to cut their travel expenses by 15 percent. He also used a series of executive orders

The plan for reform

At their first meeting with Congress about the budget, presidents usually just outline budget plans. These are then sent to Congress over several years as a series of bills. Reagan wanted to present his whole budget policy through to 1984 as a single bill when he met Congress on 18 February. He also wanted to present a tax bill in the same session. His Council of Economic Advisers (CEA) had no time to follow the usual procedure for budget planning. Normally, they would ask each department for budget plans. They would debate the plans and produce a draft budget, to be discussed with the president and re-drafted. This wasn't possible in the time. However, it meant that Congress had to vote on the whole package of spending cuts, so the administration would have approval for all its measures and control over the timetable up to 1984.

Reaganomics

Reagan's *Program for Economic Recovery* (his economic strategy) was presented to Congress on time. The plan had four parts and stressed the importance of passing the legislation quickly.

- **Cutting the federal deficit.** It was accompanied by a budget bill and a proposal for cuts on domestic spending. The budget bill aimed to reduce the federal deficit from 22 percent of the gross national product (GNP) in 1981 to 19 percent in 1986. This plan had been put together so hastily that it had a significant number of errors and a footnote that admitted that the plan included 'as yet unidentified' cuts of $74 billion, to be decided later.

- **Personal and business tax reductions.** It was accompanied by the Economic Recovery Tax Act of 1981.

- **Deregulation** (removing federal control) in industry, state and local government.

- **Planned control of the money supply** to keep inflation down while expanding the economy.

The suggested cuts in domestic spending came almost entirely from federal grants for specific projects, set up under Johnson's 'Great Society' reforms. These included grants to state and local government bodies for slum clearance and highway repair. They also included local initiatives in education, housing and the provision of various services, such as the Aid to Families with Dependent Children (AFDC) programme.

Getting the legislation passed

For the first time in decades there was a Republican majority in Senate and almost a Republican majority in the House of Representatives. The White House only had to win the support of 26 Democrats in the House to pass its legislation, which made pushing through the budget and tax bills easier. The Senate passed the budget and it was sent to the House and, after some revision, was passed and became law in August as the Omnibus Reconciliation Act of 1981 (ORA).The tax legislation was more of a battle. The Senate passed it with only one change. It cut the tax reduction for personal tax from 30 percent to 25 percent. It was a harder fight in the House. The Democrats felt they had been manipulated over the budget and saw the tax bill as a fight over control of the House. They made significant changes to the bill. The White House offered tax concessions to some Democrats to swing the vote.

The Democrats counter-offered incentives in areas they controlled and the process became an undignified scramble over concessions. In the end, a reshaped bill was passed and became law in August, as the Economic Recovery Tax Act 1981 (ERTA), at the same time as the budget. The Act cut marginal income tax by 23 percent over three years and linked the tax bands to inflation. It applied to all tax bands, so those paying the higher tax benefited most. Also, the highest income tax band rate fell from 70 to 50 percent, the lowest fell from 14 to 11 percent. ERTA also allowed all working taxpayers to set up untaxed IRAs (Independent Retirement Accounts). Business tax rates were cut and businesses could revise their depreciation (wear and tear) costs. These were usually calculated years in advance so suffered from inflation. Business tax rates were reduced and various business tax breaks were offered, skewed to favour small, innovative businesses.

EXTRACT

From 'Reaganomics and economic policy', an article about Reagan's economic policy, written by Joseph J. Horgan in 1990.

Within less than five months the Congress had enacted the main outlines of the president's economic strategy. The political attractiveness of his programme was complemented by an astute political strategy. The reconciliation procedure offered the administration an integrated and expedited means to enforce Congress to consider the President's spending reductions as a package on his terms. The administration maintained impressive unity among the ranks of the Republicans in both houses. The key to the administration's victory lies in the fact that the House Democrats enjoyed a majority of 51 seats, which required the White House to gain only 26 defections. The President's legislative strategists concentrated their efforts upon conservative Democrats, mainly from the South and West, and freely dispensed concessions. As Representative John Breaux commented, his vote could not be bought but it could be 'rented'. President Reagan skilfully used the media to mount a grass-roots lobby for his policies and capitalised upon the second honeymoon effect created by an attempted assassination on his life to convert the nominal Democratic majority in the House into a minority on economic policy votes.

SOURCE 2

This photo was taken just moments before the attempted assassination of President Reagan on 30 March 1981. The way he behaved during, and after, the shooting made him very popular with the American people, the media and politicians. Some people have suggested that the wave of sympathy and admiration that followed may have helped him to pass the Economic Recovery Tax Act and the Omnibus Reconciliation Act.

REAGAN'S ECONOMIC LEGISLATION AND OTHER ECONOMIC MEASURES

2 March 1981 Executive order setting up the President's Economic Policy Advisory Board
Sets up the EAB with economics experts from outside the government advising directly to the president, as well as the CEA

13 August 1981 Economic Recovery Tax Act (ERTA)
Cuts marginal income tax by 23 percent over three years, links the tax bands to inflation and offers other incentives (see page 119)

3 September 1982 Tax Equity and Financial Responsibility Act (TEFRA)
Makes changes to the budget in response to the economic situation, tightening up tax rules, especially for businesses; it also temporarily raises taxes on cigarettes and the telephone service

22 October 1986 Tax Reform Act
Revises the tax codes, reducing the number of tax brackets; is supposed to close a lot of tax evasion loopholes and ease the pressure on poorer families

16 June 1981 Executive order setting up the President's Commission on Housing
Set up to investigate all aspects of housing, including how it should be financed, but mainly to find ways of saving money on federal low-cost housing schemes

13 August 1981 Omnibus Budget Reconciliation Act (ORA)
Proposes a variety of tax cuts that will take $35 billion out of federal spending; the initial bill presented by the White House had proposed $45 billion-worth of cuts

7 April 1986 Consolidated Omnibus Budget Reconciliation Act (COBRA)
Revises the budget in many minor ways to save the federal government money and to move costs to state or private bodies: the most significant change shifts the responsibility for many healthcare payments from the federal government to the employer

EXTEND YOUR KNOWLEDGE

EXTEND YOUR KNOWLEDGE

Assassination
Reagan was well liked as he began his presidency, but his popularity was given a big boost by the assassination attempt of 30 March. A man called John Hinckley Jr shot at President Reagan as he was leaving a meeting at a Washington hotel. Hinckley shot Reagan's press secretary dead and Reagan was hit in the chest by a bullet ricochet as he was pushed into the car by Secret Service agents. He was driven to hospital and insisted on walking into the building unaided. He was also heard apologising to Nancy that he 'forgot to duck' – a remark that was widely reported. He made a quick recovery and his cheerful demeanour throughout impressed many people.

Reagan was 69 when he was elected, the oldest person ever to be elected president. Some people had doubted his stamina, but this event changed many minds. Reagan showed himself to be tough and determined and won himself more support.

KEY ECONOMIC TERMS

In this section on the economy, the following terms will be used.

Constant 1987 dollars OR in 1987 dollars
If a wage for 1982 (for example) is given in 'constant 1987 dollars' or 'in 1987 dollars', the actual wage is adjusted by the amount of inflation or otherwise to produce a wage that can be directly compared with a 1987 wage.

Real disposable personal income
Disposable income is the amount of money people have left to spend or save after tax. Real disposable income links disposable income to the movement of prices. So, a family might have the same disposable income in 1982 and 1984, but if prices have gone up they are, in real terms, worse off.

Real GNP
Adjusted gross national product to match inflation.

Data series
Types of statistical information.

Per capita income
Gross domestic product (GDP) divided by the number of people in the country.

Gross domestic product
The value of all goods and services produced in a country in a year.

Marginal income tax
US income tax is organised into brackets (margins), with the amount of tax rising as you move from one bracket to a higher one. The higher tax is only paid on the income in the higher tax bracket.

ACTIVITY
KNOWLEDGE CHECK

Passing Reagan's policies

1 Explain the advantages and disadvantages of Reagan's decision to bring his budget legislation to Congress as a finished package on 18 February. Explain Horgan's (Extract 2) view on the decision, using the extract.

2 Why might public sympathy over the attempted assassination of President Reagan affect politicians' decisions about how to vote on ORA and ERTA?

Interpretations of the effect of Reagan's policies

There are various interpretations of the effects of Reagan's economic policies. Most measurements of the effects of an economic policy will involve using statistics. Looking at different statistical data will produce a different view of the situation. Statistics can be considered from the point of view of the historian, sociologist or political analyst. This will also affect the conclusions.

Reagan's policies of tax cuts and money supply control were intended to stop inflation; reduce unemployment; increase personal wealth; increase productivity; encourage personal saving and investing; and encourage businesses and service providers to produce more. He also wanted federal spending and the federal deficit to fall.

Did the policies stop inflation and unemployment?

Reagan's first aim was to stop inflation. While ORA and ERTA were going through Congress, he put pressure on the Federal Reserve Board (FRB) to put tighter restrictions on the money supply. It did: even tighter restrictions than the White House asked for. Reagan's administration, unlike previous administrations, didn't ask the FRB to lift these restrictions when unemployment rose. The money supply restriction led to a sharp rise in interest rates. This hurt industries that had to buy supplies on credit (e.g. the car industry, farming) or had loans with a long pay-back period

(e.g. construction). Many businesses were badly hit. Reagan came to power in the middle of a recession. Then it deepened. Unemployment rates went from 7.1 percent of the population available for work in 1980 to a high of 9.6 percent in 1983. However, inflation, which had been 11.3 percent in 1979 and 13.5 percent in 1980, did begin to fall. In 1982, it was down to 6.2 percent. Although it moved up and down after this, by 1996 it had never reached double figures again and spent most of its time at under five percent.

EXTEND YOUR KNOWLEDGE

Interpreting unemployment statistics
In 1979, unemployed people made up 7.2 percent of the population. By 1988, the rate had gone down to 5.5 percent.

However, the percentage of people in part-time or temporary work had risen in the same period. These people were employed, but not earning at their full capacity. Businesses were reorganising to pay out as little as possible; temporary or part-time people were not paid on yearly salary rates and the insurance and other extra payments made for them were lower or non-existent.

Meanwhile, the number of people *not* included in the unemployment figures – *even though* they had no job – because they were not counted in the workforce (as they were considered unemployable, for example, through drug use, or chose not to register for work) was 34.5 percent of the population in 1988.

SOURCE 3 Unemployment rates, 1980–96. Based on data from the US Bureau of the Census.

AS, Section C

Study Extracts 3 and 4 before you answer this question.

Historians have different views about the impact of the Reagan presidency on the USA. Analyse and evaluate the extracts and use your knowledge of the issues to explain your answer to the following question.

How far do you agree with the view that Reagan's economic policies in the years 1981–96 were just a way to make the rich richer? (20 marks)

Tip
Consider the effects of Reagan's economic policy that might not have helped the economy (e.g. the rising debt).

Did the policies increase personal wealth?

Personal wealth is one of the issues that have caused a significant amount of debate. Everyone agrees that the tax cuts made many people richer. In that sense, they worked. The issue is, which sectors of the population became richer? Some historians say that the answer is clear: the rich became richer and the poor did not, that the cut in the tax bracket for the rich was the deepest and that, therefore, they benefited most. Others argue that it wasn't as simple as that, that tax cuts hurt the rich most and the poor least, and that the tax payments of the rich helped the revival of the economy.

EXTRACT

3 From *The American Dream: From Reconstruction to Reagan*, written by Esmond Wright in 1996.

So many Americans had been making so much money that the term 'millionaire' became meaningless. A Georgia marketing expert, Thomas J. Stanley, counted almost 100,000 'decamillionaires' – people worth over $10 million. Back in 1960 there hadn't been that many plain-vanilla millionaires. In 1988, approximately 1.3 individual Americans were millionaires by assets [what everything they possessed was worth], up from 574,000 in 1980, 180,000 in 1972, 90,000 in 1964, and just 27,000 in 1953. Even adjusted for inflation, the number of millionaires had doubled between the late 1970s and the late 1980s. Meanwhile, the number of billionaires according to Forbes magazine [a business magazine] went from a handful in 1981 to 26 in 1986 and 49 in 1987. As of late 1988, Forbes put that year's number of billionaires at 52, and Fortune's September assessment hung the billion-dollar label on 51 American families. ... A second circumstance was that wages – the principal source of middle- and lower-class dollars – had stagnated through 1986 even while disinflation, deregulation, and commercial opportunity were escalating the return on capital. Most of the Reagan heyday, to put it mildly, was a heyday for unearned income as rents, [share] dividends, capital gains, and interest gained relative to wages and salaries as a source of wealth and increasing economic inequality.

EXTRACT

4 From 'Side-supply economics', written by Paul Craig Roberts, in *Reaganomics and After*, a collection of articles about Reaganomics, published in 1989. From 1981 to 1982, Roberts was Assistant Secretary of the Treasury on Economic Policy.

In the 58-month period from March 1975 through January 1980 (the beginning and end of the expansion from the 1974 recession), the unemployment rate fell by 27 per cent, the consumer price index (CPI) rose by 48 per cent, and gross private domestic investment rose by 50 per cent (in 1982 dollars). In contrast, during the first 58-month period of the Reagan expansion (from November 1982 through September 1987) the unemployment rate fell by 45 per cent (about twice as much), the CPI rose by 17 per cent (only one-third as much), and gross private domestic investment grew by 77 per cent (about 50 per cent more).

The Reagan economy is remarkable in many other ways. It has produced the highest manufacturing productivity growth in the post-war period, averaging 4.6 per cent annually since recovery began in 1982, compared with 2.3 per cent in the 1970s, 2.7 per cent in the 1960s, and 2 per cent in the 1950s. Since the Reagan recovery began, per capita real disposable personal income has grown by 2.6 per cent annually, compared with 1.8 per cent in the 1970s, 3 per cent in the 1960s, and 1.5 per cent in the 1950s.

Moreover, the evidence shows that the tax burden has shifted upward in the Reagan years. The latest Treasury Department data show that, between 1981 and 1986, the share of federal income taxes paid by the rich rose from 18.1 to 26.1 per cent – a 44 per cent increase – while the share of taxes paid by the bottom 50 per cent fell from 7.5 per cent to 6.4 per cent.

THINKING HISTORICALLY — Interpretations (3a)

Differing accounts

1 Read Extracts 3 and 4, which give historical interpretations of the effects of the Reagan administration's tax cuts. For each of the historians, create a summary table of their views.

a) Make a note of how they address/interpret the key issues outlined below:
- How far did the tax cuts of the Reagan administration benefit the rich?
- To what extent did they lead to economic recovery by 1986?
- To what extent did ordinary Americans benefit from the tax cuts?

b) Make a note of the evidence the historians give in support of their claims.

c) Use your notes and knowledge to give evidence which supports or challenges their interpretations.

d) In pairs, discuss which historian's interpretation of Reagan's tax cuts seems to fit best with the available evidence – which seems the most convincing?

e) Make a note of any issues which made it difficult to compare the two interpretations directly.

Challenge: Seek out another historical interpretation of the effects of the tax cuts and compare this with the views you have explored already.

ACTIVITY
KNOWLEDGE CHECK

Trickle-down theory

Outline a speech by opponents of the tax cuts, explaining why the 'trickle-down' theory isn't working. Then outline a rebuttal speech by a member of the administration.

Did the policies increase productivity?

Productivity is a complicated thing to measure and various factors can be considered. The most usual approaches are to calculate the output per worker per hour (so measuring whether people are actually producing more per hour) or to consider the GNP (measuring whether the country as a whole is producing more); both are shown below.

SOURCE
4
Productivity measured as output per worker per hour, 1980–96. Based on data from US Department of Labor, Bureau of Labor Statistics.

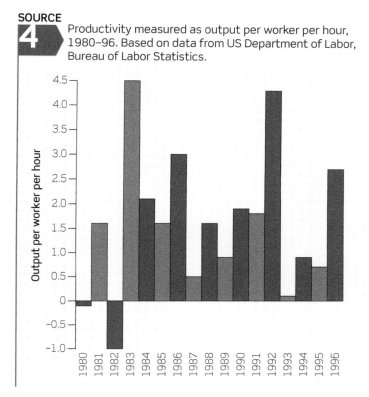

SOURCE
5
Productivity measured as GNP, 1980–96. Based on data from Knoema.

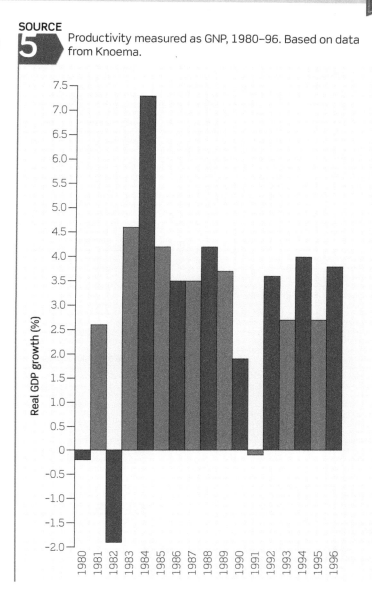

Did the policies encourage people to save and invest?

As the economy came out of the recession, towards the end of 1982, and businesses began doing well again, more people began to save and invest. However, policies to cut down 'big government' led to **deregulation** in the financial sector. Increased competition led to problems, as financial organisations took increasingly dangerous risks to win more customers (see page 126). The personal savings and investments that the policies had been designed to encourage took place in a financial environment that was increasingly unsafe. This came to a head in the late 1980s, with people losing both savings and investments during a crisis in the savings and loans industry (that only government intervention stopped), and the stockmarket crash of 1987. Recovery from this was far more rapid than the recovery from the 1929 Wall Street Crash. The FRB stepped in, encouraging banks to lend to each other and business and individual investors not to panic. Possibly because of the historical example of what damage panic could do, the crash was soon over. A significant number of individuals and businesses suffered, but not on the scale of the Great Depression.

KEY TERM

Deregulation
Removing federal restrictions from businesses: for example, setting a minimum wage.

Did the policies reduce the deficit?

The reduction of the deficit was one of Reagan's most notable failures. In 1980, it was $59 billion; paying it off cost nine percent of federal spending. In 1983, the deficit was $208 billion, taking nearly 14 percent of federal spending in loan interest payments. Worse still, it was increasingly funded by borrowing from abroad. For the first time, the USA became a significant borrowing nation, not a lending nation. This failure was partly because of Reagan's determination to cut taxes, despite the fact that it soon became clear that supply-side arguments (that the reduction in federal income from tax cuts would be covered by rising productivity and investment) didn't work. In addition, federal departments resisted cuts, while Congress toned down many welfare cuts planned by the administration. Worst of all was the defence budget. Reagan had always said increased defence spending was necessary. He had fudged the issue of how he could do that and reduce the deficit. All through the late 1960s and 1970s, governments had cut defence spending and increased spending on human resources. Under Reagan, the spending pattern reversed sharply. In 1980, human resources took 28 percent of federal spending; by 1987, it was 22 percent. Meanwhile, defence spending in the same period rose from 23 to 28 percent.

After Reagan

George H.W. Bush promised to continue Reagan's policies. However, these policies were less popular as their long-term effects and limitations became clear. Also, Bush had only just won the presidential election; political, media and public support were lukewarm. The Democrats were back in control of both houses of Congress, making life harder for his administration. Bush was often forced to back down on promises – the most famous being when he raised taxes, despite promising in his campaign that that was something he would never do.

In 1992, Bill Clinton, a Democrat, was elected to the White House. Clinton did not, however, swing back to the old Democratic policies. This was because, while Reagan's economic policies had produced problems, most voters strongly supported low taxes – a return to high taxation was not on the cards. Clinton was a 'New Democrat'. His campaign was economy-focused: low inflation; high employment; a reduced deficit; and no tariffs to regulate business and trade. His nod to older Democrats was in increasing welfare and medical care and 'investing in people'.

A memo pinned up in his campaign offices during the campaign listed three vital points to hammer home while campaigning:

- that he would address medical care

- that he would bring change

- 'the economy, stupid', which became a catchphrase inside, then widely outside, the campaign offices.

ACTIVITY
KNOWLEDGE CHECK

Effects of economic policies

1 Explain how Reagan's economic policies affected productivity.

2 Give three reasons why it was impossible to cut the deficit. Which do you think was most important? Justify your answer.

TO WHAT EXTENT WAS 'BIG GOVERNMENT' REDUCED?

SOURCE

6 From President Reagan's inaugural speech, 20 January 1981.

In this present crisis, government is not the solution to our problem; government is the problem. From time to time we've been tempted to believe that society has become too complex to be managed by self-rule, that government by an elite group is superior to government for, by, and of the people. Well, if no one among us is capable of governing himself, then who among us has the capacity to govern someone else? All of us together, in and out of government, must bear the burden. The solutions we seek must be equitable, with no one group singled out to pay a higher price.

We hear much of special interest groups. Well, our concern must be for a special interest group that has been too long neglected. It knows no sectional boundaries or ethnic and racial divisions, and it crosses political party lines. It is made up of men and women who raise our food, patrol our streets, man our mines and factories, teach our children, keep our homes, and heal us when we're sick—professionals, industrialists, shopkeepers, clerks, cabbies, and truck drivers. They are, in short, 'We the people,' this breed called Americans.

It is my intention to curb the size and influence of the Federal establishment and to demand recognition of the distinction between the powers granted to the Federal Government and those reserved to the States or to the people. All of us need to be reminded that the Federal Government did not create the States; the States created the Federal Government.

Now, so there will be no misunderstanding, it's not my intention to do away with government. It is rather to make it work – work with us, not over us; to stand by our side, not ride on our back. Government can and must provide opportunity, not smother it; foster productivity, not stifle it.

Was 'big government' reduction clearly beneficial?

Reagan believed reducing 'big government' under New Federalist policies would benefit the USA. New Federalism would produce less federal interference in state and local affairs, business (including world trade), finance and all aspects of people's lives. These measures sounded positive, especially to a nation that had become suspicious of government intervention. However, they could also be interpreted as less funding for state and local government projects and less regulation of business expansionism and greed, as well as less control over foreign imports and less social welfare for the most needy.

How was 'big government' reduced in the short term?

Reagan saw deregulation as a key tool in reducing big government. In his 1982 State of the Union address, Reagan said he was already winning the fight against big government. He said that, since he came to power, the administration had:

- cut federal regulations almost in half, removing 23,000 pages from the Federal Register (which contains all federal regulations). This had 14,500 pages in 1960 and 87,000 when Reagan came to power.

- helped to bring down the cost of petrol and heating fuel by deregulation

- created a federal strike force to combat government fraud and waste that had saved $2 billion in six months

- replaced federal agencies with private sector ones and federal employees with volunteers.

Reagan's first days in office (page 116) show how he could become focused on the small details of federal spending, while the rising deficit shows how he failed to control the overall rising debt. However, it was part of his media spin to use everyday images when he discussed change. Small-scale savings were more real to the public, in many ways, than cuts of $2 billion. Equally media-focused was his discussion of deregulation as if it was something he had instigated. In fact, Carter had begun deregulation – by the time Reagan got to office, Carter had deregulated the airlines and drafted bills on deregulating trucking, the railways and some areas of finance, including banks (though they had to obey FRB rules). However, he had also introduced more across-the-board regulations, for example, on working conditions and environmental issues.

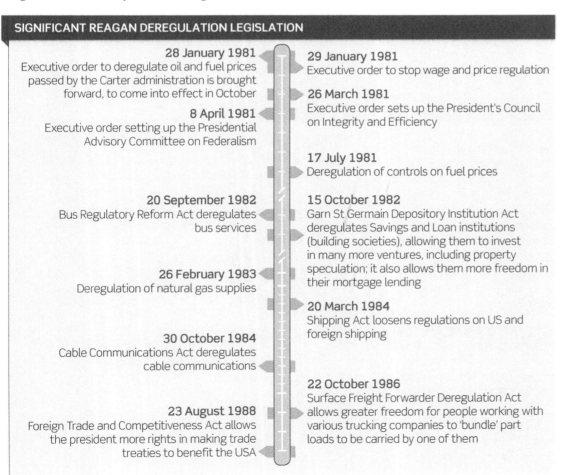

SIGNIFICANT REAGAN DEREGULATION LEGISLATION

28 January 1981
Executive order to deregulate oil and fuel prices passed by the Carter administration is brought forward, to come into effect in October

29 January 1981
Executive order to stop wage and price regulation

26 March 1981
Executive order sets up the President's Council on Integrity and Efficiency

8 April 1981
Executive order setting up the Presidential Advisory Committee on Federalism

17 July 1981
Deregulation of controls on fuel prices

20 September 1982
Bus Regulatory Reform Act deregulates bus services

15 October 1982
Garn St Germain Depository Institution Act deregulates Savings and Loan institutions (building societies), allowing them to invest in many more ventures, including property speculation; it also allows them more freedom in their mortgage lending

26 February 1983
Deregulation of natural gas supplies

20 March 1984
Shipping Act loosens regulations on US and foreign shipping

30 October 1984
Cable Communications Act deregulates cable communications

22 October 1986
Surface Freight Forwarder Deregulation Act allows greater freedom for people working with various trucking companies to 'bundle' part loads to be carried by one of them

23 August 1988
Foreign Trade and Competitiveness Act allows the president more rights in making trade treaties to benefit the USA

The problems of removing controls

Deregulation had problems. One was that, when smaller companies were struggling, big companies could, and did, buy them out. During the 1980s, big companies expanded, while small, independent businesses struggled. The period saw a rise in the number of **conglomerates** in the USA. Businesses set their own standards of safety (physical and financial) and set them lower than government regulators. Initially, deregulation brought lower prices through competition; however, as big businesses grew, it was more likely that several big businesses would 'fix' a price structure, so that they did not have to compete. Finally, many businesses, from phone companies to airlines, cut services provided (or areas covered by their services) to maximise profit. In most cases, it was rural areas that suffered.

> **KEY TERM**
>
> Conglomerate
> An organisation that controls several businesses of different types. General Electric was set up in 1892, selling electric light appliances and parts. In the 1980s, it expanded into the medical equipment, water, oil and gas industries by buying up businesses in those fields.

The Savings and Loan collapse

Carter had put some banking deregulation in place. The Reagan administration applied it to **Savings and Loan institutions (S&Ls)** in 1983. When banking restrictions were lifted, banks could offer high interest rates on savings. This was good for savers, but bad for struggling businesses and people with long-term loans (who could not switch to the lower-interest loans then on offer), such as many farmers. Banks and the newly deregulated S&Ls competed for custom. In some ways this was beneficial. Those who had savings, and who were able to understand the various offers, benefited most. However, there were problems. S&Ls were run by people used to making safe investments. Before deregulation, they had mostly provided mortgage loans at a regulated rate of interest. When they began to compete with banks and other financial institutions, they had to make increasingly risky investments, lend at very low rates and offer high rates of savings to savers. Many S&Ls failed through incompetence. The federal government was forced to pass the Competitive Equality in Banking Act in 1987, providing money to cover the money lost by closed S&Ls. It wasn't enough. By 1988, S&Ls had lost $10 billion. Then, in 1989, the property market collapsed, making the situation of all institutions that lent money on property even more difficult. In 1989, Bush had to sign the Financial Institutions Reform, Recovery, and Enforcement Act (FIRREA), which bailed out some failing organisations, closed others and set up new federal regulators — all at the cost of $150 billion.

> **KEY TERM**
>
> Savings and Loan institution (S&L)
> This was the equivalent of a building society in the UK – traditionally a conservative, financial institution that mostly lent money for mortgages.

What were the effects of the policies on trade?

Big government could also be reduced by not intervening to affect markets: trade markets as well as the stockmarket. The balance of world trade shifted against the USA, as the buying power of the dollar weakened. This meant that foreign imports became cheaper, so imports of foreign goods rose. American companies lost business. The textile industry was particularly badly affected; between 1980 and 1985, about 250 textile plants were forced to close and over 300,000 workers lost their jobs. Some political economists said that cheaper foreign products were damaging the economy. They also complained that the USA was a global borrower for the first time, rather than 'the world's banker' (a name given to the USA in the 1920s). Even worse, American companies were being bought up by foreign companies. In November 1987, one finance magazine said Britain was getting the colonies back by buying them!

Supporters of Reagan argued that the rise of foreign imports was a good thing, because it gave consumers more choice. They also argued that it made the USA an attractive place for other countries to trade with and invest in. They pointed out the levels of Japanese investment in the USA, saying it was bringing money into the country; ignoring the fact that many Japanese re-invested their profits, made in the USA, in Japan.

> **EXTEND YOUR KNOWLEDGE**
>
> A Japanese invasion?
> Britain was not the only country to be seen to be mounting a takeover. Japanese companies began, in the late 1970s, to increase their sales of cars in the USA. The two fuel crises had led people to want cars that used as little fuel as possible – small Japanese cars, not American 'gas-guzzlers'. Thanks to advanced technology, Japanese car firms could make a car and ship it to the USA, and still sell it at a profit for less than a US-manufactured car.
>
> In the 1980s, Japanese firms began to establish themselves in the USA. They did this by:
>
> - buying up a US firm entirely
>
> - investing heavily in a US firm, usually a small one; the small company got start-up help, but was dependent on its Japanese stockholder
>
> - running a company jointly with the American owners, sharing the risk, the investment, the knowledge and ideas.
>
> Japanese companies were careful about the places they offered to invest in. They often chose parts of the country where federal government and US businesses were not investing, such as South Carolina and Ohio. However, buying up or investing in US companies didn't result in much job creation. In 1987, there were around three million Americans working for Japanese companies, but most were not in newly created jobs. However, they weren't unemployed because the company had gone under, either, which might have happened without the investment.

SOURCE

7

Textile workers in Chicago, demonstrating in 1985 over how foreign imports were affecting the industry. Congress tried to introduce regulations to help the textile industry in 1985 and 1988. Reagan used the presidential veto to stop the bills.

EXTRACT

5

From *The American Dream: From Reconstruction to Reagan*, written by Esmond Wright in 1996. Wright was British, a conservative and a historian. He specialised in US history and helped to make it a popular subject in British universities.

Under Reagan, leading investors around the globe renewed their commitment to the US economy. US investors happily ended their reckless role as 'net lenders' to the world, stopped pouring their money into Third World and Communist ratholes, and repatriated their funds to the United States. Foreign investors also spurned their own economies and focused on the United States.

This capital flight from abroad and capital repatriation by Americans allowed the US to become the world's leading importer of advanced goods and equipment. Much decried by misinformed mercantilists and xenophobes, this influx of imports and investments was a thoroughly positive reflection of US success in integrating the world economy in the interests of the Americans.

EXTRACT

6

From *The Power of Presidential Ideologies*, written by Dennis Florig, published in 1992. Florig lectures in US history in Seoul, Korea.

The decline of the U.S. in the world economy was the main reason for the loss of 15 percent of all manufacturing jobs in the U.S. economy during the Reagan years. … Ironically, the shrinking of the trade deficit in the late 1980s and the early 1990s was as much a sign of weakness as strength. It was true that U.S. exports were up. But more important, due to the recession, the ability of American consumers to buy any goods, foreign or domestic, was severely restricted, and thus imports fell along with the sale of domestic goods. … In order to finance the huge budget and trade deficits and to maintain current standards of living, the United States has been borrowing massively from foreigners and increasingly selling American assets to foreigners. When the Reagan administration took office, the United States was the largest creditor nation in the world. Americans were owed $140 billion more by foreign institutions and individuals than they owed to foreigners, more than any other people in the world. By the time the administration left office, the United States was the largest debtor nation in the world. On net, Americans owed roughly $400 billion to foreigners, more than any other nation in history. Besides borrowing, another way to finance a deficit is to sell one's assets, and Americans have increasingly been selling their properties to foreign buyers. Highly publicised purchases like those of Colombia Pictures and the Rockerfeller Centre complex in New York are just the most visible cases of the U.S. liquidating its capital in order to pay for current consumption.

THINKING HISTORICALLY **Interpretations (4b)**

Method is everything

Bad history	Good history
• Based on gut feeling • Argument does not progress logically • No supporting evidence	• Based on an interpretation of evidence • Argument does progress logically • Evidence deployed to support argument

Figure 5.1 A spectrum of historical methodology.

Historical writing can reveal much about the methods by which it was constructed. Read Extract 5, and, in pairs, answer the questions below.

1 Look carefully at Figure 5.1.

   a) Where would you place each source on the spectrum of historical practice?

   b) What evidence would you use to support your choice?

2 Look at Extract 5. How would you change it to make it the same quality of historical writing as Extract 6?

3 Use a dictionary. Explain the following words in their relation to historical writing: substantiation, deduction, inference, cross-reference.

4 How important is it that historians understand and evaluate the methods used by other historians?

Conclusion

Big government was not reduced as much as Reagan had hoped. There were various reasons for this. Congress agreed to deregulate oil prices, but blocked plans to remove regulations on environmental issues such as pollution and working conditions at nuclear power stations. Another reason was that state and local governments were unwilling to take over areas of government and projects under federal control. This was because they did not want to pay for something that would otherwise be federally funded. On the other hand, unlike Carter's administration, the Reagan administration didn't introduce many new regulations. It was Congress that persuaded Reagan to pass the Food Security Act on 23 December 1985. This gave federal help to farmers who were struggling with falling prices and the falling value of farmland. Even then, he made it clear that this help was an exception, forced on him by Congress.

By the time Bush came to power, people were less keen on deregulation and federal withdrawal from state and local affairs. Industry and banking deregulation had been running for long enough for people to see the negative effects of lifting regulation. It had become clear that many deregulated businesses were more interested in their own benefit than public benefit. For instance, pre-deregulation aeroplanes flew to all over the USA and were often only half full. By 1989, the big companies had corrected the initial price fall from competition. Prices were high; planes flew to fewer places, less often and were tightly packed. Federal withdrawal from state and local programmes often meant the collapse of programmes through lack of funding. Some states and local areas suffered more than others; poor rural areas found themselves at the back of the queue for communications services, transport services and basic maintenance such as road repair.

ACTIVITY
KNOWLEDGE CHECK

Reducing big government

1 Prepare a 'prep sheet' to brief a US administration press spokesman for a television interview the day after Reagan's inauguration speech about the administration's plans for reducing 'big government'.

    a) Pick four key phrases from the speech that you want to air on television, with a note about why they are important.

    b) List the key aims of New Federalism.

    c) List two questions you want to avoid, together with the best replies you could give if the questions are asked.

2 Explain why federal control, or the lack of it, in finance has such an impact. Use examples from trade, banking or other financial institutions to illustrate your points.

WHAT WAS THE NATURE AND EXTENT OF SOCIAL CHANGE?

The Reagan years produced significant social change. The gap between rich and poor widened; family life, so praised by Reagan, came under strain. Business and industry (therefore work) changed: both the kind of work and where it was done.

Rich and poor

Between 1981 and 1996, the situation of the poorest American families worsened considerably. It is hardly surprising because Reagan made it clear that he saw a difference between 'deserving poor' and 'welfare scroungers'. The scroungers, he said, weren't willing to work; they thought the government owed them a living. Reagan repeatedly told the story of a black woman in Chicago who was defrauding taxpayers out of hundreds of thousands of dollars a year by welfare fraud, using a variety of names, welfare cards and benefits for supposedly dead war veteran husbands. A press search never found her. His OBRA finance cuts targeted mainly federal spending on projects for the poorest. OBRA also altered the Aid to Families with Dependent Children (AFDC) programme. Fewer people were eligible and many of the payments were **capped**. These moves hit the poorest working families hard, the opposite of Reagan's stated intentions.

The effect of Reagan's policies on welfare provision

- **Workfare:** Reagan's administration was the first to state, in the legislation, that claiming benefit was buying into dependency, therefore undesirable. The administration wanted to change 'welfare' to 'workfare', by requiring at least one working parent before it paid out family benefit, for example. However, much of the work provided paid below minimum wage, sometimes less than benefit, so families struggled. Another problem was that, despite government promises of childcare, many single parents found childcare impossible to find, making it impossible for them to work. OBRA tightened up previous legislation that provided work projects tied to benefits for welfare claimants. It allowed states to make working on state projects an absolute requirement for welfare payments. By January 1987, there were 42 states running work programmes. While none of them made working on a programme a requirement for benefit, most required the claimant to be looking for work.

- **Social housing:** In 1970, there were almost 2.4 million low-income homes available to families that applied for them. By 1985, there were 3.7 million families who qualified for a low-income home, but could not move into one because there were none available. This happened because Reagan's administration slashed federal funding for building low-cost homes. In 1978, the federal government spent $32.2 billion on low-cost housing projects. By 1988, it was spending just $9.2 billion. This led to a significant rise in the number of homeless people in the country, something the public found increasingly difficult to accept. They felt that it made the USA look bad and Americans feel bad; it was a direct contradiction of the American Dream.

- **Homelessness:** By the mid-1980s, the Reagan administration could no longer ignore the growing problem of homelessness. In 1987, Congress pushed through a bill giving some federal help to projects for the homeless. In 1984, federal funding available to the homeless was $300 million; in 1988, it was $1.6 billion. The 1987 McKinney Act set up the Federal Emergency Management Food and Shelter Program to be run by the Federal Emergency Management Agency (FEMA). FEMA matched state grants to local homeless projects half-and-half and the state had to choose the project and put the funding in place before the federal money was given. The state or local government funding could be raised through taxes, charities or donations. FEMA set up a federal housing project for transitional housing (with the possibility of using under-used federal buildings), with special emphasis on the elderly, disabled, veterans, families with children and Native Americans. It also gave emergency medical care to the homeless and provided education for homeless children and job training that favoured homeless veterans.

REAGAN'S WELFARE MEASURES

13 October 1982 Job Training Partnership Act
Shifts job training from federal hands to state and private schemes and removes any need for the trainees to have their incomes made up to the minimum wage

20 April 1983 Social Security Reform Bill
Delays the linking of payments to inflation from July to December; raises the amount the government takes from wages to cover the benefit; sets up a study of running the Social Security Agency as a privately run agency; makes part of benefit payments taxable; changes the earnings test for eligibility; retirement credits are now not fully payable until 1967 (rather than 1965)

22 July 1987 McKinney Vento Homeless Assistance Act
Sets up the Federal Emergency Management Food and Shelter Program to be run by the Federal Emergency Management Agency (FEMA)

13 October 1988 Family Support Act
A family is only to be eligible for benefits if at least one parent is working for at least 16 hours a week; single parents are expected to finish education and undergo job training, the state to provide childcare

The impact on living and working conditions

Working families not on welfare, or only entitled to some allowances because of their earnings, did benefit from lower taxes. However, they were hit even harder by the changes to the family credit regulations. They were also hit by rising interest rates that pushed up housing costs, mortgage costs and rent. Between 1980 and 1987, the average mortgage debt increased by 30 percent and the rate of **foreclosure** quadrupled. Many families found both parents had to work to make ends meet.

KEY TERM

Foreclosure
The repossession of a home by the mortgage lender because the borrower can no longer meet the payments.

Workers found themselves stretched in other ways, too, by the removal of many federal regulations on working conditions. Many had to work longer hours and so had less leisure time. In 1973, workers had, on average, 26 hours of leisure time a week; by 1987, it was 16 hours. Worse still, some people felt pressured to work even harder, to take work home, in constant competition to be the most productive person. Reagan's stress on productivity was emphasised by businesses. It became harder for working mothers, who might need time off if a child was sick, or had to leave on time to pick children up, to hold anything but low-level jobs. Many were persuaded to move sideways and down into part-time or temporary contract work. These workers were not part of any benefits schemes and were only paid for the hours that they worked.

Yet another change in the workforce was that under Reagan younger people, just coming into the workforce, became worse off than their elders had been. A two-tier wage structure emerged in many businesses. Established workers kept the wage rates and benefits that were negotiated when they took the job. Workers joining the business could be offered a lower salary, and fewer benefits, for doing the same job. This was offered on a take-it-or-leave-it basis. It was offered to young people and to people with experience too: it was the fact they were new to the business that put them on the lower tier. Many people, worried about job security as employers shifted to hiring part-time and temporary employees, felt they had to take the jobs.

The impact on minorities

Reagan's desire to cut back on federal involvement meant that the administration was unwilling to extend civil rights legislation or push for affirmative action. While Reagan vowed he wasn't racist or sexist, his administration did little to support minority rights. For example, in the first six months of Reagan's presidency, the Civil Rights division of the Justice Department filed five racial discrimination lawsuits. In the first six months of Nixon's presidency, they had filed 24. In 1982, *The Crisis*, the magazine of the NAACP, pointed out that the Reagan administration's inaction was harming all minority groups. It pointed to his abandonment of busing students into various schools (to promote racial segregation) as something particularly harmful to black and Hispanic Americans. This was because it virtually guaranteed that children in the poorest and most deprived areas would have to attend schools in these areas, therefore creating segregated schooling. The administration also withdrew 40 percent of its funding for bilingual education, saying that it was in the interests of children from minority groups to use English as soon as possible, to have a better chance in the workplace. The 'planned shrinkage' of inner cities that had begun under Carter continued and was made worse by the cuts to federal spending on low-cost housing.

While Reagan did appoint a woman, Sandra Day, to the Supreme Court, women's rights floundered under him. Reagan did not support the Equal Rights Act and spoke out against abortion – although he was persuaded not to introduce anti-abortion legislation. While most people agree that Reagan was lukewarm towards women's rights, there is disagreement over his reaction to the gay rights movement, especially towards AIDS.

Some people have accused him of ignoring the epidemic until his friend, actor Rock Hudson, died of AIDS. Others point out that he addressed meetings on the epidemic, and that the administration provided funding for AIDS research from 1982. What is clear is that many Republicans and conservative Reagan supporters opposed gay rights and might have opposed the administration if it was too 'gay friendly'.

Under Reagan there were, as before, winners and losers among black Americans. Hard-working, well-educated, middle-class, conformist black Americans could get ahead, especially women – they filled two minority 'quotas' for cynical businesses. Undereducated young, poor black men often went under. Even successful black people felt the constant pressure of being in a minority – of being held back and not promoted; of being seen as the 'quota' hire, not someone hired for their abilities. Black people felt increasingly less a part of the political environment. The civil rights movement was scrabbling to regain ground, fighting to retain rights (such as affirmative action appointments) that the conservatives were campaigning to remove. It was in this environment that young black Americans turned increasingly to angry, violent and defeatist rap music as their anthem, rather than the civil rights anthem 'We Shall Overcome'; they were no longer sure that they would do so.

EXTEND YOUR KNOWLEDGE

Bari-Ellen Roberts

Bari-Ellen Roberts was a high-achieving black American woman. She was working in the pensions department of Chase Manhattan bank when she was head-hunted by Texaco in 1993. Despite the fact that the company had deliberately asked her to join, Roberts felt she wasn't being allowed to rise in the company. Also, her suggestion that the company might hire more non-whites met with the accusation that she was trying to fill the place with Black Panthers. The last straw was when a white man less experienced than Roberts was promoted to be her boss – and she was told she would have to train him. In March 1994, Roberts and five other co-workers took Texaco to court for discrimination, on behalf of all the workers at Texaco. Their lawyers showed that black Americans were paid less for doing the same jobs and were confined to the less senior jobs in the company. The case dragged on. Then, in 1996, the *New York Times* was sent an audio tape of three Texaco executives discussing the case in crude and racist terms. Civil rights leaders threatened a nationwide boycott of Texaco petrol stations. With its stockmarket value falling, Texaco agreed on a $176 million pay-out and improved hiring and promotion practices. Roberts became almost as big a heroine as Rosa Parks and went on to run her own company.

EXTRACT

From *We Ain't What We Ought To Be*, a history of black Americans, written by Stephen Tuck, a historian at Oxford University, published in 2010.

After Reagan's victory, civil rights leaders saw the federal government as foe rather than (potential) friend. This was not the first time. In his last months, [Martin Luther] King had complained bitterly about the Johnson administration, and the NAACP felt at war with Nixon. But the unrelenting condemnation of a president by civil rights leaders called to mind the days of Woodrow Wilson. Reagan's campaign had set the tone. His New York speech did not mention civil rights. He then turned down a request to speak to the NAACP (he had already booked a holiday in Mexico). After winning the nomination, Reagan gave his first speech in Neshoba County, Mississippi – site of the unresolved murder of three student activists in 1964. Carter's team criticised Reagan for not mentioning the murders. What Reagan did instead was dust off old segregationalist rhetoric, asserting, 'I believe in states' rights'. The Imperial Wizard of the Klan endorsed the Republican ticket. ... He [Reagan] appointed conservative judges to the federal bench; he promoted black conservatives who opposed affirmative action; and his Justice Department proved reluctant to protect minority rights. Black leaders were angry at the racial slights, too. Reagan famously failed to recognise Charles Pierce, the sole African American member of his cabinet, at a meeting of black mayors. Above all, Reagan's mantra was, 'Government is not the solution to our problems; government *is* the problem'. By contrast, civil rights leaders had long seen federal intervention as key to solving racial equality. ... The inequality gap in wages and employment that had been closing since World War II held steady from the mid-1970s through the mid-1990s. Inner-city poverty, family breakdown, and gang violence seemed entrenched. The arrival of crack cocaine in the mid-1980s compounded the problem. New get-tough measures led to an astonishing rise in the numbers of young black men in prison. During the 1980s, sociologists popularised the term 'underclass' – a group with no opportunity, or even desire, to break out of poverty and dependency. By the 1990s large majorities of African Americans – including the black middle classes – told pollsters they did not expect the problem of racial inequality to improve in their lifetimes.

EXTRACT

From *The Declining Significance of Race: Blacks and Changing American Institutions*, an analysis of the position of black Americans in US society, written by William Julius Wilson, a sociologist at Harvard University, in 2012.

It would be shortsighted to view the traditional forms of racial segregation and discrimination as having essentially disappeared in contemporary America; the presence of blacks is still firmly resisted in various institutions and social arrangements, for example, residential areas and private social clubs. However, in the economic sphere, class has become more important than race in determining black access to privilege and power. It is clearly evident in this connection that many talented and educated blacks are now entering positions of prestige and influence at a rate comparable to or, in some situations exceeding, that of whites with equivalent qualifications.

THINKING HISTORICALLY   Interpretations (4a)

The weight of evidence

Work in pairs. Read Extracts 7 and 8, then answer the questions below:

1 Use highlighter pens to colour-code copies of the extracts. Use one colour for 'evidence', another colour for 'conclusions' and a third for language that shows the historian is 'reasoning' (e.g. 'therefore', 'so'). Alternatively, draw up a table with three columns, headed 'Evidence', 'Conclusions' and 'Reasoning language' and copy the relevant parts of the extracts into the columns.

2 How do the extracts differ in terms of the way that the evidence is used?

3 Which of these extracts do you find more convincing? Which has the best-supported arguments?

4 What other information might you want in order to make a judgement about the strength of these claims?

5 Write a paragraph of 200 words explaining the importance of using evidence to support historical claims.

Business and industry

Under Reagan, business and industry changed in size, scope and location. This had a significant impact on where people lived and the work they did, as well as which parts of the USA thrived and which struggled.

Changing businesses and farms

Reagan may have been against 'big government', but his policies favoured big businesses, even though his administration said it would encourage small ones. Big businesses profited from reduced federal regulation over wages, working hours and working conditions. Deregulation meant they could buy up or merge with other businesses. In 1983, in a radio broadcast during small business week, Reagan said his administration was helping small businesses with tax breaks, such as allowing them to pay personal, not corporate, tax. He did admit that many small businesses had gone under in the 1981–82 recession, but said that over 500,000 new small businesses had been set up in each of those years. He avoided the issue of the rising interest rates on long-term loans that many small businesses held: a key reason why many of them went under.

Farming was also badly affected by high interest rates and federal non-intervention. In the 1970s, the USA had supplied wheat to the USSR and encouraged farmers to expand (often with bigger and bigger loans) and grow wheat (with wheat-growing subsidies). When the USSR invaded Afghanistan in 1979, the USA stopped exporting wheat in protest. At the same time, interest rates rose as the money supply was tightened. Things worsened in the 1980s, not helped by a bad drought in 1983. Many smaller farms failed and were bought out by agri-businesses, or even companies that didn't farm at all. So, in 1980, 17 percent of farmers were getting 60 percent of the subsidy fund. The National Save the Family Farm Coalition was set up in 1986 by farmers themselves. It organised demonstrations and campaigns to highlight the plight of small family farms, using tactics such as traffic-slowing **tractorcades** in cities. Iowa was hit particularly hard. In 1983, there were about 500 farms sold every month. Farmers were committing suicide at four times the rate of any other workers, and there were also incidents of farmers shooting the lenders who called in loans.

KEY TERM

Tractorcade
A deliberately slow procession of tractors on urban streets; used as a protest tool.

EXTEND YOUR KNOWLEDGE

Supporting the farmers
In 1984, two Hollywood movies about the farm crisis, *Country* and *The River*, sparked widespread support for the farmers. The stars of the films testified to Congress about what they had seen while researching and filming. Advice hotlines were set up to help farmers understand their debts and work out how to restructure them. In September 1985, a Farm Aid concert was held to raise money to help the farmers and raised millions of dollars.

Changing production

During the 1980s, there was a shift in what the USA produced. Farming was not the only industry in difficulty. Older manufacturing industries, such as the car and textile industries, were doing badly against foreign imports (which could be made more cheaply) and exports dropped with the change in value of the dollar. The Reagan administration would not impose tariffs on foreign imports. Towns and cities, such as Detroit, where car manufacturers were the main employer, were badly hit by this decline. In Baltimore and Cleveland, well over 20 percent of the population was living below the poverty line, and unemployment and poverty was hitting all workers, white and non-white. It also had an effect on the industries that supplied the raw materials, as demand for those raw materials dropped. This pattern was repeated in the textile industry.

While older manufacturing industries were failing, new industries were doing well. The Reagan administration's increased spending on defence meant that the defence industry, and all the services that supplied a growing military, did well. So did the new technologies, such as the computer industry. These technologies were based in different parts of the country and had a significant effect on population and migration within the USA, following the work opportunities in the new industries. Manufacturing and the provision of raw materials may have been in decline, but service industries were expanding. Everything from estate agencies to coffee shop chains and computer goods stores did well.

The bi-coastal boom

The industries that did well in the 1980s created more employment. As a result, people were eager to move to the areas of the country where these industries were located. This resulted in a population shift from the North and East to the South and West, especially to the coastal states. Those families that could afford to make this move, for example, from Chicago to San Diego, fuelled a growth of the suburbs in these areas. Here were places where people felt their lives were improving and people in these places were consistently more likely to vote for Reagan and, after him, Bush. For them, the policies of the Reagan administration had worked. In 1987, California and the states on the East coast had 5.6 percent unemployment, compared to 7.8 percent in the rest of the country. These areas had almost 75 percent of all new businesses and about 60 percent of new jobs. The part of the country that stayed worst off was the central Great Plains area, which had always been a predominantly farming area.

ACTIVITY
KNOWLEDGE CHECK

Rich and poor

1 Write brief summaries of the effects of the Reagan years on:

 a) the rich

 b) people dependent on welfare

 c) minority groups.

Business and industry

2 What evidence is there that the administration's policies:

 a) helped big businesses

 b) helped small businesses?

3 What, in your opinion, was the most significant change in business and industry during the period? Justify your answer.

EXTEND YOUR KNOWLEDGE

'Dual economies'
The bi-coastal effect was clear in broad terms, but even the generally well-off coastal areas had pockets of more rural areas, often with an old industry base, that did less well than the rest of the areas. North Carolina had metropolitan areas specialising in banking, research, property development and insurance, but it also had many small towns in rural areas that had grown cotton for the failing textile industry and did not benefit from their coastal position.

TO WHAT EXTENT WERE THE PRESIDENCY AND US POLITICS REVITALISED?

Reagan was charismatic, and had media and popular support. In the early years of his presidency, many people felt that he had brought in a new era. They were willing to trust both the president and government again. However, a consideration of the extent to which the presidency and politics were actually revitalised needs to look at both in the longer term, beyond Reagan, as well as back towards Carter and earlier presidents.

The presidency

There can be little doubt that Reagan revitalised the presidency. He became president after Nixon and Watergate, Ford's pardon of Nixon and Carter's awkward management of the presidency. By the time Reagan came to power, many Americans didn't trust any part of the government. Many felt helpless, as if it didn't matter whom they voted for, as things would carry on declining regardless. Reagan promised to bring change, and began by doing so. His first few years set the image that people retained of him. The fact that he then did less than he, and many of his more conservative supporters, had hoped was less noticeable. The slowdown in change was hidden behind the way he projected a presidential image and his foreign affairs successes. His followers were less able at playing the role. Bush didn't get re-elected for a second term, despite having a higher average approval rating than Reagan: 61 to 52 (however, Reagan had started with an approval rating of 68 compared to Carter's 28 before the election). Bill Clinton, Bush's successor, had an average approval rating of 55.

Presidential involvement in legislation

Reagan's initial success with Congress was not repeated. Some of the legislation that he wanted to introduce, urged on by the religious right, was blocked by Congress, such as laws to cut back on busing children from poorer areas to integrated schools. However, the reason that not all of the changes he had promised were brought in was not simply because of opposition in Congress.

Reagan was also advised against some legislation, and was prepared to listen to this advice and be pragmatic and flexible about policy. For example, he believed, along with the religious right, that daily prayer should be introduced in schools, but he was advised it would never get past Congress, so he didn't bring in a bill on it. Bush was less pragmatic and flexible. He was a poor communicator and was less able to charm the public or Congress, or present them with a clear vision of his policies. He had less support in Congress – in his first term, he had 45 Republicans in the Senate (Reagan had 54 in his first term) and 175 Republicans in the House of Representatives (Reagan had 189), so he had to struggle more and was less adept at managing Congress. He promised to continue Reagan's most popular policies, keeping taxes low and defence spending up, but had to give in to the demands of Congress and raise taxes. Clinton also struggled to get legislation passed after his first big healthcare legislation package failed: increased presidential involvement in legislation did not last long.

Public image and the Iran–Contra affair

Reagan looked and played the part of the kind of president that Americans thought they had lost. He spoke of the American Dream, of family values and of confidence in the future. The public felt Reagan may not have done everything right, but he was sincere and capable.

This feeling took a jolt when, in the autumn of 1986, the Iran–Contra affair was uncovered. White House officials had supplied arms to Iran in order to free several US hostages. The officials had used the money from the arms sales to Iran (along with money raised from private sources) to support Contra rebels in Nicaragua, who were fighting the existing government. The White House had also supplied the rebels with weapons. All this was done, not just without the agreement of Congress, but against policies of neutrality in the Iran–Iraq war and of not supplying the Contras with weapons laid down by Congress. Worse, just as in Watergate, the president lied to Congress and the public by saying, first, that these things had not been done, and then, that he hadn't known about it. The officials involved destroyed documents and other evidence in an attempted cover-up. People were asking themselves what was worse – a president who ordered this and then lied, or a president who was so unable to control his officials that they could do it without him knowing? Reagan's involvement, when it became clear, did damage the presidency. Reagan himself did better than Nixon. He was more popular at the start and so many people told themselves that, because he had had an operation when he gave the orders, he could have been confused. Also they felt he was doing it to save hostages, not his own neck.

SOURCE

8 The Iran–Contra hearings went on for over a year, along with the Tower Commission investigation, set up by Reagan, and the trial of Oliver North and others who arranged the financing of the aid given to the Contras. Reagan was questioned by the press constantly and sometimes held briefings, like the one shown in the photo below, mainly refusing to comment until the hearing was over.

US politics

Reagan's presidency did affect the political environment, as outlined below, but did not bring a long period of Republican control. Instead, control of Congress shifted to and fro, bringing in more political competition. By 1988, the Democrats had a majority in the House and the Senate, although they lost this in the 1996 elections and the Republicans gained control of both.

'New Right' thinking

One of the most significant political changes was introducing 'New Right' thinking into politics. This rejected many assumptions in place since the New Deal about how involved in society, how liberal, government should be. In Reagan's first term, he united a significant number of politicians, Republican and Democrat, under a conservative coalition banner. It was this that enabled him to push through his early legislation. The coalition was reacting against the political climate of the 1970s, as they saw it. They objected to the increase of 'lazy' and 'welfare dependent' poor; the rising number of strikes and demonstrations; the increasing lack of 'law and order'; the support given by the government to issues such as gay rights, women's liberation, affirmative action and abortion. However, there was a split, in the public mind and in the reactions of politicians, between support for these ideas in general terms and accepting Reagan's more extreme policies. Time and again, polls showed that people thought the welfare system was being exploited, but also thought the poor needed more help. Meanwhile, Congress and the states managed to block a lot of legislation suggested by the Reagan administration on 'social' issues and on 'big government' handovers of control, for example, moving funding for road building from federal to state control.

EXTRACT

From 'Ideological images for a television age', written by Charles W. Dunn and J. David Woodward, in *Reaganomics and After*, a collection of articles about Reaganomics, published in 1989. Dunn is an academic; Woodward has written a biography of Reagan.

Such [tax] reforms had effects that were more symbolic than real, but in the world of media impressions such illusions are often important. Reagan was seen as a helmsman who was turning the ship of state in a new direction. Even when his changes were shown to be illusory, ... Reagan was seen as an effective leader. Going for tax cuts in the first year of the administration gave the appearance of change. ...

A popular conservative messenger with a popular conservative message has altered the landscape of political debate and public policy. The word *conservative*, no longer anathema in American political discourse, has replaced the word *liberal* as the most popular of the two words, forcing the political opposition to search for other ways to express their ideas, sometimes using the word *conservative* itself. Liberal Democrats are now reacting to the successes of the conservative Reagan agenda rather than conservative Republicans reacting to the successes of liberal New Deal policies that dominated America's political landscape for three decades.

ACTIVITY
WRITING

Evaluating Reagan

Analyse Extract 9.

1 What words and phrases do the authors use to suggest that they doubt the effectiveness of Reagan's actions?

2 What words and phrases do they use to suggest they feel that the impact on public debate and policy was effective?

3 Write a short paragraph summing up what you think the authors felt about Reagan's overall effectiveness, using quotes from the extract to back up your points.

EXTRACT

10 From 'Domestic policy in an era of "negative" government', written by Dilys M. Hill, in *Reaganomics and After*, a collection of articles about Reaganomics, published in 1989.

It would be wrong, however, to judge the record a failure from the administration's perspective (David Stockman's criticisms notwithstanding) or to believe that the territory of domestic policy has remained unchanged. The major achievement of the Reagan presidency has been to alter the terms and nature of the debate about domestic issues and thus the political agenda itself. As in Britain, political discourse was influenced by the new right perspective; liberty, the market, the moral and social evils of dependency, the obligation to work for benefits ('Workfare'). The success of the new right in shaping the policy agenda by its influence on the terms of political discourse was further revealed by the defeat of the previously dominant problem-solving approach. The expert was in retreat; the claim to solve problems by the application of rational analysis followed by collective societal solutions had failed. Problem-solving was the hallmark of the 1960s and 1970s: the result had been the 'welfare mess', rising crime and a permissive culture. The Reagan administration did not need to be told by professional or sectional interests what policies should be followed since the new policies had already been determined by belief in the market and in the reduced role of the state. What was needed was determined implementation.

ACTIVITY
KNOWLEDGE CHECK

Reagan's impact on politics

1 Study Extracts 9 and 10.

    a) What is the focus of Extract 9's analysis?

    b) What is the focus of Extract 10's analysis?

2 Explain the similarities and differences between their views on the impact of Reagan's presidency on the political scene.

Revitalised politicians?

It could be argued that the Reagan administration didn't change Republican politics enough. Many political analysts claim the problem with the Republican Party was that Republicans saw their victories as a sensible swing to their way of thinking, rather than (as it often was) a temporary reaction to Democrat mistakes, so they didn't feel the need to change their thinking. In fact, more Americans in the 1980s and 1990s cared about liberal ideals, even if they didn't call them that, than Republicans thought. People wanted a fair society, even if it wasn't equal: one closer to the American Dream than Republican big business would ever want.

The fact that Reagan could swing enough Democrats in the House to get his 1981 legislation passed was seen as a danger sign by the Democrats. However, they were a divided party and were even split about candidates. Jesse Jackson, a civil rights activist and Baptist minister, ran to be chosen as their presidential candidate in 1984; he wasn't chosen and their candidate lost. Jackson ran again in 1988. He lost again and the Democrat candidate who beat him lost heavily to George H.W. Bush.

After their defeat in 1984, they were forced to regroup: they had lost, badly, too often. They formed the Democratic Leadership Council (DLC) to revitalise the party. The 'old' liberal order of Kennedy and Johnson was tarnished. A 'New Democrat' ideology was born, promoted by the chairman of the Council in 1990: Bill Clinton. The new ideology accepted the need for low taxes and low federal intervention. This shifted Democrats closer to conservative thinking. However, they stressed the need to provide social welfare. As 'welfare' became increasingly synonymous with 'supporting the lazy', the Democrats evolved a new take on it. They said that they would abolish welfare and provide support. Clinton campaigned on this promise in 1992. He offered a 'New Covenant' to the people. He would bring change and replace policies that weren't working, the same offer Reagan had made in 1984.

Other changes to the political environment

*   Reagan brought business back into government. Businesses were bigger and money was no longer something to be shy about having. From sponsorship in sport to influence in politics through huge campaign contributions, businesses made their mark on the USA far more strongly than they had done for decades. This had knock-on effects when they supported particular political candidates. Candidates with funding can buy more air-time on television. They can run slicker, more appealing campaigns. This will give them a competitive edge that has nothing to do with their political ideas or skills.

*   The Christian right became more outspoken and involved in political issues under Reagan. It became more outspoken about issues such as abortion, teenage pregnancy and what should be taught in schools. Its view was that it had given Reagan support and brought in a lot of votes. It expected, as a reward, government legislation on these issues. However, while Reagan was outspoken in his views that coincided with the Christian right, he was advised against any actual legislation and was careful to make it clear that he was expressing a personal opinion. He was a successful president because of his willingness to adapt. He might not change his mind over abortion, but he wasn't going to try to force legislation through that would make him unpopular and be rejected by Congress anyway.

EXTEND YOUR KNOWLEDGE

The 1984 LA Olympics
The Los Angeles Olympic Organising Committee (LAOOC) was told to organise the Games without spending taxpayers' money. Most other Olympics had been largely sponsored by the government of the host country (and so by the taxpayers). The LAOOC did this partly by using existing venues (it helped that they already had sports venues that were of Olympic quality), but mainly by turning to big business. Money came pouring in, but tightly tied to sponsorship. The LAOOC made a profit of about $215 million, significantly more than any other Olympics before or since. Coca Cola, Samsung and McDonald's all became 'official' sponsors of the event, gaining in advertising and in concession sales at the sites.

Public interest and involvement

If US politics was revitalised, this ought to show itself in public interest in political issues and involvement in politics, but this wasn't happening up to 1996. The first televised presidential debate in 1960 drew 70 million viewers. Television ownership grew after this, but viewing figures for the debates dropped, even though they were seen as the events that most affected public voting. Viewing figures were around 60 million during the 1970s. However, the Reagan–Carter debates broke through this. They drew 80.6 million viewers. Did this level of interest and political involvement carry on? The 1984 debates drew 67.5 million; the 1988 debates 65.1 million; the 1992 debates 69.9 million; and, in the 1996 debates, only 36.3 million tuned in – the lowest figures in the debates' history.

So, Reagan was a popular president and changed the view of the public, media and political parties on the role of government, even if he didn't make the sweeping changes in legislation that he had hoped for. He made the presidency look as if it was a proper political role again, becoming the leader who could affect policy and guide the nation. He made people feel as if the system of government was basically sound; it just needed the right people to be in the government to make it work.

SOURCE
9
Voter turnout in US elections, 1970–90. Based on data from Center for Democracy and Election Managaement, School of Public Affairs, American University, Washington DC.

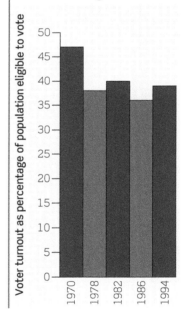

ACTIVITY
KNOWLEDGE CHECK

Effects of the Reagan presidency on politics

1 List the ways in which Reagan's presidency revitalised US politics.

2 List the ways in which its effects were limited.

3 Which factors do you think are more significant in this respect: voter behaviour or the behaviour and policies of politicians?

A-Level, Section C

Study Extracts 9 and 10 before you answer this question.

In the light of differing interpretations, how convincing do you find the view that the main achievement of Reagan's presidency was 'to alter the terms and nature of the debate about domestic issues' (Extract 10)?

To explain your answer, analyse and evaluate both extracts, using your own knowledge of the issues.

Tip

Consider the other achievements of the presidency against the suggested one.

ACTIVITY
SUMMARY

Reaganomics

1 Prepare for a debate on Reagan's economic policy and its effects. Make notes on:

a) supply-side theory and its policy of tax cuts

b) monetary control and the Federal Reserve Board

c) deficit reduction.

For each of these, define the impact it was supposed to have, the effect it did have and any unintentional consequences it had. Consider points in favour of and against the theories.

A changed society

2 How do you think the Reagan administration's policies changed life for:

a) a rich white person living in New York

b) a white car worker in Baltimore

c) a black university lecturer in California

d) a white farmer on the Great Plains?

WIDER READING

Ehrman, J. and Flamm, M.W. *Debating the Reagan Presidency*, Rowman & Littlefield (2009)

Reaganomics in Plain and Simple English, Book Caps Study Guide (2012)

Wiegand, S. *US History for Dummies*, John Wiley (2014). Despite the off-putting title, this provides helpful summaries.

BBC, *People's Century*, Episode 26: *Reaganism*

You can find footage of many of Reagan's speeches online by searching for 'Reagan' and the topic you want or 'inaugural speech'.

Preparing for your AS Paper 1 exam

Advance planning

- Draw up a timetable for your revision and try to keep to it. Spread your timetable over a number of weeks, and aim to cover four or five topics each week.

- Spend longer on topics which you have found difficult, and revise them several times.

- Above all, do not try to limit your revision by attempting to 'question spot'. Try to be confident about all aspects of your Paper 1 work, because this will ensure that you have a choice of questions in Sections A and B.

Paper 1 overview

AS Paper 1	Time: 2 hours 15 minutes	
Section A	Answer 1 question from a choice of 2	20 marks
Section B	Answer 1 question from a choice of 2	20 marks
Section C	Answer 1 compulsory interpretations question	20 marks
	Total marks =	60 marks

You should familiarise yourself with the layout of the paper by looking at the examples published by Edexcel. The questions for each section are followed by eight pages of lined paper where you should write your answer.

Section A questions

Section A questions ask you to analyse and evaluate either cause or consequence. You should consider either the reasons for, or the results of, an event or development. You will be asked for coverage of a period of around ten years, possibly a little longer. For example, a question for Option 1F might be 'Was the involvement of President Truman the main reason for the changing status of black Americans in the years 1945–55?' Your answer should consider the reason(s) given in the question, then look at other relevant points and reach a conclusion.

Section B questions

Section B questions cover a longer timespan than in Section A, at least one-third of the period you have studied. The questions take the form of 'How far…', 'How significant…,' 'To what extent…' or 'How accurate is it to say…'. The questions can deal with historical concepts such as cause, consequence, change, continuity, similarity, difference and significance. Again, you should consider the issue raised in the question, consider other relevant issues, and then conclude with an overall judgement.

Section C questions

There is no choice in Section C, which is concerned with the historical interpretations you have studied linked to the question 'What impact did the Reagan presidency (1981–89) have on the USA in the years 1981–96?' You will be given two extracts totalling around 300 words (printed separately) and the question will take the form 'How far do you agree with the view that…' There is no need to use source analysis skills such as making inferences or considering provenance for Section C answers. You will need to use the extracts and your own knowledge to consider the view given in the question.

Use of time

This is an issue which you should discuss with your teachers and fellow students, but here are some suggestions for you.

1. Do not write solidly for 45 minutes on each question. For Section A and B answers you should spend a few minutes working out what the question is asking you to do, and drawing up a plan of your answer. This is especially important for Section B answers, which cover an extended period of time.

2. For Section C it is essential that you have a clear understanding of the content of each extract and the points which each extract is making. Read each extract carefully and underline important points. You could approach your answer by analysing the first extract, then the second, and then using your own knowledge before reaching an overall judgement. You might decide to spend up to ten minutes reading the extracts and drawing up your plan, and 35 minutes writing your answer.

Preparing for your AS Level exams

Paper 1: AS Level sample answer with comments

Section A

These questions assess your understanding of the period in breadth. They will ask you about the content you learned about in the four key themes, and may ask about more than one theme. For these questions remember to:

- give an analytical, not a descriptive, response
- support your points with evidence
- cover the whole time period specified in the question
- come to a substantiated judgement

Was the shift of tactics by the civil rights movement in the 1940s and 1950s the main reason for the passing of the Civil Rights Act in 1964? (20 marks)

Average student answer

During the 1940s and 1950s civil rights groups began to move away from chasing legal enforcement of their rights to demonstrating to protest about their lack of civil rights. This was a shift in direction, not a total change, but it was something that protesters used more and more, becoming their main tactic. They saw it as a more useful tactic because they got more media attention from it and the publicity was useful.

In the 1950s the main tactic of the civil rights movement to gain equality was to go to the law and sue someone for not giving black Americans their rights. The NAACP (National Association for the Advancement of Colored People, one of the big civil rights organisations) had lawyers who chose cases that they thought would win (so cases with people who the prosecution could not say they had a criminal record, or were not good members of society in some way) and took them to court. They were not always successful and the laws, once passed, had to be properly enforced to gain black Americans any real advantage. However, there were times when there were significant successes, such as the *Brown v the Board of Education* case, which said that 'separate but equal' didn't work in schools and that schools should be desegregated. This case is an example of the problem of getting laws enforced, though. It had to be added to set a timescale and it caused a lot of anger, not sympathy, against black Americans in the South. The children who tried to desegregate schools in the South (like the Little Rock Nine) met a lot of violence and hatred. However, even in 1957, media coverage got sympathy in the North and from some Southerners and from the rest of the world, making the USA look bad.

In the 1960s the campaigns moved to using more and more of the tactics that had media appeal – peaceful direct action such as sit-ins and marches. These tactics were developed by the SCLC and spread after Martin Luther King managed the Montgomery bus boycott in this way and stressed the rules of looking respectable, behaving respectfully, making it quite clear who the enemy was in 1955. They used this in Little Rock, the students all dressed very well and were told not to fight back even if it was really difficult because all the white kids (and some of the teachers) were being racist. These tactics were developed from Ghandi's peaceful protest methods used in India. These tactics made for good photos and, increasingly, good television footage. The fact that at the Greensboro lunch counter black Americans doing the sit-in were well dressed and polite and not aggressive made them look good – whereas the whites who

> This is a weak opening paragraph because, while it discusses the 1940s and 1950s, it doesn't address the Civil Rights Act.
>
> The point made is very generalised.
>
> It could be improved by being more specific and tying it to the question.

> The candidate has some good points, but has still not tied this to the Civil Rights Act.
>
> More analysis and less narrative are needed, too.

were attacking them, pouring food and blowing smoke and also shouting looked bad – just as they did in Little Rock. Getting arrested and filling the jails was another important tactic that caught media attention (especially if it was Martin Luther King getting arrested). This showed the police as overreacting and filled the jails (like they did in Birmingham), which made things difficult for them.

While it still has too much narrative, these paragraphs also have some analysis of why the tactics were important.

If the campaigners hadn't changed their tactics in the 1940s and 1950s, maybe the media wouldn't have been as interested and it is fairly clear that it was the media interest that put a lot of pressure on politicians to act. When a lot of people in the USA and out of it were shocked by the things that were happening then there was a reason to step in and force some changes, rather than just thinking that things would sort themselves out and hoping that the problem would just go away. It was the pressure on politicians that would get the Civil Rights Act passed.

The candidate has finally got to the Civil Rights Act and made a clear link between it and the change in tactics.

As the 1960s went on and civil rights became more of a media issue then the campaigners went a step further. The civil rights campaigners continued peaceful protest tactics – but they went to places where they were sure to get a violent white reaction (like the Deep South) – to deliberately make the news and spread images of white brutality – including police brutality. This is what they did in the Freedom rides which turned very violent and there were even bombs and it was the police behind some of it. They deliberately used mostly young people and a mix of black and white (and the young whites were often middle-class white kids, so they looked like the kids of the people watching television) which was important in getting sympathy and media coverage. Also the protests got bigger. This was significant because now politicians could see black and white, young and old, from North and South, in large numbers were all campaigning for civil rights.

The candidate extends the time period and ties the changes to why they were important.

So far, only the shift in tactics has been considered as a reason.

Also, the 1960s were a time where more people had liberal beliefs anyway and where many young people were more radicalised. So it was a time when support for the civil rights movement was likely to happen. There was more support from politicians too, like Kennedy and Johnson. Some politicians supported the movement anyway. Others were more likely to support it when they found that it had a large amount of support (as the number of protesters at events grew – as with the March on Washington). This support from politicians was important, because there were still a lot of politicians (from the South mostly, but also the North) who had no time for supporting civil rights and members of the public, North and South, who were against segregation. The Ku Klux Klan in the South were especially violent from the time they were set up in 1915. Had there been less of a push for change in Congress, they might have been even worse.

The candidate produces other possible factors, but they need to be more developed.

The 1964 Civil Rights Act happened when it did for several reasons – the change in tactics, the rise in publicity, the liberal feeling of the time and the rising number of campaigners. I think the change in tactics was the main reason for the Act being passed when it was. It was the shift in tactics that was really important in getting the campaigners more publicity, not only in the USA, but all over the world.

In the concluding paragraph the candidate reaches a judgement but doesn't clearly explain the reasons for it.

Verdict

This is an average answer because:

- it has far more narrative than analysis
- it doesn't come to a strong, reasoned judgement
- there are no inaccuracies, but many points are made without development and explanation.

However, the essay structure is good and it shapes itself to the question.

Use the feedback on this essay to rewrite it, making as many improvements as you can.

Paper 1: AS Level sample answer with comments

Section A

These questions assess your understanding of the period in breadth. They will ask you about the content you learned about in the four key themes, and may ask about more than one theme. For these questions remember to:

- give an analytical, not a descriptive, response
- support your points with evidence
- cover the whole time period specified in the question
- come to a substantiated judgement.

Was the shift of tactics by the civil rights movement in the 1940s and 1950s the main reason for the passing of the Civil Rights Act in 1964? (20 marks)

Strong student answer

During the 1940s and 1950s civil rights groups began to move away from chasing legal enforcement of their rights to demonstrating to protest about their lack of civil rights. This was a shift in direction, not a total change, but it was something that protesters used more and more, because it attracted more media attention, and this raised the profile of the issue. Also, as the campaigns attracted more attention worldwide, it meant that the USA looked bad when the world saw pictures of the police firing water cannon at children (as they did in Birmingham in 1963). This put pressure on the government to change the situation. However, there were other reasons for the Civil Rights Act being passed when it was, including an increasing liberal government attitude.

> This is a good opening paragraph because it analyses the question and sets up a framework to answer it.

Early civil rights campaigns had focused on court battles for rights, led by NAACP lawyers (such as the 1954 *Brown v the Board of Education* case which got a Supreme Court ruling on desegregating schools). But earlier campaigners also protested by marching, picketing and boycotting segregated services and shops. As early as 1947 there was the Journey of Reconciliation where people rode inter-state segregated buses to protest at segregation. A significant point of change was the Montgomery Bus Boycott in 1955. It was one of the first civil rights actions to gain wide media coverage, mainly due to the length of time the boycott went on and the willingness of black Americans in Montgomery to work together. It also showed the organisational ability and the media-management qualities of Martin Luther King, who led the committee that ran the boycott. The coverage of the boycott showed civil rights leaders that they were more likely to get media coverage if they continued to employ non-violent protest tactics and media coverage meant they became an issue that politicians had to address, not something to sweep under the carpet. Then the coverage of the moves to integrate schools after the Brown decision sent pictures of Elizabeth Eckford's brave walk to school surrounded by angry mothers and there was significant coverage outside the USA, where many people were shocked by the image. It was putting pressure on politicians to act to help civil rights and it was pressure to act that led to the Civil Rights Act.

> This paragraph gives supported description of the change in tactics, analyses why it was important and ties it to the Civil Rights Act.

In the 1960s the use of non-violent direct action increased. It was succeeding in raising the profile of the civil rights movement worldwide. The 1960 Greensboro lunch counter sit-in opened a new phase of non-violent campaigns being led by young people. The four men who started the sit-in were all from the local college and they were mostly joined by young people. The SNCC was founded as a direct result of these sit-ins and its membership was largely young people, black and white. The Greensboro lunch counter campaigners and those who followed were following the direct action rules. They were dressing well and behaving well. The SNCC trained its volunteers in how to put up with harassment without reacting badly in a deliberate attempt to create the right media image. The contrast between the campaigners and the whites who were harassing them was dramatic.

> These paragraphs develop and analyse the shifts in campaigning that happened up until the passing of the Civil Rights Act with detailed analysis and support.

If the campaigners hadn't changed their tactics in the 1940s and 1950s, maybe the media wouldn't have been as interested. It was certainly more interested in the campaigns that deliberately went to places, like Birmingham, Alabama, where there was almost bound to be violence. This wasn't starting a fight, but it was provoking the violence. On the other hand the SNCC campaigns for voter registration over several years, with a big push in Mississippi in 1964, were not so well covered by the media. They were slow, steady campaigns to persuade black people to vote and to get them ready for the voter registration test. The only large-scale coverage of this was when three students on the Freedom Summer campaign were murdered. The tone of the reporting and the slant that the media gave the campaign (by their focus on the violence) was largely sympathetic to the campaigners. As images of the police setting dogs on protesters in Birmingham (1963) or bombing buses (1961) beamed around the world, people in other countries were shocked. After Birmingham, Kennedy said he was ashamed, and that is partly because what was happening was now so public.

> These paragraphs develop and analyse the shifts in campaigning that happened up until the passing of the Civil Rights Act with detailed analysis and support.

However, the Civil Rights Act probably also came when it did because of several other factors. The growing number of campaigners, black and white, made a big impact on politicians: all these people had a vote to give to someone who supported causes they supported. Martin Luther King was probably also a factor, and not just because he was one of the leaders of the movement who supported the change in tactics. He was an excellent spokesman for the cause and he had a moderate, considered way of dealing with the mainly white politicians in Congress that won his cause significant support. Also, the general feeling of the time was becoming more liberal. There was a growing feeling in government that it was time to act on civil rights. Truman had desegregated the army in 1948 by executive order because he hadn't been able to convince Congress to pass the legislation. It was part of the shift that led Kennedy to write his book about immigration that criticised anti-immigrant feeling. More people, politicians and public were talking about the need for equality. Black and white Americans had mixed more during the war and there was a rising feeling among young white students, especially in the North, that life in the USA was too unequal for all minorities. This is not to downplay the racist views of many other white Americans, nor their violent reaction to civil rights protests, but it is more moderate Americans taking the civil rights side in large numbers for the first time.

> This paragraph introduces other factors other than the shift in tactics and it makes the link clearly, with detailed analysis and support.

The 1964 Civil Rights Act happened when it did for several reasons: the liberal feeling of the time, King's personality, the rising number of campaigners. However, all of these threads could be linked to the change in campaigning tactics and it seems to me that this was the most important reason. It probably contributed to the rising support and it is probable that, without the change in tactics, there would not have been as great a rise in media attention and so the worldwide attention on the issue which must have been a significant push to politicians to get the act passed.

> The concluding paragraph mainly restates points made earlier.
>
> Candidates need to pick out the key arguments and come to a reasoned judgement.

Verdict

This is a strong answer because:

- it considers a number of factors in reasonable depth
- it analyses the question and focuses on the right time period
- it develops and explains the points it makes and makes links
- it comes to a strong, reasoned judgement.

Paper 1: AS Level sample answer with comments

Section B

These questions assess your understanding of the course in breadth and will cover a period of 30 years or more. They will ask you about the content you learned about in the four key themes, and may ask about more than one theme. The question will also require you to explore a range of concepts, such as change over time, similarity and difference, as well as significance. For these questions remember to:

- identify the focus of the question
- consider the concepts you will need to explore
- support your points with evidence from across the time period specified in the question
- develop the evidence you deploy to build up your overall judgement
- come to a substantiated judgement that directly addresses the question set.

To what extent were the style and actions of the president responsible for the changes in levels of public confidence in government in the years 1929–80?

Average student answer

The president is a very important part of US politics, with real power and he can take a major role in government. So his actions and the way that he relates to the public and the media that present him to the public have a significant effect on public confidence in the government because he is the government, to many people. So if he lies to the public (as Nixon did over Watergate) or if he's bad at making speeches and connecting with people (as Jimmy Carter was) then the public will lose confidence. However, there were other factors that shook public confidence in government that were not tied so tightly to the president and his behaviour – the economy in general and government handling of events such as the Three Mile Island incident in 1979.

Presidential style had a big effect on the public. And as it involved how the president handled Congress and the media (it isn't just a president's personality), a president's style does affect how well the administration's government works. Because if a president isn't managing Congress well, then it is harder to pass laws and so it is harder for the government to be effective. And if the government isn't effective then people are going to lose confidence in it. As well as this, if a president handles the media badly, he won't be shown in a good light, and that will affect the reaction of the public to the government. So Nixon could have good policies (and he did well with China and also his welfare reforms) yet fail to put them over well to the media and to the public. He was a suspicious man and a poor speaker and it was hard for him to overcome these hurdles, even before the Watergate cover-up exposed how far he was prepared to go to stay in power. That said, he did get re-elected in 1972 so people must have thought well enough of him to do that. Kennedy's style, on the other hand, was very persuasive. He was young, good looking and confident and made very good speeches. So actions that might have damaged the government in the eyes of the public under a different president (such as the Bay of Pigs disaster in Cuba) were more easily forgiven because of his style. It was as if he and his family hypnotised the media and the public with their glamour.

Presidential actions were also very important in confidence or the lack of it. One of the biggest knocks to public confidence was the Watergate cover-up. It was bad enough that Nixon was prepared to spy on people and rob their offices to get re-elected. But the way that more and more revelations came about taping conversations in his own office, covering-up and trying to pretend he didn't know about the break in and then making things worse by not releasing and then doctoring the tapes ... It made people very worried that the presidential system allowed

This is a good first paragraph. It begins in a fairly clumsy, generalised way, but moves on to give examples.

It could be improved by a positive example of presidential style (e.g. Roosevelt) which as well as negatives would also help to demonstrate an understanding of the timeframe.

The candidate also understands that there are other factors that have to be considered.

The candidate still isn't using the whole timeframe and is also beginning to handle presidential style alone, and in a fairly discursive way.

More focus on the question is needed, especially on the phrase 'to what extent'.

for someone like that to get into power. This was very different to Roosevelt. He arrived and his actions were positive and decisive. He showed people he was going to tackle the Depression and got people to go along with him and have confidence in his plans and policies. His actions were vital in restoring public confidence and he had a good manner to go along with that, which helped build confidence even more.

The president definitely had an effect on how confident people were in their government – whether it was his style or his actions. The extent of it was probably variable depending on what exactly his style was (Roosevelt's confident manner) and what he was doing (Nixon and Watergate). How far it affected public confidence also depended on what else was happening that might affect public confidence. So, if you think about the economy, then the Depression was a terrible time and Roosevelt managed to affect public confidence for the better, even while there were economic problems that were making people feel the government couldn't cope. So he had an impact that overrode the impact of the economy. But when there was the fuel crisis (in 1973 and then again a few years later) it was an economic crisis and the product of the actions of groups outside the country. It was produced by other factors. But the reaction of the then president (Carter) couldn't stop it and it did have a bad effect on confidence in the government.

What other things affected public confidence in government? Well, there were outside events that were not really in the president's control (as when the oil producing countries set off the fuel crisis for Carter). You could say that wars were not really part of presidential style or actions, but people did blame the presidents who were in power during the war in Vietnam for entering the war or not pulling the troops out of the war and so war could be seen as a presidential action. There was government economic policy, which was partly driven by the president, but also by Congress and so was more a government effect. And when the government didn't seem to be handling the economy well, or seemed to be handing out too much in welfare, or letting too many immigrants into the country for some people then confidence went down in the government.

Social things, such as being liberal over welfare, but also the conditions of the inner cities, rising crime and drug problems – all of these things could also lead to a loss of confidence. If people felt less safe, or less well off, or as if the country was declining then they would feel that the government wasn't working. Some people would lose confidence if they felt that government policies were changing society in a way they didn't want society to go (as when the 1960s seemed to have too many young people going in a different direction and being radical). Confidence was something that would fall if people felt their situation wasn't any better, or was getting worse.

So the president (his style and actions) had a significant effect on public opinion. It could be a decisive effect, but it was not a steady thing. The extent of the effect depended on how bad the actions were (Watergate) or how strong the style was (the Depression). If a president wasn't effective then other factors that were not directly related to the president could have more effect.

> The candidate has now expanded their timeframe, which makes the answer better, but gives no examples of how Roosevelt built confidence by his actions and style.
>
> The full timeframe is still not covered and there isn't enough analysis.

> The candidate has made a good point here, but has not developed it fully.
>
> It would help if the candidate expanded the examples – Nixon and Watergate are appearing too often.

> Again, a good point but, especially in the second paragraph, not enough development.
>
> The candidate produces, but doesn't analyse, other important factors, so does not convincingly address 'extent'.

> The concluding paragraph mainly restates points made earlier without analysing how they support the judgement made.

Verdict

This is an average answer because:

- it doesn't consider the full time range
- there is too much narrative and not enough analysis
- there are no inaccuracies, but many points are made without development and explanation
- the grammar is poor in places
- it doesn't come to a strong, reasoned judgement.

Use the feedback on this essay to rewrite it, making as many improvements as you can.

Paper 1: AS Level sample answer with comments

Section B

These questions assess your understanding of the period in breadth and will cover a period of 30 years or more. They will ask you about the content you learned about in the four key themes, and may ask about more than one theme. The question will also require you to explore a range of concepts, such as change over time, similarity and difference, as well as significance. For these questions remember to:

- identify the focus of the question
- consider the concepts you will need to explore
- support your points with evidence from across the time period specified in the question
- develop the evidence you deploy to build up your overall judgement
- come to a substantiated judgement that directly addresses the question set.

To what extent were the style and actions of the president responsible for the changes in levels of public confidence in government in the years 1929–80?

Strong student answer

Public confidence can be affected by a whole variety of factors. The president, as the face of government, could have a significant effect on public confidence in government and has done from Hoover to Carter. Ever since Roosevelt, presidents have felt the need to work hard on their public image and at making a 'relationship' with the public to keep public confidence. This became even more necessary after TV brought not only the voices of politicians, but images too. However, there are other influences on public confidence: how well the economy is doing, how well society is doing as a whole and how well individual members of the public feel they are doing. The media has a part to play in all of these factors – how the media reacts to the president and to the effects of government policy can have a big effect on public opinion. So the extent that the president himself affects public reaction depends on the other things that are happening at the time.

Hoover's actions once the Depression hit did not make him popular. He was blamed for the Hoovervilles that sprang up all over the country and he certainly was responsible for the way the Bonus Army was treated – including sending in the military. The public didn't blame Hoover for all the problems though. It was clearly the general economic policy of government, including the laws Congress was passing. However when Hoover was replaced by Roosevelt the president was vital in the building of public confidence. It seems almost impossible that Hoover, if re-elected, would have been able to produce the New Deal, even if he had shifted to New Deal thinking. Roosevelt swept in and charmed Congress into giving him rights presidents usually only had in wartime. Then he made sure he explained carefully to the media and the public what he was doing. So he got the media onto his side so it was talking supportively about his policies then his 'fireside chats' on the radio rebuilt public confidence. The president and his actions and the media worked to build this confidence despite the huge economic problems. Often the presidential factors are closely tied to the media when thinking about public confidence. Later, Carter lost confidence in a bad economic situation that was not as bad as the Depression, because he didn't seem confident himself about the situation and because the media didn't have confidence in him either.

Presidential style and actions could make a bad situation worse, too. Nixon was a suspicious man and a poor speaker and it was hard for him to overcome these hurdles, even before the Watergate cover-up exposed how far he was prepared to go to stay in power. Watergate finished him entirely. Kennedy's style, on the other hand, was very persuasive. He was young, good looking

> This is a strong first paragraph. It shows the candidate has a grasp on the timeframe and realises that it is important to consider the extent of the influence of the president.

> In these paragraphs, the candidate uses the whole timeframe and also analyses the circumstances of Roosevelt's effect on public confidence during the Depression and Carter's effect later.
>
> The candidate also points out the links between one factor and another.

and confident and made very good speeches. So actions that might have damaged the government in the eyes of the public under a different president (such as the Bay of Pigs disaster in Cuba) were more easily forgiven because of who the president making the mistake was.

While the president was seen as 'the face' of government and responsible for foreign policy and basic policy, most people in the USA understood that general policy was driven by Congress – they knew that Congress made the laws, even though the president had a veto and could use executive orders to make some changes. So public confidence in government was also going to be affected by government policy more generally. This factor that affected confidence was the factor behind the backlash voting that switched from Hoover and the Republicans to Roosevelt and the Democrats in 1932 and behind the backlash away from liberal, Democrat policies back to Reagan's Republican ideas in 1980. In each case there was an accumulation of social factors that meant that many people just didn't want the same kind of government anymore.

In 1932, the public lost confidence in Republican *laissez-faire* policies. People saw that these policies were not working. They did not feel that the Republican government would ever do enough to help – it was against their principles. So they lost confidence in that way of running the country. In 1980 the swing was the other way. After years of liberal reforms many people felt that their confidence in the government's policies had fallen. Roosevelt's New Deal and the liberal policies it had brought had worked, and had set the standard for federal government's involvement in providing for the needs of the poor. However, by 1980, there was a feeling that Johnson's Great Society measures were not helping to solve the problem of poverty. Instead, people began to complain that they were being taxed too highly and were not benefiting from this taxation – the poor who didn't work were. While this was not what everyone felt, it was no accident that the Reagan campaign's most significant question was did people feel better off than they had been four years before.

I think that there are times when the president does something that overrides any other factor that might affect public opinion. One of the biggest knocks to public confidence was the Watergate cover-up. It was bad enough that Nixon was prepared to spy on people and rob their offices to get re-elected. But the way that more and more revelations came about taping conversations in his own office, covering-up and trying to pretend he didn't know about the break-in and then making things worse by not releasing and then doctoring the tapes … it piled awfulness on awfulness. It made a huge number of people very worried that the presidential system allowed for someone like that to get into power. This was the point where some people even began to worry not just about the government, but about the system itself. However, these times don't happen very often. The wide range of political opinion in the country means that things have to get very extreme for almost the whole country to feel the same way. People felt so strongly about Nixon that they didn't elect Ford but turned to Carter instead, despite his inexperience and Ford's competent filling in as president because Ford pardoned Nixon and Carter said he wouldn't lie.

At other times, people are probably more likely to react to their own circumstances and beliefs and prejudices. And they can lose faith in the government for not controlling events that are mainly outside the control of government. So when the oil producing countries set off the fuel crisis there was nothing the government could do to make OPEC change its mind. It wanted to disrupt things in the countries it refused to sell oil to, and it did. The way the media presented the crisis made the public blame the government and then lose confidence because the media was saying the government was handling the crisis badly.

Government economic and social welfare policies had the biggest impact on people's lives and so, in many ways, were the most likely to drive public opinion. They were partly driven by the president, but also by Congress and so were more a government effect. And when the government didn't seem to be handling the economy well, or seemed to be handing out

The candidate has picked up two alternative factors that influenced public confidence in government and explained their effects.

The candidate now needs to evaluate the various factors.

The concluding paragraph mainly restates points made earlier.

Candidates need to pick out the key arguments and come to a reasoned judgement.

too much in welfare, or letting too many immigrants into the country for some people (as in the 1970s) then confidence went down in the government. Confidence also fell when people considered the conditions of the inner cities, rising crime and drug problems. It looked as though the 'Great Society' wasn't working. If people felt less safe, or less well off, or as if the country was declining then they would feel that the government wasn't working. Some people would lose confidence if they felt that government policies were changing society in a way they didn't want society to go (as when the 1960s seemed to have too many young people going in a different direction and being radical). Confidence was something that would fall if people felt their situation wasn't any better, or was getting worse.

It seems to me that the influence of the president and his actions on public opinion varied in its extent. You can't say that from 1929 to 1980 the president influenced public confidence at, for example, 60 percent, as compared to social issues at 30 percent and so on. Public opinion had a variety of influences acting on it and it shifted depending on combinations of these. So I think that Roosevelt had by far the biggest influence of anything on the rise of confidence once he set the New Deal in motion. On the other hand, I think that when public opinion swung against the government in the late 1970s it was reacting to the style and actions of several presidents but also, and probably more so, to the liberal thinking of the previous decades and the way that they had changed society. You can pick points like this and make a judgement about the balance of the various factors, but for the whole period you can't do it – you just have to say it varied.

> The concluding paragraph gives its conclusion supported by reference to the other possible influences.

Verdict

This is a strong answer because:

- it uses the full time range for its examples
- there are no inaccuracies, and many points are developed and explained
- it comes to a strong, reasoned judgement
- it analyses the impact of the various factors throughout.

Paper 1: AS Level sample answer with comments

Section C

These questions require you to read and analyse two extracts carefully in order to develop a response which examines and makes an informed judgement about different interpretations. The best answers:

- need to show an understanding of the extracts and identify the key points of interpretation
- deploy own knowledge to develop the points emerging from the extracts and provide necessary context
- develop a judgement after developing and weighing up different interpretations.

Study Extracts 1 and 9 (from Chapter 5, pages 116 and 135) before you answer this question.

Historians have different views about the impact of the Reagan presidency on the USA. Analyse and evaluate the extracts and use your knowledge of the issues to explain your answer to the following question.

How far do you agree with the view that Reagan's administration 'altered the landscape of political debate and public policy' in the years 1981–96? (Extract 9, lines 5–6)

To explain your answer, analyse and evaluate the material in both extracts, using your own knowledge of the issues.

Average student answer

The two extracts certainly seem to be saying different things. Extract 9 says that it was the Reagan administration that shifted thinking away from liberal thinking towards conservativism. Hodgson, in Extract 1, on the other hand, talks about liberalism declining before Reagan comes to power. He sees the 1970s as a time when more and more people were becoming more conservative in their views. So one of them thinks Reagan's administration was at the bottom of the change while the other one doesn't.

Reagan came to power with some clear intentions, including cutting back on 'big government' (which is what he called federal intervention in business, state and local government and the lives of US citizens). He made it quite plain that he was against the level to which the government provided welfare benefits and social care via the systems set up by Johnson's Great Society measures which were put in place when liberal ideas still had a lot of public and political support. Reagan said that he wanted to stop people 'sponging' on welfare (as he saw it) and he also wanted to tie benefits that people received more tightly to working. He also wanted low taxes.

All this would seem to confirm Dunn and Woodward's idea that Reagan brought the shift towards conservative thinking and New Right policies, including low taxes and 'workfare'. It is certainly true that after Reagan's presidency many New Right ideas stayed in place. The impact of the Reagan administration on political debate meant that the Democrats had to reform their ideas and policies, they couldn't just promise the same commitment to social welfare as before because it would have to come with higher taxes and people showed, as the Reagan presidency went on, that they favoured the policy of lower taxes. So I think it is fair to say that *after* the Reagan administration the conservative ideas of the administration became ideas that drove both political debate and policy.

However, while both the political debate and policy can be said to have changed after the Reagan administration, that does not mean that this change was begun by the administration. So it isn't yet possible to give the administration the credit for actually starting this change. Is there evidence that before Reagan there was a move beginning towards conservative policies and conservative thinking? Dunn certainly thinks so. Extract 1 says that there was a decline in people calling themselves liberal and that many people were also coming to think that federal intervention was

---

Some overall understanding is shown and reasonable use is made of the extracts.

It could be improved by developing more detail and tying the points more tightly to the question.

This paragraph is an improvement on the first.

The candidate introduces some of their own knowledge, and it is accurate.

While the first paragraph is just descriptive, the second one shows some attempt at analysis.

The candidate has produced information from Extract 1 to counter the argument put by Extract 9.

The candidate has also produced supporting evidence from their own knowledge for Hodgson's argument.

There is still no information from outside the extracts.

not the right way to solve social problems. This is just the kind of thinking that can be found in the Reagan administration's anti 'big government' policies. So are the other moves in thinking that he gives, including an unwillingness to pay higher and higher taxes.

There is evidence outside Extract 1 for the beginning of a change in thinking starting before Reagan came to power. Many people were beginning to object to paying higher property taxes. They complained that their taxes were all getting put into welfare provision and they weren't getting any benefit from the higher taxes at all. The growing religious right was arguing for conservative measures from the early 1970s and the number of people campaigning against abortion was growing. Anti-gay groups were on the rise, too. All of this ties in with the point in Extract 1 about deriding political correctness when talking about minority groups.

Even the Carter administration, which was in power at the end of the 1970s, was beginning to shift their liberal position. Carter introduced tax cuts – this was something that the Reagan administration discussed as a new departure. So it seems likely that any president to be elected in 1980 (Democrat or Republican) would have continued to see cutting taxes as good.

Overall the balance of the argument seems to lie with Hodgson's argument. I think that it is clear that there was a significant shift away from liberal thinking even before Reagan was elected. We know that he had support from conservative groups and the radical right; we even know that he disappointed both these groups by not going far enough for these groups once he became president, due to the fact that Congress turned down some of his conservative proposals. However, I do think that the Reagan administration accelerated the change. Reagan knew he had been elected to bring change and New Right thinking, so his administration did its best to do so.

Here the candidate uses evidence from their own knowledge that is relevant to the argument to provide more support for the extract that seems to be the one the candidate favours.

However, the evidence and the conclusions are fairly basic.

This is quite a good summing up. The candidate decides which argument is most reasonable and gives some reasons for their choice.

It would be improved by expanding the supporting material.

Verdict

This is an average answer because:

- it is not rooted closely enough in the extracts and they are not linked effectively
- there is not enough context given
- however, there is no incorrect information and the candidate tries to analyse the extracts in relation to the question
- it makes a judgement but it needs more substance. It lacks the necessary sense of argument for a high level.

Use the feedback on this essay to rewrite it, making as many improvements as you can.

Paper 1: AS Level sample answer with comments

Section C

These questions require you to read and analyse two extracts carefully in order to develop a response which examines and makes an informed judgement about different interpretations. The best answers:

- need to show an understanding of the extracts and identify the key points of interpretation
- deploy own knowledge to develop the points emerging from the extracts and provide necessary context
- develop a judgement after developing and weighing up different interpretations.

Study Extracts 1 and 9 (from Chapter 5, pages 116 and 135) before you answer this question.

Historians have different views about the impact of the Reagan presidency on the USA. Analyse and evaluate the extracts and use your knowledge of the issues to explain your answer to the following question.

How far do you agree with the view that Reagan's administration 'altered the landscape of political debate and public policy' in the years 1981–96? (Extract 9, lines 5–6)

To explain your answer, analyse and evaluate the material in both extracts, using your own knowledge of the issues.

Strong student answer

The two extracts certainly seem to be saying different things. Dunn and Woodward (hereafter just Dunn) state very clearly that it was the Reagan administration that shifted political debate and policy lines away from liberal and New Deal thinking towards conservativism and what many people call New Right thinking. The implication of what they are saying is that if Reagan hadn't become president then this swing wouldn't have come about. Hodgson, on the other hand, talks about liberalism declining before Reagan comes to power. He sees the 1970s as a time when more and more people were becoming more conservative in their views. Now, if this is the case then it wasn't the Reagan administration that altered the landscape: it was changing anyway.

Reagan came to power announcing he was going to make changes. These included cutting back on 'big government', by which he meant federal intervention in business, state and local government and the lives of US citizens. He made it quite plain that he was against the level to which the government provided welfare benefits and social care via the systems set up by Johnson's Great Society measures. He wanted to stop people 'sponging' on welfare (as he saw it) and wanted to tie benefits that people received more tightly to working. He also wanted low taxes. He put himself forward as a complete change from previous administrations (all the way back to Roosevelt) who took on more and more federal social welfare responsibility. The speech would seem to confirm the Dunn idea that Reagan brought the shift towards conservative thinking and New Right policies, including low taxes and 'workfare'. It is certainly true that after Reagan's presidency many New Right ideas stayed in place – including the need for low taxes and a lower level of federal intervention. This was the case even for the next Democrat to become president – Bill Clinton. The impact of the Reagan administration on political debate meant that the Democrats had to reform their ideas and policies under the Democratic Leadership Council. So I think it is fair to say that *after* the Reagan administration left office, their conservative ideas became ideas that drove both political debate and policy. If not, then the Democrats wouldn't have had to take on the policies of low taxes and reduced federal intervention.

However, while both the political debate and policy changed after the Reagan administration, that does not mean that this change was begun by the administration. So it isn't yet possible to give the administration the credit for starting this change. Is there evidence that before Reagan there was a move beginning towards conservative policies and conservative thinking? Dunn

An effective opening paragraph which focuses on the extracts and identifies their key arguments. It cites some of the evidence put forward and begins to set up the debate.

This paragraph provides context by considering Reagan's intentions on coming to power and what they suggested in terms of policy and political issues.

It also analyses how this relates to the policies of the Reagan administration and what happened after.

This paragraph and the next analyse Hodgson's argument, with contextual points well developed to show that there is evidence outside the extract to support his point of view.

certainly thinks so. Extract 1 says that there was a decline in people calling themselves liberal (presumably this is from census evidence) and that many people were also coming to think that federal intervention was not the right way to solve social problems. The extract also suggests there was a move towards 'free markets'. All of these shifts in thinking can be found in the Reagan administration's anti 'big government' ways of thinking. So are the other moves in thinking that he gives, including an unwillingness to pay higher and higher taxes to fund welfare.

There is evidence outside Extract 1 for the beginning of a change in thinking starting before Reagan came to power. Because the economy was in trouble and the government seemed to be unable to cope (for example, during the two fuel crisis periods in the 1970s), people were losing confidence in the government, were more critical and outspoken about their lack of confidence and so encouraged Republicans to think they could win an election by appealing to this new conservative reaction. In 1978 California's Proposition 18 was a revolt against higher property taxes and raised the debate on taxes in general to a higher level. The growing religious right was arguing for conservative measures from the early 1970s (groups like Phyllis Schlafly's STOP ERA) and the numbers of people campaigning against abortion was growing. Anti-gay groups were also on the rise (with Proposition 6 against gay teachers) and this ties in with the way that more people were being critical of affirmative action for non-whites and women, which supports the point in Extract 1 about deriding political correctness when talking about minority groups.

Even the Carter administration, which was in power at the end of the 1970s, was beginning to shift their liberal position. Carter had, for instance, begun to deregulate some businesses. Deregulation (removing federal controls from a business) was one of the policies Reagan presented as 'new' for reducing big government. Carter also introduced tax cuts in the last two years of his presidency – this was something else that the Reagan administration discussed as a new departure. So it seems likely that any president to be elected in 1980 (Democrat or Republican) would have continued these tactics.

> This section introduces some accurate recall to support the idea of the changes having begun in the 1970s.

Overall the balance of the argument seems to lie with Hodgson's argument. I think that it is clear that there was a significant shift away from liberal thinking even before Reagan was elected; indeed, it was one of the reasons he was elected. We know that he had support from conservative groups and the radical right; we even know that he disappointed both these groups by not going far enough for these groups once he became president, due to the fact that Congress turned down some of his conservative proposals. However, I do think that the Reagan administration accelerated the change. Reagan knew he had been elected to bring change and New Right thinking, so his administration did its best to do so. Because of this, I think that the *extent* of the change probably is due to the Reagan administration, although the change would probably have come anyway, perhaps more slowly, under a different administration.

> The concluding paragraph comes to a clear judgement based on the balance of the evidence.

Verdict

This is a strong answer because:

- it identifies and illustrates the arguments of the two extracts
- it deploys a sound range of specific evidence to develop points emerging from the extracts
- it provides a sense of the context
- it develops an argument which considers both interpretations and tries to provide balance
- there is a clear judgement.

Preparing for your A Level Paper 1 exam

Advance planning

- Draw up a timetable for your revision and try to keep to it. Spread your timetable over a number of weeks, and aim to cover four or five topics each week.

- Spend longer on topics which you have found difficult, and revise them several times.

- Above all, do not try to limit your revision by attempting to 'question spot'. Try to be confident about all aspects of your Paper 1 work, because this will ensure that you have a choice of questions in Sections A and B.

Paper 1 overview:

AL Paper 1	Time: 2 hours 15 minutes	
Section A	Answer 1 question from a choice of 2	20 marks
Section B	Answer 1 question from a choice of 2	20 marks
Section C	Answer 1 compulsory interpretations question	20 marks
	Total marks =	60 marks

You should familiarise yourself with the layout of the paper by looking at the examples published by Edexcel. The questions for each section are followed by eight pages of lined paper where you should write your answer.

Section A and Section B questions

The essay questions in Sections A and B are similar in form. They ask you to reach a judgement on an aspect of the course you have studied, and will deal with one or more historical concepts of change, continuity, similarity, difference, cause, consequence and significance. The question stems which will be used will include 'To what extent...', 'How far...', 'How significant was...' and so on. You should consider the issue raised by the question, develop your answer by looking at other relevant points, and reach a judgement in your conclusion.

The main difference between Section A and Section B questions will be the timespan of the questions. Section A questions will cover a period of ten years or more, while Section B questions will be concerned with at least one-third of the period you have studied.

A Section A question for Paper 1F might read 'How far do you agree that it was Hoover's failures that lost him the 1932 presidential election?' Your answer should consider the ways in which Hoover could have been seen to fail, the factors outside his control (for example, the actions of Congress and the impact of Roosevelt's campaign), before reaching an overall judgement on the question.

A Section B question on the same paper will cover a longer period of time, but have a similar shape. For example, 'To what extent was US involvement in the Second World War responsible for improvements in the position of women in the years 1945–60?' Here you should consider how the position of women improved in the stated period, the limits of that improvement and how they might be related to the war (for example, was the economic boom tied to the war?). You should conclude by reaching a judgement on the question.

Section C questions

There is no choice in Section C, which is concerned with the historical interpretations you have studied linked to the question 'What impact did the Reagan presidency (1981–89) have on the USA in the years 1981–96?' You will be given two extracts totalling around 400 words (printed separately) and the question will take the form 'How convincing do you find the view that...?' There is no need to use source analysis skills such as making inferences or considering provenance for Section C answers. You should approach your answer by analysing both extracts separately, and then use your own knowledge to support, and to counter, the view given in the question, before reaching an overall judgement.

Use of time

This is an issue which you should discuss with your teachers and fellow students, but here are some suggestions for you.

1. Do not write solidly for 45 minutes on each question. For Section A and B answers you should spend a few minutes working out what the question is asking you to do, and drawing up a plan of your answer. This is especially important for Section B answers, which cover an extended period of time.

2. For Section C it is essential that you have a clear understanding of the content of each extract and the points which each extract is making. Read each extract carefully and underline important points. You might decide to spend up to ten minutes reading the extracts and drawing up your plan, and 35 minutes writing your answer.

Preparing for your A Level exams

Paper 1: A Level sample answer with comments

Section A

These questions assess your understanding of the period in breadth. They will ask you about the content you learned about in the four key themes, and may ask about more than one theme. For these questions remember to:

- give an analytical, not a descriptive, response
- support your points with evidence
- cover the whole time period specified in the question
- come to a substantiated judgement.

How far do you agree that the position of American women had changed significantly for the better between the years 1917 and 1980? (20 marks)

Average student answer

Women in the USA were not really considered equal to men in this period. Just like the civil rights movement, there was a difference between women having rights in law and women having the rights in actual fact. Discrimination was not always stated but it was almost always there. They were paid less for doing the same job and there were all sorts of jobs that they were not supposed to do. In big companies, very few women made it to the most important jobs in the organisation.

> This is a weak start to the answer. The candidate's focus is on narrative rather than explanation, though there are some implied links to the question here.

In 1920 the 19th Amendment to the Constitution gave women the vote. This was a significant victory and something that women had been campaigning for a long time. However this change was only significant to those women who wanted to vote – usually white middle-class or even better off women. Women who were poor and struggling often saw the vote as irrelevant. So the vote, while a huge change for some, and in the law, did not affect the lives of all women.

> This is a much better section, with a focus on the question and good support for the first point. There is some analysis, not just narrative.

While women had worked during the war there was an expectation that they would give up their jobs once the men came home. They were to give the jobs back to the men who were returning from the war. Even if a man didn't come back for his job, employers wanted to find a man to fill it. Most people expected women to go back to the way they had behaved before they war. They would work until they married and then give up work and stay home to raise and run a family. The social pressure on women to do this was great and some women wanted to do it anyway. So the situation was that, although they had got the vote, there were not as many changes in the way of work post-war as many women might have hoped for.

> It could be improved by more support for the point about post-war work.

The Second World War saw women going into war work again, and proving themselves again. After the war, there was an expectation that women would give up their jobs and return to family life, as before. However there was also a significant change. Many jobs that had been barred to married women had the ban lifted over the war and the ban was not reinstated. Also, shortages meant that black women were allowed to train for some jobs that they hadn't been accepted for before. So their situation changed.

> These paragraphs discuss changes during and after the Second World War.

In the 1950s the story stayed the same. Women were shown everywhere as wives and mothers, or as young, unmarried shopgirls or office workers looking to 'catch' a man. There were exceptions, mostly white, educated women from middle-class families. They could pursue

> The paragraphs are mostly descriptive, although there is some general analysis.

careers as long as they were unmarried. But careers were still the exception for married women, even after the ban was lifted. Non-white women often found they needed to work, unmarried or married and many did, but not in good or well-paid jobs.

In the 1960s and 1970s the women's liberation movement thrived and, to begin with, the pressure that it exerted did win some gains for women. Along with the Civil Rights Act (which called for gender equality as well as racial equality) came calls for 'affirmative action' to iron out inequality. This was very patchily applied. The arrival of the pill and legalised abortion gave women more control over pregnancy as employers were asking in interviews if a woman intended to get pregnant over the next few years. Women campaigned vigorously for the Equal Rights Act. This was passed in Congress several times, but in 1980 had still to be ratified by enough states to pass into law (it still hasn't been). Women got more radical in the 1970s and some of them developed extreme principles, such as saying all men were the enemy. As with the civil rights movement, opponents of women's rights latched onto what the most extreme groups were saying and used this to dismiss the whole movement.

> The information here is accurate but not very detailed.
>
> There is still too much narrative and not enough analysis.

The 1970s were a time when there was a general swing away from liberal ideas and this affected support for equality for women, too. The conservative backlash of the late 1970s found groups springing up to stridently oppose abortion, family planning and women in the workplace. The feeling against equal rights was so strong that in 1979 the USA did not sign a UN resolution to work against gender discrimination.

The position of women definitely changed between 1917 and 1980. Women could vote. They were supposed to be able to get equal pay for doing the same job as a man. They were able to apply for a wider range of education opportunities and jobs. They had more control over pregnancy. There were more women in the professions and running businesses. Not all women benefited to the same degree from the changes – they had to be in a position to take advantage of them – to get an education or training for a better job. Just as with civil rights the legal position of women in 1980 was far better than their actual situation. The backlash of the late 1970s showed that there were many people, including women, that thought women were not really equal.

> The concluding paragraph mainly restates points made earlier.
>
> Candidates need to pick out the key arguments and come to a reasoned judgement.

Verdict

This is an average essay because:

- there is too much narrative and not enough analysis
- there are no inaccuracies, but many points are made without development and explanation
- it doesn't come to a strong, reasoned judgement.

However, it does focus on the question.

Use the feedback on this essay to rewrite it, making as many improvements as you can.

Paper 1: A Level sample answer with comments

Section A

These questions assess your understanding of the period in breadth. They will ask you about the content you learned about in the four key themes, and may ask about more than one theme. For these questions remember to:

- give an analytical, not a descriptive, response
- support your points with evidence
- cover the whole time period specified in the question
- come to a substantiated judgement.

How far do you agree that the position of American women had changed significantly for the better between the years 1917 and 1980? (20 marks)

Strong student answer

In 1917 the war was about to end. Women had done the work of men during the war, yet they didn't have the vote. In 1980 women did have the vote – they had had it since 1920 and no-one was trying to stop them using it. However, by 1980 a proposed change to the Constitution giving women equal rights (the Equal Right Act) had still not been ratified in all states. The fact that women felt the need for such an act to reinforce the 1964 Civil Rights Act shows that women had not achieved full equality by the end of the period. There had been significant changes for women by 1980. Married women were able to find work in many more jobs; in 1917 married women had not been able to teach, for example, whereas by 1980 many teachers were married women. Women could run their own businesses and become highly paid lawyers and surgeons. However, I think that it is important to remember that 'women' covers a wide variety of people, from a variety of backgrounds.

> This is a good opening paragraph because it establishes the timeframe, analyses the question and suggests a direction for the answer.

In 1920 the 19th Amendment to the Constitution gave women the vote. This was a significant victory and something that women had been campaigning for a long time. However this change was only significant to those women who wanted to vote – usually white middle-class or even better off women. Women who were poor and struggling often saw the vote as irrelevant, especially older women. They might vote, but often as their husband told them to. Meanwhile, in the South, all black Americans had trouble voting, because most whites didn't want them to and in some places beat them up if they tried. So the vote, while a huge change for some, and in the law, did not affect the lives of all women.

> The candidate discusses, clearly and with examples, the extent of change post-war and which groups were affected by those changes. It develops points made in the weaker answer and analyses their impact.

While women had worked during the war there was an expectation that they would give up their jobs once the men came home. Many of them had been doing war-work in munitions factories and so on. These jobs disappeared anyway. Most people expected the return to 'normalcy' to include women returning to the way they had behaved before they war. They would work until they married, in a selection of 'suitable' jobs and then, when they married they would give up work and stay home to raise and run a family. The social pressure on women to do this was great and some women wanted to do it anyway. So the situation was that, although they had got the vote, there were not as many changes in the way of work post-war as many women might have hoped for. At best, individual employers were more willing to employ women once they had employed women during the war and saw what they could do. It wasn't a large scale change.

The Second World War saw women going into war work again, and proving themselves again. After the war, there was an expectation that women would give up their jobs and return to family life, as before. However there was also a significant change. Many jobs that had been barred to married women, such as teaching, had the ban lifted over the war and the ban was not reinstated.

Shortages meant that black women were allowed to train for some jobs that they hadn't been accepted for before, such as nursing. Once these nurses showed their ability, they stayed in the system and more were trained. These were significant changes and they were beginning to affect women outside the WASP group.

In the 1950s the story stayed the same. Women were shown everywhere as wives and mothers, or as young, unmarried shopgirls or office workers looking to 'catch' a man. Non-white women found they needed to work and most had to take domestic work, agricultural work or low level work such as waiting at the diners that were springing up on the highways. There were exceptions to this. For example, there was a rising black middle class, usually city-based and a very few black young women with a good education began to make their way in professions such as law and medicine. Most non-white women were still only able to find low-paid, unskilled work and a report made in 1963 for Kennedy points out that, non-white women, no matter what their skills, were being discriminated against and forced into the worst kinds of employment.

> This section continues the discussion of changes, analysing who might have felt they were significant.

In the 1960s and 1970s the women's liberation movement thrived and, to begin with, the pressure that it exerted did win some gains for women. Along with the Civil Rights Act came calls for 'affirmative action' to iron out inequality. However, this was very patchily applied after Johnson passed an executive order calling for this in federal employment. More non-white women went to college and trained for the professions, so there were non-white surgeons as well as nurses. Many women found they were excluded from career progress by the motherhood argument. College graduates with good degrees were losing out in interviews to less well qualified men because of this. Women, even those best placed to advance, were not making as much progress as they should have. More jobs were open to women, and they had more training opportunities; but still for less pay, in many cases, and with restricted chances of advancement.

The arrival of the pill and legalised abortion gave women more control over pregnancy as employers were asking in interviews if a woman intended to get pregnant over the next few years. Women campaigned vigorously for the Equal Rights Act. This was passed in Congress several times, but in 1980 had still to be ratified by enough states to pass into law (it still hasn't been). The conservative backlash of the late 1970s was a blow to equality with groups springing up to stridently oppose abortion, family planning and women in the workplace (for example Phyllis Schlafly and STOP ERA). The feeling against equal rights was so strong that in 1979 the USA did not sign a UN resolution to work against gender discrimination.

> It is important for candidates to spell difficult names correctly. 'Schlafly' is a name you are likely to need to use and candidates regularly spell this wrong.

The position of women changed between 1917 and 1980. The changes were significant for some groups of women: mainly educated WASPs. Women could vote. They were supposed to get equal pay for doing the same job as a man. They were able to apply for a wider range of opportunities. They had more control over pregnancy. There were more women in the professions and running businesses. For other women the changes were less significant and depended more on them being in the right place at the right time. The more discriminated against group you were in, the worse your situation was – non-white women with little education had a hard time of it. Just as with civil rights the legal position of women in 1980 was far better than their actual situation. The backlash of the late 1970s revealed a worryingly high level of feeling that women did not deserve equality with men. Even civil rights groups acted as if they felt this. There was, in 1980 as in 1917, a significant feeling that women were not really equal.

> The candidate has restated the question and offered a supported judgment on the issue.

Verdict

This is a strong answer because:

- it considers a number of factors in reasonable depth
- it analyses the question and focuses on the right time period
- it develops and explains the points it makes and makes links
- it comes to a strong, reasoned judgement.

Paper 1: A Level sample answer with comments

Section B

These questions assess your understanding of the course in breadth and will cover a period of 30 years or more. They will ask you about the content you learned about in the four key themes, and may ask about more than one theme. The question will also require you to explore a range of concepts, such as change over time, similarity and difference, as well as significance. For these questions remember to:

- identify the focus of the question
- consider the concepts you will need to explore
- support your points with evidence from across the time period specified in the question
- develop the evidence you deploy to build up your overall judgement
- come to a substantiated judgement that directly addresses the question set.

How significant was the growth of credit in the USA in the 1920s in producing the Great Depression of the 1930s?

Average student answer

The Great Depression had a huge effect on the American people. It was set off by the Wall Street Crash in 1929. Millions of people lost their jobs, some lost their homes, too. They just couldn't afford to keep going. So there were lots of homeless families desperately looking for work and living rough in shanty towns or sleeping in their cars. The whole thing was made worse by a lack of government intervention at the start.

The boom of the 1920s was run by credit. The post-war demand for goods would have let the new industries, like electrical goods, grow anyway – but there would not have been nearly as many customers for all these goods if it had not been possible to borrow money. It was possible to buy a huge range of goods on easy credit terms, from the manufacturers themselves. It was also possible to borrow money easily from banks. The chance to borrow on hire purchase, paying off the sum in regular, smaller, payments, meant that more people bought consumer goods, so the manufacturers made more money and hired more workers and this turned into a boom cycle. People kept buying, so manufacturers kept on making the goods. They expanded their factories and took on more workers. So then these workers, with a wage to spend, could buy all the consumer goods too.

It wasn't just goods and property that people bought in the boom. They started buying shares too, and treating them not as savings that brought a dividend, but as a way of making money by buying shares, selling quickly at a profit, buying more, selling quickly and so on. This was only ever going to work as long as prices went on rising and that couldn't happen. Many ordinary people, who didn't really understand how the stock market worked, bought shares. This would become a problem when prices began to fall, because their panicked reaction made things worse. Too many people selling drove the prices down and then more people felt they had to sell and it became a downward spiral.

So, borrowing in the 1920s certainly contributed to the extent of the Great Depression. However, there are other factors to consider. First, there was the fact that there was an atmosphere of overspending and overconfidence, even without borrowing. Manufacturers, investors and many ordinary US citizens began to believe that the economy was going to stay in a boom cycle forever, bringing the American Dream to more and more people. They were encouraged in this by the media (for example, it was the media who pointed out how easy it would be for even an ordinary person with only a few dollars to invest and get rich). Also, some industries, such

> This paragraph provides some accurate information about the Depression. However, credit is only introduced in a very oblique way.
>
> It could be improved by a clearer tying of credit to the problems that people were having and a tighter focus on what caused the Depression.

> The candidate is using a good deal of narrative and not much analysis.
>
> More focus on the question is needed, especially on the phrase 'how significant'.

as coal mining, had been failing all though the 1920s. This was less noticeable when newer industries were doing well and absorbing some of the workers who lost their jobs in the older industries – but it was happening all along. Farmers' difficulties were there all through the 1920s too. Prices were falling and farmers grew more to make enough money to cover the falling prices, but this meant that they drove the prices down further. These were long-term factors that built up through the 1920s.

However, once the boom collapsed there was a more short-term factor that led to the Depression being as extensive as it was. The government didn't intervene. Harding's administration believed in *laissez faire* and felt that the Depression would put itself right quite quickly – as the brief depression after the First World War had done. But this time it was no good saying that people had to help themselves if they were entirely without resources and there was no work. When the government eventually did decide to act they found that the problem had just got far too big for them to deal with and they were not prepared to take the kind of measures that were needed to stop the downward spiral (for example, taking federal responsibility for social policies). So they let things get worse and worse and people lost confidence in them.

So the Great Depression had several factors contributing to it. They all had an effect and some of them set others off – the stock market got so very overheated because people were able to borrow money to buy and sell shares. It gave them the chance to get involved in something few of them understood – so then when they found that prices were going down (something they knew might happen in theory, but didn't really believe ever would) they panicked and sold and made things much worse.

> This section produces other factors than credit for the Depression.
>
> It considers types of factor.
>
> However, it doesn't consider the significance of these factors against the factor of available credit.

> The concluding paragraph does not reach a clear judgement about significance at all; although there is one made by inference.

Verdict

This is an average answer because:

- it doesn't consider the full time range
- there is too much narrative and not enough analysis
- there are no inaccuracies, but many points are made without development and explanation
- it doesn't come to a strong, reasoned judgement.

Use the feedback on this essay to rewrite it, making as many improvements as you can.

Paper 1: A Level sample answer with comments

Section B

These questions assess your understanding of the course in breadth and will cover a period of 30 years or more. They will ask you about the content you learned about in the four key themes, and may ask about more than one theme. The question will also require you to explore a range of concepts, such as change over time, similarity and difference, as well as significance. For these questions remember to:

- identify the focus of the question
- consider the concepts you will need to explore
- support your points with evidence from across the time period specified in the question
- develop the evidence you deploy to build up your overall judgement
- come to a substantiated judgement that directly addresses the question set.

How significant was the growth of credit in the USA in the 1920s in producing the Great Depression of the 1930s?

Strong student answer

The Great Depression of the 1930s probably affected many more people in the 1930s because of the growth of credit in the 1920s. That is not to say that there would not have been a Depression anyway. There were other factors at work to undermine the boom: rising unemployment, falling farm prices, failing older industries, the fact that spending during the boom was largely on consumer goods (and that market could get exhausted). However, the significance of all the borrowing of the 1920s was that so many people who were hit by the other problems were also trying to keep up with credit payments in some form or another which meant they were hit harder and it was harder for them to recover.

> This is a strong first paragraph. It shows the candidate has a grasp on the timeframe and realises that it is important to consider the *significance* of the borrowing of the 1920s.

The boom of the 1920s was as rapid and expansive as it was because of the possibility of easy credit. It was possible to buy a huge range of goods, from toasters to cars, on easy credit terms, from the manufacturers themselves. It was also possible to borrow money easily from banks to buy homes, finance businesses or buy farm machinery. The chance to borrow on hire purchase, paying off the sum in regular, smaller, payments, meant that more people bought consumer goods, so the manufacturers made more money and hired more workers and this turned into a boom cycle. However, there were problems with this. First, the demand for toasters, fridges and so on was going to wind down. Secondly, hire purchase relied on people being able to meet the regular payments, just as bank loans did. When people stopped buying goods and when they could not meet their credit payments, this created big problems for businesses.

> In these paragraphs, the candidate clearly explains how credit was connected to the boom of the 1920s and how this would make the situation worse once there were problems.

It wasn't just goods and property that people bought in the boom. They started buying shares too, and treating them not as savings that brought a dividend, but as a way of making money by buying shares, selling quickly at a profit, buying more, selling quickly and so on. This was only ever going to work as long as prices went on rising and that couldn't happen. Many ordinary people, who didn't really understand how the stock market worked, bought shares. This would become a problem when prices began to fall, because their panicked reaction made things worse. Too many people selling drove the prices down and then more people felt they had to sell and it became a downward spiral. Many people would never have become involved at all if they had not been able to borrow to buy the shares.

So, borrowing in the 1920s certainly contributed to the extent of the depression – making it the Great Depression of the 1930s, not just a shorter, smaller depression. However, there are other factors to consider. First, there was the fact that there was an atmosphere of overspending and overconfidence, even without borrowing. Even banks got caught up in the stock market boom and used investors' savings to gamble on the stock market. Also, some industries, such as coal mining, had been failing all though the 1920s. This was less noticeable when newer industries were doing well and absorbing some of the workers who lost their jobs in the older industries – but it was happening all along. Farmers' difficulties were there all through the 1920s too. Prices were falling as there was less market for US farm produce after the war. Many farmers grew more to make enough money to cover the falling prices, but this meant that they drove the prices down further. The extent of this crisis was masked by the fact that farmers could borrow money – but as they borrowed more and more money they were putting themselves in a position where they would not be able to pay the interest regularly, let alone pay it back all at once, if the banks demanded it. These were long-term factors that built up through the 1920s.

> The candidate has picked up several other factors that contributed to the Depression and analysed their role in its growth with developed examples in most cases.

However, once the boom collapsed there was a more short-term factor that led to the Depression being as extensive as it was. The government didn't intervene. Hoover's Republican administration believed in *laissez faire* and felt that the depression would put itself right quite quickly – as the brief depression after the First World War had done. They did not take into account that the credit-driven boom had masked the underlying problems that had not gone away after the first depression. Nor did they realise at first how deeply credit had fixed itself in the economy and how many people it would hit hard. It was no good saying that people had to help themselves if they were entirely without resources and there was no work. When they did decide to act they found that the problem had outgrown their ability to cope with it and they were not prepared to take the kind of measures that were needed to stop the downward spiral (for example, putting the country into debt to plough more money into relief for the poor, or taking federal responsibility for social policies).

It seems to me that the boom of the 1920s was always unlikely to continue. There were problems, such as falling farm prices and failing older industries, that were likely to bring about a depression anyway. However, I think that the credit explosion of the 1920s was highly significant for several reasons. Credit drove the boom to greater heights than it could have achieved otherwise. This masked the underlying problems and created levels of overconfidence. This allowed manufacturers to keep on producing, even when demand tailed off – if they hadn't been as confident they would probably have noticed the tailing off sooner. Credit also allowed for the stock market boom and overheating, to a point where even the banks (which should have understood the stock market) were using customers' savings to buy shares, expecting prices to keep rising. Too many people were borrowing, and that was only going to work in the economy if they could keep up repayments. I think credit made the Great Depression what it was and the most important other factor was the fact the government didn't intervene at the start. We have no way of knowing exactly how much difference it would have made, but Roosevelt's New Deal policies did improve things, and from a point where things were worse than when the Depression began.

> The concluding paragraph gives its conclusion supported by reference to the other possible influences.

Verdict

This is a strong answer because:

- it uses the full time range for its examples
- there are no inaccuracies, and many points are developed and explained
- it comes to a strong, reasoned judgement
- it analyses the impact of the various factors throughout.

Paper 1: A Level sample answer with comments

Section C

These questions require you to read two extracts carefully to identify the key points raised and establish the argument being put forward. For these questions remember to:

- read and analyse the extracts thoroughly remembering that you need to use them in tandem
- take careful note of the information provided about the extracts
- deploy own knowledge to develop the points and arguments that emerge from the extracts and to provide appropriate context
- develop an argument rooted in the points raised in the extracts and come to a substantiated conclusion.

Study Extracts 5 and 6 (from Chapter 5, page 127) before you answer this question.

In the light of differing interpretations, how convincing do you find the view that increasing foreign imports, investments and loans was both positive and a sign of US success in making world business serve its needs (Extract 5, lines 4–6)?

To explain your answer, analyse and evaluate the material in both extracts, using your own knowledge of the issues.

Average student answer

Wright is saying, very clearly, that the switch in the US import/export balance in the 1980s was beneficial. He is aware that some people think otherwise, but describes them as 'misinformed mercantilists and xenophobes'. The positiveness for him lies in the fact that other countries wanted to be involved with the USA – selling it goods and lending it money. But I'm not sure that increasing borrowing from other countries is a good thing. Wright also says that the USA stopped lending money to countries that were a bad risk – he seems to be saying that anyway. That makes sense, third world countries are very unlikely to be able to pay loans back. That seems to make more economic sense.

When Reagan came to power he laid out his intentions for government very clearly. They included a strong foreign policy and fixing the economy. He gave declining industries as one of the big problems and said he wanted to help industry grow. He also said that it was important to control government spending. This suggests that becoming a large scale borrowing nation wasn't one of the things he wanted, nor was turning the country into a consuming nation rather than a producing one. However, just because it wasn't what he wanted to achieve doesn't mean it wasn't good for the country. Wright seems to think that by not lending money by attracting foreign investment meant the USA was better off and making the world economy work for the benefit of the USA.

Wright suggests that a shift to borrowing from lending was a way of making use of the world economy because other countries were investing in the USA. Investment in the US economy is definitely good. However, it is only a good thing if investors put their money back into the US economy. But we know that the Japanese, one of the biggest investors, were not doing this. They were buying up US businesses and then putting the profits back into Japan. So that doesn't sound like making the world economy work for the USA. It sounds more like being exploited by these countries. We know that many people at the time were very unhappy with the number of businesses and other landmarks (Florig talks about the Rockefeller Center in New York) that were being taken over by companies from Japan and Europe.

Wright's second point is that the USA stopped lending money to 'Third World and Communist ratholes' and that had to be a good thing, suggesting they wouldn't be able to pay the money back. Well, it would be good for the country not to be lending money it wouldn't get back. It is hard to see that being a creditor nation is always a good thing (which is what Florig seems to

The candidate makes the mistake of tackling the extracts separately and not addressing the specific question from the start.

Some overall understanding is shown and reasonable use is made of the extract, although it looks as though the candidate is working through sentence by sentence.

The candidate is still only referring to Wright, but has produced some valid contextual detail from their own knowledge.

The candidate is now using both extracts and some own knowledge.

The answer could be improved by developing the examples more and explaining the issues in greater depth.

It could also be improved by a more balanced use of both extracts.

suggest when he contrasts being the top creditor nation in 1980 against being the top borrowing nation in 1989) because there will be countries that don't pay back what they borrow. It is also very difficult to see how ending up owing $400 billion can be good for an economy. You also need to consider that Reagan himself was always admitting that borrowing was out of control, so it seems that he didn't see borrowing hugely as a positive thing for the country.

Florig points out in his first paragraph that 15 percent of jobs in manufacturing went under while Reagan was president. It seems to me that that is a sign of US businesses doing badly, which Reagan hadn't wanted to happen. And it is hard to see this as something that could really benefit the USA. He also said imports went down – but that just means people were buying less all round. It is probably that the balance of what they did buy had shifted to imported goods – they were buying more Japanese cars after the fuel crisis of the 1970s, for example.

In conclusion, I can't really see how a high level of debt was a good thing for the country or a successful manipulation of the world economy. However, foreign investment might have been useful to the USA. Even buying up buildings and so on isn't necessarily bad if the people who buy it up (even if they are foreign) maintain the building and so on. The issue of imports is less convincing because we know that there were huge problems in car and textile manufacturing as a result of foreign imports and that businesses that had to import parts from other countries rather than making something from scratch (such as transistor radios) didn't make such significant profits.

Here the student is producing evidence from their own knowledge that is relevant to the argument and is trying to address the question using the extracts and own knowledge.

However, the evidence and the conclusions are fairly

This judgement is based mainly on the candidate's knowledge of the subject.

The essay has not managed to use both extracts and their own knowledge in a coherent way.

Verdict

This is an average answer because:

- it is not rooted closely enough in the extracts; they are not linked effectively
- there is not enough context given
- it makes a judgement but it needs more substance
- it lacks the necessary sense of argument for a high level.

However, there is no incorrect information and the candidate tries to analyse the extracts in relation to the question.

Use the feedback on this essay to rewrite it, making as many improvements as you can.

Paper 1: A Level sample answer with comments

Section C

These questions require you to read two extracts carefully to identify the key points raised and establish the argument being put forward. For these questions remember to:

- read and analyse the extracts thoroughly remembering that you need to use them in tandem
- take careful note of the information provided about the extracts
- deploy own knowledge to develop the points and arguments that emerge from the extracts and to provide appropriate context
- develop an argument rooted in the points raised in the extracts and come to a substantiated conclusion.

Study Extracts 5 and 6 (from Chapter 5, page 127) before you answer this question.

In the light of differing interpretations, how convincing do you find the view that increasing foreign imports, investments and loans was both positive and a sign of US success in making world business serve its needs (Extract 5, lines 4–6)?

To explain your answer, analyse and evaluate the material in both extracts, using your own knowledge of the issues.

Strong student answer

The two extracts have very different perspectives and their evidence is selected to support their views. They are both considering the change in the economy under Reagan where the USA turned from being the world's biggest lender to being a country that was borrowing hugely from other countries. At the same time the country was exporting less and importing more: so selling less and buying more. Wright says, very clearly, that the switch in the US import/export balance in the 1980s was beneficial. He is aware that some people think otherwise, but describes them as 'misinformed mercantilists and xenophobes'. He thinks that the shift in the situation was good for the USA. Florig, on the other hand, argues that the switch was a terrible thing, turning the USA from being the country that lent most abroad (when Reagan took power in 1980) to the country that owed the most money in the world economy. Florig feels that this can be nothing but a bad thing. He certainly wouldn't agree that it was getting the world economy to serve the USA, because the USA was putting itself in the position where it was owing more and more money.

When Reagan came to power he laid out his intentions for government very clearly. They included a strong foreign policy and fixing the economy. He gave declining industries as one of the big problems and said he wanted to help industry grow. This suggests that he certainly didn't want American businesses to be selling less. On the other hand, he was committed to letting business go its own way and not hampering it with federal intervention. The other side of it being given more freedom was it being given no support when it was in difficulty. Reagan also said that it was important to control government spending. This suggests that becoming a large scale borrowing nation wasn't one of the things he wanted, nor was turning the country into a consuming nation rather than a producing one.

Wright seems to think that by not lending money by attracting foreign investment meant the USA was better off and making the world economy work for the benefit of the USA. He suggests that a shift to borrowing from lending was good for several reasons. The first reason is that other countries were investing in the USA. Investment in the US economy is definitely good. However, it is only a good thing if investors put their money back into the US economy. But we know that the Japanese, one of the biggest investors, were not doing this. They were buying up US businesses and then putting the profits back into Japan. This supports Florig's view that foreign involvement wasn't always good for the US economy. You could argue that by buying up these factories (and we know they did this in parts of the country that US

An effective opening paragraph that focuses on the extracts and identifies their key arguments.

It cites some of the evidence put forward and begins to set up the debate.

The candidate had produced some valid contextual knowledge and tied it to the extracts.

businesses were ignoring) they were at least saving the factories from going under and stopping the unemployment that might have resulted from that. However, this isn't the same as the US getting a huge benefit from the changing economy. And if Florig is right that 15 percent of all manufacturing jobs were lost (and we know that the textile manufacturers had a hard time – they weren't being bought out, they were losing trade to cheaper imports of textiles from abroad) then it seems unlikely that takeovers like the Japanese takeovers of car firms would have benefits that would outweigh this level of job losses. So I think the evidence I know of supports Florig's point of view rather than Wright's.

Wright's second point is that the USA stopped lending money to 'Third World and Communist ratholes' and that this development had to be a good thing. The implication he is making is that these places weren't good places to lend money to and, possibly, were unlikely to pay the money back. Well, it would be good for the country not to be lending money it wouldn't get back, because that is money that the government won't be able to use. We do know that the government was getting deeper and deeper in debt, so it would be a good thing to shake off all the bad debts that it could. This would be support for Wright's point of view. However, the government didn't really stop uneconomic foreign loans when they had a political purpose – they even did it without Congress' permission (look at the Iran Contra affair). On the other hand it is hard to see that being a creditor nation is always a good thing (which is what Florig seems to suggest when he contrasts being the top creditor nation in 1980 against being the top borrowing nation in 1989) because there will be countries that don't pay back what they borrow. It is also very difficult to see how ending up owing $400 billion can be good for an economy. You also need to consider that Reagan himself was always admitting that borrowing was out of control (but that the money was needed for defence, etc.). So it seems that he didn't see borrowing hugely as a positive thing for the country.

In conclusion, I think both Wright and Florig take up extreme positions (indeed Wright's language seems very extreme for a historian). Not even the Reagan administration, which (like all other administrations) was keen to show itself in a good light, ever suggested that the level of US indebtedness was a good thing for the country or a successful manipulation of the world economy. On the other hand, foreign investment was probably useful and not all investors would have been as focused on ploughing profits back into their own country as the Japanese. The foreign loans, I think can't be seen as positive. The issue of imports is less convincing because we know that there were huge problems in car and textile manufacturing as a result of foreign imports and that businesses that had to import parts from other countries rather than making something from scratch (such as transistor radios) didn't make such significant profits.

> These paragraphs consider Reagan's inaugural speech and what it meant for his economic policy, tying it back to the question, providing context.
>
> The candidate then analyses the position of one of the extracts against both the candidate's own knowledge and the points raised in the other extract to arrive at a balanced view.

> The concluding paragraph comes to a clear judgement based on the balance of the evidence.

Verdict

This is a strong answer because:

- it identifies and illustrates the arguments of the two extracts
- it deploys a sound range of specific evidence to develop points emerging from the extracts
- it provides a sense of the context
- it develops an argument that considers both interpretations and tries to provide balance
- there is a clear judgement.

India, c1914–48: the road to independence

INTRODUCTION

By the beginning of the 20th century, the British **Raj** was at its height. In 1911, the newly crowned King George V and Queen Mary travelled to India to hold their coronation **durbar** in Delhi, symbolising the strength of British power in India.

KEY TERMS

Raj
British rule in India. British involvement in India began as early as 1600 but it was not until 1858 that Britain took over direct rule of India. In 1877 Queen Victoria was proclaimed Empress of India, linking the monarchy more closely to the Indian empire and binding India more closely to Britain. Victoria's son, Edward VII, used the title King-Emperor in respect of India, and her grandson, George V, also King-Emperor, attended his own 1911 coronation durbar in Delhi. Largely symbolic, this involvement of the monarchy emphasised the importance of the Raj to Britain.

Durbar
A public audience at which a ruler appeared before his subjects. The British adopted durbars from Indian rulers and made them into large, elaborate ceremonies.

SOURCE 1

A painting by an unknown artist of the 1911 coronation durbar, published in a French journal in 1911.

1914	
August: Outbreak of First World War, over 800,000 Indians enlist	
1919	
March: Rowlatt Acts impose wartime controls on Bengal, Bombay and Punjab	
April: Gandhi calls for first civil disobedience campaign	
April: Amritsar Massacre	
December: Government of India Act enables unequal power sharing between Indians and British in provinces	
1923	
Members of Congress permitted to stand for election to councils established by the Raj	
1927	
Muslim League's proposals for protection of Muslim interests rejected by Congress	
1929	
March: All-India Muslim League endorses Jinnah's 14 Points designed to protect Muslim interests in an independent India	
October: Viceroy Irwin issues report saying India should aim for dominion status	
December: Lahore Congress decides on *purna swaraj* (complete independence)	
1931	
Gandhi–Irwin Pact	
Lord Willingdon replaces Irwin as Viceroy	
Second Round Table Conference	
1935	
Government of India Act constitution for India rejected by Congress and Muslim League	
1940	
March: Congress demands complete independence and constituent assembly	
Muslim League demands separate Muslim homeland	
1945	
May: VE Day – end of war in Europe	
August: VJ day – end of war in Far East	
1947	
March: Mountbatten arrives in India as Viceroy	
July: Indian Independence Act sets up two independent dominions of India and Pakistan, mass carnage begins	

Not only would most British people have agreed that India was the 'jewel in the crown', hugely benefiting the British economy, but they would have regarded British rule in India as unassailable. Laws affecting India were made in the British parliament and implementing these laws in India was managed more or less efficiently. How had this come about?

The connection between Britain and India began through trade, and the growth in prosperity and power of the **East India Company** (EIC). In 1858, the British Government, concerned about the power of the EIC and mindful of the problems involved in subduing the **Indian Mutiny** of 1857, passed the **Government of India Act**. This transferred all the powers of the East India Company directly to the British Crown. From then on, Britain was responsible for the governance of India. This involved far more than straightforward administration. India was a land of opportunity, where young British officers and civil servants played polo, indulged in tiger hunts and joined gentlemen's clubs, while at the same time subduing rebellions and running a vast country, teeming with people, wealth and promise. India was also a land of *maharajahs*, Indian princes with fabled fortunes, glittering palaces, harems and private armies. It was a land, too, where thousands of Indians worked for and with the British, and British companies profited enormously from their links with India.

KEY TERMS

East India Company
A British company formed to trade with India in 1600. It grew powerful enough to control thousands of square kilometres of territory in the subcontinent.

Indian Mutiny, 1857
A mutiny of Indian soldiers (sepoys) serving in the East India Company's army. Also known as the 'Great Rebellion' or the 'First War of Independence'.

Government of India Act (1858)
Disbanded the East India Company and placed India directly under British government rule.

What most British people failed to realise was that their perceived control over India was an illusion, relying on the tacit consent of the Indian people. The first decades of the 20th century were spent in dispelling that illusion with cataclysmic effects for both Britain and the Indian subcontinent. On 14 August 1947, Jawaharlal Nehru, India's first prime minister, addressed the **Indian Constituent Assembly**. Source 2 is part of what he said.

KEY TERM

Indian Constituent Assembly
A body set up in 1946 to draft a constitution for an independent India. Its members were leading politicians from across India.

SOURCE 2 Part of a speech made by Jawaharlal Nehru to the Indian Constituent Assembly, 14 August 1947.

Long years ago we made a tryst with destiny, and now the time comes when we shall redeem our pledge. At the stroke of the midnight hour, while the world sleeps, India will awake to life and freedom. A moment comes, which comes but rarely in history, when we step out from the old to the new, when an age ends, and when the soul of a nation, long suppressed, finds utterance.

India had finally won independence from Britain. Two independent countries, India and Pakistan, stood where once had been Britain's Indian Empire. Independence was won by way of vision and planning, intrigue and betrayal, desperation and ambition, violence and bloodshed. How these toxic ingredients combined to bring independence to the Indian subcontinent in the vital years after 1914 is the subject of this option.

1918	November: Armistice and end of First World War
1920	Gandhi emerges as leader of largely Hindu Congress Party
1920–22	Second civil disobedience campaign
1922	Gandhi imprisoned by British
1924	Gandhi released from prison
1928	Simon Commission arrives in India to report on effectiveness of Government of India Act (1919)
	All-Parties Conference produces Nehru Report, setting out constitutional basis of an independent India
1930	March: Start of the Salt March
	November: First Round Table Conference in London
1932	January: Terrorist activity in India, Gandhi arrested, Congress outlawed
	November: Third Round Table Conference
1939	September: Second World War breaks out
	Viceroy Linlithgow announces India at war with Germany
1942	April: Failure of Cripps Mission, offering full dominion status after the war
	August: Congress endorses Gandhi's 'Quit India' campaign, Congress leaders arrested
1946	March: Cabinet Mission fails to break deadlock between Congress and Muslim League

2a.1 The First World War and its impact on British India, 1914–20

KEY QUESTIONS

- India in 1914: loyal to the Raj or ripe for rebellion?
- What was the cost to India of the subcontinent's contribution to the First World War?
- To what extent did the First World War change British rule in India?
- How did nationalism develop in India?

INTRODUCTION

The British, in their view, had ruled India more or less successfully from 1858. True, there had been outbreaks of unrest and minor revolts, for example, in times of famine and against Viceroy Curzon's unwise attempt to **partition Bengal**. Despite outbreaks of rioting and terrorism, the British were able to restore order in Bengal and other regions without too much trouble.

However, in the years to 1914, the concept of nationalism was beginning to grow in the minds of many Indians. In 1885, 73 individuals, representing every province of British India, met in Bombay for the first annual meeting of the Indian National Congress. Membership increased steadily, from around 600 in 1888 to about 100,000 in 1914. It is important to emphasise that, in the early days, Congress was simply a forum for discussion and was dominated by Hindus, most of whom were high-caste. It was not a political party and could not even be called a movement. Later, in the years after the First World War, it was to become the organisational vehicle for India's first great nationalist movement.

In December 1906, the All-Indian Muslim League was founded at the annual Muhammadan Educational Conference held in Dhaka. About 3,000 delegates attended with numbers growing steadily at each annual meeting. All delegates supported the establishment of a political party, primarily to protect Muslim interests in a Hindu-dominated country. Both Congress and the All-Indian Muslim League were originally intent on working with the Raj in order to enable Indians to play a greater role in running their country. Independence – releasing themselves from foreign rule – was a step very few Hindus or Muslims even dared to contemplate.

1914
August: Outbreak of First World War
Over 800,000 Indians enlist

1916
March: Lord Chelmsford becomes Viceroy of India
July–November: Battle of the Somme
December: Lucknow Pact agreement made between Congress and Muslim League to pressurise British into giving Indians more autonomy

1914	1915	1916	1917

1917
July: Edwin Montagu becomes secretary of state at the Foreign Office
July–November: Battle of Passchendaele
August: Montagu Declaration says British government will involve Indians more in governance of India

The First World War was to change the perceptions of both the British and Indians. The Allies, in rallying support for their cause, frequently referred to the war as being fought to defend the rights of nations and stressed the importance of democracy and **self-determination**. This sat uneasily with the reality of the Raj. Indians, those fighting alongside British and white colonial battalions as well as those remaining at home, assimilated these values and began to apply them to their own situation in India.

KEY TERM

Self-determination
The right of countries to
determine their own affairs.

INDIA IN 1914: LOYAL TO THE RAJ OR RIPE FOR REBELLION?

The political geography of India: the British Raj

The viceroy, the secretary of state and the Council of India

These three institutions provided the 'top down' structure of the governance of India and were intended to ensure British control of the subcontinent. The viceroy was a political appointment made in Westminster, and as such represented the British Crown in India. He worked from Delhi with a staff of 700 and a salary twice that of the British prime minister, such was his importance. In a similar way, the post of secretary of state for India was a political appointment, responsible for the development of government policy toward India and answerable to parliament. The secretary of state didn't work alone: he was guided and advised by the Council of India, based in London. This consisted of 15 men, none of them Indian, but most of whom had had some experience of living and working in India. This meant, however, that their experience was often alarmingly out-of-date and occasionally dangerously inappropriate.

The Indian Civil Service

The Indian Civil Service ensured that British laws, rules and regulations were implemented in India. It was hierarchical in structure, with power filtering down from the Crown to the humblest local official. The Indian Civil Service was renowned for its efficiency and was the model for administrators throughout the British Empire. Young men wanting a career in the Service had first to pass a competitive examination and then spend time in India working with a district officer. Leadership and all-round intelligence were prized more than academic qualifications because members of the Indian Civil Service had to turn their hands to anything, from tax assessments to dealing with rogue elephants. While it was possible for Indians to enter the Service, the route to acceptance, involving exams in London and higher education at a British university, made this virtually impossible. It wasn't until 1919 that the examinations for the Indian Civil Service were held in Delhi and Rangoon as well as in London. Nevertheless, thousands of Indians helped administer the Raj in other ways: as policemen, lawyers and soldiers, for example. But, whatever they did, they were always answerable to a British officer or official.

1919
March: Rowlatt Acts impose wartime controls over Bengal, Bombay and Punjab
April: Gandhi calls for *satyagraha* and *hartals* in response to Rowlatt Acts;
         Amritsar Massacre
December: Government of India Act enables dyarchy – limited and unequal power-sharing

1918	1919	1920

1918
July: Montagu Chelmsford Report recommends
limited power-sharing, particularly in provinces
November: Armistice and end of First World War

1920
Gandhi emerges as
leader of Congress

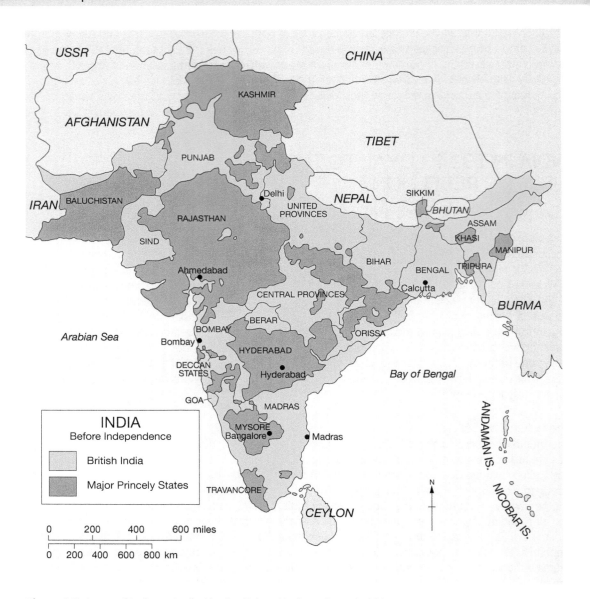

Figure 1.1: Areas of India controlled by the Raj and Indian princes in 1914.

The princely states

The British provinces of India, such as Bombay, Punjab and Madras, were ruled directly by the British government through the viceroy and the Indian Civil Service. But there were vast areas of the Indian subcontinent (see Figure 1.1) that were not directly subject to the British Raj. The Indian princes ruled about 35 percent of the country, consisting of 562 separate states. Some of these states were large. Hyderabad, for example, covered 77,000 square kilometres and contained 14 million people. Others were tiny: Kathiwar was only a few square kilometres in size and had fewer than 200 inhabitants. Rulers of these princely states had, in theory, complete authority over those whom they ruled. Practice was, however, somewhat different. They all had treaty arrangements with Britain and these treaties allowed a certain degree of local autonomy. Each state kept its own laws, languages, holidays, ministers and rulers. But each state was under the 'protection' of Britain so, in reality, couldn't instigate any action that ran counter to the interests of the British Raj.

Indian society and religion

Indian society was complex and hugely varied. Central to the way in which it operated was the caste system within which Hindus, who made up 70 percent of India's population, lived out their lives. With a population of over 300 million in 1914, this obviously had a tremendous impact on society in the subcontinent.

The significance of the caste system

The assumptions underlying the caste system were those of purity and pollution. Certain substances, such as human and animal waste and dead bodies, were believed to be pollutants, and so the closer Hindus came to them in their work, the lower in the caste system came that occupation. Some people, such as women after childbirth, became temporarily polluted and could be purified. Others, because of their occupation, could never be completely purified. In order to protect the purity of the caste above them, the castes had to be kept as separate as possible, and so there were strict rules about who could touch whom. At the very bottom of the hierarchy were the 'Untouchables'. Although this system was one of separation, it was also one of interdependence. Everyone needed the support of those in the castes above and below them, and so a system of patron–client relationships between families was established, often existing over many generations.

How did the caste system affect individual Hindus? Every Hindu was born into a specific caste and lived out their life within that caste. All social relationships were pre-determined by caste, which no one could leave unless they were prepared to become an out-caste with no place in society.

SOURCE 1

Marjorie Cashmore, who lived in India under the Raj, described what happened when she found a dead bird and asked her gardener to remove it. This is part of a collection of memories of the Raj, edited by Charles Allen and published in *Plain Tales from the Raj* in 1975.

So I told the bearer to call the masalchee [lowest person in a household, usually employed to wash dishes], but the masalchee wouldn't touch it. Then I called for the sweeper [member of the untouchable caste, usually employed to clean lavatories] and he wouldn't touch it, so I asked the bearer [house servant] who could move it and he told me to send to the bazaar for a dome, a man of very low caste. So we had to pay to get this lad to come and take the bird away.

[The domestics were there] not because you needed them, but because they were very strict about their own little trade unions. The man who waited at table might not be prepared to bring your tea in the morning; the cook would perhaps cook but he wouldn't wash up; there would be a special man to dust the floor; another special man to sweep out the verandah and so on. If you had a man to look after the horses he would need to have an assistant who went and cut the grass. As you rose in your career so the number of servants increased, not because you wanted them but because they insisted on it.

ACTIVITY
KNOWLEDGE CHECK

The caste system

To what extent does Source 1 explain the caste system?

The importance of religion

It was only the followers of the Hindu religion that were both bound and separated by the caste system. The other religions in India held different value systems and frameworks for dress, diet and social customs, as well as rituals associated with particular forms of belief. But, as well as being a binding force, religion in India, as elsewhere, was also divisive, setting different groups apart from each other often in mutual misunderstanding and distrust.

Muslims formed the largest minority religion (around 20 percent). Although, in some parts of the subcontinent, mostly in the north east and the north west, they were in the majority, they were in a minority in most states. However, while in the north west Muslims tended to hold influential positions, in the north east, especially around Bengal, Muslims were more likely to be found forming the peasant class. There were fewer Muslims in the south of the subcontinent, except in Hyderabad, which had been a stronghold of the Muslim Mughal Empire that had ruled much of the subcontinent in the 16th and 17th centuries.

Sikhs and Christians were the other two sizeable minority religious groups. Sikhs formed a highly localised group, living mainly in the Punjab, and grew out of the interaction between Hindus and Muslims in the 17th century. In the far south of India, there was an ancient denomination of Christians, claiming to have been founded by St Thomas. However, most Christians in 20th-century India were the result of 19th- and 20th-century missionary work.

Religion was to be a powerful force as the different groups and communities struggled to adjust and retain their identities in the long battle for independence. Hindu temples, for example, became the focal points of political activity for different castes, while to proclaim that certain policies and plans endangered Islam was a powerful motivating force for Muslims to engage in political activity.

EXTEND YOUR KNOWLEDGE

What do Hindus and Muslims believe?
Hindus believe that all existence comes from an eternal spiritual truth, *Brahman*. The purpose of life is to understand this eternal truth and to understand one's eternal identity as the *atma*, or soul. The soul is eternal and lives many lifetimes in a human body or in different forms of life. *Samsara* is the name given to this cycle of birth and rebirth. When true understanding is reached, the soul will be released from the cycle of rebirth.

Muslims believe that there is one true god (Allah) and that Muhammad is his final prophet. There are five pillars of Islam: a declaration of faith in Allah and belief that Muhammad is the messenger of Allah (*Shahadah*); to pray (*Salah*) five times a day; to fast (*Sawm*) during Ramadan from dawn to sunset; to pay a welfare tax (*Zakah*) for distribution to the poor; and to make a pilgrimage to Mecca (*Hajj*) at least once in a lifetime.

What was the importance of India to Britain?

No country acquires an empire out of a sense of altruism (an attitude of unselfish concern for others). Although many individuals, both privately and publicly, assured each other and the world that their mission was to 'civilise' the 'native Indians', this was certainly not the driving force of empire, nor the driving force that kept the British in India. True, India was costly to run, but that was nothing compared to the economic benefits India brought to Britain.

The importance of trade

India's economic role was vital to Britain's position in the world, both as a provider of raw materials for British industry and as a market for British manufactured goods. Initially, these were cotton goods but, by the early years of the 20th century, it included significant amounts of iron, steel and engineering products, all of which were very important for the continued prosperity of British staple industries. But the trade was not all one way: India supplied Britain with jute and raw cotton, rice, tea, oil-seed, wheat and hides. The transportation of goods, raw and finished, was greatly helped by the opening of the Suez Canal in 1869, which, running between the Mediterranean Sea and the Red Sea, greatly reduced travelling time between India and Britain, thus reducing the cost of transporting freight. This, in turn, impacted on British foreign policy: securing the Suez Canal route to India was always given a high priority.

SOURCE 2

UK imports from India by value, 1854–1913, in £1,000s. From W. Schlote, *British Overseas Trade from 1700 to the 1930s*, published in 1952.

Commodity	1854	1876	1900	1913
Raw cotton	1,642	5,875	657	1,226
Rice	884	2,639	1,625	1,281
Raw jute	510	2,799	4,101	9,182
Tea	24	2,429	5,576	7,839
Leather	18	444	2,820	2,839
Wheat	0	1,647	2	7,999
Oil-seed	0	0	50	398

SOURCE 3

UK exports to India by value, 1854–1913, in £1,000s. From W. Schlote, *British Overseas Trade from 1700 to the 1930s*, published in 1952.

Commodity	1854	1876	1900	1913
Manufactured textiles	7,191	15,961	19,069	40,729
Iron and steel goods	584	1,864	3,280	9,801
Machinery	101	724	1,529	4,558
Chemicals	67	232	683	1,309
Locomotives, railway carriages	10	155	867	2,200
Electrical engineering products	0	145	76	362
Soap	0	22	114	433

ACTIVITY
KNOWLEDGE CHECK

How could Sources 2 and 3 be used to explain:

a) the importance of India to the British economy

b) the exploitation of the Indian economy by the British?

Tariffs and investment

One way in which newly developing countries could protect their own emerging industries was to impose tariffs on goods coming into the country. In this way, imported goods became more expensive than domestically produced ones, thus allowing home industries to grow and develop. Australia and the USA used this method at the beginning of the 20th century to encourage their own domestic industries.

Nothing of the kind happened in India – quite the reverse as it would hardly be in Britain's interests to have tariffs slapped on British goods it wanted to sell in Indian markets. Indeed, towards the end of the 19th century, the British government unashamedly made India subordinate to the needs of the Lancashire cotton industry. In 1879, all import duties on Lancashire cotton cloth were removed, allowing it to flood the Indian market at a time when the Indian cotton industry desperately needed support and famine stalked the land. Three years later, all tariffs on all British goods were removed, although in 1917 some protection was given to Indian industries. Unsurprisingly, tariff control was one factor fastened on by Indian nationalists as the 20th century progressed.

Because of confidence in the ability of the Raj to control unrest in the subcontinent, in the early years of the 20th century India received about one-tenth of all British overseas investment – about £360 million by 1910. Nearly half of this was in the form of government loans to subsidise railway development and tea and coffee plantations.

Investment in India came in the form of people, too. Clearly, India provided employment for the British people who went out to work in government service as members of the Indian Civil Service (ICS) and other civilian enterprises, such as forestry, education, medicine and engineering. As well as receiving salaries when they were working, almost all colonial employees went back 'home', to Britain, when they retired. There, they received pensions paid for by India and these were one of the main 'home charges' on the Indian revenue. It was to the Indian army that the biggest manpower commitment was made, enabling Britain to have a secure presence in Asia.

What were British and Indian attitudes to each other?

It is impossible to over-estimate the impact of the Indian Mutiny of 1857 and the level of racial mistrust it raised between the British in India and the Indians. Although it occurred nearly 50 years before this option begins, its ramifications were profound. Shocked at what they perceived as disloyalty and ingratitude, the British reacted by removing themselves from their previous easy, relaxed contact with Indian society and, in effect, forming a separate caste. This separation of rulers from ruled was to lead to terrible problems as the 20th century progressed.

A separate society?

Wealthy Raj officials, as well as people in high-earning professions such as bankers and lawyers, lived in the great 18th-century houses built for the East India Company merchants; lesser officials occupied newly built bungalows in the suburbs of the important

Indian cities such as Bombay, Calcutta, Madras and Delhi. All, including the children, were looked after by a veritable army of Indian servants.

Home, for most British people, was Britain, or, more specifically, England. They sent their children back 'home' to school when they were old enough; they went 'home' for holidays when they were not spending the hot season in the hill station resorts of Simla (also the Raj's summer capital) or Poona, and some wives even chose to go back 'home' permanently with their children. In India, the British did their best to establish the sort of homes they would have had back in Britain. Furniture and furnishings, books and china, for example, were all shipped out, making the separation from Indian society even more obvious.

Living close to the edge

Not all the British in India were similarly privileged. Living close to the edge were the missionaries, whose poverty and desire to live among the Indians made them deeply suspect to the ruling classes. Businessmen and those engaged in the lower echelons of trade were automatically barred from the hierarchical society that was the British Raj by their social origins.

Anglo-Indians were equally suspect. Numbering about 110,000 at the beginning of the 20th century, they were accepted by neither the British nor the Indians. The nearest they came to acceptance by polite British society was at church, where they were consigned to the lowliest pews, and with dubious charitable gestures like children's Christmas parties. They themselves identified with Britain, usually referring to it as 'home' although they had never been there, dressing in European clothes and with the women using make-up to try to lighten their complexions. Nevertheless, it was this underclass that formed the backbone of labour on the railways and postal and telegraph services. The British, who so spurned them, could not administer India without them.

KEY TERM

Anglo-Indian
A person of mixed Indian and British descent.

Indian attitudes to the Raj

In many ways, it is very difficult to discover with any accuracy what the majority of Indians thought of the British and what their attitudes were towards them. At the beginning of the century, millions of Indians owed their livelihoods to the Raj. It provided them with a roof over their heads, food on the table, an occupation, and in some cases the makings of a career structure. Most Indians were unlikely to be openly critical of their 'masters' but this was nonetheless an alien rule and not one arising from their own culture.

British rule brought with it the English language. A good command of English was necessary for Indians (once entry was permitted) to pass examinations that allowed access to the prestigious Indian Civil Service. In one sense, the English language was a unifying factor as dozens of languages were spoken across the subcontinent. The English language also brought with it words

like 'democracy', 'imperialism' and 'nationalism' as well as the concepts that lay behind them.

An underlying groundswell of discontent and resentment did sometimes find violent expression in, for example, riots against the ill-fated partition of Bengal and in the more measured emerging nationalist movement.

ACTIVITY
KNOWLEDGE CHECK

Indian society under the Raj

1 How far do you agree with the view that the British in India formed a separate caste?

2 What were the strengths, and what were the weaknesses, of the ways in which British society in India was structured?

Indian nationalism

The Indian National Congress

Delegates at the first meeting of the Indian National Congress in 1885 were mainly high-caste Hindus, all of whom spoke English. Most were lawyers, although there was a smattering of teachers, journalists, landowners and businessmen. The delegates were not exclusively Indian: there were British delegates, too. Only two Muslims attended; three years later, Muslims numbered 83 of the 600 delegates and this domination of Congress by Hindus continued to build in the following years. The Indian National Congress met every year until the outbreak of the First World War in 1914 and became a powerful voice for Indian nationalism. At this stage Congress was a discussion forum and not a political party. The early resolutions of Congress were framed within a spirit of cooperation with the Raj, suggesting some form of power-sharing. There were, however, some who wanted to push the agenda further and harder, as seen in Source 4.

 SOURCE 4 From an address made by Bal Gangadhar Tilak to the Indian National Congress in 1907.

We have perceived one fact, that the whole of this administration, which is carried on by a handful of Englishmen, is carried on with our assistance. We are all in subordinate service. We want control over our administrative machinery. We don't want to become clerks and remain clerks. At present, we are clerks and willing instruments of our own oppression in the hands of an alien government, and that government is ruling over us, not by its innate strength, but by keeping us in ignorance and blindness to the perception of this fact. Every Englishman knows that they are a mere handful in this country, and it is the business of every one of them to befool you into believing that you are weak and they are strong. This is politics. We have been deceived by such policy for so long. What the new party wants you to do is realise the fact that your future rests entirely in your own hands. If you mean to be free, you can be free; if you do not mean to be free, you will fall and be for ever fallen.

Bal Gangadhar Tilak (1856–1920)

Indian nationalist, social reformer and first popular leader of an Indian independence movement, Tilak was born into a middle-class Hindu family. After a modern college education, he first taught mathematics and then became a journalist. Tilak founded the Marathi-language daily newspaper *Kesari* in which he strongly criticised the Raj for its suppression of freedom of expression, especially after the partition of Bengal.

Tilak joined the Indian National Congress in the 1890s, where he opposed the moderate approach of Gopal Krishna Gokhale (see page 186). When Congress split into two factions, Tilak led the extremists (*Garam Dal*). Arrested on charges of sedition in 1908 and defended in court by Muhammad Ali Jinnah, Tilak was convicted and imprisoned in Mandalay, Burma, until 1914. On his release, he rejoined the Indian National Congress.

Tilak criticised Gandhi's strategy of non-violent civil disobedience as a way of gaining independence for India. Mellowing in later life, he favoured political dialogue as a way of moving forward. Although he wanted independence for India, he wanted this independence to be exercised within the British Empire.

The Muslim League

Muslims never felt comfortable under the Congress umbrella and this led them to create alternative political organisations, which pursued a different sort of political agenda. Initially formed in 1906 in Dhaka, the Muslim League was to be the voice of the Muslim community.

The Muslims' main problem, politically, was that in nearly every state they were in the minority. In the heady days of the Raj, this was not too much of a problem. As long as the governing elite ruled *for* the people, and political decisions were not made *by* the people, the numbers didn't matter too much. However, the situation changed radically once the Raj began to move tentatively toward a more democratic situation. Unless protected, the Muslim minority would be out-voted by the Hindu majority at every level. Thus, most Muslims, right from the start, strongly opposed any extension of a democracy that was based on the principle of 'one man, one vote'. If this principle was to become the norm throughout India, there would be few, if any, Muslims elected to provincial or national assemblies. In this, the more conservative members of the British administration gave them tacit support. Congress, on the other hand, was less willing to do so. It was this dichotomy (between individual and group rights) that was to plague all negotiations as India moved closer to independence and was eventually to end in Partition.

The Indian Councils Act 1909

The Indian Councils Act was the outcome of a series of reforms agreed between John Morley, secretary of state for India, and the viceroy, Lord Minto, reflecting an understanding of the problems faced by Hindus and Muslims as they moved to have a greater say in their country's affairs.

- Sixty Indian representatives were to be elected to serve on the viceroy's Executive Council; 27 of these were to be elected from territorial constituencies and special interest groups. However, officials remained in the majority.

- The provincial councils were to be enlarged so as to create non-official majorities.

- Separate electorates were provided for Muslims and Hindus in order to allow the minority Muslims to have a voice in the various councils.

Additionally, Morley appointed two Indians to his London-based group of advisors. When Morley urged Minto to do something similar, he appointed Satyendra Sinha, the advocate-general of Bengal, to be his law advisor on his Executive Council. However, Minto and his officials in Calcutta, although believing the reforms to be essential, thought of them as a defensive action. Morley, on the other hand, regarded them as a significant step toward colonial self-government. This would not be the first time that officials agreed to the same actions but for entirely different reasons.

This Act was in force when India went to war in 1914. As a result of the war, the political landscape underwent tremendous change.

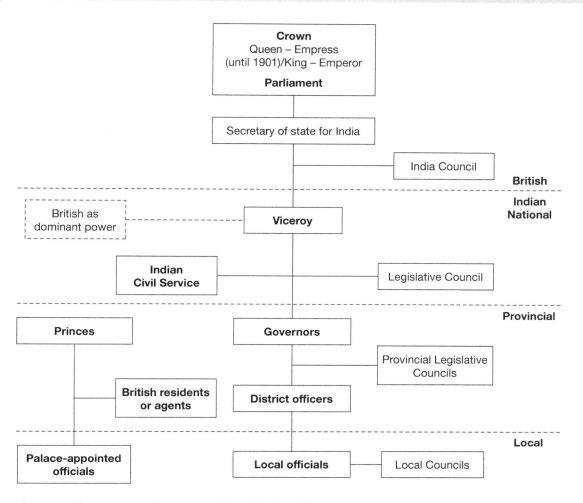

Figure 1.2: The structure of government in India before 1914.

Governing India before 1914

1 What were the strengths and weaknesses of the structure Britain established for governing India?

2 How far were the concerns of Tilak (Source 4) met by the Indian Councils Act of 1909?

3 To what extent were Muslim concerns accommodated by the Indian Councils Act of 1909?

WHAT WAS THE COST TO INDIA OF THE SUBCONTINENT'S CONTRIBUTION TO THE FIRST WORLD WAR, 1914–18?

On 3 August 1914, Germany declared war on France and swept into Belgium as a forerunner to invading France. Britain was bound by treaty obligations to defend the integrity of Belgium and declared war on Germany the following day. By the end of August most of Europe was at war. It was a war that was to draw in the countries of the British Empire and, finally, the USA.

India's response to the outbreak of war

The outbreak of war in Europe was met with instant declarations of loyalty and support for Britain from all sections of Indian society. Offers of support poured in from Congress, the Muslim League and the princely states. Twenty-seven of the largest princely states put their armies at the disposal of Britain and commissioned, fitted and provisioned a hospital ship, *Loyalty*. Even Bal Tilak, the leader of the extremist faction in Congress, declared his loyalty. Mohandas Gandhi, then a little-known lawyer, urged Indians to give such service as they felt capable of performing in order to show their desire to share in the responsibilities of membership of the British Empire.

Recruitment campaigns exceeded all expectations, and Indian troops were soon sailing for Flanders, Gallipoli and Mesopotamia, serving overseas as combatants and support staff, dwarfing all other imperial contributions to the war effort. By November 1918, some 827,000 Indians had enlisted as combatants in addition to those already serving in 1914 when the First World War began. It seems from official figures that around 64,500 Indian soldiers died in the war.

Attitudes to fighting

For most Indian soldiers, going to war was part of their well-established ancestral tradition of obligation to whoever was their emperor. Interestingly, few claimed to be fighting for India. Most cited the king or the Empire as legitimate causes for which they were fighting, an attitude that was reflected in many letters written home from the Front.

SOURCE

5   A First World War recruitment poster issued in India. The wording is in Urdu and reads 'Who will take this uniform, money and rifle? The one who will join the army.'

Indian military and economic contribution to the war

Military contribution

India poured men and materials into the war effort and, in doing so, became a crucial source of supply for the Allied cause. The first Indian expeditionary force, made up of some 16,000 British and 28,500 Indian troops of the Lahore and Meerut divisions and the Secunderabad cavalry, embarked from Karachi on 24 August 1914, reaching Marseilles on 26 September. They got to the Western Front in time for the first Battle of Ypres (19 October–22 November 1914). There, their losses were heavy. The average Indian battalion comprised 764 fighting men. By early November, the 47th Sikhs, for example, were down to 385 fit soldiers.

In early 1915, the Indian regiments were rested, but were soon back in the trenches. They provided half the Allied fighting force at Neuve Chapelle (10–13 March 1915) and the Lahore division was thrown into the counter-attack at the Second Battle of Ypres in April 1915.

SOURCE 6

Sikh soldiers arriving at Marseilles, en route for the battlefields of northern France and Flanders.

In December 1915, two infantry divisions were withdrawn from France and sent to serve in the Middle East. Some have argued that this was because the Indians were suffering low morale and the War Office feared that they could not survive another winter on the Western Front. However, it made perfect sense to concentrate the Indian army in the Middle East, where they were better suited to the climate and it would be easier to send supplies and reinforcements from India.

In the event, the move was to end in disaster for the men involved. The Indian troops took part in a campaign against the Ottoman Turks in Iraq. They were badly led and under-equipped as Indian industry was not geared up to the production of weapons or vehicles and the Allies could not afford to divert supplies from Europe. In December 1915, the British force was besieged at Kut-al-Amara and eventually surrendered to the Turks on 29 April 1916. Thousands of Indian and British troops had to endure a forced march across the desert to Turkish prisoner-of-war camps. Hundreds died on the march and in the camps.

Two Indian cavalry divisions remained on the Western Front until March 1918, when they were transferred to Palestine to take part in operations against the Turks. By the end of the war, in November 1918, some 1.5 million Indians had been recruited into combatant and non-combatant roles, and nearly all of them, together with 184,350 animals, had been sent overseas, where over 60,000 Indian troops died. This level of contribution and sacrifice dwarfed all other imperial contributions to the war effort.

SOURCE

7 A letter from Daya Ram of the 2nd Lancers, to Subadar Mahomed Kham at 'Depot 24th Punjabis, Haiderabad, Scinde' (Hyderabad, Sindh), dated 5 July 1916. Daya Ram was fighting on the Western Front; Mahomed Kham was an officer in the Indian Army. The letter was passed by the military censor.

On 16 June I went into the trenches and came back all safe on 29th. The fight is very severe. The fire of bombs descends all night long and the rain of machine guns never stops. I live in a dug-out. They are splendidly built and have wire beds and in some places these underground rooms are large enough to contain many men at once. I saw one such place at the bottom of a hill in which three full regiments could have lived. Everybody sleeps, eats and drinks underground. These trenches used to belong to the French but now belong to us. I am alive up to date through your kindness but God knows what will happen. There is great discomfort in the trenches and the lice swarm on the men. The Cavalry can't move about much in the winter and so get an easy time but in the warm weather they are always moving about from one front to another.

ACTIVITY
KNOWLEDGE CHECK

Recruitment

1 Study Source 5. How far does the source suggest that support for the Allied cause in the First World War was based on considerations apart from loyalty?

2 What use could a historian make of Source 6 in an investigation into India's military contribution to the First World War?

AS Level Exam-Style Question Section A

How much weight do you give the evidence of Source 7 for an enquiry into the role played by Indian soldiers on the Western Front?

Explain your answer, using the source, the information given about it and your own knowledge of the historical context. (12 marks)

Tip

The letter was passed by the censor; does this mean that it does not give a true picture of what the Western Front was like?

A Level Exam-Style Question Section B

'Indian contribution to the Raj in the years 1914–18 was strong and successful.'

How far do you agree with this opinion? Explain your answer. (20 marks)

Tip

Think about the positive contribution made by India to the First World War, and the impact this had on India in both positive and negative ways.

Economic contribution

By the end of the war, Indian revenues had contributed over £146 million to the Allied war effort. About half of this amount was made up of war loans, which in 1917 raised £35.5 million and in 1918 a further £38 million. Military expenditure had risen dramatically, too, and revenue demands in India were raised by 16 percent in the years 1916–17 and 10 percent in the years 1918–19.

The economic impact in India and the consequences for British rule

Economic impact

Most ordinary people in India felt the effects of war through increased taxation, shortages of fuel and rising prices, along with worry for the safety of loved ones away fighting. In this, they suffered in the same way as all people living and working on the home front in western European countries. Insofar as India was concerned, the war disrupted normal trading, created exchange rate problems and imposed the demands of the military. As a result, prices of food grains rose by 93 percent, of Indian-made goods by 60 percent and imported goods by 190 percent. The government tried to control prices, but were too often frustrated by profiteers and speculators. The situation was exacerbated by the failure of the monsoon rains to arrive in 1918–19 and consequent grain shortages and famine.

However, the war did benefit many, and not just profiteers and speculators. Indian manufacturing industries, particularly cotton, iron and steel, sugar, engineering and chemicals, expanded in order to replace goods normally imported. Shareholders saw their dividends rocket. In Bombay, for example, dividends from cloth mills jumped from six percent in 1914 to over 30 percent in 1917. In Ahmedabad, the cotton manufacturing centre of India, one mill owner reported a trebling of profits.

It was against this background that the viceroy had to juggle the demands of London for more resources, and the concerns of his district officers at localised distress and disturbances. By 1918, the viceroy's office was receiving regular reports from provincial legislatures of food riots, petty violence and rioting; some expressed concern that support for the Raj was crumbling. It was fortunate for British rule in India that these outbreaks were sporadic and never coalesced into a general campaign. If they had done, the withdrawal of so many troops to Europe, along with hundreds of Indian Civil Service men and British civilians, would have made the domestic Indian situation very tricky. Indeed, by March 1915, there was not a single British battalion left in India. Any sort of uprising would have been very difficult to contain.

It was hardly surprising that the economic effects of war were to have serious political consequences for the Raj.

AS Level Exam-Style Question Section A

Why is Source 8 valuable to the historian for an enquiry into the importance Congress placed on the First World War?

Explain your answer using the source, the information given about it and your own knowledge of the historical context. (8 marks)

Tip

Think about Banerjea's relationship with Congress, and what had happened to Indian nationalism during the First World War.

SOURCE

8 From a speech made to Congress in 1915 by Surendranath Banerjea, its president.

Brother delegates, the idea of re-adjustment is in the air, not only here in India but all the world over. The heart of the Empire is set upon it: it is the problem of problems upon which humanity is engaged. What is this war for? Why are these enormous sufferings endured? Because it is a war of re-adjustment, a war that will set right the claims of minor nationalities, uphold and vindicate the sanctity of treaties, proclamations – ours is one – charters and similar 'scraps of paper'. They are talking about what will happen after the war in Canada, in Australia; they are talking about it from the floor of the House of Commons and in the gatherings of public men and ministers of the State. May we not also talk about it a little from our standpoint? Are we to be charged with embarrassing the government when we follow the examples of illustrious public men, men weighted with a sense of responsibility at least as onerous as that felt by our critics and our candid friends?

ACTIVITY
KNOWLEDGE CHECK

Readjustment

1 Read Source 8. Which aspects of this speech would the British find (a) alarming and (b) reassuring?

2 In the years 1914–18, was the political or economic impact of the war in India more significant?

TO WHAT EXTENT DID THE FIRST WORLD WAR CHANGE BRITISH RULE IN INDIA?

The dilemma faced by the British government was seemingly intractable, unless compromises were made by the Raj and by those in India seeking greater autonomy over their affairs. The British government could not ignore the enormous sacrifices made by the Indian people in the First World War and were aware that most Indian people and politicians were looking for recognition in respect of this loyalty. They could not ignore, either, their own belief in the rights of people to democracy and self-determination. However, they faced the spectacle of the overthrow of the monarchy in Russia, seen by many Indian politicians as a sign that a new day was dawning and by many British politicians that anarchy was just around the corner. Could the Raj reach a rapprochement with India that would satisfy both parties?

The Montagu Declaration, August 1917

On 20 August 1917, Edwin Montagu, secretary of state for India, announced in the House of Commons a fresh approach to the governance of India. A passionate Liberal, Montagu had worked closely with John Morley at the India Office before the war and had become convinced that a straightforward statement of British policy toward India was essential. Working closely with the viceroy, Lord Chelmsford, the Montagu Declaration was formulated and agreed to by the British government.

SOURCE

9 Announcement of the secretary of state for India, Edwin Montagu, made in the House of Commons, 20 August 1917.

The policy of His Majesty's Government, with which the Government of India are in complete accord, is that of the increasing association of Indians in every branch of the administration, and the gradual development of self-governing institutions with a view to the progressive realisation of responsible government in India as an integral part of the British Empire. They have decided that substantial steps in this direction should be taken as soon as possible, and that it is of the highest importance as a preliminary to considering what these steps should be that there should be a free and informal exchange of opinion between those in authority at home and in India. His Majesty's government have accordingly decided, with His Majesty's approval, that I should accept the Viceroy's invitation to proceed to India to discuss these matters with the Viceroy and the Government of India, to consider with the Viceroy the views of local governments, and to receive with him the suggestions of representative bodies and others.

I would add that the progress in this policy can only be achieved by successive stages. The British Government and the Government of India, on whom the responsibility lies for the welfare and advancement of the Indian peoples, must be judges of the time and measure of each advance, and they must be guided by the co-operation received from those upon whom new opportunities of service will thus be conferred and by the extent to which it is found that confidence can be reposed in their sense of responsibility.

Ample opportunity will be afforded for public discussion of the proposals, which will be submitted in due course to Parliament.

ACTIVITY
WRITING

Analyse this announcement made by Edwin Montagu, secretary of state for India.
a) Identify any words or phrases you don't understand and research their meanings.

b) Identify words and phrases that show the British government's attitudes towards granting limited self-government to India.

The Montagu Declaration implicitly committed the British government to granting some form of self-government to India. But no timescale was given and this would seem to imply that the British government was in no hurry. Nevertheless, the Montagu Declaration ended by stating that Montagu would visit India to take soundings and this, indeed, he did.

Montagu travelled extensively through the subcontinent between November 1917 and May 1918. A keen ornithologist and wild game hunter, he found much to amaze and delight him in the activities arranged for him by the Indian princes. He was, however, alarmed to find that the British administration of India was both slow and complex, with a tendency to stifle innovation and oppose radical reform. He was very much afraid that Viceroy Chelmsford would succumb to the reactionaries among his administration. Interestingly, Montagu was particularly critical of Michael O'Dwyer, governor of the Punjab, who was adamantly opposed to any more Indian participation in government.

The Rowlatt Acts, the Amritsar Massacre and the political aftermath

In 1915, India had been placed under the Defence of India Act, enacted as a temporary measure for the duration of the war and for six months afterwards. It was intended to put a stop to what could be perceived as anti-war and possibly revolutionary activities. Protest was forbidden: there was a war to be won. In this, the Defence of India Act was similar to the Defence of the Realm Act, which applied to the United Kingdom. Insofar as India was concerned, the Act gave the viceroy the power to issue regulations in order to secure public safety and to ensure India was appropriately defended. Most Indians expected the Defence of India Act to be repealed early in 1919. The British government, however, had other ideas.

The Rowlatt Commission and the Rowlatt Acts

In 1917, the Government of India, afraid that economic and political turbulence was creating a potentially dangerous situation for the Raj, appointed a Scottish judge, Mr S.T. Rowlatt, to head a commission that was to investigate revolutionary conspiracies. In July 1918, the Commission reported. Their report isolated Bengal, Bombay and the Punjab as centres of revolutionary activity, and recommended that the old wartime controls should be continued in order to control the situation. These included imprisonment without trial, trial by judges sitting without a jury, censorship and house arrest of suspects.

The Commission's proposals were incorporated into the Anarchical and Revolutionary Crimes Act, commonly known as the Rowlatt Act. Montagu sanctioned the Act with extreme reluctance, although acknowledging the need to stamp out rebellion and riot he made it clear to the viceroy that, in his view, the Act was extremely offensive. Nevertheless, Viceroy Chelmsford went ahead. Every single one of the 22 Indian members of the Indian Legislative Council opposed the measure, but they were out-voted by the appointed officials and the Act became law in March 1919. The Muslim leader, Muhammad Ali Jinnah and several of his colleagues resigned from the Council. Indeed, Jinnah wrote a furious letter to Chelmsford, in which he accused the administration of the Raj of being neither responsible to the people nor in touch with Indian public opinion.

In reality, the new powers were not needed and the Act was repealed in 1922. However, the damage had been done. The Raj was seen as being duplicitous: supporting the Montagu Declaration on the one hand, but on the other reacting to potential trouble in the only way they knew how – by repression.

The Amritsar Massacre: events

TIMELINE: THE AMRITSAR MASSACRE

1919
30 March: First *hartals* organised

6 April: More *hartals* organised

10 April: Rioting in Amritsar, Marcia Sherwood brutally assaulted

11 April: British women and children take refuge in Gobindgarh Fort

12 April: Dyer heads up a show of force in Amritsar

13 April: Proclamations read throughout Amritsar; massacre at Jallianwala Bagh

14 April: Martial law imposed in Amritsar, Dyer invents Crawling Order

11 November: Lord Hunter and colleagues arrive in Lahore, Hunter Committee sets to work hearing evidence, Indian National Congress Punjab Sub-Committee published

1920
25 March: Report of the Indian National Congress Punjab Sub-Committee published

3 May: Dyer arrives back in England

26 May: Hunter report published

8 July: Commons debate the Amritsar Massacre

19 July: Lords debate the Amritsar Massacre

Hartal
A stoppage of work, usually accompanied by a lock-out, and used as a political protest.

Opposition to the Rowlatt Act flared up throughout India, but nowhere more fiercely than in the Punjab and nowhere more frighteningly than in its administrative capital, Amritsar. *Hartals* were organised for 30 March and 6 April 1919, resulting in an impressive display of Hindu–Muslim solidarity and no serious unrest. However, the arrest of the two organisers, Dr Saifuddin Kitchlew and Dr Satya Pal, triggered rioting, initially in their support but quickly becoming a general anti-Raj protest. Banks were stormed, buildings fired at and three Europeans killed. A mission doctor, Marcia Sherwood, was brutally beaten and saved from certain death by Hindus who found and treated her. By 11 April, over 100 terrified and exhausted European women had taken refuge in the Gobindgarh Fort, trying to find a place of safety. The British had lost control of Amritsar.

The governor of the Punjab, Michael O'Dwyer, was convinced that the rioting in Amritsar was part of a carefully planned uprising, luring Indian soldiers into a mutiny. So, his reaction to the situation in Amritsar was to treat it as the first stage in a general insurrection aimed at overthrowing the Raj. He sent in the troops.

Brigadier-General Rex Dyer led a force of some 1,000 soldiers (one-third of whom were British) into Amritsar on 12 April. A show of force in the streets was met by jeering crowds and this, linked with news of similar rioting in the Punjab cities of Lahore and Kasur, convinced Dyer that a coordinated uprising was under way. This partly explains his reactions the following day.

The following day, 13 April, was Baisakhi Day, marking the beginning of one of the most important religious festivals in the Punjab, which generally lasted for several days. Thousands of pilgrims flocked into Amritsar to worship at the Golden Temple; thousands more came to participate in horse and cattle fairs that were traditionally part of the festivities. Hundreds of these people and their families converged on the Jallianwala Bagh, a large park close to the Golden Temple. The park was surrounded by high-walled buildings and had only four exits. The people at Jallianwala Bagh intended to stay there for the duration of the festival, talking, resting and meeting with the residents of Amritsar. Arrangements were also made for a political meeting in part of the bagh so that people could voice their opinions and make their feelings known about the Rowlatt Act.

Fearing trouble, Dyer ordered proclamations to be read at various points in the city, warning against the holding of 'meetings and assemblies' and establishing a curfew. Between 10,000 and 20,000 Punjabis ignored the curfew and gathered in the Jallianwala Bagh. The political meeting began by passing two resolutions, one calling for the repeal of the Rowlatt Act and the other expressing sympathy with the dead and bereaved in the previous day's riots.

Without a word of warning, Dyer and a posse of infantrymen appeared in the narrow entrance to the bagh. Once inside, they knelt and fired 1,650 rounds of live ammunition into the crowd in ten to 15 minutes, killing around 400 and wounding 1,500 more. Just as suddenly, the troops left, leaving the wounded to fend for themselves or wait for help from friends and family brave enough to risk the curfew. When Dyer reported his actions to his superior officer, General William Beynon told him he approved of his decisions.

Martial law
Very restrictive rule, enforced by a military presence.

Salaam
A greeting accompanied by a low bow.

Dyer now set about establishing **martial law** in Amritsar. It was, however, martial law specially adapted for Amritsar and was designed to humiliate the Indians living there. For example, any Indian who passed a European had to **salaam**. Public floggings were common, with little attention being paid to the guilt or innocence of the victim. Possibly the worst punishment of all, and which probably roused the Indians to even greater anger than the massacre itself, was the Crawling Order. Dyer decided that any Indian who wished to pass along the Kucha Tawarian, the narrow street where Marcia Sherwood had been assaulted and left for dead, had to crawl along it on all fours in the muck, filth and general detritus that collected there. Dyer's version of martial law was particularly offensive to Hindus, living as they were in a structured caste system based on purity and pollution. He intended it to be so.

From the report on the Amritsar Massacre written by General Dyer for his superior officers, 25 August 1919.

I fired and continued to fire until the crowd dispersed, and I consider this is the least amount of firing which would produce the necessary moral and widespread effect it was my duty to produce if I was to justify my action. If more troops had been at hand, the casualties would have been greater in proportion. It was no longer simply a question of dispersing the crowd, but one of producing a sufficient moral effect from a military point of view not only on those who were present, but more especially throughout the Punjab. There could be no question of undue severity.

The crowd was so dense that if a determined rush had been made at any time, arms or no arms, my small force must instantly have been overpowered and consequently I was very careful of not giving the mob a chance of organising. I sometimes ceased fire and redirected my fire where the crowd was collecting more thickly. By the time I had completely dispersed the crowd my ammunition was running short. I returned to the Ram Bagh without counting or inspecting the casualties. The crowd was free now to ask for medical aid, but this they avoided doing lest they themselves be proved to have attended the assembly.

ACTIVITY
KNOWLEDGE CHECK

Reporting Amritsar
How would Source 10 be regarded by (a) the Raj and (b) Indian nationalists?

The Amritsar Massacre: impact in Britain

Details of the massacre were slow to arrive in Britain and, when they did, they divided public opinion and the Commons and Lords in Westminster. Some saw Dyer as the brave and courageous upholder of the Raj. Others felt that Dyer had destroyed all possibility of Indian nationalists and the Raj working together to create a secure future for the subcontinent. Furious debates in the Commons ended with a motion to censure Dyer being carried; furious debates in the Lords ended in support for Dyer.

From part of a speech made in the House of Commons on 8 July 1919 by the secretary of state for India, Edwin Montagu.

When you pass an order that all Indians must crawl past a particular place, when you pass an order to say that all Indians must salaam any officer of His Majesty the King, you are enforcing racial humiliation. When you take selected schoolboys from a school, guilty or innocent, and whip them publicly, when you whip people before they have been convicted, when you flog a wedding party, you are indulging in frightfulness. Are you going to keep your hold on India by terrorism, racial humiliation, and subordination, and frightfulness, or are you going to rest it upon the growing goodwill of the people of the Indian Empire?

Montagu pushed ahead with plans for an inquiry into the massacre, insisting that the inquiry should be completely fearless in its search for the proof. On 11 November 1919, Lord Hunter (former solicitor-general for Scotland) and his colleagues arrived at Lahore to ask questions, listen to evidence and reach a conclusion about the events of 11 April. Witnesses arriving to give evidence were alternately booed and cheered by the crowd; censorship having been lifted and martial law ended, journalists wrote at length. The trained lawyers on the Committee tied many witnesses, including Dyer, in knots. Dyer admitted that he would have used machine guns if he could have got armoured cars into the Jallianwala Bagh; that he had not issued a warning before opening fire; that he had continued firing until his ammunition was exhausted; that he had wanted to punish the Punjabis because they were disobedient; and that he had considered razing Amritsar to the ground. Dyer considered that he had given his evidence truthfully. He had, and it was damning. After questioning hundreds of witnesses, the Hunter Commission's report concluded that they could find no evidence of a conspiracy to overthrow the Raj; Dyer was roundly censured, but O'Dwyer was only gently reprimanded. The three Indian members of the Commission condemned the actions of both men.

SOURCE 12 From the Hunter Commission report, published in May 1920.

The action taken by General Dyer has been described by others as having saved the situation in the Punjab and having averted a rebellion on a scale similar to the mutiny. It does not, however, appear to us possible to draw this conclusion, particularly in view of the fact that it is not proved that a conspiracy to overthrow the British power had been formed prior to the outbreak.

After carefully weighing all the factors, we can arrive at no other conclusion than that, at Jallianwala Bargh, General Dyer acted beyond the necessity of the case, beyond what any reasonable man would have thought to be necessary, and that he did not act with as much humanity as the case permitted.

Dyer, summoned to Delhi and forced to resign, was unrepentant; a deputation from the organisation Ladies of the Punjab presented him with an illuminated address expressing their gratitude for what he had done. The entire garrison turned out to cheer him as he and his wife boarded the train for Bombay. Arriving in Southampton, he insisted he had acted in accordance with his duty.

A Level Exam-Style Question Section A

How far could the historian use Sources 10 and 12 together to investigate the Amritsar Massacre?

Explain your answer, using both sources, the information given about them and your own knowledge of the historical context. (20 marks)

Tip

Think about what the sources do not tell you, as well as what they do.

The Amritsar Massacre: impact in India

The Punjab Sub-Committee of the Indian National Congress set up its own inquiry. It heard evidence in advance of the Hunter Committee and completed its own report some time earlier. The Committee examined 1,700 witnesses and published 650 verified statements. Their final report, which included graphic photographs, amounted to a savage indictment of the way in which India was governed and was calculated to arouse deep feelings of anger and resentment among the Indian subjects of the Raj.

SOURCE 13 From the Indian National Congress Punjab Sub-Committee's report published in March 1920.

The people of the Punjab were incensed against Sir Michael O'Dwyer's administration by reason of his studied contempt and distrust of the educated classes, and by reason of the cruel and compulsory methods adopted during the war, for obtaining recruits and monetary contributions and his suppression of public opinion by gagging the local Press and shutting out nationalist newspapers from outside the Punjab …

The Rowlatt agitation disturbed the public mind and should be repealed …

The Jallianwala Bagh massacre was a calculated piece of inhumanity towards utterly innocent and unarmed men, including children, and unparalleled for its ferocity in the history of modern British administration.

ACTIVITY
KNOWLEDGE CHECK

How could the differences between Sources 12 and 13 be explained?

Interpretation (5c)

Good questions/Bad questions

Below are approaches attributed to three famous historians. They are generalisations for the purpose of this exercise.

Herodotus	Leopold von Ranke	Karl Marx
He looks for the interesting story, the drama and the colourful characters.	He is interested in how great men use their influence to bring about change.	He looks underneath events in an attempt to see patterns of behaviour over long periods of time.

Work in groups.

1 Devise three criteria for what makes a good historical question.

2 Consider what you know about the Amritsar Massacre.

  a) Each write a historical question based on that subject matter.

  b) Put these in rank order, with the best question first, based on your criteria.

3 On a piece of A3 paper, write the names of the three historians at the points of a large triangle.

  a) Write your questions from 2(a) on the triangle so that their positions reflect how likely the historians are to be interested by that question. For example, General Dyer's role in the Massacre would interest Herodotus and Ranke but not Marx and so would be somewhere between Ranke and Herodotus but nowhere near Marx.

  b) Add some further questions. Try to think of questions that only one of the three would be interested in.

4 Take it in turns to answer the questions you have created in the style of one of the historians. See if other members of the group can guess which one it was.

Answer the following questions individually, using examples created by the above activity.

5 Does one method of constructing history lead to better reasoning than the others? Explain your answer.

6 Explain why all historians who deploy rigorous methodology are, to an extent, useful sources for the study of the past.

Significance of 1919 for British rule: the Montagu–Chelmsford Report and the Government of India Act 1919

Meanwhile, Edwin Montagu, secretary of state for India, and Viceroy Lord Chelmsford had been working on a report that fleshed out the Montagu Declaration of 1917. Their proposals were published in July 1918 and became law as the Government of India Act in December 1919. The Act created a **dyarchy**, a division of power, albeit an unequal one, between Indians and British. The dyarchy worked like this:

- The viceroy was to be advised by a council of six civilians, three of whom had to be Indians, and the commander-in-chief of the British Army in India. The viceroy could enforce laws even if the legislative councils rejected them and he could choose his own officials.

- The provincial and central legislative councils were enlarged.

- The provincial councils were given control over Indian education, agriculture, health, local self-government and public works.

- The British retained control of military matters, foreign affairs, currency, communications and criminal law.

- The franchise was extended, although it was still linked to tax payments. After 1919, about ten percent of the adult male population was enfranchised.

KEY TERM

Dyarchy
Government by two independent authorities. In India, this system divided power in the provinces between the Indians and the British from 1919 to 1935.

- Provincial assemblies could enfranchise women if they so wished, and some did. Even so, the number of women voters was less than one percent of the adult female population.

- There were 'reserved' seats in all provincial legislatures for different religious groups (for example, Sikhs, Muslims and Christians) and special interest groups, such as landowners and university graduates.

The intention of the Government of India Act was to shift more and more decision-making from the centre to the provinces and to involve more Indians in the government of their own country. There were, however, problems. Montagu saw the Act as a welcome further step towards Indian self-government and so did his horrified critics. In the House of Commons, India became a contentious issue. Right-wing members of parliament (MPs) were convinced the government was losing its nerve and would soon lose India. Left-wing MPs protested that the reforms had not gone far enough. Members of the Indian Civil Service, concerned about their authority and their mandate to administer India, felt their strength and influence was slipping away. They knew, more than anyone, that Britain governed India only by the consent of the Indian people.

ACTIVITY
KNOWLEDGE CHECK

Reactions to Amritsar

1 Why did the government pass the Rowlatt Act? Were their fears justified?

2 Who was to blame for the Amritsar Massacre?

3 How far did the events in Amritsar influence reaction to the Government of India Act of 1919?

HOW DID NATIONALISM DEVELOP IN INDIA, 1914–20?

The political problems posed by the war were infinitely more complicated than attempting to deal with local protests against intolerable local conditions. Broad national shifts in the political spectrum had been created and were to present serious challenges to the Raj. Indian soldiers fought side-by-side with white British and colonial troops, strengthening their self-esteem. Indian political arguments that the war should be a turning point in Indian–Raj relationships were also strengthened as a consequence. Indians were beginning to bring to their own situation the concepts of freedom and democracy for which their European and, later, American allies said they were fighting.

The Indian National Congress and the emergence of Gandhi

In the years to 1914, Congress was a political party for the privileged few, supported by wealthy Indians. It most certainly did not have a mass following throughout India. Congress debated issues, was consulted by various agencies of the Raj and its members regularly argued among themselves. The most notable tensions were those between Gopal Krishna Gokhale, who believed Indians should respect the Raj and move slowly toward the distant goal of self-government, and Bal Gangadhar Tilak, who was prepared to use force to reach the same end. The role of Congress was to change with the emergence onto the political scene of a previously little-known lawyer, Mohandas Karamchand Gandhi.

Gandhi's work as a young lawyer in South Africa gave him wide experience that was to stand him in good stead when he arrived back in India in 1914. He had gained experience in working with a wide range of Indians from all castes and religions; he had learned to cooperate with and confront individuals in positions of authority and, most importantly, he had begun to experiment with a wide range of protest techniques, particularly with direct, non-violent opposition.

Gandhi had formed a strong friendship with Gokhale, who had visited him in South Africa and admired his work there. It was Gokhale who advised Gandhi, newly arrived in India on the outbreak of war, to keep a low profile while he developed an understanding of the dynamics of the Indian situation and of the ways in which his ideas of *satyagraha* could chime with growing Indian nationalism.

KEY TERM

Satyagraha
A word made up by Gandhi, based on words from the ancient Sanskrit language meaning 'truth' and 'obstinacy'. Gandhi used *satyagraha* to mean 'truth force' or 'soul force' and he and his followers applied it to non-cooperation with the British authorities.

Gandhi gradually familiarised himself with Indian politics and proceeded cautiously. In 1917, he intervened in local situations where, for example, the peasant farmers of Champaran in north Bihar were forced by white planters to grow indigo on disadvantageous terms and in Ahmedabad in Gujarat where cotton mill workers were earning a pittance. In Bihar, *satyagraha* took the form of his refusal to leave the district; in Gujarat, he fasted until the situation was resolved. This was a novel way of dealing with industrial problems. In both these cases, the positive outcome was probably due more to other political re-alignments than to Gandhi's *satyagraha*, but nevertheless his was an impressive performance.

During the war years, Gandhi worked on forging relationships with up-and-coming regional leaders, such as the Bihari lawyer, Rajendra Prasad, the mayor of Ahmedabad, Vallabhbhai Patel, and the young Jawaharlal Nehru. He seems to have been developing an astute awareness of those who would be useful to him in future struggles. Gandhi worked on developing connections with two important communities that had previously been largely neglected by Congress politicians: Muslims and businessmen. This paid off hugely: the Muslims by supporting his take-over of Congress in 1920 (see page 195) and businessmen by bank-rolling his non-cooperation campaign.

The Lucknow Pact and the role of Jinnah

Although originally conceived as an anti-Congress body, there were instances where the Muslim League and Congress worked together and pursued the same objectives. In December 1915, Congress and the Muslim League held sessions in Bombay at the same time, and both committed themselves to pursuing the political objective of self-government. This was just the beginning. The following year, at a joint meeting of Congress and the Muslim League held in Lucknow, the two organisations reached an agreement over the knotty problem of separate electorates. How had this come about?

- The Muslim League, believing that the annulment of the partition of Bengal implied that the British were no longer sympathetic to separate electorates, changed their stance of cooperation with the Raj. In 1913, demand for separation from the Raj was included in their objectives, which brought them closer to the aims of Congress.

- The declaration of war against Turkey in November 1914 caused resentment among those Muslims who regarded the Sultan of Turkey as their Caliph – their most important spiritual leader.

- Muhammad Ali Jinnah, a member of Congress as well as the League, worked tirelessly to bring about a rapprochement between the two organisations in the pursuit of a common aim: self-government. A Bombay-based barrister, he was the League's chief spokesman in the discussions leading to the Lucknow Pact. It is ironic that the proposals to create a separate Muslim electorate with reserved seats not only guaranteed Muslims a voice, it also gave them an enhanced sense of Islamic identity that sat uneasily with the sincere secularism of men like Jinnah. Indeed, Jinnah himself did not like the idea of separate electorates.

The Lucknow Pact of 1916 was the result: a pact whereby it was agreed that the number of Muslims in the provincial legislatures should be laid down province by province, and that there should be separate electorates for all communities until and unless they requested a joint one. Thus the Muslims believed that they had been given assurances by the Hindus that were similar to those obtained earlier from the British government and felt able to work with Congress.

Congress itself was strengthened, not only by cooperation with the Muslim League in what seemed like a joint enterprise, but by healing rifts in its own membership. The deaths of the moderates Gopall Krishna Gokhale and Pherozeshah Mehta enabled Congress to find a formula whereby the extremist, Bal Tilak, could re-enter Congress. It was hardly surprising that one of the first resolutions passed by the newly united Congress was to urge the British to issue a proclamation stating that their aim was to confer self-government on India in the near future.

EXTEND YOUR KNOWLEDGE

The Partition of Bengal

In 1905, against the advice of all his British and Indian advisors, Viceroy Curzon organised the partition of Bengal into two provinces: East Bengal and Assam, with its capital in Dhaka, and West Bengal, which would include the cities of Bihar and Orissa. East Bengal had a predominately Muslim population while West Bengal was predominantly Hindu. Bengal had traditionally been an unruly province and dividing the province along religious lines, Curzon argued, was the way to calm the situation.

The Hindus immediately opposed this partition because it would create a province, East Bengal, that was dominated by Muslims. Muslims, on the other hand, tended to support partition because it freed them from Hindu control, at least in one of the two new provinces.

Unsurprisingly, partition resulted in rioting and general unrest in Bengal and other parts of India. This unrest ranged from violence to more-or-less passive resistance. A Bengali terrorist movement carried out a number of murders, and a boycott of British goods was started. A massive petition was presented to the viceroy, urging him to bring partition to an end, but to no avail.

At a stroke, Curzon had managed to spark a nationwide protest movement, introduce direct confrontation into British–Indian relationships, provoke sectarian conflict, and suggest to the perceptive that partition was a 'solution' the British were not afraid to impose.

In 1911, in an attempt to placate the Hindu majority, who had been outraged by the deliberate creation of a Muslim-dominated province, Bengal was reunited. The significance of these manoeuvrings was that they set a precedent for partition being a 'solution' the British were ready to try.

SOURCE

14 Planned seats for Muslims in provincial councils as part of the Lucknow Pact of 1916.

Province	Muslim population (%)	Planned seats (%)
Punjab	Over 50	50
Bengal	Over 50	40
United Provinces	14	30
Bihar	13	25
Central Provinces + Madras	11	15
Bombay	20	33.3

ACTIVITY

KNOWLEDGE CHECK

The growth of nationalism

What problems did the Lucknow Pact hope to solve? Use Source 14 in your answer.

Of course, this working out of separate electorates was simply an agreement between Congress and the League. They had no power to impose it. However, Jinnah's statement that cooperation should be their guiding principle cemented the (albeit temporary) alliance between the two organisations and signalled to the British that the Indian nationalist movement was gaining in strength.

EXTRACT

From John Keay, *A History of India*, published in 2000.

The 1916 Lucknow Pact, by which Congress and the League agreed a joint programme, would see the League accept Muslim under-representation in Muslim majority areas (like east Bengal) in return for Congress' acceptance of Hindu under-representation in Hindu majority areas (like the United Provinces). Here was precisely the political horse-trading essential to the working of a plural society. Both sides embraced it; so even did an 'extremist' like the lately returned Tilak. At this stage, with one partition having failed, another was unthinkable. It was eminently avoidable.

EXTRACT

2

From Judith M. Brown, *Modern India: the Origins of an Asian Democracy*, published in 1994.

The Congress-League pact was emphatically not an agreement between Congress and the whole Muslim community, any more than the foundation of the League had signified the emergence of a unified Muslim Community with a single political voice. At the time of the pact, the League probably had between 500 and 800 members, and the Lucknow agreement did not even represent all of them because the negotiations were carried on by a clique.

EXTRACT

3

From Percival Spear, *A History of India, vol. 2,* published in 1965.

At the end of the year [1916] Tilak captured Congress and electrified India by concluding the Lucknow Pact with the Muslims. The essence of this was Muslim support for the Congress demand for self-government in return for the recognition of separate Muslim constituencies. Tilak had lost none of his tactical skill and now showed that he could think on an all-India scale.

THINKING HISTORICALLY   Evidence (6a)

Arguments and facts

You will be working with Extracts 1, 2 and 3.

1 Why are facts important in history?

2 Read Extracts 1 and 2.

  a) How do these extracts disagree?

  b) Which one do you think is correct? Explain your answer.

3 Read Extracts 2 and 3.

  a) How do these extracts disagree?

  b) Which one do you think is correct? Why?

4 These three sources detail arguments about the significance of the Lucknow Pact, but only briefly, if at all, mention facts like the dates and terms of the Pact. Which do you think is more important, facts or arguments?

5 If we accept that Extract 2 is wrong, do we discount it as being useful?

Home Rule Leagues

The launching of two mutually supportive Home Rule Leagues in 1916 brought the whole concept of home rule to masses of Indian people who were otherwise somewhat disinterested in the doings of Congress and the League.

- Bal Tilak's Home Rule League operated in western India, mainly in Maharashtra and Karnataka and rapidly gained 32,000 members.

- The All-India Home Rule League, started by Annie Besant, grew more slowly but soon had a network of committees that covered most of India.

Home rule, for both Besant and Tilak, did not necessarily mean separation from Britain. Defence and foreign policy matters would remain the responsibility of Britain. Home rule was simply focused on domestic affairs. Besant and Tilak toured widely, giving public lectures, and joined each other's leagues. Both organisations used newspapers, rallies, pamphlets and songs to generate interest and support, along with fiery speeches to whip up enthusiasm for home rule. The Home Rule Leagues attracted members of Congress and the Muslim League: Jinnah joined Besant's All-India Home Rule League in 1917. Excitement and enthusiasm were widespread, and hundreds of thousands of Indians signed petitions that were presented to the British authorities, demanding home rule and other concessions. Perhaps the most important impact of the leagues was that they spread political awareness in previously unpoliticised provinces. This was to be built upon by Gandhi and his *satyagraha* approach to protest, which was found by many living in rural India to be a more attractive alternative.

Provincial assemblies were alarmed by the rapid growth of the Home Rule Leagues and the British Raj even more so. Tilak was arrested for sedition and required to put up 40,000 rupees as surety of good behaviour; Besant was interned [confined] in June 1917. These moves were counter-productive: both the Muslim League and Congress swung behind home rule.

EXTEND YOUR KNOWLEDGE

Annie Besant (1847–1933)

Annie Besant was English, a free-thinker, a socialist and social reformer. In 1889, she converted to theosophy, a philosophy based on an understanding of the nature of God, seeing this as the link between socialism and spirituality. She visited India in 1893, where the headquarters of the Theosophical Society were located. Deciding that India was her one true home, she settled there for the rest of her life.

Annie learned Sanskrit, studied Hindu religious books and was determined to raise Hindu self-esteem in the face of the imperialism of the British Raj. She founded the Central Hindu College in 1898 and a network of schools throughout India, which were administered by the Theosophical Society. After 1913, Annie turned her attention to Indian independence and, in 1917, was appointed president of Congress, a post she held until 1923. Gradually, however, she lost nationalist support and was eclipsed by the campaigns of Gandhi.

Response to British legislation and the significance of Amritsar, 1919–20

Reaction to the Government of India Act of 1919

The Government of India Act was an attempt to enlist the cooperation of India's educated middle class in governing India by shifting more and more decision-making from the centre to the provinces. However, many people, particularly the Hindus, hated the idea of 'reserved' seats, believing these to be divisive, anti-democratic and inappropriate in a society that was working towards democracy on the Western European model. Those hoping for home rule were bitterly disappointed. Many reflected on the contrast between the weeks it took to pass the Rowlatt Act and the four years that elapsed between the Montagu Declaration and the Government of India Act, believing that the repression of the former more accurately represented the attitude of the British government towards India than the more liberal terms of the latter. Indeed, the Rowlatt Act very nearly wrecked the Government of India Act. Significantly, the Indian National Congress rejected the Montagu–Chelmsford reforms and boycotted the first elections held under the 1919 Act.

The significance of the Amritsar Massacre, 1919

The official responses to the Amritsar Massacre were the Hunter Commission and the report commissioned by the Indian National Congress (page 184). There was, however, a response within India that had far wider-reaching significance than either of these reports.

Horrified by the repressive nature of the Rowlatt Act, which ordinary political protest and a unanimous vote by the Indian representatives in the Imperial Legislative Council had failed to stop, Gandhi called for a *satyagraha* in April 1919. As far as he was concerned, it was a technique that had worked in Bihar and Gujarat to resolve industrial issues (or so Gandhi thought), so it should work against the Rowlatt Act and persuade the government to withdraw it. Gandhi's idea was to hold a series of *hartals* throughout India, using this form of direct, non-violent action to break the impasse between politicians. It failed. *Hartals* were held, to a greater or lesser extent, in most of India's provinces. However, the degree to which they were observed varied from region to region within and between provinces. More seriously, the stoppages erupted into violence in Gujarat and the Punjab. Gandhi immediately called a stop to the Rowlatt *satyagraha* but, even so, that failed to stop the violence. It was a dreadful lesson. *Satyagraha* would only work if everyone involved understood its basic tenets and did not use it as a pretext to follow other agendas.

By the end of 1919, Amritsar and its aftermath had turned thousands of loyal Indians against the Raj. They believed that Amritsar had revealed the true face of British rule and that any British reform that tended toward Indian independence was a sham.

ACTIVITY
KNOWLEDGE CHECK

The growth of nationalism

1 In your judgement, which would Raj officials find more threatening: the 1916 Lucknow Pact or the activities of the Home Rule Leagues? Explain your answer.

2 Write brief reports about the condition of India in 1919 from the point of view of:

  a) a member of the Indian Civil Service

  b) a member of the Indian National Congress.

ACTIVITY
SUMMARY

The Raj 1914–19

1 To what extent did the problems surrounding the Government of India Act 1919 highlight the weaknesses of the Raj?

2 Why was the issue of separate electorates for Muslims such a problem?

3 What does the Amritsar Massacre reveal about Anglo-Indian relationships?

WIDER READING

Allen, C. (ed.) *Plain Tales from the Raj*, Abacus (2000)

Brown, Judith M. *Modern India: The Origins of an Asian Democracy*, Oxford University Press (1991)

Colvin, I. *The Life of General Dyer*, Blackwood (1929)

Copland, I. *India 1885–1947*, Routledge (2001)

Draper, A. *The Amritsar Massacre*, Ashford, Buchan and Enwright (1963)

Furneaux, R. *Massacre at Amritsar*, Allen and Unwin (1963)

Moraes, F. *Witness to an Era*, Weidenfeld and Nicolson (1973)

2a.2 Changing political relationships, 1920–30

KEY QUESTIONS

- Why, and with what success, did Congress adopt Gandhi's policy of civil disobedience?
- How successfully did Congress consolidate its position, 1922–30?
- To what extent did the Muslim League become a political force, 1920–30?
- How effective was the British response to the changing political landscape in India, 1920–30?

INTRODUCTION

The years from 1920 to just after 1930 saw Congress transformed from being little more than a middle- and upper-class talking shop to a force to be reckoned with on the Indian political scene. By the mid-1920s, Congress had become a political party with mass appeal and a following of millions throughout India. It had sharpened its ideals and focused its impact, and the Raj could not afford to ignore its power and influence. That this happened was largely due to the hard work, vision and charisma of Mohandas Karamchand Gandhi, who was developing his unique response to the Raj. However, set against this essentially Hindu development was that of the increasingly organised and vocal Muslim minority that found its voice in Muhammad Ali Jinnah, and in the actions of the Muslim League and the Khilafat Movement. The heady days of the 1916 Lucknow Pact were forgotten in the increasingly politicised climate of the 1920s, and relationships between Muslims and Hindus worsened at both local and national levels. It was during the 1920s that the concept of a separate Muslim state in the Indian subcontinent began to grow and develop in the minds of Hindus and Muslims alike. The 1920s were a time for re-thinking, too, on the part of the British government, as they desperately worked to keep the Empire and the British Raj intact, while at the same time conciliating Indian opinion. It was a difficult, if impossible, tightrope to walk.

WHY, AND WITH WHAT SUCCESS, DID CONGRESS ADOPT GANDHI'S POLICY OF CIVIL DISOBEDIENCE?

Gandhi spent the years between his return to India in 1914 and the emergence of the Indian people from the horrors of the First World War in forging links with businessmen and with the Muslim community. Equally importantly, he spent the time refining and developing his philosophy, informed by attempting to put it into action when helping to resolve local disputes. It was this philosophy that underpinned his aims and beliefs and was to have a profound effect upon India in the years to 1947.

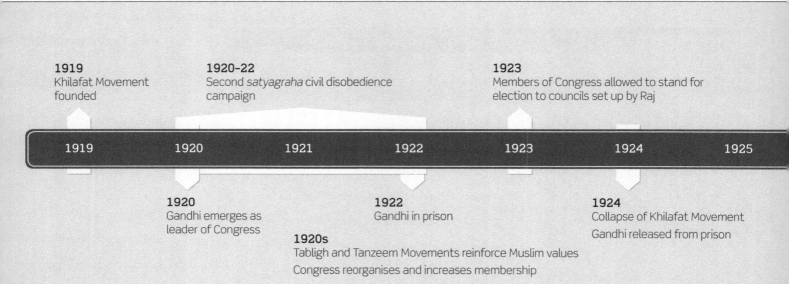

1919
Khilafat Movement founded

1920-22
Second *satyagraha* civil disobedience campaign

1923
Members of Congress allowed to stand for election to councils set up by Raj

1919 | 1920 | 1921 | 1922 | 1923 | 1924 | 1925

1920
Gandhi emerges as leader of Congress

1922
Gandhi in prison

1924
Collapse of Khilafat Movement
Gandhi released from prison

1920s
Tabligh and Tanzeem Movements reinforce Muslim values
Congress reorganises and increases membership

What were Gandhi's aims and beliefs?

The concept of *satyagraha*

Gandhi's philosophy was underpinned by his concept of *satyagraha*. He created the word by joining the Sanskrit words for 'truth' and 'obstinacy' and used it to describe non-violent resistance to injustice or evil. Every single individual, Gandhi believed, was created to search for the truth. This truth permeated the universe and was present in the deepest part of everyone's being. In order to be fully human, each person had to reach that truth within themselves. Since all individuals are at different points on their own personal journey to this truth, those with a weaker grasp of the truth should never be forced to accept a more strongly held truth. Violence would inhibit their search for ultimate truth and so non-violence between individuals and groups is essential.

It is important to note that Gandhi hated the term 'passive resistance', which is sometimes used to describe his campaigning style, and never wanted it applied to his methods. Passive resistance means just that: resisting authority by doing nothing, for example, by taking part in a sit-down protest. Gandhi advocated non-violent but active non-cooperation, for example, removing children from school.

Winning hearts and minds

Gandhi may have been out of touch, in the years to 1914, with the complexity of events in India, but this didn't stop him from having a very clear vision of the sort of society he wanted India to become or from creating a plan to achieve this. He started from the premise that Western technology had failed. It had not added to the sum of human happiness and had, indeed, made man slave to machines.

Gandhi believed that people would be much happier, and so best enabled to continue on their journey to truth, if they lived in small, self-contained communities. Freedom for India, he hoped, would be accompanied by the dismantling of the state and the return to the small simple communities of the past. Of course, the idea was completely unworkable. Delhi and Calcutta, Bombay and Madras, were bustling modern cities, teeming with millions of people who couldn't possibly return to their rural origins. But the idea of self-sufficient rural communities caught on, and the Indian peasant masses began to take notice of Gandhi and to see in him someone with whom they could identify.

Gandhi increasingly adopted a peasant lifestyle. He discarded the Western clothes of an English-educated lawyer and began wearing the Indian *dhoti*, a traditional Indian men's garment (see Source 1) emphasising as he did so that all Indian clothes should be made from the locally made cotton cloth known as *kaddar*. Always a vegetarian, he began eating more and more frugally, again as the peasants did. Like the peasants, he walked everywhere he could. He began a routine of daily spinning, believing it would bring him into closer contact with the millions of Indian peasants for whom spinning with a **charka** was a daily task. No other Indian politician behaved like this. The Indian masses now began to identify, not only with his ideas, but also with Gandhi himself. His renunciation of contemporary values and his search for truth led to people calling him **Mahatma**.

KEY TERMS

Charka
A spinning wheel. This became the symbol of the Congress party. Gandhi believed that daily spinning by India's leaders would not only bring them into closer contact with the realities of peasant life, but would also enhance the dignity of labour in the minds of India's intellectuals, who had never had to do hard physical work.

Mahatma
Usually translated as 'the Great Soul'. In India, this title is bestowed on someone who is deeply revered for wisdom and virtue.

1926
Irwin appointed Viceroy of India

1927
Congress rejects Muslim League's Delhi proposals for protection of Muslim interests in a new Constitution

1928
'Young hooligans' enter the political arena
Simon Commission arrives in Bombay
Nehru Report sets out basic constitution for an independent India

1929
Congress rejects Jinnah's '14 Points' intended as the basis of new constitution for India
Irwin Declaration asserts India should aim for dominion status
Lahore Congress decides on *purna swaraj* (complete independence)

1930
Salt *satyagraha* begins in March
Civil disobedience campaign

1931
Gandhi-Irwin Pact – civil disobedience suspended and political prisoners released
Gandhi agrees to attend London Round Table conference

| 1926 | 1927 | 1928 | 1929 | 1930 | 1931 |

EXTEND YOUR KNOWLEDGE

Ashram living

Gandhi rejected the lifestyle of Indians of his caste and profession, preferring instead to live in *ashrams*. These were austere communities of fellow believers and followers. Living in an *ashram* involved renouncing all sexual relationships as part of an individual's move towards purification. By living in *ashrams*, Gandhi was identifying himself with those traditional Indian beliefs that regarded emission of semen as a loss of strength; therefore, not to engage in the sexual act was a sign of power.

SOURCE

1 A photograph, taken in 1925, of Gandhi spinning cotton thread at Sabarmati Ashram, in Ahmedabad.

SOURCE

 In 1956 the BBC broadcast four documentary radio programmes in which people who knew Gandhi well chatted informally about him. Transcripts of the programmes were made into a book published in 1969: *Talking of Gandhi*, edited by Francis Watson and Hallam Tennyson. In this extract, Jawaharlal Nehru remembers Gandhi's immediate impact on the political scene after the First World War.

Jawaharlal Nehru: [He said] it's up to you to choose me as your leader or not. It's up to you to throw me out when you want to. It's up to you to cut off my head if you want to, but so long as I am your leader, I am the leader and there's martial law. So this curious mixture of extreme modesty and simplicity, with an iron will, an iron command always put across in a soft way.

Narrator: Gandhi himself, Mr Nehru feels, formed a link between diverse individuals.

Jawaharlal Nehru: The fact that stood out about Gandhiji [an affectionate term] was how he attracted people of different kinds - completely different kinds - and thereby he became, as you might say, a link between different groups, different individuals from the poorest peasant whom he always sought to represent to princes and rich industrialists and others - they were all attracted in their own way, and no doubt influenced by him to some extent.

Narrator: In the beginning, Mr Nehru says Congress politicians looked upon Gandhi as a respected crank.

Jawaharlal Nehru: Then when he came into the political field in a big way and made - well, rather astounding proposals asking, for instance, lawyers to give up their practice, and live simply and on next to nothing; everybody to wear hand-spun clothes made in the villages, and the whole atmosphere changed, and many of our older leaders, who wanted to co-operate with him, nevertheless were not quite clear what all this meant, because they'd been thinking differently. There was a conflict for some months, maybe a year. But he caught on well with the Indian people, the masses, and that brought some conviction to older leaders, who were pulled then towards him.

Jawaharlal Nehru (1889–1964)

Jawaharlal Nehru was the son of Motilal Nehru, an Indian barrister and leading Congress politician. Born into a wealthy Kashmiri household, he was educated in England, at Harrow School and Cambridge University, where he read law.

Nehru returned to India, where the Amritsar Massacre and the impact of Gandhi on Congress changed his life and he began to hope for Indian independence. A popular orator and deeply involved in the Non-Cooperation Movement, he was in and out of prison in the 1920s and 1930s. He refused to compromise with the Muslim League and, throughout his negotiations with the British during the Second World War, was held by many to be largely responsible for the intransigence of Jinnah, which led to Partition.

He became head of the interim government in 1946 and helped Louis Mountbatten to negotiate the final stages of independence. He remained prime minister of India until his death in 1964.

How did Gandhi emerge as leader of Congress?

When Gandhi left South Africa in 1914, he was not vehemently anti-Raj. Indeed, many of his speeches in the years from 1915 to 1918 were in support of British involvement in the First World War and of India's contribution to that involvement. But three things led Gandhi to change his mind and to develop the idea of *swaraj* or self-rule for India:

- The Rowlatt Acts, which aimed at continuing indefinitely repressive wartime restrictions (see pages 181–82).

- The Amritsar massacre of April 1919 and its tacit endorsement by large sections of the British community in India (see pages 182–83).

- One of the outcomes of the Paris peace conferences that ended the First World War was that Turkey had to pay a huge indemnity and lose its territories. This confirmed the worst fears of Indian Muslims – that white Europeans and Americans had little concern for Islamic nations. It made Gandhi realise that this could increase the idea of separateness among Muslims.

It was Gandhi's reaction to these three events that propelled him to the forefront of Indian politics. Believing that Britain no longer had the moral right to rule India, he captured the popular imagination through his style of campaigning and succeeded in winning mass support for Congress. His methods, combining spiritual strength with political awareness, had immense popular appeal. Congress, although not yet a political party and still very much a forum for discussion, could not help but be impressed. By 1920, unsurprisingly, Gandhi emerged as the leading Indian politician. There was no other all-Indian political leader or group who could challenge his influence over the Indian people nor organise opposition to him. Gokhale had died in 1915, Annie Besant was seen as a woman of little consequence and Tilak died in 1920. Members of Congress were so divided about which path was the best way forward that they couldn't unite to oppose Gandhi. Members of social and religious groups who had

previously exercised little influence at meetings of Congress now appeared as delegates supporting Gandhi. In addition, there was wide geographical support for Gandhi because of the many local disputes in which he had been involved.

So it was that members of Congress had little alternative but to ally with Gandhi. They were prepared, provided they could influence its pattern and timing, to support Gandhi, *satyagraha* and *swaraj*.

How effective was the Congress non-cooperation campaign, 1920–22?

Congress's 25th annual meeting, held in Nagpur in December 1920, was of immense significance. Gandhi dominated the proceedings and, by the force of his arguments, his ability to bind together Hindus and Muslims and by his sheer charisma, he persuaded the delegates to vote for his policy of non-cooperation with the Raj. They did so by a majority of just over two votes to one. Gandhi's aim was, quite simply, to make the Raj ungovernable. If this happened, Gandhi predicted that the Raj would wither and die within a year and *swaraj* would follow. Gandhi had written to the viceroy (Source 3) explaining why he was proposing a campaign of non-cooperation and he had now persuaded Congress to support non-cooperation in their pursuit of independence. It all seemed so simple. But was it?

SOURCE

3 Part of a letter written by Gandhi to the viceroy of India, dated 1 August 1920.

Your Excellency's light-hearted treatment of the official crime [the Amritsar Massacre], your exoneration of Sir Michael O'Dwyer, Mr Montagu's dispatch and above all the shameful ignorance of the Punjab events and the callous disregard of the feelings of the Indians betrayed by the House of Lords, have filled me with the gravest misgivings regarding the future of the Empire, have estranged me completely from the present government and have disabled me from tendering as I have hitherto whole-heartedly tendered my loyal co-operation. In my humble opinion, the ordinary method of agitating by way of petitions, deputation and the like is no remedy for moving to repentance a Government so hopelessly indifferent to the welfare of its charge as the Government of India has proved to be.

In European countries, the condoning of such grievous wrongs would have resulted in a bloody revolution by the people. They would have resisted at all cost the national emasculation such as the said wrongs imply. But one half of India is too weak to offer a violent resistance and the other half is unwilling to do so. I have therefore ventured to suggest a remedy of non-co-operation, which enables those who wish to dissociate themselves from the Government and which, if it is unattended by violence and undertaken in an ordered manner, must compel it to replace its steps and undo the wrongs committed.

SOURCE

4

From the Government of India's Resolution on the Non-Cooperation Movement, published in the *Gazette of India*, 6 November 1920.

Although in their opinion, the movement is unconstitutional in that it has as its object the paralysis and subversion of the existing administration of the country, Government has hitherto refrained from instituting criminal proceedings against those of its promoters who have advocated simultaneously with non-cooperation abstention from violence, and they have instructed local governments only to take action against those persons who have gone beyond the limits originally set by the organisers and have by speech or writing openly incited the public to violence or have attempted to tamper with the loyalty of the army or of the police. In adopting this policy, Government has been influenced by several considerations:

They have been reluctant to interfere with liberty of speech and the freedom of the press.

Government is at all times reluctant to embark on a campaign against individuals some of whom may be motivated by honest, if misguided, motives.

The third, and chief consideration, is Government's trust in the common sense of India, their belief that the sanity of the classes and the masses alike would reject non-cooperation as a visionary and unrealistic scheme, which if successful could only result in widespread disorder, political chaos, and the ruin of all those who have any real stake in the country. The appeal of non-cooperation is to prejudice and ignorance.

ACTIVITY
KNOWLEDGE CHECK

The non-cooperation campaign

1 How far does Source 3 explain why Gandhi began his non-cooperation campaign?

2 To what extent does Source 4 explain the British government's dilemma?

What did non-cooperation entail?

Gandhi and, through him, Congress, urged all Indians to:

- boycott elections to the new legislative assemblies

- hand back all titles and decorations awarded by the Raj

- remove their children from government schools

- refuse invitations to social events run by the Raj

- boycott the law courts

- withhold taxes

- refuse to buy imported goods

- leave all government posts.

Some of this was completely unrealistic. Lawyers, for example, were unlikely to leave their lucrative practices, neither would parents want to deprive their children of an education. However, many areas of non-cooperation were realistic and could quite easily bring the machinery of government to a shuddering halt. Mass refusal to pay taxes, for example, would eventually stop most government departments functioning.

Non-cooperation in action

Gandhi, mindful of what happened to his earlier *satyagraha* campaign against the Rowlatt Acts, was terrified that the movement would again fall into the hands of the mob. Accordingly, he targeted those areas of government where Indian non-cooperation was unlikely to bring them into conflict with the police. Fortunately for the campaign, these happened to be in areas such as taxation and administration, which were vital to the smooth functioning of the Raj. There were some initial successes. For example, students boycotted their examinations, taxes were not paid, a large number of qualified voters stayed away from the 1920 elections, around 200 lawyers stopped work and, during the visit of the Duke of Connaught to Calcutta in 1921, shops were closed throughout the city and few Indians attended the official ceremonies.

However, millions of Indians were unwilling or unable to understand the morality underpinning the concept of *satyagraha*. They followed their own agendas, mostly paying off old scores and attempting to drive through new initiatives. Violence broke out at different times in different provinces. In Bombay, for example, a *hartal* designed to coincide with the visit of the Prince of Wales turned into four days of looting and rioting, leaving 53 dead and hundreds injured. In Rangpur, the mob attacked moneylenders. The Muslim Moplahs of Malaba declared a **jihad**, killing British people and wealthy Hindu and Muslim landlords and moneylenders, as well as forcing Hindu peasants and labourers to convert to Islam. In the Punjab, and later in the Gangetic Plain, the Deccan and other parts of India, Hindus forced Muslims to 'purify' themselves by total immersion in water tanks and rivers, resulting in many drownings. The always fragile Hindu–Muslim alliance was in serious jeopardy. *Satyagraha* was spiralling out of control.

KEY TERM

Jihad
An Arabic word meaning 'struggle' or 'resisting'. It has come to mean a Muslim holy war.

The end of the campaign

Matters came to a head in February 1922 when a mob of Congress supporters torched a police station in Chauri Chaura, a village in Gorakhpur, burning alive 22 Indian policemen. Gandhi immediately withdrew to his *ashram* to fast and meditate, emerging a few days later to call an end to the non-cooperation campaign. His supporters were horrified that he would throw away so many gains just for a few acts of violence, but Gandhi was adamant. He turned away from political agitation to work on a social welfare programme in the villages with, of course, an emphasis on self-sufficiency and spinning and weaving. Less than a month after calling off the campaign, Gandhi was arrested and charged with promoting disaffection with the legally established government. Pleading guilty, he was sentenced to six years' imprisonment. Was it all over?

Something lost and something gained?

Gandhi's idea that *satyagraha* could, of itself, bring about *swaraj* had been discredited, but Gandhi himself was clear that the concept wasn't wrong. What was wrong, he believed, was that the Indian people were not yet ready for the sort of self-discipline that was necessary to make it effective.

One outstanding feature of Congress's commitment to *satyagraha* was the way in which members had acquired a deeper understanding of peasants' needs. Peasants had, hitherto, been more or less ignored by members of Congress. For example, Jawaharlal Nehru, a barrister with a privileged background and a member of Congress, decided in the summer of 1920 to travel extensively in Awadh, a region in the centre of what is now Uttar Pradesh but was then known as the United Provinces of Agra and Oudh – and the province of his birth. What he found there was miserable poverty, but combined with a sense of excitement that change was in the air. It was this sense of excitement that Gandhi had created and which Congress, with their growing ability to understand local grievances, was to exploit and to link, not always successfully, with the broader campaign for *swaraj*.

The significance of Gandhi's imprisonment

The ending of the non-cooperation campaign and Gandhi's imprisonment gave everyone concerned, the British and Indian governments, Congress, Gandhi and the Indian people, a breathing space. Everyone involved had to stand back and reflect on the appropriate way forward. Gandhi was released from prison in January 1924, having served nearly two years of his sentence. During this time:

- Congress became more involved in peasant communities and gained a greater understanding of peasants' needs and aspirations.

- Congress became more ready to understand and exploit local grievances and explore how these could be linked to the broader campaign for *swaraj*.

- Leadership of Congress passed to the moderate lawyers C.R. Das and Motilal Nehru. Both favoured taking advantage of the Government of India Act 1919 and, in 1923, members of Congress were allowed to stand for election to the councils set up by the Raj. Many congressmen were successful in local elections and their presence on the local councils lent those bodies an air of respectability as well as boosting the popularity of the Congress party itself. Many middle-class Indians, alienated by Gandhi's non-cooperation campaign, returned to the fold.

- The Raj returned to its traditional policy of attempting to balance the need to keep control while, at the same time, making concessions to India. Considerable support was given to the local assemblies, where, for example, a cholera and smallpox inoculation programme was started.

ACTIVITY
KNOWLEDGE CHECK

Gandhi and non-cooperation

1 Why did Gandhi wear a *dhoti* and spend time spinning cotton thread?

2 In what ways did Gandhi believe *satyagraha* would lead to *swaraj*?

3 Who, or what, was to blame for the failure of Gandhi's non-cooperation campaign?

4 How far was *satyagraha* a sensible way to achieve *swaraj*? Discuss this in a small group.

HOW SUCCESSFULLY DID CONGRESS CONSOLIDATE ITS POSITION, 1922–30?

Following the collapse of Congress's non-cooperation campaign, the 1920s were largely a period of regrouping and consolidation. Congress refined and developed its structure and increased its membership and appeal by reaching out to groups and areas hitherto untapped. Gandhi's release from prison and his 'back to basics' policy did much to increase support for Congress in rural areas. Indeed, by the end of the decade, Congress members were poised to embark on their most extensive *satyagraha* to date – one that was to have profound effects on Indians and on the Raj.

TIMELINE: CONGRESS RETRENCHMENT 1922–30

1920s Congress reorganises and increases its membership

1922 Gandhi in prison

1923 Congress allows members to stand for election to councils set up by the Raj

1924 Gandhi released from prison

1928 'Young Hooligans' enter political arena

December: Nehru Report recommends dominion status for India

1929 Lahore Congress decides on *purna swaraj*

1930
26 January: Designated Independence Day

March: Start of Salt March

April: Jawaharal Nehru imprisoned for six months

May: Gandhi arrested

June: Entire Congress Working Committee arrested

Extending the appeal of Congress

Membership

During the period of non-cooperation, membership of Congress grew by leaps and bounds. From a base of 100,000, it rose to around two million by the end of 1921. There had been withdrawals. The more conservative elements of the membership had objected to seeing Congress transformed from being a pressure group into one that demonstrated open defiance of the Raj. A large number of Muslims left because of what they regarded as Gandhi's failure to support them over their concerns about the break-up of the Islamic Ottoman Empire after the First World War (see page 206). However, overwhelmingly, the membership trend was upwards.

Congress had achieved this support in two main ways. Firstly, it extended its appeal into a wider spread of geographical areas throughout the subcontinent. Secondly, it began wooing interest groups that had hitherto been neglected. Many of its new supporters came from the richer peasantry and the commercial castes, but Congress was also beginning to recruit support from railway workers, mill-hands and poorer peasants, some of whom had organised themselves into peasant leagues.

Organisation

When Gandhi emerged as leader of Congress in 1920, the party organisation consisted of three administrative levels: local branches, provincial committees and an All-Indian Congress Committee (the AICC). This structure was revitalised in 1920 because of Gandhi's perception that a new sense of direction and purpose was needed. Cooperation with the Raj was to end and was to be replaced by non-violent non-cooperation. Membership of the All-Indian Congress Committee was increased from 161 to 350 and seats were re-allocated on a regional population basis. Great emphasis was placed on recruiting women and from hitherto untapped groups like trade unions. Around 100 additional provincial committees and several hundred more local branches were set up.

Gandhi, on his release from prison, set up a new unit within the All-Indian Congress Committee. This was the Congress Working Committee (CWC) and its job was to formulate policy. It was mirroring what a cabinet was to government. Clearly, Gandhi intended Congress to develop an alternative administrative structure that could take over when, as he hoped, the Raj withered away.

'Back to basics'

On his release from prison in 1924, Gandhi went back to basics. He set up the All-India Spinners' Association, with the intention of spreading the word about hand spinning and weaving as well as promoting the general cause of self-sufficiency. This was entirely congruent with what seemed to be his basic belief that the way forward for India was to dismantle the structure and organisation of the state and return to the simpler, self-sufficient communities of the past. He persuaded a willing Congress to embark on campaigns of mass literacy and for the improvement of village sanitation. Gandhi himself began to campaign vigorously on behalf of the 'Untouchables' in order to enable them to enter fully into Indian society.

Gandhi really did seem to have abandoned his confrontational programme of non-violence and Congress seemed to be emerging as a responsible political party, determined to improve the lot of the Indian people without embarking on the dangerous path that had independence as its goal. Those who believed this were to be proved terribly wrong.

EXTRACT

1 From *Raj: the Making and Unmaking of British India*, by Lawrence James, published in 1997.

For all his humility, Gandhi was at heart a vain man who wanted Indian freedom on his own terms and through his own methods. When both had failed, he stepped down and turned his attention to spinning and Hindu education, giving the impression that he considered these equally important as the achievement of Indian nationhood. They were, for both were part of Gandhi's programme of national redemption, which was a vital part of the struggle for independence. So was he; his semi-monastic retirement in February 1922 was followed by six years in which Congressional energies were largely consumed by sterile internal debate. The Raj breathed again.

Enter the 'young hooligans'

Many members of Congress would have been happy to let the process of constructive development continue almost indefinitely. But two events changed all this:

- Three energetic, charismatic young men, whom Gandhi was later to call the 'young hooligans', burst upon the political scene.
- The British government set up and sent out the Simon Commission (see pages 211–12).
- The two events were not unconnected.

Who were these 'young hooligans'? They were Subhas Chandra Bose, Jayaprakash Narayan and Jawaharlal Nehru. Relentlessly, together and separately, they lobbied the All-Indian Congress Committee and the Congress Working Committee. They wanted renewed action and they wanted it now. Independence, and the freedom that it would bring the Indian people, was their ultimate objective and they were impatient with what they perceived to be Congress's reluctance to confront the Raj. Congress had, in fact, for some time been discussing the limited independence and freedom that would come if they negotiated with the Raj for **dominion status**. This the 'young hooligans' fiercely opposed. It had to be independence.

KEY TERM

Dominion status
Dominions were self-governing countries within the British Empire.

SOURCE

5 From Jawaharlal Nehru's speech to Congress in Calcutta on 27 December 1928.

I submit to you honestly that if I have energy to serve the country, that energy oozes out of me at the very thought of dominion status. I cannot go about spending my energy and strength for dominion status. I do submit to you that there are many like me in this country who feel like that. You will find in all India groups of organisations that are springing up full of energy and militant spirit and they promise to attain an early freedom for India. The question is, are you going to help the development of the militant spirit in the country? Are you going to help the development of this revolutionary spirit in the country or are you going to damp it and kill it in trying to bring about a compromise? Certainly it damps my spirit if you talk of dominion status and I can only judge others by my standard. The real thing in the world is not so much the question of the struggle between India and England, the real conflict is between two sets of ideals; and the question is, which set of ideals are you going to keep before the country? This is a conflict between imperialism and all that is not imperialism, and if you look at it from that point of view, you cannot for one moment think of dominion status so long as Great Britain has the Empire around her.

ACTIVITY
KNOWLEDGE CHECK

Dominion status?
Why was Jawaharlal Nehru so opposed to India having dominion status?

Why did Gandhi label these young men hooligans? He did this because they were attracted to socialism, a doctrine they found resonated with their own anti-imperialist sentiments. Gandhi, deeply conservative, regarded socialism as dangerously radical.

EXTEND YOUR KNOWLEDGE

Subhas Chandra Bose (1897–1945)
Anti-British and very militant in his ideas, Bose opposed Gandhi's tactics of non-violence. He also opposed the idea of liberal democracies, instead preferring totalitarian regimes and believing that India would benefit from a strong totalitarian leader.

Bose was born into an affluent Bengali family in Cuttack, Orissa, and had a European education in India and at Cambridge University. He took the Indian Civil Service examination in 1920, coming second, but resigned from the Service a year later because he wanted to work for Indian independence. In the years between 1921 and 1939, Bose was imprisoned 11 times by the British for terrorist activities.

During the Second World War, Bose broadcast anti-British propaganda from Nazi Germany. He also formed an army of Indians who had been taken prisoner by the Germans; they invaded eastern India and attacked British positions there. Seen by many as a traitor and a puppet of the Germans and Japanese, Bose was killed in an aeroplane crash over Japan in 1945.

The Nehru Report, 1928

The 'young hooligans' were going to be disappointed, at least in the short-term.

At an All-Parties Conference held in 1928, a sub-committee produced a report that was really the first draft of a written constitution for India. It was the work of two eminent lawyers, Tej Bahadur Sapru, the leader of the Liberal party, and Motilal Nehru, father of Jawaharlal Nehru and a member of Congress. The Nehru Report, named after Motilal Nehru, recommended dominion status for India on the same terms as those laid down for white self-governing countries within the British Empire, like Canada and Australia. It suggested that the princely states and British India were to be joined in a federation. There would be no further devolution of power to the provinces. However, this meant in effect that Hindus would form a permanent majority within central government. Despite vague promises that religious freedoms would be safeguarded and new Muslim states created, most Muslims were deeply unhappy. Under the Nehru Report, they would lose the protection of their separate electoral status, perpetuated by the British as a result of the Lucknow Pact of 1916 (see page 187). This was only a report, but the fragile Hindu–Muslim alliance hung in the balance.

How did Congress react?

Congress organised a boycott of the Simon Commission, a parliamentary delegation sent from Britain to investigate the working of the Government of India Act 1919. It then took the initiative. In December 1928, when Congress met in Calcutta under the leadership of Motilal Nehru, delegates backed two motions. They demanded instant dominion status, as recommended by the Nehru Report, even though Jawaharlal Nehru expressed grave misgivings. He, along with Subhas Chandra Bose, proposed a second, far more radical motion: that the British were to withdraw completely from India by 31 December 1929. Congress delegates supported both motions. To expect the British meekly to withdraw from India in a matter of months was, of course, completely unrealistic. But it was a clever political manoeuvre. When withdrawal did not occur Congress would have the excuse to embark on a further course of non-cooperation if they so wished.

SOURCE

6 From the Nehru Report, published 1928.

1 India shall have the same constitutional status in the comity of nations known as the British Empire as the Dominion of Canada, the Commonwealth of Australia, the Dominion of New Zealand, the Union of South Africa and the Irish Free State, with a Parliament having powers to make laws for the peace, order and good government of India, and an executive responsible to that Parliament, and shall be styled and known as the Commonwealth of India. …

4(i) All powers of government and all authority, legislative, executive and judicial are derived from the people and shall be exercised in the Commonwealth of India through the organisations.

4(iii) Freedom of conscience and the free profession and practice of religion are, subject to public order and morality, hereby guaranteed to every person.

4(iv) The right of free expression of opinion, as well as the right to assemble peaceably and without arms, and to form associations or unions, is hereby guaranteed for purposes not opposed to public order or morality.

5 Legislative power shall be vested in a Parliament which shall consist of the King, a Senate and a House of Representatives, herein called the Parliament.

6 The Governor-General shall be appointed by the King and shall have and may exercise, during the King's pleasure but subject to this constitution, such powers and functions of the King as His Majesty may assign to him.

Communal representation

I There shall be joint mixed electorates throughout India for the House of Representatives and the provincial legislatures.

II There shall be no reservation of seats for the House of Representatives except for Muslims in provinces where they are in a minority and non-Muslims in the N-WF Province. …

IV Reservation of seats where allowed shall be for a fixed period of ten years.

A Level Exam-Style Question Section A

How far could the historian make use of Sources 5 and 6 together to investigate attitudes of Congress in the 1920s to independence from the Raj?

Explain your answer, using both sources, the information given about them and your own knowledge of the historical context. (20 marks)

Tip

Think about the impact of the split between supporters of Gandhi and those supporting the views of the 'young hooligans' and the way in which they were resolved.

ACTIVITY
KNOWLEDGE CHECK

The Nehru Report
What is there in the Nehru Report recommendations to alarm:

a) the Raj

b) Indian Muslims?

The Lahore Congress 1929 and *purna swaraj*

Gandhi's dilemma

Gandhi was aware that, when Congress met in Lahore in December 1929, his charisma and standing was such that his was the voice all delegates would listen to; his views as to the way forward would carry the day. Despite the motions passed in the Calcutta meeting of Congress, Gandhi knew that Congress members were deeply divided over what to do about the Raj. Threats were one thing, putting them into action was quite another. He was aware that to embark on another programme of mass civil disobedience would alienate the more moderate members of Congress and could end, again, in bloodshed and bitterness. On the other hand, the 'young hooligans' had considerable support in the districts, and particularly among the young and trade unionists, and were building up a steady following among the younger members of Congress. Was he to back the young militants against moderate conservatives and risk wave after wave of bloodshed, or was he to back the moderates, push for dominion status and risk dividing Congress, potentially for ever? Added to Gandhi's problems in deciding strategy and tactics was the general problem of the need for Congress to re-assert its authority. It was essential, given the proliferation of small groups that were finding a voice, for Congress to re-emphasise its claim to speak for all of India. Not to do so would run the risk of allowing the British to settle with individual factions and, in doing so, play them off against each other.

Congress decides

When Congress met in Lahore, a policy decision could no longer be shelved. Gandhi had made up his mind: he would support the young hooligans. He steered his policy through the various Congress committees and a militant open session, and ended up with a working committee of his own choosing to direct Congress's actions in the months ahead. Henceforward, *purna swaraj* (total independence) would be India's new political demand. Congress left it to their Working Committee to decide how and when the non-violent confrontation was to begin, and the Working Committee left the decision to Gandhi.

 THINKING HISTORICALLY   Cause and Consequence (6a)

Seeing things differently

Different times and different places have a different set of ideas. Beliefs about how the world works, how human societies should be governed or the best way to achieve political aims, can all be radically different from our own. It is important for the historian to take into account these different attitudes and be aware of the dangers of judging them against modern ideas.

Gandhi's methods of obtaining concessions from the British Raj were underpinned by his concept of *satyagraha*. This involved a belief that everyone was on a journey to find this ultimate truth that permeated the universe. The weaker were on different stages of their journey from the stronger and should not be forced to accept their views. Non-violence was therefore essential if everyone was to find the truth within themselves and within the universe.

Answer the following questions:

1 What attitudes do you think had given rise to the idea that *satyagraha* was the only way for Indians to achieve independence?

2 If they had known how events would progress, for example, that *satyagraha* often ended in violence, do you think that those who took part would have changed their attitude?

3 Gandhi's attitudes to the ways in which political outcomes could be achieved are different from current attitudes in the UK.

a) Are there any other ways in which his attitudes differed dramatically from those that are current in the UK now?

b) Why do you think they are that different?

4 How important is it for historians to deal with events in the context of the beliefs and values of people in the past as well as seeing them as part of a greater pattern?

The salt *satyagraha* and the consequences of civil disobedience

Opposing the salt tax

In many ways, deciding to oppose the government's tax on salt was the most sensible decision Gandhi could have made. The government tax on salt brought in little by way of revenue (about four percent of its total revenue) and cost the average Indian relatively little (about three *annas* a year, the equivalent of 1.5p). Nevertheless, it was an emotive issue. Salt was the one commodity everyone, from the poorest Indian to the richest, needed for cooking and is one of the elements the body cannot do without. Yet in India its production was controlled by the Raj, who exacted tax from its sale. This made it an ideal issue over which to oppose the Raj.

On 12 March 1930, Gandhi set out from his house in Ahmedabad, intending to walk the 240 miles to Dandi on the Gujarat coast. Accompanying him were 78 carefully chosen supporters including, at his request, Untouchables, selected to demonstrate the universality of his mission. However, a prayer meeting held the day before the march attracted 10,000 people, and a gathering held by Gandhi on the day the march began attracted 75,000. It was therefore not surprising that the original 78 were themselves followed by thousands, some of whom stayed for the whole distance, others for a day or two at a time. The march took on the character of a pilgrimage: every day the 78 participants were supposed to spin cotton thread, pray, keep a diary and at all times behave in a non-aggressive, peaceful manner. Also accompanying Gandhi was a posse of reporters and cameramen from the world's press who faithfully reported his message of non-violence. While the march was a great publicity exercise, it was also a challenge to the Raj. The challenge came when Gandhi reached the sea and symbolically picked up a piece of sea salt from the shore. He issued a public statement confessing that he had broken the law by picking up tax-free salt, and urged Indians to do the same by helping themselves to the natural salt found in creeks and along the sea-shore. The challenge developed, as across India thousands of peasants followed Gandhi's advice, breaking the law by using tax-free salt that was not government produced. It was tantamount to a declaration of war against the tax and the government that produced it.

This was a challenge the Raj could not ignore. Hundreds of peasants were arrested and imprisoned; there were mass arrests of local and national Congress leaders, including Jawaharal Nehru. But it was the arrest of Gandhi in May that sent shockwaves through India and triggered a wave of strikes and protests. Particularly worrying for the government was the number of moderate people who seemed to be sympathising with Gandhi. The government continued its programme of repression: in June, the entire Congress Working Committee was arrested.

Civil disobedience

The campaign entered its second phase after Gandhi's arrest. Unlike the non-violent campaign of 1920–22, it was not master-minded and directed centrally. Congress authorised provincial committees to organise their own *satyagrahas*, including their nature and timing. Congress did, however, recommend an order of priority: salt, the boycott of foreign cloth, non-payment of taxes and, finally, the refusal to cooperate with the authorities when they tried to prevent the *satyagraha*. In organising the civil disobedience campaign in this way, Congress cleverly papered over the cracks of potential divisions among its members as to just how disobedient civil disobedience should be. Furthermore, by allowing provincial committees such a large degree of autonomy, Congress hoped to demonstrate that it really was a universal umbrella organisation, sensitive to local needs. Most importantly, the campaign was much more difficult for the Raj to stop because there was no central organisation to take out.

SOURCE

7

Photograph taken in 1930 of women boiling water to make salt in defiance of the Raj's salt production monopoly.

 Evidence (5a)

Context is everything

Work in groups.

Take an A3 piece of paper. In the middle draw a circle about 8 inches in diameter. Label the circle 'evidence' and the area outside the circle 'context'.

1 Think of a question that Source 7 could be helpful in answering.

2 Inside the circle, write a set of statements giving information that can be gleaned only from the source itself, without any contextual knowledge.

3 Outside the circle, write down statements of contextual knowledge that relate to the source.

4 Draw annotated lines to show links between the contextual statements and the information from the source. Does context change the nature or meaning of the information?

Now answer this question:

5 Explain why knowledge of context is important when gathering and using historical evidence. Give specific examples to illustrate your point.

Was the campaign a success?

In 1930, the civil disobedience campaign became a formidable psychological weapon used by Indians against the Raj and, in places, an actual physical threat. By the middle of the year, all provinces in India had been affected, with Bombay and Gujarat being the most turbulent. For example, parts of Bombay were in the hands of the mob and were no-go areas for police. In the Bengal district of Midnapore, a salt *satyagraha* was followed by attacks on police and magistrates, intimidation of officials and a refusal to pay local taxes. In the United Provinces a peasant anti-land-tax campaign was particularly successful. In the majority of areas, civil disobedience was frequently used by people as a vehicle for expressing local grievances. In the Central Provinces, for example, local politicians decided to back opposition to forest laws that protected the interests of local landowners and encouraged peasants to fell trees and graze animals where they wished.

AS Level Exam-Style Question Section B

How accurate is it to say that Congress consolidated its position in the 1920s?
(20 marks)

Tip

Think about the re-structuring of Congress and also the ways in which Congress operated in practice.

Replicated on a national scale, the level of disturbance was impressive. Civil disobedience became the vehicle whereby a whole range of people, from students to middle-class businessmen, became politically aware and articulate. Women, in particular, became actively involved, often because the men in their families had been imprisoned, but in their own right, too, and not as substitute males. By November 1930, nearly 360 women were in jail for their participation in different *satyagrahas*.

However, by early 1931, the Raj had more or less restored law and order. Official estimates say that around 60,000 people passed through India's jails in 1930. This had put an immense strain on the civil service, police and magistrates of the Raj, as well as causing intolerable overcrowding in the jails. Indeed, by the end of 1930, there were still some 29,000 people in India's jails, including 300 women and around 2,000 youths under the age of 17. There had been a point in mid-1930 when Viceroy Irwin had seriously considered imposing martial law on the most disaffected regions. However, the memory of the disaster at Amritsar and the feeling that to bring in the army would be an admission of failure made him keep his nerve. This paid off because, by the end of the year, Congress was also feeling the strain. Local *satyagrahas*, though initially successful, could not be sustained once local grievances were settled. Furthermore, an economic upturn later in 1930 made people anxious to return to normal business relationships. Civil disobedience had simply run out of steam. By the end of 1930, the Raj and Congress had reached a stalemate.

ACTIVITY
KNOWLEDGE CHECK

Congress re-organised

1 In what ways would the new structure of Congress enable it to challenge the Raj more effectively?

2 'Gandhi was sensible to side with the "young hooligans".' Set up a debate to argue for and against this proposition.

HOW FAR DID THE MUSLIM LEAGUE BECOME A POLITICAL FORCE, 1920-30?

Muslims and Hindus had, for many years, lived and worked side by side in the Indian subcontinent, with only the occasional flare-up when religious differences and animosities came to the fore. However, as the Indian people became more politicised at the beginning of the 20th century, differences between the followers of each religion were thrown into sharper relief and too often no areas of mutual toleration could be found. However, there were possible points where rapprochement seemed possible. There were Muslim members of the Hindu-dominated Congress party and the Lucknow Pact of 1916 demonstrated a mutual understanding of the need to address Muslim fears. These fears were dominated by the Muslim minorities' concern that they should have a guaranteed voice in any new constitutional arrangement that would inevitably be dominated by the Hindu majority. Gradually, the idea of separateness began to take hold.

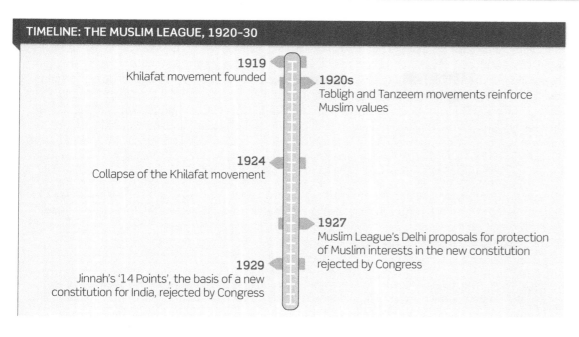

TIMELINE: THE MUSLIM LEAGUE, 1920–30

1919
Khilafat movement founded

1920s
Tabligh and Tanzeem movements reinforce Muslim values

1924
Collapse of the Khilafat movement

1927
Muslim League's Delhi proposals for protection of Muslim interests in the new constitution rejected by Congress

1929
Jinnah's '14 Points', the basis of a new constitution for India, rejected by Congress

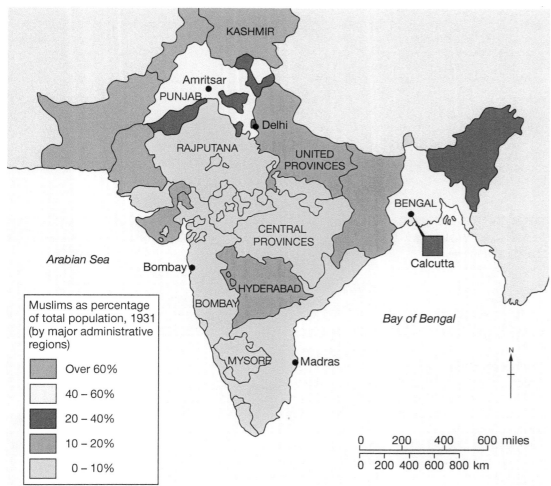

Muslims as percentage of total population, 1931 (by major administrative regions)

- Over 60%
- 40 – 60%
- 20 – 40%
- 10 – 20%
- 0 – 10%

Figure 2.1: Map of India, showing Muslims as a percentage of the total population in 1921.

The Khilafat movement

Events in the outside world impacted upon the Muslims' perception of themselves as a political as well as a religious community. Many Indian Muslims had long regarded the Sultan of Turkey as their caliph, their most important spiritual leader. Turkey's decision to fight on the side of Germany during the First World War, and therefore against Britain and the British Empire of which India was a part, challenged Muslim loyalties to the extreme. The 1919 peace settlements did nothing to ease the tension, as the Treaty of Sevres greatly reduced the size of Turkey and forces within Turkey removed the Sultan from power. The Khilafat movement, set up to support the caliph, spread rapidly throughout India. Using Islamic symbols to unite the diverse Muslim communities, it repudiated British rule in India and legitimised Muslim participation in any nationalist movement.

Muslim leaders joined with Gandhi in mobilising the masses for the 1920 and 1921 civil disobedience and non-cooperation campaigns in response to the Amritsar Massacre and the Rowlatt Acts (see pages 181–83). At the same time, Gandhi endorsed the Khilafat movement, thus bringing the weight of Hindu opinion behind what had originally been a solely Muslim movement.

SOURCE

8   From *The Collected Works of Mahatma Gandhi volume 17*, published 1960–94. Here, in an extract dated 7 March 1920, Gandhi gives his views on the Khilafat.

The Khilafat question has now become a question of questions. It has become an imperial question of the first magnitude. I trust the Hindus will realise that the Khilafat question overshadows everything else.

Briefly put, it is that the Turks should retain European Turkey, subject to full guarantees for the protection of non-Muslim races under the Turkish Empire and that the Sultan should control the holy places of Islam and should have the suzerainty over Arabia as defined by the Muslim wise men, subject to self-governing rights being given to the Arabs if they so desire. This is what was promised by Mr Lloyd George. The Mohammedan soldiers would not have fought to deprive Turkey of her possessions.

To restore to Turkey, subject to the necessary guarantees, what was hers before the war is a Christian solution. To wrest any of her possessions from her for the sake of punishing her is a gun-powder solution. The Allies of England, in the hour of triumph, must be scrupulously just. To reduce the Turks to impotence would be not only unjust. It would be a breach of solemn declarations and promises. It is to be wished that the Viceroy will take his courage in both his hands and place himself at the head of the Khilafat. But the situation rests more with us Hindus and Mohammedans than with the Viceroy and still more with the Muslim leaders than with the Hindus or the Viceroy.

ACTIVITY
KNOWLEDGE CHECK

The Khilafat movement
Read Source 8 and use your own knowledge to explain why:

a) Gandhi, a Hindu, supported the Khilafat Movement

b) Jinnah, a Muslim, opposed the Khilafat Movement.

Jinnah's attitude

By supporting the Khilafat, Gandhi gained the support of a large number of Muslim spiritual and political leaders for his policy of non-violent non-cooperation. Jinnah was left out in the cold. He opposed Gandhi's support for the Khilafat movement, believing it not only to be an opportunistic move on Gandhi's part but also that it caused schism amongst Muslims, threatening the existing political structures and an orderly progress towards independence. Indeed, at the Congress's Nagpur session in December 1920, Jinnah spoke out openly against non-cooperation. The extent of the violence that accompanied the civil disobedience, some of which involved Hindus and Muslims settling old scores, would seem to give some credence to Jinnah's desire for an alternative approach.

The collapse of the Khilafat movement

By 1923, the Khilafat movement had all but collapsed. How had this happened?

- Turkey rejected the caliphate and became a secular state. Thus an important spiritual leader for the Muslims, and the main reason for the Khilafat movement's existence, was gone.

- The religious, mass-appeal aspects of the movement alienated Western-orientated politicians like Jinnah, who resigned from Congress.
- Many Muslims became uncomfortable with Gandhi's leadership.

The re-emergence of Muslim values

The precarious alliance of the Muslim League Khilafat committees and Congress collapsed once the non-violent campaigns ended. Hindu members of Congress began to regret the generous electoral arrangements agreed for Muslims under the Lucknow Pact and Muslims began to drift away from Congress. In 1921, 10.9 percent of Congress delegates were Muslims; by 1923, this had fallen to 3.6 percent.

What were the Muslims to do? The Khilafat movement, with its focus on support for the Sultan of Turkey, as their caliph, had faded. Congress was no longer seen, by many Muslims, as an appropriate body to push for the sort of independence that would guarantee their political place in a newly independent India, and the Muslim League's voice and ability to put pressure on the Raj was far weaker than that of Congress.

In the early 1920s, two movements that had origins in the years before 1914 came to the fore in order to give direction and purpose to the Muslim community. The *Tanzeem* and the *Tabligh* movements aimed to strengthen the Muslim communities, the former focusing on organisation and the latter on the promotion of religion. The plan was that Islam would be rejuvenated and the conversion of Muslims to Hinduism would stop. The Muslim communities would regain their sense of purpose. To this end, every town was to have an ***Anjuman Tabligh-ul-Islam*** to ensure more vigorous preaching, better religious education, regular observance of religious duties and the renovation and construction of mosques.

KEY TERM

Anjuman Tabligh-ul-Islam
A gathering or association (*anjuman*) for the promotion of Islam.

These *anjumans* developed their religious focus to concentrate on the economic plight of various Muslim groups who were constrained by the power and influence of Hindu commercial communities. Anti-Hindu sentiment grew rapidly, particularly in the poorer urban areas where Muslims' anger at their poor economic conditions came to be directed against Hindus and not, as previously, the Raj. This resurgence of Muslim consciousness was rooted in the provinces and tended to be characterised by martial overtones and anti-Hindu sentiment.

The concept of separateness

Hindus and Muslims clearly represented two very different religious communities, with different belief systems and practices. While this, in itself, created the concept of separateness, it was only in the 20th century that the somewhat uneasy co-existence that had existed for hundreds of years seemed to be breaking down. This was partly due to the position of strict neutrality officially adopted by the Raj. This encouraged both Muslims and Hindus (and all other religious groups) to believe that they had equal rights to carry out their own religious practices, no matter what offence they gave. Some of the princely states experienced less religious friction; this was probably because the princes didn't see the need to maintain a neutral position on the subject and came down firmly in support of one religion or another, and everyone was clear about how much apparently extreme behaviour would be tolerated.

Worship and festivals as creating separateness
It is clear that local communities were sharply divided by the very different belief systems held by Hindus and Muslims. These offered plenty of opportunities for irritation and petty disruption. For example, Hindus liked to use gongs, bells and cymbals to create loud music when they were worshipping. Muslims preferred to pray in silence. Sometimes Hindus stopped playing music during the Muslim times of prayer and sometimes they did not. When they didn't, verbal abuse and violence resulted.

Festivals were another source of friction. At the Muslim festival of Bakr'Id, cows were ritually slaughtered. But the cow was sacred to Hindus. On the other hand, the Hindu festival of Holi was particularly noisome and troubling to Muslims. It was a very lively festival, lasting over two days. On the first day, bonfires were lit at night; on the second, people danced in the street, throwing coloured powder and water at each other and drinking a liquid laced with cannabis. There were plenty of opportunities here for irritation and mutual distrust to spill over into violence, and they frequently did.

Organisations emphasising separateness

The Hindu organisation *Arya Samj* was proactive in the Muslim community in parts of northern India. Members openly criticised Islam and sought converts to Hinduism. They argued for the protection of cows, sacred to Hindus, and established the Cow Protection Society, which brought them into open conflict with Muslim butchers and tradesmen; they attempted to have Hindi replace Urdu as the language of administration, which frightened Urdu-speaking Muslims, who began to feel more and more threatened by the Hindu majority. But it wasn't all one way. The Muslim *Tabligh* and *Tanzeem* movements were seen to be provocative by Hindus in the same way as the *Arya Samaj* was by Muslims. The situation was worsened when it became known that the major donors to the *Arya Samj* cause came from the Hindu merchant and money-lending class on whom lower class Muslims depended for their economic security.

In 1906 a Hindu 'ginger group', *Mahasabha*, was established that aimed to make the Hindu community powerful and independent. It was quite prepared to use force against people they thought were diluting the purity of the Hindu faith. It was a member of this group that was to murder Gandhi in 1948.

The Raj as emphasising separateness

Throughout the proposals the Raj put forward to enable Indians to participate in government at all levels, there was a common thread of protecting the rights of minorities by making provision for separate electorates. This can be seen in the Montagu Declaration of 1917 (page 180) and the Government of India Act of 1919 (pages 185–86). In doing this, while ensuring that Muslims had a voice in local and national affairs, the Raj ensured that the concept of separateness was further emphasised and enshrined in the political solutions they had to offer.

Breakdown of relations with Congress

It was against this background of separateness and of growing Muslim consciousness that Jinnah continued to work to try to bring Congress and the Muslim League together to work out an agreed position for India's future. Was he pursuing a lost cause? Had the emergence of a new Muslim consciousness, with its anti-Hindu overtones, meant that rapprochement was impossible?

At the Muslim League's 1927 meeting in Delhi, Jinnah persuaded members to make a bold offer to Congress in the hope of bringing Congress and the League back together again. The League offered to end its support for separate electorates (which Jinnah had never liked, anyway) in exchange for a guaranteed one-third of the seats in the Central Legislative Assembly and the separation of Sind from Bombay in order to create just one Muslim-dominated province. Congress rejected the offer out-of-hand, believing it to be the result of Muslim awareness of the weakness of their position. Viceroy Irwin had his doubts, too.

AS Level Exam-Style Question Section A (a)

Why is Source 9 valuable to the historian for an enquiry about Viceroy Irwin's attitude to Jinnah and the Muslim League?

Explain your answer, using the source, the information given about it and your own knowledge of the historical context. (8 marks)

Tip

Tease out what Irwin is actually saying about Jinnah and the Muslim League, and whether this is supported by the facts.

SOURCE

9 Part of a communication from Viceroy Irwin to the secretary of state, dated 26 March 1927.

The whole position is one of obscurity. The meeting of Muslims held on 20th in Delhi was only an informal conference. The conclusions were communicated semi-officially to the press by Jinnah. It is therefore not clear in the first place how far they represented the real views of those present. In the second place, it remains to be seen what reception they will have from representative Mahomedan bodies.

From what I have heard, there are two very different forces at work. Firstly, Jinnah finds his position as nominal leader of what is practically a Mahomedan Party most precarious. Some form of compromise with the Hindus is not only demanded by his political beliefs, but is probably an essential condition of his retaining position as a political leader. Secondly, some Mahomedans may possibly have thought this move a useful means of sowing dissentions among the Hindus, reckoning the Congress party must welcome it while the nationalists would be unlikely to agree to the separation of Sind from Bombay.

It would show the Muslims in a reasonable light, and the subsequent failure to reach agreement would be attributed to the stubbornness of the Hindus.

At present, my impression is that it is largely a question of manoeuvring for position, and that there is not much prospect of a real agreement emerging.

In 1929, Jinnah tried again. This time, he offered a compromise plan of 14 points, eight of which are listed in Source 10.

SOURCE

10 Extracts from M. A. Jinnah's draft resolution of March 1929, published in the *Indian Quarterly Register* 1929.

The League, after anxious and careful consideration, most earnestly and emphatically lays down that no scheme for the future constitution of the government of India will be acceptable to the Mussalmans of India until and unless the following basic principles are given effect to and provisions are embodied therein to safeguard their rights and interests:-

(1) The form of the future constitution should be federal, with the residuary powers vested in the provinces.

(2) A uniform measure of autonomy should be granted to every province.

(3) All legislatures in the country and other elected bodies should be constituted on the definite principle of adequate and effective representation of minorities in every Province without reducing the majority in any Province to a minority or equality.

(4) In the central legislature, Muslim representation should not be less than one third.

…

(6) Any territorial redistribution that might be necessary should not affect the Muslim majorities in the Punjab, Bengal and the North West Frontier Province.

(7) Full religious liberty should be granted to all communities.

…

(11) Provision should be made in the constitution for Muslims to have an adequate share, along with other Indians, in all the services of the state and in local self-governing bodies, whilst at the same time having due regard for the need for efficiency.

(12) The Constitution should embody adequate safeguards for the protection of Muslim culture, and for the protection and promotion of Moslem education, language, religion personal laws and Moslem charitable institutions and for their due share in the grants-in-aid given by the State and by local self-governing bodies.

> **AS Level Exam-Style Questions Section A (b)**
>
> How much weight do you give the evidence of Source 10 for an enquiry into Jinnah's attempts to reach agreement with Congress in the 1920s? (12 marks)
>
> Explain your answer, using the source, the information given about it and your own knowledge of the historical context.
>
> **Tip**
>
> *Think about whether Jinnah's demands were realistic in the context of the time.*

This offer was, again, rejected by Congress. Jinnah despaired. Believing that the situation represented a parting of the ways, he left for England to follow a lucrative career as a barrister.

In fact, the Muslim League and Congress continued to negotiate right down to independence in 1947. Even so, never again would Congress receive a better offer for a peaceful settlement; never again would there be a Lucknow-like rapprochement. It was at this point that the concept of a separate Muslim state began to develop.

ACTIVITY
KNOWLEDGE CHECK

The concept of separateness

1 Study the map showing Muslims as a percentage of the total population of India in 1931. Discuss in your group how far this explains the difficulties in relationships between Muslims and Hindus. If there was to be a separate homeland for Muslims, where should it be?

2 How far were the *Tanzeem* and the *Tabligh* movements responsible for the breakdown in relationships between Hindus and Muslims?

3 Read Source 9. Was Viceroy Irwin justified in rejecting the Muslim League's 1927 proposal for a constitutional arrangement?

4 Read Source 10. Which points were the most important in protecting the interests of Muslims living in India? Which would be most likely to alarm Hindus? Discuss this in a small group.

5 How far do you agree that, in the 1920s, Jinnah displayed sound political judgement?

Jinnah's beliefs and aims

SOURCE

11 From F. Moraes, *Witness to an Era*, published in 1973. Frank Moraes, a European-educated Indian, was born in Mumbai and worked briefly as a lawyer. For most of his adult life, however, he lived and worked as a journalist and newspaper editor in India, Sri Lanka, Burma and China. He knew Jinnah well.

[Jinnah] was tall, thin and elegant, with a monocle on a grey silk cord and a stiff white collar, which he wore in the hottest weather. Jinnah was one of the very few intellectually honest politicians I have known. Humility was not one of his strong points, but there was no humbug in his make-up. Like every decent-minded, thoughtful Indian, he wanted his country to be politically free. The British completely misread the character and aims of this dedicated man. They had been accustomed to deal with a type of Muslim leader whose dislike for the Congress could be encouraged by official favours. But Jinnah had no purchase price.

Jinnah, unlike Gandhi, did not develop a unique belief system that permeated his actions and inspired his followers. Indeed, he disapproved of Gandhi's powerful mix of religion and politics. In many ways Jinnah was not an orthodox Muslim: he rarely went to a mosque, wore European clothes and openly drank alcohol. His first wife died when she was very young: his second wife was a non-Muslim, a Parsi Indian, and his close political colleague Liaquat Ali Khan was married to a Christian. Thus it is possible to suggest that he led the Muslim League because of his effectiveness as a lawyer and leader, not primarily because he was a dedicated orthodox Muslim.

Up until the end of the 1920s, Jinnah can be seen as a committed Congress nationalist, a moderate who disapproved of mass campaigns of non-cooperation. Indeed, he was distrustful of the masses, believing them to be fickle in their loyalties. He much preferred to deal with educated Indians, and preferably around a conference table. Determined to preserve election quotas for Muslims, he was nevertheless secular in his outlook. The rejection of what Jinnah saw as his 14 Point compromise drove him out of politics, but the pressure of Indian-based Muslims persuaded him to return after the 1937 elections. Increasingly, Jinnah supported separatist demands. He started learning Urdu and appeared at formal events in traditional Muslim clothing. In these ways Jinnah identified himself more and more closely with the Muslim cause and with the League's determination to preserve separate electorates for Muslims so that their voice would be heard at all levels of government. Partition and the formation of the state of Pakistan gradually became a reality. It will never be known for sure whether or not Jinnah really wanted a separate Muslim state. It is more than possible that Jinnah was simply bluffing when he suggested this as an outcome of the talks with Nehru and Mountbatten. If it was a bluff, it was one they successfully called.

ACTIVITY
KNOWLEDGE CHECK

Jinnah

What weight should be given to Source 11's description of Jinnah?

EXTEND YOUR KNOWLEDGE

Muhammad Ali Jinnah (1876–1948)
Born on 25 December 1976, Jinnah's family was part of the prosperous business community of Karachi. Educated there, Jinnah went to England for further studies in 1892 and in 1896 qualified as a lawyer.

He started his political career by attending the Indian National Congress in 1906. In 1909 he became a member of the Imperial Legislative Council, resigning in protest ten years later. He joined the Muslim League in 1913 and the Home Rule Movement under Annie Besant in 1917.

Jinnah worked hard to create a situation in which Hindus and Muslims could create a united, independent India together. However, a widening gulf opened up between Jinnah and Gandhi on the subject of protecting the Muslim position as a minority in a country dominated by Hindus and over Gandhi's civil disobedience programme. Resigning from Congress in 1920, Jinnah became the main spokesman for the Muslim cause within India.

Jinnah pursued the separatist line on his return from England in 1935. In 1940, the Muslim League passed the Lahore Resolution, calling for a separate Muslim state somewhere in the Indian subcontinent. With Indian independence in 1947 came partition. Jinnah became the first governor-general of Pakistan in 1947, dying from a combination of lung cancer and tuberculosis a year later.

HOW EFFECTIVE WAS THE BRITISH RESPONSE TO THE CHANGING POLITICAL LANDSCAPE IN INDIA, 1920–30?

British policy in the 1920s consisted in balancing the need to keep control at the centre while at the same time making concessions to Indian aspirations. The lines to be followed were those laid down by the Montagu–Chelmsford reforms (see page 180). This meant that Britain retained responsibility for foreign policy and India's defence, and India's elected provincial and national assemblies took on responsibility for some financial and all social and welfare matters.

EXTEND YOUR KNOWLEDGE

Inoculation programme

This was a systematic and well-organised programme aimed at protecting people from the killer diseases of cholera and smallpox. Those working on the programme inoculated thousands of men, women and children against cholera and vaccinated them against smallpox.

Gandhi regarded vaccination as a manifestation of the evil that the British had unleashed on India. He advised smallpox sufferers that they would be cured if they used enemas, made sure they had plenty of fresh air, wrapped themselves in a wet sheet at night and changed their diet.

The Simon Commission

British governments, in dealing with the developing situation in India, had to be mindful of political developments in London.

What was the political situation at Westminster?

The Government of India Act of 1919, which embodied the Montagu–Chelmsford reforms, was due for review in 1929. But 1929 was the year scheduled for a general election. The Conservative government was worried that if the review was held after the general election and the Labour Party won the election then policies on India would veer to the left. Labour Party politicians had strong links with Congress and Conservative party politicians were afraid that any review undertaken under a Labour government would give Congress more or less what they wanted. What was to be done? The secretary of state for India, Lord Birkenhead, had a solution. He simply brought the review forward so that it happened before the general election and under a Conservative government.

The Commission in India

In 1927, the government sent a parliamentary delegation, headed by Sir John Simon, out to India to find out how the Government of India Act was working and to make recommendations for any necessary review. The Labour MP Clement Attlee, who later led the Labour Party to victory in the 1945 general election, was a member of the seven-man delegation. Significantly, there were no Indian members. The 'message' was loud and clear. The future of India was to be decided by British politicians based in Westminster. Indians were to take no part in deciding their own future. This was not lost on the Indians themselves.

SOURCE

12 From the presidential address made by Sir Tej Bahadur Sapru on 27 December 1927. He was the leader of the Indian Liberal Party, opposed to Congress, the non-violent campaigns and Gandhi. The Liberal Party favoured a dialogue with the British and sought self-government reforms but not independence.

I do not think a worse challenge has been thrown down ever before to Indian nationalism. Indian nationalists of the moderate school have been compelled to ask if the only way of recognising the spirit of co-operation is by telling Indians that their lot is to be none other than that of petitioners; that they cannot be trusted to participate in the responsibility of making recommendations to parliament for the future of their country; and that all that they may aspire to is to put their proposals before the Commission, which may accept them or reject them, and again to repeat the same process of persuasion, argument and discussion before the Joint Committee of Parliament. Now, if this is what is meant by co-operation, if this is the new idea of equality of status on which we are to be fed, if our patriotism is a prejudice, and if the patriotism of the seven members of parliament is to be treated as impartial justice, then we Liberals feel justified in telling the government here and in England, 'You may do anything you like in the assertion of your right as supreme power, but we are not going to acquiesce in this method of dealing with us. Neither our self-respect nor our sense of duty to our country can permit us to go near the Commission.'

ACTIVITY
KNOWLEDGE CHECK

The Simon Commission

Sir Tej Bahadur Sapru was opposed to Congress and wanted Indian self-government, but not independence. Why, then, was he so opposed to the Simon Commission? Summarise his argument.

Unsurprisingly, the Simon Commission was received badly. When the delegates arrived in Bombay, they were greeted by booing, jeering crowds carrying banners, waving black flags and shouting slogans like 'Simon, go home!' It was the same in Calcutta, Delhi, Lahore, Lucknow, Madras and Patna. Everywhere the Commission went, they were met with mass demonstrations, which the police could hardly control.

SOURCE

13 A demonstration in 1928 in Madras against the Simon Commission.

Indian opinion divided

A wide range of Indian political opinion was clearly opposed to the Simon Commission. Members of Congress, Hindu leaders, liberal thinkers and a large section of the Muslim League led by Jinnah decided to boycott the Commission and refused to give evidence to its commissioners. On the other hand, Muslims from the provinces where they were in a majority decided to help the Commission's enquiries, as did a number of Anglo-Indians, Sikhs and Untouchables. All of these minority groups hoped for a better future than that which they were anticipating under a Hindu-dominated Congress. However, the Simon Report, when it finally emerged in draft form, did little more than reassert the status quo. It was abandoned before publication.

The Labour government and the significance of the Irwin Declaration

In May 1929, a Labour government was elected in Britain. Their response to the Nehru Report and to the demands of the December 1928 Congress conference was very different from the response that the previous Conservative government might have made. The new prime minister, Ramsay MacDonald, was sympathetic to the demands of Congress and so was the new secretary of state for India, William Wedgwood Benn.

Lord Irwin, a viceroy determined to bring about conciliation, travelled back to England on his mid-term leave with two suggestions to put to the new Labour government: a conference to discuss future reforms and a declaration that the Raj's goal for India was dominion status. He met with a supportive response from both MacDonald and Wedgwood Benn as well as, somewhat surprisingly, from Stanley Baldwin, the leader of the Conservative Party.

The Irwin Declaration, 31 October 1929

It was therefore with some degree of optimism that the viceroy, Lord Irwin, issued what became known as the Irwin Declaration. This reiterated the Montagu Declaration of 1917 (see page 180) and added that the attainment of dominion status would be a natural development of this. Thus, insofar as the British propaganda machine was concerned, there was absolute continuity in British policy toward India: dominion status was now officially the natural outcome of all that had gone before. Furthermore, Indian representatives were invited to London to a Round Table Conference where details of a new Indian constitution would be hammered out.

The Congress Working Committee officially welcomed the announcement and called upon the British government to demonstrate its good faith by declaring an amnesty for all Indian political prisoners. This was a step too far for Irwin, who refused. Indian frustration at what they perceived as British stubbornness led to more terrorist attacks, including the bombing of the viceroy's train and the destruction of the carriage next to the one in which he was travelling.

Gandhi's dilemma

Gandhi, like the rest of the Congress leadership, knew that to attend the London conference would be political suicide. Not only would they be on 'foreign' soil, but they would also be forced to follow a British agenda. What was worse, the British weren't just expecting representatives of Congress to attend the proposed conference. All representatives of Indian opinion were expected to be there: Sikhs and Untouchables, for example, as well as the princes, whom Gandhi regarded as nothing better than pawns of the British. The chances of Congress getting what they wanted would, Gandhi believed, be severely compromised. On the other hand, not to go to London would probably result in a settlement being made to which Congress – and Gandhi – could not possibly agree.

The Gandhi–Irwin Pact, 1931

The violence that accompanied the Congress civil disobedience following the salt *satyagrahas*, and the Raj's attempts to combat that violence left both the Raj and Congress exhausted. Some way had to be found out of the stalemate. The only way out would seem to be some sort of truce that would save the face of Congress in general, and Gandhi in particular, and that of the Raj, to enable them to move forward.

The end of 1930 saw Gandhi in prison, developing his spiritual life, and Congress desperate to find some way of revitalising the civil disobedience campaign. Jawaharlal Nehru, released from prison in October, thought he had the answer when he announced that the conquest of power was about to begin. He went straight back into jail.

Viceroy Irwin was afraid that Congress would find a way out of the stalemate by resorting to a campaign of violence. He wanted to create a situation in which Gandhi could leave prison and participate in the London Conference as the representative of Congress, yet he himself couldn't be seen to negotiate openly with someone the authorities regarded as a terrorist. Furthermore, he had to be seen to support the Indian Civil Service and those who stood aside from confrontation. And, possibly the biggest hurdle of all, he had to persuade Gandhi that his presence at the Round Table Conference was in Congress's best interests.

A meeting between Gandhi and Irwin was brokered by Indian businessmen, who were worried at the effect the civil disobedience campaigns was having on the Indian economy. They first approached Gandhi in July 1930, but it was only in February 1931 that Irwin and Gandhi met face to face.

SOURCE 14

A comment made in 1931 by Winston Churchill to the House of Commons about the meeting between Viceroy Irwin and Gandhi.

It is alarming and also nauseating to see Mr Gandhi, a seditious Middle Temple lawyer, now posing as a fakir [a religious person who practises self-denial] of a type well known in the East, striding half-naked up the steps of the viceregal palace while he is still organising and conducting a defiant campaign of civil disobedience, to parley on equal terms with the representative of the king-emperor. Such a spectacle can only increase the unrest in India and the danger to which white people are exposed.

Irwin had done his homework and recognised in Gandhi both a spiritual being and a shrewd politician, and was able to appeal to both sides of his nature. Discussions were frank and open, and helped by the fact that both men genuinely wanted to find a way out of the impasse. In the end, this was the pact to which both signed up:

- Congress's civil disobedience campaign was suspended
- Gandhi agreed to attend a second London conference
- 19,000 Congress supporters were released from jail
- confiscated property was returned to its owners.

The Gandhi–Irwin Pact brought everyone some breathing space.

SOURCE 15

In 1956 the BBC broadcast four documentary radio programmes in which people who knew Gandhi well chatted informally about him. Transcripts of the programmes were made into a book published in 1969: *Talking of Gandhi*, edited by Francis Watson and Hallam Tennyson. Here, Viceroy Irwin remembers what happened immediately after the Pact was agreed.

Well, when I was finishing my talks with Mr Gandhi, we finished, I remember, at two o'clock on a Thursday, and at nine or ten o'clock he came back to me, and said that he had had a dreadful evening when he returned to his ashram – that he had met others of his Indian friends and Jawaharlal Nehru had said that he had betrayed India and that he had – he, Jawaharlal, had wept on his shoulder, as Gandhi said that he had never wept when his mother died – over this tragedy of the betrayal of India, and the little man was quite upset with all that, and so I said: 'Well, don't be too discouraged because you happen to live on the spot, but in a few hours' time, I shall be getting furious cables from Mr Churchill and others in England, saying that I have betrayed England and your friends think you've betrayed India, we are probably about right – in the middle.' So that cheered him up a little bit.

ACTIVITY
KNOWLEDGE CHECK

The British response

1 Why was the Simon Commission such a disaster?

2 How far did a change of government in Whitehall affect British relationships with India?

3 Read Source 14 and explain how attitudes like this hindered the search for a resolution of the situation in India.

4 Read Source 15 and use your own knowledge of the events that led to the Gandhi–Irwin Pact. Irwin said of the Pact between himself and Gandhi that 'we are probably about right'. Was he correct?

A Level Exam-Style Question Section B

How accurate is it to say that the 1920s in India were years characterised by distrust and a hardening of attitudes between Britain, Congress and the Muslim League? (20 marks)

Tip

Think about the times when rapprochement seemed possible and compromises were made, as well as the times when distrust and mutual misunderstanding polarised attitudes.

ACTIVITY
SUMMARY

Changing political relationships

1 Assess the success of Gandhi's policy of civil disobedience.

2 To what extent did the Muslim League become an effective political force in the 1920s?

3 How far did British attitudes to India change in the years 1920–31?

WIDER READING

Allen, C. (ed.) *Plain Tales from the Raj*, Abacus (2000)

Brown, J. *Modern India: The Origins of an Asian Democracy*, Oxford University Press (1991)

Copland, I. *India 1885–1947*, Routledge (2001)

James, L. *The Making and Unmaking of the British Raj*, Abacus (1998)

Keay, J. *India: A History*, Harper Press (2010)

Leadbeater, T. *Britain and India 1845–1947*, Hodder (2001)

Moraes, F. *Witness to an Era*, Weidenfeld and Nicolson (1973)

Watson, F., Tennyson, H. *Talking of Gandhi*, BBC (1969)

2a.3 Consultation and confrontation, 1930–42

KEY QUESTIONS

- Why did the Round Table Conferences, 1930–32, fail?
- How far was a political compromise reached in the years 1932–35?
- To what extent did the Government of India Act 1935 impact on Indian and British politics?
- How united was India's reaction to the outbreak of the Second World War in 1939?

INTRODUCTION

The 1930s saw the gradual emergence of the idea that the dream of independence for India could become a reality. In reaching this point, the British government, the Raj, Congress and the Muslim League were the main players. Proposals were made, countered and adapted; sometimes they were adopted, sometimes they were thrown out and sometimes they were ignored. Individuals followed their own agendas; compromises did not always seem possible but sometimes broke a deadlock. All this was being played out against a background of riot and repression, death and revolt, in the Indian subcontinent. However, by the end of the 1930s, Indian independence was seen by all parties as achievable.

WHY DID THE ROUND TABLE CONFERENCES, 1930–32, FAIL?

One of the recommendations of the Simon Commission was that a conference of all interested parties should be held in order to discuss possible constitutional reforms. Accordingly, the Round Table Conferences were organised by the British government, with the first one being held from November 1930 to January 1931. By the 1930s, many British politicians believed that India should move towards dominion status. On the other hand, there were significant disagreements between Indian politicians, and between Indian and British political parties.

1932
Third Round Table Conference, no representatives from UK Labour Party or Congress

January: Gandhi arrested, Congress outlawed, terrorist activity in India increases

August: Ramsay MacDonald announces Communal Award, Gandhi begins 'fast-unto-death', Yeravda Pact between Gandhi and Untouchables accepted by British government

1930
First Round Table Conference in London, Gandhi does not attend

1936
Lord Linlithgow becomes Viceroy of India

| 1930 | 1931 | 1932 | 1933 | 1934 | 1935 | 1936 | 1937 |

1931
Lord Willingdon replaces Lord Irwin as Viceroy

Second Round Table Conference, Gandhi attends representing Congress

1935
Government of India Act

1937
Provincial elections in India, Congress sweeps the board, surge of support for Muslim League

SOURCE

A cartoon 'A Question of Control' published in the British magazine *Punch* in January 1931.

A QUESTION OF CONTROL.

INDIA. "WHAT ABOUT CHANGING PLACES?"
JOHN BULL. "WELL, YOU'RE WELCOME TO SEE WHAT YOU CAN DO AT THE WHEEL;
BUT I THINK I'D BETTER SIT BESIDE YOU—WITHIN REACH OF THE BRAKE."

ACTIVITY
KNOWLEDGE CHECK

Who is in charge?
What is the message of the *Punch* cartoon (Source 1)? How accurately does it reflect the British position at the time it was published?

1938
Militant Bose elected president of Congress

Bose–Gandhi–Jinnah talks about conciliation collapse when Congress refuses to accept Muslim League as sole voice of Muslims in India

Bose leaves Congress and forms Forward Bloc Party, dedicated to revolutionary overthrow of the Raj

1940
20 March: Congress demands complete independence and constituent assembly

23 March: Lahore resolution of the Muslim League demands separate Muslim homeland

7 August: August Offer from viceroy on India's constitutional development

15 September: Congress rejects August Offer

28 September: Muslim League rejects August Offer

1938	1939	1940

1939
3 September: Viceroy Linlithgow announces that India is at war with Germany

14 September: Congress Working Committee declares it will not support Britain in war unless self-determination is granted to India

23 October: Congress asks all Congress provincial ministries to resign

22 December: Observed by the Muslim League as Deliverance Day from Congress rule

The first, second and third Round Table Conferences, November 1930–December 1932

The first Round Table Conference

The first Round Table Conference was opened by Lord Irwin in London in November 1930 in the House of Lords, London, and was chaired by the British prime minister and Labour Party leader, Ramsay MacDonald. The three British political parties were represented by 16 delegates. The Conservative group was led by Sir Samuel Hoare and the Liberal group by Lord Reading, who had been the Indian viceroy between 1921 and 1926. Some 58 delegates represented most shades of Indian political opinion, with the exception (see pages 219 and 223) of Congress. The delegates were all the viceroy's nominees, men of eminence, although they had no formal mandate from the groups they were supposed to represent. The princes sent 16 representatives. This was an unexpected delegation and their support for the concept of dominion status strengthened the case being made by the Labour group for granting dominion status to India on the same basis as it had been granted previously to Canada, Australia and New Zealand. This support strengthened the arguments that were put forward in the House of Commons by the minority Labour government. They were able to establish a clear policy here, backed by evidence, and so potentially freed MacDonald from the threat of Tory and Liberal opposition to granting India dominion status in parliament. Despite the absence of Congress, or perhaps because of it, considerable progress was made. It was decided that:

- India would be run as a type of dominion

- the dominion would take the form of a federation that would include the princely states as well as the 11 British provinces

- there would be Indian participation in all levels of government.

The Conference closed in January 1931 on a note of optimism.

SOURCE

2 Delegates at the first Round Table Conference, London, 1930.

The inauguration of New Delhi

In February 1931, the British formally inaugurated New Delhi as the administrative capital of the Raj amid formal celebrations led by the viceroy Lord Irwin. Calcutta had been the capital of India until 12 December 1911 when King George V, during his Delhi durbar (see page 166), announced that the capital of the Raj was to move to Delhi and laid the foundation stone for the viceroy's residence. Edwin Lutyens and Herbert Baker, two leading 20th-century British architects, were responsible for the planning and design of large parts of the new city, which grew southwards from 'old' Delhi that had been the political and financial centre of several empires of ancient India.

Of immense significance, more so than the wide streets, new housing and shopping arcades, were the administrative buildings of the Raj. Classical in design, the new secretariat buildings and viceroy's residence were designed to convey the solemnity and permanence of the Raj. They flanked an acropolis consisting of four columns representing the four dominions of Canada, South Africa, Australia and New Zealand. The message was unmistakable: India was, at some point in the near future, to be welcomed into the 'family' of British dominions. The timing was unfortunate: the British seemed to have made a crystal clear statement, set literally in stone, at a point in time where the London Round Table Conferences were supposedly about conciliation and compromise.

It is important to appreciate that each of these dominions comprised a federation of various provinces that had agreed to a single central government. Would this be the way forward for India? Certainly the symbolism of the New Delhi acropolis seemed to be pointing that way. To progressive sections of British opinion and moderate Indian opinion, federation seemed a workable way forward, as evidenced by the first Round Table Conference. However, it was not a solution favoured by diehard imperialists like Churchill, who resolutely resisted any infringement of British sovereignty. Neither was it a way forward that was acceptable to Gandhi or Nehru.

The second Round Table Conference

The second Round Table Conference, held between September and December 1931, had a similar mix of delegates to the first and there was hope that progress could be made, building on the foundations laid the previous year. There was, however, one major difference. The Gandhi–Irwin Pact had made it possible for Congress to be represented and Gandhi took this upon himself as Congress's sole representative. In doing so, he hoped to symbolise the unity of the Indian nationalist movement, claiming that Congress alone represented political India. He was also well aware that he had swung his support behind the 'young hooligans' and *purna swaraj*, and could not accept any solution that involved a form of dominion status. Thus he was effectively opposed to the outcome of the first Round Table Conference. Gandhi had also failed to consider what the impact of the attendance of other Indian delegates, with different agendas from his, would be.

Iqbal, the **Aga Khan**, and Muhammad Jinnah attended the second London Conference representing the Muslim League, Master Tara Singh represented the Sikhs and Dr Ambedkar the Untouchables. All of them demanded separate electorates for their communities and it was at this point that the Conference began to unravel. Gandhi took particular exception to the Untouchables being considered for a separate electorate, claiming that, as they were Hindus, they should come under the Hindu umbrella and he would speak for them. The well-known and well-rehearsed arguments began again, focusing on the desirability, or otherwise, of reserving seats for racial and religious minorities and how this would affect the resulting balance of power. Again, Hindus and Muslims could not agree and Gandhi, representing Congress, had the additional worry of the position of the princes and the possibility of the emergence of an alliance between them and the Muslims that could outweigh any recommendations that might be made by Congress. Unsurprisingly, this second Round Table Conference couldn't agree on a workable constitution.

KEY TERM

Aga Khan
The spiritual leader of the Ismailis, a small Muslim sect.

SOURCE

From a letter written by Devdas Gandhi to Jawaharlal Nehru on 2 October 1931. Devdas was Mahatma Gandhi's son, and was in London with his father who was attending the second Round Table Conference. Devdas Gandhi refers to his father as 'Bapu', an affectionate name used by his family and close associates.

MacDonald has agreed to the Muslim request that he should call together representatives of the various groups in order to discuss the whole communal question. Bapu has decided to give one week to these discussions, after which he is going to have nothing to do with the question. If the discussions fail, as he fears they will, he intends to make a statement next week, giving a bit of his mind to the government. He feels that the communal question is being brought deliberately to the forefront and magnified by the government because they did not intend to part with power. He has, in private conversation, already made that clear to government spokesmen. He told the Premier [Ramsay MacDonald] that there was no meaning in bringing Dr Ambedkar [representing the Untouchables] here unless it was to create difficulties. He represented the depressed classes [Untouchables] better than Dr Ambedkar. He expressed similar views about the other small minorities. They did not need special representation and Congress did not contemplate any for them. He said that the only Communities to which he would give special representation, for historic reasons, were the Muslims and the Sikhs. These ideas were intensely unpopular with most of the delegates. One after another they got up and said that the depressed classes must have special representation. Dr Ambedkar himself is extremely rude in Committee meetings as well as in private conversation.

SOURCE 4

Part of a speech made by Gandhi at the second Round Table Conference, 30 November 1931.

All the parties at this conference represent sectional interests, Congress alone claims to represent the whole of India, all interests. Congress knows no distinction of race, colour or creed; its platform is universal. And yet here I see that Congress is treated as one of the Parties. I do not mind it; I do not regard it as a calamity for the purpose of doing the work for which we have gathered together here.

ACTIVITY
KNOWLEDGE CHECK

The second Round Table Conference

How useful is Source 4 as evidence of Gandhi's position as a negotiator at the second Round Table Conference?

SOURCE 5

From F. Moraes, *Witness to an Era*, published in 1973. Frank Moraes, a European-educated Indian, was born in Mumbai and worked briefly as a lawyer. For most of his adult life, however, he lived and worked as a journalist and newspaper editor in India, Sri Lanka, Burma and China. Here he is writing about the second Round Table Conference.

Gandhi made the fatal error of claiming to speak for the Muslims and depressed classes. The spokesmen of both communities repudiated him, and since the Muslims then numbered nearly thirty per cent of the population and the depressed classes about twenty per cent, it was difficult for him to sustain his claim that he represented ninety-five per cent of India. Gandhi had, in fact, come to a tentative agreement with the Muslims on the basis of joint electorates for Hindus and Muslims, but when it came to an apportionment of seats between Hindus, Muslims and Sikhs, he yielded to the extremist Hindu leader, Pandit Madan Mohan Malaviya, who insisted that the only seat in dispute should go to the Sikhs and not to the Muslims. That Gandhi's efforts at a Hindi–Muslim settlement should have failed was bad enough. That they failed over the allocation of one seat made the attempt ridiculous. The minorities, comprising the Muslims, depressed classes, a section of Indian Christians, the Anglo-Indians and the British community then confronted the British government with a document embodying an agreement arrived at between themselves. Whitehall had no alternative but to announce that the government would make its own award.

AS Level Exam-Style Question Section A (b)

How much weight do you give to the evidence of Source 5 for an enquiry into the failure of the Round Table Conferences, 1930–32? (12 marks)

Explain your answer, using the source, the information given about it and your own knowledge of the historical context.

Tip

Consider whether Frank Moraes was directly involved in the events about which he is writing.

SOURCE 6

Gandhi leaving a session of the second Round Table Conference, September 1931.

SOURCE 7

Part of a letter written by M. R. Jayakar in January 1942 to a colleague, C. Rajagopalachari. Here Jayakar, a liberal Hindu politician who had attended the second Round Table Conference in 1931, is reflecting on Jinnah's role at the Conference. Rajagopalachari did not attend the Conference. A former chief minister of Madras (1937–39), in 1942 he was practising as a lawyer.

Jinnah's attitude at the Round Table Conference surprised every one, including the British Delegation. His one effort was, and a deceitful one too, to accept all the concessions that were made to him on behalf of the Hindus and subsequently to take them privately to the Prime Minister of England, Ramsay MacDonald, and to say to him in a bargaining spirit: 'This is what the Hindus are prepared to give; how much more will the British Government give the Muslims?' This method of bargaining became in course of time so notorious that ultimately MacDonald telephoned me, asking me to stop this process of bargaining, for it was most deceitful and led nowhere. I am citing this incident as proving the unscrupulous way in which Jinnah will bargain for the Muslim cause. As you are dealing with him, I have to warn you to be very careful.

ACTIVITY
KNOWLEDGE CHECK

The roles of Jinnah and Gandhi at the Round Table Conferences

1 How far do Sources 3 and 5 explain the weakness of Gandhi's position as a negotiator?

2 Look at Source 6. It was clearly wet and cold in London at that time. Why, then, did Gandhi dress as he did?

3 How reliable is Source 7 as evidence of Jinnah's activities at the Round Table Conferences?

AS Level Exam-Style Question Section A (a)

Why is Source 7 valuable to the historian for an enquiry into the role of Jinnah at the Round Table Conferences, 1930–32?

Explain your answer using the source, the information given about it and your own knowledge of the historical context. (8 marks)

Tip

Consider the position of the two men in connection with the Conference and the likelihood that they were showing bias against Jinnah.

The third Round Table Conference

The third Round Table Conference, held in London from November to December 1932, was doomed before it started. Only 46 delegates attended, and none from the British Labour Party or Congress. The Conference discussed the franchise, finance and the role of the princely states, but, again, couldn't reach any definite conclusions and it collapsed in confusion. There were no more Round Table Conferences.

THINKING HISTORICALLY   Cause and Consequence (6b)

Attitudes and actions

Individuals can only make choices based on their context. Prevalent attitudes combine with individual experience and natural temperament to frame the individual's perception of what is going on around them. Nobody can know the future or see into the minds of others.

Context	Action
• Gandhi's success at the 25th annual meeting of Congress in Nagpur in 1920 in binding Hindus and Muslims in support for his campaign of non-cooperation with the Raj • Combined opposition to the 1927/8 Simon Commission from Congress leaders, including Gandhi, and a large section of the Muslim League, led by Jinnah • The Muslim League's continued attempts to bring about a rapprochement with Congress (e.g. Jinnah's 14-point compromise plan of March 1929) • The 1930 salt *satyragraha*, which included Untouchables among the original 78 participants • The Gandhi-Irwin Pact of 1931	• Gandhi's decision that, at the second Round Table, held in London, September–December 1931, he alone spoke for all Indians

Answer the following questions individually then discuss your answers in a group:

1 Why might Gandhi have believed that all Indians would support his decision?

2 Why could Gandhi have thought that the British government would negotiate with him alone?

3 What other information would have been useful to him to help him decide on his course of action?

4 How reasonable was Gandhi's course of action, given what he knew about the situation at the time?

5 How far should the historian try to understand the context of the beliefs and values of people in the past when explaining why individuals make choices in history?

Why did the Round Table Conferences fail?

The situation in Britain

Between November 1930 and December 1932, the British political situation changed considerably and this had some impact on the Round Table Conferences.

In August 1931, the first Labour government resigned after splitting and replaced by a Tory-dominated coalition (the National Government) facing a depression, unemployment and the collapse of the economy. The government was tackling huge problems that, to them, were more pressing than settling the Indian question. Furthermore, the new secretary of state for India, Sir Samuel Hoare, had more reservations about self-government for India than his predecessor, William Wedgwood Benn. These reservations were shared by many in the Conservative Party. Indeed, Winston Churchill campaigned around Britain against Congress. He set up the India Defence League, with support from around 50 Conservative MPs, and made no secret of the fact that he thought Indians were totally unsuited to democracy and should remain subordinate to the white British Empire for ever.

By the time the third Round Table Conference was held at the end of 1932, Prime Minister Ramsay MacDonald had lost the support of his own Labour Party. He was able to continue in office only through a National Government, supported by his political opponents. The British Labour Party, embroiled with their own internal problems, didn't send any representatives to the Conference.

Congress

Congress was not represented at the first Conference; Nehru and Gandhi were in jail and it took the Gandhi–Irwin Pact before Gandhi was able to travel to London for the second Round Table Conference. Once at the Conference, Gandhi maintained that he alone could speak for all India, including the Muslims. While this was an attempt to establish Congress as the umbrella organisation capable of representing the whole subcontinent with himself as its sole spokesman, he only succeeded in alienating all the groups seeking separate representation, and especially the Muslims.

Divisions over separate electorates

Jinnah, representing the Muslim League and determined that the Muslim voice would be heard in any 'new' India, was firm in his support for separate electorates. In this he was supported by representatives of the other minority groups, especially the Untouchables, who were outraged that Gandhi claimed to speak for them because they were Hindus. The situation was further complicated by Jinnah's tactics, usually conducted behind the scenes, of playing one group off against another as he sought to gain greater and greater concessions for the Muslims. The British government supported the idea of separate electorates and this drew them into contention with Gandhi.

ACTIVITY
KNOWLEDGE CHECK

Why did the Round Table Conferences fail?

1 List the reasons the Conferences failed.

2 Working with a partner, agree a list of priorities.

3 Write a paragraph explaining why you have chosen that particular order.

HOW FAR WAS A POLITICAL COMPROMISE REACHED IN THE YEARS 1932–35?

The viceroy, Lord Irwin, was replaced by Lord Willingdon, who had previously been governor-general of Canada and had had earlier experience in India as governor of Bombay and of Madras. While Willingdon was governor of Bombay, and dealing with India's contribution to the First World War, Gandhi arrived from South Africa and was invited to a formal meeting at Government House. There, Willingdon was left with the impression that Gandhi was a dangerous Bolshevik; this coloured his later attitude to nationalist agitation. He made no secret of the fact that he despised the Gandhi–Irwin Pact as a weak document, and regretted that, in public at least, he was forced to treat Gandhi with respect. Largely because of these pre-conceptions, once installed as viceroy, Willingdon adopted stricter measures against protestors than his predecessors and, in doing so, alienated nationalist opinion.

Lord Willingdon 1866–1941 (viceroy April 1931–April 1936)

Freeman Freeman-Thomas, 1st Marquis of Willingdon, was a Liberal politician and administrator. Educated at Eton and Cambridge University, he served as a soldier in the Sussex artillery before being elected to the House of Commons in 1900, representing the borough of Hastings. He worked as a junior lord of the Treasury in the Liberal government and for some time worked as secretary to the prime minister, Herbert Asquith. Willingdon had royal connections, and often played tennis with the king, George V. He was reputed to be the monarch's favourite tennis partner.

Willingdon held a range of government posts in the British Empire, including the governorship of Bombay, a post he took up in 1913, just before the outbreak of the First World War. It was during this time that Gandhi arrived in Bombay from South Africa and Willingdon invited him to a formal meeting at Government House. Willingdon did not form a favourable impression of Gandhi, believing his ideas to be dangerous. The famine of 1917, which left farmers unable to pay their taxes, resulted in Willingdon confiscating property by force and Gandhi employing non-violent resistance.

Willingdon's appointment as governor of Madras came just after the Government of India Act 1919 that set up the controversial system of dyarchy in the major provinces, and again had to deal with a series of communal riots that broke out in 1921 and a general strike, which ran in parallel with the non-cooperation movement.

Proposed by the king for the governor-generalship of Canada, Willingdon took up office in October 1926. After enjoying a peaceful, cultural time in Canada, in less than five years Willingdon was back in India as viceroy, replacing Lord Irwin. On familiar ground, Willingdon was faced with dealing with the consequences of Gandhi's nationalistic non-cooperation movement. Here, he adopted much stricter measures than his predecessors, ordering the arrest of Gandhi and thousands of members of Congress. As a result he faced many threats on his life. Despite this, he commissioned the Lloyd Barrage across the Indus River that provided work for thousands and brought large areas of desert under cultivation, and established the Willingdon Sports Club in Bombay, open to Indians and British, as a direct result of being refused membership of the Royal Bombay Yacht Club because he was accompanied by Indian friends. In April 1936 he was replaced as viceroy by Lord Linlithgow.

Indian reaction to the failure of consultation

In India, the situation was deteriorating and Viceroy Willingdon decided to take a tough line. Lacking the temperament or, indeed, the willingness to engage in discussions with Gandhi, he followed the British government's instructions that he should conciliate only those elements of Indian opinion that were prepared to work with the current administration. So:

- on 4 January 1932, just one week after he returned to India from the second Round Table Conference, Gandhi was arrested and imprisoned

- Congress was outlawed

- all members of Congress's Working Committee and the Provincial Committees were rounded up and imprisoned

- youth organisations were banned.

Within four months, over 80,000 Indians, mostly members of Congress, were in prison. Reaction on the part of the Indian population was swift but, in the absence of Congress leaders locally and nationally, and especially Gandhi, was uneven and disorganised. Boycotts of British goods were common and so was non-payment of taxes; youth organisations, although officially banned, became very popular; and terrorist activity increased, with more and more women becoming involved. Indeed, the United Provinces and the Northwest Frontier Province became little more than armed camps, and troops in Peshawar and Meerut were kept on armed alert. But, by and large, the authorities kept control of the situation and the police never lost control of the streets or rural areas for very long.

The Communal Award and Gandhi's response

On 16 August 1932, Ramsay MacDonald, the British prime minister, announced the Communal Award, which was to be incorporated into any new Indian constitution. This designated Sikhs, Indian Christians, Anglo-Indians and Untouchables as separate classes, along with Muslims, which as such were to be entitled to separate electorates in any new Indian constitution.

Gandhi was furious. He wasn't in favour of separate electorates anyway, but the inclusion of Untouchables he regarded as the final straw. The removal of the stigma of Untouchability had long been one of his missions and, furthermore, in his mind all Untouchables were Hindus. This had been one of the stumbling blocks in the second Round Table Conference. Thus, Gandhi reasoned, the British government was further trying to weaken Congress by separating off the Untouchables. Furthermore, he feared that to separate out Untouchables in this way would fragment Hindu society. He reacted in a dramatic fashion, launching a **fast-unto-death**, believing he had no other course of action. Of course he had, but he chose in this way to blackmail the government into withdrawing the Communal Award.

Authorities almost invariably hate this form of protest, believing it creates martyrs, especially if the individuals concerned take it to the end and die. But the authorities always face the problem as to whether to be seen to give in to blackmail or to hold out and risk the unrest caused by allowing individuals to die as a form of protest. In this case, given the stature and influence of Gandhi, what was to be done?

SOURCE

Part of a letter written by Gandhi to Ramsay MacDonald on 18 August 1932.

I have read the British government's decision on the representation of the minorities and have slept over it. In pursuance of my letter to Sir Samuel Hoare and my declaration at the meeting of the Minorities Committee of the Round Table Conference on 13 November 1931, at St James' palace, I have to resist your decision with my life. The only way I can do so is by declaring a perpetual fast unto death from food of any kind, save water, with or without salt and soda. This fast will cease if, during its progress, the British government, of its own motion or under pressure of public opinion, revise their decision and withdraw their scheme of communal electorates for the Depressed Classes whose representatives should be elected by the general electorate under a common franchise, no matter how wide it is. The proposed fast will come into operation in the ordinary course from the noon of 20th September next, unless the said decision is meanwhile revised in the manner suggested above.

ACTIVITY
KNOWLEDGE CHECK

Fast-unto-death
To what extent was Gandhi taking a risk when he threatened to start a fast-unto-death until the Communal Award was withdrawn? Discuss this strategy in groups.

The Yeravda (Poona) Pact: a way out of the impasse?

Neither Viceroy Willingdon nor Congress wanted Gandhi to die. Willingdon didn't want to make Gandhi a martyr and, so, in his view, inflate the importance of his cause. He had plans in place to release Gandhi once he got to the point of no return so that at least he would not die in prison. Congress, of course, did not want to lose their iconic leader.

Gandhi's fast – and his threat to continue it until he died – exerted tremendous emotional and political pressure on Untouchables and other Hindus. A wide spectrum of Hindu leaders met in Bombay including representatives of the Untouchables. Together, they hammered out a set of proposals that they took by train to Poona, where Gandhi was fasting in the Yeravda jail, having refused Willingdon's offer to move him to a more comfortable private house.

Although weak and in danger of physical and mental collapse, Gandhi discussed the proposals with the delegation for several days. Finally, agreement was reached. The British government Communal Award proposal was for an allocation of 71 seats on the provincial legislatures to the Untouchables; Gandhi and the delegation settled on a total of 148, elected by a system of primary and secondary elections for seats allocated to Untouchables, with only Untouchables being able to vote in the relevant primary elections. Additionally, they agreed that Untouchables would be allocated 18 percent of the Central Assembly seats, as long as they stood for election by the votes of the general electorate. In essence, these agreements meant the abandonment of separate electorates because although there were reserved seats the voting for them was by the general electorate. Furthermore, Hindus and Untouchables reached agreement that a specific sum of money should be set aside by every provincial assembly for the education of Untouchables.

The British government accepted the Yeravda (Poona) Pact; Gandhi ended his fast a week after it began and the following week was celebrated as Untouchability Abolition Week. Although Hindu leaders declared that, henceforth, among Hindus, no one should be regarded as an Untouchable by reason of their birth and that they would have the same rights as other Hindus to use public wells, public schools, public roads and other public institutions, it took another 20 years before Untouchability was abolished by law.

The British government made the necessary amendments, as determined by the Yeravda (Poona) Pact, to the Communal Award and had already stated that the Communal Award would be incorporated into a new Indian constitution. However, agreement between Hindus and Untouchables was not enough. The London Round Table Conferences had demonstrated the wide divergence in long-term aspirations, short-term aims and tactics of, for example, Muslims, Sikhs, Christians and the princes. Believing the Indians unable to reach agreement on their own constitution, the British politicians decided to create one for them with the Government of India Act.

Support and opposition in Britain for constitutional change

A determined group of Conservatives fought the Government of India Bill every inch of the way. They joined forces with ex-generals and former civil servants, some of whom had served in India, and together they formed the India Defence League (see page 223). Rudyard Kipling was a vice-president and Winston Churchill its most vociferous supporter. Churchill's views on India were formed when he had been stationed there as an army subaltern in 1897, and they hadn't changed since. Having problems with accepting equality between the races, he refused to accept that Indians were capable of running their own affairs.

EXTEND YOUR KNOWLEDGE

Joseph Rudyard Kipling (1865–1936)
Born in Bombay, at the age of five he was sent back to England to stay with a foster family before going to boarding school in Devon. In 1881, aged 16, Kipling returned to India, where he worked as a journalist in Lahore. Back in England eight years later, he had a series of short stories published before settling down to write many longer books, for example, *The Jungle Book*, the *Just So Stories* and *Puck of Pook's Hill*. Another, published in 1901, was *Kim*, which told of the adventures of an orphaned boy, Kim, in India in the 19th century. Kim is recruited into the British Intelligence Service as a spy, and on one adventure meets up with a lama – a holy man from Tibet. Espionage and spiritual threads permeate the book and the reader is left to decide which path, the prideful or the spiritual, Kim will follow.

A strong patriot and conservative by nature, Kipling became friends with Alfred Harmsworth, the newspaper baron, Cecil Rhodes, a South African politician and Alfred Milner, a colonial administrator and member of the Cabinet during the First World War. King George V became a personal friend. After the First World War, in which his son John was killed at the Battle of Loos (1915), he became involved in the work of the Imperial War Graves Commission.

Media support for the India Defence League came from the *Daily Mail*. Its proprietor, Lord Rothermere, wrote a series of outrageous articles under the general heading, 'If We Lose India'. These were laced with entirely erroneous 'facts', such as the 'fact' that Gandhi and Congress were an insignificant group of semi-educated Hindus, and fake photographs of British troops quelling riots with lorries piled high with corpses. The message was clear: Indians were unfit to govern themselves and only the paternalistic British could effectively manage the subcontinent. If Britain were to leave India, carnage would follow. Furthermore, the *Daily Mail* warned, India was essential to the British economy and to lose India's trade, at a time when every economy in the Western world was struggling, would be the height of folly.

Harold Harmsworth, 1st Lord Rothermere (1868–1940)
The younger brother of Alfred Harmsworth (who became 1st Baron Northcliffe), Harold became the business manager in the newspaper empire they founded together. As a newspaper proprietor, he started by launching the *Daily Record* in Scotland, then bought out his brother's interest in the *Daily Mail* and launched the *Sunday Pictorial*. He used this opportunity to write a series of articles supporting Hitler and defending the retention of the British Empire as a collection of dependent territories unable to run their own affairs.

SOURCE

Extracts from Winston Churchill's speech, made in the House of Commons, on the second reading of the Government of India Bill, 11 February 1935.

We have as good a right to be in India as anyone there except, perhaps, the Depressed Classes, who are the original stock. Our government is not an irresponsible Government. It is a government responsible to the Crown and to Parliament. It is incomparably the best government that India has ever seen or ever will see.

We are confronted with the old choice of self-government versus good government. We are invited to believe that the worst self-government is better than the best good government.

Our protection and security cannot be removed from India. They have grown with our growth and strengthened with our strength. They will diminish with our diminution and decay with our decay. If this external aid is withheld, India will descend into the squalor and anarchy of India in the sixteenth and seventeenth centuries. It seems to me that the present infatuation of the liberal mind, and I must say of the more intellectual part of the Socialist mind, is at this moment very serious. Their error is an undue exaltation of the principle of self-government. They set this principle above all other principles; they press it to the destruction of all other principles.

I still think that, after all these five years of discussions and inquiry, no advance or improvement of any sort has been made upon the report of the Statutory [Simon] Commission. There has been no advance towards efficiency, no advance towards finality, and, above all, no advance towards agreement. All these protracted, tumultuous confabulations, which followed Lord Irwin's unfortunate Declaration in 1929 – all this labyrinth through which we have been led has brought us nothing that has been good for this country or for India.

SOURCE

10

Extracts from Clement Attlee's speech in the House of Commons on the Government of India Bill, 4 June 1935.

The question that we should be putting is this: does this Constitutional scheme provide a medium through which the living forces of India can operate, for what we have to deal with are the forces of modern India, a living India, and not the dead India of the past. For good or ill, the Congress Party is one of the dominating factors in the situation. It is no use ignoring it, and it is useless and futile merely to abuse it. We may disagree with it, but within it are very many of the forces that are going to make for modern India.

My first objection to this Bill is that I think it is deliberately framed so as to exclude as far as possible the Congress party from effective powers in the new Constitution.

Another serious objection is the provision with regard to the exclusion from effective political life those who have been sentenced to prison, although that has been slightly bettered during the Committee stage. But all the way through the Government have yielded time after time to the States and time after time to minority communities, but have always stood strongly up against any yielding to Congress or the Nationalists.

In this Bill provision is made by means of upper chambers representative of wealth, privilege, power and land to weight the scales all the time in favour of wealth against the poorer sections of the community.

Is this bill going to be accepted and worked by the people of India? I do not think so. The indications are that if it is to be worked at all it will be in a grudging spirit and that it is only too likely that its provisions will be used, not for seeing how far it can be made useful for self-government, but as a means of getting something more.

Prime Minister Stanley Baldwin steered the bill through the Commons with quiet determination. He stuck to the position he had taken up when he supported the Irwin Declaration (see page 213) and never wavered from it. A pragmatic prime minister, he managed to convince the majority of his party that the British Empire was an organic organisation that had to change and develop, or die. In the Commons, the bill was attacked by Winston Churchill and by Clement Attlee, but for different reasons. In the event, fewer than 50 MPs followed Churchill into the 'No' lobby and the bill became law in August 1935. The secretary of state for India, Sir Samuel Hoare, while acknowledging the furore created by the bill, countered it by arguing that no one in India had been able to produce a workable alternative to the Government of India Act.

ACTIVITY
WRITING

The strength of an argument

1 Read Source 9.

   a) What are the main points of the argument Churchill is making?

   b) What is weak about this argument?

   c) What could be added to it to make it stronger?

2 Read Source 10.

   a) What are the main points of the argument Attlee is making?

   b) What is weak about this argument?

   c) What could be added to it to make it stronger?

3 Now reflect on each argument.

   a) What techniques is Churchill using to persuade his audience to his point of view?

   b) What techniques is Attlee using to persuade the same audience of his point of view?

   c) Which argument, in your view, is the stronger? Why?

A Level Exam-Style Question Section B

How accurate is it to say that, in the years 1930–35, the British government totally misjudged the situation in India? (20 marks)

Tip

Consider the traditional aims of British policy in India and the extent to which politicians in Westminster were able to be flexible.

ACTIVITY
KNOWLEDGE CHECK

A new constitution for India

1 Why did the Communal Award give rise to such passions among Congress supporters?

2 Why was there so much opposition in Britain to the Government of India bill as it progressed through parliament?

TO WHAT EXTENT DID THE GOVERNMENT OF INDIA ACT IMPACT ON INDIAN AND BRITISH POLITICS?

The Government of India Act 1935 was the final British-written constitution to be imposed on India by the British government. A Federation of India was proposed but never put into effect. Only the clauses dealing with provincial governments were actually implemented. These were the main features:

- India was divided into 11 provinces, each of which had a legislative assembly and a provincial government. The provinces would control almost everything, except defence and foreign affairs.

- Each province would have a governor, who retained the power to act in an emergency.

- Dyarchy, the system in which provincial government was divided between appointed officials and elected representatives, was abolished.

- Separate electorates were to continue as before.

- Burma was separated from India and given its own government.

- Two new states, Sindh and Orissa, were created.

The viceroy would still be appointed by the British government and would be in control of defence and foreign affairs. However, he would have to follow the advice of an Executive Committee, which was made up mostly of Indians.

Partial implementation of the Government of India Act

The response in India to the Act explains why it was only partially implemented by the time the Second World War broke out.

Congress objected to the Act because the Party wanted *purna swaraj* (full independence from Britain and the British Empire) and members were not interested in what they saw as a half-way house. Congress wanted India to have a strong central government, which would inevitably be strongly Hindu; they could not support strong provincial governments as laid down in the Government of India Act because some provincial governments might end up being Muslim-dominated or controlled. Congress also had strong objections on a closely related issue: that of reserving seats for minority groups.

SOURCE

11 Lord and Lady Linlithgow, photographed in 1940, leaving their official residence to attend a garden party.

The Muslim League objected to the Act primarily because it did not offer enough power to Muslims in either central or provincial legislatures. No guarantees were offered for the protection of the rights of Muslims.

Congress's fears that the new provincial assemblies could be dominated by Muslims were thus far only theoretical. At the time, the provincial assemblies were dominated by Hindus. However, new elections were designated for 1937 and, should Congress and the Muslim League decide to participate in these elections, no one could be certain what the results would be.

The princes represented different interests that, in many ways, ran counter to both the Muslim League and Congress. The Government of India Act was, in reality, proposing an all-India federation that would inevitably result in a diminution of the power of the princes and they were prepared to bargain hard to protect their fiscal rights. Indeed, the government in London warned Delhi not to push the princes too hard, fearing they would refuse to cooperate altogether and the Act would fall. Furthermore, Lord Zetland, the Conservative government's secretary of state for India, was afraid that the princes would join with Tory die-hards, like Winston Churchill, to prevent the complete implementation of the Government of India Act. This potential alliance would not only virtually kill the full implementation of the Government of India Act, but it would cause severe embarrassment for the government in Westminster. This fear hampered any negotiations the two men, Lord Linlithgow (who became viceroy in 1936) and the secretary of state Lord Zetland, were conducting with representatives of the princely states, Congress and the Muslim League. Indeed, by 1939, only two-fifths of the states had agreed to the form of federation required by the Act.

EXTRACT

1 From Judith M. Brown, *Modern India: the Origins of an Asian Democracy*, published in 1994.

For all its limitations, the 1935 Act was a major experiment in the devolution of power in a non-white part of Britain's empire. Its imperial framers hoped it would channel the interests and forces in Indian public life through institutions that would protect Britain's diminishing interests on the subcontinent and require from Britain a much lighter exercise of imperial control and decreased expenditure of resources. However, by the time of its enactment it seemed a battered and much cobbled measure, disliked by most Indian politicians and a significant group of British MPs.

Despite the long-term failure to provide a federal solution to the imperial problem of ruling the subcontinent, the 1935 Act succeeded as a temporary solution to the problem of governing British India. For two years the British tactic of retreat to the centre, leaving the provinces to run themselves under Indian ministers, paid off spectacularly.

SOURCE

12 From Viceroy Linlithgow's report to London, 15 June 1936, on progress toward implementing the Government of India Act of 1935.

It is vital that the impetus of the new Statute and the consummation of Provincial Autonomy should carry us straight on into Federation. For indeed there would be grave danger in allowing any prolonged interval of time to elapse between Provincial Autonomy and the final phase. Federation has few enthusiastic friends. The Princes, I believe, for the most part regard it as inevitable but do not welcome it. Congress hates it, and Provinces will soon. Whether as regards their bureaucracies or their public opinion, they will develop a degree of local patriotism which would view with easy acquiescence the progressive weakening of central authority, such as would most certainly happen if the reconstruction of the Centre is unduly delayed.

ACTIVITY
KNOWLEDGE CHECK

The Government of India Act 1935

1 What conclusions can be drawn from Source 11 about the Raj in 1940?

2 Read Extract 1 and Source 12. How far do you agree that the 1935 Act succeeded as a temporary solution to the problem of governing India?

The princes faced problems of varying magnitude from their own subjects in their own states. There was increasing pressure for reform and greater representative government before any federal agreement was reached and confirmed the autocracy of the princes. Unrest and some limited rioting broke out in states as large as Hyderabad and as small as Khasi. Congress in general was officially opposed to the idea of the princes' nomination to any federal legislature and wanted to end their autocracy. However, the central Congress leadership was afraid that splinter groups of Congress supporters would use the agitation in the princely states to build up a power base of their own and challenge the central Congress leaders.

Outcome of the 1937 elections

Both Congress and the Muslim League were faced with an immediate dilemma: should they participate in the provincial elections, set for 1937? Not to participate would be consistent with their rejection of the Act, but the elections were going ahead anyway and who knew what way-out group would achieve power? A total boycott would cut them off from government. Furthermore, to participate might give them the opportunity to work within the system to create change. Both Congress and the League decided to take part.

SOURCE 13

Results of the elections to provincial lower houses, 1937.

Province	Total seats	Seats won by Congress
Madras	215	159
Bihar	152	95
Orissa	60	36
Central Provinces	112	71
Uttar Pradesh	228	133
Bombay	175	88
Assam	108	35
North-West Frontier Provinces	50	19
Bengal	250	54
Punjab	175	18
Sind	60	8

How did these results impact on the governance of India?

Congress, as Source 13 shows, was highly successful. The party gained overall control of the United and Central Provinces, Orissa, Bombay and Madras, and it became the largest single party in Assam and the North-West Frontier, although a combination of opponents could out-vote them. It was only in Bengal, Punjab and Sind that Congress was outvoted. Though less than half of the 1,585 provincial legislative seats contested throughout India were open to the general electorate, Congress won them all, together with 59 more from the separate electorate contests, ending up with 716 legislative members.

The Muslim League fared badly. This was largely because it had had no strong leadership until 1935, two years before the elections, when Jinnah returned to India from self-imposed exile in England. To attempt to rally co-ordinated and focused support from supporters and potential supporters for the Muslim League was a very big task. Jinnah worked hard before the elections to build up a power base but, in the limited time available to him, he wasn't able even to find enough candidates to contest all the reserved Muslim seats. An analysis of polling figures shows that Muslims gave little support to Congress candidates, even though they had to be Muslim to stand for the restricted seats. Indeed, the only overwhelmingly Muslim province that voted strongly for Congress was the North-West Frontier.

Non-Congress ministries were formed in Assam, Bengal, Punjab and Sind, and here governance worked as well as it did in the provinces with Congress ministries. There was legislative reform and much was done to protect tenants, relieve peasant poverty and control the activities of money-lenders. The only observable difference was that, in the Congress-led provinces, due to the influence of Gandhi, basic education centred on crafts was given a high priority.

How did the Muslim League revitalise itself?

Jinnah realised that the Muslim League had two alternatives. It would have to attract mass support in order to win control in some provinces, especially the Punjab and Sind, where Muslims were in a majority, or it would have to enter into some kind of power-sharing agreement with Congress. This Congress refused to contemplate. And then Congress party members played straight into the Muslim League's hands.

Many of the new Congress provincial council ministers, starved of power and recognition for so long, threw caution to the winds. They took advantage of their new offices and appointed relatives and fellow caste members to jobs they controlled; they ignored minorities and often behaved spitefully to their enemies. In some provinces, fiscal policies were drawn up to hurt Muslim landowners; in Bihar, cow-slaughter was banned; Congress flags were hoisted on public buildings where there was a substantial Muslim minority. Many Muslims felt that they were living in a Hindu Raj. Now, as never before, many Muslims believed they needed the electoral safeguards that Jinnah and the League had long been demanding.

Jinnah rose to the occasion. He began a series of carefully orchestrated personal appearances, mass rallies and press interviews. The rallies and processions deliberately harked back to the glory days of the Mughal Empire. Among other memorabilia, a 'Tipu Sultan Day' was inaugurated in honour of the Muslim sultan of Mysore who defeated the British in 1782. But Jinnah and his advisors looked to the future, too, as they deliberately targeted university students, persuading them that success in their future careers would only come about if they supported the Muslim League, with its promise of protection for Muslims via separate electorates. A Hindu-dominated India would have, the Muslim League argued, no place for them. Jinnah himself became the embodiment of Muslim identity, hopes and dreams. In spite of all the endeavours of Gandhi, Nehru and even, in the early days, Jinnah, Muslims could never be persuaded that the Hindu-dominated Congress party was their natural home. In the late 1930s, they turned to the Muslim League in their thousands. Jinnah had at last given the Muslims a sense of identity and purpose.

EXTEND YOUR KNOWLEDGE

Fateh Ali Tipu (Tipu Sultan) 1750–99

In the 1930s, Tipu Sultan became a symbol of what Muslims, given the chance and the right conditions, could achieve. In the 18th century this Muslim ruler and Sultan of Mysore had challenged British power by developing a new state and an army that could, and initially did, defeat the British.

Taught European military and administrative skills by French officers, he defeated the British at the Battle of Coleroon River in 1782 and then negotiated with them for recognition as Sultan of Mysore. He turned Mysore into a strong and wealthy state by introducing new crops and industries, for example, growing pineapples and manufacturing silk.

In 1789, Tipu attacked the adjacent British protectorate of Travancore. The resulting war ended in humiliation for Tipu in 1792, when he lost half his lands to the British East India Company. He sought revenge by allying himself with the French, but even so the Mysore wars ended in defeat and his own death.

Rapprochement between the League and Congress seemed impossible. However, there was one last-ditch stand to achieve Congress and League unity under the Congress presidency of Subhas Bose. In 1938, the year Bose was elected president, Jinnah met briefly with Gandhi, Nehru and Bose, but talks broke down because of Jinnah's insistence that the Muslim League be recognised by Congress as the sole party of India's Muslims. Congress liked to think they were an inclusive party, capable of representing the entire nation – even Muslims. Jinnah, as evidenced by his presidential address to the Patna session of the Muslim League in December 1938, thought differently.

SOURCE 14

From Jinnah's presidential address to the Patna session of the Muslim League, December 1938.

The Congress has now killed every hope of Hindu–Muslim settlement. The Congress does not want any settlement with the Muslim of India. There are four forces at play in this country. Firstly, there is the British Government. Secondly there are the rulers and peoples of the Indian States. Thirdly, there are the Hindus; and, fourthly, there are Muslims. The Congress press may clamour as much as it likes; they may bring out their morning, afternoon, evening and night editions; the Congress leaders may shout as much as they like that Congress is a national body. But I say it is not true. The Congress is nothing but a Hindu body. That is the truth and the Congress leaders know it. The presence of the few Muslims, the few misled and misguided ones, and the few who are there with ulterior motives, does not, cannot, make it a national body. I challenge anybody to deny that the Congress is not mainly a Hindu body. I ask, does the Congress represent the Muslim? I ask does the Congress represent the Christians? I ask does the Congress represent the Scheduled Castes? I ask does the Congress represent the non-Brahmans? I say the Congress does not even represent all the Hindus. What about the Hindu Mahasabha? What about the Liberal Federation? The Congress, no doubt, is the largest single party in the country. But it is nothing more than that. It may arrogate to itself whatever titles it likes: the Congress High Command, in the intoxication of power, like persons who are drunk, may make any claims it pleases them to make. But such claims cannot alter the true character of the Congress. It remains what it is – mainly a Hindu body.

ACTIVITY
KNOWLEDGE CHECK

The Muslim League
What problems does Source 14 suggest about the future governance of India?

Congress divided against itself

To all intents and purposes, Congress was a partner in government with the Raj. The partnership was, however, not always an easy one. Congress's central leadership was uncertain as to how much control it could exercise over the provincial leaders, even though they nominally supported Congress. Some ranged behind Gandhi, who favoured using parliamentary tactics even though it might mean temporarily cooperating with the Raj and the princes in order to achieve their ultimate aim of *swaraj*. Others backed Jawaharlal Nehru, hating working within a constitution they disliked and having to accept that ultimate power still lay with the British. In the end, Gandhi negotiated with the British and gained an assurance that provincial governors would not interfere with normal administration. To a considerable extent, this worked. However, in some provinces there was a clear refusal to accept not only the Raj but also the rights of Muslims.

At the end of 1938, Congress itself was torn apart by in-fighting over its presidency. There was considerable pressure on Bose to quit: Gandhi didn't trust him and neither did the old guard. However, Jawaharlal Nehru refused to stand in his place and Bose himself refused to step aside for the Gandhi faction's nominee, Pattabhi Sitaramayya. Bose knew he had the support of student, peasant and worker delegates and, in the first contested election ever for the presidency of Congress, won by 1,580 votes to 1,375. Twelve members of the Gandhi faction resigned immediately from the Working Committee in protest against the democratic election of their own president. Bose was left as president of a party that could not function because of the huge rift in its senior echelons. Gandhi ignored Bose's pleas for help and Nehru's attempts at mediation failed. Finally, Bose was forced to resign and he was replaced by Rajendra Prasad, 'elected' by the Working Committee of which he was a member. Bose and his brother, Sarat Chandra, walked away from Congress altogether. Back in their homeland of Bengal, they formed their Forward Bloc Party, dedicated to the revolutionary overthrow of the Raj.

Attitudes towards the British Raj

Throughout this period, between the passing of the Government of India Act in 1935 and its partial implementation in India up to 1939, the Raj experienced a brief period of popularity. As the 1930s progressed, and the Raj seemed less and less the natural government of India, no obvious alternative was accepted by all Indians. The vague promises of nationalism that, in previous decades, had helped to weld diverse peoples together were now seen to be inadequate as a structure for the government of the subcontinent. More and more people, and in particular Congress chief ministers, looked to the administrative structures of the Raj for practical guidance and professional help on a daily basis. For all the potential leaders of an independent India, the realisation that freedom alone would not solve the subcontinent's complex problems was sobering.

Meanwhile, the administration of British India had to continue. The new structure of provincial governance in India had little impact on British recruitment to the Indian Civil Service. Indeed, recruitment boomed in the 1930s. However, this boom in recruitment did not make up for earlier shortfalls. The ICS struggled at a time when the Service needed its greatest political and personal flexibility and skill in managing the demands of the new provincial assemblies. Many ICS men formed strong working and personal relationships with Indian politicians; their problem was their workload. This was heavy at the best of times and was to become intolerable as the major crisis of another world war loomed.

ACTIVITY
KNOWLEDGE CHECK

Strengthening the Muslim League
1 List the reasons why (a) Congress and (b) the Muslim League opposed the Government of India Act of 1935.

2 How significant, in your opinion, was the issue of separate electorates in trying to find a way forward for the future governance of India?

3 How far had the Muslim League become a force in Indian politics by the end of the 1930s?

EXTEND YOUR KNOWLEDGE

Lord Linlithgow (1887–1952)
Born in South Queensferry, West Lothian, Scotland, Victor Alexander John Hope succeeded his father as the second Marquess Linlithgow in 1908. He served as an officer in the Royal Scots battalion during the First World War, followed by various minor roles in Conservative governments in the 1920s. He was heavily involved in public life. For example, he was chair of the Medical Research Council, chair of the governing body of Imperial College, London, and chaired the Royal Commission on Agriculture in India.

He turned down the governorship of Madras and the governor-generalship of Australia, accepting the position of viceroy of India in 1936. He was the longest-serving viceroy, remaining in office until replaced by Wavell in 1943. During his time as viceroy, he attempted to implement the 1935 Government of India Act and took India into the Second World War. Disputes between the British administration and Congress ultimately led to the Quit India Movement in 1942. A traditional imperialist, he is remembered by Indian politicians for his rigorous suppression of nationalist campaigns and for his refusal to intervene in the Bengal Famine of 1943.

A staunch Presbyterian, after his retirement from India Linlithgow served as High Commissioner to the Church of Scotland.

HOW UNITED WAS INDIA'S REACTION TO THE OUTBREAK OF THE SECOND WORLD WAR IN 1939?

The First World War (1914–18) had had the effect of driving Hindus and Muslims together and so unifying India's nationalist movement. Events in the 1920s and 1930s had driven Congress and the Muslim League further and further apart, while at the same time making it clearer that India's independence from the Raj was achievable. India's reaction to the outbreak of war in 1939 reflected this, and highlighted the innate contradiction of fighting a war for liberty and democracy with a power that was denying these principles to the Indian subcontinent.

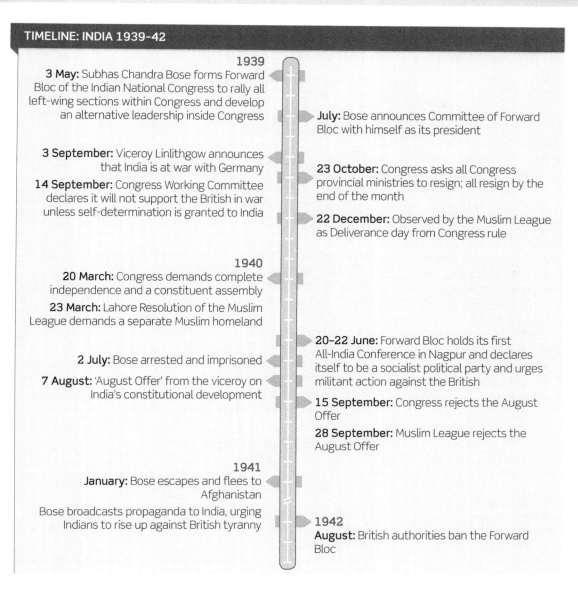

TIMELINE: INDIA 1939–42

1939

3 May: Subhas Chandra Bose forms Forward Bloc of the Indian National Congress to rally all left-wing sections within Congress and develop an alternative leadership inside Congress

July: Bose announces Committee of Forward Bloc with himself as its president

3 September: Viceroy Linlithgow announces that India is at war with Germany

14 September: Congress Working Committee declares it will not support the British in war unless self-determination is granted to India

23 October: Congress asks all Congress provincial ministries to resign; all resign by the end of the month

22 December: Observed by the Muslim League as Deliverance day from Congress rule

1940

20 March: Congress demands complete independence and a constituent assembly

23 March: Lahore Resolution of the Muslim League demands a separate Muslim homeland

2 July: Bose arrested and imprisoned

7 August: 'August Offer' from the viceroy on India's constitutional development

20–22 June: Forward Bloc holds its first All-India Conference in Nagpur and declares itself to be a socialist political party and urges militant action against the British

15 September: Congress rejects the August Offer

28 September: Muslim League rejects the August Offer

1941

January: Bose escapes and flees to Afghanistan

Bose broadcasts propaganda to India, urging Indians to rise up against British tyranny

1942
August: British authorities ban the Forward Bloc

War!

On 3 September 1939, Neville Chamberlain, the British prime minister, declared war on Nazi Germany. Lord Linlithgow, India's viceroy, followed suit. On the same day, and acting (just) within his legal powers, he committed over 300 million Indians to war without consulting a single one of them.

SOURCE

15 Part of Viceroy Linlithgow's announcement that India was at war with Nazi Germany.

Confronted with the demand that she should accept the dictation of a foreign power in relation to her own territory and her own subjects, Poland has elected to stand firm. Nowhere do these great principles mean more than in India. There is no country that values them more highly than India, and none that has at all times been more concerned to safeguard them.

ACTIVITY
KNOWLEDGE CHECK

India goes to war

Discuss in your group whether or not you find Linlithgow's comments in Source 15 surprising. Which do you think Indians would have resented most: that war was declared without consulting them, or that they were being committed to fighting for liberty and democracy by a power that was denying them these very principles?

How did Congress and the Muslim League react to the outbreak of war in 1939?

What did Congress do?

Congress's first reaction was one of shock and horror. What was the Government of India Act 1935 about if not some form of power-sharing? How could the Raj behave as if India was still in the 19th century? Was Viceroy Linlithgow not demonstrating clearly that Britain still considered itself to be master in India? Had the previous 20 years been in vain? This initial reaction was complicated by a feeling of deep sympathy with Britain in its struggle with European fascism.

Gandhi urged the British government to negotiate with Hitler, using peaceful means, of course. Those members of Congress, like Nehru, who were at all familiar with events in Europe knew just how futile this suggestion was. As hostilities commenced, Gandhi gave his wholehearted support to the British people. Nehru and other Indian socialists sympathised completely with the British approach to fascism. They were not, however, prepared to commit themselves openly to support a government that had not consulted them prior to the declaration of war, nor, or so they said, were they prepared to fight unless they were granted immediate *swaraj*.

SOURCE

16 Part of the Resolution passed by the Indian National Congress at Ramgarh, 20 March 1940.

The Congress considers the declaration, by the British Government, of India as a belligerent country, without any reference to the people of India, and the exploitation of India's resources in this war as an affront to them, which no self-respecting and freedom-loving people can accept or tolerate.

The recent pronouncements made on behalf of the British Government in regard to India demonstrate that Great Britain is carrying on the war fundamentally for Imperialist ends and for the preservation and strengthening of her Empire, which is based on the exploitation of the people of India as well as of other Asiatic and African countries. Under these circumstances, it is clear that the Congress cannot, in any way, directly or indirectly, be party to the war, which means continuance and perpetuation of this exploitation.

This Congress, therefore, strongly disapproves of Indian troops being made to fight for Great Britain and of the drain from India of men and material for the purpose of the war. Congressmen and those under the Congress influence cannot help in the prosecution of the war with men, money or material.

The Congress hereby declares that nothing short of complete independence can be accepted by the people of India. The people of India alone can properly shape their own constitution and determine their relations to other countries of the world, through a constituent assembly elected on the basis of adult suffrage.

Congress withdrew the ministries from provinces where it had a majority in order to dissociate India from the war and to enforce the Congress determination to free India from foreign domination.

A Level Exam-Style Question Section A

How far could the historian make use of Sources 15 and 16 to investigate the reaction in India to the outbreak of the Second World War in 1939?

Explain your answer, using the sources, the information given about them and your own knowledge of the historical context. (20 marks)

Tip

Consider the reaction of different communities within India to the outbreak of war as well as whether the two sources were typical of the attitudes of the British and Hindu communities.

In the early months of the Second World War, however, British politicians had other preoccupations and demands for *purna swaraj* fell upon deaf ears. As a consequence, as can be seen from Source 16, Congress's leaders ordered all Congress members to resign from provincial ministries throughout India. This was not necessarily the most sensible thing they could have done: it removed hundreds of Indians from official positions where they had been in a position to ease the effects of war for their people and, to some extent, influence events internal to India. India's provinces reverted to a form of direct British government, something that they hadn't known since 1919.

What did the Muslim League do?

Jinnah could hardly believe his luck. Congress had, of its own volition, virtually retired from the political scene. The way lay open for the Muslim League to strengthen its position.

The last Congress provincial ministry abandoned its posts on 22 December 1939, as required by Congress leaders. Jinnah had earlier designated this day as Muslim India's Day of Deliverance and called on all Muslims to celebrate their release from Hindu bondage. He suggested that the Muslim League branches all over India should hold public meetings and offer prayers of thanksgiving for deliverance from the Congress regime. This they did with gusto. Most Muslims heeded Jinnah's request that they cause no offence to ordinary Hindus – Muslim argument was with those who led Congress, not their Hindu neighbours.

Jinnah's appeal, was, of course, delivered for public consumption and to revive the Muslim League. Privately, it would seem that he and Nehru were looking for the possibility of some sort of rapprochement. Certainly, Nehru wrote to Jinnah in early December expressing sadness that their political objectives, as well as their values, seemed to differ so greatly and expressing the hope that common ground could be found. Jinnah's reply emphasised the need for Congress to treat the Muslim League as the authoritative representative organisation in India before any reconciliation could occur. He expressed the desire to discuss the matter should Nehru so desire. It is impossible to say whether or not Jinnah and Nehru were simply engaging in gesture politics. On the surface, it would seem that there was no way back now. With Congress out of the political picture, it was left to the League to work with the Raj and the British government to support the war effort and to strengthen their own position within India.

Rapprochement?

In the light of what you know about the situation, how likely is it that Jinnah and Nehru were looking for a compromise? Discuss this in your group.

The Lahore Resolution, March 1940

Freed from the necessity of coping with Congress, Jinnah focused on the Muslim League and the challenging problems of formulating the League's constitutional goals – goals with which all Muslims could agree. He called a meeting of the League in Lahore in March 1940 that was attended by approximately 100,000 Muslims.

SOURCE

17 From the Resolution of the Muslim League at Lahore, 24 March 1940.

Resolved that it is the considered view of the session of the All-India Muslim League that no constitutional plan would be workable in this country, or acceptable to the Muslims unless it is designed on the following basic principles, viz., that geographically contiguous units are demarcated into regions which should be so constituted with such territorial readjustments as may be necessary that the areas in which Muslims are numerically in a majority, as in the north-western and eastern zones of India, should be grouped to constitute independent states in which the constituent units shall be autonomous and sovereign.

That adequate, effective and mandatory safeguards should be specifically provided in the constitution for minorities in these units and regions for the protection of their religious, cultural, economic, political, administrative and other rights and interests, in consultation with them, and in other parts of India where the Muslims are in a minority.

This session further authorises the Working Committee to frame a scheme of constitution in accordance with these basic principles, providing for the assumption, finally, by the respective regions of all powers such as defence, external affairs, communications, customs and such other matters as may be necessary.

The Resolution set out what the Muslim League, under the strong guidance of Jinnah, considered to be the basic principles of any new constitution for India. The Resolution made two main proposals:

- that those areas of the subcontinent where Muslims were in the majority should be grouped to form separate independent states

- that minorities had to be protected, whether the people concerned were living in Muslim- or Hindu-dominated states.

A working party was to be set up to frame a constitution based on these two principles.

The word 'separate' had not only been said at Lahore, it had also been driven home relentlessly. The genie was out of the bottle. It seemed that Jinnah could no longer see any possibility of a Hindu–Muslim rapprochement. It is, however, by no means certain that the Muslim League at this point envisaged that two separate states of East and West Pakistan would eventually emerge. Nor is it certain that Jinnah himself wanted this: he may have been using the idea of separate states as a bargaining tactic to gain separate representation within a united subcontinent. If so, he was playing a dangerous game, risking his bluff being called. However, the involvement of the eminent Bengali politician and strong proponent of a separate Pakistan, Fazul Huq, in the drafting of the Lahore Resolution, makes it more than likely that this was a possibility in the minds of the drafters when they wrote of 'independent states in which the constituent units shall be autonomous and sovereign'.

What was the reaction of Congress?

A battle of words between Jinnah and Gandhi ensued, with Gandhi maintaining that the Lahore Resolution was tantamount to the vivisection of India and appealing over the head of Jinnah to the common sense of Muslims to draw back from the obvious suicide that partition would mean for India. Mini-*satyagraha* campaigns broke out, protesting against the Lahore Resolution. The Raj acted swiftly and the perpetrators were jailed.

Nehru denounced the idea of a separate Muslim state as a mad scheme and toured India trying to strengthen the will of Congress supporters. The young were already drilling and wearing pseudo uniforms, ready for the supposed conflict with the Muslims. Nehru inspected one such body, carrying an imitation Field Marshal's baton, and was promptly thrown into jail for his trouble. In reality, Congress was suffering from a self-inflicted wound: the withdrawal of Congress representatives from positions of authority and influence in the provinces had completely weakened their hand politically.

Nationalist reaction to the August Offer

In May 1940, two months after the Lahore Resolution, Linlithgow invited Jinnah to Simla, with the aim of discussing with him a whole range of issues relating to India and the war. Jinnah later submitted a list of tentative proposals to Linlithgow, which were welcomed. Linlithgow made these proposals the basis of his 1940 August Offer:

- 'Representative' Indians would join his Executive Council.

- A War Advisory Council would be established that would include the princes and other interested parties.

- There was an assurance that the government would not adopt any new constitution without the prior approval of Muslim India.

The viceroy accompanied this offer with a statement that seemed to place the Muslim League at the centre of any decision-making about the future of India. He made it clear that the British government could not contemplate any transfer of power to a system of government where significant elements in India's life were denied making a meaningful contribution. The message was clear. The wishes and needs of the Muslim community would have to be taken into account in any post-war settlement. It was obvious that the vital role played by Muslims in the Indian army at home and abroad greatly strengthened Jinnah's hand, particularly

AS Level Exam-Style Question Section B

How accurate is it to say that the August Offer of 1940 was a misjudgement on the part of Viceroy Linlithgow? (20 marks)

Tip

Consider the outcomes of the August Offer, both intended and unintended.

when compared to what was perceived by the British government as being the obstructive attitude of Congress. The secretary of state for India, L. S. Amery, told the House of Commons how much easier the situation would be if Congress spoke for all the main elements in India's national life. Here, indeed, was recognition of the fact that Congress did not speak for the whole of India and an understanding that the millions of Muslims had to have their interests safeguarded. The huge problem that remained for the British was not so much whether power should be transferred, but to whom?

Bose and the Axis powers

In 1939, Subhas Chandra Bose (see page 233) left the Congress party. Out-manoeuvred by Gandhi, Bose formed the Forward Bloc Party, which was basically a terrorist organisation aimed at getting the British to quit India. Initially, the aim of the Forward Bloc was to rally all the left-wing sections within Congress to develop an alternative leadership within Congress, but it quickly developed into a strongly anti-British organisation, particularly after the outbreak of war. The Forward Bloc's newspaper, *Forward Bloc*, was first published in the month war was declared and Bose travelled India, rallying support for his new party. The party's first all-India conference was held the following year in Nagpur. Declaring themselves to be a socialist political party, the conference passed a resolution urging militant action against British colonial rule.

Suspecting treason and fearing uprisings, on 2 July the authorities arrested Bose, holding him first in the Presidency Jail in Calcutta and then under house arrest. In January 1941, he escaped and clandestinely went into exile. Travelling to the Soviet Union via Afghanistan, his attempt to persuade Stalin to support the Indian independence struggle failed. Stalin was coping with the first stages of the Nazi invasion of the Soviet Union and supporting Indian independence was not one of his priorities. Having tried to gain support from Britain's new wartime ally, Bose then turned to Britain's enemies and travelled to Germany.

Meanwhile, back in India, the British authorities banned the Forward Bloc and its publications. The party's offices around the country were ransacked in an attempt to destroy seditious material and obtain membership lists. However, anti-British activities continued, but intermittently and without central direction. In Bihar, for example, Forward Bloc members were involved with underground resistance groups and distributed anti-British propaganda.

Bose's reception in Berlin was lukewarm: Hitler feared that any collapse of the British Raj in India would lead to Russia moving into the power vacuum created in the subcontinent. However, Bose was encouraged to broadcast propaganda to India urging Indians to rise up against British tyranny. Finally having no more use for him, the Nazis agreed that he could work with the Japanese on a possible land invasion into India. Bose was moved to Japan, where he formed the Indian National Army (INA) from Indian prisoners of war taken by the Japanese. Initially, Japan used the INA as a source of agents for behind-the-lines sabotage and spying in mainland India. Most of these agents were picked up by the Indian authorities. Many became double agents and some simply took the train home.

Bose still planned for a full-scale invasion of India. The Japanese, however, had more limited objectives, centring on taking Imphal, the capital city of the Indian state of Manipur, situated on the frontier with Burma, a country that had fallen to the Japanese in 1942. In the spring of 1944, some 6,000 soldiers of the Indian National Army went into action with Japanese troops. Of these 6,000, some 600 deserted to the British, 400 were killed, 1,500 died from dysentery and malaria and a further 1,400 were invalided out of the war zone. The rest surrendered. It was not a successful operation. Bose himself died on 18 August 1945 from third-degree burns after his over-loaded Japanese plane crashed in Japanese-occupied Formosa (now Taiwan). After independence, the Indian government instigated three inquiries into the circumstances of his death. Two confirmed that he had died in the plane crash, but a third found that Bose faked his own death. Conspiracy theories about these events abound.

Conclusion

The 1930s did not see a dramatic change in the by now familiar pattern of proposal and counter-proposal, deadlock and riot. It saw little change in India's economic and social structure and little change in the daily life of India's teeming millions. But the early years of the Second World War saw a discernable shift in that Indian independence seemed achievable. Congress was showing that it still had control and influence over millions of Indians and that these Indians had irrefutably demonstrated that the Raj no longer had the consent of its Congress-supporting Indian subjects, and should go. The Muslim League had greatly strengthened its position, gaining tacit agreement from Britain that some sort of separateness for the Muslim community was possible and possibly even desirable. However, the Raj, in turn, had demonstrated that it could hold India by force if necessary, and that it was more resilient than any had thought possible.

ACTIVITY
KNOWLEDGE CHECK

India and the Second World War

1 Why was Congress opposed to involvement in the Second World War?

2 What was the purpose of the Muslim Day of Deliverance?

3 Both Bose and Congress wanted Indian independence. Why, then, was Bose and the Forward Bloc treated differently by the authorities from Nehru and Congress?

ACTIVITY
SUMMARY

Consultation and confrontation in the 1930s

1 How far had Jinnah consolidated his position by the end of the 1930s?

2 To what extent was Gandhi holding the British government to ransom in the 1930s?

3 'In the 1930s, the only obstacle to Indian independence was the Indians themselves.' How far do you agree with this opinion?

WIDER READING

Brown, Judith M. *Modern India: The Origins of an Asian Democracy*, Oxford University Press (1991)

Copland, I. *India 1885–1947*, Routledge (2001)

James, L. *Raj: The Making and Unmaking of British India*, Abacus (1998)

Leadbeater, T. *Britain and India 1845–1947*, Hodder (2008)

Moraes, F. *Witness to an Era*, Weidenfeld and Nicolson (1973)

Watson, F. & Tennyson, H. *Talking of Gandhi*, BBC (1969)

2a.4 The road to independence, 1942–48

Key questions
- To what extent did the Second World War impact on Indian politics?
- How far did the relationship between Britain and India change in the years 1942–45?
- Why, in the years 1945–46, did attempts at a political settlement fail?
- Why did independence for the Indian subcontinent involve Partition?

INTRODUCTION

The First World War (1914–18) had the effect of driving Hindus and Muslims together and so unifying India's nationalist movement. Events in the 1920s and 1930s drove Congress and the Muslim League further and further apart, while at the same time making it clearer that India's independence from the Raj was achievable. The Second World War (1939–45) confirmed both of these developments: the ending of the Raj and the separation of Muslims and Hindus. It shattered all hopes of Congress and the Muslim League co-existing in an independent India.

Field Marshal Wavell, viceroy between October 1943 and March 1947, tried to pave the way for the independence of the subcontinent as a whole and the British government, by sending out the Cabinet Mission in 1946, to make one final attempt to resolve India's constitutional problems. They failed. Wavell was replaced as viceroy by Lord Louis Mountbatten of Burma, great-grandson of Queen Victoria and close friend of the British royal family, whose 'charm offensive' was supposed to smooth the way to a peaceful handover of power. It didn't work. The withdrawal of the Raj from India after imposing Partition resulted in terrifying rioting, mass destruction of property and the uncontrollable bloodletting and murder of thousands upon thousands of Hindus, Muslims and Sikhs.

TO WHAT EXTENT DID THE SECOND WORLD WAR IMPACT ON INDIAN POLITICS?

The Second World War had a profound effect on Indian politics. As Britain fought almost to the point of economic exhaustion, the maintenance of the Indian Empire was worrying British politicians. To what extent could, or indeed should, the Raj be maintained in India? The British were desperate to find a compromise that would satisfy all parties. Indian politicians rose to the occasion, pressing the interests of their own communities in trying to work towards a satisfactory constitutional solution. Meanwhile, there was a world war to fight and Axis forces, aided by Bose, who had found a different and dangerous way of opposing the Raj (see Chapter 3), were getting perilously close to the Indian subcontinent.

1942
March: Cripps Mission arrives in India
April: Congress and Muslim League reject Cripps proposals, Cripps leaves India
August: Congress endorses Gandhi's 'Quit India' campaign, Gandhi, Nehru and Congress leaders arrested

1945
May: VE day marks the end of war in Europe
June–July: Simla Conference considers Wavell's proposals for Indian self-government but fails to reach agreement

1942	1943	1944	1945

1943
June: Field Marshall Wavell becomes viceroy of India

July: Labour government elected in Britain
August: Japan surrenders

The threat of invasion

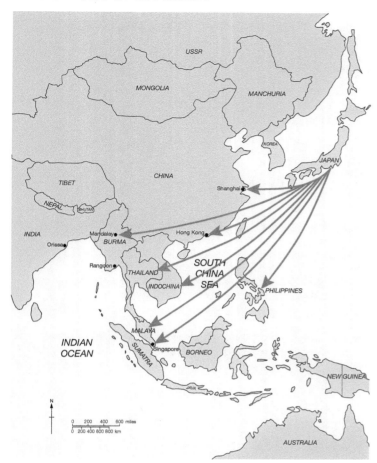

Figure 4.1: The advance of the Axis forces in the Pacific theatre 1941-42.

By the beginning of 1942, the Allies' position in all war zones was desperate. Hitler's armies controlled the Balkans and had invaded Russia; Rommel was within striking distance of the Suez Canal in Egypt, and France had fallen to the Nazi onslaught, as had most of Western Europe.

In the Pacific theatre, Japan launched a lightning strike on the US naval base of Pearl Harbor in December 1941. This had, insofar as the Japanese were concerned, the unintended outcome of propelling the USA into the war. But, meanwhile, the Japanese swept through South East Asia and, in a series of actions, took Shanghai, Hong Kong, the Philippines, Malaya, Indochina and Thailand. On 15 February 1942, the island of Singapore, previously believed to be unconquerable, fell, with the loss of a British battleship and battle cruiser two weeks after the island fell. The whole of Asia now lay open to the Japanese. They pushed on into Burma, capturing Rangoon in March and Mandalay six weeks later. With Japan's declared aim of freeing Asians from European rule, Malays and Burmese welcomed the invading troops as liberators. The Japanese ships cruised at will around the Indian Ocean, once the unchallenged province of the Royal Navy. Japanese forces were lapping at India's eastern boundaries. Calcutta, Madras and other ports along the Bay of Bengal came under attack from Japan's ships and aircraft. The situation was so desperate for the Allies in the Pacific theatre that, early in March, Viceroy Linlithgow confessed that he did not have sufficient armed forces in India to hold out against a Japanese landing on the Cuttack coast and could not prevent an advance into Orissa. All he could suggest, in response to a possible land-borne invasion through Bengal, was a scorched-earth policy.

The sea-borne threat to India was only removed when the US Navy defeated the Japanese at the Battle of the Coral Sea at the beginning of May 1942. There remained, however, the fear of a land-borne invasion, and of German and Japanese forces linking up in the Middle East.

The Cripps Mission

It was against this background that Winston Churchill, by then the British prime minister, appointed the lord privy seal, Sir Stafford Cripps, to lead a delegation to India in order to secure full Indian cooperation and support for the war effort. The British government recognised that an offer of some sort of self-determination would be necessary. Churchill himself had always opposed any form of Indian independence, but reluctantly bowed

1946

Winter: Indian general election

March: Cabinet Mission arrives in India

May: Second Simla Conference results in conditional agreement between Congress, Muslim League and British government

July: Muslim League denounces Congress and declares Direct Action Day

1947

January: Viceroy Wavell removed, replaced by Admiral Viscount Lord Louis Mountbatten

February: British Prime Minister Attlee sets time frame for Indian independence – no later than June 1948

March: Mountbatten arrives in Delhi

June: Final plan for Partition of India accepted by Congress, Muslim League and Sikhs; Boundary Commission arrives in Delhi

1946	1947

August: Deaths in Calcutta as a result of Direct Action Day

September: Congress forms interim government with Nehru as prime minister, Muslim League joins interim government

July: Indian Independence Act creating separate states of India and Pakistan receives royal assent, mass carnage begins

August: Jinnah sworn in as governor-general of Pakistan, Lord Louis Mountbatten sworn in as governor-general of India, Liaquat Ali Khan becomes prime minister of Pakistan, Jawaharlal Nehru becomes prime minister of India

to pressure from war cabinet colleagues such as Clement Attlee and Leo Amery, and from the Allies, principally the USA, USSR and China.

Sir Stafford Cripps and his delegation initially seemed to have everything going for them. He was a Labour Party minister, a friend of Nehru and Gandhi, and personally sympathetic to Indian aspirations. Well known and well liked in Congress circles, there was much optimism on the Indian side when he arrived in New Delhi on 23 March 1942. Viceroy Linlithgow, however, was less than impressed, aware of his own status and fearing that the British government would impose some sort of settlement over his head and against his advice. But Cripps's mission was doomed. It was doomed because what he had to offer was not what Congress wanted to hear. He came to offer what the British government believed was a bargain (see Source 1).

SOURCE 1

From the Draft Declaration on the Constitution of India, 30 March 1942.

His Majesty's Government, having considered the anxieties expressed in this country and in India as to the fulfilment of the promises made in regard to the future of India, have decided to lay down in precise and clear terms the steps which they propose shall be taken for the earliest possible realisation of self-government in India. The object is the creation of a new Indian Union, which shall constitute a Dominion, associated with the United Kingdom and the other Dominions by a common allegiance to the Crown, but equal to them in every respect, in no way subordinate in any aspect of its domestic or external affairs.

His Majesty's government therefore make the following declaration:

(a) Immediately upon cessation of hostilities, steps shall be taken to set up in India, in the manner described hereafter, an elected body charged with the task of framing a new Constitution for India.

(b) Provision shall be made, as set out below, for the participation of the Indian States in the constitution-making body.

(c) His Majesty's Government undertake to accept and implement forthwith the Constitution so framed subject only to:

(i) the right of any province of British India that is not prepared to accept the new Constitution to retain its present constitutional position, provisions being made for its subsequent accession if it so decides.

(ii) With such non-acceding Provinces, should they so desire, His Majesty's government will be prepared to agree upon a new Constitution giving them the full status as Indian Union and arrived at by a procedure analogous to that here laid down.

(e) During the critical period that now faces India and until the new constitution can be framed, His Majesty's government must inevitably bear the responsibility for, and retain control and direction of the defence of India as part of their world war effort.

In return, because there are two parts to every bargain, all Indian parties were invited to join in an interim government of national unity under the viceroy and his Council, which would operate until the end of the war.

Gandhi was furious, suggesting that Cripps took the first plane home if this was all he had to offer. There was nothing new here. Congress rejected the first part of the bargain – they were not willing to accept a situation where states were allowed to opt out of a united India. They were, however, willing to join the proposed interim government provided it behaved like the Westminster one, with the viceroy acting as prime minister and with the defence ministry under the control of an Indian. Churchill and Linlithgow were having none of it. The Raj had to remain in control while the war against Germany continued. Indian opinion was affronted, believing that this was yet another sign that Britain would cling on to India at all costs and would not accept Indians as equal partners. Jinnah, on the other hand, while ready to accept the Cripps bargain because of its implication that a separate state would not be a problem, had to reject it too if the Muslim League was to remain part of the constitution-making process. Cripps flew home to Britain on 12 April, empty-handed.

THINKING HISTORICALLY   Evidence (5b)

The importance of context

Documents (texts) are like small pieces of paper torn from a large tapestry (context). Historians have to reconstruct the larger pattern into which documents might fit in order to use them to construct accounts of the past. The problem is that texts can have multiple contexts. Historians often debate how best to contextualise the documents that they interpret.

The Draft Declaration on the Constitution of India (Source 1), brought to India by the Cripps Mission on 30 March 1942, set out the basis of a new constitution for the Indian subcontinent, as determined by the British government.

1 a) Summarise the key points in the Draft Declaration.

  b) What concessions is the British government making to Indian nationalists?

  c) What level of control is the British government retaining?

The timeline below provides a possible context for the document, in the wider context of the British government's response to the growing demands of Indian nationalists. Look at this timeline and then answer the question that follows.

August 1932
Communal award announced

August 1935
Government of India Act

February 1942
Fall of Singapore
Japanese troops sweep through SE Asia, threatening India

March 1942
Cripps Mission arrives in India with the Draft Declaration

March 1946
Cabinet Mission arrives in India

May 1947
Plan Balkan

July 1947
Indian Independence Act receives royal assent

2 a) How does the Draft Declaration fit into the pattern of events?

  b) Why was the Draft Declaration made in March 1942?

The document might have one kind of meaning when interpreted in the context of the British government's policy towards India, and quite another if we locate it in a different context.

Consider this timeline:

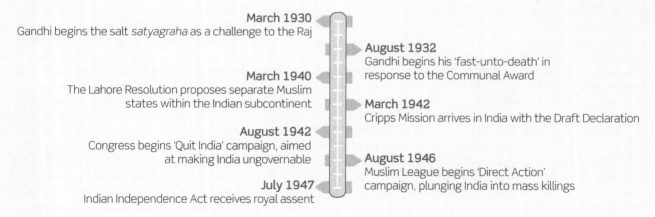

March 1930
Gandhi begins the salt *satyagraha* as a challenge to the Raj

August 1932
Gandhi begins his 'fast-unto-death' in response to the Communal Award

March 1940
The Lahore Resolution proposes separate Muslim states within the Indian subcontinent

March 1942
Cripps Mission arrives in India with the Draft Declaration

August 1942
Congress begins 'Quit India' campaign, aimed at making India ungovernable

August 1946
Muslim League begins 'Direct Action' campaign, plunging India into mass killings

July 1947
Indian Independence Act receives royal assent

3 a) How does the Draft Declaration fit into this pattern of events?

  b) Why, using this pattern of events, was the Draft Declaration made in March 1942?

Consider both timelines together and answer the following questions:

4 Use information from both timelines to construct a possible context for the Draft Declaration of March 1942.

5 Why is it important for historians to spend time thinking about possible contexts for a document before they start to use it to draw conclusions about the past?

ACTIVITY
KNOWLEDGE CHECK

The Cripps Mission

1 What was there in the Cripps Mission's Draft Declaration that was (a) unacceptable to Congress and (b) acceptable to the Muslim League?

2 Why did Jinnah not accept the offer laid out in the Draft Declaration?

The Quit India campaign and its repercussions

One result of the failure of the Cripps Mission was that both sides hardened their approaches to constitutional change.

Linthligow stepped up press censorship and intercepts, by Special Branch, of Congress communications. By the summer of 1942, the British government was aware that a new campaign of civil disobedience was being planned. Linlithgow's somewhat misguided plan to arrest all the Congress leaders and deport them to Uganda, with Gandhi being sent to Aden, collapsed when the governor of Aden said if it was implemented he would object strongly to the presence of Gandhi in Aden. Colleagues pointed out that arrest warrants would lapse on board ship. Nevertheless, crazy though Linlithgow's plan was, it is indicative of the level of panic felt in Whitehall.

Gandhi, meanwhile, was pressuring Congress to support a new *satyagraha*. He argued that, since Japan's aggression was aimed at Britain, if India became free it could make peace with Japan. Congress disagreed, Nehru in particular refusing to have anything to do with supporting fascism. Nevertheless, Gandhi persisted, drawn as always to an idyllic rural life, isolated from the rest of the world that, in reality, had never existed. Indeed, he maintained that India should be left to God and, if that was not possible, to anarchy.

What was Congress's reaction?

Taken by surprise, Congress prevaricated. To commit to a *satyagraha* at such a critical time in Britain's struggle against Nazi Germany and the Axis powers seemed, on the one hand, like an act of great folly, even treachery. It would set Raj against Congress and make any reconciliation after the war (assuming an Allied victory, which in the dark days of 1942 seemed fairly unlikely) very difficult indeed. On the other hand, to remain quiescent now might give the upper hand to Jinnah or to Bose. Congress had to make its position clear and had to rally its supporters to the cause of *swaraj*. Finally, on 8 August 1942, Congress officially sanctioned Gandhi's *satyagraha*, and his great Quit India campaign was launched.

SOURCE

2 A resolution of the All India Congress Committee, 8 August 1942.

The All India Congress Committee would yet again, at this last moment, in the interest of world freedom, renew this appeal to Britain and the United Nations. But the Committee feels that it is no longer justified in holding the nation back from endeavouring to assert its will against an imperialist and authoritarian Government, which dominates over it and prevents it from functioning in its own interest and in the interest of humanity. The Committee resolves, therefore, to sanction for the vindication of India's inalienable right to freedom and independence, the starting of a mass struggle on non-violent lines on the widest possible scale, so that the country might utilise all the non-violent strength it has gathered during the last twenty-two years of peaceful struggle. Such a struggle must inevitably be under the leadership of Gandhi and the Committee requests him to take the lead and guide the nation in the steps to be taken.

'Quit India' was the shout that greeted every British man, woman and child as they went about their daily lives in India. 'Quit India' was shouted at the troops who were desperately trying to defend India's frontiers against the Japanese. Correctly guessing that the response of the Raj would be repression, Congress leaders, before they could be imprisoned and silenced, called on their supporters to make India ungovernable.

Repercussions

Congress had spent three months arguing as to whether the party should, or should not, support Gandhi's Quit India *satyagraha* and the Raj had plenty of time to prepare contingency plans. On 9 August, the day after Congress officially sanctioned the campaign, Gandhi, Nehru and most of the Congress party's leaders were arrested and interned. Within the next fortnight, thousands of local activists were rounded up and imprisoned. Offices were raided, files taken and funds frozen.

Gandhi, anticipating that this would happen, and realising that it would thus be impossible to organise the *satyagraha* from above, urged every demonstrator to become his or her own leader. So began a horrific round of riots, killings, attacks on Europeans and damage to, and destruction of, government property. There were the usual targets: revenue offices and police stations but, alarmingly in time of war and with India daily expecting an invasion from the Japanese troops massing on its borders, stations and signal boxes were wrecked, railway tracks were torn up, and telegraph and telephone lines pulled down. Over a thousand deaths and over three thousand serious injuries were directly attributed to the Quit India campaign.

By November 1942, the worst of the attacks were over. What, if anything, had been achieved? The Quit India *satyagraha* had failed to paralyse the government, even in militant Hindu areas like Bihar. The military had remained loyal to the Raj. Even among Indian regiments, only 216 soldiers had gone absent without leave. The campaign had not attracted support throughout India in terms of geography, religion or caste. Non-cooperation had brought detention, despair and death.

Wavell becomes viceroy

In October 1943, Field Marshal Archibald Wavell was appointed viceroy of India. Outstandingly successful in the Middle East in 1940 until he was forced to transfer troops to Greece, Wavell was appointed to India just as the Japanese struck in South East Asia. Churchill's choice could be seen as an appropriate sideways move for an able man who had been in command against impossible odds and who had been, quite simply, the wrong person in the wrong place at the wrong time. Or it could be seen as indicative of Churchill's lack of understanding that when a person with political and negotiating skills was needed he chose a military man who could, presumably, be controlled from Whitehall. But, in Wavell, Churchill was to get more than he had bargained for.

SOURCE

A cartoon, commenting on Wavell as viceroy in India, published in the *Daily Mail*, 2 September 1946. The cartoon appeared with the caption, 'British superiority?'

Wavell started his time in office by touring the subcontinent on a fact-finding mission, travelling as far as 1,500 km a week by plane and train, jeep and car. He focused particularly on troubled areas, such as the Punjab, Bengal and the United Provinces, trying to allay fears, settle disputes and boost morale.

One of Wavell's first moves was to reinstate regular meetings of the 11 governors of the provinces of British India. During his seven years as viceroy, Linlithgow had not called a single such meeting. Wavell's action enabled the Government of India to present the British government with coherent advice and a unified point of view. It also made it much more difficult for the British government to dismiss the views of provincial governors out of hand. But this was easy compared to the disaster that overcame Bengal and which was to become one of the greatest tests of Wavell's leadership of the Raj.

EXTEND YOUR KNOWLEDGE

Archibald Wavell (1883–1950)

Wavell served in the Boer War and both world wars as a soldier and administrator. After his 1941 counter-offensive in North Africa failed, he exchanged posts with Claude Auchinleck, the commander-in-chief of the British Army in India. Following the fall of Malaya and Burma to the Japanese, Wavell's main objective was to maintain India's boundaries to prevent a Japanese invasion from the east and an Axis one from the west. In this he succeeded.

In 1943 Wavell was made viceroy of India. It was made clear to him that his role was to hold the line: to keep India within the Empire to act as a bulwark against the Japanese until the war ended and some kind of settlement could be reached with the Indians regarding their independence.

As viceroy, Wavell is best remembered for the measures he took to relieve the terrible famine in Bengal in 1943 and for the Simla Conference of June 1945. Here he tried to bring about a rapprochement between Congress and the Muslim League, but failed. He hated the idea of Partition, but came to regard it as inevitable.

Wavell worked hard to prepare the ground for independence and, ultimately, for Partition. He was relieved of his post in March 1947 and replaced by Mountbatten, who oversaw the final months of the Raj and Indian independence.

ACTIVITY
KNOWLEDGE CHECK

Viceroy Wavell

1 What is the message of Source 3, published in the *Daily Mail* when Wavell became viceroy?

2 What does this suggest about the level of understanding shown in the British press about the situation in India?

3 How far was the message confirmed by reality?

The Bengal Famine, 1943–44

The Bengal Famine was caused by a multiplicity of factors: a run of poor harvests and distribution failures, loss of imports, wartime price inflation and severe weather conditions. The crop yield in 1943 was the worst that century and the recorded annual death rate rose above the average of 1.2 million to 1.9 million. Men, women and children were dying from smallpox, malaria, cholera and pneumonia, and the diseases associated with malnutrition. The starving crowded into Calcutta in their thousands, in desperate hope of finding relief, begging and dying in the streets. Fear of a Japanese invasion encouraged hoarding on the part of those who could afford to buy and there was fear, too, that the famine would work as a recruiting agent for the Indian National Army (INA, see page 238). By May 1943, the price of rice had risen tenfold, and Wavell took immediate action to coordinate rationing and to try to stop profiteering, diverting troops from the war effort to do so. Churchill originally refused to divert British merchant shipping in order to take grain to starving Bengal, and Roosevelt, the US president, refused when asked to lend American ships to bring in wheat from Australia. Both leaders were afraid of damaging their own war effort.

SOURCE
4

Part of a telegram from Viceroy Wavell to the secretary of state for India, Leo Amery, sent in February 1944.

Bengal famine was one of the greatest disasters that has fallen any people under British rule and damage to our reputation here is incalculable. Attempt by His Majesty's government to prove on the basis of defective statistics that we can do without help demanded, would be regarded here by all opinion British and Indian as utterly indefensible. They must either trust the opinion of the man they appointed to advise them on Indian affairs or replace him.

It has been estimated that between one and three million people died in the three years of the Bengal Famine and in some areas whole villages were wiped out. Jinnah accused the British government of incompetence and irresponsibility, pointing out that Churchill's government wouldn't have lasted five minutes if people had been dying of starvation in the streets of London as they were on the streets of Calcutta. Congress blamed the crisis on the diversion of foodstuffs to British troops. Both Congress and the Muslim League made political capital out of the crisis. Wavell began a running battle with Whitehall, trying to buy more grain for India. Unfortunately, Churchill, focused on the war effort, listened to the advice he wanted to hear: from Lord Cherwell (paymaster-general and one of the government's scientific advisors) in particular, who claimed that the Bengal Famine was a statistical invention. Wavell's request for a guaranteed million tons of grain throughout 1944 was met with an offer of 250,000 tons and a request for Indian rice. Nevertheless, by June 1944, Wavell had extracted 450,000 tons of grain from a reluctant government.

The failure of the Simla Conference, 1945

In the spring of 1945, Viceroy Wavell travelled to London for a series of lengthy meetings with the British coalition government. The British Cabinet was ready, for two main reasons, to make a fresh attempt at an Indian settlement. Britain was millions of pounds in debt to India for goods and services borrowed to help win the war and this, combined with terrorist activity and unrest in India, convinced Wavell and Secretary of State Amery that another attempt had to be made at a constitutional settlement. Wavell returned to Delhi with a new scheme, loosely modelled on that of Sir Stafford Cripps (see pages 241–42).

The major change Wavell was to propose concerned the composition of his Executive Council. This was to be chosen in a way that would give a balanced representation of the main communities, including equal proportions of Muslims and Hindus. All members would be Indian, with the exception of the viceroy and the commander-in-chief, felt to be essential for as long as the defence of India remained a British responsibility.

From the outset, it seemed unlikely that Congress would be happy with this arrangement. Parity with Muslims would, in their view, inflate the importance of the Muslim constituency in India. Nevertheless, a conference of Indian political leaders was held at Simla on 25 June 1945 to discuss the proposals. Congress leaders were released from prison so that they could

attend and, all in all, some 21 Indian political leaders travelled to Simla, including Gandhi, Jinnah, Nehru and Azad, the Muslim president of Congress, sneered at by Jinnah as being nothing but a token Muslim. As could have been anticipated, the Conference reached deadlock on the issue of how Muslim members of the newly reconstituted Executive Council were to be chosen. Jinnah insisted that they must all be nominated by the Muslim League; Congress could not accept such a restriction, maintaining that, as Congress was an inclusive party, Muslims should be able to represent Congress as well as the Muslim League. On 14 July, Wavell adjourned the Conference, having been unable to break the deadlock between Congress and the Muslim League.

SOURCE
5

Part of a letter from Viceroy Wavell to Secretary of State Leo Amery, 15 July 1945.

Jinnah flatly refused to cooperate unless he received a categorical assurance that all the Muslim Members would be drawn from the League and that, once the Council was formed, decisions to which the Muslims objected would be made only on a vote of a specified majority – say, two-thirds. I could not accept either of these conditions. The right of communal veto, if granted to the Muslims would also have to be granted to the Hindus, and the Sikhs and the Scheduled Caste members. The working of Council would become impossible.

Now that Jinnah had rejected a move within the present Constitution based on parity, it is not clear what he would be prepared to accept short of Pakistan. Gandhi's final comment to me was that His Majesty's Government would have to decide sooner or later whether to come down on the side of Hindu or Muslim, of Congress or League, since they could never reconcile them. A discouraging comment, but true under present leadership.

ACTIVITY
KNOWLEDGE CHECK

Looking for a compromise

1 Why did the Cripps Mission fail?

2 What, in the context of the Second World War, were the risks involved in starting the Quit India campaign?

3 What were the political implications of the Bengal Famine?

4 Work in groups of three. Each person selects either (a) the Raj, (b) Congress or (c) the Muslim League. Use the information in this section about the Simla Conference to tease out the arguments that would have been presented by each group at Simla. Whose arguments are the most convincing?

5 Who was to blame for the collapse of the Simla Conference?

HOW FAR DID THE RELATIONSHIP BETWEEN BRITAIN AND INDIA CHANGE IN THE YEARS 1942–45?

The Cripps Mission, the Quit India campaign, the Bengal Famine, the Simla Conference – all, has been seen, impacted on Indian politics and played a significant part in changing the political landscape within India. There is, however, a wider picture to consider. The relationship between Britain and India has to be seen in the context of British politics and, in particular, of the pressures resulting from fighting a global war. These years were a time, too, when the USA took a greater interest in India than it had in the pre-war years.

The impact of war on British rule and Indian nationalism

The impact of war, with an economy geared up to wartime production and with financial reserves running down fast, had a profound effect upon Britain's ability to maintain the Raj in the years to 1942–45. In many ways, though, these constraints simply intensified trends that had begun in the pre-war years and that provided a foundation for the growth and development of Indian nationalism of whatever type.

- British investment in India had fallen during the 1930s. Indian capitalists and entrepreneurs were taking the lead in investing in their own country.

- India was importing less and less from Britain. In the years 1928–29, Indians spent £83 million on imported British goods. In the years 1935–36, this had fallen to £39 million. In order to help manufacturers develop their own markets, Indian governments had put increasingly high tariffs on imported goods. Indians found that, for example, home-produced cotton goods were cheaper than imported Lancashire cotton ones. Lancashire cotton exports to India collapsed. Japanese competition further squeezed British goods out of the Indian market. This was because the cost of production in Japan was lower than in Britain and so, despite import duties, Japanese goods were selling in India more cheaply than British ones. Thus, a crisis was created for the British export trade while at the same time creating an increasingly buoyant Indian economy controlled by Indians.

- In 1931, the Reserve Bank of India had been established. This meant that India could set the value of its own currency without reference to sterling. The rupee was no longer tied to the value of sterling in the world's money markets.

- From 1933, Britain paid £1.5 million a year towards the running costs of the Indian army and, in 1939, the British government agreed to pay for an army modernisation programme. While this undoubtedly helped the Allied cause in the war, it also gave the Indian army a sense of competence and self-worth, both essential ingredients of nationalism.

- Indian troops had mobilised in the war against Japan, in North Africa and in Italy, and Britain had shouldered most of the costs. This meant that, by 1945, the Indian government had built up a sterling balance in the Reserve Bank of India of £1,300 million because they had not had to meet the cost of their troops abroad. This gave Indians the potential to provide capital for Indian-based enterprises and initiatives that, in turn, had the capacity to engender national pride.

By 1945, Britain was facing a desperate economic situation. Not only did the whole British economy have to shift focus to meet peacetime demands, but wartime debts had run at £70 million per day towards the end and, by 1945, Britain owed £2,730 million, mainly to the USA. On top of this, an enormous programme of reconstruction had to be undertaken, ranging from reforming the health and education services to rebuilding bombed and damaged ports, offices, factories and homes. How realistic was it to try to maintain a role in India, particularly given the strength of the nationalist movements?

Shifting Indian loyalties: the Raj or Indian nationalism?

The old argument that Britain needed India as a bulwark of British power in Asia no longer carried much weight at a time when Indian politicians were protesting against the deployment of Indian forces in Indonesia and Indo-China. Indian politicians regarded it as unacceptable that 'their' forces were being used, in their view, to prop up decaying French and Dutch empires at a time when they were trying to free themselves from the grip of the Raj.

Two and a half million Indian men and women had joined the armed forces and, by 1945, there were 15,740 Indian officers. But they were not all loyal to the Raj. Rather, they were loyal to their concept of 'India' as their army commander-in-chief, Auchinleck, recognised, believing that a good Indian soldier was a nationalist, but not necessarily anti-British. The Indian Civil Service, too, had undergone a considerable change. Originally (see page 169) the province of the British, by 1945 it was severely undermanned because of the need for able-bodied men to work in the armed forces and ancillary services. But, even so, there were 429 British and 510 Indian ICS officers remaining in India, indicating that, broadly, the administration of India was in Indian hands.

The influence of the USA

In August 1941, before the USA entered the war, US President Roosevelt and Prime Minister Churchill met on board the US cruiser *Augusta* in Newfoundland Bay and agreed the Atlantic Charter. This was basically an affirmation that all peoples should enjoy the right of self-determination when the war was over. Indian hopes were raised by what seemed like another commitment to their independence, only to be dashed when Churchill reassured the House of Commons that this did not apply to India, Burma and other parts of the British Empire. When this was discussed in the viceroy's Legislative Council, an Indian member, Jammadas Mehta, pointedly reminded the viceroy that Indians were dying to bring freedom to others when that very same freedom was denied to them. Vinayak Savarkar, president of the All-Hindu Mahasabha, an organisation founded in 1906 to protect the rights of the Hindu community in British India, appealed directly to Roosevelt, asking him to guarantee India's post-war freedom.

The US government, soon to become the senior partner in the war against Nazi Germany and the Axis powers, viewed the situation in India with some alarm. Roosevelt saw it as essential that India was fully behind the Allied war effort. True, thousands of Indian troops were fighting in the various theatres of war, but it was the situation within India that worried him. India simply could not fall to the Japanese, who had overrun the rest of South East Asia.

Furthermore, Roosevelt was very wary of committing American troops to fighting a war in Asia, which could be seen as a last-ditch attempt to prop up the British Empire. Americans had not forgotten that America had once been part of the first British Empire, and had run a successful revolution to be free of it in 1776.

Roosevelt began putting what pressure he could on the reluctant Churchill to agree to some form of self-government for India in order to unite the country. This was supported from within the British War Cabinet by Clement Attlee and Leo Amery, who were convinced that India's future safety depended on the creation of a popularly supported national government – not after the war but immediately. This was not the same as self-government, but they were travelling in the same direction as Roosevelt. Churchill, cornered by colleagues on whom he depended, reluctantly agreed to send the Cripps Mission to India (see pages 241–42). That the Cripps Mission failed could be seen as a victory for Churchill. But, it was a victory won at too great a cost and Roosevelt had been wrong-footed. The Indians would not accept what had seemed to both men to be a perfectly reasonable proposition.

SOURCE
6 From US President Roosevelt's message to British Prime Minister Winston Churchill, 12 April 1942.

I hope most earnestly that you may be able to postpone the departure from India of Cripps until one more effort has finally been made to prevent breakdown of the negotiations.

The feeling, held here almost universally, is that the deadlock has been due to the British government's unwillingness to concede the right of self-government to the Indians, despite the willingness of the Indians to entrust to the British authorities technical, military and naval defence control. It is impossible for American public opinion to understand why, if there is willingness on the part of the British government to permit the component parts of India to secede after the war from the British Empire, it is unwilling to permit them to enjoy during the war what is tantamount to self-government.

I feel that I am compelled to place before you this issue very frankly. Should the current negotiations be allowed to collapse because of the issues as presented to the people of America and should India subsequently be invaded by Japan, with attendant serious defeats of a military or naval character for our side, it would be hard to over-estimate the prejudicial reaction on American public opinion.

The Labour government's Indian policy

On 26 July 1945, the results of the British general election were announced: the Labour Party swept into power with a 12 percent swing and 393 seats in the Commons against the Conservative Party's 213. Nehru was jubilant at Labour's victory. He had always felt ideologically closer to Clement Attlee, the Labour Party leader, than he had to the Conservatives. Indeed, as early as 1938, leading politicians in the then opposition Labour Party had held a private meeting with Jawaharlal Nehru at Stafford Cripps's house, where they undertook to pass an independence bill as soon as they came to power. The war intervened and, by the time Britain had a Labour government prepared to honour their promise, Muslim demands for separate representation within the Indian subcontinent had become stronger and clearer. When Attlee and

his cabinet turned their attention to Indian independence, the question was not whether power should be transferred because they had agreed that it should be. The real question was, to whom?

The new India Committee
Attlee lost no time in putting his India Committee together. Lord Pethick-Lawrence, with an academic and not necessarily pragmatic approach to Indian politics, became secretary of state for India; Arthur Henderson, a junior minister, spoke on his behalf in the Commons, which enabled Prime Minister Attlee and Chancellor of the Exchequer Stafford Cripps to take parliamentary control of matters relating to India. They were joined by the education minister, Ellen Wilkinson; the former India secretary, William Wedgwood Benn, who had become Viscount Stansgate on the death of his father; and the Earl of Listowel, who had been a junior minister at the India Office during the war. This was the team, imbued with enthusiasm but lacking in experience, charged with creating and implementing British policy that would lead to an independent India.

The Labour–Congress Axis
Congress had, throughout the 20th century, forged links with the Labour Party and with individual Labour MPs. It relied on the Labour Party to give voice to the opinions of Congress in the British press and the House of Commons, and it relied on personal friendships to enable this to happen.

Perhaps the most important friendship was that between Stafford Cripps and Jawaharlal Nehru. Both men were highly educated, highly intellectual and dedicated to radical reform of their respective countries. They gathered around themselves like-minded politicians who worked well together because of their shared ideals. One such man was Khrishna Menon, a London-based Indian socialist who was the driving force behind the India League, an organisation dedicated to campaigning throughout the United Kingdom for Indian independence. He did much to create and maintain Labour–Congress links and was a strong advocate of Nehru as India's future leader.

This rapport between Congress and Labour obviously made some things easier but it created difficulties too. The Muslim League had no such relationship with any British political party and, within the ranks of their leadership, there grew the strong suspicion that Labour was anti-Muslim.

ACTIVITY
KNOWLEDGE CHECK

The impact of the Second World War

1 List the ways in which the war impacted on Indian nationalism and put them in order of importance. Share your priorities in groups and reach an order with which you all agree.

2 Did the role of the USA in the years 1941–42 have a positive or negative effect on India?

3 Why did the election, in 1945, of a Labour government in Britain bring new hope to Indian nationalists?

A Level Exam-Style Question Section B

How accurate is it to say that the Second World War was the most significant factor driving Indian nationalism in the years 1935–45? (20 marks)

Tip

Consider the ways in which the aims and methods of the different nationalist groups changed during the period, and the extent to which this was due to the war.

WHY, IN THE YEARS 1945–46, DID ATTEMPTS AT A POLITICAL SOLUTION FAIL?

The new British Labour government's India Committee, dominated by Stafford Cripps, decided to recommend that elections should be held throughout India to allow people to choose their own representatives to a constituent assembly. The Committee suggested that elections would be held to the assemblies of the 11 provinces of British India and to the central assemblies in New Delhi. This, the Labour government's India Committee reasoned, would give a clear indication as to Indian opinion and pave the way for negotiations about a final political settlement. Meanwhile, they had little to suggest beyond setting up a constitution-making body of unelected Indians serving as the viceroy's Council and to resurrect the Cripps offer of 1942.

There was some concern among the British in India that the Labour government's India Committee had not fully understood the strength of the movement for a separate Pakistan, nor had they factored in to their deliberations the animosity between Nehru and Jinnah. However, what had happened, and of which few people were aware, was that in January 1946 a small fact-finding group of MPs had made an unannounced visit to India with the aim of trying to gauge the strength of support for a separate Pakistan. In private, some of the group conceded that this would be necessary to avoid Muslim unrest. Work began in secret to determine how such a partition might be achieved, with Wavell in particular being anxious that as much groundwork as possible was done in preparation, should an official decision be made to partition the subcontinent. It was immediately clear that the Punjab, with a Muslim-dominated west, a Hindu-dominated east and Sikhs spread throughout the province, would become a focus of discontent.

Meanwhile, everyone watched and waited for the outcome of the Indian elections to the central assembly and to the provincial assemblies. They would be an almost universal test of Indian opinion.

EXTEND YOUR KNOWLEDGE

Pakistan
Pakistan is a made-up word, formed from the initials of the provinces of Punjab, Afghan (North-West Frontier), Kashmir, Indus and Sind. The suffix '-stan' means 'home' or 'place' and is derived from Baluchistan, the largest province in what is now western Pakistan.

TIMELINE: FORMING THE CONSTITUENT ASSEMBLY

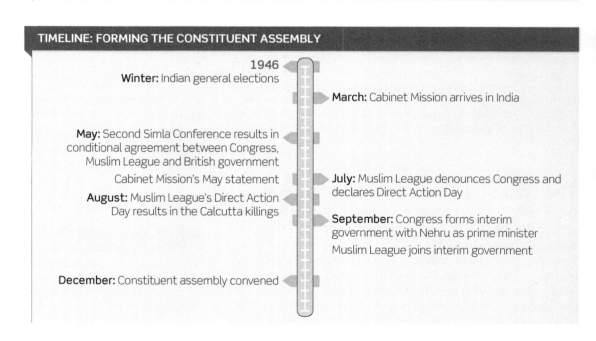

1946

Winter: Indian general elections

March: Cabinet Mission arrives in India

May: Second Simla Conference results in conditional agreement between Congress, Muslim League and British government

Cabinet Mission's May statement

July: Muslim League denounces Congress and declares Direct Action Day

August: Muslim League's Direct Action Day results in the Calcutta killings

September: Congress forms interim government with Nehru as prime minister

Muslim League joins interim government

December: Constituent assembly convened

The impact of Indian elections

It is important to realise that the elections in the spring of 1946 were carried out against a background of disorder, violence and mayhem.

The British authorities had completely mishandled the fighters captured after the defeat of the INA in 1944 (see page 238). Congress called for their immediate release, maintaining that they had, no matter how misguided, been fighting for the freedom of India. Indeed, the majority of Indians shared Congress's view. Ignoring popular sentiment, the British authorities selected a sample of senior INA officers, deliberately choosing a Hindu, a Muslim and a Sikh, and charged them with waging war against the Crown. This had the effect of uniting the three communities against the British. Sentenced to transportation for life, the three officers were then released because of fear of reprisals by the Indian army.

Seven million Indians were being demobilised from the armed services and were looking for work in industries that were already laying off workers as they returned to peacetime production levels.

Drought threatened to result in famine in southern India.

Elements within the Indian army mutinied in February 1946, as did 20,000 sailors and their officers in the Indian navy based in Bombay, Calcutta and Karachi. Congress persuaded the mutineers to surrender, which angered many of their supporters. However, Congress (and the Muslim League) saw more advantage in working with the British than against them, for the time being.

Violence is often a catalyst for fear, and fear tends to polarise voting patterns. This was true of the Indian elections, where the results in the 11 British provinces demonstrated considerable polarisation of support for Congress and the Muslim League. Overall, Congress won 90 percent of all available seats. While this may have seemed like a convincing victory, it needs unpicking. The Muslim League won 75 percent of all Muslim votes, 90 percent of all seats reserved for Muslims in the provinces (remember that not all Muslims were members of the Muslim League) and all 30 seats reserved for Muslims in the central assembly. Insofar as the provincial elections were concerned, Congress formed governments in eight provinces and the Muslim League in two, Bengal and Sind. The only province where the Congress–Muslim League polarisation was not clear was, unsurprisingly, in the Punjab where a non-Muslim coalition took control even though the Muslim League polled the largest number of votes.

What indicators were these results giving to those preparing a new constitution for India?

First, and most obviously, that the Muslim League was a powerful force within India, supported by a large proportion of the Muslim population. Any settlement would have to take account of the League's demands. There was, however, a more subtle message. In provinces where Muslims were in a minority, there was a very strong Muslim vote for Muslim League candidates as opposed to Muslims standing independently of the League. These were provinces that could never realistically expect to be part of a geographical Pakistan so implied support for a separate Muslim state to which they might travel.

The failure of the Cabinet Mission

It was into this maelstrom that Attlee sent his three-man cabinet mission to try to resolve India's constitutional problems. Given that the Labour government was pledged to implement Indian independence, there was every expectation that the new, peacetime mission would be successful. Lord Pethick-Lawrence, Stafford Cripps (now president of the Board of Trade) and A. V. Alexander (first lord of the admiralty and a Labour MP with traditional socialist views) arrived in India on 24 March 1946.

EXTEND YOUR KNOWLEDGE

Sir Stafford Cripps (1889–1952)

Born in London to wealthy parents, Richard Stafford Cripps studied chemistry at university but later switched to law and became a barrister in 1912.

During the First World War, he served as a Red Cross ambulance driver in France and then managed a chemical factory producing armaments. In 1930, he joined the Labour Party and was appointed solicitor-general in the second Labour government. In 1931, he was elected MP for Bristol East.

At the beginning of the Second World War, he worked in Moscow as the British ambassador and was a key figure in forging the alliance between Soviet Russia and the western powers after Nazi Germany attacked Russia in 1941. On his return to Britain he was appointed to the War Cabinet with the jobs of lord privy seal and leader of the House of Commons. In 1942 he led the doomed Cripps Mission to India and, later that year, was appointed minister of aircraft production. Cripps returned to India in 1946 as part of the Cabinet Mission, the failure of which eventually led to Partition.

As Chancellor of the Exchequer in 1947, Cripps was associated with the government's policy of post-war austerity, increasing taxation in an attempt to reduce consumption and boost exports, while at the same time maintaining a high level of spending on housing, health and welfare, and supporting the nationalisation of strategic industries. Ill health forced his resignation in 1950 and he died two years later.

What were the Cabinet Mission's aims?

Attlee had insisted that the Mission did everything possible to maintain a united India – a united India that could play a key role in Britain's plans for security in Asia. This would seem to rule out a separate Pakistan, but did not preclude the existence, within Hindu-dominated India, of separate Muslim-dominated states. The Mission had an additional, confidential brief that they should aim to create a positive desire for a speedy transfer of power. They needed to reverse the embarrassing failure of the 1942 Cripps Mission.

The three men stayed in India for more than three months, determined to break the deadlock between Congress and the Muslim League. They very nearly succeeded. Key Indian politicians were invited to clarify their position: Gandhi argued forcefully that power should be handed to Congress, while Jinnah, realising that a separate Pakistan could only come from a British decision, not a Congress-dominated Indian subcontinent, waited. Significantly, the Sikhs, a vulnerable minority, were ignored, as were the princes, who had separate treaties with the British and could not be forced to amalgamate with an independent India.

The Simla Conference, May 1946

A second Simla Conference was held in early May, to which Congress and the League were each invited to send four representatives. The purpose of the Conference was to work through the Cabinet Mission's proposals. These basically provided for a three-tier federal structure within a united India. Partition was not acceptable.

This is what was proposed:

- An All-India Union, responsible for defence, foreign policy and internal communication, together with powers to raise finances to fund these three elements, and governed by an executive and legislature.

- There would be three clusters of provincial governments:

  - Congress's Hindu heartland of Madras, Bombay, Orissa and the United and Central Provinces,

  - Muslim and predominantly Muslim areas of Baluchistan, the North-West Frontier Province, Sind and Punjab,

  - Bengal and Assam, where the balance of religions was slightly in favour of Muslims.

- Each provincial group would elect its own government to be responsible for the day-to-day running of provincial affairs.

- The All-India Union would comprise elected representatives from each provincial group.

Controversially, it was proposed that the regional groups could, after a period of time and a plebiscite, secede and become independent states.

The Mission suggested a second, fall-back proposition would be the creation of two separate independent states of Hindustan and Pakistan.

This did seem to be the last best hope for a peaceful transfer of power. The Mission's hope was that Congress would hate the fall-back position of two states and would opt for the main proposition, and that the Muslim League would, though obviously preferring the fall-back position, accept the first because the opt-out clause would allow for a separate Pakistan, reached by a democratic process. However, after two full Conference sessions, Congress would not agree to either option.

The May statement

Faced with the failure of the Simla Conference to reach agreement, the Cabinet Mission took matters into their own hands and announced that they could create a Constituent Assembly, comprising representatives from the 11 British provinces, who would draft a constitution for a single Indian state with regional groupings. This failed to resolve the issue: Congress flatly refused to accept the May Statement, whilst Jinnah, emphasising the compromise he had made in agreeing that the creation of Pakistan could be left to the decision of the Constituent Assembly, accepted it. The Cabinet Mission, acting unilaterally again, announced that they would set up an interim government to run India before the proposals of the Constituent Assembly could be put into effect. This interim government would be composed solely of Indians, plus the viceroy. This plan also ran onto the rocks, with Jinnah insisting that the Muslim League had to select Muslim members, while Congress insisted that they chose all the members, Muslims included. Finally, exasperated, the Cabinet Mission announced in a June statement that the viceroy would select members of the interim government. In an about turn, and not wishing to be excluded, Congress announced that that they would agree to the original plan, provided it was understood that individual states, and not groups of states, could opt out. In this way, they hoped to fragment any cohesive Pakistan that might emerge. Cripps declined to rule out this interpretation, to the anger of Wavell and Jinnah.

Direct Action

Jinnah, outraged at what he saw as the duplicity of both Congress and the Raj, convened his council of the League in Bombay on 27 July 1946 and repudiated all agreements made with the Cabinet Mission. Two days later, he called for a universal Muslim *hartal* and urged Muslims to prepare for a day of Direct Action on 16 August 1946.

SOURCE 7

From the Muslim League's call for Direct Action, 29 July 1946.

Whereas Muslim India has exhausted without success all efforts to find a peaceful solution of the Indian problem by compromise and constitutional means; and whereas the Congress is bent upon setting up Caste-Hindu Raj in India with the connivance of the British; and whereas it has become abundantly clear that the Muslims of India would not rest contented with anything less than the immediate establishment of an independent and fully sovereign state of Pakistan, the Council of the All-India Muslim League is convinced that now the time has come for the Muslim nation to resort to direct action to achieve Pakistan, to assert their just rights, to vindicate their honour and to get rid of the present British slavery and the contemplated future Caste-Hindu domination.

SOURCE 8

Viceroy Wavell's comments, recorded in his private journal on 29 July 1946.

So the Muslim League has run out, thanks to the Mission living in the pocket of Congress while out here, the dishonesty of Cripps, my stupidity and weakness in not spotting his dishonesty earlier and standing up to it, and the irresponsibility of Nehru in making the statements he has since the Mission left. I feel guilty of not seeing through Cripps' manoeuvres and refusing to be a party to Congress' insincere acceptance of the statement of May 16.

What were the effects of Direct Action?

It was not just Muslim India that was preparing for Direct Action; it was the Raj, too.

Commander-in-Chief Auchinleck, having made discreet enquiries among his Indian officers, found them to be loyal to their own concept of India, but privately warned Viceroy Wavell that he could not envisage Hindu firing at Hindu and Muslim shooting Muslim in any ensuing conflict.

Wavell had his provincial governors to worry about, too. Congress effectively controlled three-quarters of India. With the days of the Raj numbered, police loyalty would be swayed towards those who would inherit power and control. Wavell could not be sure he could contain the gathering storm.

SOURCE 9

From a statement made by Jinnah on 29 July 1946, after the Muslim League's call for Direct Action.

Never have we in the whole history of the League done anything except by constitutional methods and by constitutionalism. But now we bid goodbye to constitutional methods. Throughout the negotiations, the parties with whom we bargained held a pistol at us, one with power and machine guns behind it, and the other with non-cooperation and the threat to launch mass civil disobedience. We also have a pistol. We have exhausted all reason. There is no tribunal to which we can go. The only tribunal is the Muslim nation.

With these chilling words, Jinnah took India's Muslims into the horror and bloodletting of civil war.

In Calcutta, the police were ordered by the Muslim League to take a special holiday and the streets were given over to the mob. Within 72 hours, more than 5,000 lay dead, at least 20,000 were seriously injured and 100,000 residents made homeless. Muslim and Hindu murdered each other in an orgy of killings and bloodletting, looting and arson that spread across India.

Wavell's appeals to Congress and the Muslim League to call a halt to the killings fell on deaf ears. Growing increasingly irritated by Gandhi, whom Wavell had come to regard as a malevolent manipulator, he was genuinely appalled when Gandhi remarked that if India wanted a bloodbath, she could have it. In similar tone, Jinnah had assured him that Pakistan was worth the sacrifice of ten million Muslims. Congress, despite their numerical strength, began working outside formal negotiations, with Gandhi briefing Congress's representative in London to have private and secret conversations with Attlee. In one such conversation, Congress pressed for the removal of Wavell as viceroy, to which Attlee agreed. Wavell, hearing of this, felt undermined by Congress and by the Labour government; Jinnah, having urged Direct Action, had shown himself to be a leader who either could not control the Muslim League or had been naive in unleashing disorder.

AS Level Exam-Style Question Section A (a)

Why is Source 8 valuable to the historian for an enquiry into the failure of the Simla Conference of May 1946?

Explain your answer using the source, the information given about it and your own knowledge of the historical context. (8 marks)

Tip

Consider whether or not a private journal is likely to be accurate.

The clear outcome of Direct Action was that trust between differing communities was lost and the potential for compromise between their leaders was gone. The possibility of partition along religious lines was daily becoming a stronger and stronger likelihood.

The interim government under Nehru

It was against this background of uncontrollable violence that the interim government was sworn in on 2 September 1946, with Nehru as prime minister. The viceroy was still nominally responsible for the governance of India but in reality had to carry out the decisions of Indian ministers and the Executive Council. This effectively meant carrying out the wishes of Congress. Nehru took on responsibility for foreign affairs and Sardar Patel, Congress's general secretary, took on home affairs. Here, Patel insisted that intelligence reports were sent to the Congress administration, thus effectively sidelining the viceroy. Congress was running India. Wavell finally managed to persuade a reluctant Jinnah to join the government. Refusing to join the Executive Council because of Nehru's presence, Jinnah sent Liaquat Ali Khan instead. Hoping to give the Muslim League more power within the government, Wavell proposed that the League should become responsible for home affairs instead of Sardar Patel. When Congress threatened to bring down the whole interim government if this happened, Jinnah contented himself with the post of finance minister.

Evacuation plan

Growing increasingly concerned that India was on the brink of civil war, Wavell again warned the secretary of state that he could not contain the situation by force and requested support for his secret evacuation plan. All British civilians and their families would be moved to heavily protected safe zones near the coast and would be evacuated in an orderly way from Calcutta and Karachi. Commander-in-Chief Auchinleck would withdraw all British troops in a similarly orderly manner. Attlee refused to contemplate such a plan; playing for time, he was considering potential replacement viceroys.

Gaining the Constituent Assembly and losing a viceroy

On 7 December 1946, the Constituent Assembly met; it was never to complete its task.

Wavell was worn out. He was himself having severe doubts about his ability to cope with the increasing strains that 1947 would bring as India moved closer to independence. It gradually became clear to Cripps and Attlee, partly because of Congress's wire-pulling behind the scenes and partly through their own dealings with Wavell, that a man with fresh ideas was needed to complete India's independence. Attlee wrote to Wavell on 31 January 1947, removing him from his post and offering him an earldom in recognition of his services to the Raj. Earlier, in the first week of January, Admiral Viscount Louis Mountbatten of Burma had agreed to become India's last, and as it turned out, most controversial, viceroy.

In the middle of February 1947, Attlee announced to the House of Commons that His Majesty's government had resolved to transfer power to responsible Indian hands, no later than 30 June 1948. By responsible hands, Attlee meant an Indian government that was capable of maintaining the peace. How was that to be managed?

The race was on.

ACTIVITY
KNOWLEDGE CHECK

The Cabinet Mission

1 The Cabinet Mission clearly failed. Working in groups of four, make a case for the actions of Wavell, the British government, Jinnah or Nehru between March and December 1946, and present it to the whole group.

2 Using points made in (1) above and your own understanding of the situation, write an answer to the question: 'Why did the Cabinet Mission fail?'

WHY DID INDEPENDENCE FOR THE INDIAN SUBCONTINENT INVOLVE PARTITION?

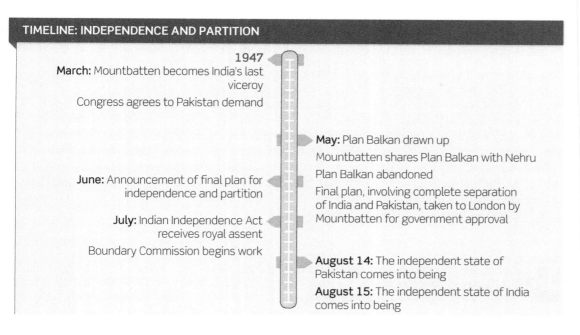

TIMELINE: INDEPENDENCE AND PARTITION

1947

March: Mountbatten becomes India's last viceroy

Congress agrees to Pakistan demand

May: Plan Balkan drawn up

Mountbatten shares Plan Balkan with Nehru

Plan Balkan abandoned

June: Announcement of final plan for independence and partition

Final plan, involving complete separation of India and Pakistan, taken to London by Mountbatten for government approval

July: Indian Independence Act receives royal assent

Boundary Commission begins work

August 14: The independent state of Pakistan comes into being

August 15: The independent state of India comes into being

The brief given to Mountbatten by Attlee and the British government was clear. Partition was to be avoided; if Congress and the League couldn't agree terms by the given deadline, then Britain would devolve power to the existing central and provincial governments and go.

Politicians, such as Ernest Bevin, the foreign secretary, together with the chiefs of staff, anticipated an attempt by Russia to expand into South East Asia in the years after 1945 and viewed with foreboding the possibility of a prolonged armed conflict should this happen. If this happened, then Indian cooperation was essential if Britain was to maintain effective contact, not only with the Commonwealth in the Pacific, but with the oil fields of the Middle East. This made the argument for a united India even stronger: Auchinleck gloomily predicted that an independent Pakistan would need a British garrison to defend it against Russian encroachments through Afghanistan.

EXTEND YOUR KNOWLEDGE

Lord Louis Mountbatten of Burma (1900–79)

A great-grandson of Queen Victoria and a close friend to the British royal family, Mountbatten was renowned for his charm, self-confidence, ambition and conceit.

Mountbatten had a spectacular career in the Navy and in London society. In August 1943, he was made supreme allied commander for South East Asia and led the campaign to rid Burma and Malaya of the Japanese.

Known for his sympathies towards nationalist movements and for his slightly left-of-centre approach to politics, Mountbatten became viceroy of India in 1947, charged with overseeing the transfer of power from the Raj to a responsible Indian government. The resultant Partition of the Indian subcontinent into India and Pakistan was accompanied by a horrendous bloodbath.

In 1949, Mountbatten resumed his naval career and was first sea lord of the admiralty at the time of the Suez crisis (1956), over which he clashed dramatically with Eden's government. He was chief of the defence staff from 1959 until his retirement in 1965.

In 1979, his boat was blown up and he was murdered by the Irish Republican Army (IRA).

Mountbatten and the decision to withdraw

The 'charm offensive' begins

One of the reasons for sending Mountbatten to negotiate the final stages of India's independence was that he was totally different from any of the previous viceroys. His flamboyance, left-wing tendencies and determination not only to be, but also to be seen, as a man of action brought a refreshing change to Indian politics and hope that the Congress–League deadlock could be broken.

Mountbatten spent his first four weeks in India consulting with Indian ministers, politicians and his own staff. With some, his charm and flattery worked, as did his clear determination to cultivate the friendship of men with whom he had to bargain. Cordial relations were quickly achieved between Mountbatten and Gandhi, Nehru and other Congress leaders. By marked contrast, Mountbatten's first meeting with Jinnah was decidedly frosty. Jinnah was not in the least seduced by the charms of the viceroy or his wife, the vicereine. Mountbatten was later to refer to him in pejorative terms that were duly relayed to Jinnah by staff who were trying to double-guess how events would turn out and where their loyalties should lie. This did nothing to improve Jinnah's view that Mountbatten had strong pro-Congress sympathies. His view was strengthened by Lady Mountbatten's very clear and much reported infatuation with the widower Nehru.

SOURCE 10

From Pamela Mountbatten, *India Remembered*, published in 2007. Pamela Mountbatten was the younger daughter of Lord and Lady Mountbatten and, then aged 17, was with them in India in the months leading to independence.

Mr Jinnah – my father rarely called him anything else – was a fastidious man. He was extremely sophisticated and, unlike the other Indian leaders, always dressed in immaculate English style rather than national dress. He was a Muslim, but only spoke in English whenever he condescended to speak. He had been intent on creating Pakistan ever since he had been introduced to the concept in London in 1933.

He did not fall for my father's charm offensive in those first days – which must have been working at full power. I was obviously ousted when the going got rough as my diary entry for 6 April reads 'Had dinner with the ADCs as Jinnah and his sister came to talk business.' At first my parents were very optimistic about the chance to mediate between Nehru and Congress, and Jinnah and the Muslim League. As my mother wrote in her diary of that same evening: 'Fascinating evening. Two very clever and odd people. I rather liked them but found them fanatical on their Pakistan and quite impractical.' Within a few meetings this optimism lapsed.

My father could talk of nothing else because he could not crack Jinnah and this had never happened to him before. He later admitted that he didn't realise how impossible his task was going to be until he met Jinnah. He has since often been accused of being anti-Muslim League, but that was not the right way of looking at the problem. Congress made themselves open to my father and courted his help. Jinnah was the opposite and rejected my father's involvement whenever he could.

AS Level Exam-Style Question Section A (b)

How much weight do you give the evidence of Source 10 for an enquiry into Mountbatten's relationship with Congress and the Muslim League?

Explain your answer using the source, the information given about it and your own knowledge of the historical context. (12 marks)

Tip

Consider the likelihood of an elderly woman remembering correctly events that took place when she was 17.

Photograph of Viceroy and Vicereine Mountbatten with Nehru in 1947.

ACTIVITY
KNOWLEDGE CHECK

The Mountbattens and Congress

What can be learned from Source 11? How far is it accurate to say that Mountbatten favoured Congress over the Muslim League when negotiating Indian independence?

Reasons for Partition and the nationalist response

What Mountbatten heard during his four weeks of consultation made him believe that Partition was the only solution. This was most certainly not what Attlee wanted to hear. For the whole of its time in India, the Raj had tried to govern impartially between Muslim and Hindu and, indeed, one of its major successes had been that its rule was secular. To fall back, now, on a primitive division of a huge land mass along religious lines was, so Attlee and his government believed, a seriously retrograde step.

So what had happened to make Mountbatten decide that Partition was the only answer? Alan Campbell-Johnson, Mountbatten's press officer, gave an explanation (see Source 12).

SOURCE
12 From A. Campbell-Johnson, *Mission with Mountbatten*, published in 1951. Campbell-Johnson was Mountbatten's press officer in India.

In his first talks with Lord Mountbatten, the Muslim League leader, Mr Jinnah, gave a frank warning that unless an acceptable political solution was reached very quickly, he could not guarantee to control the situation from his side. A similar warning was given by Congress leaders.

Unity had been Britain's greatest achievement in India, but by March 1947 the only alternatives were Pakistan or chaos. Lord Mountbatten discovered from personal discussions with the leaders of the Muslim League that they would insist on partition at all costs and fight a civil war rather than accept transfer of power to a Hindu majority union, while Congress showed themselves as champions of unity, but not at the price of coercion.

Death and destruction

While Mountbatten was talking in Delhi, riots broke out in the Punjab. Although about 56 percent of the Punjab's inhabitants were Muslim, it had been administered by a shaky alliance of Hindus, Sikhs and non-League Muslims under Khizr Hayat Khan. His resignation in March 1947 and an attempt by the League to form its own administration led to militant Sikhs calling for direct action against the League – and an explosion of violence. Amritsar and Lahore were centres of carnage, while murder, arson and looting were common throughout the province. In the North West Frontier Province, the League launched a civil disobedience campaign of its own against Congress.

What was Gandhi doing?

Gandhi was in despair. His dream of a single, united India in which all religions could co-exist seemed to be evaporating before his eyes. He fell back on his belief in the power of truth and love and began one of his long-distance walks. This time he walked through the Noakhali and Tiperah districts of East Bengal, trying through what he regarded as an act of love to stop the mass killings that had left thousands dead. As always, he aimed to communicate directly with the illiterate masses, trying to explain what the politicians were doing. He then turned his attention to Bihar, where Hindus were killing Muslims on a large scale. As a practical gesture, it was a futile one. He had become an anachronistic figure and, from this time on, was sidelined in the search for an acceptable formula for independence.

Meanwhile, back in Delhi, Mountbatten and his staff were racing against the clock. Everyone involved, Indian and British, was exhausted, tense and sometimes, inevitably, bad-tempered. Momentum had to be maintained and the deadline had to be met. Lord Ismay, Mountbatten's right-hand man and his commander-in-chief, likened India to a ship full of combustible material. The following months would show whether or not the ship would explode.

The Partition plan

The plan for Partition, and the reallocation of power, was drawn up in April and May 1947.

Plan Balkan

The first draft, known as 'Plan Balkan', basically allowed the Indian states and provinces to decide their own future. This was a recipe for total anarchy, as past history had demonstrated, and as Nehru forcefully pointed out when the plan was unofficially and improperly revealed to him in a private meeting with Mountbatten. This was yet another example of Mountbatten's perceived partiality, for Jinnah had been given no such preview.

Nehru assured Mountbatten that Congress would be sure to reject such a plan as it would both weaken India and also weaken the Congress Party itself. Furthermore, if Pakistan was to be a viable state, it needed to contain, in Jinnah's oft-stated opinion, an undivided Punjab and Bengal. To allow these states to decide their own futures would undoubtedly lead to their partition. In the face of this, and mindful of Jinnah's constant and consistent refusal to accept any arrangement that would produce an impoverished Pakistan, Mountbatten and his advisors tore up Plan Balkan and started again.

The Mountbatten plan

At great speed and with no little embarrassment, Mountbatten and his staff cobbled together a new partition plan. They were desperate to placate Congress and, at the same time, to get Jinnah's agreement. They were desperate, too, to get out of India before the subcontinent went up in flames. The remnants of the Raj were fast losing control of the domestic situation and Mountbatten was afraid the British would be swamped by events they could no longer control:

Vast areas of north west India were in a state of riot and rebellion.

The steel frame of the ICS, which had held India together in the heyday of the Raj, was now reduced to a mere skeleton of mainly Indians to whom their friends and relations looked for patronage.

Attlee's declaration that the British would be out of India by July 1948 had led to bloody contests for supremacy in mixed Hindu and Muslim areas like the Punjab.

The authorities' capacity for controlling the situation was severely compromised and collapsed altogether in Bihar. Almost the only form of authority that could go any way toward holding the situation together was the army and Partition would mean that the army would no longer be a national body, but Hindu would be split from Muslim, officers from men. When Viceroy Mountbatten asked Auchinleck how long it would take to split the army between Pakistan and India, he guessed two, possibly five, years. In the event, Auchinleck was given four weeks to complete the separation.

Jinnah, too, was in a hurry. His persistent cough and debilitating physical weakness had been diagnosed as symptoms of a terminal disease – tuberculosis. If he wanted to see the birth of a separate Muslim state, events had to move fast.

On 18 May 1947, Mountbatten carried his plan for Partition, involving the complete separation of India and Pakistan, to London for government and then parliamentary approval. On 15 July 1947, it was announced in the House of Commons that, in precisely one month's time, two separate dominions of India and Pakistan would be created on the Indian subcontinent.

The Boundary Commission

The work of the Boundary Commission was to draw a boundary between India and Pakistan that would, as far as possible, accommodate Hindus and Muslims in separate states. The Commission comprised equal numbers of Hindu and Muslim judges (chosen by Congress and the League) and a chairman, Sir Cyril Radcliffe, who was a legal expert. His impartiality was guaranteed because he had no previous experience whatsoever of India; nor, his work being done, did he ever return. Using out-of-date maps, anecdotal stories of land ownership and dusty boundary charts, the Commission was given just five weeks to complete its work.

Rumours, leaks and pressure

With so much at stake, it was inevitable that some decisions were leaked to interested parties, who then applied what pressure they could to make the Boundary Commission change its collective mind. One of the worst offenders here was Mountbatten himself. A leak would reach Nehru, who would then apply pressure on Mountbatten, who would in turn attempt to influence the Boundary Commission.

This was certainly true in the case of Firozpur. The town controlled the only bridge over the River Sutlej as well as playing a strategic part in the irrigation system of the area. Radcliffe's first draft of the boundary in the area, flown to Lahore on 10 August, placed Firozpur firmly inside Pakistan, which resulted in intensive lobbying by Nehru and Congress to have the boundary moved. On the evening of 11 August, Radcliffe had dinner with Mountbatten and Ismay. The following day, Firozpur appeared on the Indian side of the boundary.

Mountbatten was certainly not acting in an even-handed way. This may have been due in part to his personal dislike of Jinnah and to the warm relationship Mountbatten and his wife had with Nehru, but it was also due to the fact that Mountbatten simply did not believe Pakistan would last. He likened it to a temporary hut that would soon collapse and be reabsorbed into India. It may have been this belief that led him to strengthen India at the expense of Pakistan.

What about the princes?

The princes had been unstinting in their support of the Raj during the Second World War. The Maharaja of Travancore had bought the Royal Indian Navy an armed patrol boat; the Nawab of Bhopal bought fighter aircraft, as did the Nizam of Hyderabad, who bought a whole squadron of aeroplanes; and the Maharajah of Kashmir contributed 18 field ambulances. The princes invested in the war effort by buying 180 million rupees' worth of war bonds. Of their subjects, 300,000 Indian volunteers had joined India's armed forces. Now, faced with the subcontinent being split between Muslim and Hindu, India and Pakistan, they felt ignored. Worse than ignored, they felt threatened by Congress, a party dedicated to removing their sovereign powers.

Mountbatten took no notice of complaints from the princes nor of Conrad Corfield, the head of India's Political Department. Corfield had little time for India's professional politicians and sympathised with the princes' desire to remain autonomous in their own lands and to keep meddling Congress politicians out. Corfield persuaded the new secretary of state for India, Lord Listowel, to agree that neither India nor Pakistan would inherit the princely states when the Raj ended, but the princes would become, in effect, independent rulers. Having won this concession, Corfield authorised the burning of four tons of documents listing the princes' misdemeanours over the years. He wanted to prevent the papers from falling into the hands of Congress, the members of which, he suspected, would use them for political blackmail.

Nehru was furious when he heard of Corfield's manoeuvrings. If carried through, independence for the princes would mean the disintegration of India and a complete reverse for Congress, who intended quietly to take over the princely states. Mountbatten, who deeply resented being outwitted by an official, dismissed Corfield.

Mountbatten called a conference of Indian princes, held on 25 July, at which he explained that, when British rule ended on 15 August, they would have to accede to either India or Pakistan, depending on which state they were nearer. By shamelessly exploiting his royal connections and playing on the princes' loyalty, fear and superstition, by cajoling and flattering, browbeating and threatening, Mountbatten had them all signed up by the time of the transfer of power from the Raj to either India or Pakistan.

Dividing the spoils

A vast amount of administrative work had to be done before Partition could come into effect. The desk of every official in Calcutta, Delhi and Lahore was piled high with seemingly impossible paperwork. The assets and liabilities of British India had to be divided between India and Pakistan on the basis of 82.5 percent for India and 17.5 percent for Pakistan. The army and police, civil service and revenue service, all had to be dismantled and reassembled, as did everything from railways and schools through to trucks, paper, pens and paperclips. In just one month the accumulation of centuries of British hoarding, storing, building and creating was turned up, turned out and meticulously divided between the two soon-to-be dominions. These were, in essence, just things. Yet the division of these 'things' impacted on the lives of millions of people, too often with devastating effect.

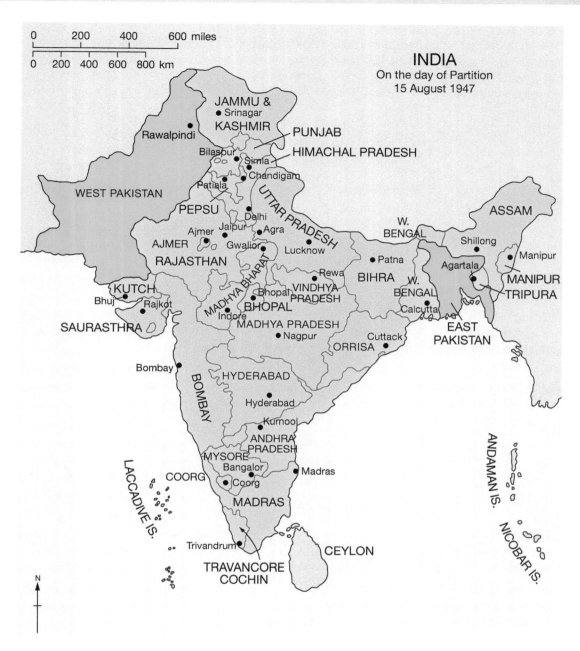

Figure 4.2: The Partition of the Indian subcontinent on 15 August 1947.

British withdrawal and communal violence

Millions of Hindus, Muslims and Sikhs were terrified that, after independence, they would wake up on the wrong side of the India–Pakistan border, living in a country hostile to their faith. They abandoned their homes, their fields and their livelihoods, packed what possessions they had, and went. They walked, crammed into bullock carts and tried to make it through to the railway system. They travelled, so they thought, to safety. And, as they travelled, Muslims heading west were butchered by Sikhs and Hindus in India. Hindus and Sikhs moving east were murdered by Muslims in Pakistan. It is reckoned that ten million people tried to change lands in that summer of 1947 and around one million Indians never made it to their promised land. They were massacred in an orgy of senseless bloodletting.

The British military withdrawal began in August 1947 and continued until mid-1948; at the very time when violence in the Punjab was at its height, the majority of British troops were kept in their barracks and then evacuated from the country. A totally inadequate force of 50,000 troops was dispatched to bring order along the new frontiers. They mostly kept their heads down in their barracks, totally unable to do anything to control the situation. Indeed, Mountbatten himself believed that the British were powerless to prevent the violence of 1946–48. Government instructions were that British troops should only be used to protect European lives. Indeed, no Indian leader would have agreed to the use of British troops.

EXTRACT

1 From Judith M. Brown, *Modern India: the Origins of an Asian Democracy*, published in 1994.

Jinnah in fact did not want the sort of partition that occurred in 1947. It was not a popular Muslim demand at the time, made little sense to Muslims secure in provincial majorities, and offered nothing to the millions of Muslims scattered as minorities throughout the subcontinent. Furthermore, it made little sense in terms of economics and defence. It probably, therefore, was designed as a bargaining counter, vague enough to unite Indian Muslims behind it, in order to achieve recognition for Muslims as a 'nation' and therefore as equal with Congress in negotiations about the future.

Independence for India and Pakistan

As midnight on 14 August 1947 approached, in Delhi's Constituent Assembly, Jawaharlal Nehru spoke. Part of his speech can be seen in Source 13. What of the other main players? Mountbatten, hoping to be the first governor-general of both India and Pakistan, had to be content with the governor-generalship of India alone. Jinnah flew from Delhi to Karachi on 7 August to become Pakistan's first governor-general himself. And Gandhi? He did not want to stay in Delhi for independence celebrations, but left for Bengal, bitterly regretting that the errors of the past had not been rectified.

SOURCE

13 From Nehru's speech to Delhi's Constituent Assembly, 14 August 1947.

Long years ago we made a tryst with destiny, and now the time comes when we shall redeem our pledge, not wholly or in full measure, but very substantially. At the stroke of the midnight hour, when the world sleeps, India will awake to life and freedom. A moment comes, which comes but rarely in history, when we step out from the old to the new, when an age ends, and when the soul of a nation, long suppressed, finds utterance. It is fitting that at this solemn moment we take the pledge of dedication to the service of India and her people and to the still larger cause of humanity.

ACTIVITY
KNOWLEDGE CHECK

Viceroy Mountbatten

1 How sensible was the British government's decision to replace Wavell with Mountbatten? Discuss this in groups.

2 Why was Mountbatten's time as viceroy accompanied by so much violence?

THINKING HISTORICALLY   Change (6a)

Separately and together

Below are some different types of history that historians may identify.

Political history	Economic history	Social history
Religious history	Military history	International history

These are thematic histories, where a historian focuses on a particular aspect of change. For example, an economic history of the British Empire would focus on trade and the economic reasons for the expansion of the empire, whereas a political history of the empire would focus on governance of the colonies and strategic reasons for its expansion.

Work in groups.

1 Write a definition for each of the six types of history.

Here are some events in our period:

1919 Amritsar Massacre	1930 Salt *satyagraha*	1935 Government of India Act	1939 India joins the Second World War on the side of the Allies	1943 Famine in Bengal	1947 Indian Independence Act

Now answer the following questions:

2 The events of 1935 and 1947 can be classified as 'political' events.

   a) What prompted the British government to pass the Indian Independence Act in 1947?

   b) What other areas of history does this cross into?

3 What political changes came about because of the 1947 Government of India Act?

4 Was the salt *satyagraha* of 1930 an economic or political event, or both? Explain your answer.

5 What was the social and political impact of the Bengal Famine of 1943?

6 The military were involved in both the Amritsar Massacre of 1919 and in India's entry into the Second World War. Does this mean that only military historians would be interested in these two events? Give reasons for your answer.

THINKING HISTORICALLY   Cause and Consequence (5b)

Causation relativity

Historical events usually have many causes. Some are crucial, while some are less important. For some historical questions, it is important to understand exactly what role certain factors played in causing historical change.

Significant factors in the timing and nature of the Indian Independence Act 1947

Election of a Labour government in Britain in 1945, members of which had prior contact with Congress and were sympathetic to Indian independence	The Muslim League's Direct Action in August 1946 leading to rioting and mass killing	The Cabinet Mission to India in March 1946 and its failure at the Simla Conference of May 1946 to bring about an agreed constitution for India
The Second World War, 1939–45	The appointment, in March 1947, of Lord Mountbatten as viceroy of India	Congress Quit India campaign, beginning in August 1942, and subsequent violence

Answer the following questions on your own.

The timing of the Indian Independence Act

1 How important was the Second World War in explaining the timing of the Act?

2 In what ways did the appointment of Mountbatten as viceroy affect the timing of the Act?

3 How could the Congress Quit India campaign have delayed the timing of the Act?

The nature of the Indian Independence Act

4 How far did the election of a Labour government impact on the attitudes of those who were drawing up the Act?

5 What role did the above factors play in the ways in which the Act affected the Indian subcontinent?

6 Would the nature of the Act have been the same if Mountbatten had not been appointed viceroy?

7 What roles did each of the above causal factors play in determining the nature and timing of the Indian Independence Act?

New beginnings?

Indian independence gave four hundred million people freedom from the largest empire the world has ever known. But it was freedom at a price. That price was partition and riot, dislocation and destruction, rape, abduction and death. The speed with which independence was granted and the way in which it was managed left a number of unresolved issues, but in many ways 1947–48 were years of transition rather than a period of abrupt closure.

Continuity

- Many British people stayed on in India after 1947 as ordinary civilians and as officials. The governors of the Punjab, Madras, Bombay and the North West Frontier Province, as well as some service chiefs and 83 civilian officers stayed in their jobs at least until the early 1950s. Indeed Mountbatten himself, at Nehru's request, stayed on for a year as India's constitutional governor-general.

- The constitutions of both India and Pakistan were framed in accordance with the old 1935 Government of India Act. There were 250 identical clauses.

- The Indian Administrative Service (IAS) took over from the old Indian Civil Service (ICS) of the Raj. It was, however, far from a clean break. Indeed, as late as the mid-1960s, when there were 23 central secretariat departments in the IAS, ICS-trained men headed 19 of them.

- The vast number of manuals and handbooks, forms and certificates, maps and gazetteers that were part of the Raj's bureaucracy, remained in place for the use of the new administrators.

- The hand-over of the Indian economy was gradual. Indeed, for at least 30 years after 1947, for example, the Indian tea industry remained in British hands.

Unresolved issues

- Partition resulted in an enormous refugee problem. Displaced people, once they had located themselves in Hindu India or Muslim Pakistan, had to find somewhere to live and somewhere to work. Enormous psychological damage was done to families who saw members decimated by violent death or they lost each other in the mass exodus and were never reunited.

- A member of the Hindu Mahasabha, angered at Gandhi's insistence that the Congress government should continue transferring assets to Pakistan, killed him. On 30 January 1948, Nathuram Godse shot Gandhi as he addressed a prayer meeting in Delhi.

- The creation of the separate state of Pakistan did not bring unalloyed joy to all Muslims living in the subcontinent. Many of them, particularly those living in the south, simply couldn't make it to Pakistan. More than 30 million remained behind in India, either through force of circumstance or through choice. Bengali Hindi-speaking Muslims had problems, too, and would mostly have preferred to live in an independent Bengal defined by culture rather than religion, and were alarmed when the Pakistan government announced that Urdu would be the official language of Pakistan.

- Muslims who did make it through to Pakistan tended to be better educated and richer than the local Sindhis and Punjabis and they filled most of the responsible posts in the new government. This caused considerable friction and many *muhajirs*, as they were called, were attacked and had their property looted and burned. One of the first victims was Pakistan's first prime minister, Liaquat Ali Khan, who was assassinated in 1951.

- The separation of the state of Pakistan into East and West Pakistan did not make for ease of government and appropriate distribution of resources. In 1971, Pakistan suffered partition again when East Pakistan became the independent state of Bangladesh.

- Conflict between Pakistan and India over Kashmir (caused largely by the inability of the Hindu maharaja, Hari Singh, to make up his mind as to whether to plump for India or Pakistan) resulted in mass killings in 1947–48 and remained unresolved for decades.

- In 1947, all the people involved in Partition agreed that power should be transferred on the basis of dominion status, hence both India and Pakistan having a constitutional governor-general. But Britain made it clear that there would be no objection if either state decided, at a later date, to sever all allegiance to the Crown. In 1950, India became a republic, followed six years later by Pakistan.

ACTIVITY
SUMMARY

Partition

1 How far would you agree that the Labour government acted with bias towards Congress throughout 1945–47?

2 How far do you agree with the view, expressed in Extract 1, that Jinnah never really wanted a separate Pakistan, but was using the suggestion as a bargaining point?

3 Why did Partition result in violence, death and destruction?

WIDER READING

Brown, J. *Modern India: The Origins of an Asian Democracy*, Oxford University Press (1985)

French, P. *Liberty or Death*, Flamingo (1997)

Mountbatten, P. *India Remembered*, Pavilion Books (2007)

Pandey, B. N. (ed.) *The Indian Nationalist Movement 1885–1947*, MacMillan (1979)

Wolpert, S. *Shameful Flight*, Oxford University Press (2006)

Preparing for your AS Level Paper 2 exam

Advance planning

1. Draw up a timetable for your revision and try to keep to it. Spread your timetable over a number of weeks, and aim to cover four or five topics each week.
2. Spend longer on topics which you have found difficult, and revise them several times.
3. Above all, do not try to limit your revision by attempting to 'question spot'. Try to be confident about all aspects of your Paper 2 work, because this will ensure that you have a choice of questions in Section B.

Paper 2 overview:

AS Paper 2	Time: 1 hour 30 minutes	
Section A	Answer 1 compulsory two-part sources question	8+12 marks = 20 marks
Section B	Answer 1 question from a choice of 3	20 marks
	Total marks =	40 marks

You should familiarise yourself with the layout of the paper by looking at the examples published by Edexcel. The sources together will total around 300 words. The questions for each section are followed by eight pages of lined paper where you should write your answer.

Section A question

Each of the two parts of the question will focus on one of the two contemporary sources provided. The sources together will total around 300 words. The (a) question, worth 8 marks, will be in the form of 'Why is Source 1 useful for an enquiry into…?' The (b) question, worth 12 marks, will be in the form of 'How much weight do you give the evidence of Source 2 for an enquiry into…?' In both your answers you should address the value of the content of the source, and then its nature, origin and purpose. Finally, you should use your own knowledge of the context of the source to assess its value.

Section B questions

These questions ask you to reach a judgement on an aspect of the topic studied. The questions will have the form, for example, of 'How far…', 'To what extent…' or 'How accurate is it to say…'. The questions can deal with historical concepts such as cause, consequence, change, continuity, similarity, difference and significance. You should consider the issue raised in the question, consider other relevant issues, and then conclude with an overall judgement.

The timescale of the questions could be as short as a single year or even a single event (an example from Paper 2F.2 could be, 'To what extent were the Round Table conferences of 1930–32 a failure?'). The timescale could be longer depending on the historical event or process being examined, but questions are likely to be shorter than those set for Sections A and B in Paper 1.

Use of time

This is an issue which you should discuss with your teachers and fellow students, but here are some suggestions for you.

1. Do not write solidly for 45 minutes on each question. For Section A it is essential that you have a clear understanding of the content of each source, the points being made, and the nature, origin and purpose of each source. You might decide to spend up to ten minutes reading the sources and drawing up your plan, and 35 minutes writing your answer.
2. For Section B answers you should spend a few minutes working out what the question is asking you to do, and drawing up a plan of your answer before you begin to write your response.

Preparing for your AS Level exams

Paper 2: AS level sample answer with comments

Section A

Part A requires you to:

- identify key points in the extract and explain them
- deploy your own knowledge of the context in which events took place
- make appropriate comments about the author/origin/purpose of the source.

Why is Source 10 (Chapter 1, page 183) valuable to historians for an enquiry about the Amritsar Massacre in 1919?

Explain your answer using the source, the information given about it and your own knowledge of the historical context. (8 marks)

Average student answer

The Amritsar Massacre was a dreadful event that took place in the Jallianwala Bagh in the city of Amritsar in April 1919. The source is valuable to historians because it was written at the time, and by someone who took part in the massacre. It was General Dyer who led the troops into the Bagh and ordered them to fire on an unarmed crowd. Dyer explained that he fired until the crowd dispersed, 'I fired and continued to fire until the crowd dispersed', and goes on to say that he did this because he felt threatened by the huge crowd. As he was reporting to his superior officer, he would take care that he got the facts right, although he could be selective in what he reported in order to present himself in the best light possible.

It is understandable that Dyer acted as he did. The situation in the Punjab was very difficult. Opposition to the Rowlatt Acts flared up all over India, but especially in the Punjab. In Amritsar, the administrative capital, the British had lost control and Dyer was attempting to regain some of that control. Indeed, the governor of the Punjab, Michael O'Dwyer, believing this was the start of a revolt, had sent Dyer into Amritsar specifically to quell the mob. He said that he intended the firing to 'produce the necessary moral and widespread effect', meaning that there was some understanding of the significance of the problem in Amritsar. He says that there 'could be no question of undue severity' meaning that he could have been as violent as he wished.

Overall the source, together with the background information, makes it clear that Dyer was acting according to his orders. Because of this it would be valuable to the historian enquiring into the Amritsar Massacre.

This is a weak opening paragraph because it states that the source is of value because it was written at the time, but at no point does it explore the possibility that Dyer was attempting to excuse his actions. The source is paraphrased rather than analysed and is accepted at face value, although with some suggestion that Dyer could have been selective in his reporting. The paragraph could be improved by explaining exactly how the source could be of value to the enquiry and what its limitations were.

Some effective points are made here about the context of the source, and there is some linkage of the source to the context. The answer would be improved if it explored Dyer's motives in writing as he did and there was more depth to the argument about Dyer's motives.

A brief conclusion that asserts the value of the source to the historian, with some indication as to why it would be valuable for the enquiry. The paragraph should be more developed, with more of the limitations of the source summarised.

Verdict

This is an average student answer because:

- the understanding of the source material lacks a clearly critical approach
- it does not use the context of the source fully enough to explain its value

- the evaluation of the source material is insufficiently related to the specific enquiry.

Use the feedback on this answer to rewrite it, making as many improvements as you can.

Paper 2: AS level sample answer with comments

Section A

Part B requires you to:

- interrogate the source
- draw reasoned inferences
- deploy your own knowledge to interpret the material in its context
- make a judgement about the value (weight) of the source in terms of making judgements.

How much weight do you give the evidence of Source 11 (Chapter 2, page 210) for an enquiry into the role played by Jinnah in the Round Table Conferences, held in London 1930–32?

Explain your answer, using the source, the information given about it and your own knowledge of the historical context. (12 marks)

Average student answer

The Round Table Conferences were held in London between 1930 and 1932. Jinnah attended the first and second one. Men, including Jinnah, who represented all shades of political opinion in India, with the exception of Congress, attended the first conference and the basis of a new constitution for India was agreed. The second conference failed to reach any agreement because Gandhi represented Congress and claimed to represent all Indian opinion, something with which others, including Jinnah, disagreed. Hardly anyone of note attended the third conference and this was largely because Gandhi was in prison and a general election had changed the political composition of the British government.

> This is a weak opening paragraph because it does not address the value of the source. Indeed. It doesn't mention the source at all, but focuses on providing the context of the source. It could be improved by explaining how the context impacts on the opinions expressed in the source.

The author of the source met Jinnah many times and knew him well. Because of this the source needs to have considerable weight put upon it. He praises him as being 'one of the very few intellectually honest politicians I have known' but also is not afraid to criticise him, 'humility was not one of his strong points', and because of this balance the source has to be taken seriously. It helps to explain why Jinnah behaved as he did at the first two London conferences by supporting the arrangements made at the first and opposing Gandhi at the second. However, it must be remembered that the author of the source was a journalist and although he knew India and the Indian political situation well, could be attempting to sensationalise what he wrote about Jinnah.

Considerable weight must be given to the source for an enquiry into the role played by Jinnah at the Round Table Conferences. It was written by someone who knew him well and explains how his personality and intellect drove what he did.

> This paragraph attempts some evaluation of the source and does address the position of the author, though without reaching any conclusion. The source is linked to the enquiry but this link is insufficiently explored and is expressed as an assertion. The response could be improved by focusing more sharply on the strengths and limitations of the source and by making a clearer link to the enquiry.

> This concluding paragraph summarises what has been written previously. It does not take the response any further. In particular, the final phrase 'explains how his personality and intellect drove what he did' needs considerable development in showing how these qualities impacted on his behaviour at the Conferences, and on what that behaviour was. This would improve the answer considerably.

Verdict

This is an average answer because:

- it does not make clear connections between the source and the question
- although accurate contextual information is provided, this is insufficiently linked to the source

- the evaluation of the source material does consider the weight that the source could bear, but this is insufficiently developed.

Use the feedback on this answer to rewrite it, making as many improvements as you can.

Paper 2: AS level sample answer with comments

Section A

Part A requires you to:

- identify key points in the extract and explain them
- deploy your own knowledge of the context in which events took place
- make appropriate comments about the author/origin/purpose of the source.

Why is Source 10 (Chapter 1, page 183) valuable to historians for an enquiry about the Amritsar Massacre in 1919?

Explain your answer using the source, the information given about it and your own knowledge of the historical context. (8 marks)

Strong student answer

General Dyer's role in the Amritsar Massacre was questioned at the time and, indeed, was the main focus of two later inquiries, one by the Hunter Commission initiated by the British government and one by the Indian National Congress. Thus for an historian to have access to a source that gives some insight into Dyer's motives in acting as he did, is of immense value.

> This is a strong introduction, contextualising the source in order to demonstrate its value to historians.

Dyer explains to his commanding officer that he 'continued to fire until the crowd dispersed' but that crowd dispersal was not his only motive driving his actions. His motive was also one of 'producing sufficient moral effect from a military point of view not only on those who were present, but more especially throughout the Punjab'. Thus it would seem that while he felt threatened by the thousands gathered in the Jallianwala Bargh, he also wanted to send a clear message to the whole of the province that the reaction to the Rowlatt Acts he had witnessed in Amritsar would not be tolerated by the British authorities. Indeed, the governor of the Punjab, Michael O'Dwyer, believed that the rioting in Amritsar that preceded the massacre was the first stage of a carefully planned uprising that would be likely to replicate the Indian mutiny of 1857. So in this sense, Dwyer could be seen, from the source, to be following what he thought were his commanding officer's orders and he is attempting to justify his actions in this report.

> Here the candidate selects specific points in the source and draws inferences from them by using the broader context. The knowledge displayed is sound and well deployed to explain the value of the source.

However, the source cannot just be taken at face value, and that makes it even more valuable for the historian. Dyer seems to have doubts that he acted correctly 'if I was to justify my actions' seems to imply that he believed might be required to do just that. In a similar way, the last two sentences show that Dyer is already preparing an excuse for leaving the injured to die by implying that the high death toll was the crowd's fault and not his.

> This paragraph identifies two very clear implications present in this source, demonstrating that Dyer had some doubts about his actions and was beginning to consider preparing his defence. The paragraph makes it clear that the inferences that can be drawn from the source make it even more valuable than the surface features.

Overall, then, the source is valuable in that it provides part of an explanation of what happened at Amritsar, of the motives prompting Dwyer to act as he did and of the doubts he had about the legitimacy of his actions. The source is valuable, too, for providing evidence that the massacre has to be seen, from the point of view of the Raj, in the whole context of the attempt to maintain control over India.

> This paragraph returns to the question of the value of the source itself for an enquiry into the Amritsar Massacre and places that within the wider context of providing an insight into the problems facing the Raj as they struggled to control the Punjab.

Verdict

This is a strong answer because:

- it makes clear connections between the source and the enquiry
- it places the source in an immediate and a wider context
- it selects and evaluates relevant parts of the source to explain its value.

Paper 2: AS level sample answer with comments

Section A

Part B requires you to:

- interrogate the source
- draw reasoned inferences
- deploy your own knowledge to interpret the material in its context
- make a judgement about the value (weight) of the source in terms of making judgements.

How much weight do you give the evidence of Source 11 (Chapter 2, page 210) for an enquiry into the role played by Jinnah in the Round Table Conferences, held in London 1930–32?

Explain your answer, using the source, the information given about it and your own knowledge of the historical context. (12 marks)

Strong student answer

This apparently perceptive description of Jinnah, written by someone who knew him well, could be applied to any of Jinnah's negotiations with the British. It is not known when the author formed his opinion of Jinnah nor on what evidence it was based. However, the pen-portrait is particularly appropriate when applied to his negotiating skills at the London-based Round Table Conferences. Indeed, the way in which Jinnah behaved may well have played a part in constructing Frank Moraes' description of his friend.

At the first Round Table Conference Jinnah, representing the Muslim League, entered into a series of negotiations with British politicians (Ramsay MacDonald and Samuel Hoare, for example), as well as Indian princes and representatives from all shades of Indian opinion from Sikhs to Untouchables with the exception of Congress, Gandhi and Nehru being in prison: 'Like every decent-minded, thoughtful Indian he wanted his country to be politically free.' The second Conference tested Jinnah's skills to the utmost. The British, wrong-footed by Gandhi's insistence that he had to be treated as the sole representative of all Indians, were taken by surprise at Jinnah's behind the scenes negotiating, wheeling and dealing to try to reach a settlement: 'The British had completely misread the character and aims of this dedicated man. They had been accustomed to deal with a type of Muslim leader whose dislike for Congress could be encouraged by official favours.' In the end, though, no matter how skilful, no matter how wrong the British were in their assessment of Jinnah, the second Round Table failed.

Some elements of Frank Moraes' assessment of Jinnah have been tested against Jinnah's role at the Round Table Conferences and have been found to be sound. Therefore the weight that can be given to all of Moraes' evidence is considerable. The assumption can be made that 'Jinnah had no purchase price' and 'humility was not one of his strong points' can be used with reasonable confidence when considering the role he played at the Conferences.

> A perceptive opening paragraph, and one that shows a clear understanding that the description of Jinnah may have been partly constructed from the role he played at the Round Table Conferences while at the same time suggesting that lack of evidence (date written and support for judgements) may affect the weight that could be placed on the source as evidence.

> A skilfully constructed paragraph, in which detailed knowledge of the first two Round Table Conferences is successfully used to test some of the statements in the source regarding Jinnah's role at the Conferences.

> A conclusion that returns to the question and considers, in a detailed and thoughtful way, the weight that can be given to the evidence provided by the source.

Verdict

This a strong answer because:

- it analyses the source material and clearly relates that analysis to the question

- it shows a deep awareness of context and relates it closely to the question
- it evaluates the evidence and reaches a substantiated conclusion as to the weight it will bear.

Paper 2: AS level sample answer with comments

Section B

These questions assess your understanding of the period in some depth. They will ask you about the content you learned about in the four key themes, but may not ask about more than one theme. For these questions remember to:

- give an analytical, not a descriptive, response
- support your points with evidence
- cover the whole time period specified in the question
- come to a substantiated judgement.

How accurate is it to say that the 'Quit India' campaign, launched by Congress in 1942, was the most important factor in the decision to grant India independence in 1947? (20 marks)

Average student answer

Congress launched the 'Quit India' campaign in August 1942 as a reaction to the failure of the Cripps mission to suggest anything new in their proposals for a new constitution for India. It was to be Gandhi's last satyagraha. 'Quit India' was shouted at every British man, woman and child, even at soldiers who were desperately trying to defend India against a possible Japanese invasion. Because Congress had taken months debating whether or not to support Gandhi's wish for the 'Quit India' satyagraha, the Raj had had plenty of time to prepare for it. The day after the satyagraha was announced, Gandhi, Nehru and other Congress leaders were thrown into prison, as were thousands of local activists. Gandhi had realised that this would happen and so urged every individual to take responsibility themselves for their actions. There was no one to lead the 'Quit India' satyagraha and mass rioting and killings swept India. The aim was to make India ungovernable.

There were many reasons why India was granted independence in 1947. The 'Quit India' campaign happened in the middle of the Second World War and at a time when it was by no means certain the Allies would win. Gandhi and Congress clearly hoped that to make India ungovernable would force the British to make promises for after the war. The war itself was another big factor in bringing about independence. Two and a half million Indians had fought on the side of the Allies and had helped bring about victory over the Axis powers. Once the war was over, the British government had to concentrate on rebuilding homes, dealing with demobilised soldiers and creating a peacetime economy while at the same time repaying war debts. The British government itself was the newly elected Labour government under Clement Attlee; before the war, Labour politicians had created some strong links with Congress.

> This paragraph gives information about the 'Quit India' campaign, but does not address the issues raised by the question. It needs to consider what is meant by 'the most important factor' by explaining exactly what would constitute 'important'. There is also too much descriptive writing, telling the story, rather than analysing it.

> This paragraph places the 'Quit India' campaign into the context of the Second World War and provides some accurate points of information. However, as well as asserting that the war was an important factor, it doesn't say how this impacted on the decision to grant Indian independence. The paragraph would be improved if this was developed and explained, and the importance, for Indian independence, of having a Labour government in Britain was explored.

There were other factors that were important, too. The British government sent a Cabinet mission to India to try to sort out constitutional problems, the main one being that the Muslim League was desperate to protect the interests of Muslims and wanted separate, protected, electorates while Congress wanted complete control. In the end, the Simla Conference failed to agree on any of the Cabinet Mission's proposals for a compromise. The confusion that followed ended up with Jinnah and the Muslim League calling for a universal hartal and urged Muslims to prepare for Direct Action, which effectively meant that riots and killings broke out throughout India from July 1946. This meant that something had to be done urgently. Mountbatten, who replaced Wavell as viceroy at the beginning of 1947, was expected to prepare the way for independence. Despite clear instructions from the British government that the subcontinent was to be kept as one unified country, Mountbatten failed to get Congress and the Muslim League to agree, and so with independence came Partition.

This paragraph identifies a range of factors but fails to explain why they were important in the process by which India became independent. In order to improve this paragraph, these factors need to be explored further and an explanation given as to how they impacted on the decision to grant India independence in 1947.

There were many factors that together brought about the decision to grant independence to India in August 1947. They ranged from the British government's inability to support an Indian Empire to the stubbornness of Congress and the Muslim League to agree a compromise earlier. The most important thing was that all the factors worked together to enable India to have independence in August 1947.

This is a weak concluding paragraph. It makes the link between a range of factors and the decision to grant independence to India in August 1947, but at no point does it answer the question, which requires a weighing of the relative importance of a range of factors. The conclusion should address the question of whether the 'Quit India' campaign was the most important factor directly and reach a supported judgement about which factor was most important.

Verdict

This is an average answer because:

- it does not give a direct and supportive answer to the question
- it does not fully explain the significance of the factors described
- it does not successfully establish criteria by which factors are to be judged important, although because a selection has been made, the criteria are implicit.

Use the feedback on this answer to rewrite it, making as may improvements as you can.

Paper 2: AS level sample answer with comments

Section B

These questions assess your understanding of the period in some depth. They will ask you about the content you learned about in the four key themes, but may not ask about more than one theme. For these questions, remember to:

- give an analytical, not a descriptive, response
- support your points with evidence
- cover the whole time period specified in the question
- come to a substantiated judgement.

How accurate is it to say that the 'Quit India' campaign, launched by Congress in 1942, was the most important factor in the decision to grant India independence in 1947? (20 marks)

Strong student answer

Many factors contributed to the decision to grant India independence in August 1947. In order to determine which was the most important, it is necessary to set out the criteria by which each will be assessed. Firstly, the factors that led directly to independence in 1947 need to be separated from those that only had an indirect impact, and then those factors that had a direct impact need to be evaluated as to whether they were necessary factors or whether independence would have happened in August 1947 without them.

It would seem, at first, that the 'Quit India' campaign was very powerful. Master-minded by Congress, the timing was critical: and was pitched to hit the Raj in August 1942 at a time when Britain was at its most vulnerable point in the Second World War. With Gandhi and Nehru's immediate imprisonment, the satyagraha was leaderless and the horrific round of riots and killings, attacks on Europeans and destruction of property seemed poised to make India ungovernable, distracting troops from the war effort as they struggled to gain control for the civil authorities. Nevertheless, the 'Quit India' movement was over within three months: Indian regiments had remained loyal to the Raj and the movement had never really gained the popular support throughout India that had been anticipated. Frightening though its immediate impact must have been, three months of riot and death could not be said to have led directly to the August 1947 independence. In many ways, the 'Quit India' campaign was similar to the Muslim League's Direct Action of July 1946. Although closer in time to August 1947, and as frightening as the 'Quit India' campaign, it should be seen more as a protest against the failure of the Cabinet mission, just as 'Quit India' was a protest against the failure of the Cripps mission.

The Second World War, dominating the period immediately before independence, cannot be ignored as a contributory factor to the August 1947 independence. The economic impact of the war, leaving Britain with debts of over £3bn, infrastructure to rebuild and industry to wind down to peacetime levels, coupled with thousands of demobilised soldiers returning home and looking for work, made any economic support for an empire in India virtually impossible. Coupled to this was the feeling in both India and Britain that India's contribution to the war effort, involving the provision of two and a half million men for military operations, needed rewarding – and that that reward was independence. The pressure for independence before 1939, with various attempts to arrive at a new constitutional framework, for example, the Round Table Conferences of 1930–32 and the Government of India Act of 1935, would probably eventually have arrived at some form of independence, but it was the catalyst of war that drove the decision to August 1947. This has to be an important factor, without which independence would not have happened when it did.

> This paragraph sets out the criteria by which the various factors are going to be assessed, and suggests an overall shape the argument will take.

> This paragraph assesses the stated factor – the Quit India campaign – against the criteria already determined and reaches the judgement that the campaign was not a necessary factor. The comparison with the Muslim Direct Action is thoughtful and demonstrates a confident familiarity with the subject matter.

> This paragraph focuses on the Second World War as a catalyst for independence in August 1947 and tests it against pre-determined criteria, deciding it was a necessary factor. The information provided is accurate and deployed analytically.

Linked closely with the war was the election, in Britain, of a Labour government in 1945. Prime minister Clement Attlee and those who were now members of the new government were known to be sympathetic to Indian independence and, in the 1930s, had made strong links with Congress leaders. This, coupled with the domestic economic situation, put early independence for India high on the government's agenda. What if a Conservative government had been elected? Churchill's opposition to Indian independence was well known, but he would have been faced with the same economic situation as Attlee was facing. It is highly likely that, given the pressure from the USA, he would have taken the same path – but more slowly. Coupled with the election of a Labour government and Attlee's perception that a speedy resolution of the Indian question was necessary, was the removal of Wavell as viceroy and the appointment of Mountbatten in his place early in 1947. This appointment, together with Attlee's announcement in the House of Commons that the transfer of power had to happen before 30 June 1948, provided the trigger that resulted in independence in August 1947.

> This paragraph discusses two linked factors – the election of a Labour government in Britain and the appointment of Mountbatten as viceroy – and tests these against the criteria, arriving at the judgement that they were the triggers that brought independence in August 1947. This is supported by evidence throughout. This, in turn, is tested against the possibility of a Labour government not being elected, and the trigger is confirmed.

A number of factors have been considered and weighed against criteria. The factor presented in the question was that of the Quit India campaign as being the most important factor. While it was clearly a contributory factor, it cannot be seen as the most important one: it focused the mind of the British on the problems of governing the subcontinent but did not of itself bring about the decision to grant independence. The conclusion has to be reached that the Second World War was pivotal in determining the urgency of the need to make a decision regarding Indian independence. It was the election of a Labour government in Britain and the appointment of Mountbatten that provided the triggers that ended with the August 1947 Indian Independence Act.

The conclusion answers the question directly. It summarises the main reasons why the Quit India campaign could not be seen as the most important factor in the decision to grant Indian independence in August 1947, explains why the Second World War was, and arrives at a judgement that has been supported throughout.

Verdict

This is a strong answer because:

- it focuses on the question throughout
- it sets criteria against which judgements can be made

- it selects relevant evidence to support the arguments being made.

Preparing for your A Level Paper 2 exam

Advance planning

1. Draw up a timetable for your revision and try to keep to it. Spread your timetable over a number of weeks, and aim to cover four or five topics each week.
2. Spend longer on topics which you have found difficult, and revise them several times.
3. Above all, do not try to limit your revision by attempting to 'question spot'. Try to be confident about all aspects of your Paper 2 work, because this will ensure that you have a choice of questions in Section B.

Paper 2 overview

AL Paper 2	Time: 1 hour 30 minutes	
Section A	Answer 1 compulsory source question	20 marks
Section B	Answer 1 question from a choice of 2	20 marks
	Total marks =	40 marks

You should familiarise yourself with the layout of the paper by looking at the examples published by Edexcel. The questions for each section are followed by eight pages of lined paper where you should write your answer.

Section A questions

This question asks you to assess two different types of contemporary sources totalling around 400 words, and will be in the form of 'How far could the historian make use of Sources 1 and 2 together to investigate…?' Your answer should evaluate both sources, considering their nature, origin and purpose, and you should use your own knowledge of the context of the sources to consider their value to the specific investigation. Remember, too, that in assessing their value, you must consider the two sources, taken together, as a set.

Section B questions

These questions ask you to reach a judgement on an aspect of the topic studied. The questions will have the form, for example, of 'How far…', 'To what extent…' or 'How accurate is it to say…'. The questions can deal with historical concepts such as cause, consequence, change, continuity, similarity, difference and significance. You should consider the issue raised in the question, then other relevant issues, and conclude with an overall judgement.

The timescale of the questions could be as short as a single year or even a single event (an example from Paper 2F.2 could be, 'How accurate is it to say that Lord Louis Mountbatten was responsible for the partition of the Indian subcontinent in 1947?'). The timescale could be longer depending on the historical event or process being examined, but questions are likely to be shorter than those set for Sections A and B in Paper 1.

Use of time

This is an issue which you should discuss with your teachers and fellow students, but here are some suggestions for you.

1. Do not write solidly for 45 minutes on each question. For Section A it is essential that you have a clear understanding of the content of each source, the points being made, and the nature, origin and purpose of each source. You might decide to spend up to ten minutes reading the sources and drawing up your plan, and 35 minutes writing your answer.
2. For Section B answers you should spend a few minutes working out what the question is asking you to do, and drawing up a plan of your answer before you begin to write your response.

Preparing for your A level exams

> ## Paper 2: A level sample answer with comments

Section A

You will need to read and analyse two sources and use them in tandem to assess how useful they are in investigating an issue. For these questions remember to:

- spend time, up to ten minutes, reading and identifying the arguments and evidence present in the sources; then make a plan to ensure that your response will be rooted in these sources
- use specific references from the sources
- deploy your own knowledge to develop points made in the sources and establish appropriate context
- come to a substantiated judgement.

Study Sources 3 and 4 (Chapter 2, pages 195–96) before you answer this question.

How far could the historian make use of Sources 3 and 4 to investigate the tensions between Congress and the Raj in the years 1920–22?

Explain your answer, using both sources, the information given about them and your own knowledge of the historical context. (20 marks)

Average student answer

There were serious tensions in India in the early 1920s. There was particular trouble in the Punjab where the Rowlatt Acts were continuing wartime restrictions in the hope of containing general unrest. Afraid that a large gathering of thousands of Indians in the administrative capital, Amritsar, was the beginning of a general uprising, the military under General Dyer killed hundreds of unarmed Indians. There was a British investigation and an Indian one.

Source 3 is part of a letter from Gandhi to the viceroy. He is respectful, but starts off by complaining about the British reaction to the Amritsar massacre. He says that the viceroy's treatment of the matter was 'light-hearted' and showed a 'shameful disregard' for the events and a 'callous disregard' for the feelings of the Indians. In saying this he is referring, not only to the actions of the military in Amritsar, but to the ways in which large sections of the British community in India supported General Dyer in what he did. Gandhi says he feels 'estranged' from the present government and can no longer offer them his loyal cooperation. This veiled threat is developed further where he says that the normal way of protest will not work any more and so he has to turn to other methods. He gives due notice that a new method of protest will be started: that of non-cooperation.

This is a weak opening because it simply provides the background to the sources without addressing the question. To improve the introduction, it needs to address the question and clarify what the issues are, both with the enquiry and with the sources.

This paragraph focuses on the first source and contextualises it. However, most is simple description or paraphrasing, where the quotes form part of that description. It does attempt to give some kind of reason for the tactic of non-cooperation, but this is taken from the source and the issue of tension is there only by implication. This paragraph would be improved if it was more analytical about Gandhi's motives and the source was placed in the context of his satyagraha philosophy. The issue of tension between Congress and the Raj should be more directly addressed with Source 4 being brought in to highlight this.

Source 4 is a response to Source 3 from the Government of India. This was effectively the body that governed India, consisting mainly of British officials with some Indian representation. Clearly they were not impressed. The document points out that non-cooperation is unconstitutional 'in that it has as its object the paralysis and subversion of the existing administration of the country', but goes on to say that, so far, the authorities have taken no action against the ring-leaders. This was because they didn't want to interfere with 'the liberty of speech' and 'the freedom of the press', and because they believed the leaders of the movement to be honest but misguided, trusting in the 'common sense of India' to reject non-cooperation.

Both these sources would be useful in an enquiry into the tensions between Congress and the Raj. The first source shows that Congress, as represented by Gandhi, is exasperated with the actions of the Raj, particularly in connection with the Amritsar massacre. They believe that the traditional methods of protest have no effect and so are going to try a new one: non-cooperation. Countering this, the government of India emphasise the tolerance towards protest they have exercised in the past, and will continue to exercise this believing that Congress's motives are honest but misguided. They do, however, hint heavily that this tolerance may not continue. So there are tensions here, now, and a very strong implication that they will continue into the future.

This paragraph provides an overview of the second source in much the same way as the preceding paragraph did for Source 3. It describes much of the content and uses quotes to support that description. There is some contextual knowledge but this is not related to the source in terms of its usefulness for the enquiry. The paragraph would be improved if the contextual information was developed and linked to the source, and if an explanation was added to show how this relates to the issue of tension between Congress and the Raj. Here, reference to source 3 would be helpful.

This final paragraph is an attempt to draw both the sources together in order to answer the question. It does little more than summarise them both and assert their utility. The paragraph would be much improved if a fuller explanation were provided as to why these sources are useful, and if the claims made by both authors were supported where appropriate with quotations from the sources.

Verdict

This is an average answer because:

- it does not make clear the connections between the sources and the enquiry
- it does not use the context of the sources to explain their value
- it does not explain the significance of the issues raised by the sources

- it does not explain why the provenance and purpose of the sources impact on judgements about their utility.

Use the feedback on this essay to rewrite it, making as many improvements as you can.

Paper 2: A level sample answer with comments

Section A

You will need to read and analyse two sources and use them in tandem to assess how useful they are in investigating an issue. For these questions remember to:

- spend time, up to ten minutes, reading and identifying the arguments and evidence present in the sources; then make a plan to ensure that your response will be rooted in these sources
- use specific references from the sources
- deploy your own knowledge to develop points made in the sources and establish appropriate context
- come to a substantiated judgement.

Study Sources 3 and 4 (Chapter 2, pages 195–96) before you answer this question.

How far could the historian make use of Sources 3 and 4 to investigate the tensions between Congress and the Raj in the years 1920–22?

Explain your answer, using both sources, the information given about them and your own knowledge of the historical context.
(20 marks)

Strong student answer

Tensions between the Raj and the Indians whom they governed were common, ranging from low level grumbling to outright riot. What would interest an historian in these two documents is that they come from a time just after the Amritsar Massacre when tensions were at a height. The support for General Dyer from large sections of British society in India appalled most Indians, whereas the Raj, intent on maintaining their administration, viewed the Punjab as a powder keg ready for rebellion. Together, the two sources, coming as they do from a pivotal moment in Indian history, shed light on past protests and riot and the ways in which the authorities dealt with them, and provide pointers for the future.

> This opening paragraph successfully contextualises the two sources, relating them clearly to the enquiry and to their value to a historian.

It was with some difficulty that Gandhi persuaded Congress to adopt his new approach to protest, moving away from 'the ordinary method of agitating by way of petitions, deputation and the like'. In reality, the 'ordinary way' as Gandhi well knew, was more than likely, as the protests against the partition of Bengal showed, to descend into riot and murder. It was this that had led him to develop his philosophy of satyagraha, the main tenet of which was that violence inhibits the individual's search for truth. It was a small step from here to believe that protest should take the form of non-violent, non-cooperation. Gandhi explains that this approach 'enables those who wish, to dissociate themselves from the Government' and clearly believes that it will lead the government 'to replace its steps and undo the wrongs committed', provided it is 'unattended by violence'. In reality, non-cooperation involved such things as a boycott of elections, a boycott of the law courts, the removal of children from schools and the withholding of taxes. Source 4, the Indian government's response, makes it clear that the authorities regard the campaign as being led by individuals 'some of whom may be motivated by honest, if misguided, motives'. But, having stated that non-cooperation was unconstitutional, the government statement goes on to say that action will only be taken against those who have gone beyond the limits set by the organisers. In this, the historian could conclude either that the authorities were either somewhat at a loss as to how to deal with this new approach or that they were trying to adopt a conciliatory approach but in any case were falling back on making the maintenance of law and order their main priority.

> This paragraph explains the philosophy underpinning the new approach taken by Gandhi and describes some practicalities of non-cooperation. It introduces Source 4 in a comparison and finishes by showing how the historian could draw conclusions from the reaction of the authorities.

This apparently conciliatory approach that Source 4 appears to be taking could be a reaction to the report of the Hunter Commission, published in May 1920. Finding that there was no justification for the actions taken by General Dyer in initiating the massacre at Amritsar, the Raj could now be seen, from this source, to be doing all that was possible not to alienate Indian opinion especially where no violence was involved in any proposed protest. This is in the face of what seems to be a deliberately provocative approach taken by Gandhi, accusing the viceroy of a 'light hearted approach', 'ignorance of the Punjab events' and a 'callous disregard of the feelings of Indians'. Angered though Congress and Gandhi were by the reaction of the British in India to the actions taken by General Dyer in April 1919, they must have known that the Hunter Commission report failed to back the actions of the military on that day. The historian might conclude that Source 3 would be useful in demonstrating Gandhi's declared motive in starting non-cooperation and Source 4 the Indian government's reaction to it, whereas experimenting with the practical implementation of philosophy of satyagraha may have been a truer motive.

> This paragraph provides the context for Source 4 and speculates about the impact the information given could have had on the Indian government's reaction. It brings in Source 3 and suggests more than one motive for Gandhi's wish to start a non-cooperation protest.

It is important to appreciate that there are some issues of which the historian should be aware when using these sources in conjunction to assess tensions between Congress and the Raj in the years 1920–22. Source 3 was written to warn the viceroy of future action, and to provide justification for it. Source 4, on the other hand, is a resolution, published as an official document in the Gazette of India, two months after non-cooperation had got under way. It is therefore a statement of what had not been done in the face of provocation – leaders had not been arrested, for example, and a warning that local governments in the provinces had been instructed to take action against specific offences. The Raj was prepared for the satyagraha to end in violence, which it did.

> This conclusion highlights the difference between the two documents, of which the historian should be aware, and shows how they can be used together to assess the motives for analysing the change in the nature of tension.

Verdict

This is a strong response because:

- it makes clear connections between the sources and the question

- it uses the context of the sources to show how they relate to each other and to the question
- it sustains focus and develops a clear and balanced argument.

Paper 2: A level sample answer with comments

Section B

These questions assess your understanding of the period in some depth. They will ask you about the content you learned about in the four key themes, but may not ask about more than one theme. For these questions remember to:

- give an analytical, not a descriptive, response
- support your points with evidence
- cover the whole time period specified in the question
- come to a substantiated judgement.

To what extent was Gandhi responsible for the failure of the London-based Round Table Conferences held in the years 1930–32? (20 marks)

Average student answer

The Government of India Act of 1919 set up a system of dyarchy to govern the provinces of India. It also stated that, after ten years of trying out this system, a commission would be appointed to determine whether or not it was working. Accordingly, the Simon Commission – a group of seven British MPs – was sent out to India in 1928. Interestingly, one of its members was Clement Attlee, who was to be the Labour prime minister when India was granted independence in 1947. Indian people in general were outraged that their future was to be determined by a group of people that didn't include a single Indian. Members of both Congress and the Muslim League boycotted the Commission. One of the recommendations made by the Commission was that a Conference should be held, to which all interested parties were to be invited, and that this would make recommendations regarding a future constitution of India.

The first Round Table Conference opened in London in November 1930. It was chaired by the British Prime Minister, Ramsay MacDonald. The British side of the debate was represented by sixteen delegates from the three political parties: Conservative, Liberal and Labour. All the fifty-eight Indian delegates were selected by the viceroy and represented all shades of Indian opinion, with one exception. That exception was Congress, and was a large omission. However, Gandhi and Nehru were in prison as a result of the violence that had accompanied the salt satyagraha and Congress was unable, or unwilling, to provide any other representatives. The Indian princes sent a delegation of sixteen. The conference made good progress. They agreed that India would be run as a dominion that would take the form of a federation that would include the princely states, and, importantly, that Indians would participate in all levels of government. However, it must be remembered that Congress, which was becoming the vehicle whereby Hindu opinion was voiced, was not represented and so did not agree to the outcome.

> This introductory paragraph sets out accurately the background to the Round Table Conferences, but fails to address the demands of the question. The paragraph would be improved if it dealt directly with the demands of the question. It needs to determine who the main participants were and how it could be possible for one individual to be responsible for the collective failure of three conferences.

> This paragraph describes what happened at the first Round Table Conference. There is an implicit link to the question in that it does comment that Congress was not represented and so did not agree to the outcome, but the question of responsibility is not addressed. The paragraph would be improved if there was a deeper analytical look at the significance of the absence of Congress and how this relates to the question.

It was clearly going to be important that Congress was represented at the conferences. Viceroy Irwin and Gandhi were anxious to find a way out of the dilemma whereby Gandhi could represent Congress at the second Round Table Conference and Irwin could not be seen to be negotiating with a man who had been imprisoned by the Raj as a terrorist. The way out was the Gandhi–Irwin Pact of 1931. Gandhi agreed to suspend the non-cooperation campaign and to attend the second London conference; Irwin agreed to release some 19,000 Congress supporters from gaol and to return confiscated property to its owners.

The second Round Table Conference was held in London between September and December 1931. There was a similar mix of delegates to the first conference, but this time with the inclusion of Gandhi, representing Congress. It was this that made all the difference. Gandhi made what seemed like a huge mistake in claiming to speak for all Indians, not just Hindus. This angered and offended just about all the other Indians who were there to speak for their own particular groups and interests. All the usual arguments began again about the desirability, or otherwise, of having separate electorates for the different communities, and if it was desirable, how it would be organised. The Untouchables were particularly angry that Gandhi claimed to speak for them and Gandhi was particularly worried that the princes might form an alliance with the Muslims and so shift the balance of the arguments being made. In the end, no agreement could be reached. Although a third conference was held at the end of 1932, it was doomed before it started. Only forty-six delegates attended; Congress did not send any delegates, nor did the British Labour party. There were some useful discussions on finance and the role of the princely states, but no viable conclusions were reached.

There were no more conferences and in the end the British government imposed the 1935 Government of India Act. Responsibility for the failure of the conferences must rest fairly and squarely on Gandhi. Without him, the first conference made good progress and there were plenty of agreements between the various Indian groupings and between them and the British government. The British government tried to be reasonable throughout, for example, by organising the Gandhi–Irwin pact. It was Gandhi's presence at the second conference that caused it to collapse because of his insistence on speaking for all Indians and his opposition to India having dominion status.

This paragraph describes what happened to enable Gandhi to attend the second conference, implying cooperation between the Raj and Gandhi himself. This paragraph would be improved if a more analytical approach was used and the significance of the roles, and hence responsibility, of the two men was explored.

This paragraph accurately covers the events of the second conference and begins to analyse the role of Gandhi, thus making a tentative link to the question. This paragraph could be improved if the roles of Gandhi and the other groups had been teased out and analysed. Responsibility for the collapse of the conference should be addressed.

This conclusion returns to the question and places responsibility for the failure of the conferences on Gandhi, and provides some evidence in support. It would be improved had the roles of the other main players been analysed throughout the essay and the conclusion weighed the evidence, reaching a judgement about where responsibility lay.

Verdict

This is an average answer because:

- it does not give a direct and supported answer to the question
- mostly accurate and relevant knowledge is included but it is not used to demonstrate an understanding of the demands of the question

- many descriptive passages are used and the attempts to provide an analysis of the main features and issues are very limited.

Use the feedback on this answer to rewrite it, making as may improvements as you can.

Paper 2: A level sample answer with comments

Section B

These questions assess your understanding of the period in some depth. They will ask you about the content you learned about in the four key themes, but may not ask about more than one theme. For these questions remember to:

- give an analytical, not a descriptive, response
- support your points with evidence
- cover the whole time period specified in the question
- come to a substantiated judgement.

To what extent was Gandhi responsible for the failure of the London-based Round Table Conferences held in the years 1930–32? (20 marks)

Strong student answer

The London-based Round Table Conferences, organised as a result of the report from the Simon Commission of 1928, presented an opportunity for all interested parties to work out the basis of a new constitution for India. The main interested parties here were the British government and its representatives in India, Congress and the Muslim League. Of course, other parties were affected and were represented, for example, the Indian princes, but it would be the aims, aspirations and actions of the main players that would determine the outcome of the conferences.

This introductory paragraph addresses the question directly and gives a clear indication as to the approach that will be taken in the answer.

The Round Table Conferences were set up under the aegis of the British government, who at the time had responsibility for the governance of India. It was the British government who had instigated the Simon Commission's investigation into the workings of the 1919 Government of India Act, and who had responded to the recommendations in the Commission's report by setting up the Conferences. The first Conference (November 1930–January 1931) was held in the House of Lords and was chaired by the British prime minister, Ramsay MacDonald, leader of the Labour party. Delegations from the other two British political parties were led by Sir Samuel Hoare (Conservative) and Lord Reading (Liberal). From the start, the government and other British political parties showed commitment to the process. They worked with Indian representatives selected by the viceroy and with the Indian princes to hammer out proposals with which they all agreed. India would be run as a dominion that took the form of a federation including the princely states, and that Indians would be present in all areas of government. The absence of Congress, with their leaders Gandhi and Nehru in prison along with thousands of other Congress members as a result of the violence that followed the salt satyagraha, presented a considerable problem. Viceroy Irwin did not want to be seen to be negotiating with a convicted terrorist and so an arrangement was made whereby Gandhi, Nehru and 19,000 imprisoned Congress members would be released from prison and confiscated property returned, in return for a cessation of non-cooperation and terrorist activities and an undertaking that Gandhi would attend the second London conference. Here, again, the British government was working hard to enable the conferences to work. However, during the second Round Table Conference, the British representatives were pushed into a difficult situation. Lobbied by Gandhi to treat him as the sole representative of all Indians, and by Jinnah to support the concept of separate electorates against the express demands of Congress, the British were unable to reconcile the two factions, and the conference ended in confusion. By the time of the third conference, the political situation in Britain had undergone considerable change. In August 1931, the first Labour government had been voted out and replaced with a Tory-dominated coalition. Indeed, Ramsay MacDonald had lost the support of his own party and Labour, the main drivers of Indian constitutional change from the British side, sent no representatives to the conference. Facing a depression, unemployment and the collapse of the economy, there was little enthusiasm for a third conference and it collapsed in confusion. How

A carefully argued paragraph that sets out the role of the British government and associated politicians and considers the weight of responsibility that can be attached to them for the failure of the conferences.

much responsibility for the collapse of the conferences could be placed at the door of Britain? Certainly, they could carry responsibility for the failure of the third conference. However, given the intransigence of Jinnah and Gandhi at the second, it was not likely that the third would have succeeded, anyway. It must not be forgotten that the British worked tirelessly at the end of the 1920s and the early 1930s to set up the conferences and ensure their smooth working.

The British government, as has been shown, worked hard to enable Gandhi to attend the second Round Table Conference. There was considerable hope that progress could be made, building on the foundations of discussions held the previous year. This was not to be. Gandhi insisted that he not only represented Congress, but claimed that Congress alone represented political India. In doing this, it seems he intended to signify the unity of the Indian nationalist movement. In making this claim, he appeared to have been unaware of what the reaction of other delegates would be, and particularly the reaction of the Untouchables and of Jinnah and the Muslim League representatives. There was a second problem, too. Back in India, Gandhi had supported purna swaraj; there was no way in which he could accept dominion status for India, as had been agreed at the first Round Table Conference. Gandhi tried to persuade MacDonald to settle the separate electorates problem, believing that the government was exaggerating the difficulty so that they could retain power once the conference collapsed. It was not surprising that the second conference could not build on the progress made at the first. How much of this was the responsibility of Gandhi? His position on separate electorates and dominion status was known before the conference; his refusal to compromise can have come as no surprise. The only way forward would have been for all non-Hindu Indians to abandon their demand for separate electorates and to abandon, too, their preferred way forward, which was to agree to dominion status. This was not going to happen.

> This paragraph analyses the role of Gandhi at the second Round Table Conference, contextualises his approach with some sound background knowledge, and links back to the question by considering his responsibility for its failure.

Jinnah was one of the ten Muslim delegates to attend the first Round Table Conference and was part of the negotiations that agreed to press for a federated India with Dominion status and Indian representation at every level of government. Interestingly, no mention was made of the separate electorates issue. This came to the fore at the second conference, and drew Jinnah and Gandhi into direct confrontation. Jinnah worked tirelessly behind the scenes with the various different groups, trying to gain concessions regarding the type and nature of separate electorates in an attempt to arrive at an agreed position. To what extent can Jinnah be blamed for the collapse of the Round Table Conferences? His bargaining techniques at the second conference certainly drew criticism, but this alone could not cause the conference to collapse. Indeed, there had been no such problem at the first conference. At the second, Jinnah was clearly trying to counter the stance of Gandhi.

> This paragraph describes and analyses Jinnah's role at the first and second Round Table Conferences and considers the weight of responsibility that he should bear.

It is clear that responsibility for the failure of the Round Table Conferences lies mainly with the British, Gandhi and Jinnah. The British government, having worked so hard to get Gandhi to the second conference, were clearly taken by surprise by his insistence on speaking for all Indians and his rejection of the outcome of the first conference; Gandhi's insistence on speaking for all Indians was clearly an enormous stumbling block during negotiations, as was the problem of separate electorates. Insofar as Jinnah was concerned, the issue of separate electorates was a similar stumbling block. All the main players were in some ways responsible for the failure of the conferences, and probably the real reason was their failure to undertake sufficient preliminary work so that the issue of separate electorates did not become such an insurmountable problem.

> A clear concluding paragraph that sums up the situation and answers the question by apportioning blame for the failure of the Round Table Conferences.

Verdict

This is a strong answer because:

- it is analytical in structure and approach, presenting a well-organised argument
- it focuses on the key issues throughout and explores them by a sustained analysis of the key issues
- sufficient knowledge is deployed to demonstrate an understanding of the of the demands and conceptual focus of the question
- valid criteria are established in order to answer the question directly and specifically.

South Africa, 1948–94: from apartheid state to 'rainbow nation'

Between 1948 and 1994, South Africa was ruled by the Afrikaner National Party, a political movement representing only part of the white population. During this period they imposed policies collectively known as 'apartheid' which defined people by race and gave different racial groups different rights. They also pursued a system of authoritarian rule in order to protect white power and Afrikaner identity. Apartheid drew on earlier segregationist policies, which discriminated against those who were not white, but contained important new elements.

From the outset Afrikaner power was opposed, especially by the growing African nationalist movement. Opposition forces were by no means united. The African National Congress (ANC), founded in 1912, split in 1959 and was banned in 1960. Most key leaders were imprisoned on Robben Island or fled into exile. Not until 1990 was it able to operate legally within South Africa again. In its place, Black Consciousness flourished among students and youths, trade unions developed among black workers and a Zulu ethnic movement emerged. In the 1980s, a United Democratic Front tried to capture the ethos of the old ANC. It was supported at a distance by the ANC in exile. At times, both Indian and Coloured South Africans had their own congresses and political groupings. The white opposition was divided between the parliamentary United Party and liberal groups. Those who confronted the Afrikaner state most vehemently suffered repression, banning, imprisonment and even death; but there was considerable scope for organisation. Understanding South Africa's opposition – and its many different strands – is essential to any study of the history of the period, and also to post-apartheid outcomes.

South Africa is not a large or populous country compared to India, the USA or Russia. In 1994 the population was about 40 million (compared with 55 million in the UK) and in 2014 was about 54 million (64 million in the UK). Yet it has been important to Great Britain. Britain fought one of its longest and most difficult colonial wars to conquer the Boer republics of South Africa in 1899–1902. South Africa was a key source of gold, most of it sent to London. And South Africa has been a touchstone for issues of race in the 20th century.

Apartheid was the subject of intense international debate. While the South African government was generally supported, or at least tolerated, by western powers, the anti-apartheid movement was based in Britain. South Africa's settlement of 1994, which brought together implacably opposed groups, was a triumph for negotiation. In the process, Nelson Mandela emerged as a global leader.

Studying South Africa

Studying a country like South Africa requires us to step outside our British experiences. There may be some familiar points and these are valuable hooks on which to hang our analysis: connections through English-speaking people, British colonialism and sport; the anti-apartheid struggle and the iconic figure of Mandela. The country is now largely an urban, consumer-oriented society easily recognisable to our nation of shopkeepers (and shoppers). Yet its people have a very different background and we need to make an imaginative leap into their world. History, especially the history of unfamiliar places, is an adventure not least for this reason.

1948 – National Party campaigns on apartheid and wins election; D. F. Malan becomes prime minister	1948
1952 – African National Congress leads Defiance Campaign	1952
1958 – H. F. Verwoerd becomes prime minister	1958
1962-63 – ANC leadership including Nelson Mandela captured and imprisoned	1962-63
1968 – Black Consciousness movement starts	1968
1975 – Relaunch of Zulu political and cultural movement Inkatha	1975
1978 – P. W. Botha becomes prime minister (later president), reform era begins	1978
1980s – Rapid urban growth as pass laws challenged and removed	1980s
1985 – COSATU trade union federation launched	1985
1990 – ANC and other movements unbanned; Nelson Mandela and other black leaders released	1990
1992 – Boipatong massacre, talks suspended; Violence in black townships	1992

1950-53	1950-53 – Major early apartheid legislation passed: Population Registration, Group Areas, Prevention of Illegal Squatting, Separate Representation of Voters, Urban Areas, Bantu Authorities, Bantu Education
1955	1955 – Freedom Charter
1960-61	1960-61 – South Africa becomes a Republic outside the British Commonwealth ANC and PAC banned
1966	1966 – Verwoerd assassinated B. J. Vorster becomes prime minister
1973	1973 – Durban Strikes Independent trade unions founded
1976	1976 – Soweto school students protest Transkei becomes first independent homeland
1983	1983 – Tri-cameral parliament and new presidential system United Democratic Front launched
1984-86	1984-86 – Insurrection and State of Emergency
1989	1989 – F. W. de Klerk becomes president
1991	1991 – Convention for a Democratic South Africa meets to negotiate transition
1994	1994 – Non-racial democratic elections ANC wins 62 percent of vote and Mandela becomes president

SOURCE 1

Former South African presidents, Nelson Mandela and F. W. de Klerk, with their Nobel Prizes for Peace, 10 December 1993.

Studying history is also a process of discovery. It offers potential to learn about a past world, different cultures, politics and societies. In South Africa, for example, we need to explore why ideas about race became so important. We also need to understand that around 1948, at the beginning of the apartheid period, roughly 75 percent of black African people were still rooted in rural lives as peasant farmers and farm workers. They spoke African languages and their lives were still partly shaped by older practices linked with the land, the homesteads, and with African customs and beliefs.

A huge amount has been written about South Africa and there is no shortage of evidence in published books and articles, autobiographies, photographs and documentaries. Using such books is an exciting journey and they also enable us to understand that no two authors share the same view of history. Each writes from their point of view, incorporating their moral and political outlook – consciously and unconsciously. This textbook distils some of the evidence and provides an interpretation of it.

South African history is highly contentious and strongly debated. The chapters that follow introduce a few of those debates and discuss different interpretations. They also touch on Nelson Mandela's life and politics and encourage you to read more about him in biographies, which are largely sympathetic, as well as his own lengthy autobiography. Mandela stands for important universal values and as a beacon against racism and intolerance. Yet it is important to remember that he was a loyal member of a political movement, the African National Congress, with its own view of South African society.

History is an adventure of the mind and can help us to discover and clarify the values we think most important, to cross social and geographical boundaries, to find new ideas, new experiences and new places.

2b.1 The response to apartheid, c1948–59

KEY QUESTIONS

- What was life like in South Africa in 1948?
- Why was the National Party victorious in the elections of 1948?
- How was apartheid codified and implemented, 1948–59?
- How did African nationalism develop, 1948–59?

INTRODUCTION

Between 1948 and 1994 the white, largely Afrikaner, National Party ruled South Africa. Successive governments aimed to ensure white domination, by defining racial and ethnic categories more rigorously than before and by allocating rights on the basis of these definitions. Black South Africans were subjected to tighter controls in respect of their political rights, their movement and the spaces that they could occupy. Ultimately, at their most ambitious, apartheid planners envisaged 11 states in South Africa, including ten for the separately defined African ethnic groups in the country.

How did white South Africans arrive at so extreme a solution?

This chapter begins in 1948, the year that the National Party won the election that brought them into office. A cornerstone of their policies was a dramatic social engineering project, known by the Afrikaans term '**apartheid**'. The first section of this chapter outlines the social and historical background, describing the composition of South African society and highlighting some existing political trends, to show how there was already a foundation for the architects of apartheid to build on. The second section explores how such an idea was able to find acceptance among the electorate. The third section examines early apartheid legislation, from laws strengthening the concept of race to those controlling the allocation of space. The chapter concludes with a look at how black South Africans responded to these challenges.

The apartheid plan was still very new in 1948, with many aspects of the project still open to debate. Politicians such as Hendrik Verwoerd were instrumental in forging the blueprint that would slowly come to fruition over the course of the 1950s and 1960s. Others vehemently opposed any designs for the separate development of racially defined groups within South Africa. New black leaders, such as Nelson Mandela and Oliver Tambo, entered into political opposition with fresh ideas and approaches that drew inspiration from successful campaigns in India, the United States and anti-colonial movements around the world.

The changes that took place during the 1950s completely shifted the social and political landscape, and set the stage for 40 years of struggle over the future of South Africa.

KEY TERM

Apartheid
An Afrikaans word meaning 'the state of being apart' or, literally, 'apartness'. Operating in South Africa, it was a system of racial segregation enforced by the dominant National Party governments.

1899–1902 – South African War between Britain and Afrikaner republics

1948 – National Party wins election, campaigning on apartheid platform

D. F. Malan becomes prime minister

United Nations issues Universal Declaration of Human Rights

1950 – Population Registration Act, Suppression of Communism Act, Group Areas Act

1952 – Pass Laws Act

African National Congress leads Defiance Campaign

| 1899–1902 | 1910 | 1948 | 1949 | 1950 | 1951 | 1952 |

1910 – Union unites Cape Colony, Natal, Orange Free State and Transvaal as Union of South Africa

1949 – Voortrekker Monument opened

African National Congress Youth League's Programme of Action adopted

Prohibition of Mixed Marriages Act passed

1951 – Prevention of Illegal Squatting Act, Separate Representation of Voters Act, Bantu Authorities Act

Walter Sisulu (1912–2003), Oliver Tambo (1917–1993) and Nelson Mandela (1918–2013)

Walter Sisulu, Oliver Tambo and Nelson Mandela, three key leaders of the ANC, all hailed from the Xhosa speaking regions of the Eastern Cape. They were all on the first executive committee of the ANC Youth League in the 1940s, and each shared a vision of a more radical, mass-based approach to liberation politics.

Sisulu was born in 1912. After leaving school at 15 he travelled to Johannesburg looking for work to help support his family. This period gave him some valuable experience that helped to forge his political identity: he worked at a gold mine, and met Clements Kadalie (the head of the Industrial and Commercial Workers Union). Finally he settled in Johannesburg where he became active in the Orlando Civic Association in Soweto, organising strikes and boycotts, before joining the ANC in 1940. After working at an estate agency, Sisulu set up his own real estate business, which evolved into an important destination for young radicals to discuss ideas and strategy. Sisulu became a mentor for several younger activists, including both Mandela and Tambo. Sisulu was a member of the South African Communist Party and developed a reputation for building bridges between political organisations.

Oliver Tambo was born in 1917. He attended missionary schools where he excelled, winning a scholarship to Fort Hare university, where he studied physics and mathematics. During his time at Fort Hare Tambo met Mandela and they both became involved themselves in student protests that led to their expulsion from the university. Tambo returned home and taught at a local high school before moving to Johannesburg. In 1942 he met Sisulu and agreed that the ANC required reinvigoration. He trained as a lawyer and set up offices with Mandela, whilst at the same time holding several elected positions within the ANC.

Mandela was born in 1918. In his teens, he became a ward at the Thembu Royal house and became familiar with the operation of African chieftaincy in the Transkeian Territories. Like Tambo, Mandela was educated at missionary schools before attending Fort Hare university. After his expulsion for his role in student protests, Mandela ran away to Johannesburg where he got a job as a mine security officer. Soon afterwards he met Sisulu, who encouraged him to join the ANC. After training as a lawyer he went into practice with Tambo.

From 1948, Sisulu, Tambo and Mandela became increasingly prominent figures in the ANC. Mandela and Sisulu were imprisoned together on Robben Island after the Rivonia Trial in 1964, while Tambo went abroad to lead the ANC in exile.

WHAT WAS LIFE LIKE IN SOUTH AFRICA IN 1948?

Race

When the National Party came to power in 1948, South Africans were already categorised in four racial groups: whites (or Europeans); Africans (or 'Natives' in the official language of the time); Coloured people; and Indians (or 'Asiatics'). They were counted in this way in censuses and these racial identities shaped key rights, such as their right to vote. It is difficult to describe South Africa's people without using the racial categories that became so entrenched, especially in the apartheid period. But we should try to do so because identities were more diverse, and multi-faceted, than these racial labels suggest.

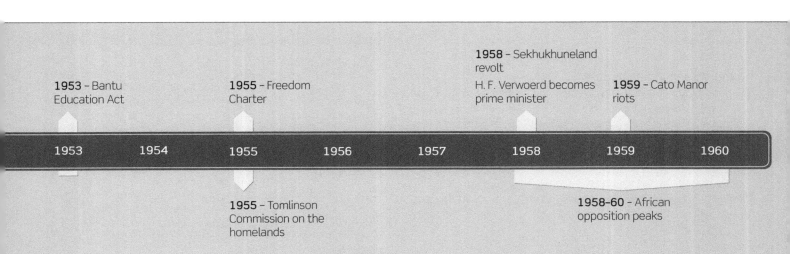

1953 – Bantu Education Act

1955 – Freedom Charter

1958 – Sekhukhuneland revolt

H. F. Verwoerd becomes prime minister

1959 – Cato Manor riots

1953 1954 1955 1956 1957 1958 1959 1960

1955 – Tomlinson Commission on the homelands

1958–60 – African opposition peaks

Africans

The original inhabitants of South Africa were San or Bushmen people, hunters and gatherers with a profound knowledge of the natural world who left a rich legacy of rock paintings. Around 2,000 years ago black African farming people migrated into the region. Some San adopted their livestock farming practices and became identified as Khoikhoi. Africans gradually formed larger and more powerful chiefdoms or kingdoms and many of the San and Khoikhoi were displaced or absorbed into these units.

In the first half of the 19th century the Zulu became the largest African kingdom. This process left a deep legacy. Although Britain conquered the Zulu kingdom between 1878 and 1885, Zulu identity remained a significant force in the 20th century and Zulu language was the most widely spoken first language in this linguistically diverse country. The Sotho, Pedi, Tswana, Xhosa, Mpondo and Thembu also became centralised states in the 19th century with distinct languages and cultures. Although they shared many social features, the difference between the Zulu and Tswana language, for example, was as wide as between French and Spanish. A major challenge facing African nationalists during the 20th century was to create a common African identity.

By the time of the 1951 census, at the beginning of the apartheid era, Africans numbered 8.5 million.

Whites

Those classed as whites in South Africa came from a variety of backgrounds. The two most dominant groups were the Afrikaners and those of British descent. South Africa's Afrikaner population, roughly 60 percent of whites or around 1.6 million in the 1951 census, was descended largely from the Dutch, French and German settlers who came to South Africa in the 17th and 18th centuries. During the 19th century, they achieved some shared identity and spoke a local version of Dutch but remained politically divided between those in the British Cape and those in two separate **Boer** republics in the interior.

The whites who spoke English as a first language in South Africa were descendants of British colonists who arrived after the Cape became part of the British Empire in 1806. Irish, Jewish and other minorities joined them, especially after the discovery of valuable minerals in the late 19th century. Numbering about one million in the 1951 census, they tended to be wealthier and more highly educated than other groups, and dominated business and the professions.

Coloured and Indian people

By the beginning of the 20th century most of those in the Cape Colony who were not classed as white or African were called Coloured. They included the descendants of the San and Khoikhoi, of slaves brought from South East Asia and other parts of Africa by the Dutch, and of relationships between whites, Africans and others. Coloured people numbered roughly 1.1 million people in 1951, nine percent of the population. They were largely based in the Western Cape and were mostly **Afrikaans**-speaking.

For fifty years, settlers in Natal imported indentured Indians, many of them Tamils from south India, to work on the sugar plantations. Some Indian traders, largely from Gujarat, were also allowed into the country; they formed another significant minority, three percent of the total population, mostly based in Natal and Transvaal, who became English-speaking.

Segregation and discrimination

Racial discrimination existed in South Africa before 1948. In handing South Africa self-government in 1910, Britain did not require whites to share power with black people despite the fact that whites were a minority of the population. Members of Parliament (MPs) and most of the electorate were white, though a small exception was made for Coloured and African people in the old Cape Colony who could meet certain property and educational qualifications. After 1930 white women were able to vote but Africans were completely disenfranchised in 1936. The 1948 election was therefore almost entirely decided by the minority white population, then about 21 percent of the total. Before 1948 most African people in the cities were forced to live in separate areas known as townships. This policy, called segregation, entrenched discrimination before the apartheid era.

Urbanisation, industrialisation and townships

Urbanisation and industrialisation

Gold was discovered in the Witwatersrand area of Transvaal (also known as 'the Rand') in 1886. The city of Johannesburg quickly grew up to provide services to the mines. The mines needed workers and the city grew from nothing in 1886 to around 100,000 by 1900. Some of the mineworkers were African migrants from rural areas, who temporarily lived in huge, male-only compounds. By 1948 the population of Johannesburg was approaching a million people with African numbers outstripping whites for the first time. Although other cities also experienced population growth, none matched the rapid increases seen in Johannesburg.

The gold mines were the motor of the South African industrial economy for the first few decades of the 20th century but gradually industry diversified from gold to producing textiles, clothing, food, chemicals and some machinery. The state developed a major iron and steel industry (ISCOR) and generated electricity, largely from coal. During the Second World War, it was difficult to import goods from Britain so South African industry further expanded to supply the home market. With around 180,000 white men serving in the armed forces employment opportunities increased for blacks. When the war was over, black and white people competed for jobs and space in the cities.

While the majority of African people lived in the countryside, the majority of whites lived in towns and cities. There were many poor white Afrikaners who had not been able to make a living on the land. The 'poor white problem' became a particular concern to government and to churches, both determined that whites should be kept as a separate and distinct group. Many were absorbed into expanding state employment, especially on the railways.

Poor whites had the vote and the nationalists appealed to their sense of insecurity with the promise of protected employment in government service and factories. Whites wished to avoid the ignominy of working under black supervision, or doing the kind of manual labour that was denigrated as black people's work.

Townships

Governments and municipal councils prior to 1948 had been keen to maintain cities as predominantly white spaces but the influx of migrants was too large. This led to the establishment of informal or shack settlements. In response, areas outside the cities, called townships, were hastily allocated to house black migrants. The biggest of these, 20 kilometres to the south west of Johannesburg, later became Soweto (an acronym for South Western Townships). The land rights of residents in these townships were tenuous, and health care and sanitation were often poor.

Rural society

South Africa had long been primarily a rural country with the majority of people living on the land and in small towns. By 1948 land ownership was deeply divided by race and by class. Whites owned over 80 percent of the land in the country, most of it as large farms held as private property. It is important to stress, however, that the land was white-owned but not inhabited only by whites. Black people were in the majority on most farms, where they worked as wage labourers and tenants. White owners and black staff lived together on the same land and worked with each other on a daily basis but generally in a strict hierarchy. In the rural areas, whites were able to maintain racial authority – sometimes called *baaskap* (bosshood) – more effectively. Whites did not usually do manual labour. Black workers looked after the livestock, drove the ox teams that still often ploughed the land, weeded the

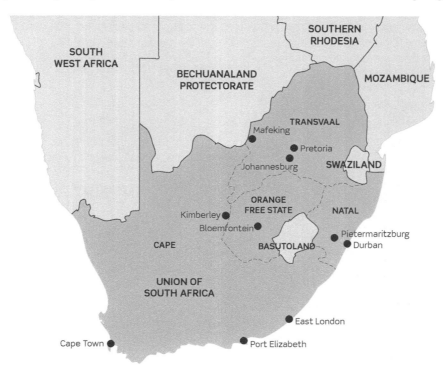

Figure 1.1: South Africa in 1948.

fields and harvested the maize (known locally as mealies) that was South Africa's staple crop. They cut cane on the sugar plantations of Natal, and picked grapes in the vineyards of the Western Cape. Wool from merino sheep was the most valuable product, much of it exported to Britain where it fed the textile industries of the northern cities such as Bradford and Leeds.

Most African rural communities either lived on the white-owned farms or on **reserves**. Life in the African reserves had changed greatly over the previous hundred years. Missionaries from a wide range of Christian denominations found their way to every corner of South Africa and Christianity had become the dominant religion. African independent churches vied for congregations with the older mission denominations, such as Catholics and Methodists. Missionaries had started schools, and many of the most successful educational establishments were in the rural areas. Taxation had forced African people into the cash economy, and consumer tastes had grown. The great majority of people wore modern clothes and even traditional dress was made from imported textiles. Women worked particularly hard and were the lynchpin of the rural economy: it was their duty to fetch water from streams (carried in buckets on their heads); to collect firewood; and to do much of the domestic and agricultural labour. On average, those in the African reserves produced about 50 percent of their food in 1948, though this varied greatly between homesteads. Men often became migrant labourers working in the cities.

It is important to emphasise that rural society was not divorced from the cities, nor from the processes of social change. But the economy of the reserves was essentially a peasant economy, supplemented by essential income from migrant workers, with very little local industry and few employment opportunities.

Afrikaner culture and politics

Between 1899 and 1902, Britain fought the South African (or Anglo-Boer) War against the two Afrikaner republics, to cement control of the region. This left a bitter legacy. After Union in 1910, politicians such as Jan Smuts attempted to unify the white population within the British Empire. Yet some Afrikaners remained resentful about the lingering imperial presence and about the role of English-speaking South Africans in supporting Britain. Smuts was opposed by J. B. M. Hertzog, who founded an exclusively Afrikaner National Party in 1913. Hertzog won the election of 1924 and secured major gains for Afrikaners, including bilingualism in the national civil service, Afrikaans rather than Dutch as a national language (alongside English), and compulsory teaching of both languages in white schools. But the Great Depression so undermined him that, in 1934, he and Smuts joined together in a United Party – in effect a government of national unity. D. F. Malan split from Hertzog to re-found the National Party. Afrikaners were deeply divided by these two political directions.

The 1920s and 1930s saw an increased pride in Afrikaner culture. In 1938 the centenary of the **Great Trek** was commemorated by a dramatic and popular re-enactment. Afrikaans bibles, Christian tracts, newspapers, books and magazines such as the *Huisgenoot* ('housemate') poured off the presses. Afrikaners were creating new communities in the towns, often in largely Afrikaans-speaking

suburbs. Studies of nationalism emphasise the importance of media and symbols that create an 'imagined community' even when old ways of life have disintegrated.

In 1948 the Afrikaner vote had become significant. It was the culmination of a rising Afrikaner sense of themselves as a people (or *volk*), with their own language, religion and culture. This sense of self could be appealed to by politicians.

The influence of Britain

In 1948 South Africa was a self-governing part of the British Empire. A Governor-General, based in Cape Town, was the representative of the British monarch, whilst a parliament sat in imitation of the system found in Westminster. People of British descent made up about 40 percent of the white population. British investors dominated mines and industries; English was the joint official language; and British sports, such as rugby, football and cricket, were popular across South Africa. These strong cultural and political links had encouraged South Africa to join in the Second World War on the side of Britain. But, by 1948, these ties to Britain provoked strong reactions among some Afrikaners, who were attracted by the possibility of a republican government.

KEY TERMS

Reserves
The heartlands of the old African kingdoms, protected for occupation by Africans in two key Acts of the white parliament: the Natives Land Act of 1913 and the Native Trust and Land Act of 1936. Although these measures stopped whites from taking the reserved land, they were also deeply discriminatory in that they forbade Africans from purchasing private land outside of the reserves. On the reserves African people held land in customary or communal tenure, meaning that land was controlled by the community rather than by an individual or organisation. Each married man had the right to a rural residential plot and also, if there was sufficient land locally, to fields for growing grain, usually maize. African families in the reserves kept a small number of livestock, usually cattle and goats, for milk and meat.

Great Trek
In the 1830s about one quarter of Afrikaners left the Cape Colony, which was then under British control, to establish independent republics in the interior of South Africa known as the Transvaal and the Orange Free State.

ACTIVITY
CONSOLIDATION

Life in South Africa

  1 a) List the advantages and disadvantages of being a poor, urban white person in South Africa in 1948.

   b) Do the same for a wealthy, urban black person in South Africa in 1948.

  You will need to think about the social, economic and political opportunities available to people at that time.

  2 On balance, who do you think had it better in South Africa in 1948, poor whites or wealthy blacks?

WHY WAS THE NATIONAL PARTY VICTORIOUS IN 1948?

The 1948 election was a major turning point – a moment when white politics and the parliamentary system mattered deeply. In 1938, on the eve of the Second World War, Afrikaner votes were almost equally split between the two parties: the United Party under Smuts and Hertzog; and the National Party under Malan. In 1939, parliament voted to support the British war effort and Hertzog resigned from the United Party, leaving Smuts in control. Malan's National Party mobilised Afrikaners behind their vision for a future South Africa. Central to their message was an idea of how Afrikaners could survive in such a culturally mixed society.

The growth of Afrikaner nationalism

The idea of Afrikaners as a *volk* (Afrikaans for 'people'), with a distinct identity separate from other South Africans, gained increasing political currency after 1939. A society of carefully chosen Afrikaner white men, called the **Broederbond** (band of brothers), provided ideological direction in favour of a Christian, nationalist, republican outlook. The Broederbond had initiated an Economic Movement to promote Afrikaner business so that nationalist interests were advanced on this, as well as political and cultural fronts.

KEY TERM

Broederbond
A secret and exclusively male Afrikaner Calvinist organisation, dedicated to the advancement of Afrikaner interests. In the years 1948–94, many important people in South African political life, including all leaders of the government, were members of the Broederbond. It sought to promote its members and supporters in state, church, education and other organisations.

Religious institutions were also at the heart of nationalism. Many Afrikaners professed a deeply held Christianity, mostly in the Calvinist Dutch Reformed Churches, which supported the idea of an autonomous *volk*. In their reckoning, black and white people played different parts in God's plan. The boundaries between the races, therefore, had to be maintained and strengthened, to avoid racial impurity that would sabotage divine designs. Inter-marrying between races was a key concern for many voters in 1948.

Many Afrikaner nationalists adamantly opposed the decision to go to war in 1939. In part this reflected their unease about fighting for the British Empire. Some Afrikaners also had fascist sympathies. A mass anti-war movement, the *Ossewabrandwag* (Ox Wagon Guard), was launched by Afrikaners and at its peak claimed 300,000 members. Uniformed militias staged mass rallies and formed shooting associations. Critics compared them with the Nazis and a few of the leaders were clearly influenced by German fascism. After the war, most joined Malan's National Party.

By 1948 the Afrikaner influence within society, as well as its political potential, was sufficient to provide a formidable base upon which to contest the election.

International context

Before the Second World War legal discrimination and segregation by race or colour was common in many countries, including British colonies. In the United States the southern states had 'Jim Crow' laws (Jim Crow was a disparaging term for black people), which restricted registration for the franchise and segregated schools and public facilities. South Africa's early segregationist legislation was harsh but not so fundamentally different from that experienced elsewhere.

Following the Second World War (1939–45), the major powers increasingly articulated a concern for universal human rights. The war against fascism and the legacy of the Holocaust underpinned a slowly growing consensus that all people had a right to self-determination and to basic human rights. The colonial empires were gradually dismantled in the two decades from 1947 when India became independent. In this context, South Africa's policies jarred.

However, in the United States, racial division remained a significant issue. While the civil rights movement gathered pace, segregation still had its supporters in the southern states in the 1940s and 1950s. White South Africans were convinced that they stood for Western, Christian and anti-Communist values and they found some international sympathy.

The 1948 election

In the glow of allied victory over fascism, and with Smuts playing a major role in the formation of the United Nations, his United Party government flirted with more liberal policies. Smuts was no liberal himself and in many respects shared the racial attitudes of his Afrikaner peers. But he was a pragmatist. If industry needed more black workers, he was prepared to facilitate this. His Minister of Health, Henry Gluckman, advocated an urgent expansion of health services in the country, along the lines of the British National Health Service, which would serve both white and black (though in segregated hospitals).

For many insecure whites these developments were threatening and in the 1948 election campaign Afrikaner nationalists harnessed everyday racism in promoting fear of the *swart gevaar* (black danger). They opposed *oorstrooming* (flooding) of African people into the cities where they competed for jobs with whites. Malan's National Party still had its major support in the countryside, and here they were able to play to a related concern, that African workers were streaming to the cities and creating a labour shortage for farmers. Nationalists stirred fears of sexual relations across the colour line – in their eyes the inevitable outcome of threats to the racial hierarchy. They accused Smuts and his Party, conservative though they were, of being sympathetic to black people, and failing to control these political dangers. In Afrikaner nationalist hands, the language of race, never absent in South African politics, was becoming more intense.

Voters listening to Jan Smuts speak at Sanderton before he lost his seat in the 1948 election.

Despite these forces swinging in his favour, Malan still only won about 38 percent of the vote in 1948. Smuts's United Party won 49 percent (with the rest going to minority parties). However the Westminster constituency system used in South Africa gave Malan his opportunity. Smuts's United Party won big majorities in many English-speaking urban seats. Most of the rural constituencies had fewer voters and Malan won many of these by small majorities.

Together with the small Afrikaner Party, Malan secured a narrow victory.

Malan and his supporters defined nationhood in cultural as well as racial terms: language and religion were central to them. They were fiercely anti-imperial, in favour of a republic, and their rhetoric attacked the old enemies: Britain, **mining capital** and Smuts – because he was an Afrikaner who worked for the British. Afrikaners were also blinded by their own sense of injustice. They had no capacity to see or understand the injustice that they and the British had meted out to Africans. They pictured themselves as bringing Christianity and civilisation to Africa.

KEY TERM

Mining capital

The gold mines were run by large corporations, headed up by wealthy individuals, commonly known as Randlords (after the Witwatersrand where the gold was mined). Many historians use the term 'mining capital' to refer collectively to mine owners and their financial backers in Europe and South Africa. They were able to shape much legislation in their favour and generally backed the United Party.

Results of the 1948 election in South Africa. Although Smuts won a larger percentage of the votes it was Malan, with more National Party MPs, who formed a government and became prime minister.

Party	Leader	Votes	Votes %
National Party	Malan	401,834	37.7
United	Smuts	524,230	49.2
Afrikaner	Havenga	41,885	3.9
Labour	Christie	27,360	2.6
Independents	–	70,662	6.6

THINKING HISTORICALLY Cause and consequence (6a)

Seeing things differently

Different times and different places have different sets of ideas. Beliefs about how the world works, how human societies should be governed or the best way to achieve economic prosperity, can all be radically different from our own. It is important for the historian to take into account these different attitudes and be aware of the dangers of judging them against modern ideas.

Segregation

Successive South African governments introduced legislation to keep the races apart. The National Party came into power in 1948 with the intention of introducing an abundance of new laws to further keep people apart.

Answer the following questions:

1 What attitudes do you think had given rise to the notion that segregation was preferable to inclusion?

2 If they had known how events would progress, e.g. that after 40 years or so apartheid would come to an end, do you think those who voted for the National Party in 1948 would have changed their attitude?

3 South African attitudes to race in the 1940s were different from current attitudes in the UK.

   a) Are there any other ways in which South African attitudes differed dramatically from those that are current in the UK now?

   b) Why do you think that they are different?

4 How important is it for historians to deal with events in the context of the beliefs and values of people in the past as well as seeing them as part of a greater pattern?

The 1948 election

Work in groups.

1 a) List as many reasons you can think of for the success of Malan and the National Party in the 1948 elections.

  b) Now put those reasons in order of importance.

  c) Compare your priorities with those of the other groups. Can you agree on a 'top three'?

2 What was the significance of Afrikaner nationalism for the outcome of the 1948 elections? Write a paragraph in explanation.

HOW WAS APARTHEID CODIFIED AND IMPLEMENTED, 1948–59?

The basic principle behind apartheid was that racially defined groups within South African society deserved tailor-made facilities. Ultimately, it was believed that via separate development all racial groups would progress. Yet apartheid was more complex than that. In 1948 the plan was not yet clearly thought through and there were many questions over how apartheid could be successfully instituted.

There was already a raft of legislation in place upon which the National Party could build. There were laws removing blacks from the franchise and limiting where they could buy land. The National Party had great respect for the law, and it was through parliament that they began fully to instigate apartheid. However, this was a gradual process rather than an instant measure. While some laws, such as that against sexual relations across the colour line, could be passed simply and quickly, there were others that required a greater understanding of the fine distinctions within South African society. As a result, commissions were formed to investigate the best ways to advance the apartheid agenda.

Strengthening the National Party

Given the narrowness of their victory, the single-mindedness of the National Party was striking. An early priority was to stay in political power. In 1949, six members of parliament were added for whites in Namibia (then South West Africa) where the Nationalists had support. South Africa ruled this former German colony as a mandate under the United Nations but it was becoming a fifth province.

The Nationalists' approach to Coloured people was indicative of the centrality of race in their thinking. Coloured people, Afrikaans- and English-speaking, shared much cultural history with whites, yet rather than pursuing them as allies, the Nationalists were determined that they should become a separate racial category, with their own institutions and spaces. This was urgent because they still had a vote in the central parliamentary elections and they voted overwhelmingly for the United Party.

South Africa largely followed the United Kingdom in that a simple majority in parliament could enact new legislation. There were

very few checks and balances. However, the Coloured vote in the Cape was specially protected and required a two-thirds majority of parliament to change it. The Nationalists passed the 1951 Separate Representation of Voters Act, removing the remaining Coloured vote, with a simple majority (i.e. less than two thirds of the vote) and seemed to be abandoning political constraint.

A bitter constitutional battle was fought out in the courts and the judges initially accepted that the Act was invalid without a two-thirds majority. The government then appointed new Afrikaner judges to get their way and packed the Senate with sympathetic Afrikaners. The Nationalists had shown that they were prepared to act ruthlessly to secure their political power. But they were also winning wider support among whites. In 1953, the National Party increased its vote from little more than 400,000 to nearly 600,000 and narrowly outpolled the United Party – though it still did not win a majority of the white vote. By now it had clearly won the support of the great majority of Afrikaners. The National Party gained a comfortable majority of parliamentary seats that was sustained for the next 40 years. Afrikaners moved quickly to capture the state including senior positions in the military, police and bureaucracy. During the 1950s, state employment increased from 482,000 to 799,000 – the majority of the new employees were Afrikaners.

EXTEND YOUR KNOWLEDGE

Afrikaner Nationalism and Fascism compared

Some South Africans compared the National Party to fascists. The African National Congress (ANC), including Nelson Mandela, used the term fascist in the 1950s and Brian Bunting, a white Communist, published a book entitled *The Rise of the South African Reich*. They pointed to similarities in racial ideology, to the centrality of ideas about the *volk* (people) rather than individual rights, and to movements such as the *Ossewabrandwag*, which seemed to support Germany in the war. The Nationalists were also deeply opposed to socialism and communism and they gradually suppressed political opposition. To this we could add a political self-assurance that bordered on megalomania.

There were, however, two major differences between Afrikaner Nationalism and the fascist parties in Europe:

- Although Afrikaners saw race as central to human difference, they did not advocate genocide of other races.

- A certain degree of political opposition was tolerated.

Apartheid laws

Afrikaner Nationalist politicians did not have a complete blueprint for apartheid when they took power. Hardliners looked for tighter separation of the races, while pragmatists recognised that the economy required African workers in large numbers. White rural communities had backed the National Party but they had no intention of dispensing with black workers on the farms. Apartheid literally meant separateness but the policy did not entail complete segregation between black and white. It was also aimed at cementing a hierarchy of rights and power.

National Party planners convinced themselves that the aspirations of African people could be met by a new political strategy:

while rights were diminished in the white-controlled areas of South Africa, they would be beneficiaries of increasingly fuller rights in self-governing territories. In nationalist terminology, the emphasis was increasingly laid on 'separate development' rather than apartheid. Over the long term, this implied increasing self-government for African people in demarcated areas based around the old reserves.

Hendrik Verwoerd

Hendrik Verwoerd, as Minister of Native Affairs (1950–58) and as prime minister (1958–66), coordinated the apartheid project. His department was increasingly staffed by sympathetic Afrikaners, pouring out of the Afrikaans universities. Verwoerd came to Native Affairs with an academic's analytical approach and a propagandist's conviction. He and his staff convinced themselves that African people still essentially saw themselves as tribal people with their primary identity and loyalty to their old kingdom or chiefdom, their language and their specific rural zone. The first step was the Bantu Authorities Act (1951), which aimed to harness the institution of African chieftaincy and ensure that such traditional authorities were appointed throughout the African reserves. The aim was to place responsibility for local government onto a conservative rural African leadership that would cooperate with the government.

In 1959, Verwoerd passed the Promotion of Bantu Self-Government Act, which envisaged self-governing African units, based around the traditional authorities. This was the truly ambitious side of apartheid. It gave Afrikaners hope that African people themselves would welcome separate development, not only from whites, but in separate ethnically defined units. Verwoerd began to argue that he was offering a form of internal decolonisation, similar to that which the European powers were pursuing in Africa as a whole.

EXTEND YOUR KNOWLEDGE

Hendrik Verwoerd (1901–66)

The credit for imagining the full implications of separate development or 'separate freedoms' is often given to Hendrik Verwoerd. He was not an Afrikaner by birth but became one by conviction. Born in 1901 in the Netherlands, his religious father emigrated to Cape Town in 1903. Verwoerd went to school in a small Free State town amid Afrikaners and then studied at Stellenbosch University. He excelled in theology, did a doctorate in psychology, and postdoctoral work in Germany and the United States, before becoming the youthful head of a new department of Sociology at Stellenbosch. His main concern at this time was the poor white problem.

The National Party was deeply concerned by Afrikaner poverty and Verwoerd increasingly devoted himself to Afrikaner nationalist politics. In 1937, he became editor of the new *Transvaler* newspaper, launched to win support amongst Afrikaners in that province. In 1948 he moved into parliament and became head of the Native Affairs Ministry, the potential key to apartheid. He also, with Afrikaner intellectuals, moved away from racist terms to more neutral and obscure language, including terms like 'separate development' and 'separate nations'.

In 1958 he became prime minister of South Africa, giving him greater powers to implement apartheid. In 1966 he was assassinated in the House of Assembly in Cape Town.

SOURCE 3 Prime Minister D. F. Malan speaking to a visiting African delegation in the early 1950s.

My government has no intention of depriving you of your rights. *Nothing will be taken from you without giving you something better in its place...* What you want is a rehabilitation of your own national lives, not competition and intermixture and equality with the white man in his particular part of the country.

SOURCE 4 Part of a speech given by M. C. de Wet Nel, Minister of Bantu Administration and Development, introducing the Promotion of Bantu Self-Government Bill to the South African parliament in 1959.

God has given a divine task and calling to every *volk* [people] in the world, which dare not be denied or destroyed by anyone... Every *volk* in the world, of whatever race or colour, just like every individual, has the inherent right to live and develop. Every *volk* is entitled to the right of self-preservation... It is our deep conviction that the personal and national ideals of every ethnic group can best be developed within its own national community. Only then will other groups feel they are not being endangered... This is the philosophical basis of the policy of Apartheid... To our *volk* this is not a mere abstraction which hangs in the air. *It is a divine task which has to be implemented and fulfilled systematically.*

Race laws

Afrikaner nationalists were deeply concerned about sex between white and black people. For some this grew from religious belief; for others it was a racial feeling. Historically many settlers, especially men, had sexual relations with black women – usually their slaves and their servants. Thus some white families had an element of black ancestry and some black families an element of white. The National Party vowed to stop such relations and immediately enacted the Mixed Marriage Act (1949) and the Immorality Act (1950), which prohibited both marriage and sex by whites across defined racial boundaries.

For race to have clearer meaning and to form the basis for new legislation, it needed to be defined more sharply. The Population Registration Act (1950) was the cornerstone for this attempt to assign everyone in South Africa one of four race categories. A national register recorded this and identity documents were issued so that race could be public knowledge. The nationalists used increasingly sophisticated technology to define and monitor the boundaries of race.

Group Areas Acts

Within the cities a series of Group Areas Acts (from 1950) had a particularly damaging effect on black communities. Typically the African 'locations' or townships were built by municipalities on the edge of town. In every city, however, there remained areas close to the centre where Coloured, Indian and African people owned houses, shops or businesses or where properties owned by whites were let out to black people. Group Areas provided the powers to eradicate these so that the central parts of the cities and the closer suburbs would be very largely in white hands. Three such zones were Sophiatown in Johannesburg, District Six in Cape Town and Cato Manor in Durban; they have become symbols of the cruelties of Group Areas and urban dispossession, as well as resistance to it.

Racist terminology

In the 1940s and 1950s whites did not use the words 'black' or 'African' and were unashamed in using pejorative terms for black people. In everyday language, they used words loaded with historic prejudice. More politely, they used the official term 'Native'. In the United States, 'Native American' became an acceptable term, chosen by indigenous people to replace the term 'Indian', because it affirmed that they were the first inhabitants of the land. In South Africa, Africans rejected 'Native' because whites instilled it with pejorative meaning. When speaking English, African people preferred to use the term 'African'. This was difficult for Afrikaners to translate into Afrikaans because they had already taken a version of the word for themselves.

So successful was the African rejection of Native that the National Party itself gave up the term soon after coming to office. In the 1950s they tried to win acceptance for the term 'Bantu' instead. This was derived from the Xhosa and Zulu word for people, *abantu*. Tied as it was to apartheid terminology, Bantu had a relatively short life as both black people and white liberals rejected it. Whites also used terms such as non-whites (*nie-blankes*) or non-Europeans. As black activists later pointed out, whites did not use non-blacks for themselves. By the 1980s, under pressure from black opinion, non-white faded away in favour of black even in official use.

SOURCE

5 Families being forcibly removed from their homes in Sophiatown, Johannesburg, under Group Areas legislation in February 1955.

KEY TERMS

African National Congress (ANC)
A national liberation movement. It was formed in 1912 to unite the African people and to become a pressure group for political, social and economic change. In the 1950s, in response to the rise of extreme Afrikaner nationalism and attacks on the rights of black people, it was transformed into a mass movement.

Drum **magazine**
Started as *African Drum* in 1951, founded by a former test cricketer Bob Crisp and ex-RAF pilot Jim Bailey. It originally had a paternalistic attitude to black Africans, emphasising their tribal origins. However, under the editorship of Anthony Sampson (1951–55) and then Sylvester Stein (1955–58) it quickly re-focused on the growing townships and became in many ways their mouthpiece.

Sophiatown

Sophiatown in Johannesburg was first to fall victim to apartheid planners. Unusually, Africans were able to hold private land there and it was not subject to the same restrictive regulations as municipal townships. Racially mixed, though predominantly African, Sophiatown housed nearly 60,000 people, with wealthier professionals, such as former **African National Congress (ANC)** President Dr Xuma, living side by side with poor tenants in squalid back-yard shacks. Relatively close to the city centre, it attracted writers and journalists working for ***Drum* magazine**. They recorded the hard-drinking, racy urban lifestyle for which it became celebrated – a venue for African politics, new music, **shebeens** (illegal bars), **tsotsis** (youthful street criminals) and gangsters. Sophiatown's reputation made it an early target for the nationalists. Planning for its removal began in 1950 and within six years, despite intense resistance, it was largely gone – bulldozed into rubble.

SOURCE 6

Can Themba, a journalist for *Drum* magazine, writing in *Requiem for Sophiatown*.

Here is the odd thing about Sophiatown. I have long been inured to the ravages wreaked upon Sophiatown. I see its wrecks daily, and through many of its passages that have made such handy short-cuts for me, I have frequently stepped gingerly over the tricky rubble. Inside of me, I have long stopped arguing the injustice, the vindictiveness, the strong arm authority of which prostrate Sophiatown is a conspicuous symbol. But the sheer fact of Sophiatown's removal has intimidated me.

Moreover, so much has gone – veritable institutions. Fatty of the Thirty-nine Steps. Now that was a great shebeen! It was in Good Street. You walked up a flight of steps, the structure looked dingy as if it would crash down with you any moment. You opened a door and walked into a dazzle of bright electric light, contemporary furniture and massive Fatty. She was a legend. Gay, friendly, coquettish, always ready to sell you a drink. And that mama had everything: whisky, brandy, gin, beer, wine – the lot. Sometimes she could even supply cigars. But now that house is flattened. I'm told that in Meadowlands she has lost the zest for the game. She has even tried to look for work in town. Ghastly.

SOURCE 7

Trevor Huddleston, recalling the sight of people being removed from Sophiatown in his book *Naught for your Comfort*, published in 1956. Trevor Huddleston was an English Anglican priest who worked as a missionary in Sophiatown. In 1978 he was made Archbishop of the Indian Ocean.

On the broad belt of grass between the European suburb of Westdene and Sophiatown (we called that strip 'the Colour Bar') a whole fleet of Army lorries was drawn up: a grim sight against the grey, watery sky. Lining the whole street were thousands of police, both white and black, the former armed with rifles and revolvers, the latter with the usual assegai [a wooden spear]. A few Sten guns were in position at various points. A V.I.P. car, containing the Commissioner of Police and a mobile wireless unit (which we afterwards discovered was in hourly contact with the minister in Cape Town) patrolled up and down.

'Where are they beginning?'

'In the yard opposite the bus station, at the bottom of Toby Street... Let's go.'

It was a fantastic sight. It looked more like a film set for an 'atmospheric' Italian film than anything real. In the yard, military lorries were drawn up. Already they were piled high with the pathetic possessions which had come from the row of rooms in the background. A rusty kitchen stove; a few blackened pots and pans; a wicker chair; mattresses belching out their coir [fibrous material from the husk of a coconut] stuffing; bundles of heaven-knows-what; and people, soaked, all soaked to the skin by the drenching rain.

Durban

Durban, South Africa's third largest city, housed about 450,000 people in 1951. Roughly a third were Indian, a third African and a third white. Indians owned substantial amounts of private property near the city centre and in Cato Manor, an area adjacent to white suburbs. Up to the 1940s Cato Manor had a semi-rural feel. Indians let land out to African tenants who built shacks and houses. Indians grew vegetables for family use and sale. But during

the 1940s, the land filled quickly with shack settlements. In 1949, African people attacked Indians who they felt were exploiting them as landlords and storekeepers. One hundred and forty-two people were killed and over 1,000 injured during riots and subsequent police suppression.

In the 1950s, the government imposed the Group Areas Act. By 1965 the shacks had largely been removed from Cato Manor and tens of thousands of African people sent to far-flung townships. About 41,000 Indian people had also been moved from the central areas, mostly to an exclusively Indian zone south of the city. It was deliberately sited as a buffer between the white suburbs and the large African township of Umlazi. Unlike the African townships, private property ownership was permitted in Indian suburbs. Apartheid worked partly by making such small gradations of rights between the different racially defined groups.

District Six

District Six was a multi-racial, largely Coloured, residential and business area near the heart of Cape Town city centre. Group Areas was enforced there a little later, from 1966. About 60,000 people were forcibly removed and resettled on the distant Cape flats; the District Six buildings were bulldozed. Not only communities but also a valuable inner city architectural heritage were destroyed in order to implement a racial ideology. Some of the site is still a vacant wasteland.

ACTIVITY
CONSOLIDATION

Apartheid laws

1 Read Sources 3 and 4. What can you learn from these sources about the South African government's apartheid policy?

2 Set up a debate about the implementation of the Group Areas Act. One group should construct an argument for the forcible implementation of the Act and the second group oppose it.

Pass laws and education

Control of space and the pass laws

Apartheid enforced a hierarchy of rights and attempted to separate public space. The typical symbols of apartheid, such as the reservation of benches, buses and beaches, were later called petty apartheid. South Africa in the apartheid era was filled with signs proclaiming such spatial separation by race. The Reservation of Separate Amenities Act (1953) entrenched and broadened this principle and made it legal to provide separate facilities for black people which were not of an equal quality.

A central element in Afrikaner nationalist policy was the focus on reducing African migration to the cities. This was known as influx control. The National Party wanted to make cities a zone where whites would be protected from cheap black labour, from African protest and from crime. Before 1948, pass laws forced all African men travelling outside the reserves to carry a pass. The National Party built on this legislation with the Natives Abolition of Passes Act (1952). This Act did not really abolish passes, but instead required a reference book for each African adult, which they had

SOURCE 8

Signs like this were commonly seen beside roadways in Johannesburg during the 1950s.

SOURCE 9

H. J. Simons, South African academic and activist, on the operation of the magistrates' courts in pass cases in 1955.

Much of the magistrate's practical experience is gained before his elevation to the bench, as a clerk of the court and as a public prosecutor. In these capacities he develops a tendency to view the machinery of justice from the standpoint of the prosecution, and, through an intimate association with the police, to acquire a dangerous confidence of their infallibility. To accept the evidence of a police witness against the uncorroborated version of the accused is very nearly a principle in the magistrates' courts. The bias, however, is not only acquired through earlier training; it is also a product of the conditions under which the courts function. Overwhelmed in the larger centres by a great mass of petty cases, most of them undefended, the courts are constrained to adopt the most expeditious methods for completing the roll. Unable for want of time to investigate cases thoroughly, they assume tacitly that the police would not have laid a charge if the accused was not guilty of some offence.

SOURCE 10

Flyer issued by the Federation of South African Women and the ANC Women's League, 13 June 1957.

Repeal the Pass Laws!

Who knows better than any African woman what it means to have a husband who must carry a pass? The women know that:

- PASSES MEAN PRISON;
- PASSES MEAN BROKEN HOMES;
- PASSES MEAN SUFFERING AND MISERY FOR EVERY AFRICAN FAMILY IN OUR COUNTRY;
- PASSES ARE JUST ANOTHER WAY IN WHICH THE GOVERNMENT MAKES SLAVES OF THE AFRICANS;
- PASSES MEAN HUNGER AND UNEMPLOYMENT;
- PASSES ARE AN INSULT.

And the Government is trying to force our WOMEN to carry passes too.

---

to present on demand. This established their identity and whether they had a right to be in urban areas. This right was specified in the Urban Areas Act (1952), which gave urban rights to a minority of African people who had been born in town, worked for ten years in town, or lived there for 15 years; these rights were extended to their children. This proved to be a significant category of people and differentiated urban insiders from the majority of Africans who were forced to keep their homes in the reserves. Despite their racial thinking, the government recognised the need for a relatively stable urban workforce in industries and services. African families, however, were not able to buy houses or land in the cities, even in the townships. This hugely undermined their security and their capacity to accumulate family wealth.

The pass laws were ferociously policed and these measures were deeply resented by African people. They were frequently stopped and searched in the streets and in their houses. In 1956, reference books were extended to women. Even those who had rights to stay in the city were victims of constant harassment. Passes caused abrasive encounters with the police on a daily basis. Most white police were Afrikaners. They were seen as brutal and cruel (and some cultivated this image) but black policemen were also essential to this system.

Convictions under the pass laws increased from 164,324 in 1952 to 384,497 in 1962. In these years, about three million people were turned into criminals for trying to exercise their right to move and pass cases clogged up the magistrates' courts.

AS Level Exam-Style Question Section A

Study Source 9 before you answer this question.

Why is Source 9 valuable to the historian for an enquiry into the operation of the pass laws in South Africa in the 1950s?

Explain your answer, using the source, the information given about it and your own knowledge of the historical context. (8 marks)

Tip

Think about the position of the author when writing this piece: are they providing information or giving an opinion?

Many of the books on South Africa assume that the pass laws were effective; the fact that they were so central an issue for the African political opposition seems to prove the point. But one of the most remarkable features of the early years of Nationalist rule was that pass laws failed to keep Africans out of the cities. The African urban population of South Africa rose from 1.8 million people in 1946 to 3.5 million in 1960: more than the whole of the white population. African rights in the cities were diminished but many people were prepared to brave the pass laws in order to find work and other opportunities. Some white employers, including householders with domestic servants, colluded with workers to bypass influx control.

Education

Education became an important issue for the apartheid lawmakers. Prior to 1948 education for Africans was for the most part racially segregated. A relatively small number of black South Africans attended elite mission schools (including many of those who became politically prominent) where they were offered a broad syllabus, taught sometimes by white as well as black teachers. The great bulk of schools, however, funded by the government and usually managed by local churches, gave only a basic primary education. Only 24 percent of black South Africans were recorded as literate in the 1951 census, a clear indication that the school system was inadequate for mass education.

The Bantu Education Act of 1953 was therefore passed in order to extend education to African children, but also to segregate the content of education. It brought schools for African students directly under state control. The government was also particularly concerned about the numbers of children joining urban gangs rather than attending school. Fear of these *tsotsis* (street youths) was one of the major drivers behind the expansion of education.

The Bantu Education Act has been heavily criticised in analyses of apartheid in South Africa, yet it did greatly increase educational opportunities at all levels. National Party policy makers believed that expanding African education was essential for the changing labour market. The need for African workers in the factories and shops was increasing rapidly and unskilled workers were no longer adequate to meet this demand. Some degree of literacy, numeracy and linguistic ability in English and Afrikaans was seen as valuable in building an efficient black workforce. Henrik Verwoerd, the Minister of Native Affairs, believed that the state should provide basic education for a greater number of people, but that Bantu education should prepare African people for only limited roles and opportunities after school.

Before the 1950s, black students who finished their matric (the final school-leaving certificate) and came from wealthier backgrounds had been able to attend the University of Fort Hare and a few hundred were admitted to the Universities of Cape Town and Witwatersrand (in Johannesburg) where they received the same training as white students. Fort Hare had become a key centre of black student opposition to apartheid and in 1959 the Extension of University Education Act was passed to ensure that Fort Hare came under government control. The Act also planned for the full segregation by race of the largely white English-language universities and set out plans for new universities for African ethnic groups and other racially defined minorities (see Chapter 3).

SOURCE
11

Statement by Hendrik Verwoerd, the Minister of Native Affairs, in 1954.

My department's policy is that education should stand with both feet in the reserves and have its roots in the spirit and being of Bantu society... The Bantu must be guided to serve his own community in all respects. There is no place for him in the European community above the level of certain forms of labour. Within his own community, however, all doors are open. For that reason it is of no avail for him to receive training which has as its aim absorption in the European community, where he cannot be absorbed. Up till now he has been subjected to a school system which drew him away from his own community and practically misled him by showing him the green pastures of the European but still did not allow him to graze there. This attitude is not only uneconomic because money is spent on education which has no specific aim, but it is even dishonest to continue with it.

ACTIVITY
WRITING

Analyse Source 11, a statement by Henrik Verwoerd on 'separate development'.

1 Identify any words or phrases you don't understand and research their meanings.

2 Identify words and phrases that are used to create an argument for separate development. How convincing an argument does Verwoerd make for separate development? How could he have been more convincing? Write a short paragraph explaining his views, using quotes from the extract to back up your points.

The Tomlinson Report and the Bantustans

In the post-war era, state planning and modernisation were seen in Western countries as the route to solving social and economic problems. It was a period of economic growth and optimism in much of the world. The Afrikaner nationalists benefited hugely from global growth in the first two decades of power. This helped in part to shape their view of the potential of the African **homelands**, also known as Bantustans. A commission was appointed under Professor F. R. Tomlinson, an agricultural economist at the University of Stellenbosch, which reported in 1955. Tomlinson believed that the economic development of the former reserves had to be at the heart of apartheid. He wrote that 'there is no midway between the two poles of ultimate total integration and ultimate separate development of the two groups' and 'sustained development of the Bantu Areas on a large scale' was 'the germinal point'.

The Tomlinson Commission believed that the Bantustans could be transformed by massive state investment of over £100 million (roughly equivalent to £7 billion in 2015). Among its many recommendations, three stand out:

- Tomlinson believed that agricultural plots had become too small and that migrant labour undermined agriculture. He recommended creating a class of full-time farmers by increasing the size of plot and turning communal into private tenure. This implied pushing many families off the land, in order to create bigger 'economic units' for farming.

- Tomlinson advocated major funding for rural industries.

- He believed that private enterprise, both South African and foreign, should be encouraged to invest in these areas.

For all his commitment to separate development, Verwoerd rejected these key recommendations. He did not believe that white South Africans would support expenditure on this scale. Nor did he want to create subsidised industries that might compete with urban white businesses. He felt that the 'Bantu' should develop 'at their own pace' and would not allow outside investment.

Verwoerd also realised that, if landholdings were enlarged, millions of Africans would potentially lose land and have little option but to migrate to the cities to find work. This would directly undermine a central tenet of apartheid. Moreover, he and his advisors believed that private land ownership would undermine the power of the chiefs on whom he relied for political support. The Native Affairs Department warned that 'individual tenure would undermine the whole tribal structure'.

'Betterment' and 'rehabilitation'

Investment in the homelands was well under the amount recommended by Tomlinson. Instead, the government prioritised a policy of 'betterment' or rehabilitation. It was cheaper but also very disruptive. 'Betterment' had its roots in the pre-apartheid period. During the interwar years there was widespread international concern about soil erosion (a concern like that about climate change today). In South Africa government officials and others were deeply perturbed about environmental degradation and soil erosion in the reserves, which they thought was undermining peasant agriculture, intensifying poverty and driving more African people to the cities.

In response officials developed a programme of 'betterment'. By 'betterment' (later called 'rehabilitation') they meant a strategy that would stop environmental degradation and enable Africans to intensify their farming without destroying the soil and vegetation. Their solution was radical. Officials believed that livestock were the main cause of degradation and thought that the most effective way of combating the problem was to divide the pastures with barbed wire into smaller paddocks. Animals would be moved from paddock to paddock throughout the year to avoid over-grazing. To create and control the space for this policy, government officials moved rural families from scattered settlements into compact villages. The National Party pursued betterment with great commitment. Perhaps over a million people were forced to move into villages during the 1950s and 1960s. At the same time, some African people were forced to sell some of their livestock in order to ease pressure on the pastures.

The removals into villages, which cut across traditional ways of living, was deeply resented. Culling of livestock was so unpopular that the government largely abandoned it in the 1960s.

The inadequacies of the Bantustans

There were problems and contradictions in the Bantustan policy. Although substantial new areas of white-owned land were bought to extend the homelands, they still made up a very limited percentage of South Africa's land area. The National Party was not prepared to divide South Africa equally, as whites would never have accepted the sacrifice. Another inconsistency in the policy was that Africans were to be subdivided into their historical chieftaincies and language groups, but whites would remain whites. There was no separate bit of 'white' South Africa for Afrikaners or English-speakers, for Portuguese South Africans, or for Jewish South Africans. Moreover, by this time most Africans conceived of themselves at least partly as Africans and not simply as members of a smaller chieftaincy or ethnic group. Certainly, they had not entirely lost their old identities and languages but all people held multiple identities. They could see themselves as members of an extended family or clan, as Zulu, as South African and as a Johannesburg worker all at the same time.

Political suppression and the Treason Trial

Although the National Party permitted a degree of opposition, it used force to suppress various protests. By the mid-1950s the government had become increasingly concerned with the growing influence of the Congress movement. In 1956, 156 members of the Congress Alliance (a broad coalition of anti-apartheid organisations, including the ANC, the Indian Congress, trade unionists and others), including most of the ANC leadership, were arrested in dawn raids. At this stage the state worked within a legal framework: those arrested were accused of high treason and subjected to a trial that was only fully resolved after five years. The prosecutors tried to prove that the Congress movement planned to overthrow the government by force and that they espoused communist ideals.

The trial brought the leaders of the Congress movement together in a special court room in Pretoria. This demonstrated to all the multi-racial nature of the anti-apartheid struggle. With fervent interest from the media, they were also able to use the trial as a chance to speak from the dock about their ideas. However, the trial also had negative effects on the ANC as its leaders were tied up in legal proceedings for several years. The prosecutors were unable to prove their case and all the accused were acquitted in 1961.

SOURCE

 12

Transcript of part of Nelson Mandela's testimony at the Treason Trial, 1960.

> BENCH: Now, the difference which I want to discuss with you, what would the reaction of White supremacy be if it was made to realise that the demands of the Congress Alliance would result in its supremacy being terminated once and for all?
>
> MANDELA: Well, that has been a problem all along, my lord.
>
> BENCH: That may be, but what do you think the reaction of White supremacy would be to that claim?
>
> MANDELA: Well, for all I know they may be hostile to that type of thing. But already political organisations are arising in this country which themselves are striving for the extension of the franchise to the African people.
>
> BENCH: Well, the question is now whether you can ever achieve that by the methods you are using?
>
> MANDELA: ...but, my lord, this is what I am coming to, that already since we applied these new methods of political action, this policy of exerting pressure, we have attained – we have achieved, we have won ground. Political parties have now emerged which themselves put forward the demand of extending the franchise to the non-European people.

ACTIVITY
CONSOLIDATION

Control of space

1 How far were the pass laws effective in reducing African migration to the cities? Explain your answer.

2 To what extent did the education reforms of the 1950s enforce apartheid?

3 Why did Verwoerd believe that the recommendations of the Tomlinson Commission would undermine apartheid?

HOW DID AFRICAN NATIONALISM DEVELOP, 1948–59?

African as well as white politics changed dramatically in these years. The African National Congress (ANC) cemented its position as the major organised black opposition movement. During these years, it made a striking transition from a relatively small, elite organisation to one that could mobilise mass support. At the same time it voiced a more radical programme of action.

Political opposition in 1948

In 1948 there was no single black opposition group, nor a single ideology uniting the different movements. They were divided by geographic zone, by race, by class and interest. It was very difficult to organise across all of these fissures. Moreover, the National Party gradually developed strategies to police and restrict protest. Nevertheless, a wide range of opposition strategies were used, occasionally to some effect.

The ANC, the principal nationwide organisation, had been established in 1912 by a group of black professionals. Initially they were spurred to action by the creation of the **Union of South Africa** in 1910. Black Africans were excluded from equal political rights in the settlement agreed with Britain and they felt they had been betrayed. They also strongly opposed the Natives Land Act of 1913 and Solomon Plaatje, the first secretary-general of the ANC, famously lamented, in his book *Native Life in South Africa* (1916), that 'the South African native found himself, not actually a slave, but a pariah in the land of his birth'. But it was difficult to unify the diverse African population or challenge white power directly. Despite many initiatives, the ANC did not succeed in winning mass support. Its leaders tended to be politically cautious, hoping that whites might change their minds.

> **KEY TERM**
>
> **Union of South Africa**
> In 1910 the British government unified the colonies of the Cape, Natal, Orange Free State and Transvaal into a single entity, the Union of South Africa, which was granted the right to self rule in the British Empire.

Outside of the ANC's organisational reach, popular politics found expression in a variety of fragmented movements. By 1948, strikes by black workers, bus boycotts, squatter movements to occupy land, street protests and mass rallies were an established feature of popular politics. Militant action was not always aimed at the state: for example, in the Durban riots of 1949 disaffected Zulu people attacked Indians.

Three examples of militant action serve to illustrate the diversity of activity in 1940s South Africa:

- Before they were erased by the Group Areas Act, shack or squatter settlements were a centre of dissidence. Squatter leaders led illegal occupations of private and municipal land and won thousands of followers who rioted when city officials tried to control them. In Johannesburg, James Mpanza, a charismatic political leader, shack landlord and religious revivalist was nicknamed Magebula, or 'slicer of land'. His movement attracted independent African urban women, who made their living from selling homemade alcohol.

- In 1946 African miners went on strike in one of the biggest and most concerted actions by black workers. They threatened South Africa's core industry and Smuts called in the army to assist police in breaking the strike. Black members of the Communist Party of South Africa played a key role in the organisation of some of the actions.

- Bus boycotts were another form of protest. Many African workers lived on the edges of the cities in municipal townships and transport costs cut deep into their meagre wages; in 1944 and again in 1949 buses were boycotted in attempts to bring fares down.

The revival of the African National Congress (ANC) and the Youth League

The great strength of the ANC, compared with any other African political movement, was organisational continuity and its capacity to attract some of the best-educated members of the African elite. However, in the 1940s there was a growing gap between the more cautious, established professional leadership and a new generation of activists.

The ANC Youth League, founded in 1944, helped to galvanise the movement into more radical action. They were inspired by the rise of global anti-colonial rhetoric and by the new confidence of African nationalists in West Africa.

The Youth League was also alarmed by white rhetoric about race and racial separation. Their politics took courage from a new phase of mass political action, especially around Johannesburg and the Witwatersrand.

The ANC Youth League tried to provide a vision for the future. Initially led by lawyer Anton Lembede, and including A. P. Mda, Oliver Tambo, Walter Sisulu and Nelson Mandela, they developed a specifically Africanist ideology, prioritising the self-determination of African people.

SOURCE 13

Nelson Mandela, in his autobiography *Long Walk to Freedom*, published in 1995.

One night in 1943 I met Anton Lembede, who held master of arts and bachelor of law degrees, and A. P. Mda. From the moment I heard Lembede speak, I knew I was seeing a magnetic personality who thought in original and often startling ways. He was then one of a handful of African lawyers in all of South Africa and was the legal partner of the venerable Dr. Pixley ka Seme, one of the founders of the ANC.

Lembede said that Africa was a black man's continent, and it was up to Africans to reassert themselves and reclaim what was rightfully theirs. He hated the idea of the black inferiority complex and castigated what he called the worship and idolization of the West and its ideas. The inferiority complex, he affirmed, was the greatest barrier to liberation. He noted that wherever the African had been given the opportunity, he was capable of developing to the same extent as the white man, citing such African heroes as Marcus Garvey, W. E. B. du Bois and Haile Selassie. 'The colour of my skin is beautiful,' he said, 'like the black soil of Mother Africa.' He believed blacks had to improve their own self-image before they could initiate successful mass action. He preached self-reliance and self-determination, and called his philosophy Africanism. We took it for granted that one day he would lead the ANC.

Lembede declared that a new spirit was stirring among the people, that ethnic differences were melting away, that young men and women thought of themselves as Africans first and foremost, not as Xhosas or Ndebeles or Tswanas. Lembede, whose father was an illiterate Zulu peasant from Natal, had trained as a teacher at Adam's College, an American Board of Missions institution. He had taught for years in the Orange Free State, learned Afrikaans, and came to see Afrikaner nationalism as a prototype of African nationalism.

The National Party victory in 1948 prompted the Youth League to launch a Programme of Action in 1949. They argued for a far more confrontational approach to white minority rule including boycotts, passive resistance, work stoppages and mass action. They believed that the squatter movements, the miners' strike and other protests showed that the mass of African people were ready for this. Their radical rhetoric was a fierce attack on the ANC old guard, as well as on white supremacy. They called for an African consciousness, nationalism and a united African people, as opposed to ideologies such as socialism or a return to African traditional leadership. Unlike Afrikaner nationalists, the new African nationalists were not significantly motivated by religious ideas.

Youth Leaguers included some of the small minority who had been to university, mostly at Fort Hare, but they saw themselves as having the potential to cross boundaries of class through their philosophy of Africanism. The Youth League helped to oust the moderate president of the ANC, Dr Xuma, and eventually in 1952 they found a more sympathetic leader in Albert Luthuli, a devoutly Christian Zulu chief.

The Youth League's Programme of Action was adopted by the ANC in December 1949. It moved away from the policy of concession-seeking from a white government, to a more militant liberation organisation. It was informed by Africanist ambitions but not completely dictated by them. Over the next few years, most of the ANC leadership adhered to the idea of non-racialism and to creating political space for alliance with others in South Africa who supported a fully democratic country, including white, Indian and Coloured activists. Mandela himself, initially influenced by Lembede, swung to this view in the early 1950s. There were thus different visions of the future, even within the ANC, of Africanism and democratic non-racialism.

SOURCE

14 Extract from a letter from Dr A. B. Xuma, ex-president-general of the ANC, to the 44th Annual Conference of the ANC, 18 December 1955.

The National Movement is disintegrating into splinters of disaffected groups... This causes much confusion in the loyalty of the Africans.

We cannot ignore these divisions whatever their respective strength. Their very existence weakens and undermines and brings mockery to our National struggle as a National aspiration of our people...

The National Congress seems to fear to face criticisms constructive and otherwise from its following and others. People who voice their reasonable and considered views on Congress policy and/or no policy and on actions in the name of the African National Congress are referred to as 'sellers-out' or 'agents' or 'friends of the Government' instead of being shown where they are wrong.

Many who dare to criticise the hierarchy have been expelled or 'liquidated' individually or en masse without a democratic hearing.

This attitude is foreign to Congress as a democratic movement and smacks of totalitarianism or authoritarianism which a movement like Congress cannot countenance and still claim to be fighting for freedom from domination and suppression.

A Level Exam-Style Question Section A

Study Sources 13 and 14 before you answer this question.

How far could the historian make use of Sources 13 and 14 together to investigate the aims and underlying philosophy of the African National Congress?

Explain your answer using the sources, the information given about them and your own knowledge of the historical context. (20 marks)

Tip

Think about the authors' backgrounds and their motives for writing. Consider where they agree and where they disagree. Sometimes, where they agree or disagree may not be explicit.

THINKING HISTORICALLY Evidence (5a)

Context is everything

Look again at Sources 2, 4, 14, and 15.

Working in groups, take an A3 piece of paper. In the middle of it draw a large circle. Label the circle 'Evidence' and the space outside the circle 'Context'.

For each source:

1 Think of a question that the source could be helpful in answering.

2 Inside the circle, write a set of statements giving information that can be gleaned only from the source itself without any contextual knowledge.

3 Outside the circle, write down statements of contextual knowledge that relate to the source.

4 Draw annotated lines to show links between the contextual statements and the information from the source. Does context change the nature or meaning of the information?

Now answer this question:

5 Explain why knowledge of context is important when gathering and using historical evidence. Give specific examples to illustrate your point.

ANC links with other organisations

By the 1940s, the Communist Party accepted that it was unlikely to find mass support among the black workers for a proletarian revolution in South Africa. Racial oppression was too central in most people's minds. The communists therefore accepted the idea of a two-phase revolution. This implied working with African nationalists to achieve first a national democratic revolution in which all could exercise full political rights regardless of colour. The socialist revolution could come later.

The National Party, which was deeply anti-communist, banned the Communist Party in 1950. The communists were an unusual organisation in South Africa because they included a socially diverse group of white and black intellectuals as well as some black workers. Although the Youth Leaguers, including Mandela and Tambo, were initially uneasy about working with communists, this alliance gradually became cemented.

Whites, Indians and Coloured people were not accepted into the ANC itself. There was already a South African Indian Congress, and white and Coloured activists formed parallel Congress organisations – strangely reflecting the racial divisions in South Africa. In this way, non-Africans became part of the Congress Alliance.

A significant grouping of white liberals also emerged who were highly critical of apartheid and believed in an extension of black political rights. Alan Paton, author of the famous novel *Cry, the Beloved Country* (1949), was one of their leaders. They formed a Liberal Party in 1953 and advocated a new language of politics based on respect and equal individual rights, rather than racial rhetoric. The Liberals attracted some black support but they were suspicious of both the ANC and communists and did not work together with them. Liberalism was a fragile flower in South Africa at the time, largely crushed by white fears and the attractions of radical African nationalism.

The Defiance Campaign

The ANC's new militancy found particular focus in the Defiance Campaign of 1952. Their strategy was for groups of volunteers to break racially based restrictions such as curfews and segregated facilities and to risk arrest. Nelson Mandela was appointed volunteer-in-chief together with Yusuf Cachalia of the Indian Congress. The Defence Campaign was influenced by the ideas of non-violent civil disobedience promoted by the Indian nationalist Mahatma Gandhi, who had lived in South Africa from 1893 until 1914.

SOURCE
15 The Defiance Campaign: black people on a whites-only train in Cape Town in 1952.

The major cities of Johannesburg and Durban were intended to be the heart of the Defiance Campaign. As it turned out, support was relatively thin in those cities with most arrests, 6,000 out of 8,000, made in the Eastern Cape cities of Port Elizabeth and East London.

Case study: East London

East Bank location, in East London, with 35,000 people, was the combative heart of the campaign. Many African people here lived in shacks. Poverty was reflected in high levels of infant mortality; an anthropologist working in the area estimated that 37 percent of babies died in their first year. The local ANC branch was led by Alcott Gwentshe (a small trader, enthusiastic rugby club member and saxophonist) and C. J. Fazzie (a particularly militant speaker).

East London was close to Fort Hare and Youth League militants found their way to the city. The Defiance Campaign began there in June 1952 with a rally of 1,500 people. The audience shouted ANC slogans such as 'Mayibuye! Mayibuye! iAfrika!' (Let Africa be returned) and sang *Nkosi Sikelel' iAfrika* ('God Bless Africa'), a hymn originally composed by an African clergyman in 1897 and adopted by the ANC. Gwentshe spoke of the overthrow of white domination, the total rejection of white rule, and the resulting era of democracy and independence.

During subsequent rallies, ANC activists and volunteers were easily distinguishable, wearing khaki uniforms – some with trench coats, black berets and neckerchiefs in the ANC colours of gold, green, and black. In July 1952, the first full month of open defiance, regular large meetings were held. There are records of these meetings in the archives from police informers who later gave evidence against leaders at trials. Protestors were arrested willingly as they hoped through sheer numbers to overload the courts and make apartheid laws unenforceable. They sat on whites-only benches in town, urinated in whites-only public toilets and refused to pay fines. Many protestors were sentenced to one month with hard labour.

As the protest rolled on, more youths came to the meetings, including those considered part of township street gangs. Some advocated violence and a police informer was stoned and chased. In October, the campaign split between the moderate Gwentshe and the radical Fazzie. Riots broke out in Port Elizabeth and the government decided to take tougher action. In early November the Minister of Justice banned all public gatherings for a month and sent armed reinforcements to stop meetings.

On 9 November 1952, activists in East London decided to go ahead with what they advertised as a religious gathering. When the police came to East Bank location in the afternoon, they found a meeting of about 800 people, who threw stones and sticks at them. The police unsuccessfully ordered the gathering to disperse and, following a baton charge, claimed that a shot was fired at them. They then opened fire themselves. The crowd dispersed and youths formed small groups to stone police and to burn buildings.

Two white people were killed by black crowds after the police shootings. Neither was specifically targeted; they were in the wrong place at the wrong time. The first was an insurance salesman who often worked in East Bank location. The second was Sister Aidan Quinlan, a Catholic medical missionary who lived in the location. Her car was set alight by an angry group as she sat inside. Allegations were made afterwards that her body was cut, and parts taken for medicine. Such killings were rare and Sister Aidan's death reverberated through South Africa.

Official reports recorded seven African deaths and 18 seriously injured; these were bodies brought to the mortuary. Many more may have been killed, dozens were mentioned in one statement and a policeman who was present later suggested that there were more deaths in East London in 1952 than the 69 at Sharpeville in 1960. The ANC leadership was so disturbed by the incident that it called off the Defiance Campaign nationally. They saw the campaign as dependent on tight discipline and non-violent action.

We have looked at the Defiance Campaign in East London in detail because it was the most sustained example of ANC mobilisation at this time. It also helps us think about history from below. Few have heard of Gwentshe and Fazzie, as compared to the ANC's national leaders. Yet they led a campaign that was more successful than that in the big cities. They showed the true potential of mass defiance, but also its dangers. They lost control of the movement as it was translated into a vehicle for unruly youths and crowd violence.

Defiance was in some respects a problematic strategy because it made the leadership of the movement so vulnerable. They had to lead by example, from the front, so that they were not accused of using others. Yet by directly offering themselves up to the police for arrest they were potentially disabling the movement. The lower echelons of activists needed to make the campaign a success did not really materialise, except in East London and Port Elizabeth. It was too much of a risk for most people to take.

But the outcome of the Defiance Campaign was hugely important for the ANC. Its claimed membership shot up from 4,000 to 100,000 people and for the first time it seemed to be attracting a mass following. Subsequently the ANC, again including Mandela, became deeply involved in resisting the imposition of Group Areas in Sophiatown, and attracted a good deal of support, publicity and moral authority from these events.

Women and the ANC

Some of the male leadership of the ANC held conservative and patriarchal views about the role of African women and women were only admitted as members in 1943. However, a Women's League was founded in 1948, incorporating existing women's organisations into the ANC, and during the 1950s they expanded their support. Women were prominent in the grass roots protests of the Defiance Campaign, especially in the Eastern Cape. The government announced in 1955 that it would extend pass laws to women as so many were moving from the rural districts to the cities. Led by Lilian Ngoyi they staged a major protest against passes, collected signatures and 20,000 marched on the Union Buildings, seat of government power in Pretoria. In 1957 they protested outside the pass office in Johannesburg. Women also led the resistance to forced removals in Cato Manor, Durban in the late 1950s.

Rural resistance

Resistance in the countryside happened alongside that in the urban centres. Bantu authorities and betterment helped to trigger a series of rural movements throughout the rural districts in the late 1950s, from Tswana-speaking communities in the north west, to Zulu-speakers on the east coast.

Case study: Sekhukhuneland

In 1957–58 people in Sekhukhuneland, home of the Pedi, tried to stave off government interference in their political and social lives.

In the 1950s, the Department of Native Affairs had planned to make Sekhukhuneland into a homeland and tried to appoint tribal authorities to run it. The people were deeply split by this intervention. Many of the men from Sekhukhuneland were migrant workers who spent long periods in Pretoria and Johannesburg. Some, such as John Nkadimeng, a factory worker and trade unionist, joined the ANC. Migrant workers also formed their own organisations to assist with transport, finding jobs, financing funerals and getting money back to their rural homes. Such men were deeply opposed to the idea of Bantustans and concerned to keep open their access to urban employment, essential for their families' livelihoods. They adapted the ANC's ideas to a rural context and were committed to the idea of equal rights and a single South Africa. They were also worried that the government would appoint chiefs who supported betterment, especially the culling of cattle. They called their organisation Sebatakgomo which meant literally, in the Sepedi language, 'a predator among the cattle'. This was clearly understood as a call to battle. They were determined that the chiefs should not become part of the state's plans.

In 1957 the government, determined to impose the Bantu Authorities Act, deposed the paramount chief and installed men who would cooperate. By May 1958, nine of those who were seen as government collaborators had been beaten or stabbed to death and others burnt out of their houses. Large numbers of police were sent in and hundreds arrested and tried. The arrest and deportation of the deposed paramount chief, who was trying to protect the interests of migrant workers and rural families, was seen as a particular provocation. He was the symbol of their identity and the way of life they were trying to defend.

ACTIVITY
CONSOLIDATION

Resistance

1 To what extent was the Defiance Campaign a failure? Discuss this in a small group.

2 Draw a Venn diagram of two interlocking circles. Above one circle, write 'rural resistance' and above the other write 'urban resistance'. Write down in each circle what would motivate people to join the opposition. Reasons that are relevant to both rural and urban resistance go in the interlocking area of the circles. Some ideas to include might be: betterment; arrests of leaders; pass laws; transport; segregation.

The Freedom Charter

In 1955 the Congress Alliance wrote a charter listing their core political beliefs. This became known as the Congress of the People Campaign, and thousands across South Africa submitted their suggestions on issues that ranged from the franchise and education to the ownership of mines and land.

The result, known as the Freedom Charter, was revealed at a rally in Kliptown, Soweto, in June 1955. The Charter gave a clear summary of the principles of the Congress movement. In its tone and vocabulary it echoed the language of freedom movements in other parts of the world, and was helpful in garnering international support for their cause. Essentially it called for a fully democratic South Africa with a fairer distribution of land and wealth. The Freedom Charter committed the movement to a non-racial South Africa and laid an important foundation for future political mobilisation.

SOURCE

The Preamble to the Freedom Charter, 1955.

WE, THE PEOPLE OF SOUTH AFRICA, declare for all our country and the world to know: that South Africa belongs to all who live in it, black and white, and that no government can justly claim authority unless it is based on the will of all the people; that our people have been robbed of their birthright to land, liberty and peace by a form of government founded on injustice and inequality; that our country will never be prosperous or free until all our people live in brotherhood, enjoying equal rights and opportunities; that only a democratic state, based on the will of all the people, can secure to all their birthright without distinction of colour, race, sex or belief;

And therefore,

We, the people of South Africa, black and white together – equals, countrymen and brothers – adopt this Freedom Charter;

And we pledge ourselves to strive together, sparing neither strength nor courage, until the democratic changes here set out have been won.

The people shall govern!

The Pan-Africanist Congress (PAC)

During the 1950s, the ANC combined within one movement the Africanist ideas of the early Youth League and the non-racial approach of the combined Congress Alliance.

At the same time a group of Africanists, largely based in Johannesburg, tried to maintain a distinct political identity and published a regular newsletter, *The Africanist*, which promoted the idea of 'Africa for the Africans'. Their biggest concentration of support was probably among teachers, including Potlake Leballo and Robert Sobukwe, who emerged as their most significant leaders.

Potlake Leballo (c1924–86)

Originally from Lesotho, Leballo was a restless and domineering figure. He trained as a teacher at Fort Hare and in Pretoria, and served in the South African army during the Second World War. War politicised African servicemen throughout the continent as it gave them a glimpse of a world outside the colonial hierarchies and they were fighting in a war supposedly for human rights and democracy against fascism and racism. Leballo was a member of the ANC Youth League and became an important figure in its Orlando branch.

Robert Sobukwe (1924–78)

Sobukwe was schooled at Healdtown, a premier Methodist mission school in the Eastern Cape, and Fort Hare, where he joined the ANC Youth League and became student president. He did so well at university and a subsequent teaching post that a very rare opportunity opened up: appointment to the academic staff of the largely white University of the Witwatersrand. Concerned to secure his professional position he remained in the background of Johannesburg politics in the mid-1950s.

The Africanists differed from the ANC leadership on a number of points:

- They thought that non-Africans were gaining too much influence in the Congress movement. The Freedom Charter (1955) was an important moment, with much of the final draft written by a multi-racial committee. Africanists believed that the ANC should be overwhelmingly led by Africans and represent the interests of Africans as the majority of the South African population. Sobukwe argued, perhaps with a little contradiction, that there was only one human race, but that Africa belonged to the Africans.

- The Africanists believed that complete independence and freedom implied the return of the land to Africans. The Freedom Charter, they felt, was too concerned with civil rights for all.

- The Africanists developed more explicitly Pan-Africanist ideas. Sobukwe proclaimed in 1959, 'We regard it as the sacred duty of every African state to strive ceaselessly and energetically for the creation of a United States of Africa, from the Cape to Cairo, Morocco to Madagascar'.

- The Africanists wanted more confrontational direct action.

An organisational split was triggered in 1958, when the leadership of the provincial ANC in the Transvaal was re-elected as a slate (a group) to their positions without debate. The reason given was that the ANC's leaders were too occupied with the Treason Trial to stand for election at that time. Leballo in particular protested at this decision and was expelled from the ANC. Later that year, at an ANC conference in Johannesburg, Luthuli compared the narrow African nationalism of the Africanists to tribalism. Sobukwe spoke to challenge Luthuli and the Africanists walked out.

The Africanists tried to form separate provincial organisations, initially within the ANC. In April 1959 they held a founding convention for a Pan-Africanist Congress (PAC) in Orlando and read telegrams of support from Nkrumah and Sekou Toure in independent Ghana and Guinea. These events were widely reported in the white and black press. Within the ANC, some felt that the government had allowed the PAC to organise freely because it was keen to split the nationalist movement, and hoped the PAC's views might be closer to 'separate development'. In fact the PAC was hostile to the division of South Africa into Bantustans.

A Level Exam-Style Question Section B

How accurate is it to say that opposition to apartheid in the years 1948–59 was largely unsuccessful? (20 marks)

Tip

Think about the criteria you would use to judge 'unsuccessful' and apply these to the actions of the urban and rural activists. Consider what was achieved as well as what was not.

ACTIVITY
SUMMARY

The response to apartheid, c.1948–59

1 a) Draw a timeline of events of the period 1948–59 from the perspective of a member of the National Party. Think about what events would have been significant to them during this period.

b) Draw a timeline of events of the period 1948–59 from the perspective of a member of the ANC Youth League. Think about what events would have been significant to them during this period.

c) To what extent do the two timelines differ? Account for the similarities and differences between the two timelines.

2 Between 1948 and 1959, what were the significant moments that would have effected:

a) a black woman who lived in Sophiatown in the 1940s

b) a black man living in a village in Sekhukhuneland?

Write a few paragraphs explaining how their lives were effected by those moments.

3 Look again at the photographs in sources 1, 5, 8 and 15 in this chapter. In your opinion, how useful are these photos in helping us understand:

a) segregation in South Africa between 1948 and 1959

b) political resistance to apartheid between 1948 and 1959?

Write a few paragraphs on the strengths and limitations of photographs as historical sources.

 WIDER READING

Beinart, William, *Twentieth-Century South Africa*, Oxford University Press (2001)

Clark, Nancy L., *South Africa: The Rise and Fall of Apartheid*, Routledge (2011)

Culpin, Christopher, *South Africa 1948–1995: a depth study*, Hodder Education (2000)

Dubow, Saul, *Apartheid, 1948–1994*, Oxford University Press (2014)

Gordimer, Nadine, *Telling Times: Writing and Living, 1950–2008*, Bloomsbury (2011)

Mandela, Nelson, *The Long Walk to Freedom*, Abacus (2013)

Mulholland, Rosemary, *South Africa 1948–1994*, Cambridge University Press (1997)

Patel, Essop, *The World of Can Themba*, Ravan Press (1990)

Paton, Alan, *Cry, the Beloved Country*, Vintage (2002)

Pinchuk, Tony, *Mandela for Beginners*, Icon (1994)

Roberts, Martin, *South Africa 1948–1994: the Rise and Fall of Apartheid*, Longman (2001)

Thompson, Leonard, *A History of South Africa*, Yale University Press (2001)

2b.2 Radicalisation of resistance and the consolidation of National Party power, 1960–68

KEY QUESTIONS

- Why did African opposition to apartheid increase during the years 1960–61?
- What factors strengthened apartheid or 'separate development' in the years 1960–68?

INTRODUCTION

The 1950s had been a turbulent decade in the history of South Africa. A raft of legislation had been introduced by the new National Party government, who continued to increase their share of the white vote at the polls. By 1960 much crucial legislation had been passed that impacted heavily upon the lives of ordinary South Africans, regardless of race.

Opposition organisations had also met with some success. Through struggles such as the Defiance Campaign, and improved methods of political communication, African nationalism had begun to take root. The newly politicised population could be tapped into by the national organisations, which had shifted away from petitions to more militant protests. While they were unable to halt the National Party's legislative programme, mass opposition by the ANC and Pan African Congress (PAC) was beginning to have some impact.

The killing of 69 protestors at Sharpeville on 21 March 1960 brought political conflict in South Africa into sharp focus. It demonstrated that the National Party intended to maintain white supremacy in the country by force; it provoked outrage around the world; and it galvanised opposition organisations, encouraging them to consider new tactics and strategies. The government cracked down on African movements, arrested and imprisoned many leaders – including Nelson Mandela – and drove others into exile. In response, opposition strategy turned to armed struggle and the leadership in exile had to navigate an international political landscape.

During the 1960s, the National Party established a secure authority, won a referendum in support of a Republic and was bolstered by a growing economy. The scope for African-led political opposition linked with the banned ANC and PAC was greatly diminished. Police and the military were increasingly important in maintaining a firm grip. Internal repression coupled with rising standards of living defused mass protests.

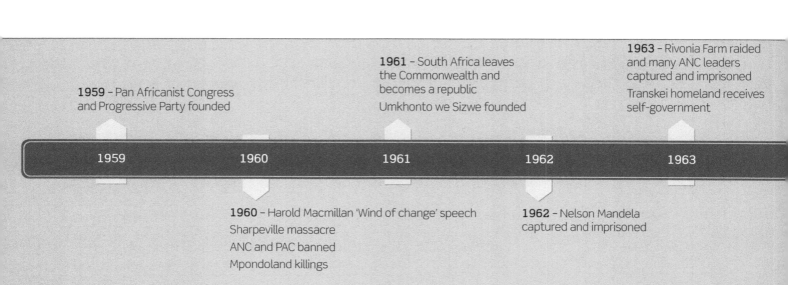

1959 – Pan Africanist Congress and Progressive Party founded

1961 – South Africa leaves the Commonwealth and becomes a republic

Umkhonto we Sizwe founded

1963 – Rivonia Farm raided and many ANC leaders captured and imprisoned

Transkei homeland receives self-government

1959   1960   1961   1962   1963

1960 – Harold Macmillan 'Wind of change' speech

Sharpeville massacre

ANC and PAC banned

Mpondoland killings

1962 – Nelson Mandela captured and imprisoned

With Verwoerd at the helm until 1966, the National Party's vision of apartheid or separate development was energetically pursued. This included ruthless implementation of discriminatory laws. However, for Verwoerd the homeland or Bantustan policy was increasingly the cornerstone of apartheid and significant moves were made to convert former reserves into self-governing territories. With African opposition scattered or contained, the 1960s may be considered as the high point for apartheid.

WHY DID OPPOSITION TO APARTHEID INCREASE DURING THE YEARS 1960–61?

During the late 1950s and early 1960s, South African opposition forces were momentarily confident – or at least hopeful – that they could make an impact. The split of the PAC from the ANC in 1959 certainly divided the major African political organisation but also helped to mobilise new communities. Simultaneously, rural political movements, based in the African reserves and with limited connections to the ANC or PAC, challenged the government at a local level.

The pass laws and restrictions over movement were at the heart of the new political dynamism. Even if many were able to bypass them, these government controls deeply constrained African people's ability to work and live legally in the cities and towns, where most jobs were available. Moreover, pass laws were the single most frequent cause of difficult encounters with the police. Police demands to see reference books were demeaning and an everyday reminder of apartheid power and injustice. Pass raids were often used by the police as a form of punishment when confronting urban protests.

The regulations also made it difficult for many to change jobs and hence to find better opportunities without losing their rights to stay in town. By 1960, the usual fine for a pass offence was between £5 and £8 or imprisonment for 5–8 weeks. It was not a huge fine, but amounted to more than two weeks' wages for the great majority of African people: 80 percent of African families in Johannesburg lived on less than £20 a month. Across South Africa, about 1,000 cases a day relating to the pass laws went through the courts and in the rushed and summary proceedings many felt they were unjustly treated. Passes, along with municipal rents and prohibitions on liquor sales, came to dominate the major urban protests in the early months of 1960.

Peaceful protest

Under the direction of charismatic younger members, the ANC had managed to mobilise parts of the population into political action during the 1950s. However, by the end of the decade, the ideology and strategy of the Congress Alliance was challenged by the PAC. The PAC was less concerned to develop a disciplined leadership and membership. They increasingly felt that if they lit the match, the people would carry the fire – mass anger would sustain a mass movement. They were more interested in an ill-defined idea of freedom than a non-racial democracy.

1969 – Winnie Madikizela-Mandela imprisoned

ANC Morogoro conference in Tanzania

1966 – Verwoerd assassinated

B. J. Vorster becomes prime minister

1964	1965	1966	1967	1968	1969

1964 – Nelson Mandela makes Rivonia statement

Afrikaner Verligte movement starts

1968 – Black Consciousness movement starts

Robert Sobukwe, leader of the PAC, had very limited experience of political campaigning but settled on the pass laws as his major focus. Despite knowing of a campaign planned by the ANC to start on 31 March 1960, Sobukwe announced that the PAC would mount its own mass action on 21 March. The PAC clearly wished to pre-empt and outdo the ANC. The ANC was deeply disturbed: Mandela later wrote that 'they sought to sabotage us', with 'blatant… opportunism'. Strangely, the PAC chose a strategy rather similar to the ANC's Defiance Campaign. Activists would offer themselves up for arrest in such numbers at police stations that they would render the pass laws inoperable. They hoped to cripple the police and judiciary through overcrowding, and the economy through a strike. Nobody seems to have counted how many pass prosecutions the state could cope with and therefore how many protestors would be needed to undermine the system.

The Sharpeville massacre and its significance

In the brief period after the PAC's foundation, some of its organisers, switching from the ANC, managed to mobilise at branch level and develop grass roots support. Cape Town and the Vaal Triangle, a heavily industrialised zone to the south west of Johannesburg, were among the most organised areas. Sharpeville, a small township near Vereeniging in the Vaal Triangle, was a centre of protest and the name became synonymous with apartheid repression. But Sharpeville was only one of many major confrontations. At the time events in Cape Town were perhaps more important in shaping the direction of South African politics.

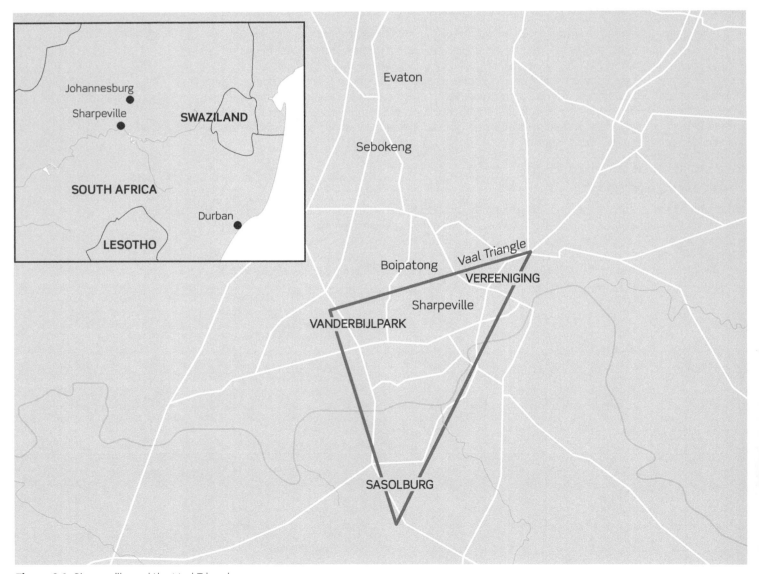

Figure 2.1: Sharpeville and the Vaal Triangle.

The Vaal Triangle was a centre of coal mining and site of South Africa's state-owned Iron and Steel Corporation factories. The African residents of Evaton, the biggest and most established township in the area, staged a bus boycott in 1956 when 15 people were killed. Sharpeville, founded in 1942, had been planned as a model township, with more facilities than usual, including a clinic and library.

Three major factors politicised the community:

- Firstly, in 1958, numbers were swelled by the arrival of about 10,000 people removed from another location by force under the Group Areas Act. Little new housing was available so there was a large and angry addition to Sharpeville's population. Rents were also increased.

- Secondly, the area was favoured by migrant workers from Lesotho, a separate British colony. They had even more insecure rights than people from the South African rural areas – yet they were equally dependent on wages. Some came illegally and pass raids were stepped up in 1959.

- Thirdly, a PAC branch was founded in Sharpeville in 1959 by a few able organisers, notably Nyakane Tsolo, a trade unionist. When Sobukwe called at short notice for the campaign against passes on 21 March 1960, the local PAC could respond quickly to spread the word through house-to-house visits and leaflets.

PAC membership in Sharpeville was probably not more than a few hundred but they set up a task force that both encouraged participation and threatened those who wanted to go to work, including bus drivers who would carry commuters. On the night of 20 March 1960, youths moved onto the streets and a policeman was stabbed. The police responded in force, dispersing crowds with baton charges and gunfire. A meeting at the football stadium was broken up by police at midnight; two protestors died.

On the morning of 21 March about 5,000 people gathered outside the fence surrounding the Sharpeville police station.

PAC leaders requested the police to arrest them all. They and some of the crowd seem to have believed that, confronted with the impossibility of this task, the government would announce the suspension of the pass laws.

The crowd were by no means all PAC members and subsequent interviews revealed that many were there out of curiosity. Some gave the thumbs up salute linked with the ANC while others shouted the PAC slogan '*Izwi Lethu*' ('the land is ours'). Journalists and photographers were also present, including Robert Sobukwe's biographer Benjamin Pogrund, who thought that the crowd was relaxed and friendly.

SOURCE 1

From *The Shooting at Sharpeville: the Agony of South Africa* written by the Anglican Bishop of Johannesburg, Ambrose Reeves, and published in 1961.

Many eyewitnesses to whom I spoke told me that the people gathered about the Police Station were in a happy mood. Very few Africans had gone to work, and an idle, holiday atmosphere pervaded the town. Some were singing and occasionally some shouted slogans. I have been told that no one was carrying weapons, and that no one was carrying stones.

This mood of relatively friendly interaction, however, changed when police reinforcements arrived, including Saracen armoured vehicles with machine guns. By 1 p.m. there were about 200 white policemen with rifles (wearing peaked caps in the photo) and a similar number of black policemen with clubs. They came from outside the area and were commanded by a more aggressive regional chief of police, Lieutenant Colonel Pienaar. By this time the police were nervous; some were inexperienced and they claimed later, incorrectly, that they had faced an angry crowd of 20,000. They knew that nine policemen had been killed at Cato Manor a few weeks before. These external police reinforcements seemed to have triggered the shooting.

SOURCE 2

Protestors running away from the police station at Sharpeville, 1960.

When Nyakane Tsolo refused to order the crowd to disperse he was arrested. This episode led the crowd to surge forward. Under examination at the subsequent inquiry, Pienaar admitted that he failed to warn the crowd of the danger of an armed response if they did not disperse. He lined up the police and ordered them to load. Those protestors at the front of the crowd could not move back. There is conflicting evidence suggesting a local gangster shot twice in the air around this time. However, it is likely that members of the police line were simply uneasy that the police station fence was under pressure. Pienaar said, probably truthfully, that he did not give the order to fire and that he did not think that the situation had merited it. It seems that shortly before 2 p.m. one of the policemen, though perhaps not a senior officer, did shout 'Fire'. There was a barrage from rifles, revolvers and a machine gun mounted on a Saracen. They fired a first round into the front row of the crowd then a second volley at people running away so that many were shot in the back. At least 69 died and 187 were injured.

The police did not behave well after the shooting. Witnesses accused them of placing stones on the station side of the fence to provide evidence that these had been thrown before police opened fire. The police were also accused of kicking and even killing wounded people. Sobukwe and some of his key supporters were arrested in Orlando, Soweto, but for the most part, the police did not arrest people.

SOURCE 3

Simon Mkutau, eyewitness at Sharpeville, cited by the historian Tom Lodge in 2009.

I went to the police station like all the others. The atmosphere was cheerful, people were happy, singing and dancing. While the people were marching through the streets, policemen were chasing them and using tear gas to try and separate them. Despite this we marched straight to the police station, still singing and shouting. Once we were there, we kind of waited for police to come and take our passes and arrest us. I was standing at the main gate, and had a clear view of what was going on inside. I actually saw the officers loading their guns.

SOURCE 4

Lydia Mahabuke, eyewitness at Sharpeville, speaking to the historian Tom Lodge in 2009.

While we were standing there singing we suddenly saw the police in a row point their guns at us. While we were still singing, without any word, without any argument, we just heard the guns being fired. I then tried to run towards the open space where the post office is now. While I was running something was hitting me in the back. After having felt this I tried to look back. People were falling, scattered. There was blood streaming down my leg. I tried to hobble. I struggled to get home.

SOURCE 5

Lieutenant Colonel Pienaar, Police Commissioner, speaking at the official inquiry into Sharpeville, 1961.

The Native mentality does not allow them to gather for a peaceful demonstration. For them to gather means violence.

SOURCE 6

From *The Shooting at Sharpeville: the Agony of South Africa* written by the Anglican Bishop of Johannesburg, Ambrose Reeves, and published in 1961.

The real crux of the police complaint about the crowd seems to be that the crowd were lacking in that respect and humility which the police apparently expect from their African fellow-citizens. There was, of course, a little police evidence that some of the crowd were waving sticks. Moreover, the police evidence is contradicted by the experience of at least three white men who passed among or through the crowd at one o'clock or shortly after one o'clock, namely, Berry the *Drum* photographer, Hoek the *Rand Daily Mail* photographer, and Labuschagne the superintendent of the Sharpeville Township. Berry walked through the crowd to the fence. The crowd seemed to him to be friendly. Hoek did not get out of his car, but he stopped among the crowd near the Police Station. He thought the crowd was noisy and excitable but he saw no signs of hostility. Labuschagne was the personification of officialdom and authority responsible for the practical application of the pass laws. He had been standing quietly for an hour or more with Captain Coetzee's men, but at about one o'clock he decided to leave them and to enter the Police Station.

SOURCE 7

This report appeared in the British left-of-centre newspaper, *The Guardian*, with the headline 'Dozens killed in Sharpeville' on 22 March 1960, the day after the shootings.

'I don't know how many we shot,' said Colonel Piernaar, the local police commander at Sharpeville. 'It all started when hordes of natives surrounded the police station. My car was struck by a stone. If they do these things they must learn their lesson the hard way.'

An official at Vereeniging hospital put the casualties at 7pm to-night at 56 dead and 162 injured.

A great roar echoed across the square as 60 police, carrying Sten guns, riot sticks and revolvers, left the vehicles and faced the crowd.

Suddenly, the Africans turned about screaming and ran from the police, who waded into them, striking out with their sticks. As the police advanced, a barrage of stones, sticks, and bottles rained on them and the crowd from surrounding buildings. The police returned to their vehicles and were followed slowly by the crowd.

A fresh barrage of stones struck the policemen, some of whom picked them up and hurled them at the crowd. Africans yelled at the police, 'Cowards' and 'Kill the white men.'

The first African was shot dead after the police had been stoned. The Africans retaliated, causing casualties among the police. The police then opened fire with sub-machine-guns, Sten guns, and rifles, and eye-witnesses said that the front ranks of the crowd fell like ninepins.

Mangled bodies of men, women, and children lay sprawled on the roadway in the square. One policeman described the scene as 'like a world war battlefield'. The police seemed to be rather shocked themselves at the scene.

AS Level Exam-Style Question Section A

Study Source 4 before you answer this question.

How much weight do you give the evidence of Source 4 for an enquiry into events at Sharpeville in 1960?

Explain your answer, using the source, the information given about it and your own knowledge of the historical context. (12 marks)

Tip
Think about how reliable people's memories are, years after an event they are describing.

EXTEND YOUR KNOWLEDGE

Protests in Cape Town

Cape Town was another major centre of protest on 21 March 1960. The African population there, alone among South Africa's major cities, was still a minority in 1960, though there had been a big influx of migrant workers after the Second World War. African migrant labourers in the Western Cape were in a particularly vulnerable position because the government was keen to limit their entry and protect jobs for Coloured people. Most lived in townships, called Langa (Sun) and Nyanga (Moon), separated from Coloured people. Of Langa's 25,000 inhabitants in 1960, 18,000 were male.

Two dynamic young men in their 20s, Philip Kgosana and Christopher Mlokoti, took over the Cape Town PAC branch in January 1960. The PAC organised mass meetings and Robert Sobukwe spoke in Cape Town. He focused on very material concerns, especially the large disparity between wages and educational provision for whites and blacks, but also spoke about municipal rents, bus fares, pass laws and police repression. Mlokoti linked these to poverty and social ills of African urban society including gangs, alcoholism and prostitution. Pan-Africanism and the independence of Ghana were also potent themes because they illustrated African liberation. Sobukwe was cautious about anti-white rhetoric but grass roots speakers less so: 'when I say the Dutch people hate us', one said, 'I do not mean only nationalists [the National Party], I mean all whites. I have no mercy for these people... we must teach our children to hate the Europeans.' The struggle, in this view, was between white and black and every white person was an oppressor.

On 21 March, a crowd of about 6,000 gathered in Langa, as well as others in Nyanga. In Cape Town, as in Sharpeville, the police refused to make arrests. Rather, they attempted to disperse the protestors with baton charges, Saracen armoured vehicles and a volley of live ammunition. Twenty died and rioting spread throughout the night. Protestors mounted roadblocks and patrols to stop police activity. By 25 March an estimated 50 percent of Cape Town's African workforce was on strike, and PAC organisers, including Philip Kgosana, led a demonstration to central Cape Town. On 27 March an estimated 95 percent of Africans were on strike, and a crowd of approximately 50,000 attended the funeral of those killed in Langa.

Except for Cape Town and the Vaal Triangle, the planned national mobilisation by the PAC on 21 March largely failed but the well-reported shootings at Sharpeville sent ripples through the country and triggered waves of criticism overseas. Unlike other instances of police repression, such as East London in 1952, or Cape Town on 21 March 1960, many photographs were taken of the Sharpeville shootings. These provided graphic evidence that was quickly circulated in the national and international press.

The massacre provoked international denunciation. On 1 April 1960, the United Nations Security Council passed a resolution condemning Sharpeville and calling for a reversal of apartheid and racial discrimination. The UN had been a theatre for criticism of apartheid since 1948, led initially by India, but this resolution represented a new level of international concern. Although Britain and France abstained, both Britain and the US supported a later resolution declaring apartheid to be a violation of the UN charter.

Meanwhile, the ANC continued to plan its own anti-pass protest. On 28 March they organised a mass pass-burning and Albert Luthuli, in Pretoria for the Treason Trial, burnt his in front of the media. The ANC called for a further **stayaway** at the end of March and a day of mourning.

KEY TERM

Stayaway
Similar to a strike in that workers are encouraged to 'stay away' from their workplace. However, rather than protesting at their workplace they would not go to work at all, to avoid reprisals, police action or arrest.

On 30 March, faced with turbulence at home, and criticism abroad, the government declared a State of Emergency (see below). On the same day 30,000 Africans marched in an orderly and non-violent demonstration six miles along the main highway from Langa to the edge of central Cape Town. Some, led by Kgosana, gathered at the police station in Caledon Square. Nearby, the whites-only parliament was in session, debating the protests. They were protected by a cordon of Saracens, armed police and troops. The police promised that the Minister of Justice would meet a PAC delegation if the crowd dispersed.

Anxious to avoid a violent confrontation, Kgosana persuaded the marchers to turn back. He was double-crossed by the police and the meeting never happened. On returning with a small group later that afternoon, Kgosana was arrested. The PAC leadership had been faced with a difficult choice. Had they tried to march a few blocks further to parliament, they would probably have met a barrage of fire-power akin to that at Sharpeville. It is remarkable in retrospect that they were allowed to reach central Cape Town. The armed forces were subsequently deployed to break the strike and impose order; they used gratuitous violence.

Next day a further protest was mounted at Cato Manor in Durban and activists tried to stop workers from going to town. A series of clashes ensued over the next few days between police and protestors and between protestors and those wishing to go to work.

Though the PAC was trying to light a fuse, they were still committed to peaceful confrontation. Significantly, the government had shown that they were prepared to enforce their authority and the National Party, if anything, became more determined to impose apartheid in the next few years.

AS Level Exam-Style Question Section B

How accurate is it to say that the anti-apartheid protests of the 1960s served only to strengthen the determination of the authorities to enforce apartheid? (12 marks)

Tip

'Only' is a key word here – as well as considering the role of the authorities, consider what else the 1960s protests achieved.

EXTEND YOUR KNOWLEDGE

Rural rebellion: Mpondoland

The government's clampdown disabled the ANC and PAC but did not entirely defuse protest. During 1960–61, a new momentum was building in parts of the countryside.

Control of forests was a major source of conflict. Timber was central to rural African life, used to build homes, fence cattle pens and gardens, provide firewood, and make essential everyday implements like the hollowed logs used to crush grain for cooking. The government took control of Mpondoland's rich coastal forests and, in order to conserve them, tried to stop regular use as well as settlement around the forest fringes. Rather than confronting a powerful government, people simply ignored the restrictions and in the 1950s there was a silent fight for the forests. Matters came to a head in February 1960 when a local magistrate came to meet a headman of one of the areas where forest encroachments were taking place. Chiefs and headmen were required by government to enforce the law but some also tried to represent the people. The magistrate and his police escort arrived at a local trading store to find 200 men had assembled. A spokesman shouted: 'You are not taking our Headman with you. He is our Headman… White man go back.' Such small-scale protests simmered throughout the rural areas and raised fundamental questions as to who had the right to control forests and other vital natural resources in the African areas: government or people?

Botha Sigcau had been paramount chief of Mpondoland since 1938. He had been imposed by the government and was unpopular. People accused him of 'selling' the people to the government. They were concerned that betterment would be imposed, forcing many to move their homes and sell some of their cattle.

In March 1960 a rebellion began, when the house of one of Botha Sigcau's advisors, Saul Mabude, an advocate of betterment, was burnt down. Solomon Madikizela and a committee of four others organised the rebellion. Initially Madikizela's goals were local: reverse Bantu Authorities, allow people to have their own chiefs, stop betterment and convictions for settling in or taking wood from the forest. Passes and taxes were also issues but essentially this was a fight for local autonomy and control. From March to June, the rebels burnt down the homesteads of chiefs who were seen as cooperating with the government and organised a boycott of trading stations run by white and Coloured families.

On 6 June 1960, the rebels organised a meeting at Ngquza Hill and a rumour spread that they were planning to attack Botha Sigcau's home. The government sent the army, which moved in around the base of Ngquza hill while a military plane flew overhead. As at Sharpeville, people claimed that there was no clear instruction to disperse. As they tried to run away towards a wooded valley, 11 were shot and many more injured.

An inquest was held in the nearby town of Bizana in June. By this time, the rebels were in touch with the ANC in Durban, which arranged legal representation. Some of the key leaders, including Solomon Madikizela, absorbed ANC ideas about the urgency of ending apartheid as a whole. Their aims broadened and the sustained revolts in Sekhukhuneland and Mpondoland gave some ANC leaders hope that rural areas could be mobilised against the government as well as the townships.

For the next few months, rebels attempted to control their local areas and set up local committees and courts; when necessary they took refuge in the forests. But large army and police contingents swept through these rural districts, arresting over 5,000. By November 1960, the rebellion had been quelled. Twenty-three rebels were hanged for murder and Madikizela was sentenced to banishment under police surveillance in the Transvaal.

Environmental history

Over the last few decades historians have mapped out a sub-discipline called 'environmental history', which looks at the changing relationship between human beings and nature. Environmental history includes discussion of the ways that humans have transformed nature to procure food and energy, destroyed habitats for wild animals, triggered soil erosion, and caused climate change. Environmental historians have also examined the question of who has the right to natural resources such as land, forests and water. This approach reflects growing global environmentalism; one of its major concerns has been the history of forests and deforestation.

The banning of political parties and the state of emergency

These were dramatic times for South Africa, but popular protest was not sufficiently widespread, nor sufficiently militant, to threaten white rule. The state had overwhelming force at its disposal and the police and armed forces were loyal. While the core of the police was white, considerable numbers of black policemen participated not only in combating crime and imposing the pass laws, but in direct suppression of political mobilisation.

The state of emergency, declared on 30 March 1960, strengthened police powers. Public meetings were outlawed, and the police could detain people without fear of restriction by the courts. Police arrested thousands of opposition political leaders in a widespread clampdown throughout the country. They used the Public Safety Act 1953, which required no warrants.

Though African political leaders did recognise their vulnerability, the sudden clampdown took many by surprise. Nelson Mandela was arrested at home in Orlando before dawn while he was preparing for the ANC stayaway and pass protest. He and some other ANC leaders were still involved in the Treason Trial and were taken to Pretoria prison to appear in court. Albert Luthuli, president of the ANC, was assaulted after his arrest. Joe Slovo, a leading white communist lawyer, was detained as he was about to appear in court for the families of 434 black miners, and six white, who had died in a coal mine disaster in the Free State.

On 8 April, soon after the Sharpeville massacre and Cape Town protests, the government, with the support of the main white opposition United Party, passed the Unlawful Organisations Act, banning parties that threatened public order. It was aimed at the ANC and PAC. Mandela recorded in his autobiography: 'we were now, all of us, outlaws'. A day later, on 9 April, Verwoerd was shot after giving a speech at the Milner Park showgrounds in Johannesburg. The attempted assassination was not by a radical black activist but a middle-aged, English-speaking white man. He said he was unhappy with the conflict in South Africa but, declared unfit to stand trial, he was committed to a psychiatric hospital where he later committed suicide. Verwoerd survived and despite a lengthy period of recuperation, he was able to keep control of the National Party and of the country.

ACTIVITY
CONSOLIDATION

African opposition to apartheid

1 What were the main methods of peaceful protest employed by the ANC?

2 Sharpeville received more media coverage than the protests in Cape Town and the Mpondoland uprising. Why do you think that was? What impact does this have on the writing and study of history, especially among those who do not rely on primary source material?

3 What difficulties did the banning of African political parties create for opposition leaders? Write a list, then suggest ways they could modify their activities to counter these difficulties.

WHY DID SOUTH AFRICA BECOME A REPUBLIC IN 1961?

The National Party came to power advocating that South Africa should be a republic, freed from the remnants of British constitutional authority in which the head of state was the British monarch. In fact, as the implementation of apartheid demonstrated, there was little that Britain could do, or was prepared to do, in order to constrain apartheid policy. The republican issue was therefore not a priority in the 1950s. The National Party did gradually renegotiate its relationship with Britain. For example, the Simonstown naval base, which had long been a focus for British naval power in the south Atlantic and Indian Ocean, passed to South Africa in an agreement of 1955, though British ships were still able to use the facilities.

Verwoerd's aims

By early 1960, Verwoerd felt sufficiently confident to announce a whites-only referendum on the question of a republic. The 1958 election had given the nationalists a secure majority, with 66 percent of parliamentary seats and 55 percent of white votes. Verwoerd saw the referendum as an opportunity to rally support beyond the constituency that usually backed the National Party. Within the Party he was determined to stamp his authority as a representative of hardline Transvalers, against the influence of the more moderate Cape nationalists. Although the latter supported apartheid, they were unhappy with his aggressive style of leadership, his arrogance and his intransigence on issues such as the republic.

Verwoerd also bolstered his support in the Afrikaner Christian nationalist association, the Broederbond. A Cape stalwart, Hendrik Thom, Rector of the University of Stellenbosch, was displaced as head of the Broederbond by a Transvaal radical, Dr P. J. Meyer, a former member of the *Ossewabrandwag* (the Afrikaner organisation that had campaigned against supporting Britain in the Second World War). Meyer was also appointed to the influential position of head of the South African Broadcasting Corporation where the nationalists increasingly took control of the broadcast media. They did not, however, introduce television because they did not feel they could adequately control the output. South Africa had no television until 1976. This helped the government to curtail the influence of global news and opinion at the height of apartheid.

Macmillan's 'wind of change' speech

Harold Macmillan, the Conservative prime minister of Britain, visited South Africa in February 1960 as part of a month long tour of Africa. Remarkably, it was the first tour of Africa, and first visit to South Africa, by a British prime minister in office – though British royals had visited, most recently King George VI and his family in 1947. Macmillan started in Ghana, independent since 1957. His visit was in part to confirm Britain's decision to decolonise more broadly, to celebrate African self-government and strengthen Commonwealth ties. Macmillan was also deeply aware of the **Cold War** between the West and the communist countries. His tour was also an attempt to keep African countries on the side of Western democracies.

> ### KEY TERM
>
> Cold War
> After the Second World War, global politics divided increasingly into three major camps. The United States and western Europe, together with Japan, saw themselves as defenders of democracy, liberty and capitalism. The Soviet Union and its allies in eastern Europe defended communism as a political system that promoted the interests of the working class and promised greater equality. They believed in powerful centralised states to achieve this goal. India and other newly independent nations started a non-aligned movement, attempting to avoid taking sides with the West or the communist bloc. The term Cold War was used to describe the tension between the West and the communist East, which dominated international politics at the time.

For all that the United States had become the most powerful nation, Britain was still the major imperial power and it was the most significant external reference point for South Africans. Macmillan's trip had already been planned when Verwoerd announced the South African referendum on republican status. It was in this context that Macmillan gave his famous 'wind of change' speech. In fact he gave some of the same speech in Ghana but it did not make much impact there because Ghana was already independent. In South Africa, the media was more attentive and the speech was heard differently.

Macmillan was attempting to steer a careful line: celebrating 50 years of the Union of South Africa; responding to Verwoerd's call for a republic; and anxious not to polarise the position. He was aware of the criticism from Indian and African leaders for visiting South Africa and being hosted by the National Party. He was equally keen to keep South Africa within the Western mainstream.

Macmillan spent much of his speech to the white members of parliament in Cape Town praising South Africa's achievements and the beauty of its countryside. He noted that much of the progress in industry was a result of British investment and that in 1956, nearly two-thirds of external investment was from Britain and a third of trade with Britain. He emphasised that 'our economies are now largely interdependent'. He highlighted the value of partnership and praised General Smuts, as well as South Africa's contribution to the War and the Commonwealth, and noted its capacity to offer technical assistance to Africa.

Macmillan's memorable phrase, 'the wind of change blowing through Africa' was not intended to call for radical change but articulated the conservative realism that was guiding his government to pursue decolonisation. This process had been set in train by the Labour government under Clement Atlee (1945–51) but only India had achieved independence under Labour. It was the British Conservatives under Macmillan (prime minister from 1957 until 1963), along with the conservative nationalist Charles de Gaulle in France, who were responsible for the most rapid decolonisation in Africa.

Macmillan saw the problems of an aggressive defence of the empire after the **Suez Crisis** in 1956. Britain was also faced with major wars against insurgents in Malaysia and Kenya. The costs of empire were rising and American pressure on Britain to decolonise was increasing. During Macmillan's premiership, most of Britain's former African territories achieved or were promised independence. He hoped that rapid decolonisation would facilitate strong links between Britain and its former colonies. These newly independent countries could then remain important markets and sites for investment.

KEY TERM

Suez Crisis, 1956

The Suez Crisis saw British and French troops sent to Egypt in 1956 to protect their interests in the Suez Canal, a vital transport link between the Mediterranean and Red Sea. The new president of Egypt, Nasser, had taken control of the canal in July. The USSR, USA and UN persuaded Britain and France to withdraw. Independence movements across the empire saw this as a significant climb down by Britain.

Macmillan attempted to present African nationalism as natural and to indicate that white South Africans needed to accept it. They were part of it: 'Indeed in the history of our times', he said to the white parliament, 'yours will be recorded as the first of the African nationalists.' He did not directly say that white South Africans should give black South Africans political rights, but this was implied; he did explicitly query 'some aspects of your policies'. He warned South Africa against trying to go it alone. Verwoerd, as well as many commentators, heard his speech in this way. In a brief response, and in later speeches, Verwoerd emphasised the white determination to stay in power, but Macmillan's visit, together with the changing face of Africa, cemented in his mind the idea of an internal decolonisation of South Africa through the Bantustan or homeland policy.

SOURCE

 From Harold Macmillan's 'wind of change' speech, delivered to the House of Assembly at Cape Town, 1960.

In the 20th century, and especially since the end of the war, the processes which gave birth to the nation states of Europe have been repeated all over the world. We have seen the awakening of national consciousness in peoples who have for centuries lived in dependence on some other power. Fifteen years ago this movement spread through Asia. Many countries there, of different races and civilizations, pressed their claim to an independent national life. Today the same thing is happening in Africa, and the most striking of all the impressions that I have formed since I left London a month ago is of the strength of this African national consciousness. In different places it takes different forms, but it is happening everywhere. The wind of change is blowing through this continent and whether we like it or not, this growth of national consciousness is a political fact. And we must all accept it as a fact, and our national policies must take account of it.

As I see it the great issue in this second half of the 20th century, is whether the uncommitted people of Asia or Africa will swing to the East or to the West. Will they be drawn into the Communist camp? Or will the great experiments in self-government that are now being made in Asia and Africa, especially within the Commonwealth, prove so successful, and by their example so compelling, that the balance will come down in favour of freedom and order and justice?

The struggle is joined and it is a struggle for the minds of men.

 EVIDENCE (5b)

The importance of context

Documents (texts) are like small pieces torn from a larger tapestry (context). Historians have to reconstruct the larger pattern into which documents might fit in order to use them to construct accounts of the past. The problem is that texts can have multiple contexts. Historians often debate how best to contextualise the documents that they interpret.

Reread Source 9, the so-called 'wind of change' speech made by Harold Macmillan, prime minister of the United Kingdom, during a visit to Cape Town on his tour of Africa in 1960.

1 Summarise some key points from the source – how did Macmillan understand the world in 1960? What were the possible futures?

As well as noting the contents of the speech, it is important to consider Macmillan's audience when he was speaking. The speech was heard by MPs sitting in the Houses of Parliament at Cape Town on 3 February 1960. The speech was also heard outside the parliament by many African activists.

The timeline below provides a possible context for the document in the wider story of political change in Africa. Look at this timeline and then answer the question that follows.

Sequence of events 1

1952	Defiance campaign in South Africa	
1957	Ghana gains independence	
1960	Sharpeville Massacre Nigeria becomes independent	Harold Macmillan makes 'wind of change' speech
1961	ANC adopts the armed struggle South Africa becomes a republic	
1961–64	Tanganyika, Uganda, Kenya, Zambia and Malawi gain independence	

Continued

2 How does the 'wind of change' speech fit into the pattern of events? Why might Macmillan have spoken to the South African parliament at this time, with this language?

The document might seem to have one kind of meaning when interpreted in the context of decolonisation. A contrasting interpretation appears if we locate it in another context.

The wind of change speech provided Verwoerd with an opportunity to assert his power. Standing up immediately after Macmillan had spoken, Verwoerd told the MPs that white South Africans were equally in need of justice and protection. The speech was used to reinforce the need for apartheid policies.

Sequence of events 2

1950	Communist Party banned in South Africa	
1959	Cuba becomes a communist country	
1960	ANC and PAC banned South Africa votes to become a republic	Harold Macmillan makes 'Wind of change' speech
1962	Nelson Mandela arrested	

3 How could Macmillan's 'wind of change' speech be made use of by Verwoerd and the National Party?

Consider both timelines together and answer the following questions:

4 Use information from both timelines to construct a possible context for the impact of Macmillan's 'wind of change' speech in 1960.

5 Why is it important for historians to spend time thinking about possible contexts for a document before they start to use it to draw conclusions about the past?

Establishing the republic, 1960–61

In October 1960, white South Africans (including those in South West Africa) voted by a narrow majority of 52 percent for a republic. The vote was close in the Cape and the Transvaal, where small majorities voted for a republic, but a large number rejected it in Natal, which contained a sizable population of British South Africans. The black opposition parties rejected the move, mainly because it was done without consultation with the majority of South Africa's population. For the largely English-speaking white opposition, the link with Britain and the Commonwealth remained an important part of their identity and an influence for moderation in South African politics.

South Africa became a republic on 31 May 1961. The office of the state president became the ceremonial head of state, replacing the Queen and the Governor-General. A new decimal currency, called the rand (short for Witwatersrand, site of South Africa's gold mines) replaced the British pound. There were many other symbolic changes that accompanied the shift to a republic. The 'crown' was replaced in statutes by the 'state', while 'royal' was removed from the names of various organisations and institutions. By and large, however, it could be argued that the move to a republic did not have a dramatic effect on South Africa as leaving the Commonwealth.

SOURCE 10 Part of a letter from Nelson Mandela to Hendrik Verwoerd, 20 April 1961.

I AM DIRECTED by the All-In African National Action Council to address your Government in the following terms:

... This conference was attended by 1,500 delegates from town and country, representing 145 religious, social, cultural, sporting, and political bodies.

Conference noted that your Government, after receiving a mandate from a section of the European population, decided to proclaim a Republic on 31 May.

It was the firm view of delegates that your Government, which represents only a minority of the population in this country, is not entitled to take such a decision without first seeking the views and obtaining the express consent of the African people. Conference feared that under this proposed Republic your Government, which is already notorious the world over for its obnoxious policies, would continue to make even more savage attacks on the rights and living conditions of the African people.

AS Level Exam-Style Question Section A

Study Source 10 before you answer this question.

Why is Source 11 valuable to the historian for an enquiry into the ANC's attitude to South Africa becoming a republic?

Explain your answer using the source, the information given about it and your knowledge of the historical context. (8 marks)

Tip
Consider who is writing the letter and also who the letter is to.

SOURCE
11

Part of a letter from Nelson Mandela to Sir De Villiers Graaff (leader of the United Party), 23 May 1961.

In one week's time, the Verwoerd Government intends to inaugurate its Republic. It is unnecessary to state that this intention has never been endorsed by the non-white majority of this country. The decision has been taken by little over half of the White community; it is opposed by every articulate group amongst the African, Coloured and Indian communities, who constitute the majority of this country.

Government's intentions to proceed, under these circumstances, has created conditions bordering on crisis. We have been excluded from the Commonwealth, and condemned 95 to 1 at the United Nations. Our trade is being boycotted, and foreign capital is being withdrawn. The country is becoming an armed camp, the Government preparing for civil war with increasingly heavy police and military apparatus, the non-white population for a general strike and long-term non-cooperation with the Government.

[...] We have called on the Government to convene an elected National Convention of representatives of all races without delay, and to charge that Convention with the task of drawing up a new Constitution for this country which would be acceptable to all racial groups.

Leaving the Commonwealth

In March 1961 a special Commonwealth Conference was called, largely to consider South Africa's position. Verwoerd attended with an application to remain as a republic in the Commonwealth. Other countries, such as India, had done so. The Asian and African heads of state were strongly against South Africa remaining in the Commonwealth as long as apartheid was government policy. Britain, Australia, New Zealand and the Federation of Rhodesia and Nyasaland supported South Africa. However, the new Commonwealth leaders, such as Kwame Nkrumah of Ghana, were not keen to polarise the position and split the organisation while there was still some hope that South Africa would shift direction.

A compromise might have been possible but when Verwoerd was asked whether he would allow diplomatic representation for newly independent African states in Pretoria he was quoted as saying that he could not have the capital crowded with so many embassies. In the face of such undiplomatic behaviour, even the Australian and British negotiators advised that they could not keep South Africa as a republic in the Commonwealth. Verwoerd withdrew the application. As in the case of Ireland in 1949, South Africa left the Commonwealth and the Afrikaner nationalist dream was achieved even more completely than they wished. South Africa became a state fully independent from Britain and the Commonwealth.

International relations after leaving the Commonwealth
White-controlled South Africa was not left entirely isolated. On the one hand, Britain was keen to keep some pressure on South Africa, both through international and regional channels. Britain was still the colonial power in the three High Commission territories that neighboured South Africa: Bechuanaland Protectorate, Basutoland and Swaziland. These territories (which became independent states within the Commonwealth, as Botswana, Lesotho and Swaziland, in 1966–68) became occasional havens for South African political dissidents and routes for escape. The United Kingdom itself was the major destination for those fleeing South Africa and the British Anti-apartheid Movement (AAM), founded in London in 1960, became a global focus for opposition.

On the other hand, as Macmillan had noted, South Africa was economically and strategically important for Britain. The Conservative Party included a strong right wing that was uneasy about decolonisation and keen to support white settlers from Britain, living in Rhodesia and South Africa. The Conservative Party Monday Club was established as a direct result of the 'wind of change' speech to debate decolonisation: they saw Macmillan as undermining the Party's commitment to empire.

As the Cold War intensified, Britain and the United States were keen to have allies against communism. The South African government never lost a chance to emphasise its role as a bastion against communism in Africa and to point to the links between the ANC and the Communist Party. The **Cuban Missile Crisis** in 1962 affirmed the Western sense that the benefits of white minority rule in South Africa outweighed the costs, at least in the short term.

British companies thought much the same. Sharpeville and Cape Town triggered a brief withdrawal of investment from South Africa but by the time the Republic was founded, in May 1961, the government had been rewarded rather than punished for repressing African nationalism. The scene was set for massive overseas investment in South Africa during the 1960s and British companies remained the largest external investors. Left wing critics such as Ruth First, wife of Joe Slovo, attributed Britain's caution in taking any action against apartheid to such economic interests, and wrote a book on the topic called *The South African Connection*. Gold supplies remained important for Western economies and in the 1960s still provided a global backing for currencies. Equally important, South Africa was the major global supplier of uranium, a by-product of gold mining that was essential for nuclear weapons and nuclear power stations. In any case there was little that the Western powers could do about apartheid short of a major economic boycott.

The ANC first called for sanctions against South Africa in 1959. In 1962 the UN passed a resolution to ban imports and exports to and from South Africa. These were voluntary, and western powers with strong interests in the South African economy did not take up sanctions. In 1963 the UN passed a resolution advocating an arms embargo against South Africa so that external powers were not supporting the government with weapons to suppress its people. Again this was a voluntary, not compulsory, measure but in 1964, the British Labour government under Harold Wilson decided to impose it.

ACTIVITY
CONSOLIDATION

Creating a republic

1 Imagine you are a National Party member and part of the welcoming committee to receive the British prime minister Harold Macmillan on his visit in 1960. Make notes planning how you would explain to him why apartheid is necessary in South Africa.

2 Write a timeline of events leading to South Africa becoming a republic in 1961. Which were the most significant? Circle the top three and write a short paragraph to explain why you chose them.

DID THE ANC AND PAC RADICALISE AFTER 1960?

Both the ANC and the PAC had to rethink their political strategies after they were banned in April 1960. They could not operate legally and those who openly declared themselves members were subject to criminal proceedings. It was illegal to spread or quote written material from the movements. The State of Emergency was lifted in August 1960 when the government thought that it had stopped the momentum of popular protest and most political detainees were released. The question for African political leaders was how to respond.

Moves to armed struggle

Throughout the 1950s and early 1960s, individual African activists had occasionally expressed themselves through violence against property or people – at East London in 1952, Durban in 1959 and Mpondoland in 1960. Political protests against apartheid had not, however, been mounted with violence against whites in mind. Mpondoland was in some senses an exception in that headmen and chiefs identifying with the state were deliberately killed and the rebels asked the ANC to assist in finding arms to fight the government. The ANC was not ready to do so. It held to its commitment to peaceful protest and civil disobedience. The movement recognised that government retaliation was likely to be particularly harsh if it resorted to violence as a political strategy.

Mandela and Sisulu claimed that they had discussed the possibility of armed struggle as far back as 1952 and the issue came up regularly among activists in the 1950s. Violence was occasionally mentioned as an option in speeches. The banning of the movements in 1960 and their inability to operate peacefully made a decision all the more urgent. Recent examples of successful armed revolutions included China in the 1940s and Cuba in 1959, and Algerian nationalists had turned to armed struggle against the French. But ANC leaders had to be cautious, especially while the Treason Trial continued. Their lawyers had managed to establish that the organisation was not committed to the violent overthrow of the state; this was a major reason for their acquittal in March 1961.

In the meantime, those linked to the ANC held an All-in African Conference to advocate a national constitutional convention. All South Africans, they argued, and not only whites, should participate in decisions about the constitutional future. A similar movement started in Cape Town spearheaded by Coloured political leaders. The ANC also decided on a three day stayaway in May 1961 to coincide with the moment that South Africa would become a republic.

The South African Communist Party (CP), already operating underground and in secret, was the first to adopt the armed struggle in principle, even though some members such as the trade unionist Moses Kotane were doubtful. Sisulu, Kotane and other African communists were also members of the ANC so that both parties were fully informed about what was happening. Mandela himself was close to them and attended secret meetings. In June 1961 the ANC itself explicitly decided on armed struggle. Some, including Luthuli, and most members of the South African Indian Congress, were still against violence out of principle. Others were concerned that the movement was not ready for this strategy, uncertain about wider support and felt that they would open themselves to even harsher retaliation by the state. But key leaders believed that they could develop an underground organisation. Oliver Tambo and others had escaped into exile where they were beyond the power of the South African state.

SOURCE 12

Albert Luthuli, president of the ANC, was awarded the Nobel Peace Prize in 1961. The following is an extract from his acceptance speech given at the award ceremony in December that year.

This golden age of Africa's independence is also the dark age of South Africa's decline and retrogression, brought about by men who, when revolutionary changes that entrenched fundamental human rights were taking place in Europe, were closed in on the tip of South Africa – and so missed the wind of progressive change. In the wake of that decline and retrogression, bitterness between men grows to alarming heights... government becomes increasingly dictatorial and intolerant of constitutional and legal procedures, increasingly violent, and suppressive; there is a constant drive for more policemen, more soldiers, more armaments, banishments without trial, and penal whippings. All the trappings of medieval backwardness and cruelty come to the fore. Education is being reduced to an instrument of subtle indoctrination. Slanted and biased reporting in the organs of public information, a creeping censorship, book banning, and blacklisting – all these spread their shadows over the land. This is South Africa today, in the age of Africa's greatness. But beneath the surface there is a spirit of defiance. The people of South Africa have never been a docile lot, least of all the African people. We have a long tradition of struggle for our national rights, reaching back to the very beginnings of white settlement and conquest 300 years ago. Our history is one of opposition to domination, of protest and refusal to submit to tyranny.

SOURCE 13

Extract from Nelson Mandela's address to the Conference of the Pan-African Freedom Movement of East and Central Africa, held in Addis Ababa on 3 February 1962.

But we believe it would be fatal to create the illusion that external pressures render it unnecessary for us to tackle the enemy from within. The centre and cornerstone of the struggle for freedom and democracy in South Africa lies inside South Africa itself. Apart from those required for essential work outside the country, freedom fighters are in great demand for work inside the country. We owe it as a duty to ourselves and to the freedom-loving peoples of the world to build and maintain in South Africa itself a powerful, solid movement, capable of surviving any attack by the government and sufficiently militant to fight back with a determination that comes from the knowledge and conviction that it is first and foremost by our own struggle and sacrifice inside South Africa itself that victory over White domination and apartheid can be won.

A Level Exam-Style Question Section A

Study Sources 12 and 13 before you answer this question.

How far could the historian use Sources 12 and 13 together to investigate opposition to apartheid in South Africa in the 1960s?

Explain your answer, using both sources, the information given about them and your own knowledge of the historical context. (20 marks)

Tip
Think about the provenance (nature, origin and purpose) of the sources and how this would impact on the use the historian could make of them.

The ANC and uMkhonto weSizwe

The armed organisation uMkhonto weSizwe (Zulu for 'Spear of the Nation' and abbreviated to MK) was set up as an organisation that was not formally linked to the ANC or the CP. It was, in theory, an independent military wing acting in support of the liberation movement, led jointly by Mandela representing the ANC and Joe Slovo for the CP. This was done partly to protect the ANC against further repression and partly because it was not fully united behind this decision. Over the long term, communist links proved important for the armed struggle. The Soviet Union made the largest financial contribution and other communist governments, such as East Germany, helped with training and education. In 1961 five African men were sent to China for training in guerrilla tactics. Attempts were made to set up MK regional commands within South Africa. It was decided that targets would include strategic sites, such as communications posts and power units, rather than places where loss of life was a risk. The first major act of sabotage was planned for 16 December 1961. This was the public holiday called Dingaan's Day when white South Africa commemorated the Boer victory over the Zulu at the Battle of Blood River in 1838. Ironically, it also coincided with Luthuli's return from Norway where he had received the Nobel Peace Prize in December 1961.

SOURCE 14

Nelson Mandela, in his 1995 autobiography *Long Walk to Freedom*, writing about moves to armed struggle.

At the meeting [of the ANC in June 1961] I argued that the state had given us no alternative to violence. I said it was wrong and immoral to subject our people to armed attacks by the state without offering them some kind of alternative. I mentioned again that the people on their own had taken up arms. Violence would begin whether we initiated it or not. Would it not be better to guide this violence ourselves, according to principles where we saved lives by attacking symbols of oppression, and not people? If we did not take the lead now, I said, we would soon be latecomers and followers to a movement we did not control...

In planning the direction and form that MK would take, we considered four types of violent activities: sabotage, guerrilla warfare, terrorism and open revolution. For a small and fledgling army, open revolution was inconceivable. Terrorism inevitably reflected poorly on those who used it, undermining any public support it might otherwise garner. Guerilla warfare was a possibility, but since the ANC had been reluctant to embrace violence at all, it made sense to start with the form of violence that inflicted the least harm against individuals: sabotage. Because it did not involve loss of life, it offered the best hope for reconciliation among the races afterwards. We did not want to start a blood-feud between white and black... Our strategy was to make selective forays against military installations, power plants, telephone lines and transportation links: targets that would not only hamper the military effectiveness of the state, but frighten National Party supporters, scare away foreign capital and weaken the economy.

The PAC and Poqo

The PAC also turned to underground organisation. Its grass roots networks among migrant workers in Cape Town provided a vehicle for covert action. For example, an informal PAC cell was founded among Africans from the Eastern Cape working at a Jewish old age home in the city. In the African townships, the focus was on political education through small meetings, with an emphasis on history, the violence of colonial conquest and the loss of land. They managed to get hold of texts by Nkrumah, Jomo Kenyatta and Franz Fanon and those with education explained them to those without. Mau Mau in Kenya was an attractive model for the PAC – more for the fear it seemed to instil in whites, than for any detailed knowledge of its strategies. The PAC's leader Robert Sobukwe was kept in prison and unable to influence the new direction of strategy. At this stage, he was clearly regarded as particularly dangerous. But Leballo and Kgosana escaped into exile and the PAC attempted to establish a new headquarters in neighbouring Lesotho.

In 1961 Poqo was formed as a movement that would, like MK, be prepared to go beyond non-violent protest. The origins of the name are uncertain but the best substantiated view is that it came from an African praise poet at a meeting in Cape Town who used the Xhosa phrase *Umbutho Wami-Afrika Poqo* ('a regiment of Africa-alone'). Praise poetry was an ancient form of performance. Traditionally poets recited praise poems ad lib for important chiefs, but the practice was now adapted for new political purposes.

Poqo was essentially a movement among migrant workers with little central control by the PAC. It maintained its Africanist ideologies and justified violence against whites. PAC cells spread to other Western Cape towns and back to the Eastern Cape. One cell planned to blow up the Blue Train, which provided a luxury railway journey from Pretoria to Cape Town. Another aimed to kill Kaiser Matanzima, who was leading the Transkei homeland to self-government. Poqo was responsible for the Paarl march in 1962, which led to the killing of two whites, and five protestors. In 1963 a Poqo cell in the Transkei staged the notorious Mbashe Bridge killings of a white family staying in a caravan.

Although relatively few whites were killed in the Poqo campaigns, Poqo was not committed, as in the case of MK, to selective sabotage of non-human targets. Poqo killings were well-publicised and described in lurid terms in the white press which saw them as examples of African savagery. In fact, both the PAC and Poqo understood their actions, like Mandela, as entirely political. They were an expression of radical African nationalism and armed struggle against a state that gave them no alternative. But they attracted particular hostility from the state when the PAC members were brought to trial. Of the men executed by hanging after political trials in the 1960s, 62 were in Poqo, 23 were Mpondo rebels, nine from Cato Manor, and seven from the ANC and MK.

Despite some dramatic moments of violence against property and people, neither the ANC nor PAC had the capacity for a sustained armed struggle. There were many factors at work: they had no physical base in South Africa or any adjacent country, they had little training, and as yet little support from abroad. The chief reason, however, was the repressive power of the state. Mandela was able to travel abroad for six months and operate underground but was arrested in 1962. The headquarters of MK, at a small farm in Rivonia, north of Johannesburg, was raided in 1963 and most of the key leaders arrested and tried.

The Rivonia Trial and its significance for Nelson Mandela

Mandela and the MK leaders were tried at the Pretoria Supreme Court in Johannesburg. Altogether there were ten leading lights of the ANC in the dock, and the trial lasted from 1963 to 1964. They were accused of recruiting fighters, attempting to commit sabotage, having links with communist organisations, and soliciting money from foreign states. Rivonia was another gruelling trial for sections of the ANC leadership. Nevertheless Mandela gave a resounding speech from the dock that has echoed down the years as a major statement of political courage and hope. He did not deny that he had espoused armed struggle and again explained why. He used the opportunity to sketch the disabilities suffered by Africans.

The Rivonia accused were defended by an able group of white lawyers sympathetic to the liberation struggle. They were led by Bram Fischer, an Afrikaner who, after a period in Oxford on a Rhodes scholarship, joined the CP in South Africa. The prosecutor called for the death penalty but the Afrikaner judge, perhaps influenced by Mandela's speech and the morality of the defence, and

Cause and consequence

Causes never simply come one after another. They are often present simultaneously and have an effect on one another. Sometimes new causes develop and interact with existing ones.

Work in groups to produce a diagram of reasons for the creation of uMkhonto weSizwe (MK) and the ANC's move to violent tactics, and the links between them. On an A3 piece of paper, write all the reasons behind the ANC's move to violent tactics including:

- State use of violence
- Failure of non-violent methods
- Apartheid legislation
- New younger activists
- The breakaway of the PAC
- The example of other liberation movements

Draw boxes around the causes. Make the size of each box reflect how long the cause was a relevant factor. For example, if you argue that 'legislation' had been an important factor for a long period then this will be quite a big box. Make links between all the causes. Draw lines between the boxes and annotate them to explain how the causes are connected and in what ways each affected the other. For example, between 'state use of violence' and 'failure of non-violent methods' you could write something like, 'events like Sharpeville showed that the state did not shy away from using violence'.

Now answer the following questions:

1 How do the causes differ in their nature? (Think in terms of events, developments, beliefs, etc.)

2 How do the causes differ in the roles they played in bringing a shift in strategy? (Think about whether each cause created the right conditions, was a trigger for events, or acted in some other way.)

3 Write a 200-word paragraph explaining how important it is to recognise the relationships between causes. Give examples from your diagram. Try to include connective phrases such as: 'this created conditions conducive to...', 'this triggered an immediate reaction...', or 'this made the development of that situation more/less likely'.

perhaps sensing the possibility that the core ANC leadership might be needed for negotiations in the future, gave life imprisonment. Sobukwe had already been incarcerated on Robben Island, a former leper colony in Table Bay off Cape Town. The black (but not the white) ANC leaders joined him there.

While the imprisonment of Mandela, Sisulu and the others was major news, one must be careful not to overstate its significance at the time. The 'Free Nelson Mandela' movement in the 1980s can distort the lens through which we look back at 1964. The government was neutralising Mandela and the others by placing them on Robben Island. Their communication, both with the outside world and with each other, was limited and censored. They were particularly isolated for the rest of the 1960s. Mandela had been the co-founder and first leader of MK. Now in prison, he was unable to lead the MK in exile, and that responsibility passed to Joe Modise, who commanded MK from 1965 until 1984. Slovo, also in exile, remained a major strategist.

SOURCE 15

Extract from a flyer, entitled 'The ANC calls on you – Save the Leaders!' issued by the ANC, October 1963.

The Government is putting the 'Rivonia' men on trial. Vorster claims he has caught the 'trouble-makers'...

WHITE MAN – DOES THAT MAKE YOU FEEL SAFE?

Vorster seeks the death sentence for some of them, imprisonment for the rest...

WHITE MAN – WILL YOU SLEEP BETTER AT NIGHT?

The prosecution will make your flesh creep with stories of 'hellish' military plots, sabotage, threats to the safety of the state...

WHITE MAN – DO YOU KNOW WHAT THIS MEANS?

LET US TELL YOU WHAT IT MEANS... South Africa is in the first stage of civil war. Apartheid has brought that war. Over 3,000 men and women, mostly Africans, but including all races, are in jails for resisting apartheid. More will be tried. They come from all over South Africa. They are not criminals. Most of them are people of the highest integrity, intelligence and courage, gentle and compassionate, vitally concerned with problems of justice and freedom. In any normal society these people would be the rulers.

SOURCE 16

Part of the speech Nelson Mandela gave from the dock during the Rivonia Trial, 1964.

Above all, we want equal political rights, because without them our disabilities will be permanent. I know this sounds revolutionary to the whites in this country, because the majority of voters will be Africans. This makes the white man fear democracy.

But this fear cannot be allowed to stand in the way of the only solution which will guarantee racial harmony and freedom for all. It is not true that the enfranchisement of all will result in racial domination. Political division, based on colour, is entirely artificial and, when it disappears, so will the domination of one colour group by another. The ANC has spent half a century fighting against racialism. When it triumphs it will not change that policy.

This then is what the ANC is fighting. Their struggle is a truly national one. It is a struggle of the African people, inspired by their own suffering and their own experience. It is a struggle for the right to live.

During my lifetime I have dedicated myself to this struggle of the African people. I have fought against white domination, and I have fought against black domination. I have cherished the ideal of a democratic and free society in which all persons live together in harmony and with equal opportunities. It is an ideal which I hope to live for and to achieve. But if needs be, it is an ideal for which I am prepared to die.

> **A Level Exam-Style Question Section B**
>
> To what extent was the Rivonia Trial a political opportunity for the ANC? (20 marks)
>
> **Tip**
> *Consider how the Rivonia Trial fitted into the wider schemes of the ANC. The question is asking you to balance the gains and losses provided by the trial.*

The impact of exile and imprisonment on the ANC and PAC

Oliver Tambo, deputy president of the ANC, went into exile in 1960 in order to salvage the movement, establish the 'external mission' and win international support. He was driven secretly to Botswana by Ronald Segal.

EXTEND YOUR KNOWLEDGE

Ronald Segal

Ronald Segal became an anti-apartheid activist in London and editor of the Penguin African Library. The series published *A Short History of Africa* by Roland Oliver and J. D. Fage as well as *Struggle for a Birthright*, a history of the ANC, the *Peasants' Revolt* by Govan Mbeki and *Class and Colour in South Africa* by H. J. Simons and R. E. Simons.

Based initially in London, Tambo travelled widely in Europe and in Africa. He was invited to address the United Nations (which recognised both the ANC and PAC as representative South African political organisations) in New York and focused on the plight of political prisoners in South Africa; the UN responded with a resolution calling for their release. After a trip to the Soviet Union he was able to secure significant funding for the movement from that source. The Soviet Union made the most important financial contribution to the ANC in exile in the 1960s and early 1970s. Also from that time, Swedish contributions became vital for the non-military activities of the ANC. Tambo's tireless travelling, and his obvious sincerity and commitment, gave the ANC significant international legitimacy in the early years of exile.

But by the end of 1963 there were few active members of the African political leadership still living free in South Africa. Those who had avoided prison sentences had gone into exile or accepted that open politics was too dangerous. Without leadership on the ground, the ability to organise opposition within South Africa became very difficult, and stifled much ANC and PAC activity. However, protest did not die down entirely and within a few years, new currents of black opposition would surface.

The global Anti-apartheid Movement in the 1960s

The Anti-apartheid Movement (AAM) was formally founded in 1960 in London. This was a global movement against apartheid rather than an organisation within South Africa or the ANC in exile. It had many different roots. In Britain, perhaps the most important were Christians in the Anglican Church who had worked in South Africa. Trevor Huddleston had served in Sophiatown and witnessed its destruction; over the long term he was a central figure in the AAM as vice-president from 1961 to 1981 and president from 1981 to 1994. Ambrose Reeves, who wrote so effectively about Sharpeville, was Bishop of Johannesburg from 1949 to 1961.

He had to resign when he was deported from South Africa. They saw apartheid as morally wrong and in conflict with Christian teaching that all were equal before God. Reeves emphasised the 'unity that is ours in Christ … whatever may be our differences of colour, culture, and class'. To these were added Labour and Liberal politicians and many activists who opposed colonialism and white rule more generally. In 1959 they started a boycott movement, focussing on South African products such as sherry, which gathered pace after Sharpeville. It was supported by newspapers such as the *Guardian* and the *Observer*. As political exiles came to Britain, the major destination for dissident South Africans, the momentum grew. Those directly involved as office-holders in the ANC, such as Oliver Tambo, did not participate formally in the AAM, but met regularly with activists and shared platforms at meetings.

Internationally, E. S. Reddy, an Indian who worked at the United Nations in New York, played a key role over many years in highlighting apartheid. He found increasing support as newly independent Asian and African states were admitted to the UN and he became the first secretary of the Special Committee against Apartheid founded in 1963. The Swedish government gave direct support to the AAM in that country and the United States, Canada and the Netherlands also housed important anti-apartheid movements.

Despite some success in boycotts of South African goods, and the launch of an *Anti-Apartheid News*, the movement struggled to find widespread support. Sport proved to be an important new area for mobilisation against apartheid.

Sport was identified by campaigners as an issue dear to white South African hearts. South Africa had ceased to send teams to the Commonwealth Games from 1961 and was excluded by FIFA from international football in 1963. In 1962, Dennis Brutus formed the South African Non-Racial Olympic Committee inside the country. Together with external supporters the Committee was successful in persuading the Olympic movement to exclude South Africa from the 1964 Games. The proposal to send an all-black team to the 1970 Football World Cup was rejected. The Anti-apartheid Movement and its allies played a key role in increasing pressure on international sporting bodies.

In the 1960s South Africa's teams remained completely segregated and in effect only white teams represented the country and even visiting teams were required to be racially segregated. These issues came to a head when Basil D'Oliveira was selected for the English cricket team in 1968. D'Oliveira was born in Cape Town but emigrated to England in 1960 because he was classified as Coloured and could not achieve his cricketing ambitions in apartheid South Africa. He played county cricket for Worcestershire and, after becoming a British citizen, was selected regularly for the English national team between 1966 and 1968. A tour to South Africa was planned at the end of 1968. Although D'Oliveira had not always been a star performer, he was at that stage top of the English batting averages. The England selectors nonetheless excluded him from the tour, saying his style of play was unsuitable for South African conditions. D'Oliveira's exclusion provoked a huge outcry as it was so patently unfair. He received 20,000 letters of support and there were resignations from Marylebone Cricket Club (MCC). When an English player had to withdraw because of injury, D'Oliveira was belatedly selected. Vorster then refused to allow the tour. He said 'it is the team of the Anti-apartheid Movement'. It was a very British crisis, with the cricketing authorities hoping to muddle through, but it brought home the costs and implications of apartheid to a far wider range of people.

ACTIVITY
CONSOLIDATION

Moves to armed struggle

1 In the move to armed struggle, what were the main targets of the ANC and Poqo and how did they differ? What were the advantages and disadvantages of the different approaches?

2 Working in groups of four or six imagine you are the organising committee of the ANC at the house in Rivonia, debating armed struggle as a political tool. With half of the group for the use of violence, and the other half against it, have a discussion and come to a conclusion on how the ANC should move forward. Would you reach a different conclusion if you knew the immediate consequences of a move to armed struggle?

WHAT FACTORS STRENGTHENED APARTHEID OR 'SEPARATE DEVELOPMENT' IN THE YEARS 1960–68?

During the 1960s, white political authority seemed secure and to some degree African opposition was suppressed. The South African economy grew quickly, and while whites were the major beneficiaries, some black people also benefited. Given the effectiveness of policing, the majority of African people temporarily accepted the hard realities of white power. Social and political divisions with black society also served to defuse the challenges to apartheid.

In 1966 Verwoerd was murdered by a parliamentary messenger of Greek origin. As with the previous shooting there was no clear political motive and his assailant was confined to a psychiatric hospital. The National Party was sufficiently entrenched for his death to make little impact on policy and on white support. He was succeeded by B. J. Vorster, the tough-talking Minister of Justice who had been responsible for much of the security legislation under which African leaders were detained and convicted.

Economic recovery

After a difficult period between two world wars, the world economy as a whole grew quickly after the Second World War and especially from about 1950 until the oil crisis of 1973. South Africa shared in global development with overall economic growth at about 4.6 percent a year for the period as a whole, and over five percent a year in the 1960s. This was faster than Europe but slower than many other middle-income countries. For example, Brazil and Mexico in Latin America as well as Japan, South Korea and Taiwan in Asia all outstripped South Africa. Even in the 1960s, problems were evident. South Africa was still very dependent on mining and agriculture, especially for its exports. Low levels of productivity and acute skill shortages hampered diversification. This was in part a result of the discriminatory education system. The government failed to invest adequately in education for the great bulk of the population.

The domestic economy

Manufacturing and agriculture benefited particularly in this era of growth. Employment in manufacturing, mostly of black people, roughly doubled between 1951 and 1975 from 855,000 to 1.6 million. The number of Africans doing white collar work (professional, technical and clerical) spiralled from 75,000 to 420,000 – African people were no longer simply manual labourers on the mines and the farms. The numbers employed in gold mining rose from about 300,000 to 400,000, but in the 1960s roughly 80 percent of them were migrant workers from outside South Africa.

A colour bar remained entrenched in law. Certain jobs were reserved for white people only – especially in the mining industry and in skilled artisanal work. African people could not be trained plumbers or electricians or welders and they could not be in control of whites at the place of work. Yet there was in some respects a 'floating' colour bar, shaped by the needs of various industries.

The complexity of apartheid in practice also made it possible to circumvent some restrictions. One example was the construction industry. Although the apartheid government tried to restrict African migration to the cities, it was also determined, in the 1950s and 1960s, to put an end to slums and shack settlements near the city centres and to move African people to large new townships on the urban margins. Urban municipalities received budgets to build a huge number of cheap (or 'sub-economic') homes. For example, state-built housing in Johannesburg increased from 10,000 in 1946 to 62,000 in 1965. By 1970, the new township of Mdantsane near East London housed perhaps 70,000 people in 12,000 new four-roomed family dwellings. The Native Building Workers Act of 1951 enabled municipalities to use African workers, even at a skilled level, on African houses. They were paid far less than white building workers, whose jobs were protected within the building industry more generally. This enabled basic township houses to be built more quickly and cheaply. It also provided employment, skills and wages to African people. In the rural areas also, those moving to denser settlements and betterment villages were beginning to employ African builders.

Apartheid bureaucracies opened up some new opportunities for black South Africans. In many of the cities, whites moved out of government jobs in the townships. Native Affairs offices, schools, creches, nurseries, hospitals and welfare organisations all absorbed more Africans. They joined the rising numbers in private sector work to become increasingly significant consumers of a wide range of goods.

Manufacturers and marketers began to identify an African market, and advertised heavily in newspapers and magazines to sell cigarettes, soft drinks, cleaning materials, clothes and radios. In turn companies and retailers needed African sales personnel, not least for the furniture and cookers that went into the new homes. Financial services such as insurance were also an expanding market.

Per capita income in the 1960s increased by about 23 percent for black South Africans – a substantial rise even if it was from a low base. The African population alone surged from 11 to 15 million and the total population from 16 to 22 million. Industrial workers were among the beneficiaries with wages rising about 50 percent in that decade. These figures point to a striking increase in economic opportunity for African people, especially those in the cities, despite the hardships of apartheid.

National Party spokesmen still articulated their intention to reduce the number of Africans in cities, and to make as many as possible migrant workers. In 1968 prosecutions for pass offences reached 700,000, nearly twice that in 1960 at the height of protests. But economic forces undermined Afrikaner strategy and in this single decade of the 1960s, the number of Africans in the cities probably rose by 1.5 million to over six million. Many did not have rights to live in the cities but they chose to take the risk. Tomlinson, the author of the recommendations regarding the Bantustan policy in the 1950s, had argued that only a massive programme of investment and development in the homelands would make any difference to the rate of urbanisation. As we have noted, Verwoerd refused to do this.

Whites benefited far more from these decades of growth. After a single year in 1960 in which white emigration exceeded immigration, the 1960s as a whole saw an overall increase of about 250,000 white immigrants. The Nationalists had been uneasy about encouraging non-Afrikaner immigration, which might undermine their electoral majority, but by the 1960s, English-speakers voted in some numbers for the National Party. The Nationalists changed their minds about immigration and white immigrants from all over Europe brought skills and capital and, in a context of falling white birth rates, they also brought numbers. Even so, the percentage of white South Africans, which peaked at 22 percent in 1921, fell to around 17 percent by 1968. Immigrants from all over Europe were immediately classified as white, receiving all of those benefits denied to Coloured, Indian or African South Africans.

The 1960s were in many ways the best of times for white South Africans. White incomes increased by 50 percent in ten years and they were on average 12 times black incomes. One of the strongest indicators of wealth was car production. South Africa produced 95,000 cars in 1960 and 195,000 in 1970. Among whites, per capita car ownership ranked about fourth in the world, behind the United States, Australia and Canada with more than one car for every three people. African people probably owned about one car per 100 people. Cars shaped society in many different ways. Whites increasingly lived in suburbs and commuted to work in their own vehicles. African people largely had to rely on public transport – buses and trains. Cars were a symbol of leisure and freedom of movement for whites.

The burgeoning townships and African women
The discussion of Group Areas above focused on the destruction of urban communities and this has been a primary emphasis of historical research on apartheid in the cities. However, new urban African communities were being formed just as the old were destroyed and social historians have focused increasingly on these processes too. Social change in part shaped African life and politics in the 1960s. Some of the new townships became the base for a less politicised urban culture, where people's lives were more focused on work, commuting, consumption, associational life and getting ahead.

EXTEND YOUR KNOWLEDGE

Social history
Social history has become a significant component of professional historical studies since the 1960s. It is an approach that emphasises 'history from below' focusing on the everyday experiences of ordinary people. Social historians study work, the working class and the lives and organisations of poor people who are the majority in most societies. They also examine popular protest movements, from strikes to rural rebellions, and popular culture from peasant life to pop music. Social historians argue not only that this is a route to understanding the experiences of the majority of people, but also that these shape social change and politics more broadly.

The major organisations in Witwatersrand townships were churches, choirs, saving societies, temperance associations and football clubs. Women's associations in the churches were particularly strong. Savings clubs or *stokvels* were ubiquitous. Members, usually a small group, contributed money regularly to a central pool and each member would then receive a payout in turn, enabling them to buy bigger consumer items or deal with emergencies. *Stokvels* suited communities where incomes were not usually sufficient to allow major purchases and women found this was a good way of keeping men from spending money on alcohol. In some types of *stokvel*, however, members would take it in turn to brew traditional maize and sorghum beer and sell this at parties.

EXTEND YOUR KNOWLEDGE

Apartheid alcohol restrictions

Until 1962, Africans were not allowed to purchase manufactured liquor such as bottled beer, wine or spirits, and sales of home-brewed beer, traditionally made by African women, were also banned. In 1961, 300,000 customers and sellers were prosecuted under the liquor laws. Next to the pass laws, these were among the most deeply resented regulations. Many African women particularly resented the monopoly over sales by municipal beer halls, especially in Durban, where the council tried to finance township development from this source – this was a major issue in the Cato Manor resistance in the late 1950s. In both countryside and town, women brewers found ways of getting round the regulations by using *stokvels* and community gatherings for sales of home-made sorghum beer as well as specialist beverages such as honey and prickly pear beers. Sometimes problematic ingredients were added, from sugar to acid, in order to ferment the beers more quickly and give them a punch.

The liquor industry was strongly in favour of deracialising liquor sales to expand their market, as were many African consumers. Conservative white politicians feared that alcohol would fuel crime and racial violence and the powerful Afrikaner Dutch Reformed Church opposed any relaxation. There was also a strong African Christian temperance movement. The Independent Order of True Templars spread from the United States and Britain to South Africa and many Africans joined. Next to the churches, it was perhaps the largest African urban association. But the interests of the liquor industry won out and the restrictions were lifted in 1962. A British journalist joked that it was one of the few enlightened and non-racial measures that Verwoerd's government had passed.

In 1965 sociologist Leo Kuper published *An African Bourgeoisie*. The study was based on extensive interviews with urban Zulu-speakers and found that far from all Zulu people being traditionalist descendants of a warrior nation, they were transforming themselves into urban consumers. Kuper's use of the term bourgeoisie was not strictly accurate because this usually refers to owners of factories and property. His African subjects in Durban were not generally in this category but mostly teachers, nurses, white collar employees or small businessmen. Nevertheless, Kuper showed the rapid growth of a new middle-class African community running football and boxing clubs, participating in ballroom dancing and absorbed in churches and choirs. They were part of an increasingly global culture. The study cut across apartheid ideas that African people belonged in the rural areas and like other studies in anthropology and social sciences at the time emphasised social change, cultural adaption and, despite apartheid, membership by black and white of a common society. The book was banned in South Africa.

Social change in the 1950s and 1960s was also benefiting African women, who were able to assert a new freedom from rural patriarchal society by migrating to town. There they could make a precarious living as domestic servants for whites, in factories or in the informal sector, selling beer, running small businesses or doing washing. Jobs were opening up for educated women in the municipal services, and especially in teaching and nursing. By the end of the 1960s the barriers to higher education were still formidable with only 342 African girls passing matric (the highest school-leaving exam) out of about 3,000. Yet there was a discernible new class of skilled and professional women and a broader determination to express new freedoms.

Drum magazine, launched in 1951, captured the changes of life in the townships in the 1960s as well as broader political developments. Alongside articles and photographs about Sharpeville and independence in Kenya and Zambia (1963–64), *Drum* covered fashionable people and urban styles (including the dress-conscious Mandela) and celebrated African prowess and masculinity in such fields as boxing and football. *Drum* was hardly feminist, but black bathing beauties in bikinis on the front cover broke the mould, both traditional and Christian. Dolly Rathebe acted as Agony Aunt to write openly about emotional problems and the words of Mary Serfontein (or Aunty Sammy), a resident of District Six, were used to provide humorous and scurrilous commentary on South African racism, especially the Mixed Marriages Act, and upright moral values in general. So popular did she become that the BBC *Panorama* programme came to interview her in Cape Town in 1965.

SOURCE

Aunty Sammy's response to the Vatican's attack on the contraceptive pill in *Drum*. Aunty Sammy's words were recorded and written up as an article by a ghost writer from *Drum*.

I have a momentous announcement to make. From here on I am not going to use the pill... The Pope said, no more pills and your Aunty Sammy obeys. His Royal Holiness said it was okay to practise birth control as long as the natural 'rhythm method' is used – and this is right up my alley.

Now, to all my sisters who also wish to use this system but do not know what the rhythm method is all about, here is my instruction. All you got to do is put rhythm into everything you do.

While in your kitchen busy cooking you must attack the pots with rhythm. Put your favourite record on the turntable of your gram and cha-cha-cha as you springclean your house... Rope your husband into the action. Get him to fix the broken chairs or do the garden in mambo-time. And then at night, when the big moment comes to climb into bed, you will both be so tired that you will fall fast asleep. And that, my sisters, is 'the rhythm method' of birth control.

By and large these social freedoms were not the rewards of apartheid, they were gains made in spite of apartheid. Had South Africa been a free society, such developments – and economic development as a whole – would surely have been even more rapid. But in the 1960s authoritarian white rule did ensure a temporary period of political peace. Black economic gains, unevenly shared, did not in themselves preclude political activity and in subsequent years, black middle-class people, especially students, became key protagonists of a renewed militancy. Yet these years of growth did defuse the most urgent political conflict and to some degree black people channelled their aspirations in the direction of consumer culture, churches, new associations and survival in the cities.

Developing the Bantustans

The 1959 Bantu Self-Government Act set in motion attempts by the government to transform the homelands into self-governing African states within South Africa. Each of ten ethno-linguistic groups defined by Pretoria was to have its own government, bureaucracy and infrastructure. In December 1963 the first self-governing homeland was established when the Transkei Legislative Assembly was opened in Umtata. The Transkei was the largest contiguous area of African settlement and Pretoria found an able, well-educated and ambitious chief, Kaiser Matanzima, to support their policy. Matanzima had been to university at Fort Hare and knew many of the Eastern Cape nationalists. But he believed that there was no option but to work with the apartheid government.

The National Party required that elections be held in the homelands before they could achieve self-government. At this stage, opponents of the Bantustan policy believed that they could make their voices heard. An opposition Democratic Party, led by Chief Victor Poto, won the elections for the Transkeian assembly. They believed that South Africa should remain one nation. However, Matanzima was not prepared to give up power. With Pretoria's support, he ensured that sufficient conservative chiefs were appointed ex-officio (simply because they were chiefs, and without being elected) to the assembly to ensure control by his Transkei National Independence Party. The Transkei government was rewarded with substantial funding from Pretoria and provided a model for homeland development. The bureaucracy, education system and health provision expanded quickly. These poor black rural areas, the former reserves, had been starved of central government funds in earlier years. Homeland development brought considerable economic benefits and opportunities for employment to a rising rural middle class. Trading stations, formerly owned largely by whites and Coloured people, were purchased by homeland government agencies and redistributed to African owners. African businessmen were able to start retail outlets in the rural towns. Similar processes followed in the major homelands of KwaZulu, Bophutatswana (for the Tswana speaking people) and Lebowa (previously Sekhukhuneland) and in the other smaller units.

Diplomatic ties

Within Africa, South Africa's position became more isolated during the 1960s. While strong relations were maintained with Western countries, most newly independent African states were reluctant to deal with the National Party. In 1963 the Organisation of African Unity, made up of independent African states, was formed, and immediately initiated a series of procedures against South Africa, including a fund for liberation. However, within the region, Pretoria was shielded by South West Africa (Namibia), under its direct rule, Rhodesia (Zimbabwe) under white rule, and the two Portuguese colonies of Mozambique and Angola.

When Vorster became prime minister in 1966, he acted pragmatically on the diplomatic front. He tackled South Africa's isolation by reaching out to several African countries, offering trade relations, technical training and economic advice in an attempt to win friends. Pretoria was concerned to expand trade with Africa, cut off potential bases for the ANC, as well as stifle criticism of apartheid and white rule. Botswana, Lesotho and Swaziland were all economically dependent on South Africa and tens of thousands of migrants from each worked in South Africa – usually on short term contracts in the mining industry. They had little choice but to maintain connection with their powerful neighbour. While most African countries were loath to accept South African advances and assistance, Vorster was successful in cementing links with Hastings Banda, the president of Malawi, whose ministers visited Pretoria in 1967 and established a strong economic relationship. Malawi was a poor country, with high rates of migration to Zimbabwe and South Africa, and Banda – a doctor trained in Scotland – adopted a more conservative approach than most other African leaders.

Despite pressure from the Anti-apartheid Movement and the United Nations, diplomatic ties with western powers, including Britain, the United States and much of western Europe continued. Japan became an increasingly important trading partner and established motor vehicle factories in South Africa. Sharpeville had been viewed by governments as a distasteful use of force, but little economic pressure was exerted. Many familiar British, German and American companies, from Barclays Bank to Volkswagen and Coca-Cola, were well established in South Africa and advertised heavily. In addition to the interest in minerals, particularly gold, uranium and coal, South Africa's booming consumer economy remained attractive to Western investors and companies. South Africa's role in the fight against communism globally, and especially in Africa, were important reasons for maintaining open, if not amiable, relations.

Vorster's use of police powers

During his time as Minister of Justice, Vorster had overseen an increase in police powers. With the threat of communism as a frequently cited explanation, he steered ever tighter security legislation through parliament. The police were given legal authority to detain suspects without trial for up to 180 days. Under the Terrorism Act of 1967 suspects could be detained without trial indefinitely.

In 1968 a new central police headquarters was opened in Johannesburg, named John Vorster Square. Inside, two floors were reserved for the security branch of the police, where they could interrogate detainees. The police station, and the security branch floors in particular, became the location for numerous acts of violence against those suspected of illegal political affiliations. Torture, disfigurement and sustained abuse were all used to garner information from suspects. Many opponents of the regime were kept in the special branch quarters for weeks or months at a time. In all, eight detainees lost their lives during detention there.

ACTIVITY
CONSOLIDATION

'Separate development'

1 Make a list of ways in which living standards for urban black South Africans improved during the 1960s.

2 Make a list of ways in which government repression increased during the 1960s.

3 Which do you think was more influential in defusing political opposition to apartheid?

4 What other factors were involved?

ACTIVITY
SUMMARY

1 Using the information in this chapter, write down ways in which you think the South African economy experienced radical change in the years 1960 to 1968?

2 How serious was the threat of communism to South Africa during this period?

3 Compare South Africa's international position in 1960 with its international position in 1968.

4 Draw a graph with one axis for time (from 1960–68) and another for intensity of protest. Plot and label significant opposition events on the graph. Are they more concentrated at one time than another? Suggest some reasons why this might be.

WIDER READING

Beinert, William, *Twentieth-Century South Africa*, Oxford University Press (2001)

Clark, Nancy L., *South Africa: The Rise and Fall of Apartheid*, Routledge (2011)

Culpin, Christopher, *South Africa 1948–1995: a depth study*, Hodder Education (2000)

Gordimer, Nadine, *Telling Times: Writing and Living, 1950–2008*, Bloomsbury (2011)

Lodge, Tom, *Sharpeville: An Apartheid Massacre and its Consequences*, Oxford University Press (2011)

Malan, Rian, *My Traitor's Heart*, Vintage (1991)

Mandela, Nelson, *The Long Walk to Freedom*, Abacus (2013)

Mulholland, Rosemary, *South Africa 1948–1994*, Cambridge University Press (1997)

O'Meara, Dan, *Forty Lost Years: the Apartheid State and the Politics of the National Party, 1948–94*, Ravan Press (1996)

Roberts, Martin, *South Africa 1948–1994: the Rise and Fall of Apartheid*, Longman (2001)

2b.3 Redefining resistance and challenges to National Party power, 1968-83

KEY QUESTIONS

- What was Black Consciousness and how did it influence the Soweto uprising?
- How did the ANC strengthen its position after the reverses of the early 1970s?
- What problems did the National Party face within South Africa, 1974–83?
- What pressures from beyond South Africa threatened National Party authority, 1974–83?

INTRODUCTION

The 1960s had been a damaging decade for black opposition groups: the ANC and the PAC, along with the Communist Party, were all officially banned. Any sort of political organising was restricted by tough legislation and severe policing. The state itself was growing in confidence, bolstered by a burgeoning economy and a continued majority for the National Party within parliament. Although Verwoerd had been assassinated in 1966, the foundations for furthering the apartheid project had been well and truly laid.

The possibilities for black resistance to apartheid seemed limited in 1968. With opposition unable to organise themselves via traditional channels or processes, it was the student movement that took up the mantle of struggle. Under the leadership of Steve Biko and others, a new conception of black identity was forged to counteract the negative portrayals that contributed to the subjugation of black people in South Africa. This new consciousness would eventually provoke explosive responses from students across the country in the 1970s.

The ANC, meanwhile, had to work from their bases in exile, building alliances and avoiding state attacks. By the late 1960s black opposition could count upon a growing global antipathy towards apartheid, centred around the Anti-apartheid Movement, which had branches in several countries throughout the world.

With political opposition at arm's length, the National Party was initially in a position to continue its plans for a divided country. However, several destabilising developments, at both the national and international level, severely hampered attempts to realise their vision of an apartheid state. Crises surrounding natural resources, disturbances in the townships, and controversies within the Party all curtailed government effectiveness, while dramatic changes beyond South Africa's borders demanded an increasingly military role within the region to ensure the survival of white supremacy.

1968 – Prime Minister Vorster requests that Basil d'Oliveira, a Coloured player, does not take part in an England cricket tour

Ciskei homeland is created

1970 – New Zealand rugby team tour South Africa with several Maori players

1973 – Global oil crisis

Banning orders against leaders of SASO, including Steve Biko

South Africa rugby tour to New Zealand is cancelled

Strikes take place across Natal

1975 – End of Portuguese rule in Mozambique and Angola

| 1968 | 1969 | 1970 | 1971 | 1972 | 1973 | 1974 | 1975 |

1969 – South African Students' Organisation (SASO) is formed

1972 – Black People's Convention founded to direct the Black Consciousness movement

PUTCO strike

World Council of Churches sells holdings in companies with interests in South Africa

1974 – Transvaal Bantu Education Department decides Afrikaans should be used in African schools

Prime Minister Vorster tours West Africa

The developments that took place between 1968 and 1983 caused a growing number of whites to begin to doubt the possibility of implementing apartheid. By 1984, the political situation had become increasingly fraught, and moves to find alternatives to apartheid became necessary.

WHAT WAS BLACK CONSCIOUSNESS AND HOW DID IT INFLUENCE THE SOWETO UPRISING?

Black consciousness proved to be a major force within South Africa, at a time when the opposition movement's political leadership was severely hamstrung by government repression. Its impact would be felt most keenly in 1976, when students responded to laws insisting upon the use of Afrikaans in their schools with a wave of protest.

Steve Biko and the South African Students' Organisation (SASO)

African higher education in the 1960s

In the late 1960s a new momentum developed within opposition circles, rooted first in the universities where apartheid had been applied following the Extension of University Education Act passed in 1959. The National Party was keen to segregate higher education completely.

'Bantu education' was heavily criticised – I. B. Tabata wrote a book evaluating the system called *Education for Barbarism*. It proved to be a doubled-edged sword. Designed to cut down the African elite's aspirations to join a common society, it also greatly extended higher education for black people. The nationalists realised that whites could not provide all of the skills needed for economic development within South Africa. They also recognised that the new homelands would need a large echelon of officials and professionals if they were ever to function as effective self-governing territories. Their aim was to create ethnically specific universities that encouraged the use of African languages and

identification with the homelands. As a result, higher educational provision for black students in the region expanded quickly in these years.

After the 1959 Act, Africans seeking a university education from the huge populations in Johannesburg, Pretoria and Witwatersrand townships were increasingly directed to the University of the North (called Turfloop). This was also the route for students from the homelands of Lebowa, Gazankulu and Venda. Turfloop became a melting pot, linguistically, ethnically and politically. Some came from families with ANC and PAC connections. By the late 1960s, students there and at other universities were becoming increasingly politicised. They were also encountering radical Christian and black American ideas.

Many of the students who came to the new black universities were from Christian backgrounds. The mission schools had been the main route to education in African communities. In the 1960s, at least two-thirds of African people professed Christianity. The biggest number, well over two million, were in a wide range of African independent churches that had broken away from the major Christian denominations.

North American civil rights successes, the militant Christianity of Martin Luther King and black power slogans drifted back to the students through newspapers, books and talks. Bobby Kennedy, brother of the assassinated United States president, visited South Africa in 1966 at the invitation of the National Union of South African Students (NUSAS). He gave some resounding and well-publicised speeches at the white campuses and staged a highly symbolic meeting with the ageing, banned Albert Luthuli.

SOURCE 1

Speech by Robert Kennedy at the University of Cape Town, 6 June 1966.

We must recognize the full human equality of all of our people before God, before the law, and in the councils of government. We must do this, not because it is economically advantageous, although it is; not because of the laws of God command it, although they do; not because people in other lands wish it so. We must do it for the single and fundamental reason that it is the right thing to do.

1977 – Death of Steve Biko
Bophuthatswana becomes an independent homeland

1979 – Congress of South African Students formed

1982 – ANC headquarters in London bombed

| 1976 | 1977 | 1978 | 1979 | 1980 | 1981 | 1982 | 1983 |

1976 – Student revolts in Soweto begin and are met with government repression
Transkei becomes an independent homeland

1978 – Vorster steps down as prime minister and is replaced by P. W. Botha

1980 – UN cultural and academic boycott of South Africa
'Free Nelson Mandela' slogan adopted by the Anti-apartheid Movement (AAM)

1983 – Nelson Mandela birthday concert held at Alexandra Palace
Tricameral parliament constitutional reform

Steve Biko and SASO

Steve Biko, a medical student at the University of Natal's segregated medical school, attended NUSAS and University Christian Movement congresses and drew on these ideas. NUSAS had long prided itself as a vehicle for liberal and non-racial expression, but it was dominated by white students. Biko led the black delegation during the 1967 NUSAS Congress at Rhodes University. They were a growing group and beginning to feel that they needed their own political vehicle. The University refused to allow black students to stay in residences on campus or use other facilities equally during the conference. Black students asked for the meeting to be suspended or moved to the township but the white delegations accepted the situation. This incident helped to trigger the formation of a separate black student movement during 1968–69. After the University Christian Movement was banned on some campuses, they founded the South African Students' Organisation (SASO) in July 1969 at Turfloop, with Biko as the first president.

A new phase of South African resistance was born. In some ways it took up the Africanist ideas expressed in earlier years by the ANC Youth League and the PAC; to these were added elements of black and **liberation theology**, African nationalism and American black power. Calling their views and movement 'black consciousness' Biko and his colleagues argued that black people should lead themselves, and not be led by whites, however sympathetic they might be. Whites were 'claiming a monopoly on intelligence and moral judgement and setting the pattern and pace for the realisation of the black man's aspirations'. Black people needed to rethink their position in society and liberate first their own minds.

KEY TERM

Liberation theology
A term used to describe a religious school of thought that argues religion can and must take a leading role in struggles against social and political oppression.

Black consciousness

Black consciousness was less an organised political movement and more an intellectual orientation. It asserted self-assurance in being black at a time when white South African society was most confident of its power. Black consciousness was an attitude of mind, and aimed to ensure that black people 'self-defined' rather than being defined by others. The use of the word black was a challenge in itself to the negative terms 'non-white' and '*nie-blanke*', which were so common in everyday language and proclaimed in the signage on benches and beaches.

'Black' probably derived from the United States, where activists used it in place of Coloured but it was also an older term of self-description in indigenous African languages. Another purpose behind using the word black was to kill off the much-disliked government term Bantu as well as other racial categories. It went beyond the term African, which had been used by both the ANC and PAC. Blackness referred in some senses to colour, but it was also a political and psychological identity. Coloured and Indian

people could identify with the idea of being black and some did participate in the movement, especially at the University of Durban Westville and the University of the Western Cape.

Black universities such as Turfloop and Fort Hare produced activists who became central in South African protest politics. Ironically, the apartheid universities gave them this opportunity: they did not have to interact daily with white students or compete for political space on campuses dominated numerically by whites. White students certainly tried to maintain contact with SASO and there was by no means an end to communication.

Although some of its leaders were detained during the early 1970s, SASO was able to maintain a strong presence on the black campuses by influencing or controlling the Student Representative Councils. SASO used the opportunity of the end of direct Portuguese colonial rule in Mozambique in 1974 to stage mass protests. In Mozambique, FRELIMO (*Frente de Libertação de Moçambique* or the Mozambican Liberation Front), had been fighting an armed struggle since 1964 and this was an important moment of liberation in the region. At Turfloop, student leaders organised a rally attended by 1,200. When the police arrived to break it up, they were confronted by students shouting 'Viva Frelimo' and 'Freedom'. Perhaps 700 congregated on the sports ground and sang the ANC anthem *Nkosi Sikelel iAfrika* (God Bless Africa). In Durban, SASO staged a march and rally at a public stadium, ignoring a government ban. The leadership had moved within a few years from ideological mobilisation to direct confrontation.

By 1972 a Black Consciousness Movement and a Black People's Convention were launched. While in certain respects black consciousness activists drew on the Africanist heritage of the PAC, its leaders were careful to distance themselves from direct connection with that banned organisation. There were also key differences. The PAC had been a movement largely of migrant workers, while black consciousness was a movement of students and youth. Black consciousness did not look primarily to the rest of Africa for its inspiration. By the early 1970s, a decade after many African countries achieved independence, the excitement of decolonisation and nationalism had given way to military coups, one-party states and dictators. Biko and his colleagues did not focus on African tradition and directly attacked the idea of homelands.

SOURCE

2   Extract from Steve Biko, *I Write What I Like: Selected Writings*, first published in 1978.

The actual intentions of the Bantustan practices are the following... to boost up as much as possible the intertribal competition and hostility... so that the collective strength and resistance of the black people can be fragmented... No, black people must learn to refuse to be pawns in a white man's game... At this stage of our history we cannot have our struggle being tribalised through the creation of Zulu, Xhosa and Tswana politicians by the system... These tribal cocoons called 'homelands' are nothing else but sophisticated concentration camps where black people are allowed to 'suffer peacefully'... Above all, we black people should all the time keep in mind that South Africa is our country and all of it belongs to us.

Protests by white students

International influences touched white as well as black students. In 1968, students in the United States and Europe staged major protests against the Vietnam War and took up both university reform and broader social issues. They were influenced to different degrees by civil rights protests, by new left wing thinking, by libertarian ideas that were expressed in greater sexual freedom, by folk and rock music, and the hippie counter-culture.

By coincidence, in that same year, the University of Cape Town (UCT) appointed Archie Mafeje as a lecturer in the Anthropology Department. The government, however, felt that this appointment of a black man, and a political radical, to a university they wished to be white was a direct challenge. They threatened UCT that if they did not rescind the appointment, some of their funding would be withdrawn. UCT's council capitulated. In response, white radical students organised a mass meeting and a sit-in. Supported by NUSAS, the protest spread. These events signalled a new dynamism in white student politics at the height of the apartheid era.

Although the withdrawal of black students into SASO was a major blow, the NUSAS leadership also incorporated radical ideas and tried to reach beyond the campuses. They campaigned on the issue of segregated and unequal education in general and mounted increasingly confrontational protests, using innovative strategies for publicity such as street theatre. In 1972 a mass gathering on the steps of the Anglican cathedral in central Cape Town was broken up by police.

Black consciousness looked to the future – it was a generational movement of students and youth in search of a new identity that transcended apartheid and subservience. Turfloop was particularly important. In 1972, the student president, Abraham Onkgopotse Tiro, was allowed to make a speech at the graduation ceremony. A staunch Christian, influenced by black consciousness, he made a stinging attack on the university authorities for the poor facilities, discrimination against African staff and the inequalities in South African society more generally.

His speech was by no means the most radical delivered by black consciousness student leaders, but the context was explosive as he spoke in front of the assembled white university authorities, black staff, parents and students. The Afrikaner rector of the university expelled him after a protest on campus. Tiro found a post teaching at Morris Isaacson High School in Soweto. Some pupils there had already formed a branch of the South African Students' Movement (SASM), the black consciousness organisation in the schools. Tiro acted as a SASO representative as well as a teacher. One of his pupils was Tsietsi Mashinini, who became a key leader of the 1976 students' revolt.

Although largely focused in educational institutions, black consciousness groups helped to launch community organisations and self-help groups. Newspapers such as *The World* in Soweto, while not directly promoting black consciousness, increased their coverage of its emerging politics. Growing literacy among African youth provided an important vehicle for political ideas.

By March 1973, the government decided that SASO was becoming too dangerous. Banning orders were issued against the most prominent leaders including Steve Biko. Tiro was dismissed from his teaching position. The state had briefly permitted a degree of tolerance for SASO in its earlier years, perhaps because black consciousness initially seemed to have some potential for reinforcing apartheid. Now it clamped down and arrested the remaining SASO leaders. At the subsequent trial in 1975 on charges under the Terrorism Act, the SASO 9 – as the defendants were dubbed – managed to secure a high profile for their ideas. They were not an illegal organisation, so the press was free to quote them. They sang freedom songs and raised clenched fists in the courtroom. Steve Biko, giving evidence for the defence, outlined the philosophy of black consciousness.

The mobilisation of school children

In 1975 the momentum of protest was shifting to the schools. The high schools were expanding quickly at this time. Between 1950 and 1975 the number of African children at school increased from around one million to over 3.5 million, with 280,000 at secondary school. In Soweto alone high school numbers increased from 12,600 to 34,000 in the four years between 1972 to 1976. This huge expansion put pressure on buildings and on teaching staff. Soweto schools often had classes of over 60. Whatever Bantu education may have intended, schools became sites of expectation, deprivation and explosive political potential. The students in Soweto's best high schools such as Morris Isaacson were highly receptive to black consciousness because it was a new and fashionable language, one geared to the youth.

High school pupils were still a minority among their age cohort in South Africa. In Soweto they had to confront the everyday reality of gangs that dominated the streets. Gangs such as the Hazels, the Dirty Dozen and the Bandidos, collectively called *tsotsis* in street language, were violent, unscrupulous and often hostile to the high school children. In his later interviews in Soweto, historian Clive Glaser heard that members of the Soweto youth gangs would hang around the schools and the shops, threatening school students, and even demanding sex with girls. School students faced a real danger of violence, including stabbing, if they crossed or challenged the gangs. The school students, increasingly militant, were fighting on two fronts – against the government and the gangs. They also had to weather criticism from their parents who had shouldered the burden of apartheid and were uneasy about their militancy. Black consciousness gave the students a stronger sense of identity.

By 1976, they were combining against the gangs and formed self-defence units that were prepared to use violence themselves. It was a tough world and it is important to illustrate this context because it helps us to understand the growing collective consciousness, the intensity of anger that such students could muster, and why some were prepared to take major risks. Events in Soweto in the mid-1970s were a key turning point in the history of apartheid and in black resistance.

The Soweto uprising, its significance and suppression

In 1974 the Transvaal Bantu Education Department decided to expand teaching in Afrikaans at African schools. Both Afrikaans and English were compulsory at high school level for white and black pupils. However, the government wished African students to learn other subjects in Afrikaans, including mathematics. The idea of greater emphasis on Afrikaans was anathema to school students in Soweto high schools. Afrikaans was seen as the language of the oppressor, used by the agents of apartheid at a national level and by the white police who harassed their parents. They experienced Afrikaans, more than English, as the language of racism. English was the language of advancement, a global language, the language of black American people and the language of black consciousness. Aside from antipathy to Afrikaans, African school children would now have to master not one but two languages in addition to their African first language. This language policy, enforced by a particularly conservative deputy minister, Andries Treurnicht, was a measure of Afrikaner confidence and short-sightedness at the height of apartheid.

Towards the end of May 1976 SASM, which was based in the schools, tried to organise boycotts in protest. An action committee announced a demonstration on 16 June in which protestors from many different schools were to converge and march to Orlando stadium. Perhaps 2,000 marching pupils were confronted by about 50 police at Orlando West School. Stones were hurled and the police released dogs and fired, leaving a few dead and others wounded. The pupils then attacked government buildings, killed two officials and threw up barricades. Anything related to the 'system' was fair game. This word had previously been used for government, or the system of power more broadly, and it was absorbed into the students' rhetoric. The government responded with force and all in all an estimated 138 were killed over the first few days of protest. Treurnicht remained intransigent on Afrikaans and denied that there was any problem with the policy. Pupils boycotted schools, tried to destroy African local government buildings and pushed the community as a whole to support them.

SOURCE
3

A speech by the character Micky, a student activist in the novel *The Children of Soweto*, written in 1982 by exiled Soweto resident Mbulelo Mzamane.

He said, 'we must destroy the snake and not just scorch its head... As everyone knows, when people mourn they don't go to work... Of course for us school is out of the question now. But what I'm saying should also take care of this other question of your parents, who continue to work for whites and so on. Suspend all sports and shows as well, so that people can sit back and think a little. Then there are lots of guys who continue to enjoy themselves at shebeens, beerhalls and so on while others suffer. These drinks are made to drug people's minds so that they don't ask too many questions or do something about their oppression. We need to be one people. I also think there are far too many offices belonging to the government in Soweto... Something must also be done about blacks who serve as police, school board members, the guys in the Useless Boy's Club, you know, the Urban Bantu Circus, and all the other sell-outs, maybe our Principals and teachers, too.'

On 17 June, 300 Wits University students marched in sympathy and Turfloop students tried to burn down the Afrikaans department on their campus. On 18 June official buildings, shops and liquor stores in Alexandra township, in Johannesburg, were attacked. Over the next few weeks, incidents spread through much of the country. Students formed a Soweto Students' Representative Council in August, after a meeting at Regina Mundi Catholic

Church, led initially by Tsietsi Mashinini from Morris Isaacson School. A charismatic figure during the critical months of June to August, he then fled into exile. Over the next few months scholars tried to trigger stayaways by workers but with limited success. In addition to targeting liquor stores, they boycotted white-owned shops and threatened, in one leaflet, vengeance against 'sell-outs and traitors of the Black Struggle'. They also organised litter collection because this service had ceased after 16 June, and rubbish was beginning to pile up. Winnie Mandela and Dr Nthatho Motlana formed a Black Parents' Association to take on the role of organising funerals and these in turn became politicised occasions.

EXTEND YOUR KNOWLEDGE

Winnie Madikizela-Mandela (formerly Winnie Mandela)
Winnie Madikizela-Mandela was born in 1936 and brought up in Transkei. Her family were educated Eastern Cape Methodists. She moved to Johannesburg in 1953 to train as a social worker and then worked at Baragwanath hospital in Soweto, the largest serving African people. In 1957 she met Nelson Mandela and they were married in 1958.

Winnie Mandela was harassed by police from the moment of Mandela's imprisonment and her visits to him on Robben Island were restricted. She was dismissed from her job as a social worker, depriving her of an income. In 1969 she was detained under the Terrorism Act, interrogated and put into solitary confinement for six months before she was charged. She was accused of working for the ANC and only released after 17 months. The government was clearly intent on victimising her. In August 1976, when involved in the Black Parents' Association in Soweto, she was imprisoned without charge for five months in Johannesburg Fort. She had become particularly popular among the Soweto youth. In May 1977, she was subjected to a quintessentially South African form of punishment – banishment to a remote township in the Free State. The intention was to isolate her politically.

Nevertheless she played a major role in keeping Mandela's name, and the ANC legacy, in the public eye in South Africa. Both because of her husband, and her own charismatic personality, as well as the vindictiveness of the state, she attracted considerable media attention. She associated herself with key new developments in the political opposition, from the Soweto student revolt, to the foundation of the United Democratic Front (UDF).

A government commission of inquiry calculated that 575 died in the Soweto revolt and its aftermath. It was the single most violent episode of state repression since Sharpeville and similarly attracted global attention. At this time, the Soweto schools could operate only sporadically. In a certain sense, the armed struggle had reached South Africa. The school students were not armed but they were increasingly prepared to use violence against property – the strategy of sabotage that the ANC espoused in 1961. On a few occasions, crowds acted violently against individuals, sometimes in revenge for police shootings. The latter were overwhelmingly the most significant cause of death. In April 1977 when the local administration declared a rise in rents, partly because they had lost money through the burning of buildings and the closing of the municipal beer halls, the Soweto Student Council organised a mass demonstration, burnt down the offices of the Urban Bantu Council and secured a postponement of rent rises. The council resigned.

SOURCE
4
Young rioters surround a burning bus during the Soweto uprising in Johannesburg, 17 June 1976.

In order to avoid arrest, an estimated 4,000 youths fled the country in 1976–77. The only coherent external organisation was the ANC, by then based in Lusaka, Zambia. Some of those who fled the country were less educated street youths, rather than students, and when recruited into MK, they were reputed to make good soldiers because they were not scared of dying. Student leaders were also imprisoned on Robben Island, with the long incarcerated political prisoners such as Mandela and Sisulu. In the debates that took place on the Island, most black consciousness activists, notably student leader Terror Lekota, moved over to the ANC.

The impact of the death of Steve Biko, 1977

In 1973 the government banned Steve Biko. He was made to live in Kingwilliamstown in the Eastern Cape, his movements were restricted and he was not allowed to attend political meetings. This made it very difficult for him to be involved in the wider national anti-apartheid movement, although he remained involved in local and regional black consciousness activities. He also maintained a strong profile through his writing, some of it published and some surreptitiously circulated, which came to define black consciousness. His profile was raised in the Eastern Cape because his ideas were taken up by Donald Woods, white editor of the *Daily Dispatch*, a liberal East London newspaper. The relationship between Woods and Biko was later portrayed in the film *Cry Freedom*, directed by Richard Attenborough (1987). In August 1977 Biko left Kingwilliamstown, breaking his banning order, and was arrested, interrogated and severely beaten. A few weeks later, when he was close to death, he was rushed 1,000 km by road to a prison hospital in Pretoria. He died on 12 September 1977.

The police claimed his death was related to a hunger strike; however Woods challenged this cover-up and made allegations of police brutality. He produced convincing evidence, including photographs taken in the morgue, to contest police claims. The nature of Biko's death in police custody provoked international disapproval, particularly in Western countries that still maintained

diplomatic and commercial relations with South Africa. Biko's funeral was attended by over ten thousand people, including several foreign ambassadors, in a huge show of support for the man and his ideals.

SOURCE
5
Mourners at the funeral of Steve Biko, 1977.

SOURCE
6
Report for international distribution on SABC, South Africa's government-sponsored radio station, published on 16 September 1977.

However, numerous detainees, who have been detained following communist training and indoctrination, have testified that they receive specific instructions to commit suicide rather than divulge information to the police. The result is that in the past 18 months seven detainees have died as a result of hanging and three others have jumped from the windows of high buildings. Police say it is virtually impossible to stop a man determined to commit suicide from doing so and, in any event, the suicides are sometimes totally unexpected.

To their critics the police point out that so far a court of law has never established that the police have been responsible for torturing or killing a single detainee, although all cases are thoroughly investigated. For any reasonable person confronted with this type of anti-South Africa propaganda the question must arise: where South Africa is spending millions and moving mountains to improve her image would she willfully and purposefully allow something like this to happen to destroy all the good work that has been done? The answer must be: No.

AS Level Exam-Style Question Section A

Study Source 6 before you answer this question.

How much weight do you give the evidence of Source 6 for an enquiry into the government's reactions to the death of Steve Biko?

Explain your answer, using the source, the information given about it and your own knowledge of the historical context. (12 marks)

Tip
Think about who wrote the source, for what purpose and how it was distributed.

Black consciousness and Soweto

1 Write two headings: 'Similarities' and 'Differences'. Under each header list ways in which black consciousness was similar to and different from previous African nationalist ideas. Review your lists. How radical do you think black consciousness in the 1970s was compared to older views on African nationalism?

2 Why was Afrikaans in schools the issue that ignited protest? What alternative issues could have stimulated similar levels of activism?

HOW DID THE ANC STRENGTHEN ITS POSITION AFTER THE REVERSES OF THE EARLY 1970s?

Now operating in exile, the ANC faced the challenge of remaining relevant to ordinary South Africans. The president, Oliver Tambo, was responsible for ensuring that the organisation did not lose its focus or significance in the struggle against apartheid. Recently, historians have argued that we must be careful not to overstate the ANC's decline during this period, and that we should acknowledge the operations conducted overseas as well the undercover work within South Africa.

Difficulties in exile

During the early 1960s, the ANC established a number of offices abroad and London remained an important centre for the movement. Within Africa, ANC activities were largely concentrated in Tanzania and Zambia. A number of exiles settled in Lusaka, Zambia, and Tambo (who became acting president after Luthuli's death) was largely based there from 1967. The movement thought that it would be appropriate to work from an African country, relatively close to South Africa, where the president, Kenneth Kaunda, was sympathetic to their cause. It was also cheaper to provide for the growing exile political community in an African country.

MK also moved to Zambia and this was the base for two attempts at major military incursions – the Wankie and Sipolilo campaigns in 1967 and 1968. In the first, a group of about 50 trained MK guerrillas, including Chris Hani, crossed the Zambezi and attempted to create a route through Zimbabwe to South Africa. After a couple of skirmishes in which they held their own, one of the detachments was largely destroyed by Rhodesian government forces. Others were forced to retreat into Botswana. The Sipolilo campaign lasted for longer, but also resulted in heavy losses. These events had important repercussions. The Zambian government became concerned about its role as a base for armed struggle and the potential for South African retaliation. In 1969 a Lusaka Manifesto was adopted by many African states that reiterated their antipathy to apartheid. But Kaunda demanded that Tambo find new bases for MK.

Hani survived the Wankie campaign and with other young members of MK issued a memorandum critical of the ANC leadership. The memorandum accused the ANC leaders of 'careerism' and becoming middle-class 'globe-trotting' bureaucrats. They were particularly critical of Joe Modise, commander-in-chief of MK, for being undemocratic, arbitrary and preoccupied with his own 'mysterious business enterprises'.

SOURCE 7

The opening of the Hani memorandum, signed by Chris Hani and six others, 1969.

The A.N.C. in Exile is in a deep crisis as a result of which a rot has set in. From informal discussions with the revolutionary members of M.K. we have inferred that they have lost all confidence in the A.N.C. leadership abroad. This they say openly and in fact show it.

SOURCE 8

Leonard Pitso, a signatory of the Hani memorandum, in an interview with the historian Hugh Macmillan in 2011.

After Wankie and Sipolilo there was no analysis, no announcement of deaths in action, no commemoration of heroes and martyrs. We knew that inside South Africa the underground was completely broken down. We knew that there were sell-outs in the NEC [National Executive Committee of the ANC], such as Tennyson Makiwane, who was later killed. The NEC was itself divided and there was a division between the ANC and MK. We wanted the NEC to sit down and analyse... what happened. What were the mistakes? We wanted concentration on the home front, not international solidarity.

Internal reorganisation and external legitimacy

The leadership of MK responded with some hostility to the accusations by Hani, and Tambo faced a major crisis within the organisation. He took personal responsibility for the military failings and sought a route of consensus. Nevertheless the youthful rebels were called to a tribunal and expelled from the ANC. Tambo called a conference in Morogoro, Tanzania, in 1969 and resigned as acting president, but was immediately re-elected without opposition. This gave him a stronger hand to address the growing divisions. The ANC also took the decision to admit people of all 'races'. There would no longer be four separate congresses that mimicked apartheid racial definitions.

The movement adopted a 'strategy and tactics' document that affirmed the importance of armed struggle, but stressed even more the need for political leadership, political education and political unity. Increasingly this implied not attempts to send big armed detachments by long and difficult routes into South Africa, but to infiltrate individuals and small groups who could resurrect the movement on the ground. Hani and the rebels were reinstated. These decisions were clearly influenced by the memorandum although it would not be until the 1980s, and the emergence of a renewed mass protest in South Africa, before a new approach was effectively developed. After a further small military contingent was destroyed entering Namibia, attempts to make armed incursions stopped.

The Morogoro decisions had a long legacy in another way. A group within the ANC believed that the movement should remain African. In 1975 they articulated their views publicly and were expelled.

Tennyson Makiwane, one of the expelled Africanists, was a senior figure in the ANC's external affairs department. He responded with a detailed memorandum condemning the decision as authoritarian. He was equally critical of the failure to reorganise within South Africa. They started a rival ANC group and attacked Tambo as well as the CP. This alternative movement soon dissolved and some went back into the ANC but Makiwane himself returned to his birthplace in the Transkei and worked for Matanzima's homeland government. In 1980 he was assassinated there.

A further schism took place in the late 1970s when a group of left-wing white exiles in England tried to revive and take over SACTU (the South African Congress of Trade Unions, the trade union movement linked to the ANC). They wished to focus its activities on working class mobilisation and imbue it with a revolutionary rhetoric. They were also expelled.

Oliver Tambo and the ANC

Holding together a politicised exile movement, scattered in different places, prone to ideological arguments, with some in the military wing and others not, was particularly difficult. Tambo was a quiet but determined man who tried to listen as well as lead. He was deeply conscious of the need for unity. He held strongly to the ANC's philosophy of non-racialism and worked with exiles from all South African communities. He fully recognised the value of the multi-racial AAM, even though it retained a significant degree of independence from the ANC and drew in a disparate set of activists with many different views. He realised the value of international solidarity, as well as finding ways of reinserting the ANC into politics on the ground within South Africa. The PAC had no comparable figure.

AS Level Exam-Style Question Section B

How accurate is it to say that the ANC made little progress in the 1970s? (20 marks)

Tip
Don't simply write about what the ANC did in these years, but focus on the ways in which the organisation worked to achieve its aims.

The global anti-apartheid movement and international boycotts

There was no single global anti-apartheid organisation; movements were based in individual countries around the world. During the 1960s the British AAM had launched a wider range of boycotts by unions and guilds related to the arts to work alongside sporting and economic sanctions. Such boycotts were partial and uneven but during the 1970s they began to bite and South Africa became increasingly culturally isolated. In 1980, the UN passed a resolution for a comprehensive cultural and academic boycott of South Africa, supported by the ANC and the AAM.

Sporting boycotts
Following the D'Oliveira crisis of 1968 the issue of race and politics in sport took shape in a new campaign called the Stop

the Seventy Tour (1969–70). The first target was a South African rugby tour of Britain and Ireland. Peter Hain (later a UK Labour minister) organised mass demonstrations, pickets of the tourists' hotels and pitch invasions. Gordon Brown (later UK prime minister) participated in Edinburgh. The tour was disrupted but not called off. Following this protest, the 1970 cricket tour by a white South African team to England was cancelled and South Africa was expelled from international test cricket in that year.

SOURCE 9
A protest against the South African cricket tour of 1970, outside the Lord's cricket ground in London.

SOURCE 10
Leaflet by the Anti-Apartheid Movement and the Stop the Seventy Tour, distributed outside grounds hosting the South African rugby team during the 1969–70 tour.

WHY WATCH THE SPRINGBOKS?

BECAUSE:

You enjoy the game?

What happens in South Africa is not your concern?

You support racialism?

Everybody has the right to enjoy the game but in South Africa everybody does not.

Only whites can represent their country in any team sport.

Africans, Indians and Coloureds – 81% of the population – are excluded on grounds of skin colour, however good they may be.

They have separate and largely inferior facilities for training, playing and watching sport.

By inviting racist teams: by watching racist sport – we are telling the South Africans – it's OK!

We are helping to sustain APARTHEID.

Along with South Africa, New Zealand was one of the top rugby nations. A number of New Zealand players, however, came from Maori backgrounds and would have been considered as Coloured in South Africa. Surprisingly, the South African government allowed a New Zealand rugby tour to South Africa in 1970 to include Maori players. However, in 1973 a whites-only South African rugby team planned to tour New Zealand. A movement called Halt All Racist Tours campaigned successfully against this visit and it was cancelled. The British Lions toured South Africa in 1974 but in 1977 Commonwealth countries signed the Gleneagles Agreement, which discouraged signatories from playing South Africa in any sporting capacity. South Africa's tour to New Zealand in 1981 triggered widespread protest and although this did not finally curtail international contacts, cricket and rugby boycotts deeply upset white South Africans.

AS Level Exam-Style Question Section A

Study Source 10 before you answer this question.

Why is Source 10 valuable to the historian for an enquiry about sporting boycotts of South African teams during the 1960s and 1970s?

Explain your answer, using the source, the information given about it and your own knowledge of the historical context. (8 marks)

Tip
Consider the nature and purpose of the source. Who wrote it and why?

Economic boycotts

In 1970 a Conservative government under Edward Heath was elected in the UK. He initially withdrew Britain from the UN arms boycott introduced in 1964 (see Chapter 2). Economic disengagement from South Africa was not palatable to the Conservative Party, to hundreds of British and international companies with business interests in the country and even to much liberal opinion in Britain and the United States. Britain remained South Africa's most important trading partner. The Conservatives opposed the idea of South Africa's economic isolation in principle. During the 1970s, they developed strategies that came to be known as 'constructive engagement'. Proponents argued that overseas investors should both improve their own employment practices and use their influence to improve wages and conditions for black workers in South Africa as a whole. They also argued, as did liberals in South Africa, that economic growth would reveal the weaknesses of apartheid and lead to its demise. They believed that as demand for workers in the South African cities expanded, so it would be increasingly difficult to control urbanisation. Companies would need more skilled black workers and this would lead the government to realise that they had to relax the race rules on jobs and skills. This argument for constructive engagement had strong support in the UK from bodies such as the Conservative Party and the Confederation of British Industry.

The AAM and its allies advocated more systematic disinvestment and boycotts. They argued that continued economic engagement was just business as usual, enabling foreign companies to make large profits on the backs of cheap black workers. They believed that comprehensive sanctions, coupled with internal protest, could bring white South Africa to change its policies. The AAM worked with British trade unions to inform them about the conditions of black workers in South Africa and to win support for radical action. In 1972, the World Council of Churches decided to sell its holdings in companies that had interests in South Africa.

The global anti-apartheid movement

1 As a world leader in the 1970s why might you think it better to encourage 'constructive engagement' with South Africa? Why might economic boycotts be a better strategy to end apartheid? Make a list of arguments in favour of both strategies then write a short paragraph to explain which you would choose and why.

2 Look again at Sources 9 and 10. Which source accounts best for the success of the Anti-Apartheid Movement in Britain in 1969–70? Explain your reasoning.

3 List the five key obstacles facing the ANC during the 1970s? Rank them in order of significance and explain why you have put them in this order.

WHAT PROBLEMS DID THE NATIONAL PARTY FACE WITHIN SOUTH AFRICA, 1974–83?

The late 1970s was a turbulent period for the National Party. The boom of the 1960s was curtailed by the oil crisis in 1973 bringing new economic challenges and the Party faced continuing opposition to apartheid on several fronts as well as internal divisions.

Political unrest and opposition

Trade union activity

Black workers made up the great majority of miners who extracted the ore crushed for gold and uranium – still South Africa's most valuable exports in the 1970s – as well as the coal that fuelled the power stations. Most white homes had black domestic servants, often living in back rooms on the premises. About 1.5 million African people worked on the farms, more than three times those in the mines. By 1976, the number of people working in manufacturing industries, factories and workshops had reached 1.6 million, more even than the farms.

Black workers had relatively few rights but they could threaten a form of disruption that struck at the heart of the economy and white wealth. Attempts at organising black workers had produced important trade unions and some had amalgamated in SACTU, the South African Congress of Trade Unions, which was aligned with the ANC. But the movement reached only about 50,000 members and faltered in the face of state repression in the 1960s, though a few important unions committed to multi-racial organisation, such as the Food and Canning Workers in the Western Cape, did survive.

Trade unions became a significant issue for the government during the 1970s and 80s. Black workers at PUTCO, the huge transport company that ran hundreds of buses from the townships to workplaces, went on strike in 1972. In 1973 Zulu-speaking migrant workers, who lived in compounds at a brick factory near Durban, withdrew from work. Their strike spread to 150 other factories in the area and included Indian women workers in the textile industry.

In this context, former unionists and white student activists began to build new trade unions in Durban, Johannesburg and Cape Town. These were independent both from the old ANC-linked SACTU and from the white-controlled unions. Their legal status was uncertain but the government did not immediately ban them. The new independent unions decided to focus primarily on the issue of wages and working conditions, rather than broader political aims. Successful organisation at the grass roots, on the shop floor, was their priority. They tried to develop democratic control by workers and generally avoided dramatic confrontations. Despite this caution, the state targeted activists by the mid-1970s – for example during the 1974 Natal textile strikes.

The great majority of black workers were unorganised, and this provided a fertile field for the new unions. South Africa was a major producer of sugar – the coastal slopes of KwaZulu-Natal were covered for miles and miles in green sugar cane. In addition to sugar mills, sugar was used in many small factories: bakeries, dairies, brewers, sweet and chocolate makers. A Sweet, Food and Allied Workers Union spread in this sector. An African Metal and Allied Workers Union (MAWU) spread in Durban and the Witwatersrand. In Cape Town, the Food and Canning Workers expanded under the leadership of a former law student, Jan Theron, from 1976.

In 1979, food workers at a small factory owned by a South African family of Italian descent, Fattis and Monis, struck for union recognition and higher wages. It was a remarkable strike in bringing together Coloured women workers and African migrant men. Through the Food and Canning Union, well connected in opposition circles in Cape Town, they won wide support from students and community groups. The company largely produced wheat products such as bread and pasta. Activists went into supermarkets, loaded their trolleys with Fattis and Monis pasta, and then dumped them at the checkouts. African traders in the townships agreed to stop selling Fattis and Monis bread, and consumers boycotted their products. This combined action helped to win the strike. This strike and boycott was remarkable for drawing in support from all racial groups. It was a time of great political fluidity and creativity amongst opposition groupings. Groups previously divided by race and class began to work together.

By 1979, some of the new independent unions felt sufficiently confident to combine in a Federation of South African Trade Unions, FOSATU, with its main support around Johannesburg and Durban. It established a strong identity as a non-racial union, dedicated to shop floor organisation and internally democratic practices.

The re-emergence of ANC support in South Africa

Black consciousness thinking deeply influenced the Soweto protest of 1976 but even then some of the students were aware of the alternative political tradition of the ANC and non-racialism. During the next few years, this became increasingly dominant within South Africa. Those wedded to the ANC, including Winnie Madikizela-Mandela, and those coming off Robben Island, sought to influence the new generation. The Congress of South African Students (COSAS), which was launched in 1979 to coordinate school protests nationally, initially drew on both traditions but its

first leader, Ephrahim Mogale, was an underground supporter of the ANC. He and others pushed it in this direction, and COSAS committed itself to the Freedom Charter. In 1980 the *Sunday Post* launched a nationwide Release Mandela campaign which won wide support. The term Charterist was used in English to describe those who broadly supported the Freedom Charter. By implication, they also supported the ANC – although it was dangerous to declare this openly. In 1980, a wave of school protests, inspired by this new political alignment, fought against racially unequal education and closed many black schools. On this occasion, protests started in Coloured schools in Cape Town and spread nationally.

In the late 1970s and early 1980s, a great diversity of civic organisations were founded in townships and rural communities. They sought to fight against local councils and rent increases and organised for equal education and services. In the rural areas they contested forced removals. A strike at the East London factory of sweet-makers Wilson Rowntree was organised by the South African Allied Workers Union (SAAWU), which openly declared for Charterism and secretly recruited youths to join MK in exile. They helped to mobilise broader opposition in the city and revived deeply rooted support for the ANC.

Liberal opposition in South Africa

Liberalism as a political ideology and movement had deep roots in South Africa but limited support. In 1953, a Liberal Party which staunchly opposed apartheid was founded largely by white activists. Most were middle class and highly educated professionals.

In 1959, 11 of the more liberal MPs in the United Party (UP) formed a separate Progressive Party. Only one, Helen Suzman, held her seat in the next election in 1961. While opposed to apartheid, they advocated a restricted, qualified franchise for blacks and were committed to working within the whites-only parliament. The Progressives were economic liberals who argued that the South African state intervened far too heavily in protecting whites in the job market. They argued that this was not only morally wrong but greatly retarded economic development in South Africa because the country was so short of skilled workers. In 1974, the Progressives achieved a small breakthrough, increasing their seats from one to seven and their (white) vote from about 40,000 (in 1966) to 59,000.

By contrast the old opposition United Party won 41 seats with 363,000 votes in 1974. At that time, it still represented the conservative views of many English-speaking South Africans. But the UP lost direction and had no effective alternative to apartheid except a softer form of segregation policy that was still aimed at ensuring white power. The UP splintered in the next few years and by 1978, a new Progressive Federal Party became the main opposition in parliament. They tried hard to break through to the Afrikaner population and recruited a charismatic young Afrikaner intellectual from Stellenbosch, Frederik van Zyl Slabbert. He won a parliamentary seat in Cape Town in 1974 and became leader of the Progressive Federal Party in 1979. Slabbert was at the forefront of reorganising the white opposition – winning 19 percent of the vote and 26 seats in 1981. It looked briefly as if this new liberal front might make further gains, as white South Africans came to terms with the need for change in the wake of Soweto and the rise of the new unions. Slabbert convinced the Party that they needed to support a universal, non-racial franchise and hence to envisage an immediate black majority. He reached out to black leaders, such as Mangosuthu Buthelezi, who might support a moderate settlement. This proved to be too radical a step for white voters and his support gradually ebbed.

EXTEND YOUR KNOWLEDGE

Helen Suzman (1917–2009)

Helen Suzman came to epitomise white liberal politics in South Africa. Born in 1917, daughter of Lithuanian Jewish immigrants, she was educated at a Johannesburg Catholic convent school and at Wits University where she studied economics. She gave up a university lecturing career to go into politics and became the United Party MP for Houghton, northern Johannesburg, one of the wealthiest constituencies in the country. She was a founding member of the Progressive Party and between 1961 and 1974 she was their only representative in parliament.

Suzman used her position to maintain a relentless criticism of government economic policy and racial discrimination in the workplace. She highlighted corruption in the government, breaches of human rights and attacked the increasingly draconian security legislation and police violence. She also visited Nelson Mandela on Robben Island and took up the cause of improving the conditions for the political prisoners there. Because of her economic views and her focus on human rights, she won particularly strong support from Western governments. They were keen to see a political force that stood somewhere between the racial nationalism of the National Party and radicalism of the ANC, with its links to the communist bloc. Suzman stood for the liberal principles of liberty of the individual and she did not call Mandela a terrorist. But she was steadfastly against armed struggle and accepted that the Progressives would work largely within white politics. By contrast, more radical whites in student politics and the new Trade Unions saw parliament as too racist and too restrictive.

Troubles in the Bantustans

During the 1970s, the National Party pressed ahead with its homeland or Bantustan policy. Although Verwoerd had been the major proponent of the scheme, Vorster put in money on a larger scale, greatly assisted by the rise in tax revenues from gold mining during the 1970s. Vorster, and his successor P. W. Botha, pushed through the policy of granting independence to homelands. Four accepted this status: Transkei (1976), Bophuthatswana (1977), Venda (1979) and Ciskei (1981). In Pretoria's eyes they were independent countries, though they were very largely dependent on South Africa for their revenues. They were not recognised by any other country, although South Africa worked hard to present them as potentially viable states.

Homeland revenues increased fourfold during the first half of the 1970s from around R120 million to R520 million, and continued to grow quickly. Some of the growing homeland budgets went to fund the social costs of apartheid such as forced relocations. A good deal of money was used to fund the expanding bureaucracies of the Bantustans and there was a great deal of waste. While Australia, Brazil, Malawi and Nigeria built one new capital, South Africa, with extraordinary profligacy, built ten new homeland capitals and kept its existing three capitals of Pretoria (executive and civil service), Cape Town (legislature) and Bloemfontein (judiciary). Failed top-down projects proliferated. Ciskei received its own, redundant, international airport not far from East London's.

But there were some benefits from this expenditure for poor rural communities. In the early 1970s, over 50 percent of some homeland budgets went to education, roads, health and agriculture. The government was keen for educational provision to expand more rapidly in the rural, rather than urban areas, as this would discourage urban migration. Bantu education brought large new budgets and the independent homelands did not have to stick strictly with this system of teaching. The five new universities launched in these marginalised parts of the country, for all their inadequacies, represented a major investment and, as illustrated above, provided crucibles for opposition politics. In the agricultural sphere, money was poured into irrigation projects, promising a new beginning for some smallholder farmers. The government believed that successful homeland agriculture would not only raise rural incomes but keep more people out of the cities. In KwaZulu, rents and services such as electricity were subsidised and a good deal cheaper than in the townships falling within South Africa.

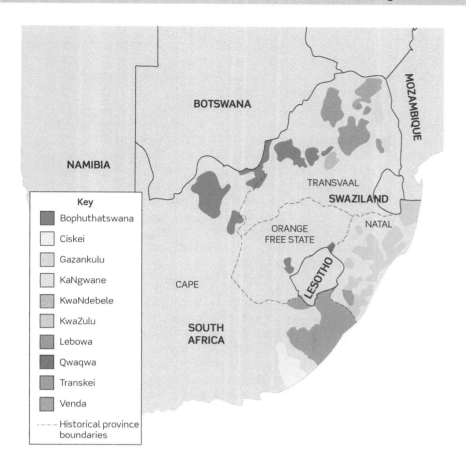

Figure 3.1: The 'Bantustan' areas of South Africa.

SOURCE

11 Speech by South African prime minister B. J. Vorster on the eve of Transkei independence, July 1976.

Since Union in 1910 successive South African Governments have consistently recognised the differences among the peoples of South Africa.

As far back as 1913 legal recognition was given to the right of the various Black peoples to the land they themselves had chosen as their own homes and where they had established their own economies within their own cultural contexts and norms which were acceptable and comprehensible to them – economies differing not only from those of the Whites, Coloureds and Asians, but also differing among the Black groups, so that each economy bore the distinctive mark of the character, culture and traditions of that particular Black people.

These facts demanded to be recognised in the policy of the South African Government, and were indeed recognised. Non-recognition would have meant a disregard of the aspirations and identity of each population group and a negation of all they are proud of.

In fact, South Africa was criticised for believing in the right of every people to have full control over its own affairs. This is no alien principle in the international community, as is evidenced by the emancipation of peoples in Africa and elsewhere.

South Africa also believes in the orderly development of every people to a stage where it feels prepared to accept the responsibility of independence. Strangely enough, this principle too, elicited criticism.

The Transkeian government put a request to the South African Government, a request which was quite reasonable considering Transkei's level of development.

In a peaceful manner and by means of political, economic and social evolution, Transkei prepared itself for the responsibility and for taking its place and holding its own as a worthy member of the international community.

Resistance

Mangosuthu Buthelezi in KwaZulu refused to hold an election or accept independence. In the 1970s, he was a frequent critic of the nationalist government and opened important space for political opposition. He gained effective access to the national media. One of the smaller homelands, Kangwane, which was supposed to provide for South Africa's Swazi population, became a centre for rural underground activism associated with the ANC. The homelands, however, were too carefully policed to become bases for a rural armed struggle led by MK. In this way South Africa was very different from Mozambique and Zimbabwe where the armed liberation movements were able to take some control over rural territory.

Some of the homeland leaders believed that they could use their new status to negotiate with Pretoria for increased rights. At a meeting in Umtata in 1973, they agreed that their long term aim should be to achieve one black nation, possibly on a federal basis. In this sense, Pretoria needed them, but could not fully control them. However, the homeland leaders could not easily find wider support. The rise of black consciousness and radicalisation of popular struggles after Soweto in 1976 had polarised African politics. For example, Buthelezi initially seemed to offer a broad national leadership but he was rejected by black consciousness activists and by those sympathetic to the ANC. By the late 1970s, he was in open conflict with the new political forces and embraced an increasingly ethnic nationalist strategy based on the KwaZulu homeland. Despite this, he survived politically to become a durable figure in post-apartheid governments.

Many of the homeland governments resorted to the same forms of repression as the South African government. Their expenditure on police and military forces, supported by Pretoria, grew quickly. Yet as noted above, homeland universities, particularly Turfloop and Fort Hare, were key centres of black consciousness and political dissidence. Eastern Cape schools were recruiting grounds for MK. Student sympathisers with the ANC who took over the Turfloop student council in the 1980s renamed the campus Lusaka, after the Zambian capital that was headquarters of the ANC in exile. Although the vanguard of political struggle undoubtedly shifted to the cities after 1976, the homeland areas also sustained their own forms of opposition politics aimed both against Bantustan leaders and the central state.

An assessment of homeland policy

The new money, pouring through a narrow funnel into homeland administrations, without sufficient oversight, created a setting in which patronage, personalised power and corruption could flourish. The homeland administrations could not be voted out and homeland politics increasingly revolved around access to the new jobs and state assets. Individual leaders such as Kaiser Matanzima in Transkei, and his brother George, gained direct financial benefit from their political positions. For example, a central element in homeland policy was to buy out white traders and hotel keepers in these rural areas and distribute the businesses to Africans. The Matanzima family had substantial interests in some of the companies that took over the small town hotels. When the Wild Coast Sun hotel and casino was developed in 1980 on the Transkei coast, senior members of the Transkei government were paid off.

It is often said that the National Party's pursuit of apartheid through balkanisation (splitting the country into smaller units) led to a reaction against political ethnicity and tribalism and reinforced commitment to a shared, non-ethnic African nationalism. Black political leaders, with a couple of exceptions, repudiated the ethnic and regional politics that bedevilled so many African countries after independence. However, the National Party did find significant support within African communities for some aspects of the homeland policy. Even if they did not think it was the end goal, some African politicians were prepared to work with the project. We should not underestimate the strength of conservative forces and support for chiefs in the countryside at this time.

The homeland policy helped shore up apartheid at an important time for the Afrikaner nationalists but it was also very expensive and wasteful of public funds. Bantustans provided a powerful focus for criticism of apartheid and by the 1980s they were becoming important centres for political opposition.

National Party division and scandal

Prime minister Vorster remained securely in power from 1966 to 1978 and comfortably won the white elections of 1970 and 1974. By this time the National Party won wide English-speaking as well as Afrikaner support. However, Afrikaners did not all think in the same way and cracks were beginning to appear in the National Party edifice. **Verligte** and **verkrampte** groupings had developed within the National Party. Their battles were fought out publicly in the newspapers.

After Soweto, in the late 1970s, the editor of *Die Burger*, a long-established Cape nationalist paper, publicly advocated that black urbanisation was inevitable and questioned the possibility of separate development. As more Afrikaners moved into business and professions, they were finding, as English-speakers before them, that the restrictions on the labour market were holding them back. The *verligtes* argued that better training should be available for black workers and suggested that if black trade unions were recognised, relations between white employers and black workers could improve. They also advocated more opportunities for the rising African middle class in the cities. Such African families were not even allowed to own their own homes. The *verkramptes*, by contrast, argued that the solution lay in more rapid and stringent implementation of separate development.

Vorster, although pragmatic in his views, tended to side with the *verkramptes*. His government pursued the policy of creating independent homelands. He rejected the recommendations of a government commission of inquiry, which he himself had appointed, that there should be greater integration of Coloured people with whites.

In 1978, Vorster had been in power for 12 years and was ageing and ill. He seemed to favour Dr Connie Mulder, a leading conservative, for the succession. Mulder, the Minister of Information and the Interior, was in charge of government propaganda and policy formulation. He was head of the powerful Transvaal National Party and worked closely with General van den Bergh, head of the Security Police and the Bureau of State Security (BOSS). Van den Bergh was a powerful and independent figure and key in the repressive and vindictive police strategies developed in the apartheid years.

Vorster gave Mulder a secret fund to wage a propaganda campaign both within and outside the country. They employed a former journalist, Eschel Rhoodie, as their chief propagandist. They tried to influence the British and American media by purchasing and publishing magazines. They cultivated overseas politicians who seemed to support white rule and smeared those who opposed them, such as Jeremy Thorpe, the Liberal Party leader in Britain, who strongly supported the AAM.

The 'information scandal'

In 1978 Vorster's government was rocked by the 'information scandal'. Newspapers published stories showing that the propaganda slush fund established under Mulder was being used in corrupt and inappropriate ways. Individuals had used some of the money for self-enrichment. The biggest slice of money had gone to establish a loss-making newspaper, *The Citizen*, designed to win English-speaking readers to the Afrikaner nationalist cause. For the English-language opposition press, this was a great opportunity to illustrate the abuse of power, corruption and dirty tricks at the heart of Afrikaner rule. Many Afrikaners had been blind to criticism and believed in the moral purpose of their government. In the face of this and other scandals, it was increasingly difficult for Afrikaners to shut their eyes. The government's own Auditor-General confirmed the misuse of secret funds.

Van den Bergh and Rhoodie resigned but when Vorster stood down at the end of 1978, Connie Mulder competed with P. W. Botha for the position of prime minister. Although Mulder's local Transvaal wing was the biggest power base in the National Party, his role in the information scandal and his attempt to deny it was already becoming known and the Transvaal nationalists split. Botha was thus elected by 98 votes to 74. Mulder lost his leadership of the Transvaal nationalists to the strongly *verkrampte* A. P. Treurnicht, who had recently tried to push through the policy of expanding the use of Afrikaans in Soweto schools.

SOURCE

12 Speech by Oliver Tambo at the Sixth Conference of Heads of State of Government of Non-Aligned Countries, September 1979, Havana, Cuba.

Within the ruling group, the military establishment is taking over all positions of political authority in the illusory hope that this will help save the regime from destruction. The so-called information scandal, on the other hand, has exposed to the white population what the oppressed people have known for a long time: namely, that the regime was bound to rely on open criminal activities to save itself, since in any case the apartheid system is itself criminal.

The regime also finds itself compelled to accelerate its already discredited separate development and bantustan programme, changing the language it is using to make this programme appear more attractive, setting up all manner of advisory committees, all intended to salvage the political option that the enemy forced upon us, an option that has been rendered bankrupt by its consistent mass rejection by the people.

Economic and population pressures

Before discussing how the political crisis unfolded, it is important to return to South Africa's economy and society. In many respects the mid-1970s was a turning point for the country.

The Western world in general went into recession following the oil crisis of 1973. Oil was essential for all industrial economies. It powered the vehicles, planes and ships that were central to mobility, global trade and internal security. In 1973 the oil price doubled. South Africa was particularly vulnerable to the oil price shock because it had no natural oil and needed to import much of its supply. During the Second World War, techniques had been developed to extract oil for petrol from coal. These had been advanced particularly by the Nazis, as they were increasingly cut off from oil supplies. The nationalists founded a state-owned corporation called SASOL, which became the biggest oil-from-coal producer in the world, and by the early 1980s produced one-third of national requirements. Nevertheless there was a big gap to fill and SASOL petrol was expensive.

Although a rise in the price of gold helped to avert a sharp economic slowdown, South African manufacturing industry ceased to grow. South Africa's factories, protected by the government, could not compete. Skilled white workers were expensive and insufficiently numerous. Black workers were held back by racial restrictions on their training and promotion and by the lack of education. The costs of apartheid were being counted. Not only did sections of the South African economy slow down, but they did so at a time when the population was increasing exponentially. Between the census years of 1960 and 1991, the white population grew from three to five million and the African population from 11 to 29 million, increasing nearly threefold. This totally altered the balance of population in the country, as the percentage of whites dwindled from around 20 percent in mid-century to barely 13 percent.

Figures from the South African census, showing population growth, 1960–91.

Census year	Total population (millions)	African population (millions)	White population (millions)	Percentage white
1960	16	10.9	3.1	19.3
1970	21.8	15	3.8	17.3
1980	29	20	4.6	15.7
1991	38.3	28.9	5.1	13.2

Massive population growth among the African people, which mirrored that in the continent as a whole, is often underestimated in analyses of South Africa. It resulted in significant social outcomes that fundamentally shaped South African society: the population, especially the black population, became younger; there was a huge surge to the cities; shack or informal settlements proliferated; and unemployment escalated, especially for the youth.

In order to understand the impact of these changes in more detail, we should turn to the rural areas where, in 1960, 68 percent of the African population still lived. We should remember that much of South Africa, about 80 percent of rural land, was subdivided into white-owned farms. Many white farmers did well in these years, from the 1950s to the early 1980s. They were at the heart of the National Party support and were assisted by government subsidies. One indicator of this was the number of tractors, which increased from 119,000 in 1960 to 302,000 in 1980. Farmers did not, however, prosper uniformly. Many smaller, less efficient farmers gave up and farm sizes doubled between 1950 and 1990. The number of white farmers fell from about 120,000 to 65,000. Growing farm sizes, greater efficiency and more mechanisation led to significant increases in agricultural production but reduced the need for African workers. Both the government and farmers' organisations were keen to limit African occupation on the white-owned farms. Between 1960 and 1980 about two million black people moved off the farms. Some were forced off; some, especially younger people, chose to leave. They hoped to find employment elsewhere and wished to escape low paid and often harsh farm labour.

What happened to these people? The Surplus People's Project, a research programme run by anti-apartheid academics, attempted to record their experiences. The term 'surplus people' was used because it suggested that the white government saw these former farmworkers as surplus to the requirements of the South African economy. They were no longer needed on the farms and yet rising unemployment meant that there were no jobs for them in the cities. In any case, the apartheid bureaucratic machine was still trying to keep black people out of the cities. Many of the surplus people ended up in far-flung and desolate settlements, within or on the edges of homelands and far away from places of employment. The anthropologist Colin Murray wrote an article about this policy called 'Displaced urbanisation'. By the early 1980s, an area called Winterveld, north of Pretoria, was probably the largest, housing over half a million people. Botshabelo (ironically meaning place of refuge) in the Free State grew from bare veld in 1979 to a settlement of over 200,000 people by 1985. The great majority came from the farms. Few houses were built for them. The government demarcated sites and provided pit toilets. Each plot was 30 by 15 metres and came with a prefabricated tin toilet hut. The number of the plot was painted on the toilet door and this number became the address for the plot.

A similar place was a small homeland called KwaNdebele in the Transvaal. It too experienced mushroom growth, from about 32,000 in 1972 to over 200,000 in 1985. In 1975, the PUTCO bus company ran two buses a day from KwaNdebele; by 1984, there were 263. In order to commute to work in Pretoria, 100 km away, African people would have to leave home at about 4 a.m. and sometimes did not get back till 9 p.m. Joseph Lelyveld, an American journalist, called the people of KwaNdebele 'a nation of sleepwalkers'. David Goldblatt, a South African photographer, visited KwaNdebele in 1983 and called his resulting photo book *The Transported of KwaNdebele*.

SOURCE
14
A photograph by David Goldblatt. 'Marabastad-Waterval bus: 8:45pm, 45 minutes to the terminal', 1983.

Population increase was so rapid, and the movement from farms and homelands so great, that these displaced towns could not cope and many people did not want to live in them. Instead, they moved to the major cities and from about 1979, informal shack settlements proliferated. Impoverished rural people literally invaded municipal land and built their own shelters from whatever material they could find – usually corrugated metal and wood. They had no decent housing, no electricity and no running water except perhaps access to communal taps. But they found it preferable to be near a big city, with the possibility of work, or of earning some income from informal trading. Khayelitsha (meaning 'new home'), near the airport in Cape Town, became perhaps the single biggest shack settlement in the country during the 1980s, mostly housing people from the Eastern Cape. The population was estimated to be over half a million. The government could not find a way of enforcing the pass laws. People resisted the logic of apartheid by ignoring it and challenging the government to move them. During the early 1980s, the pass laws were breaking down and some aspects were successfully challenged in court. Such illegal urbanisation was a massive challenge for the apartheid government because it did not wish the African population of the cities to grow. In many respects, rapid urbanisation was a direct outcome of population growth, and together with economic stagnation, presented the government with intractable problems.

Botha and reform

P. W. Botha became prime minister in 1978. Although he was not a strong *verligte*, he was committed to the need for reform. Reform from above, to accommodate opposition forces, is often a very difficult process, fraught with uncertainties; concessions can empower opposition forces and give them greater confidence and in this case they also divided the Afrikaner nationalists. Botha's aim was to keep the initiative and ensure that reform was matched with repression where necessary. He was also deeply aware of the changing regional picture as South Africa became increasingly isolated.

Reform moved along two main fronts, both of which were designed to maintain white power. Botha addressed the economy and the constitution.

The economy

Firstly, the National Party began to relax economic apartheid. Botha's period of rule (1978–89) coincided with that of President Ronald Reagan in the United States (1981–89) and Prime Minister Margaret Thatcher in the UK (1979–90). With two such powerful conservative and anti-communist leaders in key global roles, international pressure on South Africa was somewhat reduced. Both of these leaders were also advocates of free markets and deregulation. The National Party was no longer so dependent on protecting poor whites and white workers (the very success of apartheid and Afrikaner rule had greatly improved white living standards and educational levels), and Afrikaner businessmen and professionals were increasingly influential. The government therefore decided to increase the security of African workers and their ability to move into more skilled jobs and offered to recognise trade unions as long as they registered and recognised certain rules. The de Lange Commission, reporting in 1981, advocated a gradual equalisation of educational expenditure and a single national department of education (although not racial integration). After Soweto, expenditure on African education rose sharply.

In Botha's reform era, the National Party softened the language of race. He continued to promote the homelands, and in fact expenditure increased, but he also recognised that African urbanisation was irreversible and that Afrikaners should create opportunities for a black urban elite. Political powers were devolved to black urban councils and in 1979 urban African people were allowed long term leases of their properties (though not freehold) in the cities. In the same year, the national professional football league was deracialised – black and white could play in the same teams and the same league. This was an extraordinary change, because Afrikaners had been so intent on enforcing social and physical segregation, though it did not impinge directly on most Afrikaners because they largely played and followed rugby, rather than football.

These were relatively small concessions but signalled significant ideological changes. In addition to promoting homeland leaders, Botha also made overtures to conservative African church leaders. Buthelezi, the KwaZulu homeland leader, was courted by white politicians, including the National Party and Margaret Thatcher in Britain. He seemed to provide a convincing alternative black political leadership to the liberation movements. Buthelezi also shared free market economic ideas that accorded with the emerging Western consensus.

The constitution

In his second major front of reform, Botha began to reconstruct the constitution of South Africa. He wished to concentrate power in the hands of the executive, rather than parliament, and developed a presidential form of government. This would also provide a route for incorporating Coloured and Indian communities who had not been given homelands.

- In 1980, he created a President's Council, an advisory body of white, Coloured and Indian politicians.

- In 1983 Coloured and Indian parliaments were established with the President's Council as an overarching body.

- Botha became president (rather than prime minister) in 1983 at the head of a **tricameral parliament**.

The system stopped short of granting political rights to Africans outside of the homelands. But 30 years after excluding Coloured and Indian people from any influence in the central parliament, Botha's reform policy was softening the hard edges of racial exclusion. To a limited degree, the National Party was recognising that, even in its own terms, it had made a massive mistake.

Botha's reform agenda triggered a split of *verkramptes* under Treurnicht, the head of the Transvaal nationalists, into a new Conservative Party. It was ironic that it was named after the British Conservative Party because Botha saw himself as closely aligned with Mrs Thatcher's free market views while Treurnicht wished to maintain all the protections for Afrikaners. The Afrikaner Conservative Party believed, in some senses correctly, that Botha's reforms betrayed the original principles of apartheid. However, apartheid had always been to some degree a flexible ideology.

During the 1980s, Treurnicht and the Conservative Party achieved a peak of nearly 600,000 white votes. This was still considerably less than the National Party, but sufficient to win 22 white parliamentary seats and displace the liberal Progressive Federal Party as the official opposition.

KEY TERM

Tricameral parliament
The name for the new parliamentary system in South Africa from 1984. It was made up of three chambers, with representatives from the white community elected to one, members of the Indian community elected to another, and members of the Coloured community elected to the third. Each chamber could pass laws relating to their 'own affairs', in the language of the time, which included areas such as education, housing and culture.

Treurnicht mobilised those whites who felt they still needed the protection of the state – civil servants, white miners, white workers, as well as farmers and the rural Afrikaner population. This was a right wing backlash with a vengeance and throughout the 1980s, Botha always had to watch his back and constrain his reform policies in order to keep the white electorate on his side.

THINKING HISTORICALLY   Change (6a)

Separately and together

Below are some different types of history that historians may identify.

Political history	Economic history	Social history
Environmental history	Cultural history	Global history

These are thematic histories, in which a historian focuses on a particular aspect of change. For example, an economic history of apartheid would focus on the economic reasons for the segregation of South African society, whereas a political history of apartheid would focus on national governance and strategic reasons for the homelands.

Working in groups, write a definition for each type of history.

Here are some events in our period. Review this timeline and then answer the questions that follow.

1969 Formation of SASO	1973 Oil crisis	1975 Portuguese rule comes to an end in Angola and Mozambique	1976 Students protest in Soweto against Afrikaans in schools	1977 Steve Biko is killed	1983 Nelson Mandela birthday concert in London

1 Some of these events could be classified in multiple ways. For example, the fourth event could be classified as 'political'. Why were students so angry at having Afrikaans in schools? What other thematic area of history does this event speak to?

2 What political changes came about because of the end of Portuguese rule in Africa in 1975?

3 Was the oil crisis political or economic or both? Explain your answer.

4 What was the social impact in South Africa of the rise of black consciousness?

5 Was Nelson Mandela's birthday concert purely a cultural event?

Working in pairs:

6 Write a statement attacking 'thematic history'.

7 Write three statements defending 'thematic history'.

8 Explain why historians subdivide approaches to their topics into such themes.

ACTIVITY
CONSOLIDATION

1 Which of these crises was most damaging to the South African state, and which was the least: the 1973 oil crisis; the information scandal; the increase of the African population?

2 How is David Goldblatt's picture, Source 14, useful to historians?

3 What is the difference between the *verligtes* and *verkramptes*? To what extent were their political positions distinct to South Africa? What did they have in common?

WHAT PRESSURES FROM BEYOND SOUTH AFRICA THREATENED NATIONAL PARTY AUTHORITY, 1974-83?

Mozambique, Angola and Zimbabwe all went through wars of independence and civil wars during this period. These disruptions could not be ignored by Pretoria and South Africa became increasingly embroiled in conflicts throughout the region. Meanwhile, the Soweto uprising and the plight of political prisoners were taken up by the AAM and foreign media and used to help bolster anti-apartheid feeling.

Political change in southern Africa

Vorster was prime minister at a time of increasing international isolation for South Africa (1966–78), but he pursued an active foreign policy in Africa in the 1970s and tried to leave behind the '*laager* **mentality**' that had characterised earlier Afrikaner approaches.

Vorster made loans available to several states, particularly those on South Africa's doorstep such as Lesotho and Swaziland, ensuring that countries remained dependent upon South African economic support. Further afield, a strategy of dialogue was developed and in the early 1970s South Africa received over 40 representatives from African countries in Pretoria. In 1974 and 1975, Vorster toured West Africa, meeting with the leaders of Ivory Coast and Liberia.

Botha's reform policy was accompanied by a far more aggressive foreign policy based around the idea of a 'Total Strategy'. He wanted to establish regional military superiority, seek regional allies and take the initiative in 'winning hearts and minds' wherever this was possible, externally as well as internally.

Southern African regional politics was changing rapidly. In 1974 a military coup in Portugal overthrew the Portuguese fascist government, not least because of its commitment to colonial wars. Angola and Mozambique, Portugal's colonies in southern Africa, found themselves on a fast-track to independence in 1975. Before this date there had been several groups in both countries fighting for independence. Now free, these groups had to decide how power was to be shared. South Africa was an interested party in this process. Mozambique, in particular, shared a long border to South Africa's east.

> **KEY TERM**
>
> *Laager* mentality
> A defensive position taken up in the 19th century by Afrikaners when trekking in a group. They would place their ox-wagons in a circle, with the people and livestock inside. This could be defended from danger or attack from every side. This idea of Afrikaners cordoning themselves off from the outside world became a helpful metaphor to describe certain policies and approaches during the apartheid era.

Figure 3.2: South Africa and its neighbouring states by 1983.

Mozambique

FRELIMO came to power in Mozambique, led by Samora Machel. He pursued a strongly socialist policy and nationalised resources including the land and many businesses. Most of the roughly 100,000 Portuguese settlers in the country left, some to South Africa. Machel sought support from communist powers. Both his internal policy and external allies alarmed the South African government. Machel enabled the Zimbabwe African National Union (ZANU) to establish military bases in Mozambique in order to pursue its guerrilla struggle against Ian Smith's minority white government in Zimbabwe. In turn Smith supported the Renamo movement, based largely in northern Mozambique, in its rebellion and civil war against FRELIMO. Botha expanded South African support for Renamo in order to destabilise Mozambique and to discourage its government from providing a safe haven for MK and the South African armed struggle. ANC activists were already established in Maputo, the Mozambican capital. Like Swaziland, it was a convenient place from where guerrilla fighters could slip over the border to conduct raids. The Mozambican civil war was protracted and devastating for that country. In the early 1980s it was compounded by a severe drought.

Angola and Namibia

Angola became independent in 1975 under the Marxist MPLA. The South African government was concerned that it would become a base for SWAPO, the liberation movement that was attempting to free Namibia from South African rule. South Africa therefore built up a military presence on the northern Namibian border and sporadically sent its own troops into Angola in 1975–76. South Africa, as well as the United States, increasingly lent their support to the Angolan UNITA movement in its civil war against the ruling MPLA.

Extended talks were held to try to reach an internal settlement in Namibia. These were sponsored by the United Nations and supported by Western powers, which were keen to promote moderate African governments that were neither revolutionary nor Soviet-oriented. But South Africa was reluctant to give up control. The significant white population of the country included a majority of Afrikaners, and the National Party feared that African majority rule in Namibia was likely to mean a SWAPO government, which might provide succour and support to the ANC along an extended border. So Botha built up South Africa's military presence in northern Namibia. White youths were required to do long periods of compulsory military service, largely in Namibia, and the standing army expanded. South Africa also recruited African allies, including San or Bushmen, who felt vulnerable as a minority in this region and were particularly skilled in bush war.

Zimbabwe

Throughout the 1970s a conflict raged in Rhodesia (Zimbabwe) between Ian Smith's white minority regime and the liberation movements of ZAPU and ZANU. ZANU gradually emerged as the most effective military force, relying upon Chinese assistance for military hardware and training. The white minority government, meanwhile, sought help from South Africa. Pretoria was in a predicament regarding Zimbabwe. The National Party feared communist governments taking power in the neighbouring states, but recognised that Zimbabwe could not last with a white minority government. They provided enough assistance for Ian Smith's government to survive and encouraged an internal settlement with moderate African leaders. But by the late 1970s South Africa accepted that Smith would have to negotiate with the Zimbabwean liberation movements.

The Zimbabwean parties met at Lancaster House in London in 1979 and agreed on a constitution that ensured democratic elections. ZANU won a convincing victory in 1980 and the new president, Robert Mugabe, was initially supportive of reconciliation. Whites were temporarily given a minority of parliamentary seats. Land reform – a central issue in Zimbabwe – was to be based on a 'willing buyer willing seller' principle. Western governments, particularly Britain, promised substantial financial resources to underwrite purchase of land from white farmers. South Africa watched this process warily and did not directly undermine it. Botha had decided that the costs of supporting Smith's government, in the face of overwhelming Western opposition to it, had become too great. In turn, Mugabe was cautious in his dealings with South Africa and did not permit the ANC or PAC to establish military bases or a significant presence in the new Zimbabwe.

SOURCE

15

Speech by Oliver Tambo at the Conference of the International Committee against apartheid, racism and colonialism in Southern Africa (ICSA), April 1980, Stockholm, Sweden.

It has never been a part of fascist South Africa's strategic thinking that it should treat its struggle for survival as a domestic affair involving violent conflict within Namibia and South Africa only. The notorious role of the South African army in the Zimbabwean liberation war, and in the air raids and military invasions against Mozambique, Zambia and Angola is explainable only in terms of the racist regime's central objective of isolating and destroying the revolutionary movement led by the Patriotic Front alliance in Zimbabwe, by SWAPO in Namibia and the ANC in South Africa. As the enemy saw it, the struggle for the control of Salisbury was at once the struggle for the control of Pretoria and Windhoek. Terrorising the entire region of southern Africa, the Pretoria regime sought to compel the independent States of this region to withdraw their support for the liberation movements; it sought to turn these countries against liberation, making of them allies of colonial, racist and apartheid domination of the people. The attempt failed. But the intention remained.

Defence expenditure

As it was increasingly surrounded by independent African countries, and threatened at a distance by the armed struggle of the ANC, Pretoria chose to spend a great deal on defence. After the United Nations voluntary ban on weapons exports to South Africa in 1963, the government prioritised a domestic arms industry under a government corporation called Armscor. South Africa manufactured its own firearms, military vehicles and aircraft so that by 1982, 80 percent of its vastly increased store of armaments was made in the country. In this the nationalist government was assisted by France and especially Israel. Israel formed an alliance with South Africa and military links were of central importance. Both countries took a pragmatic view, and they increasingly shared political identities as isolated regimes that felt threatened by those around them.

Regional accommodations

In 1980, nine southern African states launched the Southern African Development Coordination Conference (SADCC). This excluded South Africa and was designed as a counterweight to the apartheid regime. Governments of different ideological persuasions agreed to build alternative economic and political links.

This proved difficult because South Africa controlled key transport links through its ports, roads and railways to Botswana, Zimbabwe, Lesotho and Swaziland. Through these means Pretoria could put pressure on neighbouring states to stop hosting the ANC. For SADCC the Mozambican ports, and especially Beira, were the best alternatives. Within the region, South Africa's efforts at destabilisation were primarily aimed at Mozambique because of its socialist government, its support for the ANC and its strategic importance.

However, Botha did not rely on military strategies alone. In 1982 Swaziland signed a non-aggression pact with South Africa and Lesotho had been persuaded against hosting the ANC. Mozambique suffered such serious damage from the civil war and direct South African incursions that it signed the Nkomati Accord in 1984. South Africa undertook to stop military support for Renamo if FRELIMO would cease providing sanctuary for the ANC. P. W. Botha signed this agreement personally with Samora Machel and saw it as a major breakthrough. It seemed that South Africa had at least temporarily removed much of the pressure from its borders and succeeded in creating a 'constellation of states' with which it could do business.

A Level Exam-Style Question Section A

Study Sources 13 and 15 before you answer this question.

How far could the historian use Sources 13 and 15 together to investigate the impact of apartheid in the 1970s?

Explain your answer using the sources, the information about them and your knowledge of the historical context. (20 marks)

Tip

Think about the justification for apartheid offered in Source 13 and the ways in which this justification is discounted in Source 15. Compare these to the realities of the political situation in South Africa during this decade.

International relations

1 Why was it important for South Africa to keep Mozambique and Angola unstable?

2 Draw a line with 'Allies' written at one end and 'Enemies' at the other. Place the following countries on the line depending on their relationship to South Africa during this period: Israel, USA, Mozambique, Zimbabwe, Botswana, UK, Germany, Cuba, USSR. Write a couple of sentences to summarise South Africa's relationship with each state.

International condemnation of the National Party regime, 1974-83

South Africa was to some degree protected from intense external pressure by relatively sympathetic governments in the UK, the United States and Germany. However, the global consensus against apartheid was solidifying.

Economic sanctions and political alignments

During the first half of the 1970s, calls for economic sanctions against South Africa were falling on deaf ears among the leaders of South Africa's major trading partners. In 1973, reports of starvation wages paid by British firms in South Africa made national headlines. Rather than disinvestment, a British parliamentary select committee and the Trade Union Congress advocated a formal code of conduct for British firms operating in South Africa. In the United States, similar measures were promoted by a group of black Congressmen and by Rev Leon Sullivan, an African-American minister, who was appointed to the board of General Motors. He was approached in 1975 by anti-apartheid activists and, after Soweto catapulted South Africa into global news, he formulated a series of principles and practices around wages and conditions to guide American firms in South Africa.

The AAM generally opposed these initiatives as they felt they gave succour to the South African government. The movement organised a demonstration of 6,000 in London after Soweto, but it was uncertain about some of the new developments in South Africa. Linked so strongly to the ANC and its allies, the AAM was uneasy about supporting black consciousness and the student movement. When Tsietsi Mashinini, the SASM leader, arrived in London, he was not given a platform. Similar difficulties arose over the new independent trade unions. The AAM and ANC were still guided by SACTU, the ANC's trade union arm. Although individual SACTU members went into the new unions, SACTU no longer had a presence on the ground in South Africa. But the ANC was suspicious of the new unions because they focused on shop floor politics and not national liberation and it could not control their political direction. The AAM was reluctant to promote them in its newspaper or assist in fundraising. Rather, from 1980 onwards the AAM strongly encouraged the moves to Charterism (support for the Freedom Charter principles) within South African internal organisations.

Political prisoners

In the 1970s the AAM found it could win wider support by concentrating partly on human rights issues rather than the broader political aims of liberation. British governments and most of the British public were uneasy about the armed struggle. In 1974, AAM and linked organisations launched the SATIS (South Africa, The Imprisoned Society) campaign. SATIS focused initially on all political prisoners, but found that British activist and student groups had already begun to take up Mandela's name. The AAM and the ANC felt that the focus on prisoners would be more effective if they found one iconic figure and that a personal story would also enable them to avoid difficult issues such as the armed struggle.

In 1975 Mike Terry, formerly the secretary of the British National Union of Students, became executive secretary of the AAM and provided new energy and new connections in British politics. SATIS took up the case of Solomon Mahlangu, a 20-year-old student from the Soweto generation who fled South Africa in 1976, underwent military training with MK, and then returned to work underground in 1977. Within a few days he and his associates were identified and in the short gun battle that ensued, two civilians were killed on a street in Johannesburg. Mahlangu was tried, sentenced to death and hanged in 1979. Supporting Mahlangu through his trial was important for the ANC and AAM because he was part of the new generation that they wished to win over. Mahlangu was taken up as a hero by the ANC, which named their school for exiled children in Tanzania after him.

From 1978 the campaign was increasingly personalised around Mandela, initially to celebrate his 60th birthday with international birthday cards. Three thousand were sent, perhaps not a huge number, but it was recognised as the most successful part of the SATIS campaign so far. The British Labour cabinet signed and sent a birthday card. The AAM released biographies and stories, as well as photographs and images from the period before Mandela's imprisonment. Mandela was taken up by the media again, which greatly emphasised his political stature and his humanity, as well his plight as a long term political prisoner. Though some conservatives still saw him as a terrorist, the tide of opinion was turning and *The Times* referred to him as 'the colossus of African nationalism'. From 1980 a global as well as South African campaign focused around the slogan 'Free Nelson Mandela'. AAM increasingly recognised the importance of making cultural connections, rather than presenting only political arguments. In 1983 they organised a Nelson Mandela birthday concert at Alexandra Palace to celebrate his 65th birthday.

A-Level Exam-Style Question Section B

How far were domestic challenges in the years 1974–83 responsible for P. W. Botha's reforming agenda? (20 marks)

Tip
Think about how you will define domestic challenges and consider the impact of the various external challenges as well as domestic challenges.

ACTIVITY
WRITING

Look up these terms and write short definitions in your own words:

anathema	cordon sanitaire	liberation	Marxist-Leninist
Pretoria	nationalist	Rhodesia	

Use the words to fill the blanks in this paragraph.

_____'s principal aim was to protect white minority rule in South Africa. However, _____ concern increased after the collapse of Portuguese rule in Africa. Before 1975, South Africa could rely upon a _____ of white-run states, from Angola in the west, through _____ to the north, to Mozambique in the east. Yet _____ movements in the Portuguese territories forced a retreat, and in so doing established Angola and Mozambique on the front line of the struggle against white minority rule. Furthermore, both Angola and Mozambique established _____ states, _____ to the apartheid capitalist establishment.

ACTIVITY
SUMMARY

1 Create a two-column table. Label the columns 'Oliver Tambo' and 'Steve Biko'. Consider who was more dangerous to the National Party during the years 1968–83 and why. Write your ideas into the table, in a way that allows for direct comparison between the two leaders. Who do you conclude was the greater threat to the National Party?

2 Look at the map of southern Africa, Figure 3.2. Why was Lusaka the best base for the ANC in exile? Why not choose Mbabane, Maputo or Gaborone?

3 On a scale of 1 to 10, with 10 as 'very significant' and 1 as 'insignificant', how important was Nelson Mandela during this period to: ANC strategy; AAM in Britain; Vorster; Steve Biko. Explain each of your ratings in a couple of sentences.

WIDER READING

Biko, Steve, *I Write What I Like*, Heinemann (1987)

Clark, Nancy L., *South Africa: The Rise and Fall of Apartheid*, Routledge (2011)

Culpin, Christopher, *South Africa 1948–1995: a depth study*, Hodder Education (2000)

Gordimer, Nadine, *Telling Times: Writing and Living, 1950–2008*, Bloomsbury (2011)

Lelyveld, Joseph, *Move Your Shadow*, Abacus (1989)

Mandela, Nelson, *The Long Walk to Freedom*, Abacus (2013)

Mulholland, Rosemary, *South Africa 1948–1994*, Cambridge University Press (1997)

Mzamane, Mbulelo, *The Children of Soweto*, Longman (1987)

Roberts, Martin, *South Africa 1948–1994: the Rise and Fall of Apartheid*, Longman (2001)

2b.4 The end of apartheid and the creation of the 'rainbow nation', 1984–94

KEY QUESTIONS

- Why did the townships revolt in the years 1984–87?
- Why did the National Party decide to begin negotiations in the years 1985–89?
- To what extent did political negotiations, 1989–91, end in compromise?
- To what extent did the new political settlement reached in the years 1992–94 create a fully democratic country?

INTRODUCTION

By 1984 the social and political landscape of South Africa had changed dramatically, even compared to a decade previously. Emboldened by black consciousness, and bolstered by economic and diplomatic conditions, resistance against apartheid had picked up momentum. Containing that momentum was becoming increasingly difficult for the authorities.

The process of change did not run a predictable or peaceful course. Activists attempted to make the townships ungovernable in the mid-1980s and attacked those who were seen to be collaborating with the state. The government countered with force and sought allies in African communities. Such conflicts resulted in moments of intense violence. Botha's reform policy was undermined by popular protest; he militarised the state and resorted to mass arrests.

Amid this antagonism, change began to take place behind the scenes. Senior members of the ANC met with business leaders and high-ranking National Party members in an attempt to pave the way for more concrete negotiations. Mandela was moved to prisons on the mainland to make discussions with him more practical. There was increasing pressure on the Nationalists to enter into a more formal dialogue.

When F. W. de Klerk replaced P. W. Botha as president in 1989, the pace of political change quickened. In 1990 he released Mandela from prison and legalised the ANC and the PAC. This enabled inclusive and expansive negotiations on the future of South Africa, but there remained a very real possibility that violence could undermine all chances of agreement. White politicians, with the support of the army and the police, still maintained control of the security forces. Conflict between different African political movements, particularly the Zulu Inkatha Freedom Party and the ANC, escalated. A civil war was a real risk.

1983 – Foundation of the United Democratic Front (UDF)
Inauguration of the tricameral parliament

1985 – Height of the township insurrection
State of emergency
Congress of South African Trade Unions (COSATU) formed

1988 – Mandela's 70th birthday tribute in London broadcast to 500 million

1983   1984   1985   1986   1987   1988

1984 – Beginning of the Vaal uprising
ANC calls for townships to be made ungovernable

1986 – Alexandra 'six day war' and people's committees
Second state of emergency and political crack-down by government

By 1993, however, it was clear that the major political groupings supported a unified South Africa and a peaceful transition. Elections were scheduled for the following April. Much compromise was required by key parties to agree on constitution. The ANC insisted on a universal franchise and fully democratic system, which was very likely to deliver them political power. The National Party attempted to defend existing property rights, which would protect white wealth. When Mandela was sworn into office, it was at the head of a coalition government representing a partnership of awkward bedfellows. Yet, despite threats of civil war and national disintegration, the goal of a democratic South Africa, freed from apartheid laws, had been achieved.

WHY DID THE TOWNSHIPS REVOLT IN THE YEARS 1984–87?

The black residential areas known as townships became increasingly tempestuous over the course of the 1980s. Although the government tried to contain and suppress the violence, its actions often served to antagonise people further and fuel the flames of resistance.

The political context of revolt

In order to understand the specific features of the township revolt, we should return to the government's reform process. Reform, as conceived by P. W. Botha and the political strategists closest to him, recognised that elements of apartheid had not been effective. Reform was designed not to end white power but to find new routes to preserve it. As noted in the previous chapter, homeland policy remained a central route and Botha's government continued to invest large amounts in the hope of making the homelands 'viable' as separate states. Attempts were made to draw in Coloured and Indian politicians through the tricameral parliament (see page 350). Botha found some significant political leaders, such as Allan Hendrickse of the Labour Party, who were prepared to work – at least temporarily – within this system.

One central strategy involved winning black allies and giving them greater political responsibility and local political power. African people in the cities were offered new urban black councils under the Community Council Act of 1977 and the Black Local Authorities Act of 1982. The state hoped that elected urban black councillors would be able to absorb and defuse discontent. But as in the case of the homelands, most urban voters refused to participate in elections that they saw as fraudulent.

Nevertheless, there were township residents who were keen on taking office, some genuinely believed that they could make a difference by working within the system and taking responsibility for local government into black hands. Sam Buti in Alexandra, for example, hoped to use the new powers to improve social conditions in the townships. For others, service in the local councils was a route to central government financial resources that were being channelled to the townships. The councils had direct power to allocate housing, to employ local officials, to award contracts and to grant licences for businesses such as liquor outlets and taxis. Councils were especially attractive to a new elite of township businessmen with entrepreneurial energy long suppressed by the apartheid system. The taxi business, for example, was expanding rapidly.

The government, however, devolved not only the task of spending central revenue but also that of raising more revenue locally. The great majority of urban black people lived in council housing and had to pay rent. Alongside food and transport costs, rents absorbed a major part of household budgets and were expensive for the urban poor. Yet they were the best potential stream of revenue for local councils. By the early 1980s it was clear that councils would have to increase rents if they were to improve public facilities or break even. Housing for poor black people was at a premium in the major urban centres and many had to live in backyards or shacks. Attempts by urban councils to control the spread of unplanned, informal shack settlements created further tension.

Councillors were often seen as 'sell outs' – not only participating in apartheid institutions but also taking advantage of their position. Among the politicised youth in particular, they were seen to be

1989 – Botha suffers stroke
F. W. de Klerk elected leader of National Party and president by white-only vote

1991 – Revocation of key apartheid legislation
CODESA negotiations begin

1993 – Chris Hani assassinated
Multi-party Negotiating Forum

1989   1990   1991   1992   1993   1994

1990 – Nelson Mandela released
ANC, CP and PAC unbanned

1992 – Negotiations stall
Violence in Natal, Boipatong, Ciskei

1994 – Non-racial democratic elections held

KEY TERM

Community
In South Africa, this term usually means a local African community settled in a rural village or section of a township. But it often has a strong political content too – a political community defined racially as black people who share in political struggle and sacrifice.

betraying their **communities** by doing the government's dirty work for them. Devolution was intended by the government to create a buffer and to pass responsibility to black allies. Yet it also fragmented authority and created confusion.

The United Democratic Front and grass roots organisations

By 1983, activists from many different organisations felt that they needed to take a stand against Botha's constitutional reforms. They were concerned that Botha was finding allies for this initiative, in the homelands, in the Coloured Labour Party and in the urban black councils. A new United Democratic Front (UDF) mobilised against Botha's measures and argued for a fully democratic South Africa. The first rally was held in August 1983 at Mitchell's Plain in Cape Town. This was a huge Coloured township, 30 km from the city centre, to which many families were forcibly resettled from District Six and the inner suburbs of Cape Town. The site was chosen in order to emphasise the non-racial character of the new movement: it would include Coloured as well as African people. Those who had identified with the ANC in the past were at the heart of the UDF, including Winnie Mandela and Albertina Sisulu, both wives of jailed ANC leaders. But it incorporated a new generation of highly articulate national leaders, especially those associated with churches such as Desmond Tutu (Anglican) and Frank Chikane (South African Council of Churches). Chikane was a former Turfloop black consciousness activist. Allan Boesak of the Coloured branch of the Dutch-reformed church had recently been elected as president of the World Alliance of Reformed Churches and gave a keynote address to an estimated 10,000 people, from over 500 organisations, at the Mitchell's Plain meeting.

SOURCE 1

Extract from Allan Boesak's speech at the launch of the United Democratic Front, Cape Town, 20 August 1983.

We have arrived at a historic moment. We have now brought together under the aegis of the United Democratic Front the broadest and most significant coalition of groups and organisations struggling against apartheid, racism, and injustice in South Africa since the early 1950s. We have been able to create unity among freedom-loving persons that this country has not seen for many a year.

I am particularly happy to note that this meeting is not merely a gathering of isolated individuals. No, we represent organisations deeply rooted in the struggle for justice, deeply rooted in the heart of our people. Indeed, I believe we are standing at the birth of what could become the greatest and most significant popular movement in more than a quarter of a century.

SOURCE 2

Extract from the UDF Declaration of Independence, August 1983.

We commit ourselves to uniting all our people wherever they may be, in the cities, in countryside, the factories and mines, schools, colleges and universities, housing and sports fields, churches, mosques and temples, to fight for our freedom.

The UDF adopted the Freedom Charter, but did not advocate armed struggle. It drew in an increasingly wide range of support and was instrumental in organising boycotts of Botha's Indian and Coloured parliaments as well as councils in the townships. Of those eligible to register, an estimated 13 percent of Indian voters and 18 percent of Coloured actually voted for those two parliaments. The UDF's success in mobilising against these key reform policies effectively rendered Botha's institutions inoperable as representative bodies. Black South Africans would only vote when they were voting on an equal basis to whites: in the first democratic election (1994) an estimated 85.5 percent exercised their franchise.

It is helpful to think of the UDF not as a distinct centralised organisation, but as a broad umbrella or political front that attempted to manage several strands of opposition to apartheid. It was an affiliation of grass roots movements, including trade unions, church groups, student organisations, residents associations and community groups. They were all opposed to apartheid but they espoused different priorities and ideologies and they deployed different strategies of resistance.

In 1983 COSAS aligned with the UDF and became its largest national affiliate. The movement established itself in the townships of the Transvaal early in 1984 through a Million Signatures Campaign, which directly echoed the ANC's similar initiative in 1955 to popularise the Freedom Charter.

THINKING HISTORICALLY   Cause and consequence (6b)

Attitudes and actions

Individuals can only make choices based on their context. Prevalent attitudes combine with individual experience and natural temperament to frame the individual's perception of what is going on around them. Nobody can know the future or see into the minds of others.

Context	Action
The ANC was a banned organisation in South Africa, and as such found it difficult to mobilise people easily. The Party operated from bases abroad, including Lusaka and London. Students had begun protesting in 1976 and the scale of disobedience was escalating. The South African state was increasingly using violence to suppress opposition in the townships. Other liberation organisations were beginning to gain influence within South Africa.	In October 1984 the movement put out a call to make South Africa ungovernable. Black people were encouraged to disobey laws and to make the streets dangerous for state security forces. The idea was to force the state into submission.

Answer the following questions individually and discuss your answers in a group:

1 Why might the ANC have put out the call to make South Africa ungovernable?

2 What problems might they have foreseen in such a call?

3 What other information would have been useful for the ANC to help them decide on their course of action?

4 How reasonable was the ANC's decision given what they understood about the situation at the time?

5 How far should the historian try to understand the context of the beliefs and values of people in the past when explaining why individuals make choices in history?

Protest strategies

The dynamics of South African protest shifted in the later months of 1984, with violent tactics becoming increasingly attractive to new waves of protesters. Several points of conflict triggered open rebellion in parts of South Africa. One of these was the Vaal Triangle, site of Sharpeville.

Compared with Soweto or Alexandra in Johannesburg, this had not been a significant centre of political organisation during the 1970s, but on 3 September 1984 – the day that the tricameral parliament opened in Cape Town – an uprising against the government erupted in the Vaal Triangle and councillors were killed in Sharpeville and Sebokeng. The Vaal Civic Association, affiliated to the UDF, had initially led the protests but lost control of the crowds. They did not advocate the killing of the councillors, which constituted a new departure and a redrawing by angry youth of the boundaries of legitimate protest. This was a break from the recent past in the Vaal Triangle at least. The crowds were prepared to vent their anger and take vengeance on councillors whom they thought had betrayed the community.

In the aftermath of 3 September, this type of violence became engrained in new forms of political protest. The new generation of rebels were younger, often at high school or having recently completed it, but with little prospect of employment. There was a rapid turnover in leadership as known members of the UDF were detained. The youth, at least initially, worked incognito. They had a deep knowledge of the backstreets and safe houses, and

tried to establish their own system of clandestine communication. They formed tight networks and political solidarity was essential because it was literally a matter of life and death.

The Congress of South African Students (COSAS), established in 1979, had become the most representative body for scholars. Along with African newspapers, it led the call to free Mandela in 1980. During 1984–85, they called for a renewed school boycott, and started branches in many high schools in the country. In effect they were asking that generation of schoolchildren to secure 'liberation before education'. COSAS itself had little organised presence in upsurges such as the Vaal uprising but it did participate in organising, with trade unions, a massive stayaway in November 1984.

In October 1984, following the Vaal uprising, the ANC in exile issued a call for 'making our country ungovernable'. The movement was banned and direct identification was dangerous, but the ANC did have some means of communication to South Africa through its Radio Freedom and other vehicles. Radio Freedom helped to shape the consciousness and language of militant youth to whom the armed struggle and mystique of MK were attractive.

In 1985 protest reached a crescendo around the country as a whole. Government and council offices in the townships became a frequent target, burnt down by groups of angry youths. The *toyi-toyi*, a jogging dance, cemented solidarity in the crowds. ANC flags began to appear at public events such as funerals and protests.

'People's power' became the slogan of the moment and many meetings resounded with cries of *Amandla* (power) by the speaker with a response of *Ngawethu* (to us the people) by the crowd.

SOURCE 3

A speech made by Oliver Tambo, head of the ANC in exile, at the Kabwe Conference in 1985. It was distributed on cassette tapes and broadcast on the ANC's Radio Freedom.

Pretoria has carried out its murderous plans to extreme. We must now respond to the reactionary violence of the enemy with our own revolutionary violence. The weapons are there in white houses. Each white house has a gun or two hidden inside to use against us. Our mothers work in their kitchens. We work in their gardens. We must deliberately go out to look for these weapons in these houses.

In 1985 the ANC called for a people's war and made more systematic attempts to send MK cadres into South Africa. ANC armed struggle was no longer restricted to sabotage. In 1983 a bomb outside the South African Air Force headquarters in Church Street, Pretoria, had resulted in 19 deaths and over 200 injuries. In 1985 a record number of MK activists came into the country, and the movement recorded 137 attacks. In that year 31 members of MK were killed. After a bomb at a supermarket in Amanzimtoti, south of Durban, which killed five people, the Durban cell was exposed and arrested. Joe Mamasela, a black policeman based at Vlakplaas, infiltrated a COSAS group on the East Rand: eight of them died from the booby-trapped hand-grenades he gave them.

Youths living in South Africa saw themselves as 'comrades' furthering the armed struggle of the ANC, even though the internal UDF was not calling for such tactics. Most of the young men involved in direct action now identified with the ANC as the legitimate liberation movement despite its lack of organisation on the ground. Popular mobilisation had largely left black consciousness behind and the American influence on thinking and strategy had dwindled. South African political activists had moved far beyond the civil rights movement and even the radicalism of the Black Power movement.

Alexandra, Johannesburg

At the end of 1985, Alexandra, a densely packed African township, became a new centre of gravity for rebellion. Once on the northern periphery of Johannesburg, by the 1980s it abutted rapidly expanding wealthy suburbs such as Sandton.

The revolt there broke out early in 1986, after a month of tension, and became known as the 'Six Day War'. It was triggered when a youth activist, Michael Diradeng, was shot by a security guard at the end of January. A night vigil was organised on 14 February and the comrades decided to mobilise mass participation by encouraging, and even coercing, people to attend. On their route around the township they petrol bombed the shop, Jazz Stores, where Diradeng had died, and set fire to others as well as stoning cars. They then burnt some houses, including those of black policemen. Early next morning they stabbed a policeman. Diradeng's funeral took place next day accompanied by attacks on the police and homes of councillors. Police tear-gassed and fired on a crowd of 6,000 youth and four residents were killed. Most police fled their homes in the township. A rally of perhaps

40,000 people was organised at the stadium. By now the township had been surrounded and sealed off by the army. This was a people's war by the 'young lions of Alexandra' but it was not led directly by the ANC. Police killed perhaps 27 people and order was reimposed.

A particularly important feature of the Alexandra rebellion was its longevity. It did not end after this intense period of violence. Youths and other comrades tried to develop an alternative order over the township in the shape of people's courts, echoing events in the rural areas around 1960.

SOURCE 4

Extract from a pamphlet distributed at the funeral of Michael Diradeng by youth activists, Alexandra 1986.

People! We have got two problems in Alexandra: disunity and problems not solved. To solve these problems the Alex people have decided to form structures that will encourage unity, comradeship and action – Street committees (avenue committees). We want people to have general meetings in their yards to elect a yard committee to unite people in the yard. The yard committee through its general meeting should elect a chairman, secretary and two representatives to the block committee... There shall be weekly general meetings for yards to solve matters. Problems will be referred to block committees.

SOURCE 5

Paul Tshabalala, a participant in a people's court in Alexandra, speaking to the historian Belinda Bozzoli in 2004.

People had no problems with the people's court. One would find that when a group of people have come together trying to solve something, they would say we were at the people's court... In the yards where people were trying to solve their problems, they would say they are in the people's courts. You would find children in their play they would say 'we are playing the people's court'.

SOURCE 6

N. Nxumalo, resident of Alexandra during the protests, speaking to the historian Belinda Bozzoli in 2004.

Drunkenness became less, because the people were now scared to be found in the streets. They were mainly scared of the very people who were busy with the anti crime activity. Most shebeens closed. When we come now to the incidents of stabbings, these stabbings in Alexandra usually takes place when people are already drunk during the night. Now this caused the reduction in drunkenness, because they were no longer finding more places where they would drink and get drunk and enjoy stabbing one another.

AS Level Exam-Style Question Section A

Study Source 5 before you answer this question.

How much weight do you give the evidence of Source 5 for an enquiry into the revolt in Alexandra, Johannesburg, in 1986?

Explain your answer, using the source, the information given about it and your own knowledge of the historical context.

Tip

Think about the provenance of the source: by whom it was written and what its purpose was.

SOURCE

7 An extract from the incident book kept at Wynberg Police Station, Alexandra, for a day in February 1986.

10 AM a car was stoned at 134 Fifteenth Avenue

10 AM police shot dead N. Ledwaba, a young girl standing at the gate of her home

10 AM a fire engine had to be escorted to a fire in Second Avenue

10:30 AM a Casspir had been petrol bombed, and a policeman injured

11:15 AM another petrol bomb was thrown at the corner of Selborne and Third Avenue

1.05 PM a private car was stoned, at the corner of Selborne and Thirteenth Avenue

2 PM a petrol bomb was thrown at a car on the corner of Selborne and Eighth Avenue

SOURCE

8 A student in Duduza township dancing around the burning car of a suspected police informer. This photograph was taken by the South African photo-journalist Gideon Mendel on 10 July 1985.

The brief rule of the comrades in Alexandra had its harsh side, in **necklacing** and in more casual violence against those who broke consumer boycotts of shops or were reluctant to participate in stayaways. The word *comtsotsis*, combining comrades and *tsotsis* (urban youth gangs), came into fashion briefly to describe those who used violence to establish what they perceived as an alternative social order. But it was an extraordinary achievement for the youth to briefly take over their world and try to impose a better, more liberated order. They did this largely without direct assistance from the UDF, which distanced itself from the excesses of the comrades. The youth were trying to move beyond ungovernability towards institution building, and running the townships themselves.

KEY TERM

Necklacing

A form of punishment devised by black youth at the height of the insurrection against those they viewed as *impimpi* (spies or informers). They forced discarded car tyres over the heads of victims, poured petrol into them and then lit them. This punishment was not frequently used but it came to symbolise both anger and excess. It should be remembered that many youths were being killed through violence.

Winnie Mandela, who had been harassed and detained by police over a long period, identified strongly with the new insurrectionary impulses – as she had with the Soweto uprising. At a rally in Munsieville township, near Krugersdorp (and Desmond Tutu's childhood home) in April 1986, she was quoted as saying, 'with our boxes of matches and our necklaces we shall liberate this country'. It was a flight of rhetoric, a call to arms, which echoed the call by Tambo for revolutionary violence and also the ANC commitment to armed struggle. Her words were widely criticised then and since as a particularly incendiary exhortation that the youth could burn themselves to liberation.

The trade unionist, Moses Mayekiso, formed a broad Alexandra Action Committee to ride the wave of protest. Many stopped paying rent but they were less keen on consumer boycotts. Street committees and civic organisations that drew all the different strands of the community together seemed to be the answer. The aim was to help people solve community problems within the community, to increase their sense of unity, and to act as a representative body for the community. Their aims and demands were around urban services, better housing, street repairs, toilet provision, lower bus and taxi fares, better education, less police harassment and the removal of the army. They named one of the few open spaces in the township Freedom Park. For Mayekiso, order and discipline was crucial to the success of the mass protest.

Rural rebellion

The mid-1980s insurrection was largely, but by no means entirely, based in the urban townships. The towns and rural high schools of the Eastern Cape, for example, were also centres of protest and recruitment routes for MK. In Sekhukhuneland (Lebowa), in Transvaal, site of a major rural rebellion in the 1950s, the youth also took matters into their own hands. Some were politicised members of the youth congresses but others turned to other and older ideas. They accused people of **witchcraft** and killed 32 of them. Such killings were unusual in protest politics at this time.

KEY TERM

Witchcraft

Sometimes blamed as a cause of social turmoil or illness in a community, accusations of witchcraft could intensify in times of social instability, such as the mid-1980s. It was associated with a belief that there was a malevolent individual trying to do an individual or community harm. Often, the malevolent individual was also a member of the local community.

Witches are not believed to do direct physical harm but send a familiar (a mythical creature such as a baboon, or a *tikoloshe*) or use medicines. In the homeland of Lebowa, old women – vulnerable people without strong social links and protection – were most commonly accused of witchcraft. A few more powerful men in the tribal authorities were also attacked.

SOURCE
9
From an editorial in *City Press,* the newspaper serving Johannesburg's black population, April 1986.

Black South Africa has experienced a cultural revolution, a metamorphosis in values and conventions of the profoundest type... Young people have experienced an unprecedented moral ascendancy. They are known universally as 'the youth', the legion of black teenagers who for the last two years have provided the shock troops of a nationwide popular insurrection. This has been a children's war.

The government response

In June 1985 Botha declared a state of emergency and sent the troops into the townships protected by armoured vehicles and prepared to use their weapons. Retaliation in Alexandra in 1986 was particularly brutal. The army sealed off the township in April. The houses of known activists were burnt, at least one with the people inside. In turn the activists barricaded the streets and dug trenches. The police vehicles, however, could bulldoze their way through. In May 1986 over 1,500 troops moved into Alexandra and made house to house searches, arresting anyone suspected of resistance. On 12 June a second national state of emergency resulted in the arrest of 3,000 in Alexandra alone. Over 25,000 were detained nationally over the next year, many of them youths. All the key leaders in Alexandra were arrested and subjected to a well-publicised trial. Botha dispensed with the black council and established Joint Management Committees of army, police and white bureaucrats to run the township.

Government suppression

State suppression

The National Party still had the power to repress, at least temporarily, black political protest. The army and police were entirely controlled by whites who remained loyal to the regime and shared its objective of maintaining white authority. In fact, some were to the right of the National Party. The police force increased from about 49,000 to 93,600 between 1981 and 1991, largely to cope with increasing political dissidence and growing urban populations. By 1994 the police force numbered nearly 140,000.

Common police tactics included mass arrests, imprisonment and banning orders, but there were cases of kidnappings, interrogation under torture and deaths. The special branch of the police kept files on local opposition leaders, and often attempted to turn them into informants against the ANC or other organisations. During Truth and Reconciliation Commission hearings after the end of apartheid, several cases were heard detailing atrocities committed against key activists captured by the special branch.

Conflict in the homelands

By no means all African people supported youth protest. On the ground in the townships those supporting the UDF met difficult challenges. Opposition was strongest in the homeland of KwaZulu and parts of Natal, where the Inkatha Freedom Party, the Zulu movement, was entrenched. Chief Buthelezi, at the helm of the Party, was increasingly hostile to radical protest politics.

He suppressed school boycotts in KwaZulu and developed an alternative Youth Brigade. While in theory Inkatha was a non-ethnic party, and sought broader support on the Witwatersrand, Buthelezi focused on his homeland base. Nevertheless, he believed that he could build an alliance for change outside of the UDF and ANC, which would protect regional identities and power, and espouse free market values. He would not accept independent homeland status from Pretoria because he believed this would undermine an argument for a single nation, and weaken his bargaining position.

SOURCE
10
A security forces armoured vehicle patrolling the KTC squatter community in Cape Town on 9 June 1986. Photograph by the photographer and anti-apartheid campaigner Dave Hartman.

EXTEND YOUR KNOWLEDGE

The South African police force

Many of the new police recruits in the 1980s were black. The great majority of black police officers developed a strong professional ethos and some were figures of authority and power in the townships. They became a target for attack by politicised black youth. Starting with Soweto in 1976, and elsewhere after the insurrection of the mid-1980s, many police had to move out of townships temporarily. But there are few examples of them joining the rebels. In the late 1980s the government expanded funding for community policing or special constables. They became known in Afrikaans by the term *kits konstabels* ('instant constables'), because their training was short and inadequate. Their confrontations with the township residents and militant youth could be particularly abrasive. Each of the homelands also had its own separate forces. Expenditure on police in the four biggest homelands increased from about R40 million in 1982 to R260 million in 1990.

Whatever his broader aims, Buthelezi's political practice included not only the use of homeland police to suppress opposition but also support for Inkatha vigilantes. At the grass roots Inkatha faced comrades (*amaqabane*) who were prepared to use violence and they responded in kind. A pattern of politicised violence amongst Zulu-speaking people emerged in Natal in the 1980s with serious incidents at Inanda, north of Durban, and Edendale in Pietermaritzburg.

Such conflicts could take on ethnic dimensions. One of the single most devastating conflicts during the mid-1980s was between Inkatha-linked vigilantes and Transkeians, mostly Mpondo people, identifying with the UDF who had migrated to Durban to work. The local Zulu chief in the Umbumbulu Tribal Authority, near Umlazi, on the southern rim of Durban, resented the informal shack settlements on local land. He told a researcher that Zulu people wanted first option on the jobs in the area, and on the water and the land. Well over 100 Transkeians were killed between December 1985 and January 1986 by Zulu *impis* (an old Zulu word for 'regiments') and thousands of shacks were razed to the ground.

In three years of township carnage in Zululand and Natal, around 4,000 were killed. In the main this was not ethnic conflict: both sides were Zulu speakers from different backgrounds and with different views. The comrades were intent that people in the urban townships should not be subject to the control of the homeland authorities and chiefs. They wanted to be part of one nation, South Africa.

Similar conflicts played out in other homelands. Kaizer Matanzima in Transkei arrested opposition leaders in the 1970s and passed a Public Safety Act in 1977 that gave him almost unlimited powers. He banned the Methodist church because it questioned the validity of Transkeian independence, tried to confiscate its property and established an alternative Transkeian state church on Methodist lines.

In 1980 Matanzima organised a show trial of Sabata Dalindyebo, senior chief of the Thembu, who opposed homelands. Although Sabata was acquitted of treason, he fled into exile in Zambia where he became 'the Comrade King', fully aligned with the ANC. In 1986, when Sabata died in Zambia, his body was flown home for burial. Matanzima arranged for the body to be stolen and buried elsewhere, and his troops stopped Sabata's supporters from coming to the funeral.

In 1987 Matanzima was ousted in a coup led by Bantu Holomisa at the head of a 2,000-strong Transkeian army. Sabata's son was now installed as chief of the Thembu. In September 1989, Sabata's body was exhumed and reburied at the Thembu royal home in front of a crowd of 6,000. This was a major anti-apartheid event which fully distanced the Transkei authorities from Matanzima. Holomisa also unbanned the ANC and PAC, in 1989, before de Klerk did so in South Africa; freedom songs were sung in the streets of the local capital Mthatha.

AS Level Exam-Style Question Section B

How far did the National Party's policy toward protest change in the years 1984–89? (20 marks)

Tip

Don't simply write about what the National Party did in these years, but focus on the degree of change, and on whether change was basic or simply cosmetic.

ACTIVITY
CONSOLIDATION

Townships in revolt

1 What is Source 3 trying to encourage people to do? Think about how Tambo's message could be interpreted. Is there a broader meaning than the literal one?

2 Reread Sources 4, 5, 6 and 7. How successfully do you think law and order was being maintained within Alexandra during this period?

3 Class discussion: Was the use of violence by the youth morally justified?

WHY DID THE NATIONAL PARTY DECIDE TO BEGIN NEGOTIATIONS IN THE YEARS 1985–89?

By the mid-1980s the National Party leadership, realising that white supremacy was under significant threat, tried not only to suppress black insurrection but also to find routes for compromise that might protect white interests.

Botha's reforms and 'total strategy'

President Botha's 'total strategy' aimed to use reform in order to appease criticism and mounting unrest. He hoped to win support within South Africa and counter the threat beyond its borders. In August 1985, in the midst of the township revolt, and in the face of considerable Western pressure to phase out apartheid, Botha made a keynote speech in which he was expected to expand the reform programme. Instead he used the opportunity to articulate a more cautious stance and to berate those who sought to influence South Africa from outside.

In certain respects, Botha did continue with reform. By 1986, the government had softened the implementation of many aspects of apartheid and the pass laws were largely abandoned. Racial restrictions on the labour force were partly relaxed. The government invested heavily into upgrading some key townships and, 40 years after trying to abolish it, reintroduced private ownership of township plots and houses. While this was very important for African families, it was not a political solution.

Botha turned to his generals and the security forces, led by Magnus Malan, the head of the army, who doubled as Minister of Defence, to restore order and regain the momentum. Increasingly he bypassed the tricameral parliament and the complicated new arrangements that he had only recently established. He created a State Security Council, which combined leading white cabinet ministers with the most senior military officers. This in turn established Joint Management Centres in different parts of the country, bringing together the military, police and officials. Some in the opposition press saw these organisations as coming close to a military takeover. Botha insisted on imposing control before further reform and made it clear that reform was not intended as a shift towards democracy. In the successive states of emergency, tens of thousands were arrested.

SOURCE
11

Speech by P. W. Botha at the National Party Natal Congress in Durban, 15 August 1985.

We have never given in to outside demands and we are not going to do so now. South Africa's problems will be solved by South Africans and not by foreigners.

We are not going to be deterred from doing what we think best, nor will we be forced into doing what we don't want to do. The tragedy is that hostile pressure and agitation from abroad have acted as an encouragement to the militant revolutionaries in South Africa to continue with their violence and intimidation. They have derived comfort and succour from this pressure.

My Government and I are determined to press ahead with our reform programme, and to those who prefer revolution to reform, I say they will not succeed. If necessary we will use stronger measures but they will not succeed.

We prefer to resolve our problems by peaceful means: then we can build, then we can develop, then we can train people, then we can uplift people, then we can make this country of ours a better place to live in. By violence and by burning down schools and houses and murdering innocent people, you don't build a country, you destroy it.

AS Level Exam-Style Question Section A

Study Source 11 before you answer this question.

Why is Source 11 valuable to the historian for an enquiry into the reasons for the National Party's 'total strategy' programme?

Explain your answer, using the source, the information given about it and your knowledge of the historical context. (8 marks)

Tip
Consider the author of the source and the intended audience.

A journalist called Brian Pottinger labelled Botha's first ten years in power *The Imperial Presidency* in his book of that name. Botha became intolerant of his own Party as well as the political opposition and tricameral parliament.

Taking total strategy beyond the borders

As noted in Chapter 3, by 1984 Botha had partly succeeded in neutralising support for the ANC from neighbouring African countries. Namibia remained under South African direct rule. Malawi under President Banda had reached an accommodation with South Africa. Mugabe in Zimbabwe was cautious about confronting South Africa directly. Swaziland signed a non-aggression pact in 1983 and Mozambique in 1984. Leabua Jonathan, prime minister in Lesotho from 1965 to 1986, initially cooperated with South Africa but became increasingly independent in the early 1980s and openly supported the ANC. As a result a South African-backed force attacked Lesotho and he was toppled in a coup in 1986.

The military was used in operations in the townships in the 1980s but was largely engaged beyond the borders of South Africa in pursuit of 'total strategy'. South Africa was engaged in the civil wars in Angola and Mozambique. Non-military strategies included parcel bombs. Ruth First, a white ANC member and academic, was killed by a bomb in Mozambique in 1981, and Jeannette

Curtis was killed in Angola in 1984. Albie Sachs, a white ANC lawyer, was severely injured by a car bomb in Maputo in 1988. The army staged direct raids on ANC bases and houses; in Mozambique in 1981, 1983 and 1987; in Lesotho in 1983, which killed 42 people and injured many more; and in Botswana in 1985 when 12 were killed. ANC targets in Zambia, Zimbabwe and Botswana were raided in 1986.

In 1979, a special counter-insurgency unit called Koevoet (Afrikaans for 'crowbar') was established to assist in fighting the border war in Namibia. Modelled on a similar Rhodesian force, it was led by whites but had a majority of black recruits and developed a reputation for effectiveness and brutality in the war against SWAPO. Tactics involved, on occasion, attacking and assassinating the civilian sympathisers of SWAPO. In 1983 Eugene de Kock, a key figure in Koevoet, was sent to establish a counter-insurgency unit within South Africa on a farm near Pretoria called Vlakplaas. In an inquiry in the early 1990s, and during the Truth and Reconciliation Commission hearings after 1994, its activities were more fully revealed. This unit, its core made up from former combatants in the Namibian border war, lost all constraint. Their special purpose was to 'turn' former ANC guerillas after they had been captured, to use them for information, and to infiltrate MK and the township movements. In this they had some success. They also captured anti-apartheid activists, torturing and killing some. In 1988 this unit assumed a larger function in a Civil Cooperation Bureau.

In sum, South Africa made life in the region of southern Africa very difficult for its enemies through direct intervention and indirect destabilisation. This helped to undermine any significant armed struggle by the ANC.

A shift in the balance of power

In the late 1980s, however, the balance of regional power shifted as the Soviet bloc collapsed and the Cold War subsided. From September 1987, the South African Defence Force engaged in an extended campaign within Angola to support UNITA, its ally in the Angolan civil war. The outcome of this campaign, which stretched well into 1988, was indecisive. Although the South African forces won some skirmishes, they could not establish military superiority against the Angolan forces and their Cuban allies who mustered stronger airpower. South African forces failed to control a key centre in southern Angola, Cuito Cuanavale, and the government became alarmed about the losses of white troops. Pretoria judged that the domestic appetite for heavy sacrifices in this long running border war was limited. A movement called the End Conscription Campaign worked hard to undermine the legitimacy of South Africa's wars in general and opposed the long compulsory national service required of white youths.

In 1988 Gorbachev, the reformist Soviet leader, offered to negotiate an end to the destructive Cold War conflicts in southern Africa and to persuade the Cubans to withdraw. South Africa agreed at the New York Accords in December 1988 that Namibia would move towards independence; all parties accepted that foreign troops would withdraw from Angola. A free election was held in Namibia in November 1989 in which SWAPO won 57 percent of the vote. The country became fully independent in 1990.

Despite the earlier successes of regional military and diplomatic initiatives, Botha withdrew from those elements of 'total strategy' that required sustained and expensive military commitments. By the late 1980s, he was exploring other possibilities.

International pressure and economic crisis

Botha faced increasing economic and diplomatic pressure on other fronts. In 1985 American banks refused to renew South Africa's loans. The currency slumped in 1985 after investors lost faith in Botha. Even the conservative US government under President Ronald Reagan began to support disinvestment. Gavin Relly, the chairman of Anglo-American, perhaps South Africa's largest private corporation, led a delegation of white South African businessmen to Lusaka in 1985 to meet the ANC.

The movement to free Nelson Mandela from prison was also gathering steam, backed by the AAM and ANC in exile. The scale of Mandela's popularity became completely clear in June 1988 at an event held to celebrate his 70th birthday at Wembley stadium in London.

SOURCE

12 Extract from an article by Tony Hollingsworth, organiser of the Nelson Mandela 70th birthday tribute concert at Wembley Stadium in London. The article was published in the right-of-centre *Daily Telegraph* in December 2013, shortly after Mandela's death.

In 1987, I met with Archbishop Trevor Huddleston, President of the Anti Apartheid Movement in Britain, and told him that… in my view, the way they were presented to the public – as protesters in the street – could only appeal to a small percentage of the world's population. If they were to appeal more broadly we had to reposition them as positive and confident.

I thought their main communications problem was that many TV and radio news organisations around the world were still referring to Nelson Mandela… as a 'Black Terrorist Leader' and while a 'Black Leader' could be released from prison, a 'Black Terrorist Leader' could not.

Trevor asked me what my plans were…

I told him that I intended to produce a global broadcast event called the 'Nelson Mandela 70th Birthday Tribute' involving many major music stars…

Trevor could see how a globally broadcast musical tribute would position Mandela and the movement in a positive and confident way but wanted to understand how it would get rid of the word 'terrorist' from the news. I told him that once their entertainment divisions had signed up to air the musical tribute, they would then hear their own newsrooms using the word 'terrorist' and put pressure on their colleagues to make the change.

I added a third string to the bow – that we would get a ratings figure so large that the ANC and the AAM could use it to show politicians around the world the public had moved ahead of them and if they too pushed for Mandela's release, they would be doing something popular with their voters.

About a year after my talk with Trevor, a record breaking world audience of 600 million people watched a Wembley Stadium event that involved 83 artists and lasted for almost 12 hours…

The show was broadcast live by… broadcasters… including the BBC, Fox Television in the US, China's CCTV, the Soviet state broadcaster Gosteleradio and India's Doordarshan. In South Africa it was banned and censored…

Getting artists was difficult as Mandela was not the figure he is today and few people in the world knew much about him or the ANC…

Dire Straits, whose records were banned in South Africa because they gave their royalties to Amnesty International, were the first artists to give a clear commitment to participate.

When Mark Knopfler started to play 'Brothers in Arms', he paused and said: 'This is for the man in question', adding: 'One Humanity. One Justice.' I've always thought that those four words captured the essence of what the global broadcast, the AAM, the ANC and Mandela stood for.

By the time of the event, the word 'terrorist' had disappeared from the news broadcasts of channels that aired it.

The effect of the state of emergency

By the late 1980s, the central South African state could no longer fully control political developments in the homelands or in the townships. But neither the ANC, nor the UDF, nor the youthful comrades had the power to threaten white military dominance in the short term. White South African life was affected, and threatened in certain respects, but whites were not in daily danger. Much of the conflict was restricted geographically to the townships and African rural areas. White consumer culture and standards of living were still very comfortable.

EXTEND YOUR KNOWLEDGE

White culture and wildlife

One small indicator of the security of white South Africa, even at this time, was the flourishing of wildlife tourism. South Africa had been rich in wildlife, but much of it was shot out in the 19th century. Reserves were demarcated to preserve what was left and a National Parks system developed after 1926. Tourism numbers in the Kruger National Park, the flagship park, rose from around 30,000 a year in the 1930s, to over 100,000 a year in the 1960s. They took off in the apartheid period as white South Africans increasingly identified with their landscape and considered wildlife to be a central part of their national heritage. In 1980 visitor numbers reached about 400,000, by 1990 about 600,000 and by 2000 nearly a million. Motorised tourism continued to grow through the insurrection in 1985–86 and violence in 1991–92. Foreign visitor numbers remained relatively low, in tens of thousands until the late 1990s. To meet the rigours of apartheid, a separate, much smaller, game reserve called Manyeleti was demarcated adjacent to Kruger for African visitors.

Yet for all the continuities this was a difficult time. Afrikaners had split politically both to the right and the left. Political protest was widely reported. Even though the state broadcasting service was controlled by the government, it was difficult to hide the truth entirely, and there remained a lively and diverse press. Many whites could see that their black allies had limited legitimacy and were regarded by some as enemies of the people. Elements within the government itself recognised from the mid-1980s that the reform strategy was unlikely to be sufficient and they began to explore, very hesitantly, the possibility of a negotiated settlement. In this, they were strongly encouraged by key Western powers – the United States, UK and Germany.

The path to talks

During the 1970s and early 1980s, Nelson Mandela had been increasingly elevated by the Anti-Apartheid Movement in their campaigns. It was clear that the government also recognised his standing, and his authority among prisoners on Robben Island. In 1982, Mandela, Sisulu and three other prisoners were transferred from Robben Island to Pollsmoor, a large general prison in suburban Cape Town. Part of the plan was clearly to give them better conditions and try to divide the political prisoners. Those who were separated were acutely conscious that they needed to guard against manipulation. The nationalists clearly thought that they might need Mandela – though they did not exactly know when and they were not in a hurry. In an indirect way, the

strategy paid off. Mandela and his immediate colleagues were more directly exposed to news and information. He was allowed more visitors and by 1985 this included emissaries from Britain and the United States, who undoubtedly took soundings about his positions. The process was monitored by the *verligte* Minister of Justice, Kobie Coetsee.

In January 1985, Botha offered to release Mandela and other political prisoners if they renounced violence and the armed struggle, as well as support for political movements that remained committed to such strategies. This was an immediate response to the insurrection. Mandela refused and the message was broadcast in a speech read out by his daughter, Zinzi, at a UDF rally of about 8,000 people in Soweto in February 1985. The rally had originally been organised to celebrate the award of the Nobel Peace Prize to the Anglican clergyman, Desmond Tutu. Although Mandela knew he had to reject conditional offers of freedom if he was to retain legitimacy and authority in the ANC, he did differ from many ANC leaders in actively seeking a negotiated settlement and tried to signal this to Botha in his response. He outlined the basic conditions that would be necessary for negotiations to take place and affirmed a potentially shared interest: 'your freedom and mine cannot be separated'.

Mandela wrote privately to Coetsee asking to discuss the possibility of negotiations. In 1985, he was separated from the other ANC prisoners at Pollsmoor and given his own flat. Although he had no authorisation from Oliver Tambo in Lusaka he decided to go ahead.

SOURCE

13   Extract from Nelson Mandela's autobiography *Long Walk to Freedom*, written after his release from prison and published in 1995.

> They questioned me extensively on the issue of violence and while I was not yet willing to renounce violence, I affirmed in the strongest possible terms that violence could never be the ultimate solution to the situation in South Africa and that men and women by their very nature required some kind of negotiated understanding. While I once again reiterated that these were my views and not those of the ANC, I suggested that if the government withdrew the army and the police from the townships, the ANC might agree to a suspension of the armed struggles as a prelude to talks. I told them that my release alone would not stem the violence in the country or stimulate negotiations.

Botha undermined any quick move towards talks in 1985 by staging an attack on ANC bases in Botswana, Zimbabwe and Zambia. He wished to show that the government was still in control and the ANC's pretensions at armed struggle were doomed to failure. Yet immediately after this raid, Mandela was taken out of prison for a three-hour meeting with Coetsee. Secret excursions into Cape Town followed. Botha had simultaneously authorised talks to start with the ANC in exile. Pieter de Lange, head of the Broederbond, met Thabo Mbeki and other ANC representatives in New York in 1986.

From this time the pace and density of talks quickened. Elements in the Dutch Reformed Church were renouncing their former support for apartheid and in 1987 a delegation of Afrikaners met the ANC in Dakar, Senegal. Willie Esterhuyse, a prolific Stellenbosch philosophy professor, reformist and public intellectual became a key emissary from South Africa. Thabo Mbeki, with Tambo's agreement, began more regular meetings with South African emissaries in the UK.

Against this background Mandela, still imprisoned, met a committee of four government members almost weekly for a few months and 47 times in all in 1988–89. Mandela was now so valuable that he was moved to a house in the Victor Verster prison precinct in Paarl at the end of 1988. There he could receive political visitors of all kinds. The senior negotiators on the government side were Coetsee and Niël Barnard, head of the National Intelligence Service (NIS). Mandela claims that he spent much of his time explaining the history and values of the ANC – of which the government seemed deeply ignorant. Two key issues for the government were the ANC's commitment to armed struggle and its links with the Communist Party. Mandela thought that even in 1988, when the Soviet Union was crumbling, the National Party adhered to an outdated Cold War analysis. Deeply imbued with a racist ideology, they believed that because many of the whites and Indians in the Congress movement were communists, they must be manipulating the African members.

Mandela may have been partly right about Afrikaner ignorance but not entirely so. They understood that the South African Communist Party subscribed to a two-stage revolution. Afrikaner reformists felt they could possibly live with the first stage – a nationalist and democratic revolution – but not with the second, socialist stage. The question was: was the ANC also committed to pursuing this second stage? Mandela had worked closely with CP activists over a long period, but he believed that the ANC was not in any way dominated by them and did not see the prospects of a socialist revolution as a significant possibility.

All of these discussions were held in private, but Botha was clearly concerned about what he could sell to his supporters. Major issues concerned nationalisation of industries and protection for the rights of minorities. In Afrikaner eyes, African governments elsewhere had tended to become authoritarian and some had ridden roughshod over civil rights and property rights. Though Afrikaners of course had used their power in the same way, they were now concerned about developing a political system that would protect them in the longer term. The ANC representatives tended to emphasise that South Africa should go forward as a unitary state with a democratically elected (and by implication African) government.

The National Party did not believe that this would give adequate protection to the white minority. The powerful Transvaal National Party, now led by F. W. de Klerk, was less concerned about further reform and more about the damage being done by the Conservative breakaway. Thus throughout the late 1980s the government sent mixed messages and maintained repression within the country. For example, in February 1988, it effectively banned the UDF and 16 other organisations under the emergency regulations and it closed down *New Nation*, the UDF newspaper, in March. They were not formally disbanded but they were no longer allowed to conduct public campaigns. In effect the UDF could not operate openly for the next two years. Many

of the individual leaders were harassed, detained and subjected to trials.

SOURCE
14 Niël Barnard recollecting his words to Nelson Mandela before a meeting with P. W. Botha, reported in the *Independent*, 2 November 2006.

Listen, this is an ice-breaker meeting. It is not about fundamental issues. Come to learn about the man. Talk about all those easy things in life. And don't mention the issue of Walter Sisulu... if you mention the release again of Walter Sisulu, Mr Botha will say no. I know him. And if he says no, it's no... Leave that aside. There's another way to tackle the issue. Furthermore, don't tackle difficult issues, that's not the reason for the first meeting.

Resistance 1988–89
By the late 1980s, the UDF, always a loose group, found it very difficult to operate. In 1985, trade unionists had formed a new national association called the Congress of South African Trade Unions (COSATU) and this became the most organised and sustained opposition movement. Within COSATU, the National Union of Mineworkers emerged as the largest union and staged a major strike in the mines in 1987. COSATU was affiliated to the UDF and sympathetic to the ANC but retained organisational independence.

With the UDF partly neutralised in 1989, COSATU became an increasingly central vehicle for resistance. This also helped to solidify the relationship between the UDF and COSATU. By the beginning of 1989 this alliance became called the Mass Democratic Movement (MDM). In many respects it was the UDF under another name – a means of getting round the government banning orders. Like the UDF, the leaders of the MDM largely conceived of it as a movement rather than an organisation. The MDM recognised, perhaps too easily, that the ANC was at the forefront in the struggle. The ANC's legitimacy was increasing rapidly. It had achieved this through its sustained role as a liberation movement, through the self-sacrifice of many members, including those who lost their lives in the armed struggle. The ANC carried the aura of Mandela and the other imprisoned leaders who did not have to confront the messy politics of the streets.

In 1988 and 1989, COSATU tried to put pressure on the government by organising massive stayaways, to which an estimated 2.5–3 million workers responded. This old weapon of the ANC seemed especially effective at this juncture: it impacted on white-owned South African businesses and it minimised the reprisals and arrests that were so frequently a result of direct confrontation and violent protest.

In August 1989, the MDM organised a new Defiance Campaign aimed at finally killing off segregated facilities and freeing political leaders. Protestors targeted the sensitive issue of racial segregation in hospitals and presented themselves for treatment at white-only hospitals. They invaded white beaches in Cape Town and Durban and whites-only buses in Pretoria. Police broke up a march in central Cape Town by using water cannons stained with purple dye. ANC flags were openly flying. Eighty thousand people marched in the Eastern Cape industrial town of Uitenhage, where a large Volkswagen factory was located. Twenty-three people were killed in Cape Town and another bout of detentions ensued, including Trevor Manuel, one of Cape Town's leading UDF activists, who was to emerge as a major figure in the ANC government after apartheid.

ACTIVITY
CONSOLIDATION

Imagine the Anti-Apartheid and UDF campaigners had the sorts of media available to us today. Would that have made a difference? What strategy would spread their message as widely as possible?

TO WHAT EXTENT DID POLITICAL NEGOTIATIONS, 1989–91, END IN COMPROMISE?

In 1989 the system of apartheid was still in place but it was in certain respects crumbling and the government could not easily contain political opposition. The country was deeply divided. With the police and military behind them, the National Party still held strong cards. But the ANC, together with the MDM, had established a powerful position at the head of opposition forces. Political groupings such as Inkatha, the PAC, the homeland governments, the Democratic (formerly Progressive) Party, the Coloured Labour Party and the Conservatives represented a diversity of other interests. Attempts to avoid further polarisation and violence were going to need compromises on all sides.

De Klerk's new course

In January 1989 Botha suffered a stroke. Although the Nationalist parliamentary party had to some degree been sidelined, it still had a key role in selecting its leader. F. W. de Klerk, chairman of the Transvaal provincial party, was voted in by a narrow margin. In September 1989, white, Coloured and Indian voters cast votes for their separate parts of the tricameral parliament.

De Klerk won the election with 48 percent of the white vote and thus also became national president. But the National Party received a shock in that this was its worst performance for many years and white support for the Conservative Party peaked at 31.5 percent. De Klerk won 94 seats compared to 39 for the Conservatives and 33 for the liberal Democratic Party, inheritor of the Progressives. De Klerk had been a cautious politician, a politically astute conservative, thoroughly embedded in the National Party. He was suspicious of the complex constitutional arrangements that Botha had pursued under the reform agenda in the 1980s and he was critical of Botha's presidentialism. He felt that the military and security forces had become too central in policy making and that Botha's strategy had polarised the position. De Klerk quickly reduced military budgets and curtailed the influence of the State Security Council and Joint Management Systems at the end of 1989.

SOURCE 15

Extract from speech by F. W. de Klerk on the opening of the South African parliament, 2 February 1990.

The general elections on September the 6th, 1989, placed our country irrevocably on the road of drastic change. Underlying this is the growing realisation by an increasing number of South Africans that only a negotiated understanding among the representative leaders of the entire population is able to ensure lasting peace. The alternative is growing violence, tension and conflict. That is unacceptable and in nobody's interest. The well-being of all in this country is linked inextricably to the ability of the leaders to come to terms with one another on a new dispensation. No one can escape this simple truth.

Botha, nicknamed the *Groot Krokodil* (big crocodile), had been forceful and ruthless. De Klerk was keener to find compromises and act as a political peacemaker. However, the implications of pragmatic politics were by no means clear. Did this mean finding a route acceptable to African political movements and ending apartheid? De Klerk clearly wished to seize the political initiative from opposition forces, to keep his Party in at the forefront of political changes, to win backing from the Afrikaans press, which had become critical of Botha, and even find some international support.

International political allies were slipping away, with conservative stalwarts such as Reagan and Thatcher beginning to pressure South Africa's leaders to negotiate. In 1989, the fall of the Berlin Wall signalled the end of communist influence in Europe. Gorbachev largely withdrew from Africa and, by late 1989, the Western need for a regional, anti-communist policeman declined.

A Level Exam-Style Question Section B

How accurate is it to say that international pressure was the main driving force behind the ending of apartheid? (20 marks)

Tip
Think about economic factors and the role of the ANC, which were also drivers of change.

Freeing Nelson Mandela and unbanning political parties

By mid-1989 it was clear that the ANC as a whole (barring some dissident voices) was committed to negotiations. Key ANC political prisoners, including Walter Sisulu, Raymond Mhlaba and Ahmed Kathrada were freed in October 1989. De Klerk and Mandela met in December 1989 and Mandela released a forceful statement arguing for a negotiated settlement. On its side, the National Party's only real alternative was to go back to some form of white domination, face tightening international sanctions, and try to repress an endless future of mass protest. Despite the conservative backlash, the bulk of whites no longer really supported apartheid as a formal policy and sought some other security for their future. Whites had done well under apartheid and they had too much to lose in a civil conflict. Negotiations seemed inevitable.

When de Klerk opened parliament in February 1990, he did resort to a form of presidentialism. Before consulting the new parliament, he announced that he would release Mandela and unban the political parties that had been prohibited within South Africa, including the ANC, the CP and the PAC. Mandela's slow walk to freedom in the unlikely rural surrounds of Victor Verster prison grounds, hand held high, with Winnie Mandela, was televised internationally and provided a moment of religious intensity and political hope. Mandela seemed to carry the promise of salvation.

SOURCE
16 Nelson Mandela with his wife Winnie, immediately after his release from Victor Verster prison in February 1990.

The ANC, for so long reliant upon clandestine activism, was now able to organise publicly and establish itself as the legitimate alternative for a future South Africa. After his release, Mandela addressed a series of meetings. The first, a rushed and poorly organised event on Cape Town's Grand Parade, was dwarfed by the second, before a crowd of 120,000 in Soweto's FNB stadium. Despite being shielded from the glare of publicity for nearly three decades, Mandela had sufficient self-confidence and inner strength to cope with a demanding schedule, as well as handling the world's media. Over the next few months he spent much of his time travelling, and trying to coordinate the ANC's response to its unbanning. The exiled Thabo Mbeki, who dealt with external relations, also established himself as a key strategist.

Mandela visited the United Kingdom twice in this period. It was a hub for the ANC in exile, and for the global Anti-apartheid Movement. In April 1990 Mandela visited London for a second televised concert which again reached an estimated global audience of 500 million people. This was to celebrate his release and he received an eight-minute standing ovation. He also made an extended speech. Although he himself was keen to meet Margaret Thatcher, the ANC was adamantly opposed. Her opposition to the liberation movements, her consistent opposition to sanctions, and her support for other black politicians, such as Chief Buthelezi, left a bitter taste. Mandela, however, insisted and met Thatcher in July 1990. He was keen to talk to opponents and believed that it was vital to do so – although the issue of sanctions still separated them.

With Tambo ill, Mandela became acting president of the ANC and in July 1991 he was formally elected to this position. Cyril Ramaphosa, the trade unionist, was elected secretary general. This was a significant attempt to bring the COSATU and UDF movements into the heart of the ANC. The movement had recruited 700,000 members – way beyond any previous figure. This was achieved through the folding of the UDF and MDM into the ANC. They continued as parallel movements during 1990 but did not envisage a separate future. The ANC was founding branches in South Africa and most supporters of the UDF joined these.

In March 1991, the UDF decided to disband and held its last meeting in August. An alternative strategy did not seem feasible at the time, but in the medium term this decision weakened grass roots political organisation in the country and it may have been wiser for the UDF to think of forming a separate wing of the alliance, similar to COSATU. In 1992, an organisation called the South African National Civic Organisation, headed by Moses Mayekiso, was founded to provide a vehicle for the remaining civic and residents associations that had sprung up so widely in the 1980s. But it proved to be relatively weak and disorganised.

The ANC also absorbed many of the youthful comrades, not least through the agency of Peter Mokaba. Born in 1959, he participated in the school protests of the 1970s and was another product of Turfloop, the powerhouse of African student politics. Mokaba, a close associate of Winnie Mandela, joined the UDF and emerged by 1987 as the leading figure in the South African Youth Congress, which attempted to maintain the momentum of youth organisation amid mass arrests. A charismatic public speaker, who used radical rhetoric, he was arrested and imprisoned twice. He called the comrades movement the Young Lions (from Isaiah in the bible) and in the early 1990s used the chant 'Kill the Boer, Kill the farmer' (*Dubul' ibhunu*) at mass meetings. This came from a liberation movement song and ANC spokesmen justified its use as metaphorical. The ANC Youth League, which had been so important a radical vehicle in the 1940s and 1950s, had faded in exile. Youth who left the country were largely absorbed into MK. Mokaba played a key role in transforming the youth and student organisations into a revived ANC Youth League.

Similarly, the ANC moved to incorporate traditional authorities into its broad umbrella through the organisation of CONTRALESA in 1987. This provided a vehicle for chiefs who were sympathetic to the UDF or who had hedged their bets in the homeland period and now saw the writing on the wall. Mandela, among others, was keen to prise chiefs away from the apartheid regime and felt they would add support to the ANC in the rural areas. When he spoke to 100,000 people at a welcome home event in Transkei in 1990, Mandela told the chiefs they had a role, as long as they broadly supported the liberation movement.

Thus by 1991 the ANC had successfully absorbed some of the key popular opposition forces.

Negotiations and dismantling apartheid

Mandela called de Klerk a man of integrity during his first public address. But negotiations were delayed. Although Mandela talked to de Klerk privately it was only in May 1990 that full negotiating teams met. De Klerk, it transpired, was not in a hurry. The National Party perceived that protracted negotiations would favour them. They believed that there were likely to be splits in the complex opposition alliance that included the ANC, the CP, COSATU and the UDF/MDM.

Many whites held the view, strongly encouraged by the homeland policy under apartheid, that African loyalties were primarily ethnic or tribal. They were encouraged to believe that African people would divide on ethnic lines and perceived that violent conflict within African communities – 'black on black' violence, as it was called – was at least in part a result of this. National Party leaders had by this time recognised that the ANC commanded the largest support among black people. But the intensification of conflict in KwaZulu and Natal, as well as on the Rand, encouraged them to think that black communities were divided. They still saw promise in Buthelezi and some other moderate black politicians, including homeland leaders, and in Coloured and Indian politicians who had bought into the reform process. Alan Hendrickse's Labour Party, which had participated in the Coloured parliamentary election in 1989 and won an easy victory, seemed to command considerable support in the Western Cape.

Although no political settlement seemed imminent, in June 1990, de Klerk revoked some racial legislation such as the Separate Reservation of Amenities Act. Breaches of the Group Areas Act were policed less fiercely. Hillbrow, an area of highrise residential flats, immediately to the north of the Johannesburg city centre, was defined as a white group area. But the government allowed it to become a mixed, or grey, area.

The ANC compromised in turn by suspending the armed struggle in August 1990. The ANC delegations which met the government included key exiles such as Thabo Mbeki, as well as former prisoners, and a few local activists. De Klerk saw his preparedness to accept Communist Party delegates, such as Joe Slovo, as a significant compromise. He admitted that the system of separate development had not worked, but he did not apologise for apartheid. His major concern was for the ANC to publicly reject sanctions but they refused to do so. Having suspended the armed struggle, the ANC felt that sanctions remained an important negotiating tool – they had at this point received no promises from the National Party about the shape of the future political system.

The ANC was keen to ensure freedom for political exiles and political prisoners. They thought that this has been assured and de Klerk agreed to lift the state of emergency in June 1990. But soon afterwards, in an apparently contradictory act, de Klerk arrested key members of the CP and MK. The government gave as their reason that the ANC had reneged on its promise to suspend the armed struggle because they had not fully disbanded Operation Vula. This was an underground initiative started in 1988, designed to resurrect the MK presence within the country and, with improved secret communications, to establish a more secure organisational structure with a steady supply of weaponry. The ANC argued publicly that they had suspended, not abandoned, the armed struggle and wanted to be ready to resume should negotiations break down. The arrests of some of those involved, including Mac Maharaj, later a minister and presidential spokesman, was designed also to split the ANC from the SACP and disrupt the imminent relaunch of the SACP in South Africa. Only in March 1991 were all charges withdrawn and those still underground indemnified against further government action.

This was one disagreement that undermined negotiations. Disagreement about responsibility for violence within black communities was another. Mandela and Buthelezi met in early 1991 in order to try to stem the violence in Natal. An accord was reached, but neither side adhered to it. In March 1991, 45 people were killed in three days of fighting between hostel dwellers and comrades in Alexandra, Johannesburg, and soon afterwards police killed a further 12 on the east Rand. In April 1991 ANC relations with the government reached a low point when Mandela accused de Klerk of colluding with or even orchestrating the violence by police and vigilantes in order to divide black society and justify government control. The term 'third force' was used by the ANC to describe this hidden network of provocateurs linked to government security forces. Evidence emerged at this time that Inkatha supporters were trained directly by the South African government. The ANC suspended talks.

De Klerk tried to maintain the momentum and in June 1991 revoked the Population Registration Act, the Natives Land Act and the Group Areas Act. Black people could now purchase land in any part of South Africa. However, there was still an atmosphere of deep suspicion between the ANC and the National Party.

SOURCE

17 Extract from the Pretoria minute, a summary of a meeting between the government and the ANC, held on 6 August 1990.

Both delegations expressed serious concern about the general level of violence, intimidation and unrest in the country especially in Natal. They agreed that in the context of the common search for peace and stability, it was vital that understanding should grow among all sections of the South African population that problems can and should be solved through negotiations. Both parties committed themselves to undertake steps and measures to promote and expedite the normalisation of the situation in line with the spirit of mutual trust obtaining among the leaders involved.

CODESA (1991)

Mandela had ceased to trust de Klerk and the latter clearly found the ANC uncompromising. After the early promise of talks about talks, all parties, including Buthelezi, felt they were being asked to give up too much. Nevertheless, all did agree to a first round of formal negotiations at the end of 1991 in a process called the Convention for a Democratic South Africa (CODESA). They met in the anodyne environment of the World Trade Centre in Johannesburg, near an airport which was then called Jan Smuts but would shortly be renamed O. R. Tambo. The South African process was distinctive in that it did not involve external mediation and it incorporated a very wide range of political groupings. The public proceedings, at least, were not simply a negotiation between the ANC and the National Party. The government's central aim was still to devise a constitutional strategy that might protect minorities, and ideally create a constitutional veto in the hands of whites.

SOURCE

18   Extract from the statement of intent behind CODESA, issued 21 December 1991.

We the duly authorised representatives of political parties, political organisations, administrations and the South African Government, coming together at this first meeting of the Convention for a Democratic South Africa, mindful of the awesome responsibility that rests on us at this moment in the history of our country, declare our solemn commitment:

a.   that South Africa will be a united, democratic, non-racial and non-sexist state in which sovereign authority is exercised over the whole of the territory;

b.   that the Constitution will be the supreme law and that it will be guarded over by an independent, non-racial and impartial judiciary;

c.   that there will be a multi-party democracy with the right to form and join political parties and with regular elections on the basis of universal adult suffrage on a common voters roll; in general the basic electoral system shall be that of proportional representation;

d.   that there shall be a separation of powers between the legislature, executive and judiciary with appropriate checks and balances;

e.   that the diversity of languages, cultures and religions of the people of South Africa shall be acknowledged;

f.   that all shall enjoy universally accepted human rights, freedoms and civil liberties including freedom of religion, speech and assembly protected by an entrenched and justiciable Bill of Rights and a legal system that guarantees equality of all before the law.

ACTIVITY
CONSOLIDATION

1 What, in your opinion, were Mandela's top three priorities? Similarly, what were de Klerk's top three priorities?

2 Using Source 18 and your own knowledge, how ambitious a project was CODESA?

A Level Exam-Style Question Section A

Study Sources 17 and 18 before you answer this question.

How far could the historian use Sources 16 and 17 together to investigate the problems facing those trying to create a new political settlement in South Africa in the years 1991–94?

Explain your answer using the sources, the information about them and your knowledge of the historical context. (20 marks)

Tip

Think about the aims of CODESA and of the ANC and how these clashed in practice.

TO WHAT EXTENT DID THE NEW POLITICAL SETTLEMENT REACHED IN THE YEARS 1992–94 CREATE A FULLY DEMOCRATIC COUNTRY?

CODESA, while stop–start, was a crucial milestone in the path to full democracy in South Africa. The decisions reached during those negotiations enabled elections in April 1994 and to some extent they also determined the outcome of those elections. However, deals were made to ensure that a government of national unity was established after the election, with ministerial posts for MPs from losing parties.

CODESA negotiations

CODESA started badly with a highly public spat between Mandela and de Klerk. The latter spoke last at the opening ceremony; Mandela claims that he agreed this, as a favour to de Klerk, in order to cement goodwill. De Klerk decided to open up the most sensitive issue, publicly condemning the ANC for failing to disband MK and remaining committed to violence. He no doubt felt that this would play well to his domestic white audience and also Western powers, for whom the armed struggle – alongside the communist link – had always been a difficult feature of the ANC. Mandela was so incensed that he broke with protocol, strode onto the podium and publicly lambasted de Klerk for misusing the agreement to have the last word: 'I am gravely concerned about the behaviour of Mr de Klerk today… Even the head of an illegitimate, discredited minority regime as his is, has certain moral standards to uphold.' In his autobiography Mandela said de Klerk 'began to speak to us like a schoolmaster admonishing a naughty child'. He claimed that the government was perpetuating violence and conflict, secretly funding covert organisations and facilitating Inkatha's vigilantes. Such encounters were suffused with tensions about race, about the different audiences with which leaders sought to connect, and with a concern to occupy the moral high ground.

Nevertheless progress was made at CODESA, meeting in five working committees, and significant agreements were reached in the next few months. There would be a single undivided country, a multi-party democracy with a universal non-racial franchise, a bill of rights, separation of powers and an end to racial discrimination. Private property including land and other assets would be protected. There would be some form of transitional executive council and an independent electoral commission. The National Party held out over the issue of minority rights. They wanted a veto over any constitutional proposals by insisting that a 75 percent majority in parliament should be required. They envisaged a form of power sharing, rather than a full transfer of power to a majority government that was likely to be dominated by the ANC.

Inkatha tried to entrench the position of the Zulu king. Buthelezi argued for a strongly **federal system** and at times seemed to favour a semi-autonomous greater Zululand. Federalism was also attractive to some homeland leaders and other minority groupings, for different reasons. The white liberal Democratic Party thought that this system would limit centralised power – a danger revealed by the history of National Party rule. Many Afrikaners thought that even if they could not win a majority, they might, with conservative black allies, achieve influence in some regions, such as the Western Cape. The Afrikaner right explored the idea of racially based, rather than regionally based, federalism but this was not acceptable to the ANC.

Given these disagreements, CODESA was suspended and de Klerk held a whites-only referendum in March 1992 on the question: 'Do you support continuation of the reform process which the state president began on 2 February 1990 and which is aimed at a new Constitution through negotiation?' White South Africans took this vote very seriously and de Klerk won a 69 percent majority of a high turnout. He held the referendum essentially to negate the challenge of the Conservative Party, which had recently won three by-elections. He also wanted to defuse right wing white vigilante groups that were beginning to form. It was an important event because the great majority of whites, in voting yes, finally turned their back on apartheid and recognised that they would have to relinquish much of their power and privilege. But the referendum angered many black people because it excluded them and seemed to suggest that the decision to proceed with negotiations was primarily a white decision. The ANC publicly opposed the referendum, but recognised that it was important for de Klerk to win.

KEY TERM

Federal system
In a federal political system political power is highly devolved to provinces, region, or local states. Federalism is the opposite of strongly unitary systems where the great bulk of decision-making and power rests with the central state. The United States is a federation because the 50 individual states have considerable local powers, their own governors and Congresses. Inkatha argued for a federal system in South Africa because, while it knew it could not compete for power at the national level, it thought it could win a majority in KwaZulu and Natal and control the local state. The ANC was in favour of a more unitary system.

EXTEND YOUR KNOWLEDGE

Violence
Explaining the violence in South Africa during the years of negotiation is important because it did at points border on civil war between African communities supporting the ANC and others. It seems totally counter-intuitive that at the very moment that political liberation seemed possible, conflict intensified. Between 1990 and 1994 about 14,000 people died in political violence in South Africa.

THINKING HISTORICALLY Cause and consequence (5b)

Causation relativity

Historical events usually have many causes. Some are crucial, while some are less important. For some historical questions, it is important to understand exactly what role certain factors played in causing historical change.

Significant factors in the timing and nature of the CODESA negotiations:

International vilification of apartheid, at a popular and a political level	Boycotts by companies of South African products	Civil disobedience in the townships
Election of F. W. de Klerk	Decline in support for apartheid from South African companies as economic problems worsen	Pressure by COSATU, the UDF and other organisations

Answer the following questions on your own:

The timing of the CODESA negotiations

1 How important was international opinion in explaining the timing of CODESA?

2 In what ways did the election of F. W. de Klerk impact upon foreign and domestic hopes for political change?

3 How could F. W. de Klerk have delayed the kind of reforms agreed to at CODESA?

The nature of the CODESA negotiations

4 How far did popular disobedience impact upon the urgency of the CODESA negotiations?

5 What role did the above factors play in the way that the CODESA negotiations re-shaped the political future of South Africa?

6 Would the nature of the CODESA negotiations have been the same if the UDF and other organisations had been banned at this time?

7 What roles did each of the above causal factors play in determining the nature and timing of the CODESA negotiations?

Violence and popular mobilisation

CODESA 2 reassembled in May 1992 but soon broke down because violence undermined negotiations. In June 1992 residents in the township of Boipatong in the Vaal Triangle were massacred by hostel dwellers. Police or 'third force' collusion was not proven but was widely suspected. The ANC thought that the government was doing little to control such violence in the hope that it would divide African communities.

The ANC and its allies believed not only that they should try to keep some potential for armed struggle, but also that mass demonstrations and stayaways were essential to keep the political initiative. Many African people were impatient with the long negotiations and groups within the ANC felt that they should have a more revolutionary approach – that they should topple the government rather than negotiate.

In Eastern Europe, for example, in Poland and East Germany, mass demonstrations had recently helped to unseat governments. In these cases, ironically, it was regimes sympathetic to the Soviet Union, that had been such staunch supporters of the ANC, which fell. Throughout the four years of negotiations, elements in the ANC argued strongly for mass action. Ronnie Kasrils, one of those arrested for his role in Operation Vula, where he was characterised as 'armed and dangerous', was particularly militant in his approach.

One of their key targets was the homeland governments – still seen as props for apartheid, and as hostile to ANC mobilisation in the rural areas. The ANC fixed on the Ciskei where the self-styled Brigadier Gqozo had taken power in a military coup in 1990 and publicly challenged the ANC. Civic organisations and residents' associations openly challenged Gqozo and the tribal authorities – they had clearly won a majority of support in this old heartland of the ANC. In September 1992 the ANC organised a huge march of 80,000 people, led by Chris Hani, head of the SACP and MK, and Ronnie Kasrils. Gqozo's troops shot at protestors, killing 29 and injuring over 200. A unit from the South African Defence Force was present but did not intervene.

The PAC had fared badly in exile, riven by leadership disputes and unable to develop a secure base. Most of the militant black consciousness youth, who might otherwise have been drawn to PAC, found their way into the ANC and MK. On returning from exile, however, the PAC's armed wing, by then named the Azanian People's Liberation Army (APLA), did succeed in recruiting locally. The PAC had never restricted itself to sabotage and it did not suspend the armed struggle as part of the negotiation process, which it largely rejected. In 1993, the APLA staged a number of dramatic attacks on white civilian targets, including a pub in the Eastern Cape where five were killed and a church in Cape Town. These incidents did not attract significant support among black South Africans, who were generally moving in a different direction.

Multi-party talks were restored at the beginning of 1993 and strong personal links forged between two of the chief negotiators: Cyril Ramaphosa of the ANC and Roelf Meyer of the NP. They were deeply conscious of being part of a historically significant process that was attracting intense international attention. The process was nearly undermined again in April 1993. White right wing renegades – an English-speaker and a Pole, rather than Afrikaners – assassinated Chris Hani, seen as one of the most central figures in the new generation of ANC and MK leaders. South Africa truly stood on the edge at that moment, with the possibility of a mass armed uprising. Mandela made a televised address, which successfully appealed for calm. The Afrikaner Weerstand Beweging, a paramilitary white movement, also threatened violent reprisals. They later briefly invaded the talks and assisted the leader of the Bophuthatswana homeland government, Lucas Mangope, in an attempt to stay in power.

These threats, together with the PAC killings, the intensity of mass protests, and the civil conflict in the townships, seemed to open the abyss of uncontrolled violence and civil war. The need for negotiations now seemed more urgent than ever.

SOURCE

19 Extract from the speech by Thabo Mbeki, ANC representative to the UN, to the General Assembly of the UN, 13 December 1993.

As the Assembly knows, there are some organizations and administrations in our country that have elected to remain aloof from the multi-party process of negotiations. Some of these are threatening to unleash a civil war to block the democratic transition. We are certain that this Assembly will continue to speak with one voice in calling on these elements to rejoin the forces of democratic change. It is also of great importance that this Assembly make it unequivocally clear that the peoples of the world will do nothing to legitimize or give sustenance to machinations which are intended to frustrate the final liquidation of the system of apartheid.

Constitutional agreement and elections

In April 1993 a Multi-Party Negotiating Forum was established to take up the agreements reached at CODESA and it quite quickly formed a Negotiating Council and six technical committees. By June 1993 they were able to set a date for non-racial democratic elections in April 1994. This was essential in providing a clear process of peaceful electoral politics around which the various parties could mobilise their resources and direct their political energies. Buthelezi proved to be the most intransigent and removed Inkatha from much of the negotiating process. In fact, his participation in the first election was in doubt until very soon before and it was only a guarantee of recognition of the Zulu king that led him to compromise.

Negotiators also established a Transitional Executive Committee in September 1993, which began to take control of government. In many respects, this accorded with the National Party's aim of power sharing rather than a transfer of power. But it was a temporary measure. Simultaneously the various parties negotiated a detailed interim constitution.

An interim constitution was established in November 1993. At its proclamation, both Mandela and de Klerk spoke passionately for national unity, while violence still raged about them. They had jointly been awarded the Nobel Peace Prize for 1993. Three such prizes were awarded to black South

Africans – Luthuli, Tutu and Mandela. This was one indication of the global significance of the fight to end apartheid.

The constitution (Act 200 of December 1993) could only be an interim measure because it had been achieved by negotiation and had not yet been approved by the people in an election. It entrenched a common citizenship for all, and particularly strong human rights. The document was regarded internationally as a model constitution in this respect.

KEY TERMS

Proportional representation
An electoral system whereby the proportion of votes is directly reflected in the allocation of seats in the parliament. So, for example, if a party receives 25 percent of the vote, then they would receive 25 percent of the seats in parliament.

Party list
The list of candidates from that party in the order that they prefer. For example, if the party wins 25 percent of the vote, which gives them 50 seats, then the first 50 names from the party list are the ones who become MPs.

Both sides made concessions in the final constitutional arrangements but ultimately it was clear that in achieving a fairly centralised, unitary state and non-racial universal franchise, in which all adults had the vote, the ANC was very likely to take power. The electoral system, based on **proportional representation**, and national **party lists**, also favoured the big parties and their leaderships, but arguably the ANC could have done even better if it had pursued a constituency-based system.

De Klerk wanted an extended transition period with a rotating presidency. This was not acceptable to the ANC, but they did compromise because Mandela, in particular, was anxious to keep the peace, foster national reconciliation, and to keep white skills in government and the country. Following a proposal by Joe Slovo, dubbed a 'sunset clause', the ANC agreed to an interim Government of National Unity. This would incorporate all the major parties, with five percent of the vote, for up to five years after the first election. Both the National Party and Inkatha Freedom Party held cabinet positions after 1994 and de Klerk became one of two deputy presidents. There were other elements of protection, for example, guaranteeing the pensions of white civil servants. This gave them security but there were advantages for the ANC. One of their primary aims was to Africanise the largely white bureaucracy without causing too much conflict and this measure was an encouragement for whites to retire.

The constitution gave the president considerable power. But the ANC agreed to other measures that would protect the compromises of 1994 and constrain a more revolutionary transformation of the country. These included a Bill of Rights, an independent Constitutional Court (strongly advocated by the Democratic Party) and a provision that constitutional amendments required support of two-thirds of the new parliament. Perhaps most important for white South Africans, the ANC agreed to the protection of property of all kinds. White South Africans would not be forced to give up their economic gains from the apartheid era, even though black South Africans had been disadvantaged in many ways in law. For example, Africans had not been able to own property in the cities and, unlike whites, were therefore not able to accumulate capital through this route in families.

South Africa's election was controlled by the domestically constituted Independent Electoral Commission. There was not time to develop a voters' roll and all that was needed was an identity card. In this sense, apartheid's bureaucratic thoroughness left a valuable legacy because the great majority of black people had an identity document. There were a number of recorded irregularities, but all parties agreed that the outcome was a reasonable representation of the support they commanded.

The ANC won 62.6 percent of the vote, including the great majority of non-Zulu-speaking Africans. The CP and COSATU retained a separate organisational identity but contested the election behind the ANC as part of a Tripartite Alliance. The National Party won 20.4 percent, broadly speaking the white vote plus a significant proportion of Coloured and Indian votes. Inkatha won 10.5 percent, probably more than half of Zulu speakers. Support for right wing Afrikaners dropped from about 600,000 to 425,000 and this now translated into two percent of the vote for the Freedom Front.

Perhaps most surprising were the weak results of the Liberal Democratic Party and the PAC. The Democratic Party received only 1.7 percent of the vote. Clearly, the National Party appealed successfully for unity among the minorities in the hope that it would secure them some protection and influence. This was in some senses surprising because the National Party had directly discriminated against Coloured and Indian people over a long period. In later years, the Democratic Alliance displaced the National Party as the major opposition.

Support for the PAC dwindled to 1.25 percent so that they barely secured representation in Parliament. Their hostility to the negotiation process, disorganisation, commitment to violence and radical policies were clearly out of tune with the moment and they did not again become a force in South African politics.

Queues of voters at a polling station in Alexandra township, 27 April 1994.

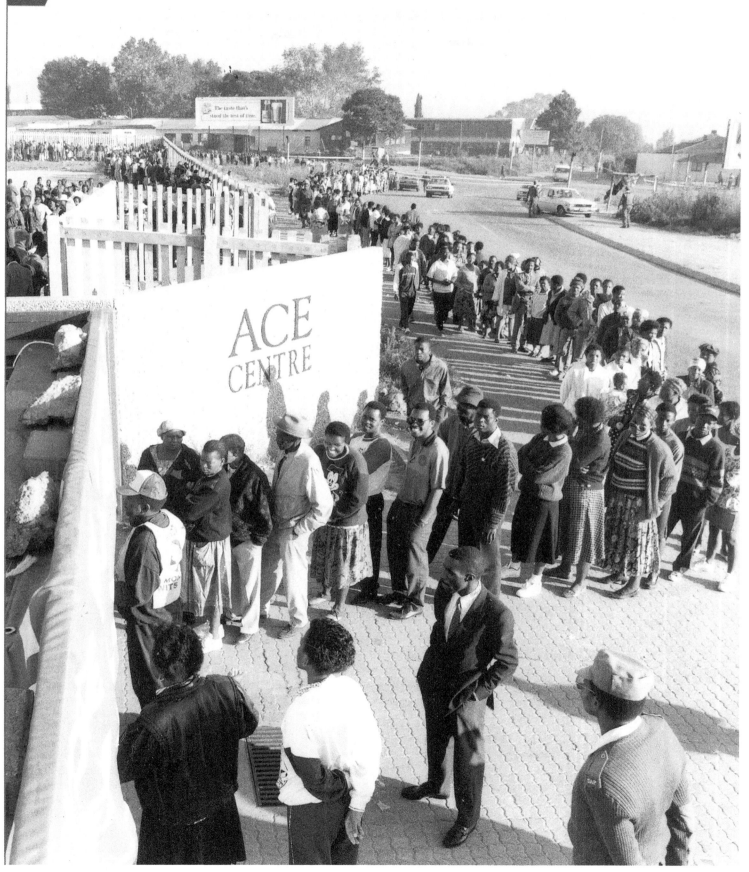

SOURCE

21 Voting results from the 1994 elections in South Africa based on data from the Electoral Commission of South Africa.

Party	Votes	Percentage of votes	Seats
African National Congress	12,237,655	62.65	252
National Party	3,983,690	20.39	82
Inkatha Freedom Party	2,058,294	10.54	43
Freedom Front	424,555	2.17	9
Democratic Party	338,426	1.73	7
Pan Africanist Congress	243,478	1.25	5
African Christian Democratic Party	88,104	0.45	2
Africa Muslim Party	34,466	0.18	0
African Moderates Congress Party	27,690	0.14	0
Dikwankwetla Party	19,451	0.10	0
Federal Party	17,663	0.09	0
Minority Front	13,433	0.07	0
Sport Organisation for Collective Contributions and Equal Rights	10,575	0.05	0
African Democratic Movement	9,886	0.05	0
Women's Rights Peace Party	6,434	0.03	0
Ximoko Progressive Party	6,320	0.03	0
Keep It Straight and Simple Party	5,916	0.03	0
Workers' List Party	4,169	0.02	0
Luso-South African Party	3,293	0.02	0
Total	19,533,498	100	400
Spoilt votes	193,112		

The Government of National Unity and international recognition

In the negotiation process, the four provinces and ten homelands were recombined as nine provinces. These were given provincial executives and legislatures as well as important responsibilities in areas of social provision such as health and education. In the 1994 election, the ANC won seven provinces while the National Party won the Western Cape and Inkatha won KwaZulu-Natal.

Given that the overall ANC victory was widely expected, the result in certain respects was a good outcome for political stability. The ANC did not win a two-thirds majority and so could not easily make constitutional changes without support from other parties. Its power was constrained by this as well as the Government of National Unity. The National Party and Inkatha both felt included in post-apartheid South Africa and could become part of the political process. Ironically, both were soon to lose support. The National Party decided to extract itself from the Government of National Unity in 1996 and, without the ballast of power and patronage, it rapidly lost support to the Democratic Party. Inkatha's vote gradually dwindled and it lost control of KwaZulu-Natal in 2004.

Mandela became South African president with Thabo Mbeki and F. W. de Klerk as deputies. Mandela, especially, saw reconciliation as a central goal. The compromises made in the negotiations ensured that, at least in the short term, South Africa experienced a political transition rather than a revolution. For some of those who had been involved in the struggle against apartheid, this was not a sufficiently dramatic transformation, and whites seemed to be left with too much influence and too much control of the commanding heights of the economy. Supporters of the National Party in particular, as well as members of the police and army, seemed to be absolved of responsibility for the past. However, the settlement did provide a period of stability for a country wracked by conflict and violence.

With a large majority in parliament, control of cabinet and of the legislative agenda, the ANC was free to dismantle the remains of apartheid and to pass a great range of legislation. For a country that had been locked in one of the most rigid systems of racial legislation, the abolition of apartheid and legal discrimination was a major victory. The majority party, supported by African people, gained political control and this immediately set the basis for more fluid racial interactions. The ANC quickly passed a Restitution of Land Rights Act, designed to compensate for the worst examples of forced removal from land, and a Truth and Reconciliation Act, designed to research and expose the worst excesses of apartheid.

Desmond Tutu, leading anti-apartheid spokesman, Nobel Prize winner (1984) and Anglican Archbishop of Cape Town (1986–96) named his book about the political struggle in South Africa *The Rainbow People of God* (1994). He offered a vision, developed by Mandela, of a rainbow nation in which people of different identities and colours could live together peacefully. It was an appealing metaphor, widely quoted, and became part of the way that South Africans talked about themselves. It was also an appropriate metaphor because – as in the rainbow – the different colours and identities in South Africa, both white and black, did not suddenly disappear.

Economic as well as racial inequalities remained a central legacy of apartheid. COSATU had grown from 460,000 members in 1985 to 1.3 million in 1994; now part of the ruling Tripartite Alliance, it secured legislation favourable to the unions and organised labour. In the early years of post-apartheid South Africa, black workers experienced rising living standards and gained enhanced rights. State employment was rapidly Africanised to provide new opportunities for hundreds of thousands of black people. These measures benefited employed and educated people, but with unemployment at over 25 percent, and deep rural poverty, many fell outside of their reach. The ANC prioritised social spending on housing, education, health and welfare, particularly state pensions, in an attempt to start the long and difficult road towards addressing poverty and inequality. These proved to be particularly intractable problems.

The transition to full democracy ensured acceptance and support from the international community including Western democracies, the Commonwealth, African nations and the rising eastern powers of China, India and Russia. The ANC and Mandela worked hard to ease the transition internationally, to pay tribute to those who had supported the struggle against apartheid and to ensure that South Africa was accepted back into the international community. In this, they were highly successful. Mandela received rapturous support on many of his foreign visits as the new head of state. Investment returned and economic boycotts were ended. South Africa was again allowed to compete in the sporting arena. The country hosted the rugby world cup in 1995 (which they won) and the cricket world cup in 1999.

After the elections, South Africa was readmitted into several regional and global initiatives. On 23 May 1994 South Africa became the 53rd member of the African Union, dramatically altering its relationship with the continent. In August 1994 South Africa became a member of the Southern African Development Community (SADC), which strengthened social, political and economic ties with other countries in the region, with whom South Africa had had a particularly fractious relationship over the previous few decades.

Conclusion

South Africa experienced an extraordinary transition. In 1948, a minority government of Afrikaners, representing barely 12 percent of the total population, had embarked on a journey which isolated the country and left a long shadow. Their policy of apartheid was based on rigid ideas about race and ethnicity. They reserved full political rights for those classified as whites and protected them by discriminating against others. In the long term, the National Party promised to subdivide the country and provide alternative independent homelands for black people.

However, most black people experienced apartheid as severely repressive. Most rejected the inequalities imposed on them. The homelands were by no means an equal division of the land and resources of the country. In any case, the great majority were committed to South Africa remaining a single country. In the 1950s African nationalism increasingly attracted a mass following as African people saw themselves as black South Africans. Although the ANC split, and was banned, this phase of political mobilisation provided the roots of the political transition during the 1990s.

The popular struggle against apartheid within and outside the country was a major and sustained global movement for human rights and political equality. It was threatened by intransigence and civil conflict. Yet most whites saw that they had little option but to relinquish political power, and the ANC leadership, particularly Nelson Mandela, understood the need for compromise and reconciliation.

The relatively peaceful negotiations in South Africa and the non-racial democratic political outcome represented an achievement not only for South Africans but for the world as a whole.

ACTIVITY
CONSOLIDATION

1 Using Source 21, choose three of the main parties that took part in the 1994 elections and research them. Make notes on their key ideas, main policies and chief promises.

2 Why do you think they were popular (or unpopular)?

3 Were they more popular in some areas of the country than others? Why might that have been?

4 Did the country vote largely on racial lines?

From apartheid state to rainbow nation

1 Write a paragraph on the ANC's bargaining power in 1985 and another on their bargaining power in 1993.

2 Make a list of key turning points that changed the ANC's negotiating position. Which turning point had the most impact? Write a paragraph to explain why.

3 What are the similarities and differences between the political interests of the National Party and Inkatha between 1989 and 1994? Which is the most important similarity and which the most significant difference?

4 What do you think were the most important forces behind the political transition in South Africa: African political protest; white self-interest and compromise; economic decline; or international pressure?

5 How successful was the ANC in uniting the South African nation?

WIDER READING

Beinart, William, *Twentieth-Century South Africa*, Oxford University Press (2001)

Clark, Nancy L., *South Africa: The Rise and Fall of Apartheid*, Routledge (2011)

Culpin, Christopher, *South Africa 1948–1995: a depth study*, Hodder Education (2000)

Gordimer, Nadine, *Telling Times: Writing and Living, 1950–2008*, Bloomsbury (2011)

Krog, Antje, *Country of My Skull*, Vintage (1999)

Lodge, Tom, *Mandela: A Critical Life*, Oxford University Press (2006)

Mandela, Nelson, *The Long Walk to Freedom*, Abacus (2013)

Mulholland, Rosemary, *South Africa 1948–1994*, Cambridge University Press (1997)

Roberts, Martin, *South Africa 1948–1994: the Rise and Fall of Apartheid*, Longman (2001)

Tutu, Desmund, *No Future Without Forgiveness*, Doubleday (1999)

Preparing for your AS Level Paper 2 exam

Advance planning

1. Draw up a timetable for your revision and try to keep to it. Spread your timetable over a number of weeks, and aim to cover four or five topics each week.
2. Spend longer on topics that you have found difficult, and revise them several times.
3. Above all, do not try to limit your revision by attempting to 'question spot'. Try to be confident about all aspects of your Paper 2 work, because this will ensure that you have a choice of questions in Section B.

Paper 2 overview:

AS Paper 2	Time: I hour 30 minutes	
Section A	Answer I compulsory two-part sources question	8+12 marks = 20 marks
Section B	Answer I question from a choice of 3	20 marks
	Total marks =	40 marks

You should familiarise yourself with the layout of the paper by looking at the examples published by Edexcel. The questions for each section are followed by eight pages of lined paper where you should write your answer.

Section A questions

Each of the two parts of the question will focus on one of the two contemporary sources provided. The sources together will total around 300 words. The (a) question, worth 8 marks, will be in the form of 'Why is Source 1 useful for an enquiry into…?' The (b) question, worth 12 marks, will be in the form of 'How much weight do you give the evidence of Source 2 for an enquiry into…?' In both your answers you should address the value of the content of the source, and then its nature, origin and purpose. Finally, you should use your own knowledge of the context of the source to assess its value.

Section B questions

These questions ask you to reach a judgement on an aspect of the topic studied. The questions will have the form, for example, of 'How far…', 'To what extent…' or 'How accurate is it to say…'. The questions can deal with historical concepts such as cause, consequence, change, continuity, similarity, difference and significance. You should consider the issue raised in the question, consider other relevant issues, and then conclude with an overall judgement.

The timescale of the questions could be as short as a single year or even a single event (an example from Option 2C.2 could be, 'To what extent was Russia's involvement in the First World War responsible for the fall of the Provisional Government in 1917?'). The timescale could be longer depending on the historical event or process being examined, but questions are likely to be shorter than the those set for Sections A and B in Paper 1.

Use of time

This is an issue that you should discuss with your teachers and fellow students, but here are some suggestions for you.

1. Do not write solidly for 45 minutes on each question. For Section A it is essential that you have a clear understanding of the content of each source, the points being made, and the nature, origin and purpose of each source. You might decide to spend up to ten minutes reading the sources and drawing up your plan, and 35 minutes writing your answer.
2. For Section B answers you should spend a few minutes working out what the question is asking you to do, and drawing up a plan of your answer before you begin to write your response.

Preparing for your AS exams

Paper 2: AS Level sample answer with comments

Section A

Part A requires you to:

- identify key points in the extract and explain them
- deploy your own knowledge of the context in which events took place
- make appropriate comments about the author/origin/purpose of the source.

Study Source 2 (Chapter 3, page 336) before you answer this question.

Why is Source 2 valuable to the historian for an enquiry into the reasons for black opposition to the Bantustans policy?

Explain your answer using the source, the information given about it and your own knowledge of the historical context. (8 marks)

Average student answer

This is a source which talks about the Bantustans. This was a policy of the white South African government to move all black people into special 'homelands' which were away from the traditional areas of settlement and which would be reserved for white people only. The Bantustans policy did not work because black people were still needed in the cities to do all the jobs that white people refused to do or to fill the vacancies that could not be filled because there were not enough people to fill them. Even people who had been relocated from the cities to the Bantustans might return to the cities because they could earn more money there.

Steve Biko was a black activist who lived and worked mainly in the Eastern Cape Province in the 1970s. He worked against the South African government as a student leader and then political activist. He founded the Black Consciousness Movement and it was his organisation that led to the Soweto Uprising in 1976. He did not like the Bantustan policy because he wanted black and white to mix as equals and not be segregated. He thinks that the Bantustans are like 'concentration camps' and that they are keeping black people away from areas of South Africa, which he says is 'our country'. He is not happy with black people being told what to do, when he writes: 'black people must learn to refuse to be pawns in a white man's game.'

The historian would clearly see that Steve Biko would not support the Bantustans policy. As a black activist, his position would be against Bantustans because he feels that it will only strengthen apartheid and keep the whites and blacks apart. His organisations like BCM and the student organisation SASO would have agreed with him. He also feels that it would be divisive for the black movement and would split black people into their separate tribes.

> The opening paragraph shows some knowledge about the issue and describes what the policy was but is weak because it talks about the Bantustan policy without really relating it to the point being made by the source.
>
> It could be improved by addressing the question more closely and stating the link explicitly rather than implying it.

> In this paragraph, there is an attempt to look at the provenance of the source. It contains some information about Steve Biko and attempts to explain why he would not like the Bantustans policy. There are attempts to use some quotes.
>
> It could be improved by using quotes to support the argument rather than as links. Some comments about the reliability and utility of the source would also improve this paragraph.

This paragraph deals partly with the question and attempts to give a direct answer. It contains an inference ('would be divisive') but this is not well substantiated.

To make this answer better, the inference needs to be fully explained and supported.

Verdict

This is an average answer because:

- it doesn't make clear connections between the source and the question
- it doesn't use the context of the source to explain its value

- it doesn't explain the significance of the issues raised in the answer, particularly where quotes are used.

Use the feedback on this essay to rewrite it, making as many improvements as you can.

Paper 2: AS Level sample answer with comments

Section A

Part B requires you to:

- interrogate the source
- draw reasoned inferences
- deploy your own knowledge to interpret the material in its context
- make a judgement about the value (weight) of the source in terms of making judgements.

Study Source 11, (Chapter 4, page 366) before you answer this question.

How much weight do you give the evidence of Source 11 for an enquiry into the effectiveness of black opposition in the 1980s?

Explain your answer using the source, the information given about it and your own knowledge of the historical context. (12 marks)

Average student answer

Botha is very angry in this source about the violent opposition of the blacks. He says that they are 'burning down schools and houses and murdering innocent people'. As the president of South Africa, he is responsible for law and order and the blacks are challenging this. Organisations like the UDF and ANC were organising violence against apartheid at the time and Botha had to declare a state of emergency. He is also very sad because he describes Africa as 'a continent that is dying at present'.

> This paragraph does not deal with the demands of the question which concerns the usefulness of this evidence about black opposition. The paragraph could be improved by making a direct connection between Botha's state of mind and black opposition.

Botha is also concerned about foreigners and their impact on ordinary South Africans. Trade bans and sporting boycotts were making ordinary white South Africans unhappy and encouraging black opposition. He shows this when he says, 'The tragedy is that hostile pressure and agitation from abroad have acted as an encouragement to the militant revolutionaries in South Africa.' The fact that he uses the word 'revolutionaries' is meant to show foreigners that they are not supporting freedom fighters but rather that they are supporting criminals against the legitimate authorities. Obviously, he feels that the link between black opposition and foreign influence is important enough to try to break.

> In this paragraph there is an attempt to look at why Botha has attempted to influence foreign opposition to apartheid and to divide it from the black opposition. It would be better if the link between black opposition and foreign pressure was made clearer. It could also explore, in more detail, how foreign pressure was affecting South Africa.

Botha is making it clear to the whites that he will not back down about apartheid. White people were becoming afraid that living in South Africa was too dangerous. When Botha says, 'I have the facts and I am not going to hand South Africa over to these revolutionaries to do the same to this lovely country', he is clearly appealing to emotions of the whites. He thinks that black parties have ruined other countries and he is not going to let them do it to South Africa. He thinks that this reassurance will keep the whites supporting him in his fight against the violence of the black opposition.

> This paragraph addresses the purpose of the speech. The paragraph could be improved by focusing on the issue of the effectiveness of black opposition and how this relates to the attitudes of the whites and the need for Botha to address the issue.

This speech clearly reveals that Botha is worried about black opposition. A historian would find this useful because if black opposition had not worried Botha, he would not have decided to make a speech about it.

> This conclusion makes an attempt at an overall judgement which relates to the demands of the question. An improved conclusion would develop the judgement and refer to the substantiating evidence quoted previously, or new quotes from the source.

Verdict

This is an average answer because:

- it doesn't make clear connections between the source and the question
- it doesn't use the context of the source to explain its limitations

- it doesn't explain the significance of the issues raised in the answer, particularly where quotes are used.

Use the feedback on this essay to rewrite it, making as many improvements as you can.

Paper 2: AS Level sample answer with comments

Section A

Part A requires you to:

- identify key points in the source and explain them
- deploy your own knowledge of the context in which events took place
- make appropriate comments about the author/origin/purpose of the source.

Study Source 2 (Chapter 3, page 336) before you answer this question.

Why is Source 2 valuable to the historian for an enquiry into the reasons for black opposition to the Bantustans policy?

Explain your answer using the source, the information given about it and your own knowledge of the historical context. (8 marks)

Strong student answer

As a black activist, Biko clearly identifies a major reason why blacks opposed the Bantustan policy. He focuses on the divisive nature of the initiative. By associating different Bantustans with different tribes, the South African authorities are re-creating the tribalism of the pre-colonial period. In doing this, according to Biko, the whites are creating conditions by which 'the collective strength and resistance of the black people can be fragmented'. Biko identifies himself as black above else, as shown by his creation of the Black Consciousness Movement and in this extract he writes 'we black people'. He sees the damaging result of the Bantustans as creating 'Zulu, Xhosa and Tswana politicians', which will divide the black opposition and make it less effective.

It is not surprising that Biko was against this policy. Bantustans were a central part of the vision of apartheid which was total segregation of whites and non-whites. As student activist who was a prominent leader of SASO (South African Students' Organisation) and the founder of the Black Consciousness Movement, Biko is bound to be hostile to Bantustans as he is fundamentally opposed to apartheid. As a leader, however, he is likely to reflect the views of those he led and thereby this is a valuable piece of evidence. There were many blacks who would also see the Bantustans as 'sophisticated concentration camps' and the fact that so many chose to stay in townships rather than move to the Bantustans is testimony to this.

Biko concentrates on the divisive nature of the Bantustans but only hints at the economic and cultural reasons. He writes of 'tribal cocoons' which implies being cut off from the rest of the world, a position which would not be acceptable to anyone who was fundamentally opposed to the apartheid policy. 'Being pawns in a white man's game' refers to the fragmentation of the black opposition but might also refer to the game of keeping the black majority poor and thereby powerless. Bantustans were poor areas, where extreme poverty was common, despite money being made available by the South African government. Part of the divisiveness of the Bantustans was to make them dependent on money from Pretoria and thereby more easily manipulated. It also goes to explain why so many felt better off making an independent living in the townships near to a major city rather than moving to a Bantustan.

> This paragraph identifies the main message of the source. It uses contextual knowledge about Biko along with inferences from the source to explain this message. It demonstrates very clearly why Biko, as a black leader, was against the Bantustans policy.

> This paragraph deals with Biko as a source and assesses how typical his views might be and thereby how useful for the historian. It sticks to the proposition given by the question in terms of this evidence being valuable as a reason for black opposition to the Bantustans policy.

> This paragraph identifies other issues that Biko tentatively hints at but does not fully explain in the source provided. How 'valuable' the source is, is judged by what the source explains explicitly but also other issues that the source touches on but does not fully explain.

Verdict

This is a strong answer because:

- it makes clear connections between the source and the question

- it uses the context of the source to show how it relates to the question
- it selects relevant parts of the source and explains why they are important in relation to the question.

Paper 2: AS Level sample answer with comments

Section A

Part B requires you to:

- interrogate the source
- draw reasoned inferences
- deploy your own knowledge to interpret the material in its context
- make a judgement about the value (weight) of the source in terms of making judgements.

Study Source 11, (Chapter 4, page 366) before you answer this question.

How much weight do you give the evidence of Source 11 for an enquiry into the effectiveness of black opposition in the 1980s?

Explain your answer using the source, the information given about it and your own knowledge of the historical context. (12 marks)

Strong student answer

The tone of this source suggests that black opposition was having a major impact on Botha and the South African authorities. 'Murdering innocent people' clearly makes the black opposition criminals in his mind, people who are not building the country but destroying it. To use these emotional phrases means that the black opposition is getting to President Botha and provoking a response. Botha clearly wants to make the blacks the 'bad guys' in this and himself the only defender of order. It is, perhaps, the extreme nature of the language used that reveals Botha's desperation and is thereby a clue to the effectiveness of the black opposition.

> This paragraph discusses the nature of the language Botha has used and what it reveals about his state of mind, then draws a conclusion from this about the effectiveness of the black opposition.

The purpose of this speech is to get people to turn against the black opposition but also to give black campaigners a clear message that they will not win. Emotive phrases like 'a dying continent' imply that the black opposition is the force that is killing it. According to Botha, 'By violence and by burning down schools and houses and murdering innocent people, you don't build a country, you destroy it.' This is a reference to the schools boycott organised by the UDF and the ANC initiative to make the country ungovernable. This is a rallying call for others (whites or moderate non-whites) to oppose the black opposition.

> This paragraph examines the purpose of the speech. It shows an awareness of the context by talking about the UDF, the ANC and the state of emergency. It also makes a judgement relating to the question.

The effectiveness of this evidence pertains to its indication of the mood of the South African government and its supporters in 1985. Botha would not make a speech of the kind without some consultation. The speech would have been written for him or perhaps in collaboration with an advisor or advisors. That others must have sanctioned this speech means that it indicates how the authorities as a whole were feeling about the situation in South Africa. Also, they are not trying to reach out to the opposition leaders in South Africa.

This evidence is very useful in what it reveals about the attitudes of the South African government, which have been directly influenced by the effectiveness of the black opposition. Without the campaigns of the UDF and ANC, Botha would not have been driven into this position and would not have felt the need to make such a dramatic speech. The hint of desperation that pervades it is indicative of how successful the opposition has been. It is as though the escalation in police activity has been matched by an escalation in rhetoric. The historian would give this great weight and use it with other examples of government initiatives and opposition activity to come to a judgement about the effective of black opposition.

> This paragraph attempts to come to an overall judgement about the value of the source and how much weight a historian would give it when forming a judgement about the effectiveness of black opposition.

Verdict

This is a strong answer because:

- it makes inferences from the source and deploys material from the source to support them
- it shows a deep awareness of context, purpose and audience and brings it into the answer when appropriate to the question
- it sticks to the question and arrives at a clear judgement.

Paper 2: AS Level sample answer with comments

Section B

These questions assess your understanding of the period in some depth. They will ask you about the content you learned about in the four key themes, but may not ask about more than one theme. For these questions remember to:

- give an analytical, not a descriptive, response
- support your points with evidence
- cover the whole time period specified in the question
- come to a substantiated judgement.

How far did economic growth strengthen apartheid 1961–83? (20 marks)

Average student answer

The South African economy was the strongest in Africa throughout this period. This was mainly due to the mining industry and farming. This meant that foreign countries would ignore apartheid because trade with South Africa was so profitable. The USA and the United Kingdom were both major trading partners with South Africa.

The South African economy was strong in the cities. This led to migration towards the cities. The apartheid system wanted blacks to move away from the cities and to live on Bantustans – areas that were reserved for them and far away from where the whites lived. This meant that the economy did not strengthen apartheid because it pulled blacks away from the Bantustans and into the cities. Black workers lived in shanty towns like Soweto rather than in the city itself. The conditions were very poor; disease was very common and the crime rate very high. As blacks were living in the city, the economy was clearly not strengthening apartheid.

Having a strong economy helped the South African government to strengthen apartheid. Having lots of money meant that they were able to pay for lots of things connected with the Bantustan policy. For example, Bantustans were very poor areas which had very low income. The South African government were able to pay the Bantustans to try and make sure that all the blacks remained there and did not go back to the white-only areas. They were also able to pay lots of security people to keep blacks out of white-only areas. The pass book laws were enforced and blacks were often prosecuted for being in the wrong place. Without a strong economy, the government could not have funded the security services and thereby strengthen apartheid.

This paragraph gives some relevant background information in explaining why foreign countries traded with South Africa despite the apartheid system. An improved paragraph would deal more directly with the demands of the question. It needs to closely examine the relationship between the economy and apartheid as a whole, not just the angle of foreign trade. The student also needs to give their own definition of 'strengthening apartheid' and how this might be measured.

This paragraph describes the link between the economy and migration and connects it to one aspect of apartheid (the Bantustan policy) but the connection is not made clearly. An improved paragraph would describe why non-white workers were so badly needed in the cities that whites would overlook the aims of apartheid. The explanation of the Bantustan policy should also be more detailed and the fact that economic reasons led to its failure should be more clearly stated.

This paragraph deals with how prosperity aided the government and helped them to strengthen apartheid. It explains the direct effect of a well-funded government on the Bantustans and then cites a second example of how having a good income can help to strengthen apartheid. A stronger answer could also give a counter-argument: only 55 percent of blacks ever went to live in Bantustans despite the government funding, and it could be argued that the pass book laws did not succeed in controlling migration.

The economy stimulated immigration into South Africa from abroad. This was not the kind of immigration that the South African authorities wanted. During the period 1961 to 1983, more white people left South Africa than came into it and yet during that time millions of migrant black workers came into South Africa illegally. Even though conditions for black workers were very poor in South Africa it was still better than the poverty that people suffered in neighbouring states. Also, having a steady job and income meant that black workers could send money home and support their families. This did not strengthen apartheid because it meant that even more non-whites were coming to live in what were officially white-only areas.

← This paragraph hints at how the prosperous economy encouraged the migration of black workers into South Africa, countering the aims of apartheid. To improve the paragraph the student could add reasons why more whites were leaving than settling in South Africa. Some figures to support the claims being made would also be helpful.

In conclusion, the economy was prosperous but it did not entirely strengthen apartheid. True, the government had lots of money and was able to spend it on measures that did strengthen apartheid. On the other hand, the need for workers meant that non-whites were needed in the cities to do all the jobs that ran the economy. Overall, economic prosperity weakened apartheid rather than strengthening it.

← This concluding paragraph reiterates the main arguments and then makes a judgement but it needs to go into more detail. It should explain the criteria by which the judgement has been made and comment on the relative significance of the arguments put forward.

Verdict

This is an average answer because:

- it doesn't give a direct and supported answer to the question
- it doesn't explain or prioritise the significance of the issues raised in the answer.

Use the feedback on this essay to rewrite it, making as many improvements as you can.

Paper 2: AS Level sample answer with comments

Section B

These questions assess your understanding of the period in some depth. They will ask you about the content you learned about in the four key themes, but may not ask you about more than one theme. For these questions, remember to:

- give an analytical, not descriptive, response
- support your points with evidence
- cover the whole time period specified in the question
- come to a substantiated judgement.

How far did economic prosperity strengthen apartheid 1961–83? (20 marks)

Strong student answer

Though economic prosperity increased in the 1960s, economic growth also declined in the 1970s and early 1980s. It gave rise to an influx of illegal migrant workers from other African states to fill positions as the economy expanded. It also created a skills shortage in certain jobs and gave blacks the opportunity to improve their lot. Across the period, apartheid was protected by the world's need for South African gold and diamonds, the tax income from which enriched the South African government and gave it a certain freedom of action. The aim of apartheid was the total segregation of whites and non-whites – whites in the urban and designated rural areas and non-whites in Bantustans. In some respects economic success did strengthen apartheid, though in some ways it also weakened it.

In many ways the economic prosperity of the 1960s strengthened apartheid. Firstly, a strong level of tax income allowed the South African government to rigorously pursue policies to strengthen apartheid. Although the Bantustan initiative pre-dates 1961, it was continued under Verwoerd and Vorster. This entailed the forced migration of black people into pre-designated homelands, the organising of which was a vast expense for the government in Pretoria. Moreover, once they were set up, the Bantustans had great difficulty paying for themselves. For example, 85 percent of the income of Transkei was funded by the South African government. Without economic prosperity, the government would have found it increasingly difficult to find this money. Also the strength of the South African economy made it a valued trading partner. While other states needed South African gold, diamonds and agricultural goods, they would have been unlikely to protest against apartheid and even less likely to pursue a policy of economic sanctions. Economic prosperity made South Africa strong and gave the government more freedom to pursue policies to strengthen apartheid.

In some other ways, the economic prosperity helped to break down the strict segregation of apartheid. As South African businesses prospered, there was a greater need for skilled workers. There were not enough white workers to fill these positions and so companies were forced to employ black workers. This meant that government policy of moving black people away from the cities into Bantustans was not working. Despite being moved from their homes, black people began to live in shanty towns like Soweto, close to the main cities, as they would still be employed by businesses in the cities. Moreover, skilled black workers could do even better for themselves. Although the law was that no white worker could be under a black worker, black workers could still be promoted. This broke down apartheid even further as all the workers under another black worker had to be non-white. This retained black workers in urban areas or drew more back from the Bantustans. An example of this is the construction industry, where a boom

This paragraph sets out an overview of the key issues without delving into the detail, the implication being that a more comprehensive treatment of these issues will follow. It sets out what would constitute a strong apartheid, a criterion that can be used later in the essay when a judgement is made.

In this paragraph, the answer deals with the aspects of economic prosperity that strengthened apartheid. It cites Bantustans as an example and describes what they were. It then explains how this links in with the question. Another example, the strength of the economy internationally, is also given.

This paragraph explains the impact of the need for workers in the urban areas and shows how this worked against apartheid. It relates directly to the previous paragraph and show how the two aspects worked against each other.

in house building relied heavily on black workers. Tax income also worked against apartheid as the government spent some of it on the education of blacks. This meant that they would be more employable and thereby less likely to leave the cities and live in the Bantustans. The economic needs of business superseded the needs of apartheid and thus the system was weakened.

The issue of migrant workers was a significant problem for the South African government and massively undermined apartheid. Rapid urbanisation had mainly been fuelled by the movement of black workers from the countryside within South Africa but also from outside the country. Though conditions were difficult for non-white workers and they had no political rights outside the Bantustans, they were relatively better off working in the cities. For workers coming from abroad this was also the case. Such were the levels of poverty in neighbouring African states that crossing illegally into South Africa was thought to be worth the dangers for the possibility of employment. This meant that from 1961 to 1983, the black population of South Africa increased. During the same period, white migration showed that more whites left South Africa than came into it. The driving force behind this change in the balance of population was the economy.

> This paragraph highlights a significant issue affecting the strength of apartheid. It explains the causes of this factor and shows how they were driven by the economy and thereby how they relate to the question.

Overall, the economy did not prosper throughout the era. In the 1970s and early 80s, the South African economy struggled, like many others in the world. This meant that any strengthening of apartheid by economic prosperity was uneven throughout the period. It could be argued that as the period progressed, world economic problems allied with the impact of economic sanctions against South Africa actually weakened apartheid. Border security was increasingly an issue and government spending on this went up and diverted from other initiatives. Though isolation may have engendered a 'siege' mentality among white South Africans by the 1980s, the Bantu policies had clearly failed, largely though economic need and much of the segregation envisaged by apartheid was non-existent. Throughout the period, the need for workers was a priority over the political needs for a pure apartheid system and because of this, economic prosperity did not strengthen apartheid.

> The conclusion answers the question directly. It gives an overview of the period and outlines the unevenness of the link between a strong economy and strong apartheid as the period progressed. It draws on arguments already made and arrives at a clear conclusion which is substantiated by the arguments given.

Verdict

This is a strong answer because:

- it answers the question throughout and analyses the key issues of economic prosperity and apartheid
- it uses a criterion that frames the issue of the question, so that a concluding judgement can be made against something tangible
- it uses a wide range of relevant historical evidence to support the points made
- it is well organised and communication of material is clear and precise.

Preparing for your A Level Paper 2 exam

Advance planning

1. Draw up a timetable for your revision and try to keep to it. Spread your timetable over a number of weeks, and aim to cover four or five topics each week.
2. Spend longer on topics that you have found difficult, and revise them several times.
3. Above all, do not try to limit your revision by attempting to 'question spot'. Try to be confident about all aspects of your Paper 2 work, because this will ensure that you have a choice of questions in Section B.

Paper 2 overview

AL Paper 2	Time: 1 hour 30 minutes	
Section A	Answer 1 compulsory source question	20 marks
Section B	Answer 1 question from a choice of 2	20 marks
	Total marks =	40 marks

You should familiarise yourself with the layout of the paper by looking at the examples published by Edexcel. The questions for each section are followed by eight pages of lined paper where you should write your answer.

Section A questions

This question asks you to assess two different types of contemporary sources totalling around 400 words, and will be in the form of 'How far could the historian make use of Sources 1 and 2 together to investigate…?' Your answer should evaluate both sources, considering their nature, origin and purpose, and you should use your own knowledge of the context of the sources to consider their value to the specific investigation. Remember, too, that in assessing their value, you must consider the two sources, taken together, as a set.

Section B questions

These questions ask you to reach a judgement on an aspect of the topic studied. The questions will have the form, for example, of 'How far…', 'To what extent…' or 'How accurate is it to say…'. The questions can deal with historical concepts such as cause, consequence, change, continuity, similarity, difference and significance. You should consider the issue raised in the question, then other relevant issues, and conclude with an overall judgement.

The timescale of the questions could be as short as a single year or even a single event (an example from Option 2C.2 could be, 'To what extent was Russia's involvement in the First World War responsible for the fall of the Romanovs in 1917?'). The timescale could be longer depending on the historical event or process being examined, but questions are likely to be shorter than the those set for Sections A and B in Paper 1.

Use of time

This is an issue that you should discuss with your teachers and fellow students, but here are some suggestions for you.

1. Do not write solidly for 45 minutes on each question. For Section A it is essential that you have a clear understanding of the content of each source, the points being made, and the nature, origin and purpose of each source. You might decide to spend up to ten minutes reading the sources and drawing up your plan, and 35 minutes writing your answer.
2. For Section B answers you should spend a few minutes working out what the question is asking you to do, and drawing up a plan of your answer before you begin to write your response.

Preparing for your A Level exams

Section A

You will need to read and analyse two sources and use them in tandem to assess how useful they are in investigating an issue. For these questions remember to:

- spend time, up to ten minutes, reading and identifying the arguments and evidence present in the sources; then make a plan to ensure that your response will be rooted in these sources
- use specific references from the sources
- deploy your own knowledge to develop points made in the sources and establish appropriate context
- come to a substantiated judgement.

Study Sources 6 and 7 (Chapter 2, page 314) before you answer this question.

How far could the historian make use of Sources 6 and 7 to investigate the reasons behind the Sharpeville Massacre in 1960?

Explain your answer, using both sources, the information given about them and your own knowledge of the historical context. (20 marks)

Average student answer

The Sharpeville Massacre took place in 1960 during a peaceful black demonstration. At some point the black crowd became animated and went to the police station. The police were afraid and they fired at the crowd causing many casualties. They claimed they were acting in self-defence. Afterwards the South African government held an inquiry though it never reached a verdict. The blacks were extremely bitter about what happened but the police led by Colonel Pienaar said that they were justified in their actions. This massacre was news all over the world and was very bad publicity for the South African government.

These sources represent both sides of the argument about the Sharpeville Massacre. Basically, the whites claimed that the blacks caused it because the crowd was out of control and the blacks say that the police caused it because they over-reacted to a peaceful demonstration. Source 7 supports the white South Africans because it talks about 'hordes of natives' and how there was 'a barrage of stones'. It chooses to quote the police chief Pienaar instead of a black sympathiser, which shows how biased it is. Pienaar felt that the blacks deserved it when he says, 'If they do these things they must learn their lesson the hard way.' the 'Guardian' is a British newspaper and so should be more towards the middle ground rather than supporting the whites. At this time, Britain was supporting apartheid and so it is natural that the 'Guardian' would look at it from a British point of view. Britain was also still a racist country and so many people might have believed in apartheid.

This is a weak opening paragraph because it simply gives an overview of some of the contextual content. It does not address the central issue of the question, which is how useful these sources are for a particular enquiry. An improved introduction would address the question directly and give a clear definition of the nature of the enquiry and an overview of the strengths and weaknesses of the sources.

This paragraph is an overview of one source. Some of it is simple description. The quotes used are part of the description and the wording and ideas expressed are not analysed. In particular the answer should acknowledge that 'hordes of natives' is a quote from Pienaar, not the journalist. The answer needs to deal more directly with the question, which is about how a historian could use this source as evidence. Also some information from Source 6 would be helpful for a direct contrast.

Source 6 supports the black view. Reeves questions the police when he says that there is 'little ← police evidence that some of the crowd were waving sticks' and states that 'no policeman was injured and no police vehicle was damaged'. This contradicts Source 7 which says that 'the Africans retaliated, causing casualties among the police'. Bishop Reeves also interprets the police evidence as showing people wishing to get away from the police station rather than laying siege to it as some of the police may have suggested. He then states how three white people have all contradicted the police evidence. Berry was able to walk through the crowd without being harmed, Hoek says they were not hostile ('no signs of hostility') and Labuschagne was able to go to the police station and leave without problem. As Labuschagne was a white official, it might have been in his interest to say how bad the blacks were, though on the other hand he might have seen the police chief as a rival and would want to make him look bad. Reeves was an anti-apartheid activist and so he would say that the police were to blame.

A historian would use both these sources to help with a judgement about how the Sharpeville Massacre occurred. Source 7 is more useful because it gives a more balanced view of the events. It acknowledges the extent of the violence when it says 'the front ranks of the crowd fell like ninepins' and that police 'waded into them, striking out with their sticks'. It also gives the authorities their chance to put their side. In Source 6, the Bishop has an axe to grind and therefore is totally biased against the police. For this reason the historian would find Source 7 more useful.

This paragraph is an overview of the second source. It describes much of the content and uses quotes to illustrate the description. There is some use of additional context and an attempt to analyse the source but the analysis strays into a discussion of someone mentioned in the source (Labuschagne) rather than the source itself. To improve this paragraph, the contextual information needs to be linked to the source throughout and an explanation added showing how this relates to the reasons for the massacre. The answer also needs to answer the question of how a historian could use this source for an enquiry into the reasons for the massacre.

This concluding paragraph looks briefly at the motivation of the authors of the sources and makes a simple judgement about their utility. To improve this paragraph, the conclusion should compare the purpose behind the writing of the two sources, i.e. the difference between a newspaper report and a book. Again the conclusion needs to deal directly with the question of how a historian would use these sources for an enquiry into the reasons for the Sharpeville massacre.

Verdict

This is an average answer because:

- it doesn't make clear connections between the sources and the question
- it makes limited use of the context of the sources to explain its value

- it doesn't explain the significance of the issues raised in the answer, particularly where quotes are used
- it does explain why the provenance and purpose of the sources impact on judgements about their utility.

Use the feedback on this essay to rewrite it, making as many improvements as you can.

Paper 2: A Level sample answer with comments

Section A

You will need to read and analyse two sources and use them in tandem to assess how useful they are in investigating an issue. For these questions remember to:

- spend time, up to ten minutes, reading and identifying the arguments and evidence present in the sources; then make a plan to ensure that your response will be rooted in these sources
- use specific references from the sources
- deploy your own knowledge to develop points made in the sources and establish appropriate context
- come to a substantiated judgement.

Study Sources 6 and 7 (Chapter 2, page 314) before you answer this question.

How far could the historian make use of Sources 6 and 7 to investigate the reasons behind the Sharpeville Massacre in 1960?

Explain your answer, using both sources, the information given about them and your own knowledge of the historical context. (20 marks)

Strong student answer

Both sources relate some of the police evidence, although from slightly different perspectives. As a newspaper report Source 7 would have had to rely on official channels to gain information about what was going on. The fact that they rely on a quote from Colonel Pienaar of the Sharpeville police indicates this. Focusing on his claim about 'hordes of natives' gives the impression that the crowd was out of control and that they were to blame for violence. 'If they do these things they must learn their lesson the hard way' shows sympathy with the white authorities from a supposedly liberal British newspaper. Bishop Reeves, on the other hand, is in no doubt about the validity of the police evidence. Although he cites some of it, he points out that 'no policeman was injured and no police vehicle was damaged', a fact which contradicts police claims of a 'riotous crowd'. A historian could use both sources as evidence of the claims made in retrospect about the incident and the police evidence, from a known anti-apartheid activist and a newspaper which was giving the official reaction in the first instance.

> This paragraph deals with a key point: both sources make claims which are either about or reliant on police evidence. It interrogates aspects of this evidence and finishes with a statement which brings the argument back to demands of the question.

The timing of the two sources is very important in judging the validity of the evidence being presented. Bishop Reeves's book was published sometime later, in 1961, though as Archbishop of Johannesburg, he would have had access to a great deal of eye-witness testimony. During the writing of the book, he would have had time to consider what information he wanted to pass on. He is keen to make clear that even white people contradicted the police evidence. As an anti-apartheid activist, it is reasonable to expect that he will find and select evidence which matches his point of view. This is not to dismiss the evidence which has much relevance to the issues which would explain the Sharpeville Massacre. the 'Guardian', on the other hand, is issuing a rapid response. It is unclear whether or not they had a reporter on the scene but given the nature of the information in the article, it could be assumed that they did not. As a newspaper, it is very important to get the story to press as quickly as possible to perhaps gain an advantage over their rivals or at very least not be left behind. Reeves points out that there was a 'Daily Mail' photographer present and so the 'Guardian' may already have been at a disadvantage. The speed of their report and the reliance on official information does not make the source invalid, though it should not be assumed that the absence of other evidence is, in itself, significant.

> This paragraph shows an understanding of the context and the significance of how time changes our interpretations of history. It relates these matters to the specific examples of these sources.

There is a danger that the dynamics of the victor's history could play a part in our analysis of these sources. In the short term, when Western powers supported the South African regime and the attitudes of colonialism were still prevalent, it is perhaps not surprising that a national newspaper in Britain would have given credence to the official story. Reverence for the authorities was commonplace and the ideas that rioting blacks might provoke an incident and that the police would not retaliate without good reason would have been acceptable. As time moved on, and the wider world came to regard apartheid as evil, then sympathy for the black victims would have increased and Reeves's book would have been accepted by a far wider readership – even the term 'Sharpeville Massacre' is heavily loaded towards this interpretation. The historian would need to be aware of this context when viewing the evidence presented by these two sources.

> This paragraph places the sources in a wider context and examines how prevalent attitudes both then and now would affect how the historian would use them.

Overall, these sources would be useful for a historian researching the reasons behind the Sharpeville Massacre. As contemporary reactions, they provide some evidence of the events as they unfolded. This would need to be corroborated by other evidence before a judgement could be made. These sources also illustrate the difference in attitude between the two sides. the 'Guardian' article shows that, although unfortunate, it is not unreasonable for the police to fire on a crowd of black people who were hurling a 'barrage of stones' and yelling 'Cowards' and 'Kill the white men'. For Reeves, there is no justification for this action. Not only does he contradict the 'Guardian' article when he questions 'this allegedly riotous crowd' but his comment on the police's point of view, 'the crowd were lacking in that respect and humility which the police apparently expect from their African fellow-citizens' would suggest that he has little respect for the police in any case nor the apartheid authorities.

> The conclusion deals clearly with the question of how the historian could use the two sources and their overall message.

Verdict

This is a strong answer because:

- it makes clear connections between the sources and the question

- it uses the context of the source to show how they relate to the question
- it sustains focus and develops a clear and balanced argument
- the judgement follows on from the arguments put forward.

Paper 2: A Level sample answer with comments

Section B

These questions assess your understanding of the period in some depth. They will ask you about the content you learned about in the four key themes, but may not ask about more than one theme. For these questions remember to:

- give an analytical, not a descriptive, response
- support your points with evidence
- cover the whole time period specified in the question
- come to a substantiated judgement.

How accurate is it to say that the violent protests of the 1980s played the main role in ending apartheid? (20 marks)

Average student answer

Apartheid was finished in 1994 when Nelson Mandela became the first black president. This followed a long period of violent protest. Protests were organised by the UDF, a movement which was created in the 1980s in order to fight against apartheid. Some of these got violent like the Vaal uprising in 1984.

> This paragraph gives information about the subject matter of the essay but does not directly address the question. To be better, the paragraph would need to define what it means by the 'main role' and explain what would constitute this, and by what criteria this would be judged. It could also suggest some other factors that could be argued to have played the 'main role'.

There were many protests that got violent during the 1980s. In 1984, the ANC called for the townships to be made ungovernable and a year later declared a people's war. This was a mixture of boycotts, peaceful protests and violent protests. Often peaceful protests turned to violence. The Vaal uprising of 1984 is an example of violent protest. The mayor shot two protestors and the crowd turned nasty. President Botha declared a state of emergency in 1986 so that he would have emergency powers. This shows how much the violence had affected him. Despite the state of emergency the violence continued and the next president F. W. De Klerk decided that he needed to end apartheid in order to put a stop to the violence. This means that violence was very important.

> In this paragraph, the material deals with violence and gives some examples. It also mentions the effect on two presidents. To improve this answer, the reasons why these things are important need to be fully explained with reference to the idea of playing a 'main role'.

The role of individuals was very important to the end of apartheid. Nelson Mandela was the inspiration for many black people during and after apartheid. Even when he was in prison on Robben Island, people all over the world talked about him and even wrote songs about him. When he was released he was able to bring together all the factions of the black protest movement and it was this that limited the violence. It was the election of Nelson Mandela in 1994 that finally ended apartheid. F. W. de Klerk was also important as he made the decision to release Mandela from prison. He knew that only Mandela could stop the violence in the townships and so he negotiated with him. Mandela and de Klerk were awarded the Nobel Peace Prize for their efforts to end apartheid.

> There is an explanation here of what Mandela and de Klerk did to end apartheid. It contains some factual detail but its link to the question is mostly implicit. To make this paragraph better, it needs to bring this information closer to the question. How does the influence of these individuals compare with the influence of violence on the authorities? How were the actions of de Klerk and Mandela shaped by the violence around them?

International sanctions were also important. In 1977, the Gleneagles Agreement was signed and the countries of the world refused to have sporting and cultural links with South Africa. International sides were banned from playing against other countries although rebel cricket tours occasionally brought international sportsmen to South Africa. Entertainment venues like Sun City attracted great stars but as the 1980s progressed fewer and fewer international acts were playing concerts in South Africa. Also, economic sanctions began to affect the South African economy. Investment was down and this caused the rand to lose its value against foreign currency and inflation was very high. This caused a problem for the authorities, who needed the economy to be strong in order to maintain their power. Violence became more widespread when the economy started to slow down due to economic sanctions.

In conclusion, violence was an important reason that apartheid ended. The violence made President Botha declare states of emergencies and so it must have been severe. Sanctions affected the economy which only added to the violence as people became poorer and more desperate. In the end, the key people who made the changes which brought about the end of apartheid were responding to the increasing levels of violence throughout the country. Violence is, therefore, more important than the other factors.

This paragraph describes the sanctions imposed by other countries and makes a brief reference to their impact on the South African government and also how they affected, at least by a knock-on effect, the level of violence. To make this better, the paragraph needs to give far more detail of the effects of foreign sanctions. It also needs to assess to what extent sanctions contributed to violence and to what extent sanctions caused change without connection to violence.

The conclusion explains the links between violence and the other factors and arrives at a judgement that violence is the most important reason. To make this paragraph better, it needs to deal with the idea of 'main role' and what that means. If the judgement is that violent protest played the main role then the paragraph needs to discuss the other factors and give reasons why those factors did not play the main role.

Verdict

This is an average answer because:

- it doesn't give a direct and supported answer to the question
- it doesn't fully explain the significance of the issues raised in the answer

- though there is an attempt to answer the question, the argument is not always substantiated with evidence.

Use the feedback on this essay to rewrite it, making as many improvements as you can.

Paper 2: A Level sample answer with comments

Section B

These questions assess your understanding of the period in some depth. They will ask you about the content you learned about in the four key themes, but may not ask about more than one theme. For these questions remember to:

- give an analytical, not a descriptive, response
- support your points with evidence
- cover the whole time period specified in the question
- come to a substantiated judgement.

How accurate is it to say that the violent protests of the 1980s played the main role in ending apartheid? (20 marks)

Strong student answer

Though apartheid was ended between 1990 and 1994, it is not reasonable to argue that violent protest was the main cause of this. There were other factors such as peaceful protest, international sanctions and key individuals also played a part. In order to be seen as the main cause, a factor would need to be identified clearly as the driving factor behind the changes that took place or the one factor without which change would not have happened. It is difficult to say this about violent protest.

Violent protest was a major part of political life in South Africa during the 1980s. It is true that violent protests affected government policy but perhaps in the long term rather than the short term. The Vaal uprising, for example, provided the sort of news-grabbing violence that could unsettle the South African government. The violence in the townships in 1985 and 1986, particularly in Alexandra during the 'Six Day War', had a similar effect. This had an effect on President Botha who talked about reform and, in 1986, declared a second State of Emergency. When Botha talked about reform, he was referring to change in order to preserve apartheid, not necessarily to emancipate the non-whites and introduce more equality. There were, however, some concessions to non-whites such as the tricameral parliament and more devolvement of government. Moreover, in the long term, violence played a key part in convincing the rulers of South Africa that the only way forward was to abolish apartheid. F. W. de Klerk was of this opinion when he became president in 1989. He had seen that the troubles in South Africa were not abating and that the full dismantling of apartheid would be the only thing to quell the violence. It is difficult to know how far Botha and de Klerk were motivated by the violence but it certainly played a role in influencing their decisions.

It is also worth noting that much of the protest in South Africa was peaceful. School boycotts, such as the one organised by the UDF in Cape Town in 1980 and strikes such as the COSATU miners' strike in 1987, are examples of non-violent ways of putting pressure on the authorities. These initiatives brought publicity for the anti-apartheid movement to a worldwide audience. Peaceful protest could be a powerful weapon, such as when non-white voters boycotted the first elections to the tricameral parliament. That only 16 percent of eligible voters turned out in 1984 was a massive humiliation to President Botha. However, it is also possible for peaceful protest to turn violent. During the miners' strike of 1984, the sight of pickets clashing with police left the viewers wondering who had initiated the violence. It is often better from a pressure point-of-view to be seen as the victim of violence rather than the perpetrator. Peaceful protest therefore had an important role in bringing about change in South Africa and may have been in many cases a precursor to violent protest.

This paragraph sets out the key factors. It attempts to give some kind of criteria against which the main role can be judged and states an overall judgement, hinting that this will be substantiated in the essay that follows.

In this paragraph the effect of violence on the South Africa government is analysed with specific examples. A judgement is made at the end regarding how far the truth can be known.

This paragraph makes claims about the impact of peaceful protest and links it to the violent protest that is in the question.

The impact of foreign pressure also played a major part in the ending of apartheid. From 1984 onwards, the US ban on new investment had a significant economic impact. The South African economy went into recession, the value of the rand fell and interest rates and inflation grew. It could be argued that the strength of the apartheid regime in the 1960s and the 1970s had been built on the strength of the South African economy and thereby a weakened economy naturally weakened the position of the government. Moreover, economic recession had its greatest impact on the poor, who under pressure may well have been more motivated to involve themselves in violent protest. F. W. de Klerk cited economic reasons for ending apartheid, though it would not be in his interest to say that it was the violence. In addition, the cultural and sporting boycotts will have had a direct impact on the white population and may have made them question whether the isolation brought on by apartheid was worth it. This psychological pressure had nothing to do with violence.

> This paragraph explains how international pressure helped to bring about the end of apartheid. It also directly addresses the question of the role violence played.

There were key individuals who played a major role in the end of apartheid. Had F. W. de Klerk not recognised that the states of emergency could not be sustained indefinitely, then apartheid would not have ended the way it did. It was his willingness to reform that paved the way for the end of apartheid. His release of Nelson Mandela opened a connection between the government and the protest movement that was able to move the process forward. It could be argued that the violence in the 1980s and the response of the security services played a part in shaping de Klerk's views about the viability of continuing with apartheid. Mandela himself also played a significant role in creating the conditions wherein the whites would feel safe dismantling apartheid. By bringing blacks together and calming the violence, Mandela was able to reassure the rulers of South Africa that apartheid could be dismantled safely. In a way, the violence affected Mandela's role as it was he who brought it under control. In this sense it could be argued that violence had been sustaining apartheid during the 1980s as the whites were afraid of ending apartheid and creating an increase in the violence.

> This paragraph indicates that key individuals, in this case de Klerk and Mandela, played a significant role. It also demonstrates the role that violence played in shaping each of their roles.

Overall, violent protest probably did play the main role in bringing about the end of apartheid. In itself, it provoked the states of emergency in 1985 and 1988, indicating that there was a high level of political and social instability, which was only ended by Mandela's election as president. Violence also had clear links with other factors. Often peaceful protest would degenerate into violence and thereby increase the pressure on the authorities. Some peaceful protests stayed peaceful and thereby contributed to the pressure without violence. The economic problems put a tangible pressure on the white community and clearly had a major impact but the natural result of this pressure was often violent protest by the poor who took the brunt of the downturn. Ultimately, it is very difficult to arrive at a certain judgement because we would need to be able to look inside the minds of those involved but it would be inconceivable that violent protest of such strength, which lasted such a long time, would not have been pivotal in the decisions that were made.

> The conclusion explains how the previous factors can be compared with the question and how they substantiate the judgement that has been made.

Verdict

This is a strong answer because:

- it answers the question throughout
- it uses the issue of the question to set criteria so that a judgement is made against something tangible
- it selects relevant evidence and deploys it to support the arguments being made.

Index

Acknowledgements

Picture Credits

The publisher would like to thank the following for their kind permission to reproduce their photographs:

(Key: b-bottom; c-centre; l-left; r-right; t-top)

akg-images Ltd: 166; **Alamy Images:** National Geographic Image Collection 6, Superstock 95; **Collection Dominique Faivre:** with thanks to In Flanders Fields Museum, Belgium 177; **CONELRAD.com:** 11l, 24; **Corbis:** Bettmann 10b, 16, 203, 304, Hulton-Deutsch Collection 212; **Getty Images:** Bernard Gotfryd 115, 127, Cynthia Johnson/The LIFE Images Collection 137, Dave Hartman/AFP 364, Eric Smith 100, Gideon Mendel/AFP 363, Hulton Archive/Douglas Miller 221, Hulton Archive/Ejor 297, Hulton Archive/Keystone 229, Margaret Bourke-White/Time & Life Pictures 88b, 93, Mike Evans 120, Paul Slade/Paris Match 105, Peter Jordan/The LIFE Images Collection 339tr, Popperfoto 339tl, Ricky Carioti/The Washington Post 48, Terrence Spencer/The LIFE Images Collection 295, Universal History Archive/UIG 313; **Goodman Gallery:** David Goldblatt 349; **Imperial War Museum:** 176; **Magnum Photos Ltd:** George Rodger 292, Henri Cartier-Bresson 257; **Mary Evans Picture Library:** Dorothea Lange/FSA/Epic 62, 65, 89t, Everett Collection 72; **National Archives:** 318; **Press Association Images:** AP 11r, 31, 37, 50, 59, 86, Neal Ulevich/AP 63, 76; **Punch Cartoon Library:** 217; **Rex Features:** British Library/Robana 218, Gallo Images 371, 379, Ron Stilling/Daily Mail 341, Sipa Press 285; **The National Library of Wales:** Daily Mail/Solo Syndication/Associated Newspapers Ltd 245; **TopFoto:** Dinodia 194, The Granger Collection 8, 10t, 20, 40, 43, 88t, 89b, 112

Cover images: *Front:* **Reuters:** Juda Ngwenya

All other images © Pearson Education

Every effort has been made to trace the copyright holders and we apologise in advance for any unintentional omissions. We would be pleased to insert the appropriate acknowledgement in any subsequent edition of this publication.

Tables

Table p. 292 adapted from http://en.wikipedia.org/wiki/South_African_general_election,_1948, Used under Creative Commons Attribution-ShareAlike License, http://creativecommons.org/licenses/by-sa/3.0/

Text

Extract p. 15 from *American Individualism* by Herbert Hoover, Doubleday, Page & Company, 1922, reproduced with permission; Extract 'Source 3' p. 17 from *Hard Times: An Oral History of the Great Depression* by Studs Turkel, The New Press, 1986, pp. 20–21, Copyright © 2000 by Studs Terkel, Reprinted by permission of The New Press, www.thenewpress.com; Extract p. 20 from *Franklin Roosevelt and the New Deal* by David Keith Adams , Historical Association, 1979, Copyright © The Historical Association, www.history.org.uk; Extract p. 22 from *The Presidential Difference: Leadership Style from FDR to Barack Obama*, 3rd ed. by Fred I. Greenstein, Princeton University Press, 2009, p. 3 © 2009 Fred Greenstein, Reprinted by permission of Princeton University Press; Extract p. 26 from *The USA and the Cold War* by Oliver Edwards, Hodder and Stoughton, 1997, p. 135, Copyright © 2002 Oliver Edwards, Reproduced by permission of Hodder Education; Extract p. 41, Extract 3 p. 48, Extract 7 p. 131 from *We Ain't What We Ought To Be, The Black Freedom Struggle from Emancipation to Obama* by Stephen Tuck , The Belknap Press of Harvard University Press, 2010, pp. 184–185, p. 282, 373, 376 Reprinted by permission of the publisher, Cambridge, Mass.: The Belknap Press of Harvard

University Press, Copyright © 2010 by Stephen Tuck; Extract 'Source 4' p. 48 With much gratitude to Don Chapman for his help for tracking down Sam Jones and many thanks to Sam Jones for his memories; Extract 4 p. 54, Extract p. 102, Extract 3 p. 122, Extract 5 p. 127 from *The American Dream From Reconstruction to Reagan, A History of the United States of America* Vol. III by Esmond Wright, Blackwell, 1996, pp. 422, 354, 489, 489, Copyright © Esmond Wright 1996; Extract 5 p. 54 from *Blacks in the 1970s: Did They Scale the Job Ladder?* by Diane Nilsen Westcott , Bureau of Labor Statistics,1982; Extract p. 57 from "Protest, Repression, and Race: Legal Violence and the Chicano Movement" by Ian F. Haney López in *University of Pennsylvania Law Review*, Vol. 150 (1), Nov., 2001, pp. 205–244, reproduced with permission; Extract p. 59 from *The Meaning of Gay: Interaction, Publicity, and Community Among Homosexual Men in 1960s San Francisco* by J. Todd Abercrombie, Lexington Books, 2010, p. 310, reproduced with permission; Extract 1 p. 68 from "A Century of Change: the U.S. Labor Force, 1950–2050" by Mitra Toossi in *Monthly Labor Review*, May, p. 18, 2002, U.S. Department of Labor; Extract 2 p. 68 from *The Politics of Women's Liberation* by Jo Freeman, Addison-Wesley Longman, pp. ix–x, Copyright © by Jo Freeman; Extract p. 83 from *Brought To You By, Postwar Television Advertising and the American Dream* by Lawrence R. Samuel, University of Texas Press, 2001, pp. ix-x, Reproduced with permission; Extract p. 87 from *Media Spectacle* by Douglas Kellner, Routledge, 2003, p. 165, Reproduced with permission; Extracts pp. 98, 119 from "Reaganomics and Economic Policy" by Joseph J. Horgan in *The Reagan Presidency* edited by Dilys M. Hill, Raymond A. Moore and Phil Williams, Macmillan, 1990, p. 135, 149–150, Reproduced with permission of Palgrave Macmillan; Extract p. 110 from *The Motel in America, Road and American Culture* by John A. Jackle, Keith A Sculle & Jefferson S. Rogers , Johns Hopkins University Press, 2002, pp. 110, © 1996 The Johns Hopkins University Press, Reprinted with permission of Johns Hopkins University Press; Extract p. 112 from *The Growth of the American Republic,* Vol. 2 edited by Samuel Eliot Morison, Henry Steele Commager & William E Leuchtenberg, Oxford University Press, 1969, p. 723, By permission of Oxford University Press USA; Extract p. 116 from *More Equal Than Others, America from Nixon to the New Century* by Godfrey Hodgson, Princeton University Press, 2004, p. 183, Copyright © 2004 by the Century Foundation, Published by Princeton University Press; Extract 4 p. 122 from "Supply-side Economics, An Assessment of the Theory and Results" by Paul Craig Roberts in *Reaganomics and After*, edited and introduction by Sir Alan Peacock, *IEA Readings* no. 28, Institute of Economic Affairs, 1989, pp. 39–40, First published by Institute of Economic Affairs, London in 1989; Extract 6 p. 127 from *The Power of Presidential Ideologies* by Dennis Florig, Greenwood Publishing Group, 1992, p. 235, Reproduced with permission of PRAEGER, in the format Educational/Instructional Program via Copyright Clearance Center; Extract 8 p. 131 from *The Declining Significance of Race: Blacks and Changing American Institutions*, 3rd ed. by William Julius Wilson, University of Chicago Press, 2012, p. 2 © 1978, 1980, 2012 by The University of Chicago Press. All rights reserved; Extract p. 135 from Ideological Images for a Television Age by Charles W. Dunn and J. David Woodward in *Reaganomics and After* edited and introduction by Sir Alan Peacock, *IEA Readings* no. 28, Institute of Economic Affairs, 1989, pp. 125, 129, First published by Institute of Economic Affairs, London in 1989; Extract p. 136 from "Domestic Policy in an Era of 'Negative' Government" by Joseph J. Horgan in *The Reagan Presidency* edited by Dilys M. Hill, Raymond A. Moore and Phil Willliams, Macmillan, 1990, p. 162, reproduced with permission from Palgrave Macmillan; Extract p. 171 from *Plain Tales from the Raj* edited by Charles Allen, Andre Deutsch, 1975, p. 72, Reproduced with permission; Extract p. 178 from Letter from Daya Ram of the 2nd Lancers (British Library reference: IOR/L/MIL/5/826/6 f.876), dated 5 July 1916, http://blog.europeana. eu/2012/11/letters-from-Indian-soldiers-in-France-1916/ © The British Library Board IOR/L/MIL 5.826.6 f876; Extract 1 p. 189 from *A History of India* by John Keay, Harper Perennial, 2004, p. 470, Reprinted by permission of Harper Collins Publishers Ltd. © 2004 John Keay; Extract 2 p. 189, Extract p. 230, Extract 1 p. 262 from *Modern India, The Origins of an Asian Democracy* by Judith M Brown, Oxford University Press, 1994, pp. 200, 293, 332, Copyright © Judith M. Brown 1994, By permission of Oxford University Press; Extract 3 p. 189 from *A History of India*, Vol. 2 by Percival Spear, Penguin, 1965 (Revised edition 1970), pp. 164–65, Copyright © Percival Spear, 1965, 1970, Reproduced by permission of Penguin Books Ltd.; Extract p. 198 from *Raj: the Making and Unmaking of British India* by Lawrence James, Abacus, 1997, p. 490, Reproduced with permission from Abacus, an imprint of Little, Brown Book Group and Andrew Lownie Literary Agency; Extract p. 208 from National Archives of India, Home Political File 6127 , With permission from Director General, National Archives of India; Extract p. 210, Extract 'Source 5' p. 220 from *Witness to an Era* by F. Mores, Weidenfeld and Nicholson, 1973, p. 74, 32, Reproduced with permission from The Orion Publishing Group, London; Extract p. 221 from M. R. Jayakar Papers, File no 408, With permission

from Director General, National Archives of India; Extract p. 256 from *India Remembered* by Pamela Mountbatten, Pavilion, 2007, pp. 74–76, Reproduced with kind permission of Pavilion Books; Extract p. 258 from *The Mission with Mountbatten* by A. Campbell-Johnson, Robert Hale, 1951, Reproduced with permission from David Higham Associates; Extract 'Source 6' p. 296 from *Requiem for Sophiatown* by Can Themba, Penguin, 2006, p. 50, Reproduced with permission from Penguin Random House, South Africa; Extract 'Source 7' p. 296 from *Naught for your comfort* by Trevor Huddlestone, The Country Life Press, 1956, p. 179, Reproduced with permission from The literary executors of Archbishop Trevor Huddleston and the Bodleian Library, University of Oxford; Extract 'Source 9' p. 297 from *Colour and Culture in South Africa* by S. Patterson, Taylor and Francis, 1953, p. 53, Copyright © 1953, Reproduced with permission from Taylor & Francis Books UK; Extracts p. 300, 320, 321, from https://www.nelsonmandela.org/omalley/index.phplv01615/06lv01616.htm, https://www.nelsonmandela.org/omalley/index.php/site/q/03lv01538/04lv01600/05lv01617/06lv01621.htm, https://www.nelsonmandela.org/omalley/index.php/site/q/03lv01538/04lv01600/05lv01617/06lv01622.htm, Reproduced with permission from Nelson Mandela Foundation; Extracts and quotes pp. 302, 312, 317, 'Source 14' p. 323, 368, 375 from *Long Walk to Freedom* by Nelson Mandela, Abacus, 1995, pp.110, 279–280, 336, 630, Reproduced with permission from Little, Brown Book Group; Extract 'Source 1' p. 313, 'Source 6', p. 314 from *The Shooting at Sharpeville: The Agony of South Africa* by Ambrose Reeves, Houghton Mifflin Harcourt, 1961, p. 38, Copyright © 1960 by Bishop Ambrose Reeves, renewed 1988 by Nicholas Reeves, Reprinted by permission of Houghton Mifflin Harcourt Publishing Company. All rights reserved; Extract 'Source 7' p. 314 from "The Archive, 22 March 1960, Dozens Killed in Sharpeville" http://www.theguardian.com/theguardian/2010/mar/22/sharpeville-massacre-eyewitness-account, Copyright © Guardian News & Media Ltd 2015; Extract 'Source 4' p. 314 from *Sharpeville: An Apartheid Massacre and its Consequences* by Tom Lodge, Oxford University Press, 2011, p.10, By permission of Oxford University Press and author; Extract p. 323 from http://db.nelsonmandela.org/speeches/pub_view.asp?pg=item&ItemID=NMS004&txtstr=african%20freedom, Reproduced with permission from Nelson Mandela Foundation; Extract p. 326 from http://www.un.org/en/events/mandeladay/court_statement_1964.shtml, Reproduced with permission from Nelson Mandela Foundation; Quote p. 327 from Bishop Ambrose Reeves in *Church and Race in South Africa* by David Paton, SCM Press, 1958, p. 30; Extract p. 331 from Jacky Heyns, 'The Wrong End of apartheid' in *The Beat of the Drum* edited by Angela Caccia, Ravan Press, 1983, p. 6 © BAHA Mary Serfontein; Extract p. 338 from *The Children of Soweto* by Mbulelo Mzamane, Longman Africa, 1995 [1982], with thanks to Nthoana Tau-Mzamane, Nomvuyo Mzamane, Thamsanqa Mazamane and Nonkosi Mzamane; Extract p. 339 from SABC, With permission from SABC Radio; Extracts and quotes on p. 340 from *The Lusaka Years: The ANC in Exile in Zambia, 1963 to 1994* by Hugh Macmillan, Jacana Media, 2013, pp. 57, 72, Reproduced with permission; Extract p. 341 from http://www.aamarchives.org/file-view/category/26-sport.html Copyright © Anti-Apartheid Movement Archives Committee; Extract p. 345 from "Message to Transkei On The Eve of Independence" , July 1976 from *South African History Online*, http://v1.sahistory.org.za/pages/library-resources/speeches/vorster-speeches/1976-transkei.htm; Quote p. 348 from "Displaced Urbanization: South Africa's Rural Slums" by Colin Murray in *African Affairs*, Vol. 86 (1), July 1987, p. 311, By permission of Oxford University Press; Quote p. 348 from Joseph Lelyveld in *Move Your Shadow: South Africa, Black and White* by J. Lelyveld, Penguin, 1986, p.127, Reproduced with permission; Extract 'Source 1' p. 360 Reproduced with permission from Dr Allan A. Boesak; Extracts 'Source 4', 'Source 5' , 'Source 6' p. 362, 'Source 7' p. 363 from *Theatres of Struggle and the End of Apartheid* by Belinda Bozzoli, Edinburgh University Press, 2004, pp. 72, 177, 176, 71; Extract p. 364 from *City Press*, 20/04/1986, Reproduced with permission; Extract p. 369 from "Mandela & Botha: The Crocodile & the Saint" in *The Independent*, 02/11/2006, Copyright © The Independent, Reproduced with permission; Extract p. 367 from "Nelson Mandela Dies: The Story Behind his 70th Birthday Concert" by Tony Hollingsworth in *The Telegraph*, 06/12/2013, Copyright © Tony Hollingsworth/Telegraph Media Group Limited; Extract p. 377 from http://www.nelsonmandela.org/omalley/index.php/site/q/03lv02039/04lv02103/05lv02117/06lv02118.htm Reproduced with permission from The Thabo Mbeki Foundation.

Every effort has been made to contact copyright holders of material reproduced in this book. Any omissions will be rectified in subsequent printings if notice is given to the publishers.